D1744292

CONTEMPORARY MEDIA ISSUES

CONTEMPORARY MEDIA ISSUES

WM. DAVID SLOAN

EMILY ERICKSON HOFF

EDITORS

VISION V PRESS
Northport, Alabama

Vision Press
3230 Mystic Lake Way
P.O. Box 1106
Northport, AL 35476

Library of Congress Cataloguing-in-Publication Data

Contemporary media issues / editors. Wm. David Sloan, Emily Erickson Hoff.
    p.   cm.
    Includes bibliographical references and index.
    ISBN 1-885219-10-5
    1. Mass media--United States.   I. Sloan, W. David (William David), 1947- . II. Hoff, Emily Erickson, 1970- .
P92.U5C64   1998
302.23'0973--dc21   98-10055
                                          CIP

Printed in the United States of America

Table of Contents

The Media and Society / 1

The Media and Politics / 121

Contents

The Media as a Business / 171

Legal Issues / 219

Media Roles and Obligations / 289

Contents

News Practices / 409

Editors and Authors / 503

Index / 509

CONTEMPORARY MEDIA ISSUES

1 THE MEDIA AND SOCIETY

his book begins appropriately with a discussion on how powerful the media have been — and continue to be — in the daily lives of Americans. David Copeland traces the question back to the 1920s, when the emergence of movies was soon followed by concern about their impact on children. Since that time, as Professor Copeland explains, a myriad of empirical studies have been conducted to see, once and for all, what kind of influence movies, music, newspapers, and television have on the individual psyche.

The elusive answer to the question of media power is important, as the subsequent chapters demonstrate. In chapters two and three, for example, Judith Buddenbaum and Val Limburg present the various sides of what some have called America's "culture wars," which have pitted liberals against conservatives in a struggle to have the media reflect their respective values. This discussion is further expanded in Douglas Tarpley's treatment of the political correctness phenomenon that was born on university campuses and has subsequently become an issue in newsrooms throughout the country. Alf Pratte and Kenneth Campbell build on this theme, outlining the changing roles of minorities in the country and in the media. Hugh Cate then shows the enduring tension that exists between members of the media and another "special-interest" group: the U.S. armed forces.

The struggles that are played out between the media and all these groups, whether they're Christians or gays or Marines, show just how powerful the media are believed to be. With each new year of our modern "information age," the attention to the media seems to increase. The news and entertainment media have become the primary means through which we share our culture with one another. This has made the "coming out" of Ellen Degeneras' sitcom character a major event; it has enabled the world to grieve for Yitzhak Rabin, Princess Diana, and Mother Teresa together — from the comfort of thousands of living rooms. It has meant we can watch, minute by minute, the fate of American soldiers in the Persian Gulf and the fate of a national sports hero charged with murdering his ex-wife. It is no accident that secret agent James Bond, no longer able to battle a Soviet empire, was forced in 1997 to face a completely different foe — a media mogul who wanted to start a war in order to boost his newspaper circulation. With such a major role in American lives, it should be no surprise that the media are pressured from all sides to present a "reality" that best suits their audience.

In each of the following chapters of this book, an author — a recognized authority on the topic — has researched an important issue regarding our modern media and then explained the various sides of that issue in order to give you a complete picture. Each chapter concludes with the author's suggested resolution to the issue. However, this book has been designed to help you consider these issues and draw your own thoughtful conclusions. Indeed, as some of the chapter authors explain in their own suggested resolutions, the issues are so complex that there usually are no simple answers. In fact, the nature of the issues themselves suggests exactly the same thing. On any issue on which disputants of integrity and goodwill believe strongly in their own views, it is likely that a proper resolution would incorporate ideas from both, or all, sides. Thus, one should beware of arguments that do not take into consideration the opposing views. Thus, we encourage you to read these chapters critically, and we hope you will be able to take away a sense of the challenges that face today's media, as well as your own assessment of those challenges.

Chapter One

Media Effects: Powerful or Minimal?

David Copeland

In 1993, a five-year-old boy set his bed on fire with a cigarette lighter. His two-year-old sister died in the bedroom blaze. Investigators blamed the fire on the youngster's television habits. He'd been watching the MTV program "Beavis and Butt-head," where the fifteen-year-old cartoon characters proclaimed, "Fire is cool."

In 1994, *U.S. News and World Report* issued the findings of a survey on the media. Ninety per cent of the respondents said they believed that motion picture and television violence contributed to violence in American society.

In 1995, Dr. Leonard Eron, speaking to a Senate subcommittee on commerce, science and transportation as part of The Children's Protection from Violent Programming Act, told senators that children who watch excessive amounts of television are more likely to be convicted for serious crimes. He also warned that even those who did not watch television could be affected by its programming. "You and your child might be the victims of violence perpetrated by someone who as a youngster did learn the motivation for and the techniques of violence from television," Eron said.

In 1996, using all of the above information and more, Congress passed the Telecommunications Act, which provided a screening process for television programming because of the potential negative effects it holds for young viewers. In July 1996, nearly one hundred congressional representatives introduced into the House a resolution calling for major American television networks to reserve the first hour of nightly prime-time viewing for "family-oriented programming" to keep younger children from being influenced by the harmful, violent fare of television. The call was just one of the many resolutions and acts introduced into the 104th Congress in 1995-1996 that sought to curtail broadcast media because of their potential for violent effects on society. And this was all in addition to the Telecommunications Act.

The actions and response of Congress and the nation to the visual media leads to the conclusion that motion pictures and television must have a powerful and lasting impact upon society. But do they? Researchers have attempted to discover the answer to this question and others since the 1920s. If media do have this potential, can society blame its ills upon them as surveys and the 104th Congress have done in the 1990s? Yes, it can, but is such blame justified?

This chapter looks at the major studies of the effects of visual media from the Payne Fund Studies of 1929 forward in an attempt to answer the above questions. Studies into visual media effects and especially into television's role in affecting society have continually increased since the 1950s. Discussing them all would be impossible. For this chapter, many of the research projects included received government funding. They are also considered the major sources of much of our knowledge into media effects. Also, because most of these studies focus upon violence and the media, this chapter does the same. Although similar studies into media effects have been done dealing with newspapers and radio, the effects of visual media upon society have generally been considered more con-troversial and the effects of film and television more powerful than those of newspapers and radio, the radio broadcast of "War of the Worlds" perhaps being the exception.

This chapter approaches visual effects studies in chronological order, explains backgrounds of the studies and divides them into two groups: those that conclude visual media produce powerful effects and those that conclude visual media produce minimal results. In some cases, researchers in one study or a clustered group of studies discovered both. In these instances, the findings will be discussed under both headings. The chapter's conclusion attempts to briefly draw conclusions from the research projects discussed and from a few studies not included in the major portion of the chapter. Before looking at the findings these studies reached, however, a brief discussion of the history of media effects studies should help in understanding the conclusions reached by each of the media effects studies.

Origins of the Issue

At the beginning of the twentieth century, scientists and inventors such as Thomas Edison and August and Luis Lumière had completed their experimentation on creating moving pictures. With the process for producing motion pictures in place and in operation, movie houses called nickelodeons opened in New York City in 1905. Within five years, theaters were operating all across America draw-ing in millions to watch. The large numbers of people attending movies in rela-tive darkness with only a common visual image and perhaps live music fed perfectly into the theories that had been developed to explain how a large, urban, detached society reacts to stimuli. The response created by a mass media message such as motion pictures came to be known as the magic bullet theory. Social scientists studying mass society around the turn of the twentieth century did not call it that, but they concluded messages reach individuals who responded identically in much the way targets respond to the impact of bullets. In other words, an audience watching a movie perceived the actions on the screen and the live, accompanying music individually but identically. The reaction of individuals to the message of the motion picture was immediate and, as a bullet hitting a target, the results were powerful. In the first two decades of the twentieth century, however, these ideas concerning the power of motion pictures, or other media for that matter, were not tested in any scientific way. Most researchers assumed the magic bullet theory to be true, and the powerful effects of motion pictures on individuals became the standard for understanding societal reaction to movie messages.

In the 1920s, the American film industry erupted in activity, and movie attendance skyrocketed. According to the U.S. Bureau of Census *Historical Statistics of the United States*, approximately 40 million Americans attended movies per week in 1922. By 1930, that number had climbed to 90 million, meaning, according to Census figures, that on average three individuals in every American household attended a movie at least once a week. The rapid rise in movie attendance raised further questions about the effects of motion pictures upon society, especially their effects upon adolescents and children, estimated by Edgar Dale in *Children's Attendance at Motion Pictures* to comprise about 44 per cent of weekly movie attendees or slightly more than 40 million young people in 1929.

The large number of adolescents and children attending motion pictures raised a number of questions that society had only speculated upon before the end of the 1920s. As W.W. Charters said in the preface to *Motion Pictures and the Social Attitudes of Children*: "Motion pictures are not understood by the present generation of adults. They are new; they make an enormous appeal to children; and they present ideas and situations that parents may not like. Consequently, when parents think of the welfare of their children who are exposed to these compelling situations, they wonder about the effect of the pictures upon the ideals and behavior of the children." Charters then posed the questions that opened up effects research, "Do motion pictures really influence children in any direction? Are their conduct, ideals and attitudes affected by the movies? In short, just what effect do motion pictures have upon children of different ages?"

In order to find the answers to these questions, Charters and a team of university psychologists, sociologists and educators were brought together in 1928 by the Motion Picture Research Council. Collectively known as the Payne Fund for the organization that provided the grant money for the study, scholars in 1929 began a series of field projects with young people. Their findings were published in a series of thirteen studies in 1933.

World War II sparked the next major research into the effects of film. Recruits were needed by the United States, and military leaders turned to motion pictures as a way to ensure a positive reaction to America's war efforts, especially among young men. Since younger Americans attended movies by the millions each week, motion pictures were a logical choice as a persuader. Hollywood producer Frank Capra was enlisted for the project, and he produced a series of seven films under the title *Why We Fight*. Because the film series was shown to recruits, researchers had ready-made research subjects, and the soldiers were divided in experimental and control groups. The results of the experiments added another chapter to the emerging controversy of media effects. The findings were published by Carl I. Hovland, Arthur A. Lumsdaine and Fred D. Sheffield, three of the researchers who conducted the testing on the servicemen, in *Experiments on Mass Communication* in 1949.

Following World War II, researchers turned their attention to the potential effects of television as it became the visual medium of choice for society. According to Wilbur Schramm, Jack Lyle and Edwin Parker in *Television in the Lives of Our Children*, the number of televisions increased from 100,000 in 1948 to one million in 1949. The number of television stations increased too, and the FCC, fearing a glut and overlapping of TV stations as had occurred with radio stations in the late 1920s, issued a moratorium on any new stations until 1952. Despite the fact that no new stations took to the airwaves, the purchase of televisions did not stop. In 1952, according to the U.S. Bureau of Census, 15.3 million sets were in place in American homes. By the end of the 1950s, according to Census figures, slightly more than 87 per cent of American homes had television. The number of actual sets in homes, according to Schramm, Lyle and Parker, exceeded 50 million. By 1970, the U.S. Bureau of Census estimated that more than 95 per cent of American homes had at least one television.

The first studies of television effects during the 1950s continued the trend begun by motion picture research of looking at the effects of the medium upon young people. Because television was not an ubiquitous medium at the beginning of the 1950s, studies tended to look at the overall intrusion of television into the lives of children and families. Eleanor Maccoby studied television's effect on children doing homework and going to bed along with TV's effect on family socialization in 1950 and 1951.

By the mid-1950s, the question of television violence and its effects on young people became the subject of congressional hearings, and a Senate sub-committee on juvenile delinquency released a report warning of the potential danger to young viewers of TV violence in 1956. The first major research into the effects of television, including violence, on children followed in Great Britain and the United States. The British study, Hilde T. Himmelweit, A.N. Oppenheim and Pamela Vince, *Television and the Child*, was published in 1958. The American study, Wilbur Schramm, Jack Lyle and Edwin B. Parker, *Television in the Lives of Our Children*, was published in 1961.

The domestic upheaval and violence of 1960s spurred the next major study on media effects in America. Following assassinations of political leaders, race riots in major American cities and growing violence on American streets, President Lyndon B. Johnson created the National Commission on the Causes and Prevention of Violence in 1968. According to *Violence and the Media*, the 1969 printed findings of the commission, media were presumed to be the principal cause of these national problems. The commission was charged "to investigate the effects of media portrayals of violence upon the public and the role of the mass media in the process of violent and non-violent change." The charge singled out television as the chief source of media effects on society.

While the results of the President's Commission on the Causes and Prevention of Violence were being published, Congress issued a call for yet another study of media effects specifically aimed at television violence and its effects upon children and adolescents. Congress placed the new study under the auspices of the Surgeon General's office. The commission, called the Surgeon General's Scientific Advisory Committee on Television and Social Behavior, planned a new series of research experiments to determine television effects, something that the 1968-1969 study, which relied extensively on previously pub-lished material, had not done. The Surgeon General's study sought specifically to find "the relationship between televised violence and the attitudes and behav-ior of children," according to the preface of the five-volume committee report, *Television and Social Behavior*, published in 1972.

Following the Surgeon General's Report, studies into television effects increased in America. In fact, 90 per cent of all research into television's influ-ences on behavior took place in the 1970s, according to Herbert Pardes, director of the National Institute of Mental Health. George Comstock and M. Fisher, in *Television and Human Behavior: A Guide to the Pertinent Scientific Literature*, listed 2,400 different publications related to television and its effects on people in 1975. The culmination of 1970s research was the 1982 two-volume *Television and Behavior: Ten Years of Scientific Progress and Implications for the Eighties*, an update and elaboration of the 1972 Surgeon General's Report prepared by the National

Institute of Mental Health. As with the Surgeon General's Report, the NIMH studies focused upon media effects on children and adolescents, but not exclusively. Television's effects on society, social beliefs and behavior, and interpersonal relations were also included as NIMH compiled the research literature on the effects of television from 1979-1981.

Following the publication of *Television and Social Behavior*, researchers into the effects of visual media on society expanded and refined their work. While media violence and effects upon children continued as a part of research, studies into the role of visual media effects on society in relation to advertising, minorities, health and sexual issues, to name a few topics, became the focus of those studying television and society. In America, as a 1994 *U.S. News and World Report* survey uncovered, 90 per cent of people *believe* that visual media contribute, or cause, a negative effect upon society. With major research into the effects of visual media stretching back to the 1920s, however, an overview of experimental results, not societal beliefs, should help in determining the degree that media have or do not have an effect on society. It is to the results of the studies this research now turns.

Media Effects: Powerful or Minimal?

In the summer of 1996, professor Ellen Wartella, a researcher in the three-year National Television Violence Study begun in the fall of 1994 and funded by the Cable Television Association, spoke to an international group of journalism and mass communication educators. "Research is clear," she said. "Media violence does have an effect." Wartella's 1996 conclusion, that media do have an effect on society, was a reiteration of what most researchers have said since the Payne Fund Studies of the 1920s. If media could not produce effects on society, would corporations such as Proctor & Gamble, Philip Morris and General Motors spend in excess of $1 billion per year in efforts to produce both short- and long-term changes in consumer buying patterns?

But the conclusion that media, specifically visual media, produce societal effects cannot be explained with a blanket statement that media can affect society. Since studies into the effects of media began in the 1920s, experiments have produced varying results; some of the experiments into visual media effects have discovered powerful effects, while other experiments have found only limited or minimal visual media effects. Research findings demonstrate just how difficult it is to ascertain media effects. Within the Payne Fund Studies, for example, some of the researchers reported finding powerful effects, while others concluded motion pictures produced very limited at best effects on viewers.

Powerful effects, as discovered by researchers, produced changes in receivers' actions and attitudes that vary noticeably from how receivers acted or believed before being exposed to the visual medium. In some cases, these changes were immediate and quite apparent but did not last. In other instances, short-term changes in actions and attitudes were undetected, but cumulative exposure to similar media messages produced a discernible change in actions and attitudes over time. Minimal effects, as discovered by researchers, produced only temporary, slight, or no changes in the actions and attitudes of receivers. The findings for minimal or limited effects may have also been inconclusive. The powerful effects discovered by researchers are discussed below.

Powerful Effects

The Payne Fund's studies reached a number of conclusions that reinforced that era's fears concerning the negative effects of motion pictures. Payne Fund researchers used thousands of America's young people and adults. In *Getting Ideas from the Movies*, Perry W. Holaday and George W. Stoddard studied more than 3,000 observers using 17 motion pictures, compiling more than three-quarters of a million individual responses to questions concerning movie effects. They concluded that retention from movies occurred three and six months after viewing a motion picture. "This retention is lasting," Holaday and Stoddard reported. "Children, even very young ones, can retain specific memories of a picture with a high degree of accuracy and completeness." The researchers said retention was between 80 and 92 per cent after three months and nearly 60 per cent after six months.

Herbert Blumer and Philip Hauser, also in a Payne Fund study, concluded that what was seen on a motion picture screen contributed to criminal activity. In *Movies, Delinquency, and Crime*, the sociologists studied training school students, ex-convicts and youth from high-crime neighborhoods. Blumer and Hauser said that visual media played a direct role in delinquent behavior and criminal activity. In their conclusion, they stated:

> Through the display of crime techniques and criminal patterns of behavior; by arousing desires for easy money and luxury, and by suggesting questionable methods for their achievements; by inducing a spirit of bravado, toughness, and adventurousness; by arousing intense sexual desires; and by invoking daydreaming of criminal roles, motion pictures may create attitudes and furnish techniques conducive, quite unwittingly, to delinquent or criminal behavior.

Studying the effects of motion pictures on the social attitudes of children, Ruth C. Peterson and L. L. Thurstone discovered a potentially even more powerful way that movies could influence viewers — a cumulative effect. Their studies revealed that taken separately, certain motion pictures had no significant effect on the actions and attitudes of test subjects. But when the same subjects viewed movies that proposed the same actions, attitudes, or themes at intervals of one week, the movies produced a cumulative effect on receivers. Peterson and Thurstone concluded in *Motion Pictures and the Social Attitudes of Children* "that motion pictures have definite, lasting effects on the social attitudes of children and that a number of pictures pertaining to the same issue may have a cumulative effect on attitude."

In yet another of the Payne Fund studies, Herbert Blumer looked at how more than 1,800 adults, adolescents and children saw motion pictures influencing their lives. What Blumer discovered, especially with adolescents, was the adoption of behavior of the actors in movies. Hair styles changed, clothes changed, mannerisms were adopted. Blumer concluded in *Movies and Conduct* that motion pictures provided a powerful effect on viewers because motion pictures affected social behavior and personal choices for extended periods of time after the behavior of actors was observed in movies.

In 1942, the U.S. Army joined researchers in human behavior and sociology and Hollywood to produce a series of films aimed at educating and motivating new soldiers about the global war that the United States entered following the Japanese bombing of Pearl Harbor in December 1941. The *Why We Fight* series used seven films in an attempt to achieve its purposes. The researchers, in order to determine how well the films succeeded in educating and motivating soldiers, set up experiments using test and control groups. Following World War II, three of the researchers, Carl I. Hovland, Arthur A. Lumsdaine and Fred D. Sheffield, published their findings in *Experiments on Mass Communication*. The researchers discovered that the use of films such as those in the *Why We Fight* series greatly affected factual knowledge. Hovland, Lumsdaine and Sheffield reported that with some factual information the use of a visual medium increased knowledge fourfold between those in the test and control groups.

The authors discovered, as will be discussed later, that the *Why We Fight* series had little effect in changing attitudes and opinions of soldiers. But with one film, "The Battle of Britain," the researchers reported that long-term changes in opinion were greater than short-term changes. In this test the short-term group was tested for opinion changes after one week. The long-term groups was tested nine weeks after viewing the film. Hovland, Lumsdaine and Sheffield called this increase in opinion change after the longer period a "sleeper effect." The researchers explained the effect by saying initial inclination toward a subject made it more probable that a long-term change would occur than a short-term one.

The authors also reported that general opinion could change over time because the individual had fewer opinions tied directly to specific facts. The sleeper effect pointed to a potentially powerful media effect, and the three researchers offered basic interpretations of why it might exist. Still, they could offer no answers as to why it may have been a result of the tests, only that it occurred.

In the 1950s visual media effects research began to focus upon television. Most studies were carried out by individual researchers or by small groups of researchers who worked with relatively small groups of children and adolescents. As will be seen later in this chapter, most research in this decade into the effects of television reported that the new medium generally produced a minimal effect upon viewers. William H. Haines, however, concluded in a 1955 *Journal of Social Therapy* article titled "Juvenile Delinquency and Television" that television and movies that played "a distinct role in the creation of anti-social behavior in susceptible teen-agers." Eleanor Maccoby, who published her study of television effects in "Television: Its Impact on School Children" in *Public Opinion Quarterly* in 1951, said television probably played a role similar to fairy stories and fantasy plays used by children for centuries. But, Maccoby pointed out, "TV has changed the quantitative impact of certain forms of fantasy to the point that it is pertinent to inquire into the long-range effects such a change will have." Most researchers, however, credited any powerful effects of television upon viewers with low intelligence, low socio-economic standing, emotional imbalance and inherent tendencies toward aggression.

By the end of the 1960s, however, many Americans viewed television and visual media in general differently. The Media Task Force, as part of a national commission to prevent violence, began hearings in October 1968, and its findings were published in December 1969. In most cases, the Media Task Force report, prepared by Robert K. Baker and Sandra J. Ball, gathered and collated the results of effects studies of the 1950s and 1960s and congressional hearings into a multivolume source. The Task Force did, however, authorize a new study of television violence based on one week of prime-time network programming each from 1967 and 1968. The new analysis of media violence was conducted by researchers from the Annenberg School of Communications at the University of Pennsylvania.

The researchers discovered that the total percentage of violence on each of the three major network stations increased from 1967 to 1968. The study found that for both years ABC's network programming contained violence 89.5 per cent of the time, while 71.6 per cent of the CBS programming for the same period contained acts of violence. It found that ABC, CBS and NBC, for the weeks of the study, had acts of violence in 81.4 per cent of their programs. The study defined violence as "the overt expression of force intended to hurt or kill."

The Media Task Force concluded that the effects produced by media violence were of "a variety that most persons would deem costly and harmful to individuals and society" and that television had the greatest potential of all media for powerful short- and long-term effects. A short-term effect of violent television programming, the committee said, was that "audiences exposed to mass media portrayals of violence learn how to perform violent acts." Consequently, audiences that have learned violent behavior from media are likely to exhibit that learning "if they encounter a situation similar to the portrayed situation, expect to be rewarded for violent behavior, or do not observe disproving reactions to the portrayal of aggression."

In terms of long-term effects, the committee said that exposure to media violence over extended periods of time socializes audiences to violence. As a result, those who have been effectively socialized by mass media portrayals of violence will probably resolve conflict with the use of violence and use violence to obtain a desired end. Long-term exposure to media violence desensitizes viewers to real violence and lowers inhibitions against the use of violence. Because long-term exposure to media violence does all of the above, the Task Force concluded, audiences become more likely to use violence and to passively tolerate its use by others. In addition, the committee said, TV violence has the effect of producing inaccurate portrayals of class, ethnic, racial and occupational groups that in turn creates reactions of fear and hatred for these groups within a society that has no direct contact with these groups. Television more than any other mass medium, the Task Force said, "is re-shaping the traditional, definitional, and socializing activities of political, economic, educational, recreational, and religious institutions" and "is the primary source of exposure to severe acts of violence for the majority of Americans."

Even though the Media Task Force had gathered the collective knowledge on media and violence to date, Congress appropriated $1 million in 1969 before *Violence and the Media* was printed for additional studies into television, its portrayals of violence, and young people. The new study was directed by the Office of the Surgeon General. The study became known as the Surgeon General's Report. The results were published in 1971 in the five-volume *Television and Social Behavior* and the accompanying *Television and Growing Up: The Impact of Televised Violence*, which contained many of the conclusions reached by the Surgeon General's committee.

The new research in the Surgeon General's Report included studies of facial expressions of children viewing violence, adolescent aggression and the violence content of Saturday morning cartoons, to name three. But the report did little except affirm what had already been discovered about visual media effects. Essentially, the Surgeon General Report reinforced that television had the potential for powerful effects in short-term aggressive behavior among young people and the potential to produce a cumulative effect toward the acceptance and use of violence.

The effects of television on aggressive behavior were studied by Robert M. Liebert and Robert A. Baron, who used a laboratory situation to find out whether watching a three-and-a-half minute clip of television violence, fights, shootings and knifings, versus sports competition, would tend to make children more susceptible to violence toward other children. The children then were placed in situations where they could help or hurt another child by pushing selected help or hurt buttons. The researchers discovered that the children "who had observed the aggressive program later showed more willingness to engage in interpersonal aggression than those who had observed the neutral program." In addition, the children who viewed the violent clip, a portion of the program *The Untouchables*, tended to hold down the hurt button longer than children who viewed the sports clip. In fact, Liebert and Baron reported, the lowest mean time in pushing the hurt button for the group viewing the aggression was higher than the highest mean time in pushing the hurt button for the group viewing the non-aggression. "[T]he primary effect of exposure to the aggressive program was that of reducing subjects' restraints against inflicting severe discomfort on the ostensible peer victim," the researchers reported. They concluded that viewing the violent material did affect the willingness to engage in interpersonal aggression.

The cumulative effects of television upon young people was the focus of a study by Monroe M. Lefkowitz, Leonard D. Eron, Leopold O. Walder and L. Rowell Huesman. The researchers looked at the aggressive behavior of a group of children over a ten-year period (1959-1969), from ages 8 to 18 and grades 3 to 13. A number of factors were used to determine individual aggression, including television programs watched, amount of time spent watching television, and subsequent aggressive behavior as reported by family and peers.

What "Television Violence and Child Aggression: A Follow-up Study" discovered was that, especially among boys, the more violence they viewed, the more aggressive they became. And, the research discovered, aggression among these individuals increased when measured 10 years later. "[T]elevision habits established by age eight influence aggressive and other behaviors at that time and at least through late adolescence," the study reported. "This is more true for boys than for girls, although many of the relations for girls are in the same direction as those for boys, though less strong." The study also discovered that it was not necessarily the type of program watched but the amount of programming that increased the aggressive behavior. They concluded "that preferring violent fare in the third grade leads to the building of aggressive habits" and that the "relation between television violence and aggressive behavior in the thirteenth grade is due to the fact that this behavior has already been established."

The study also stated that the more violent fare watched the harder it became for individuals to distinguish between television violence and real-life violence. The study said these children come to the conclusion that "this [television violence] is the way life is and the way one goes about solving problems. Inhibitions against expressing overt aggression would thus be diminished." The researchers also concluded that children who tended to be unpopular in the third grade tended to remain unpopular among their peers. These children tended to watch more television at age eight and continued to watch more television than their "popular" counterparts. The study concluded, "The more unpopular he is the more time he devotes to television."

The Surgeon General's Report commissioned in 1968 was no doubt the main initiative for media effects research in the 1970s. In fact, studies in the field increased more than 730 per cent in the decade compared to all research done on media effects beginning with the Payne Study of 1929. About 2,500 studies took place in the 1970s versus about 300 up to that time. The relationship between television viewing and violence continued to be the main subject of research, but that research now expanded to look at media effects in other areas as well. *The Effects of Television Advertising on Children* collected studies into advertising under sponsorship of the National Science Foundation. *Television and Social Behavior* collected research other than studies in violence, focusing especially on television's effect upon racism and attitudes toward minorities. The studies were part of a report to the Social Science Research Council.

In 1979, another government-sponsored study of media effects began. Under the guidance of the National Institute of Mental Health, the U.S. Department of Health and Human Services started collecting data on research that NIMH and others had been conducting for at least a decade. The two-volume *Television and Behavior* was published in 1982 and summarized the research of the 1970s, including aspects of the findings included in *Television Advertising and Children* and *Television and Social Behavior*. NIMH research concluded that media effects went beyond violence, the principal focus of studies in the 1960s, to provide potentially powerful effects in other areas. NIMH research explained that almost everyone learned from television. The study concluded that television could and did have a positive effect on the health of viewers and the pro-social behavior in children. The study cited television campaigns against drug abuse, smoking, seatbelt usage and dental health as examples of areas in which television messages changed American attitudes.

But, *Television and Behavior* also concluded, these effects could have a negative impact on society. The study concluded, "television content reflecting certain stereotypes may limit or distort how people view women, ethnic groups, or the elderly, for example, and how people interpret the extent to which there are dangers that confront them in daily life."

Even though *Television and Behavior* pointed out television's potential in many areas of society, the study returned to violence and the medium. The study stated: "In magnitude, television violence is as strongly correlated with aggressive behavior as any other behavioral variable that has been measured. The research question has moved from asking whether or not there is an effect to seeking explanations for the effect. According to observational learning theory, when children observe television characters who behave violently, they learn to be violent or aggressive themselves."

Television violence also produced an attitude of fear, the study said. Heavy viewers of television exhibited more fear, mistrust and apprehension than light viewers. The study also concluded that "the viewer learns more than aggressive behavior from televised violence. The viewer learns to be a victim and to identify with victims.... Thus, the effects of televised violence may be even more extensive than suggested by earlier studies, and they may be exhibited in more subtle forms of behavior than aggression." And, the study warned, "fast action, loud music, and stimulating camera tricks may account for changes in behavior following televised violence."

Following the NIMH study, most research in visual media effects was carried on by independent researchers and not collated by any major government or independent agency. L. Rowell Huesman and Leonard D. Eron, who followed eight-year-olds for a decade as part of the Surgeon General's Report, concluded in *Television and the Aggressive Child*, a world-wide study, that children's and adults' aggressive behavior can be influenced by exposure to television and films.

In June 1994, the National Cable Television Association commissioned the largest analysis of violence in television programming content ever to take place. The analysis will involve the evaluation of more than 2,700 hours of programming each year for three years. The study will not, however, draw any conclusions about the effects of violent programs, according to Wayne Danielson, one of the researchers on the project. But, according to researcher Ellen Wartella, the study assumes that media violence has an effect on society.

Minimal Effects

Just as some researchers have been adamant that visual media produce powerful effects in both short- and long-term situations, other researchers have reached completely different conclusions from their studies, finding a limited relationship between the interaction of individuals and media. Sometimes these conflicting results have come out of the same research reports.

While Holaday and Stoddard, Peterson and Thurstone and Blumer pointed to very strong and long-lasting media effects in their Payne Fund reports, others pointed out that motion pictures might not be the primary affecter of behavior. W. W. Charters in *Motion Pictures and Youth* said understanding the relationship between the medium and behavior was at best complicated. He questioned how one could properly rate movie effects in relation to what is taught and learned at home, school, church, community customs, peer relationships and street life. Frank K. Shuttleworth and Mark A. May in *Social Conduct and Attitudes of Movie Fans* concluded that motion pictures could have an effect on children, but "this influence is specific for a given child and a given movie. The same picture may influence different children in distinctly opposite directions. Thus ... the net effect appears small." Shuttleworth and May went on to conclude that movies only further established and confirmed behavior patterns and attitudes already in place among young people.

The *Why We Fight* film series and the studies of the series' effects also produced conflicting findings. The powerful potential for the "sleeper effect" described by researchers Hovland, Lumsdaine and Sheffield was countered by the discovery that the films had little to no effect on viewers in other areas, especially in changing attitudes and motivation. The films did little to change attitudes or increase motivation that would make soldiers want to fight, accept unconditional surrender of the enemy, think positively of British war efforts, or dislike the enemy. According to *Experiments on Mass Communication*, "The films had no effect on the items prepared for the purpose of measuring effects on the men's motivation to serve as soldiers, which was considered the ultimate objective of the orientation program.

Studies into the effect of television that began in the 1950s continued to add to the belief that visual media produced minimal effects. Maccoby 's 1950 study, as mentioned earlier, concluded that "in many ways TV probably plays a role similar to that of the fairy stories and fantasy play which have been a part of children's lives since our earliest records of man." Large-scale studies of television effects and children took place later in the decade in England, America and Canada. Himmelweit, Oppenheim and Vince published the first of these studies in 1958. *Television and the Child* studied more than 1,800 television viewers in four British cities. The researchers discovered that television did create some anxieties about growing up, but they concluded that "television exerts an influence only where views are not already firmly fixed, or where it gives information not already obtained from other sources."

Schramm, Lyle and Parker published the first major study on the effects of television on North American children in 1961. Beginning in 1958, they conducted ten studies across America, with one more taking place in Canada. The studies sought the answer to a number of questions, including 1) Does television deepen the ignorance or broaden the knowledge of children? 2) Does television distort children's values? 3) Does television cause withdrawn and addictive behavior? But for Schramm, Lyle and Parker, finding the answer to what they saw as "the most serious and frequent question raised by television" — whether violence teaches children violence and crime — was paramount.

The findings in *Television and the Lives of Our Children* indicated that it was not so much what television did to children but what children did with television. The researchers noted that television positively influenced education and that preschoolers who watched large amounts of television came to school with better vocabularies than those who viewed little television. But the researchers said that mental ability, social norms and social relationships were the chief variables in determining television use and effects. Schramm, Lyle and Parker concluded by saying that television is "neither a distinct advantage nor a severe handicap" in children's cognitive development.

In finding answers for the questions dealing with television and its effects on values, addictive behavior and violent activity, *Television in the Lives of Our Children* concluded that "very little delinquency can be traced directly to television." Schramm, Lyle and Parker also said that television broadcasters were not completely free of fault if children's values were not that of parents or if children turned to delinquency and violence. But, according to the researchers, "Television is at best a contributory cause." Television was not something to be feared or given clemency in its relationship with children, the researchers said. Schramm, Lyle and Parker explained: "For *some* children, under *some* conditions, *some* television is harmful. For *other* children, under the same conditions, or for the same children under *other* conditions, it may be beneficial. For *most* children, under *most* conditions, *most* television is probably neither particularly harmful nor particularly beneficial."

They concluded, "If a child has security and love, interests, friendships, and healthful activities in his non-television hours, there is little chance that anything very bad is going to happen to him as a result of television."

Although the findings of *Television in the Lives of Our Children* were at odds with the findings of the 1969 government-sponsored *Violence in the Media* report, the 1972 Surgeon General's Report ultimately returned to the position advocated by Schramm, Lyle and Parker. *Television and Social Behavior* found a number of potentially powerful effects of media, which are discussed above, but in *Television and Growing* Up, the separate summary volume published with the five-volume report, the committee summarized its findings this way:

> The accumulated evidence, however, does not warrant the conclusion that televised violence has a uniformly adverse effect nor the conclusion that it has an adverse effect on the majority of children. It cannot even be said that the majority of the children in the various studies we have reviewed showed an increase in aggressive behavior in response to the violent fare to which they were exposed.

The next major study of media effects, *Television and Social Behavior*, concluded that television was "the major socializing force in America" and that "the effects of televised violence may be even more extensive than suggested by earlier studies." But the research and a subsequent report collated by NIMH was not without conflicting data. In a three-year study of approximately 3,200 young people sponsored by the National Broadcasting Company, J. Ronald Milavsky, along with other researchers, could not detect with any consistency significant effects of television on aggression. The researchers admitted that television may play a "very small" role in producing aggression. "Television and Aggression: Results of a Panel Study" concluded by stating that "this study did not find evidence that television violence was causally implicated in the development of aggressive behavior patterns among children and adolescents."

Resolution

The question of the power of media effects may be just as much at question today as it was at the time of the Payne Fund Study. That visual media can and do affect viewers was assumed in 1929 and today. The question that remains is just how and to what extent these media affect viewers. A class of college students studying media and society, for example, may say it believes strongly that visual media has an impact upon viewers. The class will readily admit to viewing dozens of murders on screen, including violent attacks in so-called "slasher" movies. Yet none of the students say they would ever consider such violent acts, a concept affirmed by the 1969 Media Task Force report *Violence and the Media*. "Common sense and observation refute the claim that exposure alone makes all people think and act violently. We know millions of adults and children are exposed daily to television entertainment programming, but a majority of them do not espouse violent norms or behave violently," the study concluded.

Media studies point to individuals and differences in them as a way to determine media effects. The *Why We Fight* studies of Hovland, Lumsdaine and Sheffield found that individuals, more than anything seen in the films, were themselves the source of media effects. And the caveat offered by Schramm, Lyle and Parker, which was repeated in the Surgeon General's Report, also finds the individual at the root of media effects. "For *some* children, under *some* conditions, *some* television is harmful.... For *most* children, under *most* conditions, most television is probably neither harmful nor particularly beneficial."

Even if all researchers into media effects concluded that it is individual differences that create visual media effects, that admission would not discount the possibility of powerful media effects. From the Payne Fund Study forward, the cumulative effect that media may have has been proposed. The Media Task Force reported that repeated exposure to media violence makes violence socially acceptable and desensitizes viewers. Similarly, the Surgeon General's Report pointed out the great cumulative effect of media in acceptance of violence. Lefkowitz and associates in "Television Violence and Child Aggression" observed that aggression increased during a ten-year period, and it was not necessarily the type of visual media observed but the amount. The actions that were observed might be learned from repeated viewing; the cumulative exposure to certain actions on screen could trigger behavior that had been learned elsewhere. The same results in cumulative exposure to media have been observed in studies into racism and sexism, too.

While most of the studies into visual media effects have focused on the power to produce negative impact, the powerful effects of visual media have also been shown to produce long-term positive changes in such things as seatbelt laws, smoking and dental health. This potential to influence is why many people are again concerned about the glamorization of potentially harmful activities such as smoking on screen by actors in television programs and movies.

Perhaps one of the best ways to understand visual media effects has been explained by George Gerbner and associates. They view the relationship between visual media and viewers as an interaction between medium and its publics. Television, Gerbner says in "Growing Up with Television: The Cultivation Perspective," is a pervasive medium. Its influences on the composition and structure of the symbolic environment of viewers are often subtle, complex and intermingled with influences that have nothing to do with media. Television in this situation becomes an integral part of a dynamic process of medium, individual and other aspects of the individual's life. Television in this cultivation perspective is the main instrument of symbols and as a result shapes lifestyles and outlooks.

The cumulative exposure to television is the root here, just as it was in most studies in this chapter. The more that viewers interact with the symbols and messages seen on television, the more those perspectives become a part of life. Television may introduce new concepts or reinforce ideas gained elsewhere in society. Gerbner even hypothesizes that media effects studies that find little or no change in receivers through media-viewer interaction may actually reflect the strength of cultivation. Television's version of the world, in this instance, has in effect become the viewer's version of the world, and the two reinforce each other.

Even with all the effects studies since the 1920s, the discussion still returns to the questions of whether visual media affect individuals and society, and how powerful those effects are. To the question of visual media affecting individuals and society, most research has demonstrated at least some impact of visual media. As to the strength of those effects, cumulative exposure, individual differences and societal norms no doubt all play a part. There is an interaction between viewers and media. Can society blame its ills upon the media as surveys and the 104th Congress have done in the 1990s? Yes, it can, but is such blame justified? If all violence on television were canceled and replaced by programs espousing acts of kindness, would societal violence stop? The answer is clearly no, because the relationship between visual media and viewers is much more complex. If, as Gerbner suggests, television is but a part of a dynamic interactive process, then television cannot move away from violence or any aspect of life any more than passers-by can avoid slowing down at the scene of wreck along a highway. What does this mean? It means that the dialogue on how media affect society, the power of that influence versus the relative innocuous nature of effects, will continue with more studies, more theories and more disagreement into the future.

Recommended Readings

Books

Adler, Richard., Gerald S. Lesser, Laurene Krasny Meringoff, Thomas S. Robertson, John R. Rossiter, and Scott Ward. *The Effects of Television Advertising on Children.* Lexington, Mass.: Lexington Books, 1980. Comprehensive look at the effects of advertising on children.

Baker, Robert K., and Sandra J. Ball. *Violence and the Media*, 2 Vols. Washington, D.C.: U.S.

Government Printing Office, 1969. Reports of the presidential commission established in 1968. Volume I looks at the history and function of media and the television world of violence. Volume II contains congressional hearings.

Bandura, Albert, and Richard Walters. *Social Learning and Personality Development*. New York: Holt, Rinehart & Winston, 1963. Discusses the observational concept of media effects by using "Bobo" dolls. Found that children who saw abusive conduct with the doll imitated behavior.

Bryant, Jennings and Dolf Zillman, eds. *Media Effects: Advances in Theory and Research*. Hillsdale, N.J.: Lawrence Erlbaum, 1994. Collection of research into all media effects. Of special value to visual media effects are studies that seek to explain the relationship between media and societal actions, minorities and media, and media effects on health issues.

Comstock, George A., Eli A. Rubinstein, and John P. Murray, eds. *Television and Social Behavior*. 5 Vols. Washington, D.C.: U.S. Department of Health, Education, and Welfare, 1972. The Surgeon General's Report. The five volumes seek to find out the amount and character of television violence, the circumstances in which violent programming is created, and the formal and informal influences that affect the selection and prohibition of television content.

Cooper, Cynthia A. *Violence on Television: Congressional Inquiry, Public Criticism and Industry Response, A Policy Analysis*. Lanham, Md.: University Press of America, 1996. Looks at congressional and public scrutiny of American policymaking toward television focusing upon the political, cultural, and social aspects of this forty-year debate.

Himmelweit, Hilde, A. N. Oppenheim, and Pamela Vince. *Television and the Child*. London: Oxford University Press, 1958. First major study of the effects of television on children. Conducted in Great Britain, the study looks at the fright factor of visual violence.

Hovland, Carl I., Arthur A. Lumsdaine, and Fred D. Sheffield. *Experiments on Mass Communication*. Princeton, N.J.: Princeton University Press, 1949. Reports the results of the experiments into motion picture effects of the *Why We Fight* series.

Huesmann, L. Rowell, and Leonard D. Eron, eds. *Television and the Aggressive Child: A Cross-National Comparison*. Hillsdale, N.J.: Lawrence Erlbaum, 1986. Compares television violence and aggressive children's behavior internationally. Points out that most of the studies find a relation between violence and behavior but that not all studies have been conducted identically making comparisons difficult.

Klapper, Joseph. *The Effects of Mass Communication*. New York: Free Press, 1960. Compilation and evaluation of media effects using the work of the author and as much of the available literature as possible. Pays special attention to television studies of the 1950s.

Lowery, Shearon A., and Melvin L. DeFleur. *Milestones in Mass Communication Research,*

3rd ed. White Plains, N.Y.: Longmans, 1995. Attempts to explain what the authors consider the principal studies in media effects of the century. Looks at all media and is probably the best single source for understanding studies outside of the original research reports.

Motion Pictures and Youth: The Payne Fund Studies. New York: Macmillan, 1933. Findings of the Payne Fund published in several different volumes. The series seeks to find answers to why and how often children attend movies, how movies affect societal well-being, and the effects movies have on emotions, attitudes, ideals, crime, and delinquency.

National Television Violence Study Scientific Papers, 1994-95. Mediascope, Inc., 1996. Initial papers produced by scholars studying media violence for the National Cable Television Association. The study seeks to classify television violence and looks at violence in all television genres. Revised for publication as *National Television Violence Study.* Thousand Oaks, Calif.: Sage Publications, 1996.

Pearl, David, Lorraine Bouthilet, and Joyce Lazar, eds. *Television and Behavior: Ten Years of Scientific Progress and Implications for the Eighties,* 2 Vols. Washington, D.C.: U.S. Department of Health and Human Services, 1982. National Institute of Mental Health study that is presented as a companion and update of the Surgeon General's Report of 1972. Volume I offers summary reports of the findings. Volume II contains technical reviews and research reports.

Schramm, Wilbur, Jack Lyle, and Edwin B. Parker. *Television in the Lives of Our Children.* Stanford, Calif.: Stanford University Press, 1961. First major American study into effects of television on children. Points to children as the actors in the relation between television and viewers, citing that children use television, not vice versa.

Television and Growing Up: The Impact of Televised Violence. Washington, D.C.: U.S. Government Printing Office, 1972. Companion volume to the five-volume Surgeon General's Report. Draws out summaries and conclusions from the studies.

Withey, Stephen B., and Ronald P. Abeles, eds. *Television and Social Behavior: Beyond Violence and Children.* Hillsdale, N.J.: Lawrence Erlbaum, 1980. Studies by the Social Science Research Council into television and behavior. Work contains a number of chapters on television and race portrayals and on television's potential for racism.

Articles

Bogart, Leo. "Warning: The Surgeon General Has Determined That TV Violence Is Moderately Dangerous to Your Child's Mental Health." *Public Opinion Quarterly* 36 (1972): 491-521. Response to the 1972 Surgeon General's Report by a researcher who was "black-balled" by networks from doing research for the report.

Feshbach, Seymour. "The Stimulating vs. Cathartic Effects of a Vicarious Aggressive Experience." *Journal of Abnormal and Social Psychology* 63 (1961): 381-5. Proposes the cathar-sis theory of media effects, which states that frustrations and violent behavior are relieved by vicariously watching media violence.

Goldberg, Marvin E., and Gerald J. Gorn. "Some Unintended Consequences of TV Advertising to Children." *Journal of Consumer Research* 5 (1978): 22-9. Study of preschoolers to determine potential side effects of product advertising. Researchers suggest these include parent-child conflict and unhappy children.

Guttman, Monika. "A Kinder, Gentler Hollywood." *U.S. News and World Report* (9 May 1994): 38-46. *U.S. News* and UCLA survey of national and Hollywood perceptions of visual media. Important because Congress has used the findings of the study for much of its subsequent action.

Maccoby, Eleanor E. "Television: Its Impact on School Children." *Public Opinion Quarterly* 15 (1951): 421-44. Early study into television's effects on children. Looks at items such as homework time and the supper hour. Suggests television and fairy tales serve similar purposes, but television deserves further study to determine its long-range effects.

Malamuth, N. M. And B. Spinner. "A Longitudinal Content Analysis of Sexual Violence in the Best-Selling Erotica Magazines." *Journal of Sex Research* 16 (1980): 226-37. Looks at major erotica magazines over a five-year period. Focuses on increases in depictions of bondage, rape, and sadism in the magazines in the mid-1970s and potential effects of these depictions.

Morgan, M., A. Alexander, J. Shanahan, and C. Harris. "Adolescents, VCRs, and the Family Environment." *Communication Research* 17 (1990): 83-106. Study of three items above that concludes that television can exert an independent influence on adolescents. It also demonstrates that other factors such as the activity of families can also influence viewing.

Tulloch, Marian I. "Evaluating Aggression: School Students' Responses to Television Portrayals of Institutionalized Violence." *Journal of Youth and Adolescence* 24 (1995): 95-116. Study of students ages 9-16 on situational responses to televised violence. Concludes that age, gender, and social backgrounds affect responses to that violence.

Chapter Two

Media Influences on Traditional Values

Judith M. Buddenbaum

Americans have a love-hate relationship with their media.

In the typical American home, the television set is turned on for at least six hours every day. Millions of people read the most popular books, magazines and newspapers. New movies and videos can gross upward of $20 million in a single week; records, CDs and cassettes routinely go platinum. Computers and the accompanying modems and software that allow internet access have been among the hottest selling items at Christmas for several years running.

At the same time, people complain endlessly about the content of the media they so regularly turn to for information and entertainment. Four out of every five people who responded to a 1993 Times-Mirror survey said there is too much violence on television. A similar number said there is too much sex. Those concerns are not limited to television. In a 1994 survey, the average grade top leaders from churches representing all Christian traditions gave all mass media was a D for the quality of the entertainment they provide. The average grade for news coverage was only slightly better: a D+.

During the 1992 election campaign, Republican vice-presidential candidate Dan Quayle made headlines with his speech accusing the producers of the popular "Murphy Brown" television show of undermining traditional morality with a story line involving the lead character's out-of-wedlock pregnancy. Four years later, traditional and family values and the role of the media in upholding or undermining them were no longer just a conservative or Republican issue. As presidential candidates, both Bob Dole and Bill Clinton bashed the media. In Congress Republicans and Democrats joined together to pass legislation, which Clinton signed into law, mandating v-chips and some kind of warning labels for television programs. 1996 also saw passage of the Communications Decency Act in response to public concern about internet access to sexually oriented material.

To sociologists such as James Davison Hunter, such expressions of displeasure are evidence of a culture war. That war is often described as one being waged between those intent on upholding traditional values and an amoral media industry that, by accident or by design, would destroy them.

Origins of the Issue

But if the rhetoric about a culture war is new, the concern for media effects is not. Americans have always been highly suspicious of the media; they have always worried most about the newest and most popular media, especially when they are accessible to and enjoyed by women or children.

In colonial New England, clergy warned their flocks about the dangers inherent in music, dance and works of fiction. In the latter half of the nineteenth century, popular women's magazines routinely cautioned readers about the harmful effects of fiction on the delicate female psyche. In the 1950s Dr. Frederic Wertham, a noted New York psychiatrist, claimed comic books had practically taken over the minds of children. His book, *Seduction of the Innocent*, fueled a public outcry; Congress investigated. Wertham's testimony before a Senate subcommittee led the comic industry to develop a code to head off government regulation. Forty years later the Parents Music Resource Center headed by Tipper Gore, wife of Vice President Al Gore, focused enough attention on popular music lyrics to persuade many music companies to adopt voluntary labeling.

Since their inception, both the broadcasting and film industry have had their critics; the criticism has fueled periodic attempts at regulation. On April 21, 1926, during a campaign to mandate movie review boards, the *New York Evening Sun* quoted the Rev. William Sheafe Chase, superintendent of the International Reform Federation and vice-president of the National Civic League, as saying:

> The unregulated motion picture screen has been the school of crime in every country of the world for twenty-five years. It has ridiculed marriage and the holiness of pure sex relations, the sacredness of the home and obedience to father and mother. It has advocated theft, gambling and disrespect for law. It has justified divorce, free love and violation of the Volstead Act, and of all laws.

If that language is virtually indistinguishable from the complaints heard today, so too is George Bernard Shaw's concern, quoted in the *New York Times* a month later, about the lack of attention to any undesirable qualities other than salaciousness.

Whereas Europeans have historically considered violence the true obscenity, Americans have always been more concerned about sexually oriented material. Anthony Comstock returned from military service during the Civil War to lead the battle that resulted in making American obscenity law the most restrictive in the Western world for almost a century. Although American obscenity law today is much more consistent with that of other Western nations, the 1996 Communications Decency Act picked up language from the old Comstock laws in an effort to remove from the internet any text, graphic or sound that was "lewd, lascivious, or filthy," any information about abortions or any that would tell how to make or obtain drugs or anything else for "indecent or immoral use."

The U.S. Supreme Court ruled such sweeping content restrictions to be an unconstitutional abridgement of protected speech. The American Civil Liberties Union and the American Library Association, which had brought the case to court, applauded the decision. Others were appalled. The Christian Coalition, among others, denounced the "godless court" for what it characterized as a continuing assault on the nation's Christian heritage and its traditional moral values.

As the different reactions to the Communications Decency Act suggest, not everyone sees media or media content as threatening. Even those who firmly believe the media can undermine people's values may disagree with each other over the nature of the problem and its solution. People with similar religious and political beliefs fall into different camps and sometimes have opinions that place them in several simultaneously. Allied groups often have diametrically opposed religious or political beliefs, yet share the same basic opinion about the effect of media on values.

Those complexities and ambiguities make it difficult to identify "sides" in any debate about mass media and values. Nevertheless, it is possible to separate concerned parties into those who believe the media effectively uphold cultural values and those who believe the media pose a threat to traditional values. It is also appropriate to consider the views of those who produce and distribute the material for which they are so often criticized.

The Media Uphold Traditional Values

This is a true minority opinion. Some people of color and others whose ideologies place them outside the political or religious mainstream accept it, although they rarely speak out in ways that make them part of any public debate. Instead, this viewpoint is most often articulated by members of the academic community who examine the production of culture.

From this perspective, the media appear to be part of the power structure. Because of the industry's relationship to political, economic and religious elites, media content supports the status quo by reinforcing the ideals of individual autonomy and personal responsibility, the democratic and capitalist political and economic structure and the Judeo-Christian religious beliefs and values that undergird them.

The most strident proponents of this perspective see the media as agents of cultural imperialism. The American Marxist Herbert I. Schiller, for example, argues that the introduction of American movies and televisions into Third World cultures led inevitably to the adoption of American values in politics and lifestyle. Similarly, the Latin American critic Luis Beltran argues that American television programming supports the values of "individualism, elitism, racism, materialism, providentialism, authoritarianism, romanticism and aggressiveness" that are more in line with U.S. norms and interests than they are with those of developing nations. Because they see such effects happening in foreign countries, these critics see no reason to doubt that the basic effect of mass media in America is to undergird the democratic-capitalist system and to promote the kind of individualism and competitive spirit that democracy and capitalism require.

But if this line of argument is essentially Marxist, it would be a mistake to think that only those who are Marxist see the media as upholding American values. Quentin Schultze, a professor of communication at Calvin College and committed Christian who often writes for Christian audiences, has made similar arguments. According to Schultze,

> Television is the most popular mythology of a diverse people, so it tends to confirm those beliefs common to the masses. We watch television, in part, expecting to have our beliefs confirmed.... We assume the good guys will win and the bad guys will be brought to justice. We also anticipate that the goodness of human beings will be evident, as in the reconciliation among characters at the end of a situation comedy.

While acknowledging that television is sometimes "at odds with what many of us know to be the truth," Schultze argues that, in general, television creates and reinforces myths that are consistent with core Christian beliefs because the culture itself is rooted in Christianity.

Others, who would not be comfortable seeing themselves or their analysis labeled either Marxist or Christian, make similar points. J. Herbert Altschull calls the media "agents of power." In his book by that name, Altschull contends that all media reflect the core values of the political and economic system in which they operate. Three of his "seven laws of journalism" state:

- In all press systems, the news media are agents of those who exercise political and economic power....

- The content of the news media always reflects the interests of those who finance the press....

- Schools of journalism transmit ideologies and value systems of the society in which they exist and inevitably assist those in power to maintain their control of the news media.

In his book *Unsecular Media*, Mark Silk makes the case that news stories can be classified into a limited number of "topois" or themes that are drawn from the dominant religion and that support its values. Although the religion portrayed by the media is not always Christian, others would agree with Silk's contention that the general tendency of the media is to support conventional Christian religiosity and the values it fosters. Sociologists of religion such as David Bromley and Anson Shupe find the media consistently present non-Christian religions as false and dangerous. Like the research team of Richard V. Ericson, Patricia M. Baranek and Janet B.L. Chan, they contend that the media police the boundary between the acceptable and the unacceptable.

Where others see news stories of crime, immorality and other kinds of "deviance" as harmful, Ericson, Baranek and Chan see them as a mechanism for social control. "[W]e no longer parade deviants in the town square or expose them to the carnival atmosphere of Tyburn," according to the authors. Instead, "newspapers (and now radio and television) offer their readers the same kind of entertainment once supplied by public hangings or the use of stocks and pillories." They point out that the bulk of modern news coverage concerns crime and punishment. These stories "constitute our main source of information about the normative contours of society. In a figurative sense, at least, morality and immorality meet at the public scaffold, and it is during this meeting that the community declares where the line between them should be drawn."

From this perspective, the mass media do not threaten traditional values. As Ericson, Baranek and Chan point out in their book *Visualizing Deviance*, the media draw on key establishment sources for their information; they accept the labels those sources use and their framing of stories and thus publicize and promote what the "spokespersons within the hierarchy of credibility" consider appropriate reactions to behaviors. In the process, the media fulfill what Schultze describes as a "prophetic function." Through the totality of their content and through individual instances of "sensationalism," the media call people both to repent and return to core values and also to change those things that are inconsistent with them.

The Media Undermine Traditional Values

This is the dominant position. However, even those most vocal in their complaints about the media differ in their perceptions of the problem. On the basis of their preferred solution to it, they can appropriately be divided into two camps. "Exclusionists" would like to see the content they find threatening made unavailable. "Inclusionists" would allow objectionable content to be part of the marketplace of ideas, but they would like to decrease both its prevalence and its availability to those who might be harmed.

The Exclusionist Perspective: Whereas members of the academic community are the most public proponents of the view that the media support traditional values, those who believe that some media content is so threatening that it should not be available see intellectuals, along with journalists and the entertainment industry, at the root of the problem. To them, the "information elite" is, at best, out of touch with and indifferent to mainstream values. At worst, it is opposed to those values and intent on replacing them with an "anything goes" mentality promoted under the guise of claims to freedom of speech and press. Therefore, they see themselves engaged in a war to defend their culture from the forces that would destroy everything they hold dear.

As evidence that there is a culture war, and to buttress their claim to an enemy, they often quote almost verbatim from *Elites in Conflict: Social Change in America Today* by Stanley Rothman, S. Robert Lichter and Linda Lichter: "The cultural establishment, which includes academics, the creative elite of television and motion pictures, and the leaders of the new public interest groups, are more liberal and alienated from traditional institutions and values than are traditional elites...." Although exclusionists are more likely to be conservative Protestant clergy than social science researchers, they often turn to the work of Rothman, Lichter and Lichter to support their claims about the media. In an interview published in the book *Religious Television: Controversies and Conclusions*, the conservative Methodist minister Donald E. Wildmon, who for at least twenty years has been among the most vocal proponents of the belief that movies, network television entertainment programs and their advertisers are in the business of promoting "sex, violence and profanity," is quoted as saying that "after monitoring television for 11 years and after reading the Lichter, Lichter and Rothman Report — which said that the most striking finding in their study was that the people who controlled television want to reshape society in their own image — that confirmed every conclusion I reached but was hesitant to say because it sounded so extreme."

In most cases, exclusionists' criticisms about media content are based on the underlying fear that the content undermines parental and religious authority, promotes disrespect for traditional and orthodox conceptions of God and the Bible, and encourages casual acceptance of moral relativism. They voice concern about implicit or explicit messages in movies, popular music, rock concerts, music videos, the news media, advertising, the Public Broadcasting System, the National Endowment for the Arts and, most recently, the internet.

However, much of their concern centers on television because it comes into the home. In his 1985 book, *Home Invaders*, Wildmon argues that, because of television, "the organized church in America faces the greatest threat to its existence since our country was founded.... There is an intentional effort among many of the leaders of our media to reshape our society, to replace the Christian view of man as our foundation with the humanist view of man."

In their calls to "clean up the media," exclusionists often focus on individual instances of objectionable content: a single medium, a particular genre, a piece of information, story line, character or episode they find objectionable. Over one hundred television programs ranging from "Alf" and "All in the Family" to "Wonder Years" and the "World of Disney" have come under attack. Wildmon claimed a cartoon that showed Mighty Mouse smelling a flower depicted "drug-enhanced exhilaration" and that the television movie "Flesh and Blood" promoted incest.

To highlight the danger, exclusionists sometimes cite findings from social science research, especially that of the Family Research Council. However, just as often, they use anecdotal evidence. As illustrated by Wildmon's argument that viewing "Exorcist II" caused one child to kill another, the underlying concern is that "stories about" and "promotion of" are synonymous, and that learning about something necessarily leads to accepting and doing.

"I'm all for labels. I want to know what's in the things I eat," Cal Thomas wrote in one of his 1997 syndicated newspaper columns. "But," he continued, "most television has become like cigarettes. The content is so poisonous that labeling the product does nothing to help those who are irresponsible enough to ingest it." Wildmon has also equated television content with cancer.

To prevent people from contracting that "cancer," exclusionists want to rid the media of content they deem objectionable before it can do further harm. Their preferred strategy has been one of grass-roots organization and mobilization.

Using religious television and radio programs and magazines such as *Focus on the Family* to spread the word, and then working through local congregations and chapters of organizations such as the Eagle Forum, the Moral Majority and, more recently, the Christian Coalition to mobilize people at the local level, they have mounted letter-writing campaigns and boycotts aimed directly at producers, distributors and corporate sponsors. They have also engaged in political activities designed to elect leaders who will appoint judges or commissioners to the Federal Communications Commission who share their views.

Although conservative Christians have been in the forefront of those efforts, it would be a mistake to think that they are the only ones who want to "clean up the media" by ridding it of content they believe is a threat to traditional values. The movie critic Michael Medved, who is Jewish, holds similar views. Chapter titles in his book *Hollywood v. America* claim the movie industry is guilty of "forgetting the faithful," "promoting promiscuity," "maligning marriage," "encouraging illegitimacy" and "bashing America," among other things.

The same kind of opinions can also be seen in the speeches and writings of political leaders. Senators Jesse Helms and Orrin Hatch, who have long opposed federal funding for the National Endowment for the Arts and for public television, have been leaders in attempts to ban indecent programming from radio and television. Senator James Exon was largely responsible for drafting the Communications Decency Act of 1996.

Concern about the effects of pornography prompted President Richard Nixon to reject the findings of the first presidential commission on obscenity and pornography and appoint a new one to further investigate the problem. The Meese Commission found some evidence of harm. Those findings produced new allies for religious and political conservatives in their battle against "smut." Feminist attorneys and law professors Andrea Dworkin and Catharine MacKinnon developed the argument that pornography degrades women and thus is a threat to their equality and freedom. At their urging, city councils in Minneapolis and Indianapolis passed their model ordinance making pornography illegal. Although the Minneapolis mayor vetoed the ordinance in that city, and courts found the Indianapolis one unconstitutional, Dworkin and MacKinnon have tirelessly promoted their arguments in the classroom, in law review articles, in books, and on the lecture circuit.

In the crusade to rid mass media of sexually-oriented material, religious and political conservatives and otherwise liberal feminists have become allies, but they are uneasy allies at best. Whereas the conservatives' main concern is for traditional moral values and gender roles especially within the nuclear family, the feminists' concern is for promoting equal rights for women by making their portrayal in "subservient positions" illegal. To do that, feminists advocate new laws with broader legal definitions of discrimination and more all-encompassing definitions of obscene and unprotected speech.

The Inclusionist Perspective: This may be the majority position, but it is difficult to tell. With few clear leaders and little organization, this group is less vocal than the exclusionists. Proponents are a loose amalgam of mainline or old-line

Protestants, some Catholics and others from non-Christian faiths as well as those who are truly secular. Although they share many of the same opinions about the media as the exclusionists, there are also some differences that set them apart.

Most inclusionists do not see the problem as stemming from any kind of overt attempt by the information elite to subvert traditional values. Therefore, they rarely approach the problem with the enthusiasm of the exclusionists, who argue that they are fighting a war for the soul of America. For the inclusionists, the harmful effects are generally accidental by-products of people in a pluralistic society exercising their First Amendment rights, compounded by an economic system that usually rewards media practitioners for producing shallow information and mindless entertainment.

Like the exclusionists, they complain that there is too much sex on television, in the movies, and in rock videos. But it is not sex *per se* that bothers them so much as it is "gratuitous" or "exploitative" sex. Neither do they see sexually-oriented material as the most problematic kind of content. In *Television: Manna from Hollywood?*, a book aimed at Christian parents, Quentin Schultze argues that "[s]exually related sins are not necessarily more severe than others. Our prudishness is evident in our frequent preoccupation with human sexuality and our relative disregard for sins related to greed, covetousness, and injustice," he says. "What about lying, cheating, and stealing? What about disrespect for legitimate authority? What about racism and sexism?"

Indeed, it is those latter "sins" that people in this group are usually most concerned with. Responses to a 1994 survey of church leaders' attitudes toward the media clearly indicate that clergy from Catholic and less conservative Protestant churches were more likely than those from more conservative Protestant churches to see violence, not sex, as the primary threat. They were also more likely to criticize the rampant materialism of advertisements or the stereotypical portrayals of homosexuals, unwed mothers, the poor and religious, racial and ethnic minorities.

Most inclusionists concede that content they may personally find distasteful and potentially harmful can, as Schultze argues, "perform a prophetic function" by alerting them to problems that need to be dealt with. Therefore, they are usually more willing to tolerate the existence of content they find objectionable.

Like the exclusionists, inclusionists agree that individual instances of media content — a single story, a movie, television program or rock video — may cause harm. But what they fear most is that people will casually and uncritically accept the materialism and consumerism promoted through advertising or come to consider acceptable and normal those beliefs and behaviors most commonly described in the news or shown as entertainment that poses the greatest threat to values. Therefore, their goal is not to remove all content they find offensive, but rather to promote strategies that will mitigate the agenda-setting or cultivation effects of an overabundance of commercials or of too many movies, television programs, and rock videos featuring sex and violence.

Because most people in this category want access to a wide range of information and ideas for themselves, they reject both government censorship and citizen action that could accomplish the same thing. As William Fore, the former head of the National Council of Churches argues in *Mythmakers*, they tend to believe such efforts are usually unwise and ineffective in the long run. Therefore, inclusionists rarely mount their own boycotts or join those initiated by the exclusionists even when they agree with them about the offensiveness of a movie or television program.

Instead, their preferred strategy is to promote individual and family responsibility. "If parents dogmatically refuse to allow their kids to watch various programs," argues Quentin Shultze, "the gap between the lifestyles and values of parents and children is likely to grow. But if parents and children together discuss why particular shows are unacceptable or worthwhile, both can improve their spiritual discernment and deepen their personal relationships."

Because inclusionists are not as concerned that potentially harmful content exists as they are that people attend to it uncritically and without taking personal responsibility for their reaction to it, they are also among the strongest advocates of media literacy programs and of policies that would put more information about media content into the hands of consumers. It is this concern for informed consumption that led the Parents Music Resource Center to push for labels on popular music.

Although that rating system, like the newer one for television programs, is currently a voluntary one, many inclusionists also favor political activity designed to encourage changes in media content and in the system itself. Most would, for example, applaud the kind of change-oriented policy advocacy and involvement represented by the U.S. Supreme Court case, *United Church of Christ vs. F.C.C.*, that ultimately gave citizens standing in cases involving broadcast license renewals.

However, lawsuits like the one filed by the United Church of Christ are extremely rare. More often inclusionists lobby government officials and agencies to adopt policies that could decrease the overabundance of sex and violence and increase the availability of more varied and thought-provoking fare by reducing commercial pressures on the media. They have, for example, strongly supported federal funding for public broadcasting and for the National Endowment for the Arts.

Inclusionists have also worked to persuade the Federal Communications

Commission to require television stations to provide better programming for children and to insist on better separation between program content and advertising in children's programs. Newton Minow, the Federal Communications Commissioner who first popularized the notion of television as a "wasteland," agrees that ideally "[p]arents should monitor their children's viewing and, whenever possible, watch television with them," but he also argues that Congress should "explicitly define the Communications Act's 'public interest' standard in terms of broadcasters' service to children."

Although individuals and groups allied with the inclusionist camp have been among the leading proponents of government regulation, they have usually been quite careful to respect the right of adults to receive material they need and want. Action for Children's Television, which produces "Sesame Street," challenged the constitutionality of a total ban on "indecent" television programs, even though it has been among the most consistent supporters of legislation designed to protect children and to encourage production of "quality" programs for them.

Similarly, many inclusionists favor legislation mandating a V-chip in all new television sets; they have also supported the parts of the 1996 Communications Decency Act that would restrict children's access to sexually explicit material and that would protect them from sexual exploitation. However, just as healthcare providers and average subscribers protested bitterly when America On-Line temporarily banned use of the word "breast" on computer bulletin boards and in chat-rooms, many also opposed the part of the Hatch Amendment that had the potential for restricting adult access to medical information and to other non-obscene adult content.

The Media Response

To think of a media response is to mistake the media for a monolith. However, it probably is fair to say that most media professionals are equally uncomfortable with the idea that the media uphold the status quo and with the belief that the media are so threatening to traditional values that restrictions should be imposed. Most creative people simply do not like to see themselves as anybody's "tool." They are highly suspicious of those who believe it is writers' and producers' duty to support or promote anyone else's values. Instead, media professionals prefer to see themselves simply as contributors to the marketplace of ideas the First Amendment was intended to protect.

Like Jessamyn West, the Quaker author of *Friendly Persuasion*, they believe the news media and those who work in the entertainment industry "should be the eyes of the public, [seeing] as much as possible and [reporting] as fully and as meaningfully as [their] talents permit." West believes that any lesser role for the media is wasteful. "When the artist is made to scamp his proper work by the pressure of the community," she writes, "it is as if the community willingly lopped off a finger or bound up one eye."

Individual writers or entertainers, acting as the "eyes of the public," may have an agenda. However, as screenwriter and producer Bob Gale points out, people who work for the media "are of all types, diverse in our politics, our taste, our values our sense of what is entertainment, our religious backgrounds, our regional backgrounds, our education, our age." With such diversity, Gale argues that the media are not out to support or destroy anyone's values. Because the industry is so competitive, he contends there can be no "shared 'agenda' other than capitalism."

But that shared agenda does make the media somewhat responsive to the kind of concerns embodied in public debate over the media's effect on values. As businesses, the media cannot abide too much public controversy about their offerings. Letter-writing campaigns and boycotts or threatened boycotts convinced the Southland Corporation, owner of the 7-11 convenience stores, to stop selling *Playboy* and *Penthouse*. Networks have killed television programs, and local stations sometimes refuse to air some programs or insist on editing others. Movie theaters in Lexington, Kentucky, and elsewhere refused to show *The Last Temptation of Christ*. Choosing to sell only material it considers "family friendly," WalMart refuses to stock many popular cassettes and CDs unless the lyrics and album covers meet with the corporation's approval; Blockbuster generally does not stock adult or unrated movies.

But pressures from the public and from major distributors coupled with the market forces that require producing content that will deliver large audiences with the proper demographics to advertisers also make those who produce information and entertainment nervous. Therefore, the industry often finds itself joining with inclusionists in support of public funding for the arts and for public broadcasting. As a protective measure, the industry sometimes also supports the kind of labeling and government regulatory efforts inclusionists favor.

Resolution

It might seem the question of mass media effects on people's values is one that could be settled with empirical evidence, but there is evidence to support all sides. Even where evidence seems to favor one over the other, the correlations are never perfect. There are always the exceptions that can be used to buttress a claim.

Those who argue that the media support traditional values base their conclusion primarily on macro-level analysis. At the systems level, there is evidence that most media content reflects the political and economic interests of the power structure. The rest may be little more than the safety valve that keeps threats to the system in check.

But whatever the effect at the macro level may be, those who see the media as undermining values are more concerned about people than political and economic systems. Although they, too, sometimes make the mistake of inferring effects from content and of mistaking correlations for causation, they are right when they contend that messages do have consequences. Copycat crimes sometimes happen. Over time media emphasis on certain themes almost certainly does have a cultivation or agenda-setting effect. However, it is also true that people respond differently to the same message.

The Disney studio is known for making "wholesome" movies, but some people complained about *Pocahontas* because they thought it portrayed her as a New Age environmentalist instead of as a convert to Christianity; others complained that the movie was another instance of Disney films stereotyping women as longing for and needing a strong man to rescue them. When William Bennett, who was Secretary of Education and director of the Office of National Drug Control Policy under Presidents Ronald Reagan and George Bush, tried to redress the decline in values he perceived by publishing his *Book of Virtues*, a reviewer for *Christian Century* complained that he left out the virtues of tolerance and compassion; when he adapted chapters in his book for television, a writer for the conservative Christian news magazine, *World*, fretted because the tales of virtue were not taken from the Bible.

As those reactions suggest, resolving the debate over media and values to anyone's total satisfaction may be impossible, but it may at least be possible to reduce the rancor. Concerns about the media and media effects on values should be and must be raised. The different positions on the nature of the problem, its causes and the appropriate remedies need to be heard, understood, and taken seriously by everyone.

But all sides need to remember that as long as there are media, there will be media content and that content must necessarily be about something. In a pluralistic society differences over what that "something" should be and how the "something" should be told are almost inevitable. Therefore, the safest course may lie in encouraging individual responsibility: the media for thinking carefully about the potential effects of the material they provide and the public for the material they attend to and their response to it. Anything else invites abrogating core First Amendment values without which such a debate over media content and its effects on people's values would be both meaningless and impossible.

Recommended Readings

Books

Ball-Rokeach, Sandra, Milton Rokeach and Joel W. Grube, *The Great American Values Test: Influencing Behavior and Belief through Television*. New York: The Free Press, 1984. Reports the results of a field experiment designed to test the effects of a single television program on people's values.

Beahm, George, ed. *War of Words: The Censorship Debate*. Kansas City: Andrews and McMeel, 1993. The general thrust is anti-censorship, but this volume is noteworthy for the inclusion of different perspectives, including those of Kurt Vonnegut, James A. Michenor, Ray Bradbury, Frank Zappa, Jack Valenti, Phyllis Schlafley, Jerry Falwell and Jesse Helms.

Bennett, William J. *The De-Valuing of America: The Fight for our Culture and Our Children*. New York: Touchstone, 1992. Describes a decline in moral values, outlines Bennett's views on the cause of the problem, and explains what he thinks still needs to be done.

Falwell, Jerry. *Listen America*. New York: Doubleday, 1980. This early book by the televangelist critiques American culture and explains the conservative religious remedy for declining values.

Fore, William F. *Mythmakers: Gospel, Culture and the Media*. New York: Friendship Press, 1990. Overview of the problem and the appropriate remedies from the inclusionist perspective. The author is the former president of the National Council of Churches of Christ.

Hunter, James Davison. *Culture Wars: The Struggle to Define America*. New York: Basic Books, 1990. The classic analysis of the sources of the moral and cultural conflict confronting America. Chapter 9 deals specifically with the battle to control the mass media.

Medved, Michael. *Hollywood vs. America: Popular Culture and the War on Traditional Values*. New York: HarperCollins, 1992. In this highly influential book, the noted movie critic makes the case that traditional values are under assault from a media industry that is out of touch with and largely hostile to mainstream America.

Minow, Newton N., and Craig L. LaMay. *Abandoned in the Wasteland: Children, Television and the First Amendment*. New York: Hill and Wang, 1995. The former chairman of the Federal Communications Commission presents the case for government policies and for media literacy programs designed to protect the marketplace of ideas while decreasing the potential for harm to children and other vulnerable groups.

Schiller, Herbert I. *Mass Communications and American Empire*. Boston: Beacon Press. 1969. This early work is one of many in which Schiller makes the case that media cultural imperialism promotes and re-enforces the American political and economic order.

Schultze, Quentin. *Television: Manna from Hollywood?* Grand Rapids, Mich.: Zondervan, 1986. Takes a closer look at the values propagated by individual programs and genres and the steps parents can take to mitigate media effects.

Suman, Michael, ed. *Religion and Prime-Time Television.* Westport, Conn: Praeger, 1997. Focuses on the debate over how the media portray religion; some chapters also address issues in the debate over media's effects on values.

Wildmon, Donald E., with Randall Nulton. *Don Wildmon: The Man the Networks Love to Hate.* Wilmore, Ky.: Bristol Books, 1989. This account of Wildmon's crusade against network television presents the conservative minister as a David fighting to save America and America's traditional values from the Goliath of a media industry that would destroy them.

Articles

Beltran, Luis Ramiro. "TV Etchings in the Minds of Latin Americans: Conservatism, Materialism and Conformism." *Gazette* 24:1 (1978): 64-85. Examines the effects of imported American television programs on people's attitudes and opinions.

Denby, David. "Buried Alive: Our Children and the Culture of Crud." *New Yorker*, 16 July 1996, 48-58. Captures the dilemma faced by parents who value freedom of expression, yet welcome the V-chip because they feel a need to limit their children's access to the media if they are to pass their own values on to their children.

Dworkin, Andrea. "Against the Male Flood: Censorship, Pornography and Equality." *Harvard Women's Law Journal* 8 (Spring 1987): 1-29. Argues that pornography should be treated as a violation of women's civil rights.

Elshtain, Jean Bethke. "The New Porn Wars." *The New Republic* 190 (June 25, 1984): 15-20. The noted political philosopher analyzes the uneasy alliance between feminists and religious conservatives who would make pornography illegal, in the process addressing the strengths and weaknesses of their arguments as well as those of their opponents.

Schultze, Quentin J. "Television Drama as Sacred Text." Pp. 3-28 in John P. Ferré, ed., *Channels of Belief: Religion and American Commercial Television.* Ames, Iowa: Iowa State University Press, 1990. Argues that, taken as a whole, media entertainment is consistent with core cultural values.

Chapter Three

TV as a Reflection of American Morés

Val E. Limburg

Early in the history of broadcasting, before television was a glimmer in the networks' eyes, and when some people thought that broadcasting would never work because it couldn't keep its messages private, radio programs were still considered "guests" in families' homes. Those responsible for radio programs defined entertainment as light music performed by studio musicians. Soon there crept into the programming mix those who gave medical advice over the air, astrologers, fortune tellers and religious preachers. By the early 1930s, formats began to appear that were constant day-to-day, or week-to-week. Most notable were melodramas fantasizing romantic adventures. Eventually, their sponsorship by household cleansing products earned them the name of "soap operas." These serial dramas recounted the encounters of families in their relationships, or romance, usually in their most benign form, among other themes.

As radio drama moved through mysteries and other action drama, themes of crime became more explicit and suggestive. By the time television came along, popular radio programs included *Gangbusters, Dragnet* and *The FBI.* At the time, some thought the crime stories were too explicit. But later when they were laid out in the new visual medium of television, scenes of horror seemed even more troublesome. In the following generations, viewers' appetites for such scenes increased. Violence, coupled with language and sexual descriptions, established new standards and popularity of such programs.

Despite several Congressional hearings on violence in television, and the commissioning of the Surgeon General to report on TV and social behavior, concern about its extensive presence continues, as does concern about language and adult themes of sexuality. Such thematic values move forward in programs, often faster than the social morés they supposedly reflect.

Several questions guide the arguments on this issue of shifting values as reflected in television programming: Why are there claims of value shifts? Haven't there always been controversial and daring new values reflected in novels, comics, movies, radio, and television? Who holds the traditional values, and why are they outraged? What are their values? Who represents the values seen in the media today? What values appear to have shifted? How do we know there have been shifts? What are the moves being done to fight the shifts? What are the positions of those moving forward with ever more daring themes? And finally, are there any standards, "public morals," or any measuring base against which to judge the movement of values in today's programming?

This article examines the values in TV programming, their history, turning points, viewpoints, and rating points. Lastly, there is an examination of how this all relates to the values of major social streams.

Origins of the Issue

Changing values can only really be assessed in historical context. What was popular to our grandparents' generation isn't even on today's scene. What was unacceptable to our parents may be a major part of today's popular culture.

For example, in 1954 the Television Code of the National Association of Broadcasters stated "Respect is maintained for the sanctity of marriage and the value of the home." Such respect was reflected in programs such as *Father Knows Best, Leave It to Beaver,* and *Ozzie and Harriet.* Compare that with more recent programs such as *Married with Children* or *Rosanne.*

This 1954 code of good practice also warned broadcasters to avoid "the presentation of techniques of crime in such detail as to invite imitation." Critics of today's TV, including politicians, parents' groups, and religious organizations, would argue that the medium is abundant with such episodes. In 1954 there was a long list of taboos of subjects or depictions for TV programming, most of which are no longer of concern to most observers, except to note the ethical distance traveled since that era. For example, there were not to be depictions of the following:

- administration of illegal drugs
- gambling
- simulation of news events that may be misleading
- dramatized medical advice that may be mistaken as legitimate
- criminality that may be depicted as sympathetic
- the use of horror for its own sake
- derision of law enforcement
- justifiable murder
- acceptable suicide
- exposition of sex crimes

Needless to say, many of these elements are commonly found in today's TV programming. Discussion of the values that would determine the ethical dimensions of such changes — whether they're good or bad, proper or improper, acceptable or unacceptable — guides this discussion.

Another dimension of change to consider is the place of entertainment in our society. Amusing ourselves is easy with the television in our homes. But it's only entertainment, a passive kind of thing in our environment. Should we even worry that it ought to be subject to ethics analysis? In considering this question, media ethicist Clifford Christians cites anthropologist Robert Redfield, who served on the Hutchins Commission of 1949. Redfield argued for "the interdependency of social institutions (like the media) and social beliefs (like the sanctity of life). Yes, he would argue, the entertainment media must be put to the test of ethical reasoning."

In earlier times, to "entertain" was to hold someone's attention or to keep guests occupied — from the Latin *tenere*, to hold or to keep. A good host entertained guests. Such efforts were diversions from everyday life. Part of entertainment was to be amused — from the middle French amuser, to cause to waste time or divert attention. Thus, the etymological basis tells us something of the place of entertainment and amusement. Later, in colonial times, the "Protestant work ethic" was articulated: the idea that work was virtuous and that wasting time was evil. Idle hands were considered tools in the Devil's workshop. Or, as Isaac Watts penned,

> *For Satan finds some mischief still*
> *For idle hands to do.*

Work and the avoidance of too much idle time continued to be a dominant value in American society throughout the nineteenth century. By the end of that century, the Industrial Revolution had given Americans more time away from their traditional work setting. Leisure activities emerged: baseball, pulp novels, more staged dramas, and whatever else filled the time. Kinetoscope parlors and then movie houses occupied people with illusions of reality. Radio came along in the later 1920s, and by the mid 1930s was an important part of Americans' use of leisure time. That medium was seen at first as a "guest" in the listener's home, and accorded all the respect and honor to its host or hostess that an actual guest would in a friend's home. Much of that thinking was carried over to television.

The television industry, through the National Association of Broadcasters, stated in the Preamble to the 1954 Television Code: "It is the responsibility of television to bear constantly in mind that the audience is primarily a home audience and consequently that television's relationship to the viewers is that between guest and host." Generally, the values reflected a concern and "accountability to the American public for the respect for the special needs of children, for community responsibility, for the advancement of education and culture, for the acceptability of the program materials chosen, for decency and decorum in production, and for propriety in advertising."

However, as society changed, values changed. Concerns that were once primary to the programming themes of television drifted away, and new themes were found in programming, new themes that countered earlier, more traditional values.

Such is the context for the arguments involved in the ethics of television programming. But there are some aspects of programming that are especially offensive to those holding to more traditional values. And there are themes that more progressive observers feel ought to reflect real society. These themes offer two sides for study, one of the "traditionalist" and one of the "progressive." Long have their differences been evident:

> *Historic continuity with the past is not a duty, it is only a necessity .*
> — O.W. Holmes, Jr.

> *Tradition means giving votes to the most obscure of all classes —*
> *our ancestors. It is the democracy of the dead.*
> — G.K. Chesterton

In this discussion, four issues are examined: violence, sexual situations, language, and the media's advisory role.

Violence — the Traditionalist View

In childhood, innocence is marked by the absence of violence. Violence against children and child abuse are among the most abhorrent crimes. Concern for the problem of violence has driven social science research, the literature of which contains hundreds of studies demonstrating how children exposed to mediated violence (e.g., film and television) become "desensitized."

Some researchers, such as Albert Bandura, have devoted much of their professional careers to demonstrating the dangers of exposing children to violence and the subsequent aggressive behavior — even long-term carry-over behavior that is anti-social and often illegal. Bandura began his experimental laboratory research in the early 1960s, publishing in psychology journals, culminating in his 1977 theoretical treatise, *Social Learning Theory*. This theory, demonstrated in his research, was that children learn their personalities, including aggressive aspects, from experiences with peers, family, culture, and mediated sub-culture, such as that found on television. Children's modeling actions from seeing others' inter-actions could evoke novel behavior, including aggression and violence, thus playing a unique and striking role in a child's social development.

In the early 1970s, the U.S. Surgeon General's Scientific Advisory Committee on Television and Social Behavior reviewed all existing research, and filled in the gaps by commissioning further research on the subject. The resulting seven volumes of findings were summarized by then-Surgeon General Jesse Steinfeld, who reported that "televised violence indeed does have an adverse effect on certain members of our society." He went on to say that while most human behavior research is never absolute and certain, "[t]here comes a time when the data are sufficient to justify action. That time has come."

Some observers, such as William Bennett, cite FBI records that show that violent crime in the United States has risen from *16.1 episodes per 10,000 in 1960 to 75.8 per 10,000 in 1991.* Bennett relates that increase with television's growing fascination with violence. Further, the National Coalition on Television Violence reported in 1994 that by age eighteen, the American teenager will have wit-nessed 200,000 violent acts on TV, including 40,000 murders.

Social scientists such as Andison (1977), Hearold (1986), and Dorr and Kovaric (1980) have all done exhaustive surveys of the research literature, concluding that television violence seems to be capable of affecting viewers of both sexes and varying ages, social classes, ethnicities, and levels of usual aggressiveness. Extent of effects depends on how heavily television is viewed and acculturation to aggressive tactics.

These and other observers who read study after study seem to become con-vinced that exposure to the violence programmed on television today does indeed affect children, the socially maladjusted, and perhaps all of us, usually in subtle and undesirable ways for most families. Television, they argue, is creating a value system and a cultural ethic unwanted in home and in society.

Violence — the Progressive View

It is argued by other social scientists as well as those in the media that since violence is all around us, it is simplistic to attach blame to any single factor in a person's life. In response to the Surgeon General's Report, Robert Kaplan and Robert Singer, both respected researchers, noted:

"Instead of castigating (TV), it might be more useful to ask why the public is so fascinated by programs portraying violence. We would like to suggest investigations into the connections between violence and unemployment, racial prejudice, poor housing and lack of medical care, the prevalence of guns and the ease of obtaining alcohol, the high mobility of the population, the prevalence of broken families, the role of age, the still partly subservient role of women, the lack of public school courses in child-rearing, and a possibly declining faith in the just nature of our political judicial system."

Another argument against placing the blame on the media is that of Former FCC Commissioner Lee Loevinger, who poses a "Reflective–Projective" concept of media influence. In an article titled "The Ambiguous Mirror," he argues that the media are best understood as mirrors of society. Such mirroring simply reflects the ugliness of real life. The media, then, re-project such violence. The implication is that if you don't like what's reflected from the real world, turn off the TV or change the channel, but don't impose your values or ethics on others when you see the unpleasantries of real life.

While few would argue for more violence, the real question becomes "What do we do about it in a society that values freedom of expression?" Arguing about such freedoms, Justice William O. Douglas once noted in the 1957 case of *Roth v. U.S.* that "if the First Amendment guarantee of freedom of speech and press is to mean anything in the field, it must allow protests even against the moral code that the standard of the day sets for the community."

Ethics and the associated values are very personal by nature. One may not like what is on television, but someone from this camp would be concerned about the imposition of one individual's values from his or her ethics on a system, even if there are others who hold the same values. TV program producers and creators, like others expressing their rights of free speech, it would be argued, ought to have the right to depict characterizations and events that may not be in keeping with what some people would want to see.

For the media, which are basically businesses, fed by popularity and ratings, the issue seems simple enough. If violence, or any other supposedly unpopular issue, is really repugnant, let the public shun it. It will lose its popularity; ratings and thus sales and profits will drop, and the media will avoid it. Unprofitability is a terrible fate for ideas in the media. So it all falls back on the public and the individuals in the public: if viewers didn't want it, it wouldn't really be there.

An especially enigmatic problem is if one takes the position of somehow censoring or controlling content, where is the line drawn? Does a comedic fall or a pie in the face constitute "violence?" Are real life accounts of violence on the news acceptable, but fictitious depictions taboo? And, while certain forms of violence may not be suitable for small children, at what age are adolescents ready for which kinds of violence? After all, shouldn't the parents decide control in their own home, rather than have some kind of social, government or network control? That way, the lines and the values are from the family itself, rather than an external social agent. Isn't a better way of handling the situation in the form of education, to inform one's self and children about whatever evils there might be in violence and how to avoid it?

Sex — the Traditionalist View

Descriptions, discussions, and depictions of sexual situations have traditionally been reserved for the most private settings. Sexual relations are, after all, private acts. Part of the traditional social norm has been the handling of sex not only with discretion, but faithfulness to one partner, and heterosexuality. Legally our society has historically tabooed pornography, adultery, and sodomy. And while such taboos may have lost their potency, traditionalists argue that their presence doesn't make them right.

USA Today surveyed a sample week of programs and found that forty-one out of forty-five sex scenes involved couples who were not married to each other. Other surveys confirmed that observation, noting that the concern about adulterous relationship still runs strong among Americans.

Nevertheless, television programs have helped diminish the strength of these taboos by popularizing promiscuity and deriding chastity. For example, with a high percentage of teenagers among its viewers, *Beverly Hills 90210* seems to have had a profound influence on young viewers, including its one virginal character, Brenda. After years of being chaste, however, she chose to lose her virginity in the 1991 season. In an article run by the Associated Press, Shannon Doherty, who portrays Brenda, expressed concern about the episode. "I worried about how the audience would take it," she said. "I still believe there are virgins in this world — girls who want to say no. From now on they can look at my character and say, 'Wow, she's doing it, why can't we?'"

Other critics of progressive and daring themes in TV programs, such as those representing the American Family Association, are concerned about consequences bringing forth a new kind of "television morality." Their publication, *AFA Journal*, identifies programs each month that push the edge of sexual propriety. One recent issue gave reviews of twelve programs during the previous month wherein shows' characters were promiscuously sleeping with each other, or using vulgar jokes about kinky sex and scatological humor. The *Journal* continually reminds its readers that each season the popularity of such once-tabooed program themes and issues grows.

Others argue that we may be blind to our heritage and the direction from our history. Hilton Kramer, in *New Criterion*, relates "An overall decline in standards and good taste, coupled with rampant egalitarianism, has rendered Americans incapable of distinguishing between good and bad — the moral obtuseness in our cultural life."

Are we an oversexed society? And if we are, so what? Freud noted that civilization has been developed by the measure of sacrifices of sexual gratification. J.D. Unwin, in *Sexual Regulations and Cultural Behavior*, examined the sexual customs of a number of cultures, both primitive and advanced. He concluded that more sexually permissive behavior led to slower mental development, less creativity, and slower social progress. Pitirim Sorokin in his 1950 work on altruistic love also surveyed ninety cultures worldwide and found much the same thing.

William Stephens in his *Reflections on Marriage*, found that tribes made the least cultural progress when they practiced the greatest sexual freedom. Historian Arnold Toynbee likewise observed that a culture was the most conducive to progress when its young people postponed rather than stimulated sexual experience. Finally historians Will and Ariel Durant noted that sex in the young "is a river of fire that must be banked and cooled by a hundred restraints if it is not to consume in chaos both the individual and the group."

More fundamentally, AFA argues, the promotion of promiscuous sex in television programming has ultimately helped foster the spread of AIDS, sexually transmitted diseases, teen pregnancies, and generally an American obsession with sex. Television programs show that the need to be loved can be satisfied by the promises of yielding to our sexual appetites.

In their study, "Adolescents' Exposure to Television and Movie Sex," Bradley Greenberg and his colleagues studied the sexual content of the soap operas and prime-time television series most viewed by adolescents. They found that sexual intercourse occurred 1.14 times per hour and comprised 39 per cent of the coded sexual activity. Viewing of sexually oriented programs tended to feed on itself: the more one watched such programs, the more one was likely to be preoccupied with that topic, which then reinforced such viewing and so on. Viewers that frequently view sexually oriented programs tend to believe that sexual activity is more predominant in reality than those without such viewing habits.

It could be argued that when psychologists, anthropologists, sociologists, historians, communication researchers, as well as ethicists and religious leaders all seem to see the same kinds of dangers, the point is clear: they believe that television programmers should act more responsibly in the development of programs that affect our ethics and social mores.

Sex — the Progressive View

Yet others believe that the true mark of civilization is not to walk with our head turned backward but to go forward boldly, accept change, adapt, realize human potential to progress, and most of all, learn tolerance of perspective and values different from one's own. Isn't the distinguishing characteristic of an intelligent person the ability to learn to choose what works best for his or her own circumstances? One kind of ethics is individualistic ethics: "If Grandma was a virgin when she married, that's fine for her and her era, but says nothing for me."

In an extensive survey of Americans from every walk of life, sociologists James Patterson and Peter Kim found that a lot has happened to our sexual mores since the findings of Kinsey, Masters and Johnson, and Hite. We have also modified our awareness and activities since the AIDS epidemic that is now diminishing. Sex is widely available, widely practiced in all kinds of settings, and enjoyed more now than ever before. The figures gleaned by Patterson and Kim show that "the average American can expect to enjoy more sex with more partners for more years than any other people in history. By quite a lot, too." The progress of our society hasn't seemed much diminished for the wear, either. More than half of the respondents in a survey by Mel Poretz and Barry Sinrod revealed that they had experienced sex by the time they were eighteen years of age. At the same time, the survey disclosed that 69 per cent were in favor of their children marrying as virgins. Perhaps a fundamental feature of today's society is an individual's freedom of choice, including the choice for abstinence.

Of all the media, television is perhaps the most benign when it comes to displays of sexual activity. Sex is much more explicit, extensive, and popular in motion pictures and magazines. Look at the number of R-rated movies with either sexual themes or nudity. Now there's even a newer label, NC-17, which allows even more explicit material without violating the confines of the motion picture industry. Look at the popularity of *Playboy* and *Penthouse*. It should seem clear that television would be the least explicit and is perhaps the least influential in cultivating sexual activity in our society.

Educators point out that elected school boards have approved curricula that allow sex education and discussion about sex and sexuality, although this was a hush-hush activity earlier, as if even the word "sex" had embarrassed us then. Such educators concerned with future citizens argue that we can not educate about sexually transmitted diseases without explaining to adolescents the physiological and psychological nature of sex. Some inhibitions are self-destructive, and reluctance to talk about sex, or the use of sexual themes in television programs may be part of such self destruction.

Many in the progressive camp argue for an age of sexual tolerance. If an activity is somehow bad, or socially destructive, laws can be passed to penalize those who practice them. Such was the public sentiment found in 1970 studies by the Lockart Commission on Pornography: "when no ill effects are found, society should not be repressed, censorship should be avoided, the values or ethics of one group should not be forced on another, and tolerance should be practiced. Such tolerance leads to a happier, more harmonious world in which to live."

Language — the Traditionalist View

Language constructs reality for us. Words are the tools with which we recognize things, and see their virtue or vice. Language scholars such as Kenneth Burke have discussed how words evoke in us emotions or understanding. They reflect attitudes, values, principles or philosophies. Some words, when put together, create a great awareness of the spirit of human nature; such is the recognition of great literature. Authors, journalists, and other writers may achieve worldwide recognition and fame with Pulitzer Prizes or Nobel Prizes for literature. While words can build, instruct, and inspire, they can also demean, degrade, or reflect ignorance; and such is the nature of profane language.

Traditionalists argue that words once taboo in normal conversations have become acceptable, partly because of their repetition in the media, particularly in motion pictures, but increasingly in television as well. Television has always borrowed heavily from motion pictures, and the creative community of each is often the same. Recent television seasons, for example, have shown a tendency to include expletives not heard on prime-time just five years ago. Some speculate that it may have all started when in 1938 Rhett Butler told Scarlett O'Hara, "Frankly, my dear, I don't give a damn." By the 1960s more than the word "damn" was to be heard in movies. Today, a typical R-rated movie contains many words that were once forbidden in polite society.

Greenberg and his colleagues studied R-rated films viewed by adolescents in the early 1980s, and found that the most popular movies abounded with profanities. Five key words and their variants accounted for 79 per cent of all the swearing. His study went on to indicate the major words, their classification, and their lexicons. More recent research finds intensifications with respect to profanities.

Content analyses of popular music lyrics also finds extensive lexicons of profanity. But the nature of attending to either records and movies is different than with television. Television comes into the home. Its omnipresence (there's usually more than one set per household) leads to the difficulty of control by parents. Television is, after all, a guest in the home. It should not bring into the home language and standards unanticipated and unwanted by those in the home. Such is the basis of the federal regulations governing the broadcasting that imposes a penalty on "whoever utters any obscene, indecent, or profane language by means of radio communication." Later courts interpreted this wording to encompass television.

In *FCC v. Pacifica*, a New York radio station aired a monologue of comedian George Carlin in which he described "seven dirty words that can't be said on radio or television." When a parent objected because his young son heard the broadcast that aired in mid-afternoon, he took the matter to the FCC, which ruled the words to be "patently offensive" and fined the station, which then appealed. The Supreme Court found that the FCC was correct in recognizing that the broadcast was patently offensive, partly because it was aired "at a time when children were undoubtedly in the audience." The court went on to hint that airing the same program late at night in a "safe harbor" when children were much less likely to be present would be less egregious. The Court pointed out the potentially "invasive" nature of broadcasting, and recognized the right of listeners and viewers to be protected from affronting programs in broadcasting. Since law follows the ethics and norms of a society, such rights of protection seem paramount. These are the ethics of contemporary society.

There are many words that remain highly taboo, and other words that have become taboo, such as the "n" word in referring to African Americans. Such a language taboo is as much in place for progressives as for traditionalists. Still, the latter will wonder how much time will elapse before the indecent becomes acceptable, since the erosion is already clearly under way — even in the medium of television, perhaps the last media holdout.

Language — the Progressive View

It's true that language is a precursor to behavior. But just as we can't control each and every behavior of another human being, we are unable to control each word that comes from the mouth. Language scholar Malcolm Sillars argues that as society changes, our language changes. In his *Messages, Meanings, and Culture*, he traces the American value systems and the words, both positive and negative that reflect the dominant values. What was once taboo is now acceptable; changes in language may even reveal the unenlightenment or superstitions of earlier language styles. For example, words like "sex" and "pregnant" were once not used in polite society or mixed company. When the telephone was first invented, some people would not use the word "hello" to answer it because the greeting contained the word "hell." There are myriads of examples that show how language has changed. Society adapts to new styles. There are always those who dare to put forth that which is currently socially taboo, and those that hold out, perhaps as long as their lifetime.

Language is not reality, it only used to reflect each person's perception of reality. Such were the arguments of pragmatists such as George Herbert Mead, Charles Sanders Pierce, and William James, who held that truth was relative. And so was the language that constructed truth. This position might question why one person should censor another's perception and the language construction that goes with it? One may usually control his or her own children's use of words to a certain age. Then, with the onset of adulthood and a broader panorama of the world and the language that defines it, an adolescent designs his or her perceptions with less influence from parents. We move forward, sometimes to the dislike of those who face backwards to the past.

To constrain words, language, and perception is contradictory to the freedoms we enjoy in our democracy. One is still free to use or not use the words he or she wishes, but that freedom does not extend to determine what words others will use or not use.

Media's Advisory Role — the Traditionalist View

In a society that values information, advisories and warnings about media content are important. Many holding this viewpoint want to know of the changes that they must face and wonder how we can live in an educated society and be expected to take at face value the substance of the content of any media. We know what's in the food when we buy; ingredient labeling is required. When we take out a bank loan, we must sign a form saying that we understand the terms for our own protection. A new car tells us what the added options are and how much each costs. Such things have become a part of our enlightened culture, from caveat emptor, "let the buyer beware," to caveat vendor, "let the seller beware." Why, then aren't parents warned about the specifics of the content of record albums or television programs?

Several years ago, Tipper Gore, wife of then-Senator Al Gore, tried to organize and support a Parents' Music Resource Committee (PMRC), to encourage the labeling of records, warning of explicit lyrics. She was met with derision and rage from those who felt her activities were censorship. Her efforts were intended to get a law to place advisory labels on the music, just as other consumable products are labeled. Nevertheless, perceptions of any kind of censorship are red flags in our society. But the arguments of such music labeling seems logical enough to have been the basis for later federal legislation.

In 1997 the television industry adopted rating standards for its programming. At first, based on age, the ratings were: TV-Y for all children; TV-Y7 directed to older children; TV-G General audiences; TV-PG parental guidance suggested; TV-14 parents strongly cautioned; TV-M mature audience only.

That the Congressionally mandated "V-chip" and ratings system received endorsement by President Clinton and the cooperation of a huge television industry (in collaboration with the motion picture industry and some consumer groups) would seem to show that general advisory labeling was a viable and needed solution to addressing media content.

However, before the system had functioned more than a few months, there were clamors for more definitive programming content ratings to be added to advisories for age group ratings. The newer simple descriptors indicated presence of objectionable language (L), sexual situation (S), suggestive dialogue (D), and violence (V). The system and the push for modification demonstrated to many the need for such an advisory function.

Media's Advisory Role — the Progressive View

The problems associated with the judgments about what constitutes appropriate warnings about violence, sex, or language have already been discussed. These are all highly subjective issues. Violence, for example, may include harmless but comedic actions, often found in cartoons. Are these the kind of things that ought to be labeled when they have no bearing on real life? And what of sex, the most common of all human experiences? When do descriptions or depictions of sexual activities become objectionable and need to be labeled? Language varies so much that one can never be certain when a word is so widely used socially that it isn't really taboo, except to a few. So on what basis are the judgments about labeling made, and even more critically, who makes them? The government? Some kind of self-appointed censor? Private industry? Consumer committees? Might each of these have its own agenda? Might not it be better to avoid the whole labeling scenario completely? Arguments against labeling have been made by columnist Tom Wicker:

1. Such labels are in fact censorship, since they throw into a "warning" category all artistic efforts that someone might consider questionable and want to label.

2. Who is to decide what material requires a label? The artist? A record company? A retail store that sells the material? Law enforcement? A govern-

ment bureaucrat?

3. Most of the states' bills on such labeling would fine and/or imprison the retail seller, even if he or she feels very differently about the material from the artist who produced the work.

4. "Label, just to be safe" might become the policy of many retail sellers responsible for labeling; "better safe than sorry." This all-encompassing attitude might sweep in materials that are really not offensive.

5. In music, the focus is only on the lyrics, not the music. The pounding rhythms of rock music or even Ravel's crescendos in Bolero might be as prurient as any four-letter words in a lyric.

6. If labeling music lyrics and television programs seems appropriate, why not label everything in television, including news and commercials, and everything on radio, including the extemporaneous chatter of disc jockeys. Moreover, what about concerts and operas, traditionally accepted as they are?

7. Finally, labeling may mark the beginning of a whole crusade of muffling any kind of unconventional idea.

As to the idea of the TV program ratings: this attempt shows that even the best intentions of labeling — giving parents some guidelines — can go awry. Here, someone has made some judgments about the age at which a child may or may not view a program. Well intended as it is, there are some problems with this, as cited by Dale Kunkel, including the fact that use of simple categories with a word or two are a mealy milque-toast of equivocating language. Look, for example, at the language of TV-14 : "Program *may* contain some material that many parents would find unsuitable for children under 14 years of age." (Author's emphasis) Just what does that mean, and to which kinds of viewing families?

Moreover, ratings have been purposely designed to be benign because TV programmers do not want to tie them in with the issue of violence and the mandated V-chip system, requiring filtering of violent programs, a filtering that ought to be in the hands of parents anyway.

We've not yet seen the end of the dispute over ratings and advisory warnings.

Resolution

Any discussion of ethics is incomplete until there's an understanding that we can only know ethics through some kind of moral reasoning process, or some kind of ethics analysis. Such a process entails finding the values basic to the issues or ethical dilemmas. Then, from the values proceeds a discovery of the fundamental philosophy or principles of life, or *weltanschauung* (world view).

Once we know the philosophy of life from which we act, we will have discovered a lot about ourselves. More importantly, we will discover that everyone has his or her own philosophy. You may not agree with it, but it belongs to that person, and can hardly be seen as something that ought to be excised.

With the issues or ethical dilemmas cited above, values might reveal an appositional paradigm or diagraming of opposites, which may act to clarify why the fundamental positions differ. Such values identified here are extracted by a process of ethics analysis or moral reasoning, such as described by Ralph Potter in his treatise, "The Logic of Moral Argument." The result is a reasoning system known as Potter's Box. For our two opposite positions, such a paradigm might appear like this:

Values

Traditionalist
traditional, resolute, obedient, family security,
wisdom (especially learning from the past), love, compassion

Progressive
freedom, independence, broadminded, imaginative, equality,
pleasure, daring, courageous or unafraid

There are other variations: a comfortable life versus an exciting life, or security versus adventure. Some of these may seem far afield from the situations above, but they typify an outlook of life, a philosophy.

More traditional philosophical terms might refer to positions of noted thinkers. Thus, a traditionalist might refer to the Golden Rule or to Immanuel Kant's ideas about a categorical imperative to "Act on that maxim which you will to become a universal law." A progressive might reflect more the thinking of John Stuart Mill in his ideas about utilitarianism: "Seek the greatest happiness for the greatest number." Some observers might consider the question of "To whom is moral duty owed?" Is it to people created in the image of God, or is it to ideas about the equality of humanity — the need to equate and adjust, from the perspective of a specific point in time?

More historically, the arguments between traditionalists and progressives might be a question of whether we attempt to learn from the great thinkers of the past and pass on and preserve the wisdom of earlier generations, or take the wisdom of earlier generations and formulate it to suit the present and project it to the future.

It is possible, of course, that one may take a strictly deontological position in ethics. That is, people are ethically at their best when they follow good rules most faithfully. They have a duty to the past. Or, one may take a teleological position in regard to ethics. That is, one is more concerned with the ends, with the right consequences, and not so much the means used to get there. It's not as though such a person divorces him or herself from the past, but uses only those lesson from history that would have apparent good results.

When it comes down to it, one's philosophy or outlook in life and how it is applied to the complicated situations found in today's media is a highly personal experience. The important thing may be to know what one's own philosophy is, following the Socratic notion that "An unexamined life is not worth living."

Recommended Readings

Books

Bandura, Albert. *Social Learning Theory*. Englewood Cliffs, N.J.: Prentice Hall, 1977. Probes how violence, among other behavior, is learned from the media: observation, modeling, and desensitization.

Bennett, William J. *The Index of Leading Cultural Indicators*. New York: Simon & Schuster, 1994. Statistics in crime and social issues suggest a correlation to depictions of such issues in the media.

Comstock, G.A., and E. Rubinstein, eds. *Television and Social Behavior: A Technical Report to the Surgeon General's Scientific Advisory Committee on Television and Social Behavior*. Washington, D.C.: National Institute of Mental Health, 1972. A broad scientific inquiry about television and its impact on the viewer.

Sorokin, Pitirim A. *Altruistic Love: A Study of American "Good Neighbors" and Christian Saints*. Boston: Beacon Press, 1950. This nearly forgotten work came out of the Harvard Research Center in Altruistic Integration and Creativity in 1950. The author considers the social interaction among American demographics features as they relate to values.

Articles & Book Chapters

Andison, F.S. "TV Violence and viewer aggression: A culmination of study results 1956-1976." *Public Opinion Quarterly* 41 (1977): 314-31. Exhaustive overview of studies on violence conducted between 1956 and 1976.

Bandura, Albert. "Influence of models' reinforcement contingencies on the acquisition of imitative responses." *Journal of Personality and Social Psychology* 1 (1965): 589-95. Examines the peculiar characteristics that are modeled in subjects' responses to mediated examples.

Bandura, Albert, D. Ross, and S.A. Ross. "Transmission of aggression through imitation of aggressive models." *Journal of Abnormal and Social Psychology* 63 (1961): 575-82. Aggression and violence are imitated, especially by children.

Bandura, Albert, D. Ross, and S.A. Ross. "Imitation of film-mediated aggressive models." *Journal of Abnormal and Social Psychology* 66 (1963): 3-11. Striking instances through studies of how unique model of aggression in film are imitated by subjects.

Dorr, A., and P. Kovaric. "Some of the people some of the time — But which people? Televised violence and its effects." Pp. 183-99, in E.L. Palmer and A. Dorr, eds., *Children and the Faces of Television: Teaching, Violence, Selling.* New York: Academic Press, 1980. Examines the variables that affect when aggressive behavior is imitated.

Greenberg, Bradley S., R. Linsangan, A. Soderman, C. Heeter, C. Lin, C. Stanley, and M. Siemicki. "Adolescents' Exposure to Television and Movie Sex." Pp. 61-98, in Bradley S. Greenberg, J.D. Brown, and N. Buerkel-Rothfuss, eds., *Media, Sex and the Adolescent.* Cresskill, N.J.: Hampton Press, 1993. Examines several hundred studies looking at various influences of the media on adolescents' sexual behavior.

Hearold, S. "A Synthesis of 1043 Effects of Television on Social Behavior." Pp. 65-133 in G. Comstock, ed., *Public Communications and Behavior,* Vol. 1. New York: Academic Press, 1968. A review and summary of existing studies (in 1968).

Kaplan, Robert M., and Robert D. Singer. "Television Violence and Viewer Aggression: A Reexamination of the Evidence." *Journal of Social Issues* 32:4 (1976): 35-70. After a surge of studies on TV and violence during the late 1960s and early 1970s, this study reexamines the variables and results of many of them.

Loevinger, Lee. "The Ambiguous Mirror: The Reflective-Projective Theory of Broadcasting and Mass Communication." *Journal of Broadcasting* 12:2 (1968): 97-116. Former FCC Commissioner argues that TV project reflects and projects social values; such effects are not simply one-way.

Chapter Four

PC in Perspective:
Implications for Journalists

Douglas Tarpley

When the state of Minnesota ordered the elimination of the term "squaw," deemed offensive by some Native Americans but long used to label many historic, geographic places, Lake County's governing body formally resolved to change the name of Squaw Lake and Squaw Bay to "Politically Correct" Lake and "Politically Correct" Bay.

The Disney Corporation's apparently painstaking efforts to make the historic figure Pocohantas "politically correct" in the hit film by the same name subsequently generated considerable criticism from those who believed it sacrificed historical accuracy for the sake of cultural sensitivity.

Two graduates brought Stanford University unwanted notoriety through their well publicized book, *The Diversity Myth*, a scathing review of the "multicultural" curriculum they were forced to experience. James Finn Garner's popular *Politically Correct Bedtime Stories* spoofed serious liberal and conservative efforts to protest and censor classic literature, films, and other works of art.

Some feminists asserted Jesus Christ was more "she" than "he," and some members of the gay community inferred that the historical Jesus had a sexual orientation compatible to theirs. Christmas nativity scenes in various locales were modified to include figures chosen to reflect a diversity of races and religions as well as images of Santa Claus and Rudolph the Red-Nosed Reindeer.

"Physically challenged," "vertically-challenged," "full-figured," and seemingly thousands of similar non-offensive new terms and humorous slang have been absorbed into our national vocabulary. A successful network television program is titled "Politically Incorrect." Perfume-free environments have joined smoke-free atmospheres to free us from contamination.

Moby Dick has met Free Willy.

As these examples illustrate, political correctness and political incorrectness have emerged and stimulated considerable controversy as well as argument and creative humor throughout American culture over the past decade or so. From labels primarily used in the mid-1980s and early-1990s and confined primarily to college campuses, political correctness and political incorrectness have rapidly evolved into ambiguous terms that seem to mean many different things to many different people.

Political correctness and political incorrectness are particularly provocative concepts as they relate to the mass media, especially news organizations. Some critics claim that American news media popularized the terms, shaped and spread widespread debate, profited from public attention to the ideas in their many forms, and yet failed to understand and define them adequately for their audiences. The collective mass media, news media, or particular media organizations have also been accused of being nefarious agenda-setting, gatekeeping champions of either political correctness or political incorrectness themselves. Then there are people who suggest the mass media are merely *reflecting* ways of thinking and forms of behavior that have permeated the American culture in recent years or may have existed long before these popular terms emerged. Certainly signs of political correctness and political incorrectness can be found throughout newspaper, magazine, television, film, and other media content in recent years, as advertisers, public relations specialists, journalists, creative writers, dramatists, and other communication professionals have attempted to adapt to an increasingly pluralistic society.

Despite the fact that news media organizations, practicing journalists, and media scholars have been operating in this cloudy yet pervasive climate of political correctness and incorrectness for some time now, research dealing with how news media themselves have affected or been affected by it has been sparse. Published or public dialogue on the subject among journalists has been somewhat limited, has lacked depth, or has been couched or obfuscated within other terms, ideas, and trends such as diversity and multiculturalism.

Those in the journalistic community seem to have responded to questions about the relationship between the news media and these competing cultural forces in three basic ways: 1) Some appear to deny that PC is an issue, claiming that its impact on the news media and society is minimal or it is a matter of fashionable terms being attached to problems and issues that mass media scholars and practitioners have been dealing with for years, such as minority rights, women's rights, free speech, media bias, news objectivity, and the blurring of news and entertainment. 2) Others appear to be struggling to define what political correctness is and to understand how and to what degree it has influenced newsroom norms and policies, reporting procedures, editorial decisions, basic news values, stylebooks, traditional standards of news objectivity, hiring and personnel considerations, journalism education, and coverage of the political correctness story itself. 3) Still others seem to be viewing both left-leaning political correctness and backlash political incorrectness as an inevitable and acceptable reflection of recent trends toward advocacy journalism.

This essay will trace the origins and evolution of the terms "political correctness" and "political incorrectness" and the ideas behind them, help define what they have come to mean in today's society, and examine a variety of questions and issues surrounding these three basic ways the news media have responded to the political correctness/political incorrectness phenomenon. This will lead to more specific questions on this subject for consideration by practicing journalists, news organizations, and journalism scholars and practical recommendations about how news media may deal with the issue in the future.

Origins of the Issue

Admitting that the origins and meaning of political correctness are "muddled," D. Charles Whitney and Ellen Wartella trace the early development of the term, idea, and controversies in their article, "Media Coverage of the 'Political Correctness' Debate." They argue that the news media were greatly responsible for transforming what was a relatively innocuous 1980s clash, limited primarily to various university settings — between left-leaning proponents of multiculturalism, minority rights, and women's rights and those defending a male-dominated, largely white, mainstream culture — into a widespread, popular debate by the early 1990s.

The media brought forth this change of perspective in three ways. First, they gave considerable publicity and credence to a series of books produced by conservative authors who attacked conditions on college campuses and contemporary higher education as a whole. These include Allan Bloom's *The Closing of the American Mind*, Charles J. Sykes' *Prof. Scam: Professors and the Demise of Higher Education*, and *The Hollow Men: Politics and Corruption in Higher Education*, Bruce Wilshire's *Professionalism, Purity and Alienation*, Page Smith's *Killing the Spirit: Higher Education in America*, David E. Purpel's *The Moral and Spiritual Crisis in Education*, Roger Kimball's *Tenured Radicals: How Politics Has Corrupted Our Higher Education*, and, most of all, the highly popular *Illiberal Education* by Dinesh D'Souza. The media also dramatically increased the number of political correctness stories they carried, particularly in 1991 as the revised perspective of the issue became entrenched in the American culture. And finally, they treated specific revelations or apparent instances of politically correct thought or behavior as "crimes."

While many critics considered these leftist efforts to be elitist, potentially repressive, or both, Tom Foster Digby in *The Humanist* article "PC and the Fear of Feminism," echoed the claims of many that the political influence of university radicals, on or off campus, was highly overestimated. In "Freedom of Expression, the University, and the Media" in *Journal of Communication*, Everette E. Dennis noted that political correctness was merely a term coined by critics and journalists to reflect longstanding ideas about multiculturalism and minority rights that became threatening when they were manifested in the form of "new courses, theories of history and other considerations" by faculty members and their students who were basically recruited to add diversity to university communities. T. Kenneth Cribb agreed in "Dumb and Dumber," a *National Review* article, that it was politically correct thinking that inspired actions on college campuses, such as changing curricula, modifying reading lists, developing new speech codes, and attempting to re-define acceptable behavior outside the classroom that drew the increasing public concern and media attention in the early 1990s.

Although still a matter of conflicting viewpoints about minority rights, academic freedom, free speech, the future of higher education, and other college campus concerns, the term "political correctness" and resistance to what it is perceived to represent (i.e. political incorrectness) have spilled over from academia into every dimension of society since the early 1990s. What was a nebulous term to begin with is now linked to a variety of activities and given a number of meanings that have become widely embedded in everyday American cultural consciousness.

Current Definitions of Political Correctness

Political correctness and political incorrectness are commonly perceived today as minority-rights issues. It has been largely African Americans, Hispanics, Native Americans, Asian Americans, Arab Americans, women, the handicapped, gays and lesbians, and other groups seeking fair treatment both on college campuses and in American society as a whole who have used politically correct terms such as "diversity" and "multiculturalism" as a rallying cry. While many people support such traditional civil rights concepts as equal opportunity and even affirmative action, negative reaction to political correctness has been considerable when it has been linked to extreme efforts to demand immediate equality rather than equal opportunity, reparations for past oppression, or subjugation or revision of facts in favor of egalitarian values and goals. White males, who have traditionally dominated American culture, appear to have stirred much of the backlash to such efforts.

Political correctness in this sense relates to "radical egalitarianism," a perspective that in its extreme demands that every cultural subgroup, no matter how small, or even every individual, no matter how bizarre, has the right to be heard and demand equality in all areas of life. Political correctness has been associated, confused, and equated with a host of popular terms such as "multiculturalism," "diversity," and "pluralism." These three words are overlapping terms that represent ideals and goals. Within the mass media industries, "diversity" has been used to reflect the need to encourage or even demand through FCC rulings and other means that various minority groups and political viewpoints be heard through the limited communication channels that exist. In more recent years, it has been used by media organizations to refer to the objective of recruiting, training, and maintaining a workforce that represents all minority groups and women and of depicting them fairly and carefully in media content.

Other authors distinguish between the following terms as well:

- *assimilation*: desire of subordinate individuals or groups to take on the characteristics of and be accepted within a dominant cultural group

- *pluralism*: maintainance of differentiation or heterogeneity

- *multicultural pluralism*: belief in the idea that a common culture is possible

- *multicultural particularism*: conviction that a common culture is neither possible nor desirable

In the *Critical Inquiry* article "Boutique Multiculturalism, or Why Liberals Are Incapable of Thinking about Hate Speech," Stanley Fish makes a distinction between the person who "does not and cannot take seriously the core values of the cultures he tolerates" (i.e "boutique multiculturalism") and one who at least attempts to stretch tolerance of other cultures to its limits but finds it impossible to do so (i.e. "strong multiculturalism").

Again, it is when these goals or ideals are forced by one group or groups upon others that political correctness takes on its most common and ominous meaning. For example, "diversity" in the media may be construed as a noble cause until it is pushed through media manipulation, policies, programs, and executive decisions that are perceived by many to be unfair. It is this tendency that has caused some angry critics to label multiculturalism or diversity as "political correctness in disguise."

In *Opening of the American Mind*, Lawrence Lavine joins others who have argued that political correctness is merely the healthy product of demographic trends occurring in American society. Specifically, an increased growth rate among minority groups, the effects of immigration, and increased visibility and power of women and minorities in the workforce, he argues, inevitably exert pressure on more established social institutions.

Many define political correctness and political incorrectness in a much larger sense. In his article "Being Politically Correct in a Politically Incorrect World," Lawrence Grossberg suggests that the terms reflect a "culture war," basically a product of ongoing tensions between the worldviews, lifestyles, and agendas of liberals and conservatives. In *Politically Incorrect*, Ralph Reed views the issue as essentially a conflict between those who "no longer believe that religion can make a legitimate and rational contribution to civic discourse" and those who believe it is foolish to separate religion and politics. In this climate, politically correct and politically incorrect have become both derogatory rhetorical labels for opponents and convenient means of virtuous self-identity. The terms have also been used by both liberals and conservatives to direct people toward "correct" and away from "incorrect" positions on particular, important public issues of the time such as abortion, euthanasia, capital punishment, animal rights, creationism/evolution, and media bias.

For others in our current culture, political correctness and political incorrectness seem to be viewed in even broader terms. No longer are they just perceived as a matter of minority views or actions being forced upon others. Instead, political correctness has become attached to any group, institution, or movement. Being politically incorrect now often means standing up against any effort to silence the views of others or failure to respect their rights. It is standing up with pride against governmental entities, dominant political parties, powerful corporations, pervasive media organizations, and prominent political movements such as environmentalism or world government. It is resistance to authority of any kind.

The evolution of these terms and ideas has given them even more sweeping meaning for some people. Political correctness now often represents prevailing norms and fashions or efforts to impose them. Political incorrectness, by contrast, is any individual or collective effort to resist them. It is essentially nonconformity and taking pride in it. Furthermore, it is this manifestation of the concepts that now seems to be used most frequently. Historical figures or groups, for example, have been referred to as politically incorrect for being out of step with the norms of their time. Contemporary musical works have been judged politically correct or politically incorrect because they did or did not conform to the latest tastes, styles or techniques. Politicians have made generic use of "politically incorrect" to identify themselves and their constituents.

Political correctness and political incorrectness have also been tied to current freedom of speech issues. In a recent *USA Today* article, "Will Zealots Spell the Doom of Great Literature," W.J. Reeves calls political correctness the "McCarthyism of the 1990s" because of its attempts to censor or rewrite classic literature. In *Free Speech for Me — But Not for Thee*, Nate Hentoff bemoans the fact that both the political left and right have in recent years steadfastly and actively attempted to censor each other and redefine the limits of free speech to serve their political purposes.

Perhaps most of all, political correctness and political incorrectness have been perceived as a language issue that has affected every professional field and prompted discussion, debate, and humor throughout the American culture. Political correctness has come to mean a rigorous effort to eliminate intimidating, outdated words and jargon from media content, books, religious works and other materials and from workplace, educational and other environments. The goal has been to replace them with sensitive, extremely tolerant, non-sexist, non-racist, non-ethnic, non-religious terms that will offend no one.

On the surface, political incorrectness has involved reaction, much of it in the form of ridicule, to what have been perceived to be excessive, picayune efforts to redeem the cultural vocabulary and eliminate distinctions within sexes, races, and other cultural groups. Politically correct terms are continually being parodied, and many people are laughing at new terms created primarily for the sake of humor. Being politically correct itself has even been labeled "category challenged" and "logocentric." Beneath this particular form of resistance, again appears to reside an unwillingness to accept what one element of society is attempting to impose on another.

Politically correct and politically incorrect have also become adjectives used to describe almost any person, place, or thing. A review of recent magazine article headlines indicates there are politically correct doctors, lawyers, teachers, orthodontists, flowers, wood types, funeral arrangements, and fairy tales, to name a few. PC designations are increasingly used as evaluative terms for whatever is being observed or described. For example, in *Commentary*, Daniel Seligman suggested that boys playing with dolls, the homeless, sex education, girls in football, witches, earth, female cops, Aztecs and Seminoles, the 1970s, and "die-ins" were among those things that were "in" and thus politically correct, while IQ tests, cutting trees, "bums," dead white males, fur coats, guns, roast beef, the 1980s, and genes were "out" and thus politically incorrect.

Old Issue with New Label?

Some people have suggested that political correctness and political incorrectness are merely new terms representing old ideas and power struggles in American society. They are terms that are helping to crystallize thinking and behavior at a moment in history, but they and some of what they have come to represent will eventually fade away and be replaced by new terms and ideas. Chuck Green of the *Denver Post* contends that "political correctness is just a new label for what's been around forever." Many journalists shrug off concerns about political correctness in the newsroom, equating the political correctness criticisms with the old "liberal media bias" label. At an Association of American Editorial Cartoonists annual meeting during the height of the political correctness debate in 1992, only ten professional cartoonists in attendance publicly complained that political correctness pressures in the newsroom hindered their freedom of expression.

Even the political correctness controversy on college campuses has been dismissed by some academics as exaggerated. John K. Wilson's 1995 book, *The Myth of Political Correctness*, regards the multicultural curriculum revisions at universities like Stanford as having only a minor influence. Huntley Collins of the *Philadelphia Inquirer* claims that the influence of political correctness is "grossly exaggerated." Jeff MacNelly of the *Chicago Tribune* agrees, declaring that there is no political correctness crisis that should concern journalists.

One of the underlying assumptions of journalists who regard political correctness as a "non-issue" is that news media professionals are not personally affected by the social and political pressures of political correctness. Others suggest, however, that this assumption begs the question of news objectivity. If our postmodern society and intellectual climate have accepted the idea that objectivity is simply one person or one group's socially constructed subjective perceptions of certain phenomena, then the journalist who works within that postmodern culture cannot argue that he or she is unaffected by the preeminent egalitarian value system underlying the construct of multiculturalism so closely associated with political correctness.

Surprisingly, the media landscape is relatively devoid of open discussions among journalists of how political correctness affects the way news is conceptualized, gathered, and packaged. For example, a review of the hundreds of printed articles that discuss some aspect of political correctness reveals only a few articles that raise the question of how journalists are dealing with the pressures upon them to be politically correct. This conspicuous absence of discussion suggests either that journalists do not see this as a major issue affecting the news or that they feel they cannot openly discuss the issue.

A few examples, however, of journalistic discussions of political correctness in the newsroom do exist. David Harpe, editor of the *Louisville Courier-Journal*, acknowledged in a 1993 conference of Associated Press managing editors that political correctness does affect the newsroom. He cited an "orthodoxy" for reporting a whole range of perennial and controversial issues such as abortion, homosexuality (now a politically incorrect term), and religious faith, often referred to as "extreme fundamentalism" by journalists.

Gary North, freelance writer and co-editor of a Knight-Ridder newspaper, agrees that political correctness operates in the newsroom but states that it is nothing new, only much more "in the open." He argues that journalists should be aware of their own political bias when producing news. Robert Novak suggests that the influence of political correctness on journalists is difficult to perceive and control because journalists are elitist in nature. Innocent elitism or simple arrogance are two additional reasons why journalists may dismiss the influence of political correctness on the news.

PC Struggles in the Newsroom

While some news media professionals and critics suggest that political correctness is essentially an inflated or rhetorical issue, others perceive signs within the journalism profession that professionals are struggling to understand what political correctness and political incorrectness are and how they are influencing newsroom norms, policies, and practices. This is particularly true among those news organizations and individual journalists who are attempting to pursue or uphold traditional standards of news objectivity.

Mirroring society as a whole, the backdrop for debate among journalists is the apparent "culture war" between liberals and conservatives. Individual journalists and news organizations representing both sides have viewed each other as political correctness culprits for what they perceive to be an erosion of traditional journalistic standards. Claiming that only two conservatives exist among about 500 otherwise liberal, elitist reporters and editors who are based in Washington, D.C., conservative journalist Robert Novak, in a *USA Today* article titled "Political Correctness," charged that American journalism now prints "all the news that's 'politically correct' to print." On the other hand, Dorothy Giobbe, in an *Editor and Publisher* article, "Political Correctness," quotes one editor as saying, "Political correctness is a label foisted on dissident voices by those who want to maintain the mainstream views in media and education."

Journalists have also debated, to some extent, the nature, merits, and difficulties of political correctness within the context of minority rights issues, although the term and ideas behind it are often lost under the banner of diversity and, to a lesser degree, multiculturalism. It is clear that many in the news industry have become advocates for educating, hiring, training, promoting, and effectively utilizing African Americans, Hispanics, Asian Americans, Native Americans, gays, other minority groups, and women. They have also challenged peers and students of journalism to produce news content that is devoid of offensive language and stereotypes. Moreover, news events and issues involving any of these groups should be reported more thoroughly and fairly, they say. For example, since the early 1990s *The Quill* has run a regular column and numerous stories under the diversity label, which include tips, reports of studies and statistics measuring the progress of women and minorities in the media.

The idea of diversity in journalism has been prompted by current realities in the news business: declining readership and the threatened demise of daily newspapers; fragmentation of audiences spurred by the expansion of cable television, DBS, video rentals, and other media alternatives; shrinking viewership of major televisions networks; and other changes related to mass media and society. Tailoring new or existing media to particular minority markets is viewed as an opportunity for growth. In their *Journalism Monograph* study, "Objectivity Revisited: A Special Model of Political Ideology and Mass Communication," Ekaterina Ognianova and James W. Endersby argue that the convention of news objectivity itself is shaped more by mass media economics than political, cultural, technological, and philosophical influences. Appearing neutral and inoffensive is the best way to attract big audiences.

Like those in other professions and parts of society, many journalists perceive diversity as an ideal that goes well beyond news media economics and whose fulfillment is long overdue. A reported 50 per cent of news organizations still have no minorities on staff, and biased coverage and distorted, stereotypical depictions of women and particular racial and ethnic groups have been documented by many scholarly studies through the years. The Society of Professional Journalists recently revised the organization's Code of Ethics to include the statements: "Avoid stereotypes in covering issues of race, gender, age, religion, ethnicity, geography, sexual orientation and social status" and "Strive to give voice to all segments of society in public discourse."

As in other contexts, however, diversity has generated debate when it has been perceived as a matter of certain cultures forcing their ideas, values, and agendas into the newsroom and news content. Politically correct diversity in this sense has been opposed on a number of grounds. First, it is intolerant and insensitive to traditional news standards and those who have pursued them. It is advocacy disguised as "objectivity." Moreover, it is an attempt to promote the goals and ideals of special interest groups at the expense of striving for accuracy, facts, and a variety of sources and viewpoints. In addition, it demands extreme changes in hiring policies that threaten quality, stability, and well established, successful newsroom norms, policies, and practices. Its use is also opposed by some because they believe it imposes confusing, stringent, or even ridiculous uses of language in the reporting and editing process. In addition, it is charged, to demand that the only morally and socially acceptable perspective is tolerance for all races, genders, ideologies, cultures, and alternative lifestyles tramples on the personal beliefs, values, and freedoms of those who disagree. Finally, it is opposed by some who believe that treating all groups and viewpoints as equally newsworthy is wrong in both principle and practicality.

Many practitioners suggest that news organizations need to take advantage of diversity by utilizing the unique perspectives and understandings that minority journalists bring to the newsroom. Others, such as Gary North, in an *Editor and Publisher* article, "Being politically correct in the newsroom," have posed compelling questions: At what point should a member of the newsroom become an advocate for his or her minority? At what point should an editor in authority defer to that minority member? And at what point do several minority newsroom members become a pressure group like any other, advocating the group's preferred language or outlook be published or broadcast?

The most vociferous critics of current journalism practices contend that failure to answer these and other political correctness questions has caused many of today's news organizations to mimic politicians who are afraid to offend special interest groups and continually succumb to the pressures imposed by such groups both inside and outside the newsroom. Editorializing is no longer confined to the editorial page or the commentary segment of a newscast. Added to the debate are questions about how far minority group representation should extend in the newsroom and news content.

Journalists concerned about political correctness also view the issue in terms of freedom of speech. For example, in the recent *Editor and Publisher* article "'Homojournalist' loses his job," Allan Wolper reviews the freedom of expression debate surrounding the firing of a Canadian college journalism professor who is a self-described "gay prostitute" and published defender of pedophilia. Some news media professionals wonder what the limits of free speech are in a culture that increasingly condones views and behaviors that were once socially unacceptable — and still in the case of pedophilia — in the name of political correctness.

The political correctness dialogue among journalists who contend it is a growing problem has also been crystallized in the matter of language. Numerous articles written by journalists for other journalists deal with difficulties and extend advice about choosing inoffensive, non-stereotypical labels and terms when reporting on women, ethnic minorities, and other groups. The *AP Stylebook* and other news organization stylebooks have undergone revisions to accommodate such concerns, but there is as yet no unanimity about a politically correct style. For example, a recent edition of *The Quill* reports professional arguments over whether the term "Hispanic" should be an all-inclusive label. And in a recent *Columbia Journalism Review* article, "Unequal Terms," Louis Harris reports about use of the term "racial preference" in place of "affirmative action."

Journalists struggling with political correctness issues have generally depended on anecdotal rather than statistical evidence to support their contentions. Those pushing for "diversity," for example, regularly update and report conflicting evidence about minority hiring and refer to occasional studies dealing with treatment of women and others in news content.

There are a number of current, widely debated news media trends and issues that would appear to make those within the field susceptible to both the most innocuous and devious forms of political correctness. The include the following:

- The increasing development and influence of organized special interest groups within the field of journalism, such as the National Lesbian & Gay Journalists Association, Asian American Journalists Association, National Association of Hispanic Journalists, Native American Journalists Association, and National Association of Black Journalists.

- Well-documented evidence that news organizations are overly dependent on a narrow range of news sources, as well as "official" news sources, news releases, and other materials provided by image-conscious organizations and special interest groups.

- The decreasing competition among news media in many markets, the result of the decline of daily newspapers and great increase in mergers and crossownership in recent years. Where there are fewer outlets for diverse voices to be heard, pressure to be politically correct or politically incorrect is likely to rise.

- The growing use of diversity consultants, training, workshops, committees within news organizations, leading to a greater understanding, but also greater demand that the causes of particular groups be forwarded.

Political Correctness as Advocacy Journalism

Other journalists, critics, and scholars who perceive strong pressures of political correctness at work within the journalism field regard this trend as a reflection of a move toward a press system built on advocacy. In "Political Correctness Has No Place in the Newsroom" from *USA Today*, Robert Novak declares, "A free press is one of the foundations of a free society. Yet, Americans increasingly distrust and resent the media. A major reason is that many journalists have crossed the line from reporting to advocacy." In his *National Review* article, "PC Comes to the Newsroom," Daniel Seligman points to examples of a number of large-market, reputable newspapers that seem to "reflect increased fears in editor's offices that something might be published that would offend various movements represented in the newsroom." In "The Other Side of the Rainbow," a *Columbia Journalism Review* piece, William McGowan bemoans the departure of the *New York Times* from its "vaunted tradition of frank, fearless, and forthright exposition of the news." While it "may not be the Pravda of p.c.," he says, "it is certainly something less than a model of detached neutrality." Joseph Epstein, in a *Commentary* article, "The Degradation of *The New York Times*," agrees, noting that "the only news that stays news" in the publication are the obituaries.

Proponents of advocacy are not upset with these observations, conditions, and trends. They argue that a media system comprising many alternative voices best fits an increasingly pluralistic society that spawns a seemingly endless variety of special interest groups and causes. Opportunities for the needs and viewpoints of diverse groups to be expressed have increased because of the fragmentation of mass media in recent years, they contend. A press system built on the idea of advocacy is compatible with this trend. In addition, supporters of an advocacy press note that the whole notion of objective journalism has always been misleading, since the predisposition of reporters, editors, and other news media personnel and many other "gatekeeping" and "agenda setting" influences shape and bias news content.

This response to the tension exerted by these external and internal pressures on news journalists is to see them as an expression of the postmodern fragmentation prevalent in modern American culture. Specifically, journalists in this camp embrace these tensions as a reflection of the fragmentation of American culture, as a positive step away from traditional objective American journalism and a positive step toward an advocacy paradigm. In "PC And The Press" in *Change*, Huntly Collins concludes that this advocacy has "forced news organizations to confront their own racism and sexism," even though the journalistic attention the political correctness movement has been given is somewhat exaggerated. And in "Political Correctness In The Newsroom" from *Editor & Publisher*, David Harpe, editor of the *Louisville Courier-Journal*, says that "U.S. newsrooms operate under the sway of a politically correct orthodoxy."

Some journalists declare that the freedom to advocate particular points of view should be the norm. In "Being politically correct in the newsroom," Gary North says, "I prefer an assertive ... editor and a publication or program with a point of view." He says this is preferable to a "wishy-washy, pandering product that tries to please everyone and ends up pleasing no one." And later he says, "As to minority community members within a newsroom, I subscribe to a mild, collegial way of influencing: suggest, nudge, offer a well-stated opinion." He argues almost an "existential journalism," to borrow a term from John Merrill's *The Existential Journalist,* when he declares that "[j]ournalistic integrity means, above all, being true to yourself, be it a question of coverage or calling someone 'pro-choice' or 'pro-life' vs. 'pro-abortion' and 'anti-abortion,' or 'AIDS victim' vs. 'AIDS patient' vs. 'person with AIDS' or 'gay' and 'homosexual' or 'black' vs. 'African-American.'" And, in "PC Comes To the Newsroom," Daniel Seligman represents a lot of journalists when he declares, "The mighty American media have begun moving down the politically correct road long trodden by the colleges, and are doing so for many of the same reasons." He concludes that content analyses of big stories in recent years show that political correctness is "solidly based in scores of newsrooms." He quotes a *New York Times* editor who said that "the single most important issue this newspaper faces is diversity." He adds that "[t]he more diverse staff will do a better job of reporting."

A number of journalists in this category see a link between the economic pressures and content fare as a justification for advocacy journalism. Because of declining readership and the threatened demise of daily newspapers, fragmentation of audiences, shrinking viewership of major television networks, and other changes related to mass media and society, many journalists see the need to tailor new or existing media to selective minority markets as a means of survival and even growth. In our "hypersensitive society," John Leo argues that in response to this economic need for success in the marketplace, journalists even resort to a sensationalism, capitalizing on the public's "victim culture" mentality. He notes, for example, that stories about politically correct issues of gender and race are often displayed with sensational headlines that the story details may not even support. "This negative twist on news is really quite positive" for the circulation of newspapers by generating fear in the audience, he explains. He adds that it also enhances the continuation of influence by advocates and "is fairly common in reports on women's progress." Columnist William Raspberry, Leo notes, dealt with this "mentality quite shrewdly ... referring to 'feminist leaders' who find it impossible to acknowledge serious progress toward gender fairness — not because there has been progress, but because their power derives from their ability to keep portraying women as victims." And finally, in "The

Degradation of *The New York Times*," Joseph Epstein quotes a managing editor of the *New York Times* as saying, "we have to grab young readers by the lapels because they are less interested in reading."

Journalists and scholars following the political correctness debate often frame the discussion within the larger context of society's contemporary postmodernism. As many scholars explain, the United States is segmenting into antagonistic groups. A "tribalism" is splitting the culture. Indeed, the term "culture wars" is part of the popular culture's vocabulary, reflecting conflict among groups regarding such moral issues as abortion, euthanasia, cultural diversity, and education. In fact, the traditional values of Western civilization are being questioned, deconstructed. A number of polls indicate that the majority of Americans no longer believe that such a thing as absolute truth exists. They reject modernism because of its belief in an absolute, discoverable truth. Postmodernists do not believe in this objective truth, preferring instead to embrace a relativism and a new aesthetic framework devoid of absolutes. Postmodernist thinking results in the splintering of our culture into various subcultures based on ethnicity, sexuality, and social relationships, ultimately calling for a new social order.

This worldview has profound implications for the journalist whose social function is four-fold: 1) to inform the public of the external events and issues; 2) to interpret and analyze the meaning of those events in a way to bring some sense of their meaning to the public; 3) to entertain the audience; 4) to socialize or pass along values of the culture to new members of the community or to subsequent generations. As many scholars have explained, the mass media do not exist in a vacuum, but function as part of a social system. Journalism is no exception.

As Michael Burgoon and William Bailey declare in "PC at Last! PC at Last! Thank God Almighty, We are PC at Last!," political correctness "rejects the traditional, commonsense notion of an objective reality, and therefore rejects also the notion of external value-free criteria by which the truth or falsity of discourse can be judged. Instead, reality is socially constructed through language, and the dominant culture's ideology is imbued in that reality." And later he summarily declares, "We have bought from whole cloth the notion that we can rename a problem out of existence." For example, in "A session on political correctness," David Astor observes that many journalists are concerned that "they are getting increased pressure from angry readers and worried editors over the content" of their work. The reason? Readers are just more sensitive now than in years past. He quotes one panelist who said, "There is more division in the country, and a higher sensitivity level. Groups are splitting farther and farther apart on issues."

Another panel member observed that "many Americans strongly identify themselves as Christians, gays, blacks, or as part of some other group and want that group to be perceived favorably in the media." Hence, the pressure on the journalist mirrors what is happening in American society.

The American Society of Newspaper Editors has formally embraced a goal of proportional representation in newsrooms in the next few years. By then the newsrooms are supposed to have a minority representation of about 25 per cent, more accurately reflecting the ethnic makeup of American culture than newsrooms now do. Documentation exists to indicate that a host of metropolitan and daily newspapers have introduced hiring programs explicitly identified as "quotas" to achieve this diversity in the belief that the new personnel will change the nature of news content and its form, and thus appeal more to readers and viewers.

Other journalists, however, view this advocacy in the newsroom with concern, even fear — because of the potential impact on words and behavior. They object to what they see as a deliberate effort by special interest groups — within and outside of the newsroom — to distort, manipulate, and willfully intimidate journalists. For example, in "Political Correctness Attacks Black Right Wing," Stephen Goode charges that although the polls show that only about a third of blacks claim to be liberals, a third moderate, and a third conservative, "blacks in the media come from the same liberal one-third and editors turn to that segment for quotes." He adds that they "intimidate white editors and corporate leaders and they get away with it." And, in "Political Correctness: Speech Control or Thought Control?" Gerald Kreyche says, "Political correctness is not so much about words, as it is about action and conduct, for words lead from ideas into real life." And then he recalls several anecdotes through which newspapers and magazines influenced a number of events, including even a Smithsonian Institution's exhibit that was ultimately "pared." The real tragedy, he declares, is that political correctness "may be paved with good intentions, but so is the road to Hades. It not only hides truth, but denies it. PC insinuates untruth and sacrifices truth for compromise." He is afraid that the "backers of political correctness, also known as the 'word police,' would like to graduate to 'thought police.' Those who didn't conform would undergo re-education, as do many faculty members accused of insensitivity in the classroom."

Others agree. In "Political Correctness: Journalists attempt to define what it means today," Dorothy Giobbe quotes Margaret O'Brien Steinfels, editor of the *Commonwealth*, as saying that the "unprofessional" influence is "shaping, deforming the news." And in "A session on political correctness" in *Editor & Publisher*, David Astor quotes a journalist who charges that a liberal agenda manipulates the content of news. "[T]he media target some people but not others," the journalist said. The media have no problem talking about the 'Bubba vote' in the South but they don't go to New York and talk about the 'Jose vote' or the 'Vinnie vote'."

Other journalists suggest that this advocacy is served by withholding coverage of stories or failing to tell "the whole story." In his *National Review* article, "PC Comes to the Newsroom," Daniel Seligman fears that journalists, in an effort to accommodate concerns of special-interest groups, don't always tell "the story." A growing number of editors of newspapers with large staffs, he believes, are afraid of offending groups on their staffs that have their own agendas.

Resolution

Resolving issues related to political correctness can be a complicated task, depending on the basic views to which the audience and members of the journalistic community adhere. If political correctness is perceived as merely a rhetorical issue or a label attached to news profession problems that have existed for a long time, then it is essentially a non-issue and the term will eventually fade away — even as the recurring issues continue to be debated within and outside of the professional community. However, there seems to be considerable reason to believe that the accelerating, bold, passionate efforts of special interest groups and causes, the product of an increasingly pluralistic society, are exerting new pressures, and are changing the thinking and behavior within many newsrooms. News professionals who dismiss political correctness as an issue have underestimated its complexity and impact.

Those journalists and news media organizations who view political correctness as a reflection of and desired step toward a media system that permits greater advocacy and thus better meshes with changing cultural conditions in American society may find, like the New Journalists of the 1960s and 1970s, that mainstream journalism may ultimately continue to embrace traditional — if modified — professional conventions of form, content, and practice. Only time will tell whether or not traditional journalism will lose out to a new paradigm of "partisan" journalism. Simply, this perspective also fails to deal with the apparent fact that strong tensions between journalists who intentionally or unintentionally act as advocates for particular groups or causes and those who are committed to traditional standards of news objectivity do exist as they have historically. At the least, individual journalists and news organizations need to openly debate and determine what they want to be in this respect. If the decision is to be advocates of particular groups, causes, points of view, or agendas, they should clearly state to audiences that this is the personal or organizational mission and editorial philosophy that will shape and reflect all news content rather than misleading viewers, listeners, or readers into thinking standards of objectivity are being pursued and met.

For journalists and news organizations conscious of, concerned about, or familiar with conflicts regarding political correctness and political incorrectness in the newsroom, serious effort needs to be made to find balance in a number of contexts. For example, a balance could be struck between upholding traditional standards of news objectivity and responding to the legitimate cries of minority cultural groups. In addition, effort could be made to develop readers or audiences in a diversifying culture and an extremely competitive media environment.

A number of steps can be taken. Media practitioners need to gain a better understanding of political correctness and political incorrectness and their many underlying ideas and issues. And they need to cover political correctness stories and the "culture war" with more balanced and in-depth analysis, encouraging more substantive dialogue about the nature and implications of the issue. In addition, they need to research systematically in order to discover the extent and many specific ways in which this issue has influenced editorial decision-making, reporting practices, news values, stylebooks, personnel matters, marketing strategies, internal communication, the effects of news content on audiences, and other concerns of news organizations. Moreover, they need to pursue diversity in news organizations through representatives of various groups and views. In addition, they could refocus on the basics of good reporting by seeking facts, a fair representation of views on an event or issue and other time-tested news values. They could also avoid being either politically correct or politically incorrect by conscientiously resisting those conditions that seem to make news organizations and individual journalists susceptible to these influences. Finally, they could teach media literacy to audiences or sponsor efforts to do so in order to show them how to recognize political correctness in news content and why news objectivity is an ideal that is never fully achieved.

Whether they attach political correctness or political incorrectness to their work or not, news organizations and individual journalists practice their profession today in an atmosphere where these terms and their challenges are a prominent part of media cultures and the larger cultures in which they reside. The terms seem to beg for further debate, dialogue, questions, research, resolutions, and actions.

Recommended Readings

Books

Berman, Paul, ed. *Debating PC: The Controversy Over Political Correctness on College Campuses.* New York: Laurel/Dell, 1992.. Confined to the political correctness issue in higher education, but reflects the origins of the issue.

Bloom, Alan. *The Closing of the American Mind.* New York: Simon & Schuster, 1986. One of several popular books critical of contemporary higher education that fueled the initial political correctness debate on college campuses.

D'Souza, Dinesh. *Illiberal Education: The Politics of Race and Sex on Campus.* New York: Free Press, 1991. Controversial and highly publicized book that many suggest sparked media interest in the political correctnessissue and led to its popularization.

Jenkins, Russell, John J. Virtes, and Frederick W. Campano. *National Review Politically Incorrect Reference Guide.* National Review, Inc., 1993. A good bibliography of books and articles that relate to the political correctness issue, but selected for a conservative readership.

Kimball, Roger. *Tenured Radicals: How Politics Has Corrupted Our Higher Education.* New York: Harper & Row, 1990. One of several books critical of American higher education that prompted the initial political correctness debate.

Reed, Ralph. *Politically Incorrect.* Dallas: Word Publishing, 1994. A political conservative's effort to frame the political correctness issue within a larger culture war between liberals and conservatives, particularly religious conservatives.

Levine, Lawrence W. *The Opening of the American Mind.* Boston: Beacon Press, 1996. Argues that political correctness is nothing extraordinary, but rather a reflection of old patterns of conflict among groups and an inevitable result of changing demographics in a new era of multiculturalism.

Articles

Collins, Huntly. "PC and the Press." *Change* (January/February, 1992): 12-16. A *Philadelphia Inquirer* reporter claims that political correctness is an overrated issue made popular by news media and journalists who misunderstood or distorted the issue and events in the context of higher education.

Epstein, Joseph. "The Degradation of the 'New York Times'." *Commentary* (May, 1994): 34-9. A provocative analysis of the *New York Times* that concludes that it has succumbed to the pressures of political correctness.

Dennis, Everette E. "Freedom of Expression, the University and the Media." *Journal of Communication* 42 (Spring 1992): 73-80. Discusses the tensions between political correctness and freedom of speech and press on college campuses and calls for more meaningful communication about and study of the issue.

Fish, Stanley. "Boutique Multiculturalism, or Why Liberals Are Incapable of Thinking about Hate Speech." *Critical Inquiry* 23 (Winter 1997): 378-95. Good discussion of varying perspectives of multiculturalism and tolerance that helps define the political correctness issue.

Giobbe, Dorothy. "Political Correctness." *Editor & Publisher*, 22 October 1994, pp. 13, 44. Reports panel discussion on the subject at meeting of the Association of Opinion Page Editors.

Grossberg, Larry. "Being Politically Correct in a Politically Incorrect World." *Journal of Communication* 42 (Spring, 1992). Calls for those in the field of communication to dialogue and study the political correctness issue more meaningfully.

Hill, Monica, and Bonnie Thrasher. "A Model of Respect: Correctness in the Campus Newsroom." *Journal of Mass Media Ethics* 9 (1993): 43-55. Offers guidelines for campus newspapers and other news organizations to professionally and ethically avoid conflicts that are brought about by an atmoshere of political correctness.

McGowan, William. "The Other Side of the *Rainbow.*"*Columbia Journalism Review* (November/December 1993): 53-7. How the quest for diversity at many large newspapers has turned into "cheerleading" for racial and other groups.

North, Gary. "Being Politically Correct in the Newsroom." *Editor & Publisher*, 16 October 1993, pp. 40, 48. Raises some of the key questions news organizations must respond to when confronted with political correctness in the newsroom.

Seligman, Daniel. "PC Comes to the Newsroom." *National Review*, 23 June 1993, pp. 29-34. A conservative journalist's thoughtful arguments and examples of how political correctness has affected many news organizations.

Whitney, Charles, and Ellen Wartella. "Media Coverage of the 'Political Correctness' Debate." *Journal of Communication* 42 (1992): 87-92. Excellent review of the origins of the political correctness issue and analysis of the frequency of news coverage to support the claim that it was a media-created issue.

Chapter Five

The Media and Diversity

Alf Pratte

Diversity has been an issue throughout communications history, but it has become particularly important in the last two decades. Although the major emphasis in recent years has been related to hiring African, Hispanic, Asian, and Native Americans (AHANAs), the meaning of diversity in the media is expanding to include the disabled, gays, and other minority groups. This recent emphasis on employment diversity was preceded by steps to employ women, who are still struggling to achieve managerial and editorial positions in a "pink collar" industry dominated by white males. A related concern is the lack of diversity in coverage and content in the mass media — a concern fostered by group ownership, conglomerates, deregulation, and other policies and practices that favor the special interests of the modern corporate newspaper.

By reaching out beyond what was once primarily a field dominated by white males to attract a greater non-mainstream audience, today's media owners are strongly motivated by economic as well as moral and ethical goals. A Dow Jones publication, *Newspapers, Diversity & You*, argued that if "newspapers are to survive and thrive in the decades ahead, they must attract and serve America's increasingly multicultural readership. Their staffs must be joined and led by journalists from racially and ethnically diverse backgrounds."

Origins of the Issue

Although the trend is changing, the newspaper and broadcasting industry traditionally has been slow to employ and cover minorities. The problem has been rooted in — and exacerbated by — patterns of prejudice, racism, economic determinism, and stereotypical coverage. Addressing the failure of mass communications to adequately report on minorities, Clint Wilson and Felix Gutierrez in *Minorities and Media* describe four characteristic phases that, depending upon specific time and circumstances, have been experienced by America's ethnic minorities. In the first phase, the minority group is excluded from media coverage altogether because it isn't considered part of society. This gives way to depictions of the group as a threat to society, and to confrontational reporting. The third phase emerges at the tail end of the confrontational one and is marked by media attempts to reassure the public that the group no longer poses any threat. In the final phase, "socially integrated news reporting" enables members of the minority group to actually participate in the media's gatekeeping process.

In contrast to these phases, some historians believe that propaganda from the first presses helped contribute to America's pluralism. According to Julie Hedgepeth Williams, the promotional materials of Richard Hakluyt, Theodore deBray, and others reached and influenced people of many nationalities and religious backgrounds, producing an interesting population mix in America. Because of the writings aimed at both the well-to-do and those of the lower socio-economic classes, Williams reports a wide variety of people arrived on the continent, creating the basis for the pluralistic nature of the American populace. "That mixture of people," she writes in *The Media in America*, "would lay the foundations for democracy."

Notwithstanding the success of the press in attracting diverse social and economic groups, the colonial newspapers and magazines that followed did not reflect the diversity. From its earliest years, print journalism was designed primarily by and for a mainstream audience. Despite the cultural, political, religious, and racial heterogeneity of the colonial population that was nearly 20 per cent black at the time of the first census in 1790, diversity did not characterize the early printing press, which consisted mostly of printing official proclamations and religious pamphlets. From the late 1700s through the 1820s, however, printed matter became more diversified in type, language, ethnic origin, and content. There was also a shift from a reliance on oral delivery of messages to printed verification of rumors and news.

Even with the advent of the more populist penny press in the 1830s, newspaper publishers, editors, and reporters failed to report adequately or fairly on minority political, economic, racial, or religious groups. Such exclusion prompted the development of the first black newspapers and others outside the mainstream media. These included not only blacks but utopians, feminists, immigrants, working class radicals and war resisters ignored or stereotyped by the mainstream press. Wilson and Gutierrez have found that the first newspapers for Latinos, Blacks, Native Americans, and Asian Americans were preceded by other media targeted to minority groups, most notably the Polish and German-speaking residents of the English colonies. They developed in the same era as the first mass circulation press pioneered by Benjamin Day in 1833.

Following the Civil War, the diversity gap in the newsroom increased as fewer opportunities in education and employment were available to non-whites. This likely exacerbated the mainstream press tendency to view minorities in stereotypes or caricatures. Sterling Brown, in his pioneering work, *The Negro in American Fiction*, identified these caricatures as the "contented slave," the "wretched freeman," the "tragic mulatto," and the "comic Negro." These depictions were the most persistent African-American stereotypes to emerge from the nineteenth century and carry over into the present. American mainstream journalism also served as an active anti-Asian influence beginning in the 1870s, when newspapers drummed hostility against Chinese laborers. According to William Wong, in an article titled "Covering the Invisible Model Minority," the attitude helped create a political atmosphere that contributed to the 1882 Chinese Exclusion Act barring Chinese workers from the United States.

The legacy of derogatory racial caricatures and restricted employment opportunities reemerged in the new mass media industries that dominated the production and distribution of African-American images, as well as those of other minorities, in the twentieth century. In their history of African Americans in the mass media, Jannette L. Dates and William Barlow, in *Split Image: African Americans in the Mass Media*, record that white-owned media industries based most of the black portraits they produced on the prevailing nineteenth-century stereotypes. In addition, the press helped to shape public opinion against Japanese Americans in World War II. The majority of the all-white media supported government action permitting more than 110,000 ethnic Japanese living on the West Coast and Hawaii, most of them U.S. citizens, to be put into internment camps, without due process. James Startt in *The Media in America* claims that the wide media endorsement of the dropping of atomic bombs on the Japanese cities of Hiroshima and Nagasaki was simply the final demonstration of how popular opposition to bombing had been neutralized in the American press.

A major stimulus for change was disregarded when the media ignored the warning raised by the 1947 Hutchins Commission in *A Free and Responsible Press* concerning the ingrained policy of media exclusion. Such criticism was generally slighted by the nearly all-white, all-male press. It was not until the U.S. Supreme Court formally struck down segregation in American schools in 1954 that the white mainstream print media slowly began to report the deep rooted economic, social and cultural issues that contributed to racism. This recognition was further stimulated by the images of the civil rights movement found in motion pictures, print media, and television in Little Rock, Montgomery, Birmingham, Watts, and Washington, D.C. In 1968, the Kerner Commission provided a scathing indictment of the print and broadcast media for fostering prejudice by not reporting on racial issues and failing to address black Americans, thus contributing to the division of America into one black and one white nation. Ironically, despite the important warning about press neglect in minority coverage, the Kerner Commission report itself neglected to mention American Indians. According to James and Sharon Murphy in *Let My People Know*, that failure was itself a comment on the problem. "The call for improvement of media coverage or minorities," they wrote, "seemed targeted at blacks and chicanos. But the same criticism could have been easily applied to the media treatment of Indians."

Catch Up and Concern

After nearly two centuries of coverage marked by demeaning depictions, discrimination or neglect, America's white-majority media reluctantly embraced a policy from the 1970s forward characterized by some as "catch-up and concern." The result was a flurry of activity and goal setting to encourage newspapers, magazines, broadcast facilities, and other media to be more representative of the diverse society for a variety of economic and moral reasons. In recent years Wilson and Gutierrez report that media corporations, spurred by pressure groups, their own minority employees, or even a growing social consciousness, have come to see the growing minority population as an opportunity, not a problem. They write: "Rather than simply trying to overcome a hurdle and put the obstacle behind them, they recognize that the United States is growing as a racially diverse nation and that the changing demographics are an opportunity for them to gain new audiences and readers. It is this attitude, coupled with the growing racial diversity of the nation, that presages the greatest progress of minorities and the media of communication."

A 1990 study of the *New York Times*, the *Boston Globe*, the *Atlanta Constitution*, and the *Chicago Tribune* by Carolyn Martindale indicates some changes since the 1950s. In most of the papers the image of blacks as criminals represented a very small percentage of the coverage of blacks during the 1970s. This finding suggests that the old stereotypes of black Americans are beginning to lose their sway.

Another example of success in better reflecting minority groups can be seen in the improved coverage of Asian Americans, who have had a long history of being stereotyped by the American press. William Wong, in his work on media coverage of Chinese Americans, reports that although television coverage of Asian Americans remains spotty and sensationalized, print coverage, while retaining some of the bi-polar good-bad images, has become "increasingly nuanced, textured and true to life," thanks in part to greater numbers of Asian Americans journalists.

In an article on the improved coverage of Chinese Americans, Wong writes that the biggest reason for improved coverage is the growth and complexity of the Asian-American population itself, which has tripled to 8 million since 1970. Other census statistics indicate the non-white population will double by 2040. Some projections point to a day when the so-called minorities will be the American majority.

Precision in identifying the various Asian ethnic people in America and understanding who they are is a step toward better journalism, Wong observes. Other proven journalistic principles include good reporting, precise writing, cultivation of credible sources, knowledge of cultural traditions, histories, and experiences. "The assumption here is that journalism values the latter attributes," Wong explains, "but shrinking newsroom resources and a tendency toward `tabloidization' steal from a newsroom the wherewithal to devote reporting time to study complex communities like Asian ethnic groups."

Because it was regulated to some extent, the broadcast industry was an occasional leader in efforts to achieve a mass media more reflective of American diversity. This was stimulated in part through the re-licensing process mandated by Congress and implemented through the Federal Communications Commission. Major court rulings endorsed various community and regulatory efforts to enhance diversity in the broadcast media. In 1960, the Supreme Court ordered the FCC to recognize the "standing" or direct and substantial interest of a community group that challenged the relicensing of a Jackson, Mississippi, television station accused of racist policies Through the license renewal process, the FCC voted to strip the licenses from all public television stations in Alabama because they had discriminated against blacks in the 1960s. By 1975, when the FCC took its action, legal scholar Don Pember in the book *Mass Media Law* says, the public broadcasting stations had solved the problems, served the minority community with high quality programming, and were considered model broadcasting operations with regard to employment of minorities. For a time the government gave minority group members special preferences when applying for broadcast licenses. This practice was ruled constitutional in 1990 when the Supreme Court declared that government had the power to devise what is described as "benign race conscious" measures "to the extent they serve important government objectives."

By the end of the 1980s, William Barlow concluded, black radio in the United States had reached a new plateau. For the first time in its history, there were both network and chain operations controlled by African-American broadcasters. In general, the black public stations, along with the more progressive black commercial outlets, were on the cutting edge of the movement to establish and maintain a self-sufficient African-American presence on the airways. In 1988, Lee Thornton reported, the number of minorities in broadcast news had nearly doubled over the previous decade to about 20 per cent. The number of minority journalists in print journalism had reached nearly 10 per cent.

Wilson and Gutierrez note that two other events in the 1980s signaled the beginning of a more committed effort to increase ethnic diversity in newsrooms. Legal actions brought against the *New York Times* and the Associated Press forced them to improve their minority employment numbers. Some observers believed the move would bring more diverse coverage in the national press. That hope was founded on the premise that successful legal action, particularly when large respected institutions are involved, may spur others because of fear that they, too, may be vulnerable to similar legal actions.

Wilson and Gutierrez also give credit to a significant advocacy movement in the 1980s involving the resources of minority professionals who succeeded in white-owned newspapers but who were keenly aware of the problems that minorities encountered on the job. Faced with a majority mass media tainted by racism and insensitive to their needs, minorities had three options: seeking access into the majority media through employment; developing and maintaining their own communications media; and applying pressure to make changes in majority media content as it relates to them.

Among the professional groups formed to advance their cause were the National Association of Black Journalists, the National Hispanic Journalists Association, the Asian American Journalists Association, and the Native American Press Association. Individual activists recognized for advancing the cause of minority journalists include Robert Maynard and Nancy Hicks, instrumental in founding the Institute for Journalism Education, among other efforts; Jay T. Harris (who conducted studies for ASNE); Gerald Garcia and Gerald M. Sass, executives with Gannett Newspapers and the Gannett Newspaper Foundation); and Albert Fitzpatrick, an executive with Knight Newspapers.

Wilson and Gutierrez believe the efforts of such advocates and spokespersons for ethnic diversity in newspapers were responsible for much of the early progress fostering diversity. Such leaders prompted the ASNE in 1978 to adopt a goal to have the nation's minority newsroom population equal in percentage to the U.S. population by the year 2000. By 1985 employment rates suggested that the goal would be achieved approximately three generations late. In addition to ASNE, other professional and trade organizations such as the Newspaper

Association of America (formerly the ANPA) and the Associated Press Managing Editors (APME) have active minority committees. Minority advocates who focus their attention on the newspaper industry, however, are primarily educators or professionals who serve as advisers or catalysts for the generation of programs to meet specific needs as they are identified. Although critics emphasize that industry employment goals are far from reaching the U.S. population of 25 per cent minority, they find it encouraging that emphasis has been given to employment by institutions that slighted the issue for most of their history. In addition, Ellis Close, in an article titled "Seething in Silence — The News in Black and White," observes: "Setting industry goals is primarily an exercise in symbolism. This is not to say that taking such a stand doesn't have an impact. It does. Among other things, it serves to legitimize the goal of newsroom integration. And, though newsrooms are far from seeing the goals achieved, they are further along that route than the other major players in the news business. Television, outside major urban areas, is not a particularly integrated enterprise. And mainstream magazine staffs remain, for the most part overwhelmingly white."

Notwithstanding the progress being made in employment diversity, in a representative poll of 531 conducted by MORI Research on questions ranging from job satisfaction to hiring and promotion opportunities for the Associated Press Managing Editors, responses from whites and minorities differed starkly. White journalists, the study found, tend to think their newspapers do a good job of covering minority communities; minority journalists feel just the opposite. Whites believe standards are lower for minorities; minorities feel they're higher. Whites believe minorities move quickly out of entry level positions; minorities believe they get parked there. About half of the African Americans said they planned to leave their current job or the media business in the next five years. About 40 per cent of the Hispanics said they plan to stay at their newspapers, but they want to be in a different position within five years. By contrast, the APME report says, almost 60 per cent of Hispanics were pessimistic about their promotion chances.

Against Mandated Media Diversity

Despite the differing perspectives that have occurred as newsrooms have become more diverse, there are at least four major arguments that question the diversity agenda:

1. Although politically, ethically, and economically correct, the goal to have the newsroom reflect the percentage of minorities in society is a form of reverse

discrimination or racism against whites.

2. Increasingly militant minority reporters have difficulty in being objective and thus damage the credibility of the profession.

3. Race should not be a criterion for the way people are treated.

4. Diversity tends to divide the media, thus contributing to a disintegration of community and national unity.

The push for diversity has, according to articles and letters in journalism publications, contributed to "racial tension and "high anxiety" in the newsroom, and to "white men running scared." Many whites view the emphasis on diversity with a concern that the price of years of neglect and prejudice will be paid by them. This is particularly true where mergers, emphasizing bottom line and the marketing approach to journalism, have contributed to fewer persons being hired and more reductions in force. Minorities, while welcoming diversity, must live with the feeling that their hiring or promotion may have been at the price of a rejected white colleague who is adequately or better qualified, or that others will assume this even if it isn't true. Anthony J. Lomenzo concludes that while white managers can play the game of political correctness to remedy the ills of the past by tilting toward minorities or women, the American pursuit of social equality will take a beating. Talent and competition take a back seat to primary considerations of race and gender under the guise of fairness.

Such tensions have contributed to a political and judicial backlash seen in the passage of legislation protesting immigration policies and affirmative action programs. Some support for this trend is starting to emerge from the courts. Recently, the affirmative action programs designed to give minorities preferential treatment have been attacked as the nation's political mood has shifted. Furthermore, in a 5-4 ruling, the Supreme Court rejected its 1990 decision that the FCC's minority preference programs were not overbroad.

The second issue raised as organizations seek staffs reflecting a wider range of ethnic and social diversity revolves around the question of whether a reporter from a segment of society long discriminated against, can resist the temptation to become an advocate. Examples of such advocacy can be seen in the cases of female reporters who participate in pro-choice rallies or gay reporters who cover the AIDS epidemic. Critics of such reporting charge that such sympathy with causes being covered strikes at the heart of journalism objectivity and harms the credibility of all media individuals and institutions.

The third issue is that the diverse newsroom will not necessarily give rise to better coverage. Rather it will contribute to special-interest coverage and lobbying similar to that which exists today in government and politics. Indeed, one argument is that well-trained journalists of all races and backgrounds should be able to report objectively the news of the community. The corollary is that race, religion, or other special interests cloud the objectivity reporters should have.

The results of all this well-intended, mandated social planning, according to critics of enhancing newspaper diversity through goals and quotas, is that such practices may contribute to division rather than unity. Using quotas to better reflect the newsroom is analogous to the school busing programs of the 1960s. Although studies showed that busing the minority students to white schools to achieve racial balance contributed to better test scores for the minorities, the test scores of white students transported to less affluent areas suffered slightly. Of greater concern to both groups was the division and conflict that the busing of the children caused throughout the entire community.

Whether the example is analogous or not, the idea of mandating that certain stories, pages, photos, and positions must include a minority and/or a woman, such as is the practice of *USA Today*, contributes to the feeling of "beating back the white guys." This is because providing preferential treatment for targeted persons to the detriment of others not only breeds anxiety and tension but fosters resentment as well as alienation, polarization, and eventually hate. The very ills journalists have sought to alleviate and cure are being fostered. Quotas of sources determined by gender or race also come into conflict with news practices that recognize that the opinions of all men and women are not necessarily equal or even worthwhile. Although it is a nice marketing gesture to interview a sampling of men, women, and minorities on major policy questions at shopping centers or amusement parks, their opinions in the long run do not necessarily weigh as much as the members of the informed and influential group — even if those being interviewed are white.

Resolution

Part of the problem in increasing diversity in journalism is related to the fact that many editors see diversity as a simple and single solution to an involved and complex problem that has grown over generations. According to Wilson and Gutierrez, "Some experimented with Spanish or Asian language 'simulcasts' of news programs. Some inserted special sections geared for minority communities on a regular basis. Others did extensive special reports on the different minority communities in their circulation or broadcast area. Not all of these were successful in gaining increased readership, viewership or acceptance by the minority communities. And, as a result, some media managers were discouraged from trying other approaches."

Other critics point to the limited progress made thus far in overcoming the serious neglect of the past. In a study of minority news coverage in the *Columbus* (Ohio) *Dispatch* twenty years after the Kerner Commission report, Edward C. Pease discovered little progress. His *Newspaper Research Journal* study found that minority-related coverage became less "bad" and more "good" between 1965 and 1987; and even though there wasn't much more news about minorities in the *Dispatch* than twenty-two years earlier, less of it was negative. Minorities seem to have made little progress since 1965 in terms of having their voices and concerns heard, their problems discussed, their triumphs and sorrows reported, and their opinions considered.

More positive results can be seen in the efforts of two newspapers — one in the South and one in the North — to explore racial diversity and its ramifications. For their well-read efforts, the *New Orleans Times Picayune* won the Society of Professional Journalists' annual Sigma Delta Chi award for public service. The *Akron Beacon Journal* won the 1994 Pulitzer Prize for public service. According to Sig Gisler, the in-depth series challenge the notion that Americans are "tired" of reading and hearing about race. "Executed with honesty, integrity and imagination," Gisler wrote, "even a long series that closely and critically examines issues of race can engage and hold an audience."

Gisler says that, to their credit, both the New Orleans and Akron newspapers acted on the belief that honest dialogue, however initially painful and threatening, ultimately reduces fear, mistrust, and anger. The New Orleans and Akron examples, he says, underlie the importance of racial diversity in a newsroom's staff and leadership. More important, the cases demonstrate how the media can influence racial attitudes within communities and newsrooms.

In print news, Jannette Dates says three questions remain salient 150 years after the first black newspaper began publication: Does the majority press devote an equitable share of positive coverage to the minority community? Does the majority press employ a representative number of minority journalists? Does the majority press provide adequate minority participation at most decision making or management levels? Despite progress, Dates says none of these questions could be answered in the affirmative.

Although their hiring rates far exceeded those of companion media industries, broadcasters were caught cheating in reporting minority hiring statistics because most were hired into low category jobs, say Wilson and Gutierrez. One example was the scheme of counting female minorities twice, as "two-fers," in an effort to pad minority hiring figures. In television, minorities were found primarily in visible "on air" positions but were generally not found in decision-making management jobs.

Similar concerns are raised by Lee Thornton in an analysis of minorities coming into broadcast news. "The reality," Thornton writes, "was that, while their numbers had increased, the image problem had not been solved, for too often blacks were still chosen only to replace blacks who had been lost. The reality was that by the late 1980s, African Americans were creating their own forms to fill the coverage of issues relating directly to their lives. By then Black Entertainment Television was aiming its `BET news' with stories by, about, and decidedly for black consumption nationwide."

Although history shows that those individuals and institutions in a position to make changes procrastinated in trying to make the media more reflective of the pluralistic American society, there can be little question that the issue is now a priority on the media agenda and in journalism education. After close to two centuries of neglect the bandwagon is being filled. Hundreds of committees have been formed, speeches given, and articles and books written about the topic. Indeed, one of the backlash dangers of the diversity movement is that for some it is causing anxiety and a challenge to the credibility of the media.

A new concern about the moral and economic-motivated progress made in recent years is the slowdown in society's commitment to diversity. Some of this is reflected in the shifting rulings of the courts. Affirmative action programs designed to give minorities preferential treatment are starting to come under attack.

Leo Bogart, the former executive vice-president of the Newspaper Advertising Bureau, argues that newspapers need to maintain and accelerate their commitment to hire, train, and promote minorities. He warns against using such vague jargon as "multicultural diversity," recognizing that every minority group is unique and that most can't be defined in racial terms. He calls for more emphasis on Newspaper in Education programs that reach children in homes where parents don't read newspapers or speak English. Newspapers should also strive to give readers the feeling that the newspaper is for them and not just for some distant establishment.

Others urge that both the majority and minority should be united to assure not only that awareness and goal setting continue but that a wider range of broad-based goal setting and pluralistic planning continue. Authors such as Michael Eric Dyson, Jannette L. Dates and William Barlow emphasize that greater access to positions of power and creativity by minorities within the media industries may have a significant impact on more accurate portrayals of African Americans and, by extension, other racial and ethnic groups. Lee Thornton, in an article focusing on the strides made by African Americans between 1955 and 1990 in radio and television newsrooms, concludes that broadcast journalists in general, and African Americans in particular, have a responsibility to minorities to bring the media at all levels to greater congruence with the institutional, cultural, and intellectual diversity of American society. J. Sean McCleneghan of New Mexico State University reports that African-American newspaper opinion leaders are continuing to set standards for excellence for the next generation of media professionals.

Other ideas suggested by Frank Denton and Howard Kurtz are to include public members on the editorial board, to develop representative columnists, methodically to learn all about a newspaper's communities, and to institutionalize ways of talking and listening to them. They say two national roundtables called "Demography and Democracy" and "New Directions for News" developed some radical but doable ideas, such as a "democracy mall" to take a different kind of populist journalist into alienated communities. "We need to routinize coverage of minority communities, day in and day out," they propose, "and launch reporting projects inspired by their needs — not, for example, just the annual tribute to Crispus Attucks and Rosa Parks during Black History Month."

In addition, continued efforts need to be made in journalism education. One of the important books relating to this topic, *Pluralizing Journalism Education*, devotes about one third of its twenty-four chapters to ways in which to recruit, nurture, mentor, and retain minority students and faculty. "Clearly," says Ted Pease, "any gains that we in the academy make in terms of student and faculty diversity will translate directly into greater newsroom and news content in all the media."

This contrasts with journalism texts that for much of the twentieth century paid scant consideration to the ways the press covered — or failed to cover — racial and ethnic minorities. According to Linda Steiner's study published in *Journalism Monographs*, no pre-1970s textbook addressed race and ethnicity beyond stylebook rules on how to refer to the minority status of subjects. A study of twenty-four journalism textbooks published between 1908 and 1988 found that early reporting texts confined their discussion of minorities to addressing the use of racial designations in crime stories and prohibitions against demeaning racial terms and dialect. Native Americans were not mentioned in the early texts.

More important than the obvious race and skin-based diversity, however, will be the changes in attitudes important in both newsrooms and American society. Of particular import as a standard will be what Dr. Martin Luther King referred to as content of character before color of skin. Along with the content of character will be the growing recognition of talent, competence, and experience before race, color or gender.

Dates and Barlow believe that only a concerted systematic effort with the media mainstream, academia, and industry can ensure that the future will be different from the past for African American and other minorities with respect to the development and control of their media images. "Respect for the multicultural society that will characterize America in the twenty-first century," they argue, "must be engendered by all image makers who shape the world view of the American public, regardless of their race. America's future can be one of either relatively smooth transition or great upheaval. The task is great and the hour is late. We encourage all those of goodwill and stout heart to begin the transformation now."

Recommended Readings

Books

Beasley, Maurine H., and Sheila J. Gibbons. *Taking Their Place: A documentary history of women and journalism*. Washington: American University Press, 1994. Interprets and discusses participation of women in print and broadcast media, and how they are represented.

Dates, Jannette L., and William Barlow. *Split Image: African Americans in the Mass Media* . Washington, D.C.: Howard University, 1990. A comprehensive history of African Americans in the mass media — music, film, radio, television, advertising, and print and broadcast news.

Newspapers, Diversity & You 1995-1997. New York: Dow Jones Newspaper Fund, 1995. Booklet designed to guide minority high school and college students and young professionals in pursuing careers as newspaper journalists.

Kessler, Lauren. *The Dissident Press: Alternative Journalism in American History*. Beverly Hills: 1984. Rediscovers the needs, goals, and social impact of America's dissident journalists as alternative voices that have faced exclusion or ridicule by mainstream society.

MacDonald, J. Fred. *Blacks and White TV: African Americans in Television Since 1948*, 2nd ed. Chicago: Nelson-Hall Publishers, 1992. Although more optimistic than the first edition because of greater choice of channels, MacDonald sees the regressive forces of racism still flourishing over TV.

Martindale, Carolyn, ed. *Pluralizing Journalism Education: A Multicultural Handbook*. Westport, Conn.: Greenwood Press, 1993. Two dozen authors make philosophic and economic arguments for pluralizing journalism education and provide practical recommendations for recruiting and retaining students as well as making changes to the curriculum.

Murphy, James E., and Sharon M. Murphy. *Let My People Know: American Indian Journalism, 1828-1978*. Norman: University of Oklahoma Press, 1981. The first serious study of its kind analyzes the neglect and stereotyping of Native Americans.

Nelson, Jack A. *The Disabled, the Media, and the Information Age*. Westport, Conn.: Greenwood Press, 1994. Fifteen writers discuss images, language, ethics, civil rights, the workplace, technology, and other issues of the disabled and their role in enhancing newsroom diversity.

Weston, Mary Ann. *Native Americans in the News: Images of Indians in the Twentieth Century Press*. Westport, Conn.: Greenwood Press, 1996. History of racial and ethnic groups in mainstream press.

Wilson, Clint C. II, and Felix Gutierrez. *Minorities and Media: Diversity and the End of Mass Communication*. Newbury Park: 1985. Examines the history, relationships, and commonalities between the mass media and the four largest minority groups.

Articles & Book Chapters

Kerner, Otto. *Report of the National Advisory Commission on Civil Disorders*. New York: 1968). Chapter 15 of this official government report indicts the mass media for its role in contributing to civil disorders through lack of coverage and a staff that did not reflect American diversity.

Martindale, Carolyn. "Significant silences: newspaper coverage of problems facings facing black Americans." *Newspaper Research Journal* 15:2 (Spring 1994). Coverage of problems facing Black Americans was less than might be expected in the 1960s, but increased in the decade after that, only to decline in the 1980s.

Pease, Edward C. "Cornerstone for growth: how minorities are vital to the future of newspapers." *Newspaper Research Journal* 10:4 (Summer 1989). A comprehensive newspaper industry report on minority demographics recommends that American newspapers turn to minority readers, employees and advertisers to improve readership and circulation.

Tucker, Cynthia. "Can Militant Minority Reporters Be Objective?" *Nieman Reports* (Spring 1994. The question is reversed from the days when Blacks covered "Black" news and women wrote for "women's pages."

Chapter Six

News Media Coverage of Minorities

Kenneth Campbell

During the final quarter of the twentieth century, the news media's coverage of minorities has became one of the most controversial ongoing issues the mainstream media have faced. The respected Freedom Forum for Media Studies devoted the entire summer 1994 issue of its quarterly *Media Studies Journal* to the topic, using the title "Race — America's Rawest Nerve." Minority coverage is of enormous significance because of the potential impact media portrayals may have on readers and viewers, and because of the country's increasing population of people of color who will be the audience of tomorrow. The news media have come under sharp attack by those who argue that the news unfairly and inaccurately perpetuates stereotypes of minorities as violent, criminal, and irresponsible. And yet, others argue that when news media try to improve coverage of minorities in newscasts and newspages, particularly to increase positive portrayals, they are caving in to special interest groups and political correctness rather than reporting news fairly, objectively, and accurately. This chapter addresses both sides of the argument with an attempt to provide a context for understanding the debate.

Origins of the Issue

For minorities, coverage of their communities by the mainstream news media has been an issue since the colonial period, although most blacks in the United States then were still uneducated and could not read. Recent research shows that minorities were generally ignored by the mainstream media, and their few depictions were stereotypical. Whether as slaves, noble savages, warriors, or low-skilled workers, they were presented as being less intelligent and less civilized. The minority groups responded to the mainstream news media's portrayals by starting their own publications to present their side of the story. According to Clint Wilson and Felix Gutierrez, in their 1995 book *Race,*

Multiculturalism and the Media, the first Latino newspaper, *El Misisipi*, was founded in 1808 to rail against Napoleon's takeover of Spain; the first black newspaper, *Freedom's Journal*, in 1827 to "plead our own cause"; the first Native American newspaper, the *Cherokee Phoenix*, in 1828 to advocate a tribal identity and disseminate tribal news to the Cherokees and the native viewpoint to a wider audience; and the first Asian American newspaper, the *Golden Hills News*, in 1851 to Christianize the Chinese and to advocate respect for them among the forty-niners in the gold rush.

Samuel Cornish and John B. Russwurm expressed the sentiment of many people of color when they started the first black newspaper, *Freedom's Journal*, on March 16, 1827, in New York City. They wrote:

> We wish to plead our own cause. Too long have others spoken for us. Too long has the publick been deceived by misrepresentations, in things which concern us dearly, though in the estimation of some mere trifles; for though there are many in society who exercise towards us benevolent feelings; still (with sorrow we confess it) there are others who make it their business to enlarge upon the least trifle, which tends to the discredit of any person of colour; and pronounce anathemas and denounce our whole body for the misconduct of this guilty one.

While these newspapers became the voices of their communities, they never challenged the mainstream press. Thus, society's view of "news" and other events in communities of color has always been based on information presented in the mainstream media.

Most modern efforts to improve news media coverage of minorities began as a response to the Kerner Commission report in 1968. The commission, appointed by President Johnson, analyzed the causes of the urban riots of the 1960s, particularly riots in Newark, N.J., and Detroit, Mich., which occurred within a two-week period during the summer of 1967. Chapter 15 of the report, "The News Media and the Disorders," identified two grave concerns — coverage of minorities and employment of journalists of color — that remain the focus of the discussion today. The commission reported that its primary concern was not in the riot reporting itself, but in "the failure to report adequately on race relations and ghetto problems and to bring more Negroes into journalism." According to the report, the media had failed to communicate to its white audience "a sense of the degradation, misery, and hopelessness of living in the ghetto," and "a feeling for the difficulties and frustrations of being a Negro in the United States. They have not shown understanding or appreciation of — and thus have not communicated — a sense of Negro culture, thought, or history."

While distorted media coverage is a problem for minorities, such distortions could be an even bigger problem for white Americans who have little or no contact with minorities. What is presented in the newspaper or on television — especially in the news — becomes their reality. "By failing to portray the Negro as a matter of routine and in the context of the total society, the news media have, we believe, contributed to the black-white schism in this country," the report said.

Saying that the media report from "a white man's standpoint," the commission blamed the dismal performance on the lack of journalists of color, particularly in supervisory and decision-making positions. "The journalistic profession," the report said, "has been shockingly backward in seeking out, hiring, training, and promoting Negroes." At the time, the Kerner Commission found that fewer than 5 per cent of the nation's journalists and fewer than 1 per cent of editors and supervisors were black; and most of them worked for black-owned organizations, rather than mainstream media.

The commission encouraged news organizations to train and hire journalists of color to report on conditions in their communities before problems began to fester and explode. People from the communities would have access to sources that outsiders would not have, the report contended, and journalists of color would understand the problems of their communities better than outsiders.

Addressing the Problem

Much has changed in American journalism and its attitude toward minority coverage in the thirty years since the release of the Kerner report. David Shaw, media critic for the *Los Angeles Times*, captured the essence of the efforts to address the inadequate coverage of minorities in his 1990 report, "Coloring the News." Shaw said that in the 1960s and early 1970s, proponents of increased and balanced coverage of minorities argued that it was the moral and ethical thing to do. After little change, a journalistic argument emerged: "Better minority coverage would make for better — i.e., more complete, more sensitive and more diverse newspapers," according to Shaw. Again, there was little change. Now, Shaw said, readership is declining, minority populations are increasing, and a financial rationale is being advanced: "Cover minorities better because they're not going to be in the minority much longer, and if you don't cover them, they won't read your papers or patronize your advertisers and you're going to be out of business, scratching your head, wondering what you did wrong."

An early major industry-wide effort to increase minorities in the newsroom was undertaken by the American Society of Newspaper Editors, whose members are daily newspaper editors. The ASNE established a goal in 1978 of having the percentage of minorities in newsrooms equal their proportion of the population by the year 2000. Efforts to reach the goal have included the creation of several summer workshops — some associated with colleges and universities — and internships to train minorities for careers in journalism. These efforts have pushed the proportion of journalists of color on daily newspaper staffs to 11.35 per cent in 1997, according to ASNE, although nearly half of the dailies still had no journalists of color. Some 8.9 per cent of newsroom supervisors were minorities. TV news organizations had increased their percentage of minorities on the news staff to 18 per cent in 1994, but as newsroom directors they dropped from 10 per cent in 1990 to 7.7 per cent in 1994, according to the latest statistics provided by Vernon Stone, a University of Missouri professor who monitors broadcast employment.

Despite the increase in minority journalists, people and communities of color maintain that the news media still present a distorted picture of them. For example, in a 1994 report, a major Hispanic group called the National Council of La Raza contended that negative stereotyping in the media is halting the progress of Hispanics. The report, quoted in a 1994 *Editor and Publisher* article titled "State of Hispanic America," admitted that there was insufficient longitudinal research to support its criticism — but that anecdotal evidence showed a lack of Hispanic perspectives in the news. "Specifically," the report asserted, "such coverage appears to focus on Latinos as 'objects' of the news to be commented on by others, rather than as 'subjects' of the news who have authoritative or legitimate perspective to share." Contending that the print media tend to present Hispanics as "problem people," either as perpetrators or victims of crime, drugs, poverty, and sloth, the report noted that "these negative portrayals are exacerbated by the fact that they are rarely counterbalanced by Hispanics who appear in more positive settings in the news."

Research on the coverage of minority communities supports the contention that the Kerner concerns are still valid. Professor Carolyn Martindale researched the portrayal of African Americans between 1950 and 1989 in her book, *Blacks and the White Press*, and a series of scholarly articles. Although in general the presentation of blacks in stereotypical roles fell while everyday life portrayals increased during the four decades, she found that less than 5 per cent of the newshole of the four major dailies was dedicated to coverage of African Americans. Professor Edward Pease, in a 1989 *Newspaper Research Journal* article "Kerner Plus 20: Minority News Coverage in the *Columbus Dispatch*," found "a miniscule" increase in the percentage of the newspaper's news items regarding people of color when he compared the newspaper's coverage in 1965 and 1987.

He also found less than 4 per cent of the stories in both years related to people of color, and an increase in crime news related to them. Pease concluded that in the *Columbus Dispatch*, "minorities seem to have made little progress since 1965 in terms of having their voices and concerns heard, their problems discussed."

In other noteworthy studies, Professor Marilyn Gist in a 1990 *Newspaper Research Journal* article, "Minorities and Media Imagery," found that African American males were disproportionately involved in crime, drugs, and gangs, and in stories about low achievement. Professors Kenneth Campbell and Ernest Wiggins, in a 1992 study, "Despite Progress, African Americans Still Scarce in South Carolina Daily Newspapers," reported in their analysis of four daily newspapers that although African Americans make up nearly 30 per cent of the state's population, only 5.7 per cent of the stories related directly to African Americans. They concluded: "the most glaring shortcoming is the scarcity of stories of specific interest to or incorporating African Americans."

Broadcast research presents a similar picture. Two U.S. Commission on Civil Rights reports, the 1977 *Window Dressing on the Set* and its update in 1979, found not only that network evening newscasts rarely dealt with topics related to minorities, but also that minorities seldom appeared as newsmakers or correspondents.

Robert M. Entman, in his 1990 study, "Modern Racism and the Images of Blacks in Local Television News," in *Critical Studies in Mass Communication*, said his research showed that TV news no longer promotes "traditional racism" such as overtly condoning segregation, racial slurs, and physical violence against blacks, but TV news now supports "modern racism," which is more subtle. Examples of modern racism range from quoting sources that attack issues of specific interest to blacks, such as affirmative action, to presenting blacks in a disproportionate number and as threatening in crime stories. In a 1994 study, "Representation and Reality in the Portrayal of Blacks on Network Television News," which appeared in *Journalism and Mass Communication Quarterly*, Entman examined a year's worth of transcripts of the nightly ABC "World News" programs. He found "a dearth of blacks in stories that have as their central theme either blacks as positive contributors to American society, or blacks as human beings whose racial identity is incidental."

In 1994 the professional minority journalists organizations released "News Watch," a report that concluded that people of color still tend to be invisible in the general news media, both print and broadcast, and when presented, are frequently stereotyped. Raul Ramirez, news director at KQED public radio in San Francisco and a principal author of the report, said that the "bad news is the invisibility, the lack of coverage, that absence from the daily public discussion ... that determines public policy. This results in bad public policy because it is uninformed public policy."

In two studies, "African Americans in TV News in South Carolina," published in 1996 in *The State of Black South Carolina,* and "Still Knowing Their Place: African Americans in Southeast TV Newscasts," a research paper presented in 1997, Professors Kenneth Campbell, Ernest Wiggins, and Sonya Forte Duhe found that African Americans are often vastly underrepresented when their frequency in TV newscasts is compared to their percentage in the TV viewing area's population. Blacks were also underrepresented in higher prestige roles and, not surprisingly, overrepresented in some lower prestige roles. For example, blacks tended to be overrepresented in low-skilled jobs and as criminals.

In response to the continuing criticisms pointing out their shortcomings, some news organizations have established hiring goals for minorities, aggressive efforts to move minorities into supervisory positions, and firm rules for increasing the presence of minorities in their news reports. Along with these efforts, the news organizations have begun to monitor how their particular newsroom covers minorities and minority communities by conducting content audits. Knight Ridder and Gannett are considered two of the leaders in such efforts. Additionally, some news organizations have included sensitivity workshops or diversity training as a part of staff development in an effort to increase awareness of racial and ethnic insensitivities.

But, as stated earlier, in the eyes of the minority communities, much more effort is needed to improve the coverage. In a survey of news coverage in 1994, 62 per cent of African American respondents, 39 per cent of Hispanics and 29 per cent of Asians were disappointed with the coverage of their respective communities. Also, when asked whether having a reporter of their own race or ethnicity improves coverage of a story related to that race or ethnic group, 74 per cent of African Americans, 68 per cent of Hispanics, and 63 per cent of Asians said it made "a great deal" or "a moderate amount" of difference. Commenting on the results of the survey in the article, "Most Blacks Upset By News Coverage," which appeared in 1994 in *Editor and Publisher* magazine, *USA Today* Editor Peter S. Prichard said, "These poll results show that those of us in the media still have a significant distance to travel before we will satisfy the concerns of our nation's minority citizens."

Criticism of Research & Newsroom Diversity Practices

These studies have not gone unchallenged, nor have the newsroom practices. The research has been criticized primarily by newsroom supervisors who say it underestimates their efforts to improve coverage of minority communities; the newsroom tactics have been criticized by some journalists and critics of multiculturalism.

Newsroom supervisors who support diversity efforts do not disagree with the basic thrust of the critical research — that coverage of communities of color needs to be improved — but many do argue that a much better job is being done than research shows. They contend that studies that count the number of minority stories sources ignore minority issues and sources that have been "mainstreamed" into the total news report. Rather than publishing stories on minorities or minority issues, the goal in mainstreaming is to incorporate minorities into all kinds of stories. Such an approach moves away from a focus on identifiable minority stories, or "ghettoizing" minority sources into stories about minorities. Therefore, a reporter covering a story about banking goes beyond the call of duty to find a minority banker to use as a source, even though the story has no racial angle or implications. The source is not identified as a person of color, unless race is essential to the story, although the source's picture may be used, which would allow readers or viewers to see that the person is a member of a minority group.

Significant efforts are being made in many newsrooms to mainstream minorities, from creating data banks of minority sources to conducting content audits in which editors monitor stories to make sure minority sources are being used. Some news agencies have policies that require reporters to check each story for diversity of sources (including women). Reporters who are not including minority sources in their stories can be required to do a better job. Mainstreaming presents an accurate picture, according to its advocates, even if readers and viewers don't always know that a source is a minority group member. What is important, say mainstreaming advocates, is that the goal of diversity among sources is being reached, and that generally means a more accurate story is being presented.

Some newsroom supervisors also contend that the research is flawed and doesn't support the argument that the media inadequately cover minorities or portray them as stereotypes. The major flaw, according to these supervisors, is that the research suggests people of color are only interested in a story if it has them in it, or it focuses on an issue or event traditionally associated with people of color. But, newsroom supervisors ask, aren't minorities interested in, and affected by, most stories about politics, education, taxes, crime, and other public affairs? Don't minorities find human interest stories about local persons and major entertainers interesting? Minorities are members of the entire community, the newsroom supervisors argue, not just one part of it. And so, they are interested in stories about the entire community — local, national, and global. To suggest otherwise, according to newsroom supervisors, is to distort who people of color really are — the same criticism that is made against stories about people of color.

Similarly, just the mere presence of a person of color in a story is not an indication that minorities are, or should be, interested in the story, according to newsroom supervisors. Particularly in news stories, it is often the story topic, or information that the story might provide, that attracts the reader rather than the person or persons used as the source. It is far-fetched to think that an entire group of people will not read or view a story of interest to them simply because their ethnic group is not present, the newsroom supervisors contend.

Another criticism of counting minorities in stories to determine how well they are portrayed is that it puts too much blame on journalists for reporting what might simply be reality. It is unrealistic, newsroom supervisors say, to expect people of color to appear in the news report equal to their percentage in the population. And it is more unrealistic to expect the news report to contain persons of color in the many different societal and occupational roles in proportion to their presence in those roles. When there are relatively few minorities in a role, it follows that they are likely to be absent from the media report. The supervisors also argue that when people of color are shown in disproportionately large numbers, such as criminals and unskilled laborers, it is because they are disproportionately represented in those roles in real life. It is accurate, they contend, that minorities commit a disproportionately large percentage of crimes and minorities are disproportionately concentrated in low-skilled jobs. While such portrayals might be considered negative, they are accurate.

Finally, newsroom supervisors argue that the research on minorities does not take into account special reports they publish or broadcast. Many newspapers, as well as network and local broadcast news organizations, have done impressive in-depth stories on race relations and minority communities during the past few years. These pieces address problems in a much more substantive way than the daily news report is capable of doing. The commitment it takes to carry out such projects, according to newsroom supervisors, is evidence of the long-term commitments of some news organizations to improving the coverage of communities of color.

Newsroom supervisors find themselves defending their diversity efforts not only against criticism that they are not doing enough but also against criticism that their efforts are misguided. Critics of diversity efforts say they do not oppose the goal of improved coverage — they would like improved coverage of all segments of society — nor do they oppose the goal of greater diversity in the newsrooms. However, they believe diversity efforts have led to greater distortion of the news rather than greater accuracy.

According to critics, diversity efforts cause news coverage to be driven by politics or ideology of journalists and journalistic organizations. Critics say unqualified minority journalists are being hired and promoted in the name of diversity, and that news media are bowing to the pressures of political correctness and special interests groups, causing them to tread lightly or avoid stories involving race altogether — especially stories that would reflect negatively on minorities. Unfortunately, critics often keep a low public profile, or tend to speak anonymously. Christopher Caldwell, in "Affirmative Sourcing," an article critical of some newsroom diversity efforts that appeared in 1993 in *Media Critic* magazine, noted that few critics of diversity policies would let him use their name. Neither have the critics amassed a body of research to support their criticisms. Rather, the position of critics usually emerges as editors and other journalists respond to research on the coverage of minorities or to criticism of certain diversity efforts and their perceived impact.

The charge that diversity efforts leads to soft coverage that favors minorities stings the news media where it hurts because minorities still complain of negative coverage when journalists would like to think they are doing a better job. *Los Angeles Times* media critic David Shaw sees the two tendencies as linked: "Some critics say the press may occasionally try to overcompensate for its essentially negative portrayal of blacks and Latinos by being too soft on prominent members of those ethnic groups who deserve critical scrutiny." One of those critics is conservative writer Dinesh D'Souza, who stated in his 1995 book *The End of Racism*, that despite the criticism of black activists who say the media are racist, "many newspapers seem to tread extremely cautiously when reporting incidents in which blacks and other minorities are placed in an unfavorable light. Even while reporting such gruesome crimes as rape, *The New York Times* sometimes provides a description of the suspect but omits the crucial detail of race, apparently to avoid reinforcing public suspicions of African Americans." Howard Kurtz, media critic for the *Washington Post*, also contended in the 1991 article, "Our Politically Correct Press," that the media have gone soft on race. He said that "in an era when an ill-chosen phrase can spark a nationwide backlash, the profession seems infused with a new skittishness, a growing fear that some group or faction or minority might be offended by industrial strength opinions." He added, "Most news organizations have retreated to a kind of race-neutral posture in which race and ethnicity are excluded unless absolutely necessary."

As D'Souza and Kurtz indicate, the *New York Times'* and the *Washington*

Post's coverage of blacks in their respective cities is cited by critics of diversity efforts as examples of favorable media coverage of blacks. In the article "A great story never told," which appeared in *U.S. News and World Report* in 1996, John Leo reported that "the influence of diversity politics in newsrooms means that journalists are increasingly reluctant to report negative news about minorities ... (as well as other groups).... *[T]he New York Times'* commitment to racial justice, which is obviously a good thing, has made it increasingly hard to report racial stories accurately." An example that has been cited is the *New York Times'* coverage of the Crown Heights riots, which, according to John O'Sullivan in a 1993 issue of the *National Review*, showed that "[p]olitical correctness is already an influence in city newsrooms." Relying on an analysis by William McGowan of the Manhattan Institute's *City Journal*, O'Sullivan said that the press downplayed the anti-semitic character of black gangs. O'Sullivan contrasted this coverage with what he called the *New York Times'* prompt condemnation of the murder of Yusuf Hawkins, a black youth, by a mixed race gang, which the paper attributed in part to white racism.

In a rare public discussion of criticism of newsroom diversity efforts, Ruth Shalit, in her article "Race in the Newsroom," which appeared in *The New Republic* in 1995, raised a furor when she charged the *Washington Post* with being soft on racial issues and black politicians. She wrote that "the *Post's* coverage of the majority-black city in which it is located has grown increasingly timorous and protective over the past decade. Aggressive coverage of the social pathologies at the heart of Washington's black underclass — chronic welfare dependence, adolescent childbearing, neighborhood crime and violence — has increasingly given way to human-interest puffery." Reese Cleghorn, dean of the College of Journalism at the University of Maryland, responded to Shalit's contention in his *American Journalism Review* column in the November 1995 issue. He agreed that coverage was sometimes "being warped (or subdued) to avoid offending minority readers," but added that "the *Post* was more guilty several years ago. These days, it more often takes gusty positions in relation to its black readership, but it does sometimes still walk on eggs to avoid being pilloried as white racist." The "kowtowing" to minority readers, he said, was "probably not as much as the kowtowing to the biases of middle-class whites." The soft coverage of the middle class is precisely the reason for the soft coverage of minorities, according to a high-level *Washington Post* editor quoted by Shalit. The editor, unhappy with what Shalit calls "diversity journalism," said, "Today, with the rise of a black middle class, some of the middle-class people we offend are going to be black. What I'm trying to suggest is that diversity in the newsroom is a subset of the larger issue of middle-class America sort of being upset about what journalists do and papers increasingly caving to them. And a whole philosophy is growing up, as far as I'm concerned, to rationalize the cave."

Critics also argue that special efforts to recruit and hire minorities — the news media's affirmative action policy — lead to unprepared minority journalists in leadership positions, then to distrust and low morale. Shaw reported the contention among some journalists and critics: "[S]ome minorities who capitalize on the current climate and move 'too quickly' to big papers may not acquire the skills that they would develop under less pressure during an apprenticeship at a smaller paper, a few editors say." Ruth Shalit, in her *New Republic* article, described a "growing backlash against affirmative action" at the *Post*. Summing up the situation at the paper, she said that "[d]espite real achievements, its [the *Post's*] well-intentioned efforts have gone awry, in ways that have implications for the politics of newsrooms across America for the way that news is covered — and not covered — by newspapers in the future." Diversity hiring at the newspaper, Shalit says, "has provoked an affirmative action backlash, fanning racial tensions among white and black reporters as both groups feel aggrieved and victimized by discrimination." The hiring policy, along with the newspaper's effort to achieve "racially balanced news coverage" that does not offend the "increasingly brittle sensibilities of the relevant groups," has "compromise[d] the paper's traditional role as a gadfly in Washington, D.C., and in the nation as a whole," Shalit contends.

Several surveys of journalists in the 1990s suggest the morale problem based on racial issues is industry-wide. "The Newsroom Barometer: Job satisfaction & the impact of racial diversity at U.S. daily newspapers," by Professors Edward Pease and J. Frazier Smith in 1991, reported what Pease called "deep dissatisfaction among both minority and white journalists about newspaper performance in covering minorities." Similarly, the National Association of Black Journalists' 1994 report, "Muted Voices," found a "gulf in communication between reporters and managers" that inhibits discussion about race and leads to widespread job dissatisfaction. In 1996, the Associated Press Managing Editors Diversity Committee Report again found a "wide perceptual gap between white and minority newsroom professionals."

Finally, at least one report contends that the efforts to change the content of mainstream media to appeal to minorities may not be needed, that the efforts are based on a misinterpretation of the news media's own research. Gilbert Cranberg and Vincent Rodriguez, writing in 1994 in *Columbia Journalism Review*, argued that minorities read the newspaper in proportion to their percentage in the population, and thus no special effort is needed to increase their readership. "Certainly, diverse newsrooms and improved coverage of minorities are overdue," they wrote. "Sensitive and informed coverage of all segments of society is in the interest of all readers. But much of the talk directed at editors nowadays sounds like this: If you want to win minority readers — and you'd better — pitch them minority content. That's not only condescending, it perpetuates myths, and sells minorities short."

Resolution

Although much has changed, so much remains the same. The news media have followed the two key recommendations of the Kerner report. Employment of minorities in the news media has increased significantly, although it has levelled off during recent years. Significant progress has also been made on the second recommendation — improved coverage. The complaint is no longer that minorities are not covered, but rather the coverage tends to be negative and to stereotype minorities.

Diversity advocates and their critics agree that coverage of minorities needs to be fair, accurate, and balanced. The two sides, however, do not agree on what fair, accurate and balanced coverage is, nor how to reach it. Both sides say it is not just racial and ethnic minorities who need the accurate coverage, but everyone. They disagree, however, on whether that accurate coverage can mean intentional favorable coverage, or less emphasized coverage of the negative. When minorities disproportionately commit crimes, or hold low-skilled jobs, or are on welfare, diversity critics say, the news media should reflect it. Accuracy can be negative.

Diversity advocates, though, are looking through the lens of history. Since the news media have contributed to society's many stereotypes of minorities, diversity advocates contend that extra effort, additional context, is needed to present a true picture. A story about a violent crime committed by a black or Latino male can be accurate as the report of a single incident, but when combined with other similar stories, or in the context of previous stories, it might continue to perpetuate the stereotype of the black or Latino male as criminal. The truth, or accuracy, isn't necessarily presented in one story or picture. Since the news media helped to create the stereotype, diversity advocates say it is appropriate for the news media to use measures over a period of time to create an accurate societal image of the groups. Thus, diversity advocates call for more stories about minorities that are neutral or positive and that counter previous stereotypes of minorities. They also want to incorporate more minorities into stories where race is irrelevant. If improved coverage means withholding certain stories or presenting images of minorities that might perpetuate stereotypes, that can be done at times, when the information is not vital. For a fuller discussion of alternative methods for incorporating diversity into the news report, see "Implementation of Racial and Ethnic Diversity in the American Press: Objectives, Obstacles, and Incentives" by The Joan Shorenstein Center of the Harvard University John F. Kennedy School of Government.

An improved, more accurate portrayal of minorities in the news media is important for all of society. Minorities often feel that how they are presented in the news media is how white America sees them. And for white America, the presentation can seem to represent how minorities really are. As the Kerner report stated, "If what the white American reads in the newspapers or sees on television conditions his expectation of what is ordinary and normal in the larger society, he will neither understand nor accept the black American. By failing to portray the Negro as a matter of routine and in the context of the total society, the news media have, we believe, contributed to the black-white schism in this country." This criticism still resonates with many in the minority communities.

Nevertheless, many of the efforts of the news media to improve coverage of minority communities have shown positive results. The diversity critics notwithstanding, the minority recruitment and hiring policies have increased minority representation in many newsrooms, which has resulted in improved coverage. A greater commitment to fairness and accuracy has resulted in fewer stereotypical stories and more stories that represent the variety of experiences in the minority communities. If these improvements have been made in large part because of the increase in minorities in the newsroom, even greater improvements will be made when the proportion of minority supervisors in the newsroom increases.

Recommended Readings

Books

Associated Press Managing Editors. *Report of Committee on Minorities*. Minneapolis, Minn.: MORI Research, 1996. The report, conducted with the cooperation of the professional minority journalists associations, is the latest of several surveys in the 1990s that shows wide differences of opinion between minority and white journalists on issues involving newsroom employment and coverage of minority communities.

D'Souza, Dinesh. *The End of Racism*. New York: The Free Press, 1995. Only a few pages specifically address media bias, but they are significant in the development of D'Souza's overall argument against multiculturalism.

Implementation of Racial and Ethnic Diversity in the American Press: Objectives, Obstacles, and

Incentives, Cambridge, Mass.: Joan Shorenstein Center, Harvard University John F. Kennedy School of Government, 1996. This report concludes "that while much research has been done and the objectives are clear, there are numerous obstacles to implementation" of racial and ethnic diversity in the press.

Martindale, Carolyn. *The White Press and Black America*. New York: Greenwood Press, 1986. A content analysis of major newspapers over four decades shows little change in content.

Muted Voices: Frustration and Fear in the Newsroom: An analytical look at obstacles to the advancement of African American journalists. Reston, Va.: National Association of Black Journalists, 1994. A survey of NABJ members as well as managers in print and broadcast found: "The gulf in communications between reporters and managers is so great that the journalists are afraid to speak up about race issues and are hitting a glass ceiling of opportunity that leads to frustration early in their careers."

News Watch: A critical look at coverage of people of color. San Francisco, Calif.: Center for Integration and Improvement of Journalism, San Francisco State University, 1994. A report sponsored by the country's journalists of color organizations — Asian American Journalists Association, National Association of Black Journalists, National Association of Hispanic Journalists, and Native American Journalists Association — found continued stereotyping of minorities in the news media.

Pease, Edward, and J. Frazier Smith. *The Newsroom Barometer: Job satisfaction & the impact of racial diversity at U.S. daily newspapers*. Columbus, Ohio: Bush Research Center of the E.W. Scripps School of Journalism, Ohio University, 1991. One of several studies in the 1990s that shows significant differences in the perceptions of white and minority journalists on issues of newsroom employment, where minorities find themselves "excluded and overlooked, feel themselves undervalued and often shunned, [and think they are viewed as] second-class citizens...."

Wilson, Clint C., and Felix Gutierrez. *Race, Multiculturalism, and the Media*. Thousand Oaks, Calif.: Sage, 1995. The authors chronicle and analyze "the relationship between peoples of color and mainstream 'mass media' in the United States," including a chapter, "The Press: Adding Color to the News," and other sections on both print and broadcast news media.

Articles & Book Chapters

Caldwell, Christopher. "Affirmative Sourcing." *Media Critic* (Fall 1993): 27-37. This critique of diversity efforts muses: "Multiculturalism has invaded the newsroom as more and more papers demand that every story mirror the nation's racial, ethnic and sexual make-up. In pursuit of diversity, will newspapers attract new audiences or become bulletin boards for special interests?"

Campbell, Kenneth, Sonya Forte Duhe, and Ernest L. Wiggins. "African Americans in TV News in South Carolina." Pp. 124-45 in K. Campbell, ed., *The State of Black South Carolina*

1995-1996: An Action Agenda for the Future. Columbia, S.C.: The Urban League, 1995. This content analysis of broadcast news finds blacks underrepresented in higher prestige occupations and activities and overrepresented in lower prestige ones, which is consistent with other research.

Cranberg, Gilbert, and Vincent Rodriguez. "The Myth of the Minority Reader." *Columbia Journalism Review* (January/February 1994): 42-3. The authors contend that there is no "minority readership gap." Instead of focusing on increasing minority content, newspapers should focus on doing something about "the twin underlying causes of non-readership — low income and bad schools."

Entman, Robert. "Representation and Reality in the Portrayal of Blacks on Network Television News." *Journalism Quarterly* 71 (Autumn 1994): 509-20. One of several studies by Entmann that found unflattering portrayals of minorities in broadcast media, confirming his hypothesis that the media support subtle bias rather than overt discrimination.

Kurtz, Howard. "Our Politically Correct Press: More and More Stories Seem Too Touchy For Journalists." *Washington Post*, 20 January 1991, pp. B1, B4. Kurtz, who covers the media for the *Post*, questions whether political correctness has caused the news media to become too cautious in the coverage of issues involving race.

Pease, Edward F. "Kerner Plus 20: Minority News Coverage in the Columbus Dispatch." *Newspaper Research Journal* (Spring 1989): 17-37. This study comparing newspaper content at the time of and twenty years after the Kerner report found little difference in the small percentage of space devoted to stories about minorities.

Shaw, David. "Negative news and little else: Focusing on crime and poverty paints an incomplete portrait of minorities," in "Coloring the News," a special report in *Quill* (May 1991): 15-24. In a reprint of part of a series from his newspaper, *Los Angeles Times* media critic Shaw offers a balanced discussion of news media coverage of minorities.

Shalit, Ruth. "Race in the Newsroom." *The New Republic*, 2 October 1995, pp. 20-37. Contends that affirmative action hiring policies have led to racial tensions in the newsroom and soft coverage of the black community. Also read "Race in the Newsroom: An Exchange," *The New Republic*, 16 October 1995, pp. 14-17, which includes responses by *Washington Post's* Executive Editor Leonard Downie Jr. and Publisher Donald Graham.

Chapter Seven

Military and Media Relations

Hugh C. Cate

The relationship between the military and media is in a constant state of change. The military, attempting to protect its interests, seeks to harness the media's ability to influence the public. The media, likewise, seek to stand behind the principles of the First Amendment and provide the public with the truth. Throughout modern history, the media have endured systems of censorship and restrictions of access deemed necessary by the military during armed conflicts involving American soldiers. Both methods of control strike at the very heart of all the freedoms that most in the media hold dear. Conversely, those in the military stand by these methods of control as being integral security measures that are absolutely necessary to minimize casualties on the battlefield. The two sides have been in conflict for decades and will continue to be until each institution recognizes the unique situations of combat and the inherent roles and responsibilities of each during battle.

Understanding the relationship between the two institutions first requires an understanding of the terms used in defining the relationship. The "military" is an all-encompassing term for the men and women who serve in the United States Armed Forces. It represents the Army, Air Force, Navy, Marines, and Coast Guard. The term also represents civilians who serve the needs of the Armed Forces from positions within the Department of Defense. The myriad chains of command as well as the roles and responsibilities of each Service adds even more complexity to the term "military."

Similarly, the term "media" refers to the vast expanse of media outlets such as newsprint, magazines, television, and radio. Each outlet contains its own methods, styles, roles, and responsibilities. The media comprise everyone from journalists and reporters on local papers to editors and owners of the largest newspaper chains and television networks in America.

The relationship between these vast institutions, by virtue of their diversity, must constantly be in a state of flux. Their tenuous relationship has been evolving since a reporter first covered a battle during the Mexican-American war of 1846–1848. The media's goal to keep the public informed matched against the military's objective to fight and win wars determines the nature of the relationship between the two institutions.

The military and the media will always need to have some type of working relationship. The evolution of this relationship can be seen by examining the state of the relationship during each of our nation's major military conflicts. Examining the relationship between the two institutions during each conflict will also provide information about the nature of those relations.

Origins of the Issue

The Civil War provides a unique starting point from which to examine the relationship between the military and the media. The media, mainly newspapers during this period, were experiencing a growth in both readership and the ability to transmit news to the public. The telegraph now allowed reporters to file reports on battles and conditions with a speed never before seen. As a result of the new technological innovations, the emphasis on speed pervaded the atmosphere of combat coverage among the media. The military placed the priority on security. As such, a system of military censorship evolved attempting to ensure reporters released only information that would be of no use to the enemy. The media, overwhelmed by the new technology and growing readership, at times did release information in the forms of battle maps and troop strengths that could indeed be helpful to the enemy.

The relationship between the two institutions was off to a shaky start. The writings of General William T. Sherman exemplify the nature of the relationship. Sherman had a great animosity toward the media and based his ire on the spread of information about his units to the enemy. He revealed his dislike in a series of letters written to Thomas Ewing, his foster father. "They encumber our transports, occupy state rooms to the exclusion of officers on duty, they eat our provisions, they swell the crowd of hangers on, and increase the impedimenta," he wrote indignantly. "They publish without stint positive information of movements past and prospective, organizations, names of commanders, and accurate information which reaches the enemy with as much regularity as it does our People."

The Civil War kicked off a history of mutual distrust between the media and the military. The military established censoring systems to reduce the amount of intelligence passed to the enemy. The reporters, often blatantly disregarding the censors, continued to believe they had the right to report what they witnessed. It was the first time the military developed a system to censor the media, as well as the first time the media had to endure censorship.

Following the Spanish-American War, supporters of that war in both the military and the media had pushed for rules and regulations covering the control of the media during combat. The Army War College even published a book on the relations between the press and the military during times of war. With the onset of World War I, however, the media fell under the system of propaganda already in place in Europe. The military continued to treat war correspondents with suspicion and caution. War correspondents who wished to visit the battlefield had to pay a severe price to conduct their business. The Secretary of War personally accredited those who desired to cover the war. In addition, the correspondents had to take an oath to write the truth and submit a $10,000 bond to ensure their proper conduct in the field. Once in France, the correspondents then had to submit their releases to military censors who guardedly protected even the least important military secrets. The media, following the war, staged numerous protests over the censorship that took place during the conflict.

In the years between the first and second World Wars, the military attempted to reconcile the differences between the two institutions. Its members were beginning to understand that winning public support was just as important as winning the battles on the field. Attempts to restructure the Public Affairs systems within the military began, and the military slowly began a period of change.

World War II, however, severely tested the new structural changes. The military, although attempting to keep the public informed, continued censoring news material while relaxing some of the standards concerning access to the combat zones. Although it attempted to keep the public informed of the general trends within the war, conflicts regarding censorship continued to surface. But despite these conflicts, both the military and the media were generally satisfied with the relationship during this period. Both agreed that World War II was as honestly and accurately relayed to the American public as possible.

The success during the second World War left many in the military expecting the same results during the Korean War. American involvement in the Korean War began with the media free to report news to the public within certain guidelines issued by the military, which lacked the facilities or expertise to set up a censorship department at the beginning of the conflict. As such, there were no reports of the media abusing the system and relaying critical information to the enemy. However, the good rapport between the two institutions lasted only until the Chinese entered the conflict.

Once that happened, the military failed to issue proper guidance to the media on what was or was not critical information. Subsequently, a number of reports containing useful information to the enemy appeared in the press, and the military again deemed it necessary to invoke a censorship policy. The media did not take the censorship seriously, and there were numerous breaches of security. Reporters who were free to travel to different countries waited until they were outside the combat zone to release their information. Nevertheless, journalists reporting on the Korean War still supported the military's mission. This would not be the case in Vietnam.

Although relations between the military and the media had been strained, the Vietnam conflict set a new precedent. Trying to take a more proactive, public relations approach, the military placed voluntary guidelines on the media rather than invoke censorship. But the media's support for American involvement lasted only until the Tet Offensive of 1968. The surprise attack by the North Vietnamese during the traditional cease fire in observance of the Tet holiday stunned the American people. After this, the media became increasingly critical, and the shocking images it presented to its TV and print audience fueled the fire that led the public to denounce the entire war effort. Those in the military blamed the media for their lack of homefront support, and the bitterness of this era would seep into the decades that followed.

In 1983, the United States invaded Grenada in Operation Urgent Fury. There were no reporters on the scene to cover the initial invasion — the military had closed the entire operation off to the media and issued only its own news releases. The media finally gained access to the island nation after two days, and even then could not file reports until the military screened the information. This inflamed the media, whose members believed the military withheld information that the public had a right to receive.

Subsequent protests to the highest levels of government resulted in the creation of the Sidle commission. This commission, created by the Joint Chiefs of Staff, included fourteen journalists and press relations officials. The commission's goal was to devise methods in which future media relations could be handled more efficiently.

The commission recommended eight solutions for facilitating future coverage of military operations. These included the recommendation that the military plan for and include the media on all future missions, as well as accreditation rules, equipment requirements, and transportation requirements. The commission also recommended that the military take the initiative to increase rapport between the two institutions. The most important recommendation was the creation of a National Media Pool to cover military operations where full access to all media was not possible.

The first major conflict to use the National Media Pool was the invasion of Panama in December 1989. The pool's activation occurred in a timely manner, and media representatives arrived in the country just hours after the operation began. Although the reporters arrived on time, the rest of the operation was a fiasco. The military, whether intentionally or not, hindered the movements of the media. The media did not have access into the combat zone for several days and, once granted access, were not provided adequate transportation resources. Likewise, the media sent reporters to the combat zone with improper credentials and very little experience covering military operations. The media and the military again stumbled over the rough ground of a new alliance.

The National Media Pool received the next call to action during Operation Desert Storm. With the Iraqi invasion of Kuwait and the subsequent buildup of allied forces in Saudi Arabia, it was the pool system through which the media gained access to the battlefield. The sheer number of media in the Gulf region during the conflict, according to the military, made necessary the use of this pool system to control access and maintain security. At one time there were more than 3,000 media representatives in the region, and they again had to face the security reviews required by the military. There were many instances in which the media accused the military of changing stories for public-relations reasons, rather than security ones.

The brief war came and went, and the public seemed satisfied with the level of information controlled by the military. Many in the media, however, decried the use of censorship in the region as a violation of their First Amendment rights. They also protested the restricted access to the combat zone placed upon representatives. *The Nation* magazine even filed a lawsuit against the Department of Defense, alleging violations of the media's First Amendment rights. It was time again to discuss the rules for future operations.

In September 1991, the Secretary of Defense met with leading media executives to discuss future operations. The discussions resulted in ten principles of media coverage during times of war. The principles included the use of pools for only a limited time at the beginning of an operation as well as accreditation requirements. The principles also defined the military's requirements to support the media. The media and military representatives agreed to support nine of the ten principles outlined. The issue of contention dealt with security reviews of news in certain combat situations. The media vehemently opposed such reviews and issued a release to the Department of Defense stating their position. That issue remains unresolved to this day.

The principles were put to the test during the military's missions in Haiti and Somalia. The pools were activated and aboard the inbound aircraft for Haiti until President Clinton canceled the mission in mid-flight. The peace-keeping nature of these operations required modified use of the pools and security reviews; and, again, neither side was satisfied with the outcome. The most memorable conflict took place when the media aired pictures of American servicemen's bodies being dragged through the streets of Mogadishu in October of 1993. The military was outraged because the tape aired before the men's families were informed of their deaths.

Most recently, though, the military and the media worked toward a true common ground in Bosnia as part of the International Force (IFOR). The military, based upon attempts by the Marines during Operation Desert Storm, decided to allow media representatives direct access to the units in the field. Media representatives were "embedded" with units, and the military allowed the soldiers to answer the media's questions within guidelines issued by the IFOR Commander. The tactic received good reviews from both the media and military representatives. The problem that arises, though, is that this situation was not a real combat scenario. What will happen when the military is called to fight and win future battles?

The brief examination of the history of relations between the two institutions reveals certain issues that form the core of all previous, current, and probable future tensions. The first issue relates to the constitutional concerns of the media. The media are one of the the guardians of free speech. As such, they also have a formidable stake in the rights of access to newsworthy events. The military, though, maintains a different perspective on the importance of these constitutional rights during combat operations involving American servicemen and women. The next major issue is the military's belief that media representatives, taken as a whole, lack the necessary military experience to accurately portray events to the public. The media, however, do not believe military experience is necessary to report the news in a fair and accurate manner. The final and most important issue is the distrust and suspicion between the two institutions. The lingering suspicions of each, created over the past hundred years, pose the greatest barrier to improved relations in the future. Examining each issue in depth will illuminate the root causes of poor relations between the two institutions and must precede any proposed solutions to the causes of problems.

Constitutional Concerns

The media have always endured some type of censorship during conflicts involving American servicemen and women. The military imposed some censorship during the Civil War and continued to do so in each major conflict through

Operation Desert Storm. As a rule of thumb, the media generally accepted the military's need for some types of censorship during these conflicts. The media, however, have never truly been satisfied with the arrangements. The recent actions by the military in Grenada, Panama, and the Persian Gulf highlight the level of discontent.

The media believe the military, in restricting access to the operations in Panama and Grenada, denied one of their most basic rights: the right to inform the American public of the actions of its service members. The media, although unhappy with the military's unusual methods of restricting access, continued to accept the military's ever-present and overriding concerns for operational security. The media's protests led to the creation of guidelines to ensure no actions by the military would again restrict the media's ability to inform the public of newsworthy events.

Operation Desert Storm provided another situation in which the media had to succumb to the military's restrictive regulations and policies. Those procedures, namely the pre-publication reviews of news material and the pool system, hindered the media's ability to fairly and accurately cover the conflict. The prevailing belief among media members is that the military instituted the guidelines to protect their image. Those in the military argue that the restrictions were necessary to prevent any unnecessary injuries and protect the security of the entire operation.

The situation brings to light the constitutional concerns of the media. Do the media have a constitutional right to report freely and accurately everything that takes place within a combat zone? Does the military have the constitutional power to restrict access to a combat zone and conduct pre-publication reviews of news material? Having unlimited access to combat zones allows the media to truthfully portray the events to the American public, and an absence of pre-publication review allows them to portray the military in a more realistic light.

Meanwhile, increases in modern technology, combined with the sheer number of media representatives who want access to a combat zone, arguably require the use of restrictive regulations and policies. These policies, according to the military, reduce the likelihood of unnecessary casualties and confusion within a combat zone.

In January 1991, the media, represented by *The Nation* magazine and other plaintiffs, sought to solve the constitutional questions in a court of law. A lawsuit filed in the U.S. District Court of the Southern District of New York challenged the constitutionality of the military's regulations. The plaintiffs contended that the media had a constitutional right of access to a foreign arena where American forces were engaged. The main focus of the lawsuit was on First and

Fifth Amendment rights.

The court faced a challenge, with no clear precedents to draw on. It was the first time the court had to address the "right of access" in the contexts of military operations and national security. Previous cases, such as *Near v. Minnesota* (1931) and *Richmond Newspapers v. Virginia* (1980), dealt with prior restraint issues and access to criminal proceedings in a courtroom. The closest case the court had to the 1991 suit was *Greer v. Spock* (1976), which upheld the exclusion of the press and public from military bases.

The plaintiffs contended that the court should "recognize the right of the press to unrestricted access, and hold, as a matter of constitutional law, that DoD follow only those guidelines used during the Vietnam War." The court disagreed, and instead recognized the military's right to reasonable time, place, and manner restrictions on the media, given a legitimate government interest.

The problem with the lawsuit was that the media wished to have all regulations pertaining to access ruled unconstitutional for future conflicts. The court, unable to define all the parameters of future conflicts, decided not to rule on the issue. *The Nation's* case clearly shows the conflicting interests between the two institutions. To date, the constitutional questions surrounding the media's access to a combat zone have yet to be resolved. The issue will, at some point in the future, probably again reach the courts, unless the two institutions agree to fundamental changes in the current system of operations.

A Military Point of View

The military is a complex structure that demands precision, accuracy, and discipline. It is both a profession and a structured group. Members of the military understand the roles, command relationships, and missions of each branch of service. The inherent understanding of the operational tactics, techniques, and procedures assures an orderly, efficient fighting force that is capable of fighting and winning American battles with minimal loss of life. Thus it is common for those in the military to believe that an adequate representation of their actions requires the knowledge of an insider. The media, on the other hand, are proud of their traditional role as outside observers.

The problems, from the military viewpoint, are twofold. The military believes that a correspondent not well versed in the tactics, techniques, and procedures of the services cannot accurately relay truthful information without bias or misunderstanding of the overall concept. In the military's view, negative coverage is the result of inadequate understanding; in the media's view, this coverage is simply the best, most objective way to communicate the truth. If a report is negative, then the situation was negative.

The second facet of this issue deals with security. The military places a high premium on operational security. Human lives often depend on the military's ability to maintain that security. Security requirements within the military exist at all levels of operations. From the lone sentry providing security for a ten-person squad to the electronic encryption of messages from the Commander-in-Chief, security is second nature to the military.

To the military, the media represent a chronic security risk. There is a belief that the journalist with little or no experience may inadvertently release information that jeopardizes human life. The military view may stem from historic examples, or it may derive from the inherently different goals of each institution.

The goal of the media is to attain open and independent coverage of all conflicts. Open and independent coverage, they believe, will allow the public to gain the best possible information on the activities of the government.

The Heart of the Problem

The two previous examples provide an excellent backdrop for the one crucial issue that stands between these two institutions: distrust, the one pervasive issue within both institutions. Examining each of the issues for hidden motivation reveals the core of the problems between the military and the media.

The media maintain that the military unconstitutionally restricts access to combat zones and unnecessarily censors news reports. Media personnel have been frequently heard relating that during the Persian Gulf War, the public received only what the military wanted it to. The media maintain that it is their job as the watchdog of governmental activities to truthfully relay to the people the actions of our democratic government. The issue is a lack of trust. The media do not trust the government to accurately portray events involving the American military.

The media have long been referred to as the "Fourth Estate" of government. Their role as guardian of the truth and preserver of democracy has a long and distinguished heritage. The media are not incorrect for perceiving the military as overstepping its bounds of power. They have a necessary function in the preservation of democracy. One of those roles is ensuring that no government agency oversteps the boundaries of its power as given by the people. The media maintain a constant vigil over the ministrations of the government and act as the "great equalizer" in our democratic society.

The situation with the military, though, is unique. The conditions the military deems necessary to protect the lives of American servicemen and women dictate the changes in normal media coverage of events. The media, faced with such unique situations, are left powerless to conduct their business of keeping the public informed in the manner that they feel is necessary. Such conflicts and unique situations will of course breed a sense of distrust between the two institutions. The distrust of the military, an agent of the government, derives from the heritage and culture of the media as an institution.

The military also retains a distrust of the media. At all levels of service the perception that the media cannot be trusted exists. Even those service members who have had absolutely no contact with the media believe this to be true. The perception evolved over the course of the nation's wars and reached its apex during the Vietnam War. The military believed that the media were responsible for the terrible downswing in public opinion toward all things military, including the conflict. They felt betrayed and used. Regardless of the reasons behind these perceptions, they are still present today. Leaders in the military who experienced the relations with the media during that time have passed down the perceptions to the new generations of military personnel.

These are not the only reasons for each institution to maintain a sense of mistrust for each other. One of the major factors is the inherent nature of each institution. The military is a group of dedicated men and women who consider their job a profession. It is the profession of arms. Their mission is to fight and win the nation's battles. They have a strict code of conduct and professional ethics. They live within a very structured, disciplined world where wrong decisions can result in the deaths of fellow service members. They are, by the very nature of their business, wary of outsiders.

The media, conversely, are an institution whose foundations lie in the realm of capitalism. Their role as the guardian of truth and free speech is indeed an honorable and necessary part of a democratic society. The media maintain codes of conduct and ethical guidelines, yet their overall performance is profit driven. The two institutions are so distinctively different that the guarded perceptions of distrust may always be a part of their relationship.

The two institutions, although vastly different and wary of each other, are also inextricably linked in the requirements for positive public opinion. The media, being a profit-driven institution, rely on the public to support their business. The media must walk the fine line of truthful and accurate coverage of news events or risk a decrease in popularity among their consumers. A good example is the recent coverage of the Persian Gulf War. While the media denounced the policies and procedures surrounding the conflict, the American public remained thoroughly satisfied with the results. The media did not push the issue into the forefront of the public's agenda. The issue remained quietly, and resolutely, within the channels of communication between the military and the media. If the media were to push the issue forward, with their consumers already happy with the results of the coverage, they would risk losing the popular public opinion of the media. The resultant loss of public approval might then result in the loss of revenues from those who became disenchanted with the media.

Accordingly, the military has only recently realized the power of popular public opinion. A popular public opinion of the military relates to a popular opinion within the Congress. A popular opinion within the Congress results in increased funding for training, maintaining, and sustaining the force. A well-trained force wins battles with minimal casualties. Conversely, a negative public opinion results in decreased funding and is counter-productive to the military.

Although the two are linked within the realm of public opinion, this area is also a cause of distrust. Neither institution wishes to lose the approval of the public. Interactions between the two are then, by the very nature of each institution, cautious and watchful. Yet the wary, watchful attitude of each institution can lead to a successful relationship where both parties reap the benefits.

Resolution

The brief history of the interactions between the two institutions reveals the tension-wrought evolution of the relationship. The analysis of the core issues involved in the relationship displays the true nature of the problems. The next logical step is to provide the solution. The solution to the problems must address the central issue facing the two institutions. The solution must address the issue of trust. Both parties will always harbor some measure of distrust. A certain level of distrust, though, can be a constructive element in any proposed solution. The key, then, is to decrease the amount of distrust within each institution and establish a competent, comprehensive working relationship that benefits both parties.

The pool system is destined to fail in future conflicts due to the overbearing and restrictive nature of its rules. While the pool system may benefit the military, it does not benefit the media. Instead, it serves only to increase the lack of trust between the two institutions. The current method of embedding media correspondents in military units to allow open and independent coverage provides a good starting point for any new solution.

The "embedding" system allows for open and independent coverage of the peacekeeping operation. It allows the media correspondents to converse with the military personnel on an individual basis. The military personnel follow strict guidelines concerning the type of information that is proper to release. This system appears to meet the needs of both parties and eases tensions between the institutions. The problem, though, is that the system does not actually alleviate much of the mutual distrust. It is, however, an excellent starting point for a true solution.

Much of the distrust felt among the institutions stems from a lack of knowledge. The military really does not understand what a media correspondent's job entails. Likewise, the media correspondents do not fully understand the military system. The method of habitually "embedding" selected correspondents into military units is the key. The military uses a system of habitual relationships between units to increase trust in each other and ease the transition from peace to war. Artillery units are habitually assigned to support certain infantry and armor units. Cavalry squadrons are habitually assigned to divisions, and combat support aircraft are habitually associated with maneuver units. The habitual association allows the units to train together during peace so they will be better prepared to fight together during war. They know how the other operates and what to expect and when to expect it. The same system should be used between the military and the media.

Media personnel should be habitually assigned to cover units of their choice in peace and during war. The key sacrifice the media must make in this situation is releasing their correspondents to train with the military during peacetime. When the correspondent's habitually associated unit deploys on a major training exercise, the same correspondent, or correspondents, should accompany the unit to the field. Granted, the military operational pace will preclude correspondents from covering every deployment. Most likely, the correspondents may only participate during one, two or possibly three training deployments during a year's time. One fourteen-day rotation with a unit to the National Training Center in California would provide ample training time for both institutions.

The vital element of this plan is getting the two institutions to work together during peacetime, just as they would during war. One might say that personnel turnover rates will preclude any possible gains in the situation. That is just not true. Habitually associating correspondents with units forces both the military and the media to develop standard operating procedures for their personnel.

The military will have to change the overall concept of support. Junior leaders in all units will need training to help integrate media personnel into their unit. Transportation, communication equipment, and field gear for the media correspondents will need to be identified and prepared for their use. Plans to support the correspondents with food, water, and fuel will have to be developed to ensure that a proper integration of the media occurs. Once these basic changes occur, the media and the military can begin to interact during peacetime much the same way they will during war.

The solution calls for sacrifices to be made by each institution. The military will have to adapt to the extra personnel in the units and develop plans to allow open and independent coverage. The media will have to allow their correspondents to train with the military during peace on a habitual basis. These fundamental changes will reap benefits for both parties. The correspondent who arrives at the unit to deploy to a combat zone may not be the same one who previously trained with the unit. The correspondents should be, but other requirements or personnel turnover may prevent their participation. The important aspect, though, is that it does not have to be the same individual. Once correspondents and the military train together in peacetime, the foundations of future successful integration are laid.

The junior leader assigned as the liaison officer to the media may be brand new. The correspondent may have recently graduated from Columbia University and be on his first assignment. It will not matter. As the media and the military train together in peacetime, guidelines are written and standards published. Both institutions have the advantage of having prior relationships with each other. The correspondent arrives and is accepted into the unit just as a new military person would be after he first took the oath of service. The key is that by working together, the institutions are building trust. They become used to the way each other operates. The correspondents gain tremendous insights into the everyday life and work of the military. The military gains valuable experience integrating the necessary media representatives.

The two institutions will settle the issues surrounding the pre-publication review of news material. The integrated, habitually associated correspondent will already have the knowledge of what is crucial information to the enemy. He will be subjected to the same laws of conduct as any other citizen. The time the two institutions spend together will make the censorship issue moot. Open and independent coverage of combat situations will become a reality. Access to the combat zone will be assured through the habitual embedding of media representatives in military units. Experience should not be a factor, as the groundwork for smooth operations will be present. The two parties will understand what is required of each and will operate smoothly and efficiently in future combat situations. They will begin to build a trusting relationship between individuals within each institution. The key is to allow the actual members of the institutions to interact and develop their own relationships. These relationships between individuals will dictate the overall relationship between the two institutions.

The media and the military have long had a troubled relationship. The two institutions are vastly different, yet each is a necessary player in our democratic society. The crucial factor in improving the relationship between the two institutions is trust. The previous tensions between the two institutions result from a lack of trust. Every major tension, crisis, or disagreement between the media and the military can be traced to a lack of trust. Decreasing the lack of trust felt by each will enhance relations and provide for smooth operations during actual combat. The military will profit through the increased coverage of its forces. The media will profit through an increased understanding of the military. Each will undoubtedly maintain some slight level of distrust in the future. A small measure of distrust, though, keeps each institution on the lookout for problems and provides the impetus to provide quality solutions to any future tensions.

Recommended Readings

Books

Derrik Mercer, Geoff Mungham, and Kevin Williams. *The Fog of War The Media on the Battlefield*. London: 1987. An excellent insight into the military-media relationship on the battlefied.

Fialka, J.J. *Hotel Warriors Covering the Gulf War*. Baltimore: Woodrow Wilson Center Press, 1992. An in-depth look at the situations confronting correspondents during the Gulf War.

Hammond, William M., ed. *The Military and the Media: The U.S. Army in Vietnam.* Washington D.C.: Center for Military History, 1990. An in-depth historical account of military-media relationship during the Vietnam conflict.

Hooper, Alan. *The Military and the Media*. Great Britain: Gower, 1982. An examination of the relationship between the military and the media from a British point of view.

Kennedy, William V. *The Military and the Media: Why the Press Cannot be trusted to Cover a War*. Westport, Conn.: Praeger, 1993. An in-depth view of the problems confronting contemporary media-military relations. Also contains a brief historical review of the roots of the conflicts between the two.

Knightley, Phillip. *The First Casualty From Crimea to Vietnam: The War Correspondent as Hero, Propagandist, and Myth Maker.* New York: 1975. A useful although biased source of insights concerning war correspondents and their experiences dealing with the military and battle.

Matthews, Lloyd J. *Newsmen and National Defense: Is Conflict Inevitable?* Washington: Brassey's, 1991. An excellent book that provides a scholarly compilation of issues confronting military-media relations.

Minor, Dale. *The Information War*. New York: Hawthorne Books, 1970. A scholarly review of the situations and conflicts faced by American correspondents during the Vietnam War.

Thompson, Loren B. *Defense Beat: The Dilemmas of Defense Coverage*. New York: Lexington Books, 1991. A compilation of views pertaining to the problems encountered between the military and the media. Contains both pro-military and pro-media views.

Wyatt, C.R. *Paper Soldiers: The American Press and the Vietnam War*. New York: W.W. Norton, 1991. A precise and candid exposé covering the correspondents and the practices of media coverage during the Vietnam War.

Young, Peter R. *Defence and the Media in Time of Limited War*. Great Britain: publisher??, 1992. A compilation of views and case studies — written from a variety of viewpoints — pertaining to military-media relations in the context of limited war.

Articles

Jacobs, Matthew J. "Assessing the constitutionality of press restrictions in the Persian Gulf War." *Stanford Law Review* 44:3 (February 1992): 675-726. A legal analysis of the constitutional issues surrounding the military policies in the Persian Gulf War.

Lamb, David. "Pentagon Hardball (Persian Gulf War, 1991 and the press)." *Washington Journalism Review* 13:3 (April 1991): 33-8. An overview of the military's policies and procedures affecting the media during the Persian Gulf War.

Maitre, H. Joachim. "Journalistic Incompetence." *Nieman Reports* (Summer 1991): 10-16. An experienced war correspondent reviews the media and their portrayed ignorance during the Persian Gulf War.

Sharkey, J. "Will the New Plan Help War Coverage?" *Washington Journalism Review* (September 1992): 11-13. Describes the problems faced by the new agreement between the military and the media.

Steger, M.D. "Slicing the Gordian Knot: A proposal to reform military regulation of media coverage of combat operations." *University of San Francisco School of Law Review* (Summer 1994). An in-depth review of the legal issues surrounding the military regulations of the media during combat. The author also bases the recommendations for change upon the unconstitutional restrictions imposed.

2 The Media and Politics

Many observers today are increasingly concerned about the influence that news media have upon public attitudes toward government and the political process. The recent "media frenzy" over President Bill Clinton's relationship with White House intern Monica Lewinsky is just one instance in a long history of such controversies. The press acts as the communications middleman for government officials and American citizens. Traditionally, that role has been one of a "watchdog" for the public, or of a "Fourth Estate" of government, serving as an additional check upon government activities.

Today, however, some believe that the press has performed weakly in this duty, either because its members have their own agendas or because they have dug too deeply into the dark side of politicians' lives.

In this section, Anthony Fellow — who occupies the dual role of both a communication professor and a public offical — examines the relationship between the news media and the present state of voter cynicism. As Professor Fellow demonstrates, the Watergate scandal in the early 1970s was just the first of an apparent avalanche of deceptions and misdeeds that have marked American politics in the last quarter of this century. This has led to a public that trusts neither its government nor its news media — and it has led, arguably, to a state in which the nation's whole democracy is undermined by cynicism.

In chapter nine, Robert Fortner examines the public's perception of the media's objectivity, or lack thereof. One of the common criticisms of the press in recent years has been that its members — reporters, editors, publishers — operate from a politically liberal bias. Professor Fortner outlines both sides of this issue. Is there in fact a liberal bias in political reporting, or is there simply an institutional bias, brought about by the journalistic pursuit of conflict and both budget and time constraints? Or are the American media as close to professional objectivity as they can be, and are biases simply the perception of the readers and viewers?

Mark Popovich brings the magnifying glass even closer to media practices in his discussion of the news coverage of politicians and, in particular, of their private activities. Touching on both the legal and ethical aspects of privacy, Professor Popovich presents a debate that centers on a "right to know" about the private lives of the nation's officials and the "right to be left alone."

All three chapters pose the essential questions: What role should the media have in keeping politicians and the political process accountable to American citizens? And how far should that role extend? At what point will this modern "muckraking" result in complete cynicism and apathy?

Whether or not they want it, the news media have an enormous influence upon the public's perception of government. It is a weighty responsibility, and the issues addressed in this section are not easy ones to resolve. They are, clearly, issues that will follow us in the future.

Chapter Eight

The Media and American Democracy

Anthony R. Fellow

The odd couple of American political consultants, Mary Matalin and James Carville, are on the stump these days, bashing the press at each of their one-night gigs. The dynamic duo of politics are taking up where James Fallows left off.

It was Fallows, now editor of *U.S. News & World Report*, who laid it on the line in 1996. The American press is undermining democracy by creating an electorate that is cynical toward politicians, Fallows wrote in his bestseller, *Breaking the News*.

Carville goes even further in his indictment of the American press. If you read the nation's press, he told a Pasadena, Calif., audience, the electorate should not only have a cynical attitude toward politicians, but they ought to look at them as axe murderers. "The nation's press is destabilizing democracy," Carville said. Why? "Because the press so disallows us to be responsible citizens." Carville has even found support among media professionals. "If [citizens] are cynical, it's in large measure because of what they read or watch," says Marvin Kalb, a former correspondent for CBS and NBC. "That, in turn, is a function of the press. The process is chasing its own tail."

Have we become a nation of doubters, turning cynical? Has the American press created a nation so skeptical that the ideals of democracy are being threatened? In this chapter, we will pose the following question: Have the news media become so arrogant, cynical, and scandal-minded that they have undermined the principles of American democracy?

Just how serious is the erosion of public trust in the press or government? A recent poll by the National Opinion Research Center at the University of Chicago found that only 11 per cent of those surveyed felt "a great deal" of confidence in the press. A year earlier, a survey by the Times Mirror Center for *The People & The Press* showed that the public appeared to be far more cynical than the news media about government officials. About 77 per cent of the 1,819 Americans surveyed said they distrusted public officials in Washington. By contrast, the survey showed that journalists, in their private beliefs, were not very cynical at all. Many of them said they respected individual politicians. Some 53 per cent thought public officials as a class were more honest and honorable than the general public was.

A generational element exists to this cynicism, according to Andrew Kohut, Times Mirror Center director. The poll found that the most cynical members of the public are thirty to thirty-nine years old, followed by those forty to fifty-five. "These are people who came of age when Watergate and Vietnam dominated the news. They would have a pretty jaundiced view of their national leaders," Kohut told *Times* reporter Stanley Meisler.

Is a cynical press undermining democracy? We first must look at how the present view evolved in America. Finally, we'll attempt to answer the question: Is there any hope for the future?

Origins of the Issue

Since the birth of the United States, the relationship between the news media and the nation's politicians has been a rocky one. In his book *The American Journalist: Paradox of the Press,* Loren Ghiglione writes that the American journalist began as a part-time amateur who put partisanship ahead of professionalism. Sam Adams and his fellow propagandists for the American Revolution were followed by John Fenno, Phillip Freneau, and other mouthpieces for political parties.

Editor Freneau in his *National Gazette* wasted no time in vilifying the first U.S. president. Wielding one of the most vindictive pens in the nation's history, Freneau called George Washington the front man for the Federalists. To Washington's dismay, the hateful editor wrote: "The first magistrate of a country seldom knows the real state of the nation, particularly if he be buoyed up by official importance to think it beneath his dignity to mix occasionally with the people."

Meanwhile, opposition editors attacked Thomas Jefferson's character, opinion, and politics. *Richmond Examiner* editor James Callender charged Jefferson with dishonesty and cowardice and of having sexual relations with Sally Hemmings, a slave woman on his plantation. A disgusted Jefferson retorted with the following in 1807: "The man who never looks into a newspaper is better informed than he who reads them; inasmuch as he who knows nothing is nearer to truth than he whose mind is filled with falsehoods and errors."

Such falsehoods by vindictive newspapers, alleged Andrew Jackson, caused his wife's early death after they published articles saying his marriage was illegal and sinful. However, Jackson was the first presidential manipulator of the news. Many of the most influential members of his "Kitchen Cabinet" were journalists. According to John Tebbel and Sarah Miles Watts in their book, *The Press and The Presidency*, John Quincy Adams was so upset at these appointments that he quipped: "The appointments, almost without exception, are conferred upon the vilest purveyors of slander during the late electioneering campaign, and an excessive disproportion of places is given to editors of the foulest presses."

The sharpest sting by these "purveyors of slander" was saved for Abraham Lincoln, who was the most involved with the press, owed the most to it, and suffered the most from it, according to Tebbel and Watts. The vicious press called him a "monkey face," the "personification of evil," a "Black Republican" who would destroy the South. But it was Lincoln who refused to have a "party newspaper" and championed an independent and free press.

Not so different from modern times, this independent media found that gossip sold well. Press reports about Grover Cleveland's sexual indiscretions — which produced a son born out of wedlock — tarnished his image as a pillar of the community. It was the press that led the chant: "Ma! Ma! Where's my pa? Gone to the White House, Ha! Ha! Ha!"

But the press had a change of heart with the administration of Theodore Roosevelt. According to Tebbel and Watts, Roosevelt consolidated the power of the presidency and manipulated the media to promote himself and his causes to a degree never before seen.

By the presidency of Teddy Roosevelt's cousin, Franklin D. Roosevelt, the news was much more upbeat. The nation's political leaders were treated by journalists with deference and respect in the 1940s and 1950s, according to Ellen Hume, former executive director of Harvard's Joan Shorenstein Barone Center on the Press, Politics and Public Policy. At the start of his presidency, FDR captured the American public and the media. He was an extension of the news-gathering process, taking direct questions from correspondents, and discussing confidential policies informally. He also was not shy in telling reporters how he would fashion a story. His sexual indiscretions and physical conditions were never reported.

Also an artful news manager, Dwight D. Eisenhower won over the public and press. However, the public's confidence eroded in 1955 when Ike suffered a heart attack. According to Tebbel and Watts, the president's staff told the press he had "suffered a digestive upset in the night." It was not until six-and-a-half hours later, doctors admitted it had been a heart attack.

What changed everything were the lies of the Vietnam War, Watergate, the Iran-Contra scandal and Iraqgate, according to Hume. "Now journalists are locked into the negative assumption that the government and political leaders are lying much of the time," she said.

The Pentagon Papers showed that presidents for four decades lied about American involvement in Southeast Asia. Former Secretary of Defense Robert McNamara came clean thirty years later when he wrote that much of the information disseminated to the press and public about American involvement in Vietnam was based on official lies.

But it was Watergate that left the most lasting effects on the public, the press, and the government. In their book *Communications Ethics*, Jaska and Pritchard write that public trust had been shattered, that the deceit had been so widespread that the public wondered how long it might be before a semblance of trust in the highest levels of government could be restored.

As for reporters, this gap in trust produced an adversarial relationship between the press and public officials. For some, that may not be so bad. Says Nicholas Horrock of the *New York Times* in a *Newsweek* article on "The Legacy of Watergate," "A lot of young reporters today are more likely to ask the right questions of the right people than before Watergate."

Public confidence in government increased with Ronald Reagan's first term in office. This lasted until the *New York Times* published a Lebanese weekly magazine's report that the United States had secretly sold arms to Iran. The article explained how the United States had arranged for shipments of arms valued at $100 million to the Iranians, through the cooperation of Israel, at least seven times between August 30, 1985, and October 29, 1986. Payments from the arms-to-Iran deal had been deposited in a Swiss bank account and then redirected to aid the Contras, rebel forces fighting the socialist government in Nicaragua, circumventing official U.S. government policies and procedures.

Polls following a Joint Senate-House Investigating Committee about the arms-to-Iran deal showed a cynical public. An ABC News poll, for example, showed that 52 per cent of the public believed that the president was not telling the truth about what he had known.

According to Jaksa and Pritchard, the cumulative effect of the deceptions that occurred during Vietnam, Watergate, and the Iran-Contra affair has contributed to a crisis of confidence in public officials and makes the restoration of trust a serious challenge to U.S. society.

This dramatic transition from lap dog to watchdog to pit bull, Hume told *Los Angeles Times* reporter David Shaw, has created the phenomenon of "gotcha" journalism a "constantly cynical framework [that] doubtlessly feeds the public's cynicism and distrust of its political leadership — and of the piranha press corps which seems willing to devour anyone, at anytime, for frivolous infractions as well as for serious ones." According to Shaw, this has led, over time, to both diminished confidence in the media and diminished voter turnout at the polls.

Have the news media become so arrogant, cynical, and scandal-minded that they have undermined the principles of American democracy? Fallows and his followers say yes, because the values of journalists have changed, their current practices undermine the credibility of the press, and their actions affect the future prospects of every American by distorting the processes by which we choose our leaders and resolve our public problems.

The Changing Values of Journalists

Journalism has become more celebrity oriented, resulting in the loss of the essence of real journalism — the search for information of use to the public, media critics say. They point to *60 Minutes* as the culprit. Why? Thanks to *60 Minutes*, Fallows says, we have seen a shift from authority to celebrity in TV news. "It changed TV journalism for one simple reason: it made money."

It made money for networks and individual journalists who gained the potential to command power, riches, and prestige that few of their predecessors could have hoped for. Journalism is not known as a lucrative profession, but for the most prominent network stars there is a payoff, reported the *Frontline* broadcast of "Why America Hates the Press." For example:

- Christine Amanpour of CNN has signed for $2 million a year for three years to become the highest paid field correspondent in TV news.

- According to *USA Today*, Diane Sawyer of ABC News just renewed her contract for $7 million annually.

- Both Ted Koppel and Dan Rather reportedly earn $6 million a year.

- Barbara Walters is said to have a base salary range of $4 million with additional fees for her specials that add up to an annual salary of $7 to $8 million.

Others earn thousands on the lecture circuit.

- Columnist David Gergen earned $239,000 for fifty speeches in 1993.

- *60 Minutes* correspondent Mike Wallace gets a reported $25,000 per talk, while colleague Lesley Stahl receives $20,000.

- ABC correspondent Sam Donaldson receives a $30,000 lecture fee, while his colleague Cokie Roberts commands $20,000.

- *New York Times* columnist William Safire also receives a $20,000 lecture fee.

- CNN's Judy Woodruff earns $7,500 per lecture as does NBC News correspondent Lisa Myers.

- If you were to ask Fred Barnes of *The McLaughlin Group* to be your guest speaker, it would cost you $5,000.

But celebrity journalists have always existed. Charles Dickens reported from the American frontier; Nellie Bly raced around the world by ship, strain, horseback, and rickshaw for Pulitzer's *New York World*; Edward R. Murrow broadcast from Czechoslovakia and London as it was bombed; and Eric Sevareid, Charles Collingwood, Howard K. Smith, and Walter Cronkite became famous wartime reporters. The difference, Fallows says, is that these journalists carried with them a sense of authority, "based mainly on their on-the-scene wartime reporting, rather than sheer celebrity or the spillover importance they got by being assigned to a major beat like the White House."

Other media critics say the big bucks that journalists now command have affected the value they place on those they write about. Michael Lerner, who, to his dislike, has been called "the guru of the White House," says the current wave of cynicism in politics results from the national media's belief that human beings are rarely motivated by anything beyond material self-interest.

"Media moguls and national columnists tend toward this view with the same ferocity and irrationality that they attribute to religious fundamentalists," Lerner writes in his latest book, *The Politics of Meaning*. "Anyone who challenges this belief, the media people reason, must either be stupid or a manipulator for his or her own self-interest."

Lerner says the result of such cynicism was a no-holds-barred assault on Hillary Clinton. For example, the *New Republic* suggested that the first lady was merely reflecting on her own lack of ethical center during her ascendancy to power, saying, "If she wants to talk about the discontents of her own climb, and the spiritual emptiness she feels, congratulations to her for real candor. But that doesn't mean everyone else is a moral failure."

The Changing Practices of Journalists

Still other media critics say these best-known and best-paid people in journalism now set an example that erodes the quality of the news and threatens journalism's claim on public respect. Fallows, for one, says the star system distorts the news through the phenomenon of the "Bigfoot" at newspapers and news magazines. Bigfoot is the star columnist or writer who is paid more than most normal reporters and is happiest when writing about the main story each week.

The Bigfoot system discourages other reporters and subtly twists the news. Unlike beat reporters, regular correspondents who cover a given agency or region, the Bigfoot doesn't understand the issues. Bigfoots appear to be more interested in pure politics — the way a new proposal will "play" in the Congress, how it will help or hurt the contenders in the next presidential race.

What results is "horse-race politics," neglecting the why of issues in favor of how they'll affect the next presidential race. As Michael Robinson and Margaret Sheehan put it in *Over the Wire and on TV: CBS and UPI in Campaign '80,* "Horse-race coverage permeates almost everything the press does in covering elections and candidates." "Horse race" and "character" have become the two most newsworthy aspects of political campaigns, according to Stephen Ansolabehere, Roy Behr, and Shanto Iyengar in *The Media Game.* They write: "News reports on the candidates' standing in public opinion polls, their advertising strategies, the size of the crowds at their appearances, their fund-raising efforts, and their electoral prospects far surpass coverage detailing their issue positions, ideology, prior experience or decision-making style."

The reasons for the prominence of horse-race and character coverage in the news is that it is relatively easy to cover for the reporter with or without big feet (and fees), big attitudes, and big bylines. One reason, according to authors of *The Media Game,* is that most of the major news organizations have themselves become public opinion pollsters. "This type of information is therefore readily accessible to reporters (in many instances, at the touch of a computer key)," they explain. Another reason is that horse-race coverage produces good pictures.

However, the horse race aspects of political campaigns tend not to be what is on the minds of the typical citizen. "The citizens ask overwhelmingly about the what of politics," Fallows writes. "What are you going to do about the health care system? What can you do to reduce the cost of welfare? The reporters ask almost exclusively about the how. How are you going to try to take away Perot's constituency? How do you answer charges that you have flip-flopped?"

When ordinary citizens have a chance to pose questions to political leaders, Fallows says, they rarely ask about the game of politics. "They mainly want to know how the reality of politics will affect them — through taxes, programs, scholarship funds, wars."

A 1997 survey conducted by the Roper Center in conjunction with the Newseum illustrates the gap between what the public wants to know and what they get from the press. Some 42 per cent of those surveyed complained that journalists don't ask elected officials the kinds of questions that are important to most Americans. About 76 per cent said the press spent too much time reporting on the private lives of public officials.

If citizens are interested in policy questions, then why are the media preoccupied with the character issue? Norms of campaign journalism have shifted. According to Larry Sabato in his book *Feeding Frenzy: How Attack Journalism Has Transformed American Politics,* in the 1950s and 1960s an incident concerning a candidate's private life was considered irrelevant "unless it seriously impinged on his or her public performance."

It was Watergate and several instances of bizarre and inappropriate behavior by congressmen that caused the current shift that suggests that personal weakness can have political relevance. "Private conduct is a road map to public action," veteran political correspondent Robert Novak is quoted in *Feeding Frenzy.* Thus Ansolabehere, Behr, and Iyengar write that today the candidates' love lives (Gary Hart, Ted Kennedy, Bill Clinton) control over their emotions (Ed Muskie and Pat Schroeder), language (Jesse Jackson, Bob Kerrey), law school records (Joe Biden), avoidance of military service (Dan Quayle and Bill Clinton), and even food tastes (George Bush and broccoli) have all been deemed newsworthy.

But is this what the public wants? In their book *Nothing Sacred,* Beverly Kees and Bill Phillips reveal the results of a survey of 599 journalists, 561 politicians, and 605 members of the public. They found that the public and even some journalists and politicians have three major concerns about current coverage. They are that 1) stories are based on speculation, 2) stories are blown out of proportion, and 3) the press beats stories to death.

They found that members of the public don't trust much of what they read and hear because it is speculation, allegation, or spin. Jack Nelson, Washington bureau chief for the *Los Angeles Times* and a veteran of national political coverage, cites Whitewater coverage as an example of poor reporting. "We've lowered our standards on what we put in the papers these days. We publish stories that are based on a single source or a questionable source. We raise questions we don't answer. We jump to conclusions without having solid evidence. We let the tabloids dictate the pace. We run stories based on relatively little solid information and figure if we call up the person to ask for his reaction, we're covered."

Seattle Mayor Norm Rice knows firsthand what Nelson is talking about. In the CNN special titled "Democracy in America: In Nothing We Trust," journalists traced the horror of a rumor gone wild. For two years, Rice listened to whispers in the community about an outlandish story that a family member once caught him in bed with another man and shot him. The story was circulated on homemade fliers by a fired city employee who was bent on getting his job back, a man who sent dozens of threatening postcards and letters to the mayor and his family.

According to Michel Fancher of the *Seattle Times:* "This clearly was character assassination of the worst kind. And the mainstream press knew about that for a couple years, investigated it, found there was no substance to it, and so ignored it." But in the spring of 1996, a critic of the mayor broadcast the rumor anyway. The whispers got even louder, and before Rice could denounce the story publicly, the rumor the press had previously rejected as unfit to print was front-page news.

"The very thing that I was fearful of began to come into play," Rice told CNN, "[which was] that the articles were dealing with a lie and then making the lie have a prominence in a way that I had no control over." His denial kept the story boiling, says Brooks Jackson, special CNN assignment correspondent. Now local TV news ran with it, repeating the seamy details. Within days Mike Segal (the talk show host who first spread the tawdry rumor) was fired, but since scandal sells, whether it's true or not, he was back on the air a week later at another Seattle area station, keeping the rumor alive without any regrets.

Kees and Phillips also found that "stories are often blown out of proportion to their significance." Remember the story about Jennifer Fitzgerald, who was alleged to be George Bush's mistress although neither party ever confirmed it nor was any solid proof made public? The long-whispered story came out during the Bush-Clinton campaign and was based on a footnote quoting a dead source.

Says Deborah Mathis, Gannett News Service White House correspondent: "Sometimes where there is smoke, there is smoke. And that's all you are ever going to get."

Finally, the public, journalists, and politicians told Kees and Phillips that "the press too often beats stories to death." One such story involved Mathis. During the 1992 presidential campaign she was alleged to be a Clinton girlfriend. She denied the allegation to several reporters who then tried to build a story out of suggestive facts. "I had heard the rumors off and on about me and about 3,000 other women in Arkansas over time, and they were promptly dismissed." But she says the questions went on to build the appearance of possibility. "And that can be just as indicting as anything else," Mathis says.

Undermining Democracy

Critics say these changing values and practices of journalists undermine our democracy. The 1997 Roper Center and Newseum poll revealed that Americans have very little trust in their political as well as news leaders. About 22 per cent of those surveyed said they believed all of what a minister, priest, or rabbi had to say. Only 2 per cent said the same about newspaper reporters, and just 5 per cent said they totally trusted network TV news anchors. Local TV anchors got a 7 per cent trust rating, while radio talk-show hosts got just 1 per cent. The president got 4 per cent, and members of Congress and lawyers got 3 per cent.

What's wrong with the news media? The same poll showed:

- 64% think the news is too sensationalized
- 64% think reporters spend too much time offering their own opinions
- 63% think the news is too manipulated by special interests
- 60% think reporters too often quote sources whose names are not given in news stories
- 52% think the news is too biased
- 46% think the news is too negative

These same polls showed that the public believed that politicians' morals were worse than those of the average citizen. For example, four-fifths thought that political authorities could never be trusted to do the right thing. (In the early 1960s, 70 per cent of Americans thought the government could be trusted to do the right thing.)

Kathleen Hall Jamieson and Joseph N. Cappella, professors at the University of Pennsylvania's Annenberg School of Communication, write in the *Atlanta Journal-Constitution* that political scientists have attributed this cynicism to disenchantment with policy alternatives, overpromising and failure to deliver, and dissatisfaction with incumbents as leaders. But they say there is more to it: "A tendency on the part of reporters to filter both elections and public policy through a set of cynical assumptions," they write, "including the notions that politicians act out of self-interest rather than a commitment to the public good, and the journalistic tendency to concentrate on the clash of competing points of view rather than on consensus — on attack rather than construction advocacy."

To illustrate their point, Hall Jamieson and Cappella conducted a study to see how the tone of news coverage affected public attitudes toward politicians and government. Citizens in six cities other than Philadelphia read and watched news about the Philadelphia mayoral election. Half of the sample were shown real newspaper and TV stories that emphasized underlying strategies, poll results, charge and countercharge, and examination of candidates' potential character problems. Other readers read and heard real stories that primarily dealt with solutions the candidates were offering to the city's problems.

"The results were clear," the researchers write. "Those who read and saw the 'strategy-based' reporting were more likely to conclude that the candidates were posturing, deceptive, self-interested, and unconcerned with the welfare of the city."

In sum, media critics point out that values and practices of journalists have changed. Meanwhile, ratings experts continue to tell media managers that negative news sells and that coverage of disasters and crimes keep viewers hooked. The end result is that mainstream journalism has fallen into the habit of portraying public life in America as a race to the bottom, in which one group of conniving, insincere politicians ceaselessly tries to outmaneuver another. Politicians seem untrustworthy while they're running, and they disappoint even their supporters soon after they take office, and by the time they leave office they are making excuses for what they couldn't do. The great problem for American democracy in the 1990s is that because media people barely trust elected leaders or the entire legislative system to accomplish anything of value, they are in the end, "undermining American democracy."

Jim Squires, former editor of the *Chicago Tribune* and author of *Read All About It! The Corporate Takeover of America's Newspapers,* disagrees. "Journalists long ago lost the power to undermine democracy — although that does not mean it is not being undermined by a crisis of character that afflicts candidates, political debate and the media," he writes in "Election Chronicles — A Question of Character." Critics of Fallows are quick to point out that journalism still has values, and journalists practice their craft by writing stories that reflect the temper of the times. If anything, they say, it is the political consultants, Matalin and Carville, for example, who have undermined American democracy.

The Values of Journalists

Journalism may have more higher priced stars, but research on campaign reporting has found that the press is, on the whole, neutral toward the candidates, according to Richard Hofstetter in *Bias in the News.* Robinson and Sheehan found that news coverage of campaigns is scrupulously objective in the sense that the news conveys information about specific events, occurrences, or statements as opposed to inferences and analyses of these events, occurrences, or statements. They found that campaign news reports contained little editorial flavor and were invariably neutral.

Their study, according to *The Media Game*'s authors, illustrates that the values and norms of public affairs journalism carry over to campaign journalism. "Reporters strive to convey hard factual information rather than interpretation and commentary," they write. The authors note that news is the product of a well-developed system of reporting. This system places a premium on reporting and writing that is simple, precise, and colorful and has clear story lines. These same qualities, of course, are generally absent from the ambiguous world of politics and public affairs. In addition, news is a product that must attract an audience in order to generate revenue from advertisers. Reporters use presentations that are likely to prove interesting to a large audience.

Unlike journalism, which for all its failings still has rules, values, and a conscience, the campaign industry deliberately operates on the edge of the law and comfortably beyond all ethical bounds. No half-truth, misrepresentation, or lie "escapes utilization if polling data suggest it will move a leaning or undecided voter away from one candidate toward another," Squires says.

In his television documentary *The Public Mind*, Bill Moyers first introduced Americans to the "powerful tools of fiction" used by the campaign industry. Those tools include exaggeration, distortion, and outright lies. They are repeated in a series of images, often disguised as news and entertainment, to influence public opinion. With such techniques in hand, the campaign industry has replaced both the political parties and the press as the source of the nation's political information. "This information is designed not to educate voters on matters of public policy but to influence the 30 per cent of the electorate not loyal to either of the two major parties," Squires writes.

For Squires, the political press has been only a narrow lane on the giant highway, which includes countless sources of information other than journalism, most of it advertising or promoting something. He notes that nearly three quarters of all political contributions are ultimately spent in the preparation, production, and airing of advertising and infomercials or the planting of outright lies into the never-ending stream of information flowing to voters.

MIT professor Ansolabehere suggests in an article by *Boston Globe* writer Peter S. Canellos that negative advertising turned voters away from politics and that free media may be accomplishing the same thing. Dave Bartlett, president of the Radio-Television News Directors Association, agrees: "Don't blame us for apathy. The politicians have screwed up the political system. We've been there to report it."

Political handlers also have helped "screw up" the system, Bartlett says. It may have been Joe McGinniss, author of *The Selling of the President 1968*, who first told Americans that millions of dollars were being spent to influence our most important democratic exercise — the selection of a president. And the mainstream press, for all its valiant efforts, really didn't have much to do with it.

The Practices of Journalists

Many reporters know they sound cynical or write negative stories. They also know that people blame them for it. But most reporters say it isn't their fault. Their stories merely reflect society. Others say they are covering the issues but must compete with entertainment-driven information programs.

Robert MacNeil, former executive editor and co-anchor of the *MacNeil/ Lehrer NewsHour*, agrees. "The media reflect the temper of the times," he writes in "Regaining Dignity." "They do not create that temper, although they may shape it, crystallize it, magnify it, make it more extreme, and raise its pitch." For example, reporting on presidential elections reflects the system and the type of campaign, writes Hal Bruno, political director of ABC News, in "The System Is the Problem." The media do not invent the campaign, nor did they create this process. But critics accuse the media of treating it like a horse race.

"And the reason we do [treat it like a horse race] is that it is," Bruno writes. "They created a horse race, which is held every week on a different track. Those that finish in the money advance to the next round. Those who don't, run out of money. And under the process the reformers created, when you're out of money, you're out of the game."

The cynical tone is also justified by the relentless "spin" of the politicians they write about. If anyone is undermining American democracy, it is these "spin masters" — these political handlers — not the media. In the April 1997 issue of *Campaigns & Elections*, four top "spin doctors" teach candidates and handlers how to deal with the press and get one's earned media messages across to the right audience, at the right time, in the right way. Says Craig Shirley, one of those spin doctors: "In this 'hyperspeed' world of mass communications, the idea of a newscycle is anachronistic. News travels and changes constantly." In other words, the alternative media is no longer a gap filler when the *New York Times* won't cover a story. Another spin doctor, Robert Shrum, says, "News organizations increasingly accept negative stories without disclosing that they're obtained directly from campaigns."

Because of such actions, the press is criticized for not covering issues. Fallows and his followers, for example, say citizens want to know about the what of politics, but reporters dwell exclusively on the how. "This is probably the biggest myth since Cinderella," Bruno says. "The issues are the news of the day. We cover them on the evening news in a shorter form. We cover them in depth and detail on *Nightline*, on the magazine shows, on the weekend programs. Everything we cover is related to where the candidates stand on issues. But when people say that we're not covering the issues, I find myself wondering, What are they watching?"

What they *aren't* watching is network news. The mainstream press is slowly losing the game. Chunks of the population, and the democratic electorate, no longer get their information from the networks. According to Roper surveys, the nation once received 90 per cent of its news from the networks. That fell to 77 per cent by 1980 and 52 per cent in 1995. Instead millions of Americans are getting their news from talk shows that grow more lurid and leering, life crime and rescue shows, syndicated tabloid news, docudramas, and re-enactments. Even more disturbing, Roper says, half of the nation finds these programs "fairly credible sources of information."

Increased competition in the marketplace may be the enemy of conventional standards of journalism, according to MacNeil. "The question is whether these hot new kinds of information programming, with their high entertainment values and appeal to the young, are forcing serious journalists to follow them for survival."

Take the O.J. Simpson story, which made for great tabloid fare — a rich sports celebrity involved in an interracial marriage with a history of domestic violence. President Bill Clinton's state of the union address was even interrupted to announce the latest Simpson verdict. Would journalists have spent so much time on the story if *Hard Copy, Current Affair,* and the *National Enquirer* had not?

The public appears to have an almost insatiable appetite for such material, and the media are responding to this demand. In the 1960s Daniel Boorstin noted that American audiences wanted excitement and drama in their news and information programming. He said that since the "real" world couldn't provide this, the news media had turned to coverage of what he coined "pseudo-events" — a staged action to draw attention to an individual or event. This demonstrates that the media will get serious only when they see the country getting serious, when they see the audience for serious stuff out-rating the audience for circuses, MacNeil says.

It is not the value and practices of the mainstream media then that have undermined American democracy, say critics of Fallows, but the competition in the marketplace that has lessened the conventional standards of journalism. Is there any hope for the future?

Resolution

The answer, Fallows argues, is public or civic journalism. "Fundamentally, what it's saying is that journalists have to take seriously the effect of what they do on public life," Fallows told David Gergen in a special *Online Forum.* "For example, if they present all political issues as just being a mud fight among politicians, they have to recognize what this will do to the public sense of politics in the long run."

According to Jay Rosen in "Getting the Connections Right: Public Journalism and the Troubles in the Press," public journalism calls on the press to help revive civic life and improve public dialogue — and to fashion a coherent response to the deepening troubles in our civic climate, most of which implicate journalists. "At a time of grave doubts about the future of the press and broad concern about the health of American democracy," he writes, "those involved see this as the hour for creative experiment and piecemeal reform, for serious discussion about ultimate aims and possible ends, for innovations as bold and lasting as the arrival of the Op-Ed page." Rosen says journalists experimenting with public journalism have rediscovered the power of the democratic ideal as an organizing principle for their work. "Self government, public deliberation, participatory democracy — these familiar themes, if taken seriously, can recharge the batteries of the press and show the way to much-needed reforms."

To further illustrate this concept, let's take a chunk of the press in North Carolina in 1996 when it decided to do something about the state of political campaigns. Michael Kelly, in a *New Yorker* article titled "Media Culpa," said the North Carolina press wanted to get away from campaigns that often turned on name-calling and the exploitation of hot-button topics such as race, rather than on the issues voters really cared about. Some fifteen media organizations — six newspapers, five commercial television channels, three radio stations, and the statewide public-television channel — created a consortium to force the candidates in the gubernatorial and senatorial races to discuss the proper issues, properly.

He writes that the "Your Voice, Your Vote" consortium, as it termed itself, commissioned two polls of 1,000 North Carolinians each — one in January, for the primary season, and one in July, for the general election. Respondents were asked to identify the issues on which they felt it was "very important" to know where the candidates stood. For the general election, the list that emerged consisted of Crime and Drugs, Taxes and Spending, Affordable Health Care, and Education. The candidates were invited to sit for three-hour videotaped group interviews, in which they would be grilled on the chosen issues. What resulted from the interviews were a series of shared stories describing the candidates' positions on issues. Identical stories ran in all the newspapers, on successive Sundays, and on all the television channels and radio stations.

That experiment produced both praise and a great deal of criticism. For example, Al Hunt, in his *Wall Street Journal* column, worried about public journalists overusing marketing techniques, polls, surveys, and focus groups as replacement for "actually spending time reporting on citizens." Those who practice public journalism cede editorial judgment to pollsters or, worse, to readers or viewers in focus groups who have no particular knowledge of a state, of politics or of politicians, according to Michael Gartner in "Public Journalism — Seeing Through the Gimmicks."

In Mike Hoyt's *Columbia Journalism Review* article on "A Civic Journalist?"

New York Times columnist Max Frankel points out that newsrooms have limited resources and that developing large amounts of attention and money to big-ticket public journalism activities could shortchange (or further shortchange) basic newsgathering. But Hoyt says the best argument against public journalism, perhaps, is that its rhetoric makes such excellent cover for pandering. "A newsroom that would seek to market itself as the community's pal, meanwhile, is the kind that could reflexively refrain from doing anything that might offend that community."

In "Has Democracy Gone Awry?" *Boston Globe* writer Anthony Flint says that if the experts can't agree on whether cynicism permeates our society, and if it does, what we should do about it, then part of the problem may be the terms of the debate. "Whatever their differences, the warring Cassandras and Polyannas start out with the same premise," he says. "Both camps — those warning of civic decline and those responding that our civic impulses have simply been rechanneled — believe that any slippage from the communitarian ideals that Tocqueville observed in the early 19th century is cause for concern."

If Tocqueville were alive today, he might be surprised to learn that his observations are still held up as a standard at all. Indeed, Flint says, instead of seeing cynicism as a warning that the country is falling apart — or denying the existence of the phenomenon altogether — we might begin viewing it as a permanent, but not disabling, feature of a mature democracy. Under this analysis, Flint says citizen discontent is something that America must learn to live with, the way that Europe has. In fact, he says, disenchantment can even be seen as a sign of health.

"Since Tocqueville visited America," he says, "the country has experienced childhood growing pains, adolescent struggles, adult traumas. Cynicism may simply represent the nation's wrinkles and worry lines — not always attractive, but hardly life-threatening."

Recommended Readings

Books

Ansolabehere, Stephen, Roy Behr, and Shanto Iyengar. *The Media Game: American Politics in the Age of Television.* New York: Macmillan, 1993. Politicians speak to the media; the media then speak to the voters. The media can filter, alter, distort or ignore altogether what politicians says. The authors explore how this two-step flow of communications has radically altered the behavior of politicians and dramatically affected the relation of individual citizens to the political process.

Diamond, Edwin, and Robert A. Silverman. *White House to Your House: Media & Politics in Virtual America*. Cambridge, Mass.: MIT Press, 1997. Analyzes the presidential performers in national campaigns as well as in the period between presidential elections, formally known as governance, but now also recognized as the permanent campaign.

Fallows, James. *Breaking the News*. New York: Pantheon Books, 1996. This best-seller attempts to explain why the values of journalists have changed, how their current practices undermine the credibility of the press, and how they distort the process by which leaders are elected.

Kees, Beverly, and Bill Phillips. *Nothing Sacred*. Nashville, Tenn.: Freedom Forum First Amendment Center, 1994. Journalists, politicians, and the public agree: When it comes to coverage of political figures, the line between private life and public interest no longer exists.

McGinniss, Joe. *The Selling of the President 1968*. New York: Penguin Books, 1988. Now a classic, the book presents an insider's account — sometimes shocking and often funny — of the first electronic election.

Rosen, Jay. *Getting the Connections Right: Public Journalism and the Troubles in the Press*. New York: Twentieth Century Fund, 1996. Public journalism, at its best, leaves behind some additional capacity in the community, augmenting its ability to "recognize itself, converse well, and make choices."

Sabato, Larry J. *Feeding Frenzy: How Attack Journalism Has Transformed American Politics*. New York: Free Press, 1991. Discusses the impact of attack journalism on American politics.

Squires, James D. *Read All About It! The Corporate Takeover of America's Newspapers*. New York: Times Books, 1993. Looks at what is wrong with American newspapers — the corporatization of the press that is resulting in an erosion of its quality, integrity, and reliability.

Articles & Book Chapters

Bruno, Hal. "The Primaries: The System Is the Problem." *Media Studies Journal* 11 (Winter 1997): 25-9. The veteran broadcaster argues that the nature of the nominating system does not produce the qualities the country needs in a president.

Canellos, Peter S. "A Disdain for Politics is Becoming the Vogue: Campaign '96." *Boston Globe*, 9 October 1996. Cynicism is being marketed like a fragrance, writes Canellos. However, it is not the journalists' fault; blame it on negative advertising, handlers, and an uninformed citizenry.

Flint, Anthony. "Has Democracy Gone Awry?" *Boston Globe*, 20 October 1996. The journalist writes that some social critics say that America's civic life is disappearing, but the pessimists may be looking in the wrong places.

Gartner, Michael. "Public Journalism — Seeing Through the Gimmicks." *Media Studies Journal* 11 (Winter 1997): 69-77. "Newspapers go through waves of experimentation, and nervous editors periodically listen to goofy professors or rich foundations. This civic journalism is no different, just the trend of the moment."

Halonen, Doug. "Journalists: Don't Blame Us for Apathy." *Boston Globe,* 20 May 1996. Veteran broadcasters make it clear that they don't see themselves as the problem for the growing apathy among the electorate.

Hoyt, Mike. "A Civic Journalist?" *Columbia Journalism Review* (September/October 1995): 1–6. Despite its attractiveness to a growing number of journalists, the theory of public journalism is gaining even more critics.

Jaksa, James A., and Michael S. Pritchard. *Communication Ethics: Methods of Analysis.* Belmont, Calif.: Wadsworth. Chapter two, "A Crisis of Confidence?" discusses the effects of Watergate on politics, the press, and the electorate.

Jamieson, Kathleen Hall, and Joseph N. Cappella. "The Media and the Message: Is the Messenger to Blame, too, for a Cynical Citizenry?" *Atlanta Journal-Constitution,* 15 September 1994. The authors add another dimension to growing cynicism — a tendency on the part of reporters to filter both elections and public policy through a set of cynical assumptions.

Kelly, Michael. "Media Culpa." *The New Yorker,* 4 November 1996, 45-9. The author answers the question: What happened when the press tried to get high-minded practicing civic journalism? It fudged the most- clear-cut race in the country.

MacNeil, Robert. "Regaining Dignity." *Media Studies Journal* 9 (Summer 1995): 103-11. The veteran broadcaster says it is time for journalists to stop thinking of themselves as media, "just another of the rings in the circus, which the government and public can kick around."

Rosen, Jay. "The Propaganda of the Present: Reflections on Civic Identity in the Media Age." *Tikkun* 11 (January 1996): 19. The conflict between "journalism" and "the media" is part of a larger tension between America's civic culture and America's consumer culture, between the nation understood as a republic of citizens and the nation understood as a vast marketplace of freely associating individuals.

Shaw, David. "Trust in Media Is on Decline." *Los Angeles Times,* 31 March 1993. Polls show that the public frequently expresses the view that news outlets are biased and sensationalistic. Journalists tell their concerns about this view that they label unfair.

Chapter Nine

The Media and
Political Bias

Robert S. Fortner

To the traditional categories of things inescapable, death, and taxes, we must add a third: the inevitability of denunciations of "liberal media bias" by a variety of "watchdog" groups in the aftermath of virtually every national election. These groups, among which the Media Research Center (MRC), AIM (Accuracy in Media), and the Center for Media and Public Affairs (CMPA) are the most visible, release such conclusions regularly, claiming that the television networks and the "national" press (including the *Wall Street Journal, New York Times, Washington Post, USA Today,* and the major news magazines) fail to inform the American electorate adequately about scandals and peccadilloes, and that sustained investigation and reporting of the results might well change the outcome of an election. Although organizations representing other political quarters are less well-funded and organized, they may also denounce the media's performance, as President Bill Clinton did himself after his 1992 election.

Origins of the Issue

The concerns expressed about the portrayal of politics to the American electorate are perhaps inevitable in a polarized society where opposing factions struggle to dominate the "public culture" or, as James Davison Hunter puts it in *Culture Wars,* "the repository of the symbols of national life and purpose." This public culture includes the norms and legal codes of the state, the nature of public responsibility, the symbols of national identity, and the collective myths of a culture, all of which interpret its history and establish its future promise.

At one time the press in America was unabashedly partisan; political parties owned their own newspapers. After the creation of the "penny press" in the 1830s, however, and its rapid development of a mass readership, the media gradually developed a more distant relationship with politics, often concentrating on crime, accidents, and more sensationalistic events that would increase circulation and profit as it became increasingly advertiser-supported.

With the exception of the muckraking period at the turn of the century, the tradition of objectivity defined the press' public ideology as it reported political, social, cultural, or religious stories. As the electronic media developed into important communications channels in the 1930s, however, speeding up reporting and making it possible for politicians to speak directly to the people via radio, the stakes for politicians increased. The result was what Richard L. Rubin in *Press, Party, and Presidency* called a "political communications strategy" to deal with the press. Its first important proponent was President Franklin D. Roosevelt, who saw the press as an impediment to his New Deal. Roosevelt attacked the wire services, "claiming to detect subtle bias in their treatment of his administration," as Rubin put it. The claims put forth by Democrats about an anti-Adlai Stevenson bias in 1952 and 1956 were less subtle, and Vice-President Richard Nixon's use of the media to get his message across in the famous "Checkers speech" suggested that media could be an ally to Republicans under an ethics cloud.

The watershed event that resulted in the modern "news bias industry" occurred after the 1968 Democratic convention. The McGovern-Fraser Commission recommended changes in the nominating process that resulted in a fundamental change in the method of selecting the Democratic nominee for president. Before the change, two-thirds of the delegates to the national convention had been selected by state party conventions; afterwards three-quarters of the delegates were chosen by voters in primary elections. As state legislatures dominated by Democrats passed new rules to select convention delegates, they applied equally to both parties. Thomas E. Patterson explained in *Out of Order* that this increased the media's influence. Because candidates now appealed directly to voters, the party leadership lost influence, and the media, which connected contenders and voters, took on a key responsibility.

Two other events followed as the 1972 presidential campaign unfolded. The first was the publication of Joe McGinniss' book, *The Selling of the President 1968*, which claimed that Richard Nixon had been repackaged as a "new Nixon" and sold to the American people like toothpaste. This seemed to suggest that the press had failed in its self-proclaimed obligation to be a "watchdog" for the citizenry. The second was the Watergate scandal, which emboldened the press and established it solidly as an adversary in the political process. This scandal also suggested that control of information between political parties and campaign staffs, on the one side, and the press on the other, was a crucial dimension of presidential politics. Eventually politicians began to hire spin doctors and political and image consultants to assist them in their information management strategies and news organizations began to contract with polling organizations to determine the success or failure of each campaign's strategies. The press was increasingly interested both in 1) the candidate's rhetorical strategies, including the cultivated image, and 2) the managerial strategies for withholding or releasing information. Campaign managers countered this new investigative interest by hiring their own polling organizations to keep their candidate "connected" to the people. As Larry Sabato put it in *The Rise of Political Consultants*, this development severely damaged the party system and set the stage for the triumph of political personality cults.

The apparatus installed by both campaign and news organizations heightened the struggle between the press and politicians as each attempted to define the political activities of a presidential campaign in terms that suited its own needs: the press needed dramatic and interesting stories to report, while candidates needed to release information or define policies on a schedule calculated to increase their impact and allow their campaigns to peak at the appropriate time to enhance their election chances. As the ubiquity of television increased, political advertising, which bypassed journalistic scrutiny, began to loom larger in the arsenals of political candidates. This development further soured the press' attitude toward politicians.

With Ronald Reagan's election in 1976, the stakes were increased further still. Reagan appealed to traditional values that some groups in society declared to be under attack by congressional and court action. Reagan was successful in making the Republicans the party of traditional morality—the "pro-life," "pro-family" and "pro-American" party. Members of the public, particularly those who declared themselves "anti-liberal," included the press and media among their adversaries in the "culture war" that formed one of the themes of Pat Buchanan's address to the Republican National Convention in 1988.

The Liberal Media Bias

The research that established the foundation of the anti-liberal argument as applied to the media was conducted by S. Robert Lichter, Stanley Rothman, and Linda Lichter and published in 1986 as *The Media Elite: America's New Power Brokers*. The book was based on interviews conducted in 1979 and 1980 among newspaper, news magazine, and television journalists, mostly based in Washington, D.C. They concluded that reporters trusted "liberal sources" over "conservative" ones by a three-to-one margin, and that 54 per cent of reporters described their own political convictions "left of center," compared to only 19 per cent who said they were "right of center." A slightly higher proportion of reporters thought their colleagues were "mostly on the left" and fewer that they were "mostly on the right." In the presidential elections beginning in 1964, the authors concluded, over 80 per cent of the journalists interviewed reported that they had voted for the Democratic presidential nominee, even when the majority of voters had selected the Republican nominee.

This *Media Elite* research into the liberal bias of the press core, supporting data from Stephen Hess's *Washington Reporters*, the *Los Angeles Times*, and the Associated Press Managing Editors Association (ASME), among others, resulted in L. Brent Bozell III's and Brent H. Baker's assertion in *And That's the Way it Isn't* that "there is no such thing as an 'objective' national news media."

In a second publication of the Media Research Center, Tim Graham cited additional research on reporters' political views that had been completed for the Freedom Forum, and on press opinion of the coverage of the 1992 campaign reported by the Times Mirror Center for the People and the Press to support his argument about liberal bias. Quoting the Times Mirror study, he argued that a "substantial majority (55 per cent) of the American journalists who followed the 1992 presidential campaign believe that George Bush's candidacy was damaged by the way the press covered him. Only 11 per cent feel that Gov. Bill Clinton's campaign was harmed by the way the press covered his drive." Graham's own conclusion was that the 1992 campaign was the best demonstration in modern times of a liberal media bias and of its damage by leaving the public uninformed about the person it elects to the nation's highest office.

Graham divided his critique of the media's performance into seven categories: the primary season, coverage of the national conventions, the fall campaign, the new Clinton administration, Clinton's 1994 travails, the 1994 Republican revolution, and Clinton versus Gingrich. He argued that, while the media claimed they had "hammered Clinton with a one-two punch of Gennifer Flowers and draft dodging" during the primaries, "TV reporters actually worked hard to bury both issues." He contrasted the coverage accorded to Clinton's draft story to that over Dan Quayle's 1988 National Guard controversy: thirteen evening news stories on Clinton's draft story in the first ten days after the story broke compared to fifty-one for the Quayle National Guard story over the same period in 1988.

In his portrayal of TV news coverage of the conventions, Graham complained that "none of the networks use[d] the word 'liberal' to describe Bill Clinton, Al Gore, or the Democratic platform.... But the media found that Republicans gathering in Houston suffered from apocalyptic right-wing extremist rhetoric sure to strike a chord of fear or disgust in the average voter."

His summary of media coverage of the fall campaign was equally stark: "While the media found Democrats offering hope and solutions, they portrayed the Republicans as tired, desperate mudslingers." As for the Clinton's arrival in Washington: "some reporters ... became Clinton appointees: in the first two years of the Clinton administration, more than twice as many reporters jumped on board than in the entire four years of the Bush administration. Reporters like Martha Sherrill of the *Washington Post* and Margaret Carlson of *Time* magazine celebrated Hillary Clinton as 'our leading cult figure' and an 'icon of American womanhood.'"

The revelations of Clinton's alleged sexual misdeeds and Whitewater involvement that erupted in 1994 resulted, Graham said, in network and news magazine reporters moving "quickly to take these stories off the front burner or off the stove entirely." As for the Republican takeover of the House and Senate, "media pundits claimed the results were not a vote for the Contract with America or a desire to restrain government growth." And, in the treatment of Clinton and Gingrich, Graham charged, "the same reporters who downplayed Whitewater played up ethical allegations against new Speaker Newt Gingrich, including a book advance he rejected after controversy."

Accuracy In Media's website (http://www.aim.org/bias.htm) also argued that a liberal bias pervades the media. "Few reporters," Joseph C. Goulden wrote there, "can put their prejudices aside when they sit down before a word processor or stand before a microphone." His evidence came from quoted comments from Evan Thomas, Washington bureau chief for *Newsweek*, on *Inside Washington*. "There is liberal bias," Thomas had said. "About 85 per cent of the reporters who cover the White House vote Democratic." He also cited Bernard Goldberg, CBS News correspondent, from an op-ed piece in *The Wall Street Journal*: "The old argument that the networks and other 'media elites' have a liberal bias is so blatantly true that it's hardly worth discussing anymore."

The Center for Media and Public Affair's website (http://www.proxicom. com: 8080/cmpa/html/2600.html) carried the introduction to S. Robert Lichter's and Richard E. Noyes' book, *Good Intentions Make Bad News: Why Americans Hate Campaign Journalism*, which began by admitting that media bashing had become mainstream, coming from all sides of the political spectrum. "In many respects," they said, "the candidates and the often-derided talk shows performed better than the mainstream media did during Campaign '92."

In 1996, CMPA's Media Monitor concluded that a "majority of TV news sources have said favorable things about Bill Clinton in election news stories, while three of five comments about Bob Dole have been unfavorable. Thus, Clinton leads in the race for good press with 54 per cent positive judgments compared to Dole's 42 per cent positive." The following issue also reported that Clinton was "winning the battle for good press," and that "Since Labor Day ...

the gap between the two men's media images has widened 54 per cent good press for Clinton vs. only 30 per cent for Dole."

Some members of the press agree with the analysis of media bias. Michael Barone, for instance, writing in the *Detroit News*, claims that "most honest journalists" acknowledge that claims of "scrupulously objective" reporting are nonsense, even "laughable." Although many reporters and editors do produce "fair-minded work" and "the bias of the press does not work reliably in any one direction," there is, he says, a "tilt for all to see heading in just the direction you would expect from newsrooms staffed by very large majorities of Democrats, cultural liberals and feminists."

William Powers complained in *The New Republic*, too, that "by and large, the mainline media did not focus intense, sustained attention on the stories that could have been most threatening to the president's chances of re-election." He conceded that the key news organizations had covered the story, but had tended to play it down, from the Paula Jones case to the Whitewater investigation, "the congressional investigations became the dogs that didn't bark, or at least were not made to bark very loudly or very long. In 1996, scandal went out of fashion."

The arguments of those who claim a liberal media bias exists ultimately boil down to this: the majority of working reporters in various news organizations are themselves liberal, vote Democratic, and report the news from that particular point of view. This can be seen by examining the quantity of attention given to political candidates especially presidential contenders and agendas or platforms. This can be as simple as reluctance to use labels, such as "liberal," or the rush to label, using such terms as "right-wing," "fanatic" or "conservative." It may also be more complicated, indicated by such flags as the amount of "good news" or negative reporting received by candidates, emphasis on "horse-race" reporting that suggests which candidate is the winner or loser (thus creating a self-fulfilling prophecy), or decisions to downplay or play up issues that emerge in a campaign that could affect the perception of a candidate's viability, competence, or ethics.

As William Rusher argues in *The Coming Battle for the Media*, the major media organizations have, in the past few decades, responded "to liberal intellectual trends once dominant but now much less so," and "allied themselves with those political forces promoting liberal policies (meaning primarily the Democratic party), and have placed news reportage at the service of those policies."

The Unbiased Media

There are at least two significant arguments made in opposition to the claims about a biased liberal media. First and perhaps most obvious is that the media are biased toward the status quo, serving the interests of the giant corporations that largely control the press and broadcasting organizations. Such arguments are largely theoretical rather than empirical, however, except in dealing with the relationship between news selection or slant and the pressures created by advertising dollars.

Perhaps the best exception to this generalization is the perspective provided by Todd Gitlin in *The Whole World is Watching*. Writing from a leftist perspective, he argued that press bias against the "new left" had resulted in the undoing of the Students for a Democratic Society (SDS), which had provided an alternative political perspective to the orthodoxies of traditional politics in America. His analysis of the news fit within the theoretical framework established by Ralph Milliband in *The State in Capitalist Society*, where Milliband argued that the mass media "still contribute to the fostering of a climate of conformity" in which they present news falling outside the dominant consensus "as curious heresies" or "irrelevant eccentricities which serious people may dismiss as of no consequence." And Gaye Tuchman has noted in *Making News* that both "newspaper and television stations carry 'must stories,' items that the business office, advertising staff, or front office say 'must be carried' to satisfy either advertisers or friends of well-placed executives in the news organization."

The second argument is that the media, while sometimes flawed in their news judgment or balance, are, on the whole, professional (i.e., objective) and non-partisan in their treatment of politics. As Pamela J. Shoemaker and Stephen D. Reese conclude in *Mediating the Message*, for instance, "Academic researchers have looked closely at bias and have generally given the news media good marks for fairness and objectivity.... In general, empirical evidence shows that most news content is neutral, with little evidence of overt partisan bias in favor of one candidate or another."

Michael J. Robinson and Margaret A. Sheehan have provided one of the most cited pieces of research into news values, a sustained look at the coverage of the 1980 presidential election by CBS and UPI. They concluded that if the performance of the press is examined in historical context, then it is performing objectively. Even using "absolute standards," they say, "the national press behaves objectivistically [sic] in covering major political campaigns. There are serious deficiencies in political reporting at the national level, but overt subjectivity about issues or about candidates is not high on the list." Most "outraged complaints," they conclude, can be overruled.

Other scholars have come to similar conclusions. Herbert J. Gans in *Deciding What's News*, struggled with the issue of journalistic values, saying that journalists "try hard to be objective, but neither they nor anyone else can in the end proceed without values." Gans argued that journalists do not "deliberately insert values into the news," but that viewers and readers brings their own preconceptions to that news, "and may infer many different values from what they see and read." Based on his participant observer study of news within television network news organizations and news magazines, Gans concluded:

> [J]ournalists with conscious values were in the minority, for the news media I studied seem to attract people who keep their values to themselves.... Many of the reporters or writers constantly immersed in American politics did not seem particularly interested in it apart from their work.... They were only interested in 'getting the story.'

Likewise, in his study of the 1968 election, *The Political Impact of Mass Media*, Richard Hofstetter found little evidence of any consistent pattern of political bias in election reporting, despite the vocal complaints of anti-Nixon bias in reporting (notably by Spiro Agnew, who accused the press of being "nattering nabobs of negativism"). "If anything" Richard L. Rubins concluded in *Press, Party, and Presidency*, "the bias in news reporting remains the broad professional tendency to favor action and controversy because they attract attention and sustain interest.... If there is one journalistic value that clearly dominates others it is this professional need to generate stories of change, movement, and something happening."

Scholars provide several reasons for the inability of the media to establish a consistent pattern of bias. Timothy Crouse, for instance, in his often-cited book, *The Boys on the Bus*, provides a compelling account of "pack journalism" which, he said, was so reprehensible that "[m]any reporters and journalism professors blame it for everything that is shallow, obvious, meretricious, misleading, or dull in American campaign coverage." It was what led the campaign press corps (those who traveled with the candidates) to "believe the same rumors, subscribe to the same theories, and write the same stories." What prevented reporters from reporting from their own individual and biased perspectives was the necessity of staying with the pack, for "even the most independent journalist cannot completely escape the pressures of the pack."

Edward J. Epstein, in *News from Nowhere*, said the main finding of his study was "that the pictures of society that are shown on television as national news are largely though not entirely performed and shaped by organizational considerations. To maintain themselves in a competitive world, the networks impose a set of prior restraints, rules and conditions on the operations of their news divisions." These constraints were budgets, time schedules, and general policies, not political convictions. Gaye Tuchman, in *Making News*, noted that journalists point out that they must be unbiased since their accounts are produced independently within a variety of organizations "and so do not represent a personal bias."

Another ameliorating aspect of political reporting is what may be termed the media's "reactive posture." It is this factor that led the press, during the 1976 primary campaigns for instance, to provide more news coverage to whichever candidate had won the previous week's primary. Thomas E. Patterson explained the pattern in *The Mass Media Election*. During the week following each primary, each candidate would receive coverage in proportion to his success in that primary—usually about 60 per cent for the leader, then 20, 15, and 5 per cent respectively for the runners-up. "This imbalance," he maintained, "reflected no obvious bias by the press toward a particular candidate." Patterson argued later that the "dominant theme of presidential election coverage is one of winning and losing." So more attention is paid to candidates who win primaries, or who are leading in the polls, than to others. As the fortunes of candidates wax and wane, then, the amount of press coverage including speculation as to the reasons for the candidates' positions in the "horse race" increases or decreases. As Patterson put it in another book, writing with Robert D. McClure in *The Unseeing Eye*, television's demand for good pictures leads the networks to report presidential elections as spectacular sports events complete with "huge crowds, rabid followers, dramatic do-or-die battles, winner and losers. It is this part of the election that the networks emphasize."

The arguments against the notion of liberal media bias, then, are that journalistic values such as objectivity, along with pack journalism and a reactive posture seen in the media's obsession with winners and losers, mitigate potential political bias in reporting. So do the procedures adopted by news organizations to ensure that their financial resources are well used, their available time to produce and air or print stories are used efficiently, and that their reports fit into the matrix of reports on a given day as produced by various news organizations. To the extent that bias exists, then, the argument goes, it must either be inadvertent or the result of the way that particular campaign plays out.

Resolution

This is a dispute that will never reach a satisfactory resolution, for news is a symbolic construct over which competitive institutions contend for control. As John Hartley explains in *Understanding News*, news "is a social and cultural institution among many others," including politics. Or, as Gaye Tuchman has put it, "Because news imparts a public character to occurrences, news is first and foremost a social institution." Whenever one institution succeeds in controlling access to a symbolic construct, others who object to the nature of that construct are bound to complain. If those who argue against the liberal bias of the press were satisfied with news organizations' control, then those with other political agendas would be dissatisfied. And media definitions of what news is, and how it should be reported, as Michael Schudson suggests in *Discovering the News*, should lead to an acknowledgment that "the belief in objectivity in journalism, as in other professions, is not just a claim about what kind of knowledge is reliable. It is also a moral philosophy, a declaration of what kind of thinking one should engage in, in making moral decisions." It is also a political commitment, he says, acknowledging certain groups as "relevant audiences." This is what makes the definition of news, or the claims about bias, so contentious: the definitions, and the apparatus that controls them, are part of the cultural and moral fabric of society.

Moreover, the struggle among institutions eager to control public perceptions of candidates is a dynamic one. The definition of news, or the nature of reporting in one election, will not necessarily work in another. In the reporter's view, the nature of his or her job changes according to the nature of the contest being reported. As Carlin Romano puts it in his essay, "The Grisly Truth about Bare Facts," "the rational principles that govern coverage decisions are not 'scientific.' Unlike scientific laws, they can't be assumed to apply uniformly or to permit accurate predictions of future cases." But for those who come from a particular moral or political posture (or ideology) the terrain is absolute and unchangeable. Conflict is thus inevitable.

Thomas E. Patterson has provided three useful claims (or "themes" as he uses them in his book, *Out of Order*) that illuminate aspects of this conflict. These are:

- Journalistic values and political values are at odds with one another, which results in a news agenda that misrepresents what is at stake in the choice among the candidates.

- Journalistic values, though supposedly neutral, introduce an element of random partisanship into the campaign, which coincidentally works to the advantage of one side or another.

- Election news, rather than serving to bring candidates and voters together, drives a wedge between them.

Patterson goes on to explore the dimensions of these themes, noting that the news media's version of reality is necessarily story-bound. "The 'facts' must cohere, and they must do so in time for the daily deadline." So the news needs, as Richard L. Rubin puts it, "a strong provocative posture from which to dramatize events." This bias is a journalistic one rather than an overtly political one, which is what leads to Patterson's conclusion that partisanship "coincidentally works to the advantage of one side or another."

In other words, media have institutional biases. They search for dramatic narrative, compelling controversy, control of the symbolic repertoire of reporting. This leads them to criticize campaign advertisements and the routine of national conventions. It explains their quest for the unusual, dramatic, and compelling aspects of otherwise boring conventions—such as controversial keynote addresses or statements at variance with the party's platform positions—or for inconsistencies between a candidate's rhetorical posture and his own behavior, or the duplicity that is assumed to exist in campaign staffs dominated by consultants and pollsters.

Ultimately these dimensions of news reporting more adequately explain the actions of the press in the campaign season than do simple examination of the content of news reports or surveys of reporters' political convictions. These dimensions help explain the apparent decisions made, for instance, during the 1996 presidential race by the Dole campaign to go easy on the "character issue" because of fear that, if it were pushed, the press would feel obliged to make the most of an alleged 1968 extramarital affair to avoid being accused of a double standard. *The New Yorker,* according to Howard Kurtz's *Washington Post* story, said that "Dole feared a media frenzy that would doom his candidacy." The original story of the affair was broken by the *National Enquirer,* a paper with the same dubious credentials as the tabloids that broke stories on Clinton's alleged sexual misdeeds. Dole's position made his own past a non-story because he chose not to emphasize the character issue.

This perspective also helps explain why voters who complained about the media's treatment of Dole during the campaign were most concerned about the amount of attention paid to his standing in the polls, as Richard Morin and Mario A. Brossard reported in "So Did the Campaign Accomplish Anything?" It also explains why the amount of press coverage of the 1996 elections fell so dramatically from 1992. As Howard Kurtz put it in "Hey! Is Anyone Listening?" "Ratings for the party conventions hit an all-time low and viewership for the first presidential debate was down nearly 20 per cent from four years ago. "Network news coverage of the campaign dropped 40 per cent last month from 1992, while the number of front-page stories in *The Washington Post* declined by half." This may even explain why the press seemed so disinterested in Clinton's ethics problems. R. H. Melton and Bill McAllister excused the press' ho-hum attitude with the subtitle of their essay, "Watergate, Whitewater, Whatever": "Ethics problems have plagued every administration since the Nixon era." Ethics problems had no drama or controversy because they were so old hat.

This perspective does not necessarily excuse the behavior of journalists, who exhibit what James Fallows calls a "limited curiosity." According to Fallows, the public is interested primarily in "pure politics [and who] can be coerced into examining the substance of an issue only as a last resort. The subtle and sure result is a stream of daily messages that the real meaning of public life is the struggle of Bob Dole against Newt Gingrich against Bill Clinton, rather than our collective efforts to solve collective problems." And it matters. As Shanto Iyengar and Donald Kinder put it in *News That Matters*, "the public's view of the president's personal qualities depends on which aspects of national life television news chooses to cover and which to ignore. The terms of character are set, in part, by television news, just as the terms of performance are." This conclusion holds whether or not competence or character are raised by a candidate's opponent. The public needs information about those who run for public office, regardless of which political game is being played out by the candidate's campaign organizations. To the extent that such matters are ignored by the press and media, citizens are not served, regardless of the personal political convictions of news reporters or the partisanship that might be displayed in their stories about the election.

What requires our attention and sustained critique is the institution of news and news organizations, for this is the root of the issue. A reflective examination of the values of news professionalism and their application to what Fallows called society's "collective problems" would not only improve the quality of reporting and reduce the institutional conflict between media and politics, but it would also de-politicize debate: it would reduce partisanship and focus attention on problems and solutions. Regardless of where one stands on the issue of bias in the media, therefore, it would be good to recall the conclusion of James McCartney in "Hoodwinked!" "In every presidential election since Richard Nixon faced John F. Kennedy in 1960," McCartney observed, "the American press has fumbled the ball in some significant, often memorable way. Candidates have gotten away with outright lies, deliberate misrepresentations, phony assertions and, on occasion, ridiculous, unachievable proposals. In each instance the public and democracy have been poorly served." And this has been true of the reporting on both sides of the political spectrum. It's a competence issue; not a partisan one.

In other words, the debate about media bias may actually miscast the issue, leading us to examine the minutia of journalistic prose, camera angles, press releases, advertising claims, and media coverage of these activities rather than the serious issues that are raised by the institutional control and practices of journalism itself. This was one conclusion of the Commission on Freedom of the Press in 1947 in *A Free and Responsible Press*. It argued that when the press as an institution became so economically powerful that it might threaten democracy, it would be necessary for its members to control themselves or to be controlled by government—at which point the American people would lose their chief safeguard against totalitarianism.

So, while we might agree that from time to time political bias may exist in the reports of the press on significant public issues (including political campaigns), we would do well to attack the root of the problem rather than its symptoms. That, in turn, would require a re-examination of the role of the First Amendment protections accorded to the press, and that, as the Commission argued, would not only result in the loss of our chief safeguard against totalitarianism, but "at the same time take a long step toward it." The cure could be worse than the disease.

For that reason it is unlikely that press bias can be eliminated or reduced. The American democracy cannot do it. For that reason, too, the debate will continue, and the polemic may even become more vitriolic as the press becomes, through further consolidation, even more immune to its critics. Perhaps the ultimate irony is that those who are most keen to lambaste the press for its bias also inhabit the political camp of those most keen to see unfettered capitalism govern the activities of the media barons. It is through the development of the great media empires that the press becomes most immune to the criticism of those who attack it, and they inhabit the same part of the ideological spectrum.

Recommended Readings

Books

Bozell, L. Brent III, and Brent H. Baker. *And That's the Way it Isn't*. Alexandria, Va.: Media Research Center, 1990. A compendium of results from research studies that suggest a liberal media bias, conducted largely by S. Robert Lichter and associates of the Center for Media and Public Affairs or by the Media Research Center itself.

Epstein, Joseph Jay. *News from Nowhere: Television and the News*. New York: Vintage Books, 1973. A participant observer study of the operations of network television news operations, based on Epstein's observations at NBC.

Gans, Herbert. *Deciding What's News: A Study of CBS Evening News, NBC Nightly News, Newsweek and Time.* New York: Vintage Books, 1979. A participant observer study concentrating on the news judgments made within network news operations and national news magazines.

Gitlin, Todd. *The Whole World Is Watching: Mass Media in the Making and Unmaking of the New Left.* Los Angeles: University of California Press, 1980. Written from a New-Left perspective, this is one of the few book-length treatments of media bias that discusses a status quo or conservative bias in the media.

Graham, Tim. *Pattern of Deception: The Media's Role in the Clinton Presidency.* Alexandria, Va.: Media Research Center, 1996. A book based on some of the latest content analysis studies performed at the Media Research Center.

Hartley, John. *Understanding News.* London: Methuen, 1982. A sociological and semiotic analysis of news operations, content, and values.

Hofstetter, Richard. *The Political Impact of Mass Media.* Beverly Hills: Sage, 1974. One of the most comprehensive studies of political effects of media available.

Hunter, James Davison. *Culture Wars: The Struggle to Define America.* New York: Basic Books, 1991. A polemic work that argues for the application of traditional moral values in the cultural arena in the United States.

Iyengar, Shanto, and Donald R. Kinder. *News that Matters: Television and American Opinion.* Chicago, Ill.: University of Chicago Press, 1987. A book that reports on the results of several experimental research designs aimed at determining the effect of news on opinion.

Lichter, S. Robert, Stanley Rothman, and Linda S. Lichter. *The Media Elite.* New York: Adler and Adler, 1986. One of the earliest and most foundational studies indicating a liberal media bias among media elites (Washington, DC, based reporters).

Patterson, Thomas E. *The Mass Media Election: How Americans Choose Their President.* New York: Praeger, 1980. One of a series of content analysis-based studies on presidential elections.

Patterson, Thomas E. *Out of Order.* New York: Vintage Books, 1994. A significant work, based on Patterson's and his associate's work on presidential elections, providing a detailed and sophisticated account of the role of the press in politics.

Patterson, Thomas E., and Robert D. McClure. *The Unseeing Eye: The Myth of Television Power in National Elections.* New York: G. B. Putnam, 1976. Another content analysis-based study of the role of television journalism in national politics.

Robinson, Michael J., and Margaret A. Sheehan. *Over the Wire and on TV: CBS and UPI in Campaign '80.* New York: Russell Sage Foundation, 1983. A classic work that casts doubt on the liberal media hypothesis.

Rubin, Richard L. *Press, Party, and Presidency.* New York: W. W. Norton, 1981. A useful book that examines both media and political party impact on presidential politics.

Rusher, William A. *The Coming Battle for the Media: Curbing the Power of the Media Elite.* New York: William Morrow, 1988. A polemical book making the case against a liberal media and its impact on political life in the United States.

Tuchman, Gaye. *Making News: A Study in the Construction of Reality.* New York: The Free Press, 1978. A theoretically sophisticated examination of the ways in which journalists work and how their work creates reality.

Articles

Clayman, Steven E. "Defining Moments, Presidential Debates, and the Dynamics of Quotability." *Journal of Communication* 45 (1995): 118–46. This research focuses on one moment in the 1988 Vice-Presidential debate between Lloyd Bentsen and Dan Quayle, and how a particular excerpt dominated news coverage of the event. It argues that journalists used this excerpt because of three factors: narrative relevance, conspicuousness, and extractability.

Kaid, Lynda Lee, John C. Tedesco, and Lori Melton McKinnon. "Presidential Ads as Nightly News: A Content Analysis of 1988 and 1992 Televised Adwatches." *Journal of Broadcasting & Electronic Media* 40 (1996): 297–308. An examination of how media cover political advertising.

Lesher, Glenn, and Michael L. McKean. "Using TV News for Political Information During an Off-Year Election: Effects on Political Knowledge and Cynicism." *Journalism & Mass Communications Quarterly* 74 (1997): 69–83. This survey of a 1994 U.S. Senate campaign in Missouri argues that voters who used TV news for political information acquired information about the candidates and did not become cynical in response to that information.

Lowry, Dennis T., and Jon A. Shidler. "The Sound Bites, the Biters, and the Bitten: An Analysis of Network TV News Bias in Campaign '92." *Journalism & Mass Communication Quarterly* 72 (1995): 33–44. This content analysis of network news coverage of the Bush-Clinton election provides fodder for both sides of the media-bias debate.

Rhee, June Woong. "Strategy and Issue Frames in Election Campaign Coverage: A Social Cognitive Account of Framing Effects." *Journal of Communication* 47 (1997): 26–48. This examination of message structures in campaign news stories indicated two primary news frames for reporting: stories focusing on strategy and those focusing on issues. Both types of stories were found to be effective in influencing individual interpretations of campaigns.

Chapter Ten

The Press, Privacy and Politicians

Mark Popovich

Many argue that over the past two decades, media practitioners have deserted the time-worn principles of fairness and accuracy when it comes to political reporting. Whether it started in the 1970s after Watergate, arguably the most significant media story of the century, or as others suggest, with Gary Hart's alleged affair in the 1980s, political reporters began to abandon candidate platforms and bread-and-butter issues in election campaigns. Their focus has increasingly become the character of candidates running for public office.

"There was a time when news organizations were governed by a sense of propriety," says *National Journal* columnists Jack W. Germond and Jules Whitcover, "that kept figures in public life immune from many of the revelations that threaten to do in their political careers today."

The media have a "growing preoccupation with bedroom politics," notes Robert W. Merry in *Congressional Quarterly Weekly Report.* "With each new sexual scandal to hit the nation's political community, the old standards of fact-based journalism suffer further erosion."

"Scandal stories that used to be ignored," writes Norman J. Ornstein in *The Atlantic,* "or carried somewhere deep inside the paper, are now uniformly and routinely slated for the front page; the more salacious they are, the higher their placement."

Washington Post writer Howard Kurtz says, "In an era in which Donna Rice, Marla Maples, Tai Collins and Gennifer Flowers have each basked in 15 minutes of white-hot publicity, there seem to be no rules, no boundaries, no corner of human behavior into which prying reporters won't poke."

This state of affairs has prompted an ongoing debate among the traditional news media and on the pages of media trade journals about the state of political reporting in America today. Questions of how to deal ethically with invasions of privacy, marital infidelity, and sexual escapades in the political arena have taken on as much importance as how to cover candidate platforms, party strategy and campaign events. Examples of excessively reported private lives and public scandals have been numerous in the past two decades. Here are a few examples to consider:

- Allegations of improper sexual behavior against President Bill Clinton by former Arkansas state employee Paula Jones and a claim by White House intern Monica Lewinsky that she had an affair with him.

- Accusations against Clinton by a former state employee during the 1992 New Hampshire primary regarding his use of Arkansas state funds when he was Governor to romance five women, one of whom was identified as Gennifer Flowers.

- Disclosure of a story — nearly a decade old — about Independent-Republican gubernatorial candidate Jon Gunseth cavorting in a swimming pool with four teenage girls, which led to his withdrawal from the campaign in 1990.

- Questions by the media concerning the handling of medical records for presidential candidate Paul Tsongas, who was diagnosed with cancer a few days following the 1987 New York primary, when the public thought he had been given a clean bill of health in 1986.

- Media requests in 1988 for information about the academic record of Vice Presidential candidate Dan Quayle, his acceptance into law school and his Vietnam service in the National Guard.

- Coverage of Presidential candidate Gary Hart's travails in the 1988 campaign after the *Miami Herald* reported that he had spent the night with model Donna Rice, and a later revelation that he had gone on an overnight cruise with her.

Each of these stories focused on traditionally private areas: marital relations, academic records, medical records, and even events that transpired before the candidate had decided to run for public office. At issue here is the tenuous balance between the First Amendment rights and the privacy rights of those the press scrutinizes.

The growing disclosure of such information raises important questions: Where do the media derive their authority to report on public officials and public figures? What effect has such reportage had on media credibility? What effect has it had on the political process? Does this journalism invade the privacy of politicians? What are the legal definitions of privacy? Should politicians be judged by different privacy standards than private persons? The remainder of this chapter will present an overview of the developing legal concept known as privacy, focus on some of the ethical issues surrounding media coverage of politicians and privacy, and then provide some suggestions for how to resolve the conflict between the First Amendment rights of the press to gather information and the right of privacy extended to politicians.

Origins of the Issue

First Amendment lawyer Floyd Abrams notes that the legal concept of privacy is "a new area of law with a pedigree less than a hundred years old." Privacy is not specifically guaranteed by the Constitution, but the U.S. Supreme Court has recognized a right of personal privacy in varying contexts with roots in the First, Fourth, Fifth, and Ninth Amendments, in the first section of the Fourteenth Amendment, and in the penumbra of the Bill of Rights.

But it was not until 1890 that the legal right was proposed when two young Boston lawyers, Louis Brandeis and Samuel Warren, wrote "The Right to Privacy" for the *Harvard Law Review*. They argued for a right of privacy against other private individuals, including members of the media. Years later, now a Supreme Court Justice, Brandeis defined privacy as "the right to be left alone."

It is important to understand that the rights called for by Brandeis and Warren were distinct from a constitutional right of privacy, which protects individuals including the press from government intrusion. The Supreme Court has found opportunities in federal privacy cases to define the scope or "zones" of privacy, as the justices called them. In *Griswold v. Connecticut* (1965), for example, the Court struck down a state law that made it a crime for even married couples to use contraceptives. The justices said that such personal decisions fell into zones of privacy, which included marital activities, procreation, contraception, family relations, child rearing, and education practices. This case set the stage for subsequent Court decisions in *Roe v. Wade* (1973) and other abortion and contraception cases.

Privacy tort law developed rather slowly after its introduction, and the early cases revolved around the tort of appropriation, which was the primary focus of state laws. Many of the cases included elements of both libel and privacy. Because libel concepts were more fully developed in the law, the courts decided cases on the basis of libel evidence rather than privacy considerations. After reviewing the body of privacy case law in 1960, Dean William Prosser organized the concept into four torts: appropriation, intrusion, false light, and the publication of embarrassing private facts. Appropriation deals with the unauthorized use of someone's likeness or picture for commercial purposes without consent.

Intrusion involves the physical or technological invasion of a person's privacy. Putting a person in a false light occurs when the press, for example, portrays a person in a way that is inconsistent with the facts of a story. Publication of private information involves public disclosure of embarrassing facts about the plaintiff. It is the private-facts tort under which the press falls when it reports on the private lives of politicians.

The Supreme Court has considered the private-facts tort more often than the others, says Ellen Alderman and Caroline Kennedy in their recent book *The Right To Privacy*. But at the same time, the Court "has specifically refused to decide whether truthful publications must always be protected by the First Amendment. Rather, the Court has decided each case on its specific facts. And each case that has come before the Court has involved the quite narrow area of information that is already part of the public record." The authors suggest that very few of the privacy cases considered by the Court have pitted politicians against the media. It is private individuals who are shaping the law of media and privacy.

The differences in privacy rights accorded public officials and private individuals by the courts have been evolving since the 1964 landmark libel decision *New York Times v. Sullivan* (1964). The *New York Times* decision required public officials to show "actual malice," or reckless disregard of the truth, on the part of the media in order to win a libel suit. In practice, the decision places the burden of proof on the defendant, rather than the plaintiff. Part of the Court's reasoning for this turnaround in legal procedure was to balance the scales of power that public officials had wielded previously over the media (viz., seditious libel). The Court reasoned that the general public had a right to know how public officials conducted their public responsibilities, and that the debate on public issues should be as open, robust, and uninhibited as possible, even if it meant that unpleasant or harmful remarks were made toward public officials. The Court made it clear, however, that its decision did not extend to the private lives of public officials.

Subsequent Supreme Court decisions expanded the *New York Times* ruling from public officials to public figures, including those running for public office for the first time, and persons who had voluntarily thrust themselves into public controversies. By early in the 1970s, the public was convinced that the Supreme Court had made it nearly impossible for the news media to lose a libel suit and that the concept of a private individual was effectively dead. In *Gertz v. Welch* (1974), however, the Court backtracked to the point of recognizing the private person in libel law. After the smoke had cleared, Gertz had convinced the court that he was a private individual, even though a lawyer by profession, and that he should have a lighter standard — negligence — by which to show media fault. The court maintained its actual malice standard for public officials, all-purpose public figures, and limited, or vortex, public figures.

The actual malice standard has been linked to cases that involve both libel and privacy concerns. In *Time, Inc. v. Hill* (1967), the Court combined false light and defamation with the actual malice test. Members of the Hill family had argued that a *Life* magazine article about a play based on their nineteen-hour hostage incident had portrayed the family inaccurately. Time, Inc., which owned *Life*, had appealed the case to the Supreme Court, requesting that the Court use its actual malice standard established in *New York Times v. Sullivan*. The Court did so, reversing a lower court ruling that had given the Hill family compensatory damages. More recently, in *Hustler v. Falwell* (1988), the Court reversed an earlier jury decision awarding damages to the Rev. Jerry Falwell on the basis that he had been defamed and subjected to intentional infliction of emotional distress because of a parody ad in *Hustler* magazine. The Court determined that Falwell, as a public figure, could neither show that he had been defamed nor that actual malice actually existed.

"The media's victories in the libel arena," says Martin London and Barbara Dill, writing in *At What Price?* "seem to have shrunk privacy rights, too. Again, the press has aggressively sought special rules for itself, making the right to privacy in many ways little more than an empty promise."

More protection for the media in private facts cases is available in the form of three other defenses that have evolved in tort law: public record, newsworthiness, and consent of those involved in the story. In *Cox v. Cohn* (1975), the courts made it clear that if personal information is found on the public record, it is an effective defense for the media in privacy suits. Earlier courts had ruled that newsworthy individuals carry their newsworthy status indefinitely. In *Sidis v. F-R Publishing Corp.* (1940), a writer for *The New Yorker* magazine interviewed James Sidis, who years earlier had displayed unusual intellectual talents. When the writer interviewed Sidis, he found the former prodigy living in obscurity. The court reasoned that whether or not Sidis had fulfilled his early promise was still a matter of public concern. Legal scholars argued that the Sidis case shows that the courts take a very broad view of the "newsworthiness" test. Some would suggest that courts even shy away from determining what is newsworthy, rather leaving that to the media to decide.

Opinions about the "power" of the media in their ability to cover public officials and public figures is understandably mixed. When a group of media lawyers and journalists met in 1984 on the twentieth anniversary of *New York Times v. Sullivan*, *Editor and Publisher* reporter Andrew Radolf quoted Associated

Press executive Louis D. Boccardi, who said that the *Times* decision "is not a hunting license to get public figures, a license to lie or to attack the nation's capacity to trust its public officials. It is the basis for uninhibited, but responsible scrutiny, of public officials, public figures and public acts."

But attorney Dan Burt, who represented Gen. William Westmoreland in his libel suit against CBS, portrayed the case's legacy in a different light because it resulted in "the removal of any effective check or measure of accountability with respect to the press. The right an individual has to his reputation is something that has to be protected."

The right of the press to cover and report on the activities of politicians has come into conflict with the privacy rights of those public officials. This conflict has involved politicians, political scientists, journalism practitioners, and philosophers, all of whom understand what is at stake here for the general public and the future of political campaigns.

Leave Politicians' Private Lives Alone

In the past two decades, the media have turned coverage of political candidates into feeding frenzies, according to political scientist Larry Sabato. In his book, *Feeding Frenzy: How Attack Journalism has Transformed American Politics*, Sabato defines feeding frenzies as "press coverage attending any political event or circumstance where a critical mass of journalists leap to cover the same embarrassing or scandalous subject and pursue it intensely, often excessively, and sometimes uncontrollably." Although invasions of candidate privacy comprise only a small part of Sabato's book, it is clear that these invasions, along with gossip, rumors, and scandals, result in a loss of media credibility and a distortion of the political process.

Another interpretation of the change in media campaign coverage is explained by political scientist Thomas Patterson, in his 1994 book, *Out of Order*, which argues that the role of the press in political campaigns has changed since the 1970s. He wrote:

> The modern campaign requires the press to play a constructive role. When the parties established a nominating process (1970 McGovern-Fraser reforms) that is essentially a free-for-all between self-generated candidacies, the task of bringing the candidates and voters together in a common effort was superimposed on a media system that was built for other purposes. The press was no longer asked only to keep an eye out for wrongdoing and to provide a conduit for candidates to convey their messages to the voters. It was also expected to guide the voter's decisions. It was obliged to inspect the

candidates' platforms, judge their fitness for the nation's highest office, and determine their electability — functions the parties had performed in the past. In addition, the press had to carry out these tasks in a way that would enable the voters to exercise their discretion effectively in the choice of nominees.

Patterson provides statistics illustrating that media coverage of presidential candidates has turned increasingly negative since the 1970s. As the media began to adopt a more cynical tone in their political coverage, they began to alienate the public. Negative media coverage also began to alienate presidential candidates, who began to look for alternative ways to get their message to the public. Never was this more evident than in the 1992 and 1996 presidential elections when the candidates took their platforms to non-conventional news forums — TV talk shows, MTV, cable news, and interview shows. "There is danger to democracy," Patterson says, "in both the unrelenting negativism of the press and increased ability of candidates to avoid the press' scrutiny. These tendencies are related; the first fosters the second. And neither is healthy."

This adversarial relationship between the media and politicians has been recognized by media practitioners. Robert Merry opines that the press is asking questions today that a person would never ask his best friend "in the privacy of a corner table at the neighborhood pub." *Advertising Age* columnist Rance Crain says, "The press is getting all tangled up over whether sexual acrobatics are relevant information to pass on to voters. Reporters are agonizing over whether a candidate's peccadilloes are legitimate news or fodder for the sleazy tabloids."

One of the pitfalls of a media preoccupation with personal information during a presidential campaign is that it "depoliticizes" campaign issues by focusing on election rituals rather than serious debate of those issues, according to Patterson. Political reporters, for whatever reason, find it easier to report on the foibles, gaffs, and sexual escapades of the candidates, thereby blurring the public and private lives of the candidates. This concern with character issues, which dates back to George Washington, has become a routine reporting activity for reporters during presidential campaigns for nearly two decades, thereby evolving into an election ritual. In the meantime, the voting public finds it increasingly difficult to discern differences between the candidates, because those defining campaign issues are not adequately covered by the media.

Philosophers would argue that such a blurring of the public and private is not a healthy activity for the political system, nor is it a healthy activity for society at large. "A political perspective," says Jean Bethke Elshtain, writing in *The New*

Republic, "requires us to differentiate the activity we call 'politics' — that which is held in common and open to the public scrutiny and judgment from other activities and relationships. If all conceptual boundaries are blurred and all distinctions between public and private eliminated, no politics can exist, by definition."

The importance of privacy in a democratic society cannot be understated in this day and age. Notwithstanding the existence and intrusion of computers, listening devices, chemical tests, credit files, and data banks, "privacy represents the power to control access to one's self, and thus it conveys some capacity to resist the coercive power of the state," explains Louis Hodge in the *Journal of Mass Media Ethics.* And the more information the government has on file about an individual, the more it can use that information to the individual's disadvantage. The same holds true for politicians. Andy Stark, writing in *The Antioch Review,* adds that the value of private knowledge to each of us contributes to our own consistency and coherence of character because we can separate our public and private lives. He suggests that this separation is even more important today than it was for the Founding Fathers. "For while the increased transparency of the lives of public figures brings them ever more within the public's range of vision, their growing complexity is, at the very same time, taking them farther afield from their own [vision]," he writes.

W.A. Parent, writing in *Philosophical Issues in Journalism,* provides two other values of privacy that benefit the individual:

- As long as we live in a society where individuals are intolerant of life styles, habits and ways of things that differ from their own, and where human foibles tend to become the object of scorn and ridicule, our desire for privacy will continue unabated.

- We desire privacy out of a sincere conviction that there are certain facts about us which other people, particularly strangers and casual acquaintances, are not entitled to know.

As the list of media coverage problems that political candidates experience grows with each election campaign, candidates suffer through campaign disruptions, see election polls plummet and experience emotional pain and agony with their families and supporters. The end result, according to Sabato, is predictable: "American society today is losing the services of many exceptionally talented individuals who could make outstanding contributions to the commonweal, but who understandably will not subject themselves and their loved ones to abusive, intrusive press coverage."

Politicians' Private Lives Should be Covered

There is little question that the media provide a public service by reporting on political campaigns and the candidates who run in them. Political coverage provides insights into the primary campaigns, candidate platforms, elections, and the character of candidates who seek public office. The courts have done their part to ensure that the balance of power between politicians and the press continues to protect the interchange of ideas that would promote the political and social change desired by the people. "[W]e consider this case," wrote Justice Brennan in the *New York Times* case, "against the background of a profound national commitment to the principle that debate on public issues should be uninhibited, robust, and wide-open, and that it may well include vehement, caustic, and sometimes unpleasantly sharp attacks on government and public officials."

How do journalists balance their right to provide information about political candidates against the right of those candidates to maintain a reasonable zone of privacy? In the *Journal of Mass Media Ethics,* L. Paul Husselbee points out that because the First Amendment protects the press, the conflict between press freedom and privacy is already balanced in favor of the media. However, he adds, "The legal right to free expression does not diminish the need for journalists to exercise moral judgment in choosing what to publish, or whose privacy to invade or respect. Ultimately, respect for others and their rights cannot be legislated."

Journalists make ethical decisions every day, and as *Post* columnist Kurtz points out, most have some ethical standards. Most news organizations choose not to print the names of juveniles in criminal proceedings; they resist efforts by activists to "out" closeted homosexuals; most do not name women in rape cases without their consent; most editors will not print rumors; nor will they report on extramarital affairs by politicians unless they affect public performance.

One editor in Arkansas extended an apology to a local politician for irresponsible journalism four years after the newspaper printed lies that probably cost him an election and left a stain on his reputation. Executive Editor Mike Masterson of the *Northwest Arkansas Times* extended an apology to Dan Coody, after the newspaper had charged that the 1992 mayoral candidate was mentally unstable and hiding a criminal record. No evidence for any other those accusations was ever found. Masterson, who was not on the staff in 1992, dug into the story when he came to the newspaper, and his apology was supported by the new publisher of the *Times.*

One study shows that a majority of newspaper editors, for example, do have ethics codes for their organizations, and they are comfortable printing private information about politicians. Bruce Garrison and Sigman Splichal used a phone and mail survey to query newspaper editors in 1993 about their opinions on the ethics of privacy and political candidates. Their results, which appeared in the *Journal of Mass Media Ethics*, showed:

- Approximately 54 per cent of the responding editors had adopted a formal ethics code for their media organizations, but only 26 per cent had a formal policy regarding disclosure of intimate private information about public officials.

- About 75 per cent of the editors did not feel the private lives of public officials were out of bounds, especially when it came to marital infidelity.

- More than 50 per cent of the editors believed that the news media pay too much attention to the personal lives of political candidates.

"Years ago, the policy was simple," Garrison and Sigman concluded. "[It was to look] the other way. But, now that many news organizations look at these issues squarely face to face, they feel compelled not to ignore them. Journalists just have not figured out what to do about writing about intimate matters and, although we know there is a price to pay for it, we have not conclusively decided if the price is worth paying."

Journalists are social power brokers, according to Jay Black, Robert Steele, and Ralph Barney in *Doing Journalism in Ethics*, and as such they have a moral obligation to take information from the few and to distribute it among the masses. Journalists act in the best interests of society when they can distribute the power that information provides. Moreover, journalists have a greater responsibility than most to act ethically. L. Paul Husselbee says, "The modern journalist ties the right to know not only to a fundamental right to information for the purpose of protecting the public welfare and individual liberties, but to public curiosity about people and events in which the public has no legitimate interest."

Because journalists have a moral mandate to collect and report information, media ethicists have concluded that there are times when it is morally responsible for journalists to invade a person's privacy. *Journal of Mass Media Ethics* writer Louis Hodges proposes that invasions of privacy "are justified only when the public's need to know private things about an individual is strong enough to override that individual's need for and moral right to privacy." One such area concerns how the private morality of a candidate is related to his or her public character. "Character has always been, and will continue to be, political news," Lee Wilkins suggests. "At its most fundamental, an examination of character can reveal much about the relationship between leaders and followers on which democratic society by definition depends." Sissela Bok, in her book *Secrets*, warns journalists not to take at face value those who use claims of privacy, confidentiality, or national security to cover up abuses. She says that the press has a "much clearer public mandate to probe and to expose [secrets]."

Clifford G. Christians, Mark Fackler, and Kim B. Rotzoll in *Media Ethics* recommend that three moral principles be met to justify ethically an invasion of privacy. They say that editors and reporters should start with decency and basic fairness, which cannot be negotiated. "Redeeming social value," the second principle, should be a criterion when selecting which information should be disclosed. And third, they recommend that the individual's dignity should not be maligned in the name of press privilege. "Clearly, privacy matters cannot be treated sanctimoniously by ethicists," the authors conclude. "They are among the most painful that humane reporters encounter."

Resolution

Both media ethicists and political scientists have grappled with potential resolutions to the conflict between media practitioners and politicians. Sabato suggests a type of "fairness doctrine," which he feels can be beneficial to journalists, politicians, and the public. He says that "in most news organizations no specific guidelines exist to enable journalists to navigate successfully between these extremes when a frenzy storm hits, thereby increasing the chances that the almost irresistible competitive dynamics of the frenzy will determine the rules of coverage." His fairness doctrine would spell out the situations in which journalists should report about the private lives of politicians. Such situations would involve financial matters, health, and illness, incidents that reach the police blotter, sexual activity as long as it is related to public issues, illegal drug use, and any private behavior that compromises public resources. He suggests that any extramarital activity not be divulged if such activity is at least a decade in the past. He feels that the media should provide a substantial body of evidence for every charge they publish and that it would be appropriate for the media to vary the intensity of their scrutiny to correspond to the rank of the candidate, i.e., presidential candidates would receive more scrutiny than senatorial candidates.

Rather than waste so much energy covering the private lives of politicians, Sabato says that the media should devote more coverage to their public lives. Professor Lee Wilkins, in the *Journal of Mass Media Ethics*, agrees and thinks that "the profession has minimized — covering the historic and public political record of candidates," and that the media should "take new risks using psychological insights to inform analysis that will never fit the criterion of objective news reporting." Wilkins says that journalists cover "political character" and in order to do so they must invade the privacy of the individual — but, he cautions, not without meeting some tests first. The invasion of privacy should be placed in a context of facts and history; it should meet the traditional tests of journalistic publicity and evidence; it should be linked to public and political acts; it should further the larger political discourse; and it should be weighed against the public's need to know.

Another approach that might provide guidance to the media on this issue is the adoption of and adherence to a single national ethics code. When newspaper writer Joel Achenbach exclaimed that "we forget we have a code!" he was only half right. Journalists have more than just one ethics code. They have many ethics codes, and therein lies the problem. For every journalism organization in existence, whether it is the Society of Professional Journalists, National Press Photographers Association, Associated Press Managing Editors, or even the American Society of Newspaper Editors, there is a code of ethics. No wonder journalists have trouble subscribing to a code, and no wonder the general public cannot associate journalists with any single set of ethical precepts that might be found in a code of ethics.

Such is not the case among the traditional professions. The medical profession follows the Hippocratic Oath. The legal profession follows the American Bar Association Canons of Ethics. Members of the clergy look to the Bible for their moral guidance. The existence of a single code of ethics for each profession is one of the criteria common to professions in this country. And those who have codes also have ways to censure members who deviate from that code, even if they do most of their ethics reviews in secret. They appoint review boards of their peers to adjudicate ethical indiscretions, or violations of their codes of ethics. Why can't media professionals do the same thing?

Most in the media would say that one code of ethics for the profession would put too much stress on the First Amendment. After all, who would comprise this peer review board? There are so many media outlets in this country that a national peer review board would be unwieldy, expensive, and ineffective. Even now, how often are media practitioners penalized for ethical violations? For that matter, how many doctors, lawyers, or clergymen suffer the same fate? The failure of the National Press Council in the 1980s provides some indication of how popular the concept of self-review was with the media in general. Some media organizations publicly denounced what the council represented at its inception and never cooperated with it.

Voluntary action by media practitioners, who swear their allegiance to an ethics code created by their peers, is called for here. This action will not restrict other journalists from carrying out journalism in any way they see fit, nor will it require any kind of role definition. It probably won't make a difference in how we distinguish good journalists from bad journalists. But it will allow working journalists to align themselves with, and to live by, a code of ethics to which many of their peers also will have subscribed. One code will go a long way toward changing the negative attitudes of the public toward the media, and it might even relieve some of the resentment that the public harbors for a profession that has always been quick to criticize others while seldom turning the spotlight on its own transgressions. Even at that, former presidential press secretary Jody Powell, writing in the *Washington Post,* says that "for any real good to come of it, some of those in journalism who enjoy the respect of their peers will have to find the courage to point the finger of public condemnation at the rotten apples and shoddy behavior in their own profession."

Whether it is a reporter-politician fairness doctrine, a call for more in-depth and relevant character reporting, or an ethics code that provides some guidelines to the media concerning the information they gather about the candidates they cover, no one disputes the fact that the information the media provide about political campaigns is important to the political discourse in this country. It is ironic, however, that unless the media assume more responsibility for their conduct in reporting public and private affairs of politicians, the result may be a loss of the democratic traditions that they are morally obligated to protect.

Recommended Readings

Books

Alderman, Ellen, and Caroline Kennedy. *The Right to Privacy.* New York: Knopf, 1995. This text utilizes cases, interviews, and effective writing to present a survey of privacy case law.

Bok, Sissela. *Secrets.* New York: Vintage Books, 1989. This volume is an important discussion of secrets in our society, in many different environments, including confidentiality, whistle blowing and leaking, and investigative journalism. The author clarifies the notion of the public's right to know.

Sabato, Larry J. *Feeding Frenzy: How Attack Journalism Has Transformed American Politics.* New York: The Free Press, 1991. A well-documented look, replete with solutions, at a growing rift between the media and politicians. Sabato suggests, for example, that the media should not report any sexual activity involving politicians if the activity is more than a decade old.

The Press, Privacy and Politicians

Articles & Book Chapters

Crain, Rance. "Live by the bimbo, die.... " *Advertising Age,* 9 March 1992, 25. Crain discusses the ethics of reporting on presidential affairs, and he concludes that President Clinton is fair game for criticism considering his previous record.

Elshtain, Jean Bethke. "The Hard Questions: Bad Publicity." *The New Republic,* 12 August 1996, 25. Provides a philosophical look at the detrimental effects on democratic politics caused when the public and private lives of politicians are no longer separated.

Garrison, Bruce, and Sigman Splichal. "Reporting on Private Affairs of Candidates: A Study of Newspaper Practices." *Journal of Mass Media Ethics* (Winter 1994): 169-83. Authors report on a study in 1993 that queried 283 editors concerning their newspaper policies on the use of ethics codes, coverage of political candidate privacy, public official privacy, and other ethical questions.

Giobbe, Dorothy. "Better Late Than Never. " *Editor & Publisher,* 1 June 1996, 14-15. This article details how an Arkansas newspaper's management, four years after the occurrence, apologized to a local politician for unfair treatment during his political campaign to become mayor in 1992.

Hodges, Louis. "The Journalist and Privacy." *Journal of Mass Media Ethics* (Winter, 1994): 197-212. Presents some specific guidelines for journalists who cover public officials, public figures, celebrities, temporarily newsworthy heroes, criminals, innocent victims of crime and tragedy, and adult relatives of the prominent.

Husselbee, L. Paul. "Respecting Privacy in an Information Society: A Journalist's Dilemma." *Journal of Mass Media Ethics* (Winter 1994): 145-56. Husselbee discusses the conflict that journalists have concerning digging for information and the right of privacy enjoyed by the public, and he presents a five-part test for journalists to follow when they want to use data-base research for subsequent publication.

Merry, Robert W. "The New Journalism: Rumor and Innuendo." *Congressional Quarterly,* 8 February 1992, 338. Merry decries the loss of "fact-based journalism," which has been replaced by a preoccupation with bedroom politics. He sees a difference in reporting from the time of President John F. Kennedy to Bill Clinton.

Ornstein, Norman J. "Sexpress." *The Atlantic* (October 1991): 24-5. This media critic documents a number of cases that illustrate how mainstream media reporting techniques and values have been eroded with increased competition from the tabloids.

Parent, W.A. "Privacy, Morality, and the Law," in *Philosophical Issues in Journalism,* ed. Elliot D. Cohen. New York: Oxford University Press, 1992. Parent makes a case for the value of privacy in society but not without a thorough discussion of the validity of Prosser's four torts.

Powell, Jody. "No Consequences," in *Impact of Mass Media: Current Issues,* ed. Ray Eldon Hiebert. White Plains, N.Y.: Longman, 1995. Powell's perspective is that only journalists can rescue their own credibility that plummeted, in his opinion, after the media's shabby reporting of the death of White House lawyer Vincent Foster in 1993.

Stark, Andy. "Public knowledge, private knowledge." *The Antioch Review* (Fall 1990): 439-48. Stark argues that the public's preoccupation with the privacy of politicians has been a detriment to politicians who eradicate any differences between their public and private selves in order to define their own image to the public. The result is that the public finds it more difficult today to evaluate the real character of politicians.

Wilkins, Lee. "Journalists and the Character of Public Officials/Figures." *Journal of Mass Media Ethics* (Winter 1994): 157-68. Wilkins presents a number of ways to encourage journalists to cover the public record of politicians rather than their character. Journalists have overlooked for too long the historical and public information about politicians that they could easily access for the benefit of the voting public.

3 The Media as a Business

*O*ne of the threads running through this book is that of incredible media competition. In recent years, new technologies, corporate ownership, and proliferating media outlets have combined to transform the media industry into an arena of cut-throat competition and, for its members, an extremely high-pressure career choice.

This section explores the realities of these developments, including the rising tension that exists between traditional journalistic ideals and the forces of ratings and circulation figures that, according to some, threaten those ideals.

In chapter eleven, Clay Calvert discusses that tension in terms of the civic and corporate responsibilities that all media practitioners face. "Do journalists owe duties to the corporate owners for whom they work?" Professor Calvert asks, "or to the readers for whom they report or to both?" Are the two always contradictory? Professor Calvert presents various sides of the debate and posits public journalism as a possible answer to the dual demands of shareholders and the public.

Garrett Ray, who in his earlier career as a newspaper editor won several journalism awards, takes a step back and poses the question: Is this new trend in concentrated corporate ownership necessarily a bad one? Professor Ray outlines the two vantage points and considers corporate ownership's impact on the diversity of views presented by the media and the credibility of the press, as well as the power that media ownership brings in today's world. Does corporate ownership, for example, force media practitioners to march lock-step with its corporation's worldview and profit-motive? Or can such ownership better protect the dissemination of non-majority opinions?

One of the potential paths that Professor Ray suggests — for newspapers at least — is that of Joint Operating Agreements, which are further explored by David Coulson and Stephen Lacy. They provide a history of the 1970

Newspaper Preservation Act, an antitrust law that Congress passed to assist a newspaper industry that was already collapsing under the weight of corporate competition. JOAs enable two newspapers to merge their business operations while keeping their editorial departments independent. As Professors Coulson and Lacy explain, there have been advantages and disadvantages to this system. It has, for example, been responsible for keeping a number of daily newspapers afloat — but it has also served to create virtual monopolies, thus forcing smaller players out of the arena.

The theme of an increasingly competitive media industry is woven into many issues in this book. This section, however, presents some of the reasons why the "conglomeration juggernaut," as one liberal critc calls it, has become such an integral part of the mass media — and what implications the trend has for the industry's future.

Chapter Eleven

Balancing Corporate Duties and Civic Responsibilities

Clay Calvert

A seemingly inexorable "conglomeration juggernaut," critic Todd Gitlin writes in the *Media Studies Journal*, marches on the communications industry. More and more media outlets are falling into the hands of fewer and fewer corporations. Mergers between conglomerates with diversified media and non-media holdings that strive for goals other than producing high-quality journalism are, Gitlin observes, "taking place amid a deafening silence."

The merger mania that placed the news divisions at ABC and CBS in 1995 in the hands of Walt Disney Co. and Westinghouse Electric Corp., respectively, brings into high relief the increasing tension between the bottom-line corporate interests of businesses that control news organizations and the civic and social responsibilities of those entities. This tension is neither new nor is it likely to disappear in the future.

Joan Konner, publisher of the *Columbia Journalism Review*, recently wrote that journalism "has always existed in two different realities — the reality of the economic marketplace; and the reality of a special institution protected by law in order to serve the public interest." John E. Swearingen concurs with Konner, writing in his essay *Responsibility in Journalism: A Business Perspective* that "despite the disparities in purpose and function, business and journalism — for better or worse — are locked together in a symbiotic relationship."

The purpose and function of business and journalism *are* different. *Newsweek's* Jonathan Alter quipped in a recent column addressing Disney's takeover of ABC, "Remember that book 'Men Are From Mars, Women Are From Venus'? Well, business is from Saturn, journalism is from Jupiter. As the media monopoly grows, the culture clash between the two is becoming a source of major discomfort."

This chapter presents contrasting views about the purpose and function of news organizations owned by for-profit business enterprises. Do journalists owe duties to the corporate owners for whom they work *or* to the readers for whom they report *or* to both? Alternative perspectives of First Amendment freedoms and responsibilities granted to the press are offered with a view of some of the benefits and drawbacks of the conglomeration juggernaut. The chapter also proposes for discussion five principles for balancing the often conflicting interests journalists face in serving the needs of big business and providing the public with quality journalism. The silence described by Gitlin, although writing from a strong ideological point of view, at the start of this chapter must be broken by a loud-but-well-reasoned discussion on the responsibilities of the news media in the United States.

Origins of the Issue

"Through concentration of ownership the flow of news and opinion is shaped at the sources; its variety is limited; and at the same time the insistence of the consumer's need has increased." Those words, which easily could have been written today, were penned a half-century ago by the Commission on Freedom of the Press in its controversial 1947 report, *A Free and Responsible Press*. At the time, concentration of ownership was *already* perceived as a threat to quality journalism, and the commission, headed by University of Chicago President Robert M. Hutchins, emphasized the need for social responsibility in the news business.

Just as concerns about concentration of ownership are not new, bottom-line concerns of newspaper owners have long existed. Writing in 1996 in the *American Journalism Review*, Neil Shine observes that "there has never been a newspaper publisher who, from the moment he or she first decided to put ink to paper, did not understand that a prudent business course should probably involve making a profit." Shine, former publisher of the *Detroit Free Press*, adds that "the history of American journalism is strewn with outrageous examples of downholds and cutbacks" and that "the only thing new about bottom-line journalism is the name."

Martin Mayer concurs with this historical perspective in his 1993 book *Making News*. Noting that "newspapers have been a big business for a very long time," he states that "newspaper publishers are more or less expected to be businesspeople like other businesspeople."

Causes for Concern

Although concerns about concentration of ownership and bottom-line journalism may be nothing new, there is real cause for concern today about whether such forces threaten quality journalism. Today, as Gene Goodwin and

Ron F. Smith write in *Groping for Ethics in Journalism*, four out of five daily news-papers in the United States are group owned. By the mid-1990s, the Gannett Co. Inc. owned more than eighty daily newspapers. The picture in broadcasting is the mirror image. In 1996 President Bill Clinton and Congress gave the green light to increasing concentration of ownership in radio and television by signing the Telecommunications Act. The legislation substantially loosened restrictions on the number of radio and television stations that a single entity can own or control. Prior to this, a company could own only twelve television stations. Today, broadcasters can own an unlimited number of television stations across the nation, subject only to the caveat that the aggregate audience share for those stations does not exceed 35 per cent of the total national audience

What, if anything, is the problem with ownership concentration or big busi-nesses running news operations? Professor Stephen Lacy and his colleagues wrote in a recent issue of *Journalism and Mass Communication Quarterly* that many media scholars assume "that publicly traded companies necessarily are con-cerned with short-term profits and return to shareholders that are driven by stock analysts' reports.... The focus on profitability, some scholars argue, can result in decisions based on narrow financial goals, rather than news and public service considerations."

Potential dangers posed by letting business interests dictate news content include the self-censorship of stories that might offend or harm major advertisers. Michael Parenti observes in *Inventing Reality: The Politics of News Media* that "[a]dvertisers will cancel ads when they feel the reporting reflects unfavorably on their own product or industry."

Rather than risk offending a major advertiser, news organizations may simply *not* print or broadcast a story that is potentially damaging to that advertiser. The same story, however, may be of real public importance, perhaps concerning a dangerous or defective product. The decision not to publish or air a story because of business concerns is the essence of self-censorship.

A related problem occurs when advertiser needs dictate the addition or creation of editorial content. Business sections are created or expanded by news-papers to create space for business advertisements. Sometimes they are filled with stories favorable to major advertisers and the business community. "Today, well-run newspapers aggressively court advertisers, presenting themselves as marketing partners and jointly planning campaigns to help sell products and services," writes Conrad C. Fink in 1996 in *Strategic Newspaper Management*.

Another possible danger is the lack of self-coverage that arises when a con-glomerate with non-media holdings controls a news operation. Marc Gunter, writing in the *American Journalism Review*, observes that "all the networks struggle over how to cover themselves and their corporate interests." In some cases, *not* covering "bad news" about one's parent company or its interests makes the most business sense for that company and, no less important, for the journalist's own job security.

One might ask whether CBS news will aggressively cover or investigate its parent company, Westinghouse, or any of the fields in which Westinghouse does business, including the controversial nuclear power industry. Veteran White House correspondent Sarah McClendon was quoted in *Editor & Publisher* magazine shortly before Westinghouse's takeover of CBS as stating that "[i]f they get to buy CBS, you are going to hear news according to Westinghouse. We are going to have to take their word on radiation, and on the management of nuclear fuel."

An additional problem occurs when economic-minded owners (and editors) give readers what they *want* — or at least what marketing consultants think they want — rather than information they *need* for complex decision making in a democracy. Shorter, reader-friendly "news-lite" stories omit details and content necessary for a thorough understanding of issues. Puff pieces, light feature stories, and so-called soft news replace enterprise reporting, investigative series, and hard news.

Doug Underwood observes in his book *When MBAs Rule the Newsroom* that "daily newspapers caught up in reader-friendly journalism are in danger of losing the true spirit of the journalism mission — the commitment to community service, the passion for probing injustice, the love of good writing, and the devotion to enterprise reporting." Underwood states that "diminished coverage of government has been one fallout of the move toward market-oriented journalism."

When newspapers substitute profit tunnel vision for a broader vision of the news, some citizens are ignored. Newspapers have little financial incentive to reach out to people outside of the middle and upper-class populations who are the target of expensive and profitable newspaper advertising. A truly inclusive democracy, however, requires that *all* citizens, not just a select few, be informed about, as the Hutchins Commission wrote, the day's events in a context that gives them meaning. This is not the case, however, today. "Increasingly the coverage of the news is being shaped by the desire of news executives for upscale readers," Underwood writes.

This parade of horrors — some real, some perhaps imagined by old-guard journalists afraid of change — reveals the importance of considering what the duties of the news media and journalists should be in an era of corporate conglomeration and chain ownership. Is their first duty to shareholders and executives for whom the journalists work? Or is the first duty of journalists toward their readers? Is it possible to balance the two duties?

The following sections present two contrasting viewpoints — the business perspective and the journalism perspective — about the functions and responsibilities of news organizations controlled by for-profit businesses and the duties of journalists who work in them. Although this dialectic presents seemingly opposite views, suggestions and guidelines are made later in this chapter that enable responsible journalism without taking a naive view of the importance of profit and financial stability in corporate media.

Corporate Duties of the Press

The primary purpose of the newspaper business, writes John E. Swearingen in *Responsibility in Journalism: A Business Perspective,* is "to sell words and ideas." A similar statement can be made about the function of television news — its primary purpose is to sell the viewing audience to advertisers willing to pay for fifteen- or thirty-second commercials during a newscast to reach those viewers with messages about their products and services.

When a corporation is publicly held, its owners are shareholders who expect a return on their investment (their investment is the shares of stock in the corporation that they purchase). Conrad C. Fink writes in *Strategic Newspaper Management* that newspaper executives owe a fiduciary duty or responsibility to the shareholders to try to return a profit on shares purchased. Shareholders of publicly owned corporations, he writes, "are investors" who will sell their stocks if the return on their investment is not high enough.

From the start, then, it must be emphasized that there is nothing inherently evil or wrong about selling a product to make a profit. The United States is, after all, premised on an economic system of capitalism and a philosophy of individual libertarianism. Fink writes that although newspapers must have higher ideals than merely keeping shareholders happy, "newspapers *are* businesses. Profit is *not* a dirty word. Out-of-business newspapers can't defend the people's right to know. Just ask journalists who worked for the *Washington Star, Philadelphia Bulletin, New York Herald Tribune* and other once-great (but now dead) newspapers."

Fink's last point is important. Sound business judgment allows newspapers and television news magazines to survive. Defunct newspapers and broadcast properties serve neither the public nor shareholders. The argument takes an additional step when defenders argue that long-term survival requires sacrificing short-term journalistic goals. Economic stability (and growth) may require changes and adjustments in news and editorial content. It may require, in some cases, letting business executives dictate news judgments.

Consider a not-so-hypothetical situation. A major television network faces a $10 billion defamation lawsuit brought by a major tobacco company. The case arises from essentially true and damaging reports about the tobacco industry's process of manufacturing cigarettes that the network broadcast during one of its television news magazines. The tobacco company that filed the lawsuit claims the allegations regarding its addition of nicotine in cigarettes are false and damaging to its reputation.

The television network has options. It can fight the defamation action vigorously in court, in the name of First Amendment freedoms of speech and press. It can hire a barrage of the most talented and high-powered media defense attorneys from New York City and Washington, D. C., who probably could win the case on appeal, if not at the trial court or jury level.

Such a decision to aggressively defend the broadcasts, however, may prove exorbitantly expensive for the network, *regardless* of the ultimate outcome of the case. Costs of defending the lawsuit, including often astronomical attorneys' fees, are incurred, as are time costs on journalists and producers who must testify during depositions and perhaps at trial.

Both the economic and non-economic costs of defending the suit drain precious resources from the news gathering and reporting operation. This, in turn, hinders and harms the television network's service of the public. Although it might be nice to fight the case to the finish in the name of First Amendment, it may not be wise, economically and from a long-term journalism perspective, to do so.

The television network has an alternative to engaging in a long, protracted, and expensive fight with the tobacco company. It can settle the case for the price of the plaintiff's costs and attorneys' fees and by airing a public apology for the allegedly defamatory broadcast. This option saves economic resources that allows the television network in the future to do *other* hard-hitting investigations that inform the public. Rather than risking it all on one case, the television network can sacrifice the one story — a story that has already aired and served the public — in order to continue on in the journalism business. In brief, prudent business judgment can make sound journalistic sense.

This scenario is very similar to the situation that involved two *Day One* broadcasts on ABC television that led to a defamation action filed by tobacco giant, Philip Morris. An excellent, more detailed description of the real-life choices that faced ABC is set forth in Steve Weinberg's article in *Columbia Journalism Review*, "Smoking Guns: ABC, Philip Morris and the Infamous

---

[1] ABC settled the case for an estimated $10 million in attorneys fees and costs paid to Philip Morris. For an analysis of the ABC situation in a similar case involving self-censorship, CBS and tabacco company Brown & Williamson, see C. Calvert, "Stumbling Down Tobacco Road: Media Self-Censorship and Corporate Capitulation in the War on the Cigarette Industry," *Loyola of Los Angeles Law Review* 30:1 (1996): 139-75.

Apology."[1] The goal of producing profits for shareholders, then, does *not* include a concomitant goal of producing shoddy or poor journalism. Although some owners may ignore social responsibilities to the public described later in this chapter, increasing or maintaining the profitability of a news organization does *not* mean that shareholders and executives want or desire to produce poor journalism. In fact, under the business viewpoint, it is in the best interests of all to produce an appealing journalistic product.

For instance, from the business point of view, journalists cannot neglect what readers want to see and read. They must try to serve public wants, preferences, and desires, often as determined by marketing research techniques such as interviews, focus groups, and surveys. Stories are written and aired to satisfy what readers want to read and the viewers want to see, *not* to satisfy the wants and desires of journalists and their editors. Those stories also are written in styles that are easy to read and often are short enough to accommodate the time-constraints that busy newspaper readers face.

By serving up journalistic fare that caters to the widest public interests, newspapers and magazines survive and thrive. Newspapers that ignore readers' tastes go out of business.

Under a business perspective there *is* a check that ensures quality through free and open marketplace competition. Although there is no *a priori* standard of "good" journalism under a laissez-faire economics marketplace model of accountability, quality journalism *is* that journalism that survives in the marketplace. As Theodore L. Glasser writes in his essay *Press Responsibility and First Amendment Values*, "allusions to the power of competition and the value of free trade underscore the libertarian's abiding faith in the principle of laissez-faire; and, historically, they vivify the libertarian's enduring confidence in the relationship between economic freedom and freedom of expression."

If readers are not happy with the journalism that they read or watch, they may change the channel or cancel a subscription to a newspaper or a magazine. This direct economic impact on the now-shunned news business may force it to change its reporting practices and content to satisfy readers' and viewers' preferences. If the news organization, however, does not change, it may eventually go out of business. In this case, it can no longer serve the public. Journalists unwilling to adapt to changing economic times and to readers' or viewers' wants serve no one's interest except their own.

A benefit for quality journalism caused by increasing conglomeration is that larger businesses have greater financial resources to invest in sometimes risky hard-hitting journalism. This may be especially true when news operations comprise only a small part of the profits for the entire conglomerate or business.

Tom Wolzien, former news producer at NBC and now a Wall Street media analyst, explains in the *Media Studies Journal* that:

> [a]t the post-merger ABC television network, the total profits of the news division are only 1 per cent of the entire Disney company. That means that news is not financially material to the whole company. And that may give the news division some freedom in dealing with major investigative pieces. Where a lawsuit may be big, the company's resources are bigger. In a world of big-time news risks, only the largest of corporate parents have the resources to tolerate the risk.

Bigger businesses, in other words, may produce and nurture better journalism that a smaller, independently-owned organization might not be able to or may not be willing to risk.

The big business perspective can also increase quality journalism via its concentration of financial resources. Although a publicly owned chain or newspaper group seeks profits for its shareholders, the greater financial resources of the chain may allow a small, chain-owned newspaper to place a correspondent in Washington, D.C., or to locate a bureau in a state capital. In addition, as Steven Rattner notes in a recent edition of the *Media Studies Journal*, media mergers "have provided the capital needed to launch exciting but expensive new undertakings." Pooling financial resources and journalistic talents thus can benefit not only stockholders but also readers.

A final point about the duties of journalists and news organizations under the business perspective cannot be ignored — it is far better to owe *a duty to shareholders* than it is to *owe a duty to the government* under an alternative, non-capitalistic, non-libertarian system in which government officials dictate the type of content that constitutes quality journalism. Although private, profit-driven interests might impinge somewhat on journalists' freedom to write or report what they want in the United States, this is far less intrusive than direct government interference with editorial and news judgment. Freedom from government control allows the press to play its Fourth Estate role — to function as a watchdog that guards against and exposes government abuses of power and corruption. Journalists, in the business viewpoint that holds true today in the United States, are neither told by the government what to report nor punished by the government for criticizing it. The forces of the free market, not the government, influence news and editorial content.

Related to this argument from the business perspective is the principle that the First Amendment to the United States Constitution protects the press from government interference. The First Amendment provides that "Congress shall make no law ... abridging the freedom of speech, or of the press." That amendment does not, however, mandate or dictate some standard of quality journalism. Social or civic responsibility must be left to the consciences of the owners and executives of specific news media operations. It *cannot* be mandated or imposed by the government. A truly free press, as journalist Vermont Royster once said, is a press free to be irresponsible, or, as Theodore L. Glasser more recently put it, "a press truly free to set its own agenda."

The First Amendment, under the business perspective, thus may be seen as granting a negative liberty to the press. It is negative in the sense that it is a freedom *from* government interference with editorial and ownership operations, as opposed to a freedom *for* social responsibility. As Glasser writes, a negative view of press freedom "means a press free from public control — a press sufficiently insulated from the specter of state action."

Under the business viewpoint, in summary, serving shareholders' needs and the public's wants is *not* incompatible with quality journalism. The desire to make profits does not equate to a concomitant desire to produce shoddy journalism. Giving members of the public the news that they want to read increases circulation and viewership, which, in turn, increases dividends for shareholders. Large, publicly owned chains give journalists greater economic resources for engaging in better journalism. Journalists should give readers what they want to read; after all, it is the readers (and the advertising dollars attracted by them) that pay journalists' salaries.

Civic Duties of the Press

Questions about the responsibilities of journalism and news organizations, writes Louis W. Hodges in his essay *Defining Press Responsibility: A Functional Approach*, "focus on the nature and function of the press, on the criteria rational people might use to access press performance." The function of the press and the responsibilities of journalism, Hodges observes, extend to *more* than just the news organizations and employers for whom journalists work. Duties also flow to the readers and viewers for whom journalists report. What are the responsibilities and duties of journalists to readers and audiences?

News media organizations have social, educational, and political obligations and responsibilities that stretch far beyond producing dividends for their employers and shareholders. Robert B. Entman observes in *Democracy Without Citizens* that, at least in theory, "the press is supposed to enhance democracy both by stimulating the citizenry's political interest and by providing the specific information they need to hold government accountable." He adds that "the point of a free press is to prevent rulers from damaging the nation and destroying themselves." Entman writes that "the information necessary for intelligent voting can come only from the mass media, or from friends who themselves scan the news."

These journalistic obligations stem in part from the First Amendment protection extended to the press as an institution. Concomitant with First Amendment *rights* are *responsibilities* to serve the public's interest and its right to know information that affects democratic self-governance.

The First Amendment, in contrast to the first viewpoint described in this chapter, is more than just a shield that owners can raise to ward off government interference with their business. Instead, the First Amendment is a constitutional provision that allows the press to play important political roles in the United States that must not be subverted by profiteering owners. As the Hutchins Commission on Freedom of the Press observed in *A Free and Responsible Press* more than fifty years ago, "the freedom of the press can remain a right of those who publish only if it incorporates into itself the right of the citizen and the public interest." In other words, the Constitutional right of a free press entails the concomitant responsibility of serving the public interest.

The responsibilities included within the duty of serving the public interest require that journalists both *provide information* about events, issues, and individuals that affects self-governance (an information transmission responsibility) and *check government abuses* of power (an investigative, watchdog responsibility).

The information transmission responsibility is important. As Jay Black and his colleagues write in *Doing Ethics in Journalism*, "distribution of information is redistribution of power." Information allows members of the public to make informed choices, to make changes in society, to have power over public affairs. Information distribution thus is an especially important and powerful duty performed by the press.

The Hutchins Commission made this clear in 1947. It stated that "the freedom of the press is freighted with responsibility of providing the current intelligence needed by a free society." It emphasized that "In terms of quality, the information provided must be provided in such a form, and with so scrupulous a regard for the wholeness of the truth and the fairness of its presentation, that the American people may make for themselves, by the exercise of reason and conscience, the fundamental decisions necessary to the direction of the government and their lives."

Unpacking this statement, it is clear that part of the duty of information conveyance that journalists owe to readers and viewers relates directly to democratic self-governance. The press must provide information that allows citizens to participate in an informed, meaningful way in a democracy. As veteran journalist Edwin Newman remarks in his essay, *A Journalist's Responsibility*, "[w]e in the news business help to provide the people with the information they need to frame their attitudes and to make, or at any rate to authorize or ratify, the decisions on which the well-being of the nation rests."

Hodges further describes the political functions performed by the press. He states that "the very existence of the press serves to reduce the likelihood of usurpation of power by those who govern. Governors who know that they are being watched have to take the people into account in ways they otherwise would not. Although the press cannot itself prevent the corruption of office, it can inform the people who have the power to do so."

The responsibility for providing political information to the electorate and citizens in the United States requires that journalists deliver to readers and viewers more than just the information that they may *want* to read or watch. Although giving audience members what they want may serve corporate interests by increasing readership or viewership, this information is not concomitant with what the public *needs* to make wise and informed decisions. The distinction between *public wants* and *public needs* parallels a distinction between providing information that is *interesting* to the public and information that is of the *public interest* — that is, information that serves the public interest as defined as the collective welfare of society.

For instance, many members of the public may *want* to know more about or be *interested* in knowing more about the latest sex scandal in Washington, D.C., or the most recent run-in with the law of a drug-addicted movie star. Serving readers and viewers this type of journalistic fare not only gives them what they want but, in doing so, it also facilitates the corporate duties of journalists to their shareholders by increasing the audience. There is a problem, however, if journalists limit their responsibility to giving the public what it wants to read or watch. Plain and simple, this information may have little value in terms of what the public needs to know in terms of its collective safety and welfare. It may not in any way affect the collective-level needs of society. The responsibilities of journalists and journalism must thus extend beyond providing the public with what it wants to read and view to include supplying the public with the information that it — and democracy — needs to prosper and thrive.

The growing "civic" or "public" journalism movement takes the responsibilities of journalists one step further than providing information about self-government and keeping tabs on government corruption. Theodore L. Glasser and Stephanie Craft write in a recent article in the *Journal of Mass Media Ethics* that the central premise of public journalism is that the "purpose of the press is to promote and improve, and not merely to report on or complain about, the quality of public or civic life." Arthur Charity concurs, writing in *Doing Public Journalism* that "[p]ublic journalism is about nothing more than the conviction that journalism's business is about making citizenship work."

Journalists, according to public journalism advocates, have a responsibility to their readers and to society at large to enhance and facilitate public life. This means, in part, that reporters must listen to, diagnose, and serve the needs of the members of the communities in which they work. Stories must, as one advocate of public journalism writes, "help move the public toward meaningful judgment and action."

Public journalists also must facilitate and promote public participation in the democratic process. This occurs with the organization of town meetings or other fora that bring citizens together to discuss the needs of their communities and the nation. In brief, journalists involved in the public journalism movement carry responsibilities far beyond the duty of information transmission. They must facilitate and enhance public life and democracy.

In contrast to the corporate duties perspective, journalists also have a responsibility to serve *all* members of society, not just the elite or wealthy individuals who are demographically attractive to advertisers. This means both providing information that all citizens need *and* providing all citizens with a voice in journalism. Herbert Gans writes in *Multiperspectival News* that "in order to be comprehensive, the news must report nation and society in terms of all known perspectives; in order to be representative, it must enable all sectors of nation and society to place their actors and activities — and messages — in the symbolic arena."

In summary, journalists owe duties not only to shareholders but to the public. Specifically, journalists carry the responsibility of serving public needs and democracy. These responsibilities spring, in part, from the rights granted to the press under the First Amendment.

Resolution

Is it possible for journalists, in an era of ever-growing conglomeration, to serve both corporate and public responsibilities? Can journalists balance the two duties successfully? The answer appears to be yes, provided that corporate executives *and* journalists recognize — and respect — each other's responsibilities.

Joan Konner, publisher of *Columbia Journalism Review*, argues that "there is strong evidence" that economic interests and public responsibilities are not mutually exclusive. "We have many examples of profitability and quality today:

The New York Times; The Washington Post; The Wall Street Journal; and smaller papers like the Raleigh *News and Observer* and *The Charlotte Observer.* There are hundreds of quality magazines and book publishers. And there is quality television news, some on CNN but also on the networks and PBS."

To achieve this balance, at least five things are necessary. The first is understanding and education. Owners must understand that the businesses that they control — news businesses — produce a product that is *not* akin to soap or a refrigerator. The product, instead, is speech; and speech, in turn, carries consequences both in terms of how it mirrors and creates reality and in terms of how it helps or hinders the democratic system within which the news organizations operate.

Journalists must understand as well that they work for capitalistic enterprises that are *not* inherently evil. In fact, sometimes, as described earlier in this chapter, sound business judgment is essential for the long-term survival of news operations. News organizations that go out of business serve no one's interest.

Concomitant with each side's understanding of the other's perspectives is trust. Owners and journalists must overcome a deep-rooted distrust of each other. Just as owners and journalists ask the public to trust them in supplying the day's news in a fair, objective, and accurate manner, media owners and executives must learn to trust journalists and vice versa. Mutual distrust leads to mutually assured destruction of the news organization.

Trust does not mean that owners can "trust" journalists never to report "bad" news about the parent company or its interests. Rather, trust means that owners can trust journalists not to single out for attack the parent company, but to approach it and its interests in an objective and impartial manner, as a good journalist would with any story or issue. Trust on the part of journalists requires that they not suspect that every action made by managing executives is done to harm the quality of news.

The third requirement might be called "cooperation with separation." This requires that, once each side understands the corporate and public duties that news organizations carry, owners must cooperate with journalists by granting them the independence necessary to produce hard-hitting reportage. In other words, there must be a separation — a separation built on trust and cooperation — between the business and editorial sides of news organizations. Leonard Silk observes in *The Ethics and Economics of Journalism* that a strict separation of church and state — a strict separation of editorial decisions and business decisions — has been a hallmark of the *New York Times.* When editorial decisions are made, however, the journalism professionals who make them must take into account the perspective not only of themselves and readers, but also of their owners.

Perspective taking is crucial for ethical decision making.

The fourth requirement involves ethics codes. The ethics codes that apply in newsrooms must be matched by ethics codes for the corporate executives and owners of news operations. Although they owe a fiduciary duty to shareholders, the managing executives have ethical duties to the readers who buy their products — their newspapers, their magazines — to serve them information that they need to function in a democracy.

The fifth requirement is that journalists must give publicity to possible conflicts of interest that arise when reporting. They must inform the public — and invite feedback from audience members — about how business interests influence their journalistic decisions. The public, after all, pays the ultimate price when stories are held back or softened when business interests interfere with journalistic judgment.

These five steps are necessary elements for a lasting and well-reasoned balance between the corporate and public responsibilities of news organizations. Ultimately, the steps can be ignored, adopted or adapted to fit a particular news organization. If the steps are ignored, however, something else must be done soon to keep the journalism of the future useful to the American democratic system.

Recommended Readings

Books

Bagdikian, B. *The Media Monopoly*, 4th ed. Boston: Beacon Press, 1992. The most recent edition of Bagdikian's classic is packed with alarming numbers and analysis of the corporate conglomerations that control the communications industry. News and public information, Bagdikian argues, become little more than "industrial by-product."

Commission on Freedom of the Press. *A Free and Responsible Press*. Chicago: University of Chicago Press, 1947. Providing the seminal report of the commission led by chairman Robert M. Huthins and vice-chairman Zechariah Chafee, Jr., that articulated a number of goals for the press and a press theory of social responsibility.

Entman, R.M. *Democracy Without Citizens: Media and the Decay of American Politics*. New York: Oxford University Press, 1989. The book provides an empirically anchored theory of news and democracy that explores the interdependence of news, economics, audience, and politics.

Fink, C. C. *Strategic Newspaper Management*. Boston: Allyn & Bacon, 1996. An excellent primer on newspaper management that presents a solid analysis of the economic and business concerns that newspaper executives and owners face on a daily basis.

Parenti, M. *Inventing Reality: The Politics of News Media*, 2d ed. New York: St. Martin's Press. 1993. A left-of-center, critical analysis of the economic and political forces that shape the content of the news.

Underwood, D. *When MBAs Rule the Newsroom*. New York: Columbia University Press, 1993. The author, a practicing journalist turned professor, uses formal interviews and other social science techniques to present a scholarly analysis of the background and effects of market-driven and reader-driven journalism on newspaper content and on journalists and editors.

Articles & Book Chapters

Alter, J. "A call for Chinese walls: Why we should keep journalists out of the Magic Kingdom." *Newsweek*, 14 August 1995, 31. The brief article does an excellent job of presenting the tension that news organizations face when covering the affairs of their corporate parents.

Gitlin, T. "Not so fast." *Media Studies Journal* 10:2 (1996): 1-6. The New York University professor of culture, journalism, and sociology argues that the "potential for harm is at least as impressive as the potential for good" caused by the growing conglomeration juggernaut in the communications industry. Today's communications deals, Gitlin argues, may impact culture in the United States and the rest of the world for decades.

Konner, J. "The last nickel." *Columbia Journalism Review* (November-December 1995): 4. The author argues in this brief essay that quality journalism and the economic realities of the marketplace are not incompatible. She cites the *New York Times* and the *Washington Post* as examples of newspapers that combine quality and profitability.

Lacy, S., M. A. Shaver, and C. St. Cyr. "Effects of public ownership and newspaper competition on the financial performance of newspaper corporations: A replication and extension." *Journalism and Mass Communication Quarterly* 73:2 (1996): 332-41. A study of eleven newspaper groups concludes that the more public the newspaper company, the greater the need to manage in ways that provide earnings predictability and keep stock prices going up.

Matthews, M. N. "How public ownership affects publisher autonomy." *Journalism and Mass Communication Quarterly* 73:2 (1996): 342-53. Using survey data gathered in 1992, Matthews concludes that publishers employed by privately owned newspaper chains have greater autonomy than publishers employed by publicly owned newspaper chains.

Shine, N. "Bottom-line journalism: A newspaper tradition." *American Journalism Review* (July-August 1995): 26-8. Drawing on his own experiences, the former reporter, columnist, editor, and publisher of the *Detroit Free Press* illustrates that economic pressures are nothing new in the newspaper industry.

Silk, L. "The ethics and economics of journalism." Pp. 86-92 in R. Schmuhl, ed., *The Responsibilities of Journalism*. Notre Dame, Ind.: University of Notre Dame Press, 1984. Silk argues that two principles will preserve the quality of journalism in the news business: 1) separation of the business side from the news and editorial staffs, and 2) professionalism within journalism. He also believes that ombudsmen are a good thing for newspapers to have on staff.

Weinberg, S. "Smoking guns: ABC, Philip Morris and the infamous apology." *Columbia Journalism Review* (November-December 1995): 29-37. This article provides a thorough description of the tension between journalism and economic pressures faced recently by ABC for two broadcasts about the tobacco industry.

Wolzien, T. "The big news-big business bargain." *Media Studies Journal* 10:2 (1996): 109-14. The author, a Wall Street media analyst and former news producer at NBC, argues that the "news fraternity is the best protection for news operations within new and ongoing corporate structures." He concludes that big news needs big business.

Chapter Twelve

Concentration of Mass Media Ownership

Garrett W. Ray

Painter Norman Rockwell once focused his artistry on a small-town newspaper office. The 1946 painting "Country Editor" shows the editor in shirtsleeves at his typewriter as townspeople stop in to chat with neighbors at the front counter. Today, that scene reflects an enduring myth more than the reality of American media.

Those mid-century "hometown newspapers" were likely to be owned by local people who decided what to cover, how to cover it, what to editorialize about and how to invest the paper's profits. In addition, most cities and many small towns had at least two competing newspapers. Local ownership and local competition were common.

American media no longer fit that picture. Ownership of all businesses has moved away from Main Street. Today a relative handful of large companies own virtually all the media in America. The owners of your hometown newspaper, radio station, or cable system may be anonymous stockholders in a multinational corporation. Some companies may own non-media businesses as well.

The companies may not even have their headquarters in the United States. Most consumers have not heard of Pearson plc (headquartered in London) or The News Corporation Limited (Rupert Murdoch's Sydney-based empire), although these giant firms may control media Americans use every day.

Although media groups may buy individual media properties, growth increasingly occurs through purchases of other groups — for example, the merger of Time, Inc. and Warner Communications. So the big get bigger. As media ownership has become more concentrated, competition between specific media in specific localities has declined. Fewer than 1 per cent of America's cities now have competing daily newspapers.

Critics ask what happens when media ownership no longer rests in thousands of local hands, but with a few giant national or multinational companies. Many observers say this trend toward "group" or "chain" journalism endangers democracy. Others argue that the effects are mixed or even beneficial. These conflicting views raise important questions about control of the media: Does group ownership decrease or increase quality? How important is competition? Will groups impose their political and social views on their properties? What values drive their decisions? How will this affect the democratic process, especially the "public forum" where information and ideas are exchanged?

Origins of the Issue

Libertarianism is a double-edged sword. The philosophy of the free market has been central to arguments about control of the press since America's earliest years. The freedoms guaranteed in the First Amendment include freedom of the press from government control, making it the only business to receive special constitutional protection. In return, the press has been expected to provide an open forum for public debate and information.

The writers of the Bill of Rights looked back to John Locke and John Milton, seventeenth-century libertarian philosophers. Locke claimed that rational people needed no church or king to find the truth for themselves, and that they had the right to pursue that truth. Milton emphasized that this process depended upon diversity of ideas and freedom of expression. From this seedbed grew the metaphor of "the marketplace of ideas."

A pattern of media concentration had already begun to develop near the end of the nineteenth century. Ironically, it too was based upon the libertarian argument: Government should not interfere with the economic marketplace, but should allow open competition to determine which businesses succeed or fail. Press barons like William Randolph Hearst and Edward W. Scripps used the private enterprise argument to amass enormous power in the late 1880s. In the early twentieth century, suspension of competing newspapers, mergers of others with rivals, concentration of ownership , and creation of chains became common.

More than 150 years after the Bill of Rights was written, the libertarian philosophy emerged as an argument against concentration of media ownership. In 1947 an influential group of American scholars known as the Hutchins Commission presented a controversial report on the role of the media in a democratic society. The commission argued for diversity of opinions, and it rejected government control of the press. But the scholars also suggested that the libertarian marketplace of ideas was not open to every voice, even if the press remained free from government control.

"The owners and managers of the press determine which persons, which facts, which versions of the facts, and which ideas shall reach the public," the authors asserted in their report, *A Free and Responsible Press*. Citizens should not have to depend on the whims of media owners to determine whose arguments are heard and what information is circulated, the commission argued. It continued, "The danger is that the entire function of communications will fall under the control of fewer and fewer persons. Among the consequences of this concentration, the output of the press reflects the biases of owners and denies adequate expression to important elements in communities."

While the Hutchins Commission helped draw attention to the question of media ownership, its report did nothing to slow the growth of concentration. In fact, the most significant growth of media groups has occurred in the decades following the commission's report.

Ben Bagdikian, a prominent critic of corporate influence on the media, observes in *The Media Monopoly* that 80 per cent of America's daily newspapers were independently owned at the end of World War II. Barely four decades later, the pattern had been reversed: 80 per cent of the dailies were owned by corporate groups. The urge to merge has been even more dramatic for the magazine industry, Bagdikian indicates. In 1981 most of the country's magazines were controlled by twenty corporations; seven years later, they were controlled by three.

Benjamin Compaine, principal author of *Who Owns the Media?*, confirms a steady increase from 1910 to 1980 in the number of newspapers controlled by newspaper groups. However, ownership was not necessarily becoming more narrow during this time. Compaine reports that during the same period, the number of newspaper groups increased dramatically — from thirteen groups to 154. Groups can be huge, holding hundreds of newspapers, magazines, and other properties. Or they can be tiny. When one locally owned weekly newspaper buys the weekly in a neighboring town, that also constitutes a group. However, in the group-versus-independent argument, attention focuses on large companies, often corporately owned, that have properties in several cities, states or even countries.

The last two decades have produced an explosion of media technology, leading to rapid changes in media economics and potential social effects. Will new media bring additional companies into the market, which might diversify not only ownership but also the variety of material available? For example, in the decades when most Americans received only three network TV channels, who could have foreseen the creation of new cable television networks by Ted Turner? Or will already powerful corporations reach out to embrace — and control — new media as well? Bagdikian quotes a 1994 *New York Times* interview with a media consultant predicting that the top twenty cable television firms would merge themselves into five companies.

In spite of widely differing views, participants in the debate over media concentration agree on two points:

First, the mass media must provide diversity, both in the information they present and the public forums they offer. Bryce Rucker, whose 1968 book, *The First Freedom,* provided an early landmark attack on media concentration, draws inspiration from Thomas Jefferson. Rucker argues that "few would dispute that our press freedom is predicated on the concept of a marketplace of ideas from which the public may select." Similarly, Bagdikian describes the press as "a kind of balance wheel, bringing reason and diversity of opinion to its reporting and commentary." Compaine argues that critics have overstated the dangers of concentration, yet he recognizes the importance of diversity: "We cannot take issue with the need to maintain a vigorous flow of varied ideas and information."

Second, both critics and defenders agree that concentration is increasing across all media. *Managing Media Organizations,* a management text by John M. Lavine and Daniel B. Wackman, points out that recent decades have seen a sharp rise in concentration "in almost every information industry and at every size level." The authors also point out that acquisitions between industries have created multi-media conglomerates. The 1985 merger of Capital Cities Communications and ABC created Capital Cities/ABC, which owned literally thousands of television and radio stations, recording and publishing companies, video enterprises, motion picture producers, scenic attractions, daily newspapers, and specialized business newspapers. Now Capital Cities/ABC has merged with The Walt Disney Company to form an even larger and more diverse conglomerate.

Beyond these two areas of consensus, however, there is little agreement about the impacts of media concentration.

Critics of Media Concentration

Access to plentiful media choices does not ensure competition or diversity in specific media. "Publishers publicly like to insist that there is no such thing as a newspaper monopoly," Bagdikian writes. "So publishers created the charming concept of 'media voices' ... anything and everything printed, uttered, broadcast, seen, or heard in and by a community. Thus, no daily paper is a monopoly. Unfortunately, almost all of them are." Residents of a particular community might receive the local daily newspaper, subscribe to three special interest magazines, pick up handbills from the lawn, scan billboard advertisements, subscribe to cable television, and listen to the radio while commuting to work. All those media provide a variety of information from diverse sources. But with rare exceptions, the town's citizens cannot subscribe to two local newspapers. For that particular kind of information, only one supplier exists. Bryce Rucker explains, "To argue that *Time, Newsweek,* out-of-town newspapers, out-of-town radio and television stations somehow make monopoly ownership palatable evades the question. None of those media cover local news or comment on local issues."

Concentration reduces the likelihood of a vigorous exchange of diverse viewpoints. Morris Ernst (whose 1946 book *The First Freedom* inspired Rucker to write a book with the same title and theme) writes in the introduction to Rucker's book that monopoly in the "thought" marketplace has denied citizens the choice of ideas "or even the ability to assay for the truth." The Hutchins Commission report, issued during the same decade as Ernst's book, pursues the same argument: "Through concentration of ownership the variety of sources of news and opinion is limited. At the same time the insistence of the citizen's need has increased."

In 1890, New York City had fifteen general-circulation, English-language daily newspapers. By the 1960s, there were only seven. By 1997, New York City had only four dailies, and one of these focuses on Long Island, not greater New York City.

The values of "corporate culture" conflict with traditional journalistic values, corrupting news media standards and credibility. Journalism has always valued what Bagdikian calls "separation of Church and State." Editorial decisions are to be kept separate from advertising, circulation, and other business decisions. The corporate culture of "business first" threatens this principle.

Norman Isaacs, journalism educator and former editor, describes his perception of financial decisionmakers who may measure the media's success by only one standard — profitability. He argues in *Untended Gates* that, for money-market people, "the business of communications is no different than dealing with automobiles, computers, food, toothpaste, soap, shoes, or anything else .... They certainly have helped in making obsolete so many of the basic values that built journalism into one of the major institutions in the American society." Other veteran editors have expressed similar views. Among them is James D. Squires, former editor of the *Chicago Tribune,* the title of whose book reflects his argument that corporations have weakened the press as an institution of democracy. The book is titled *Read All About It: The Corporate Takeover of America's Newspapers.*

Some see special danger in mergers of entertainment companies with news organizations. Reflecting on the Time-Warner merger, Rinker Buck wrote in *Newsinc.* magazine in 1990, "The breakup of founder Henry Luce's old magazine empire may be just one of many cases where merged communications companies weigh the value of high-margin entertainment against the low margins of magazine publishing and beat a strategic retreat." The consequence may be that news providers become starved for resources and new investment capital as their parent companies devote more of their staffing and financial backing to enlarging their more profitable enterprises, such as movies or television comedies.

This shift in cultural values has other consequences. In 1995 ABC was in the final stages of purchase negotiations with Disney, and CBS was about to be acquired by Westinghouse. Both were also involved in bitter disputes over documentaries criticizing the tobacco industry. CBS killed a scheduled *60 Minutes* interview with a tobacco company executive who had promised to reveal company secrets. Facing a $10 billion libel suit from Philip Morris, ABC News publicly apologized for an earlier program. Some argue that the decisions reflected the triumph of business over good journalism.

Diversity is further threatened by cross-ownership and interlocking board memberships. By the 1980s, Bagdikian charges, most of America's major media were already controlled by fifty giant corporations, interlocked in common financial interest with other big industries and banks. That number has now been reduced to about ten, he says, making the dominant players "the new communications cartel." Such arrangements often involve stock in one company owned by another, as well as shared members of the boards of directors. One might argue that these practices do not necessarily destroy any company's independence. But James P. Winter, a Canadian researcher who has examined the ties between two Canadian press chains as well as between those chains and other businesses, implies that the dangers are "intuitively obvious." Winter's research appears in Picard et. al.'s *Press Concentration and Monopoly*, edited by Robert G. Picard and others. His conclusion is reinforced by Dennis W. Mazzocco, a former ABC television producer, who specifically charges in his book that because of cross-ownerships, U.S. broadcast media must satisfy the interests of a small group of banks, insurance companies, and giant institutional investor groups.

The influence of stock prices on publicly-owned companies makes them especially susceptible to pressure for strong short-term earnings. Family owners of media companies are not necessarily less eager for profits than stockholders of public companies. However, wealthy media families, relatively free from worries about the next quarter, can take a long view of the value of their investment. But it is now more common for a media outlet to be owned by a large corporation than by a family, notes Eric Gibson, reviewing the memoirs of editor Ben Bradlee in Forbes *Media Critic*.

Since 1963 many large media companies have sold their stock publicly. This has created a new and influential audience of Wall Street investors and analysts, according to Paul M. Hirsch and Tracy A. Thompson. Their study of the impact of public ownership on newspapers appears in *Audiencemaking*, edited by James S. Ettema and D. Charles Whitney. "Worried about losing their companies to hostile raiders, managers have begun basing strategic decisions and organization designs on expected impact on shareholder value," they argue, "rather than such criteria as serving the public, the community, or employees."

A few corporations may soon control all the important mass media around the globe. Viacom, Paramount, and Blockbuster are now one international company, as are Disney, Capital Cities, and ABC. Time Warner and Turner Broadcasting were moving toward a merger in early 1997. Time Warner has entered into numerous cross-media global partnerships.

Some years ago one newspaper chain owner expressed concern at the possibility that American news media could become takeover targets of foreign-owned corporations. "How would you like it if King Fahd controlled Knight-Ridder or Mitsubishi turned the dials at Gannett?" asked C.K. McClatchy, chairman of McClatchy Newspapers, in a 1988 speech. Now, many American media are owned by foreign companies.

Media companies use their power to influence political decisions from Main Street to Congress and the President's office. Public officials have good reason to listen to media lobbyists. Media affect public opinion in part through their gatekeeping role, determining what issues and information will shape the public agenda. They also can editorially endorse politicians and programs. By running or omitting a story, they can punish an enemy or reward a friend.

Bagdikian writes, "What the public learns is heavily weighted by what serves the economic and political interests of the corporations that own the media." Moreover, the media's political agenda consistently presents a distorted world view. Michael Parenti, in *Inventing Reality*, contends that the mass media deliberately distort reality to reflect the conservative economic interests of large institutions. The authors of *Manufacturing Consent* share this view.

Even if power is exercised infrequently or indirectly, political leaders as well as media employees are aware of its potential. U.S. Rep. Morris Udall (D-Ariz.) tried unsuccessfully to curtail the growing concentration of media. The overriding issue, he said, was the potential power to control public opinion. "Al Neuharth [former Gannett chief executive] ... could decide tomorrow morning that they want total control of their newspapers' editorial product," Udall said.

In spite of media firms' insistence to the contrary, editorial autonomy is a myth. Some companies directly interfere with editorial policy. Roger Wood, a top executive for Australian-born press baron Rupert Murdoch, was quoted in the *Wall Street Journal* when Murdoch's *New York Post* campaigned against vice presidential candidate Geraldine Ferraro. "His papers are right-wing newspapers," Wood said of Murdoch. "He believes he can influence people with them."

More likely, media groups will preach a gospel of non-interference while hiring executives who exercise self-censorship. Andrew Kreig was an editor and senior reporter on the *Hartford Courant* before and after its purchase by The Times Mirror Company in 1979. "Hidden corporate imperatives and taboos thwarted the newspaper's mission of truth-telling," he writes in *Spiked.* "The chain conferred power onto fiercely loyal, ruthlessly ambitious executives brought in from afar.... The chieftains were free to bungle and lie, and to suppress inconvenient facts and ideas."

After reviewing a number of studies of owners' influence, Bryce Rucker concludes that owners using mass media "as weapons for their selfish interests has been well-documented." Bagdikian adds more recent examples of interference in news decisions.

Corporate owners reduce the quality and diversity of local journalism as they seek to cut costs. Reporters and editors disparage corporate accountants as "bean counters." While emphasis on the bottom line has increased media efficiency and profits, it can have dangerous consequences.

Large media companies can crush smaller competitors. "As the size and financial power of the new dominant firms have escalated, so has their coercive power to offer a bothersome smaller competitor a choice of either selling out at once or slowly facing ruin," Bagdikian warns. Dramatic evidence appears in Richard McCord's book, *The Chain Gang.* The former investigative reporter documents the cynical, brutally efficient efforts of Gannett to kill smaller competitive newspapers in three American cities.

In a one-newspaper town, the surviving paper or new owner can set advertising and subscription rates without the restraints provided by true competition. While raising rates, the new management also often cuts the staff and reduces the "news hole" to meet demands for increased profitability.

"Many groups set high profit goals for their papers ... and these goals, in turn, push the companies to operate tightly budgeted, often miserly, news operations," says Loren Ghiglione in *The Buying and Selling of America's Newspapers.* He also notes, "The people running the papers reflect the bottom-line mentality of the ownership." Corporate executives' negative influence on papers can go beyond a focus on profits. Media groups often bring in executives who may know and care little about the community; their loyalty is to the company, not the town. Patrick R. Parsons and his colleagues, discussing editors and their roles, *Press Concentration and Monopoly,* confirm the mobility of group editors. The survey supports the view that chain editors move from paper to paper, spending less time and making fewer attachments to the community than independent editors.

Arguments for Concentration

Critics often confuse a number of diverse issues. Corporate ownership is not necessarily the same as chain ownership, and neither leads inevitably to concentration, to monopoly control, or even to a decline in competition. In his book *The Menace of the Corporate Newspaper: Fact or Fiction?* David Pearce Demers urges more clarity in describing the facts and defining the issues. He points out that "newspaper chain" is an imprecise term that leads to confusion when researchers study the effects of media concentration. Instead, he focuses on whether the media company has the characteristics of the corporate form of organization. Even this can be confusing, he points out. "In everyday conversation, the term corporate newspaper is often used synonymously with one or more of the following: a legally incorporated business, a newspaper owned by a chain, a newspaper managed by professionally trained and educated experts rather than the owners, and a large bureaucratic organization." All reflect some feature of the corporate newspaper, but no single definition will do, he says. He adds that researchers' tendency to rely heavily on one of these characteristics is responsible in part for the widely mixed findings in the field.

For Benjamin Compaine, the key question regarding ownership is, "How few is too few?" If critics truly want to encourage diversity of sources for information and knowledge, he argues, the focus should not be on concentration in any given media segment. Instead the analysis should ask, "How many media owners are there in the mass communications industry overall?" From this perspective, the newsweekly magazines compete not only with each other; they also compete with all newspapers, as well as local and national television news programs and news radio stations, for consumers' time and attention.

It is irrelevant to discuss whether concentration is good or bad or whether it should occur, as it is a natural result of broad economic trends that are inevitable. The media are subject to the same trends that influence other businesses. The power of the marketplace determines whether businesses will grow or die, and economic reality forces many industries to consolidate and concentrate.

"Media firms must continually seek new ways to earn more money ... and new ways to improve efficiency if they are to maintain high profit levels," suggest John M. Lavine and Daniel B. Wackman, in their book *Managing Media Organizations.* Compaine notes, "While it may be a pleasant fantasy to wish there could be two or three independent newspapers in every city or fifteen radio stations in every town and village, the fact is that the economic infrastructure does not support such dreams."

Moreover, savvy media owners naturally look for growth opportunities.

Compaine points out that consumers and advertisers have spent a relatively fixed percentage on all media over an extended period, and that behavior is likely to continue. So as consumers and advertisers show more interest in video and CD players, cable TV, and innovative computer programs, "it should not be surprising that owners of businesses in the mass communications industry would want to increase earnings by purchasing more properties or, even more to the point, become involved in the new media."

Public access to a wide range of information and opinion is increasing, not decreasing. In eighteenth-century America, "it is not likely that individuals had the diversity of sources, from as great a variety of producers, as we have today," Compaine argues. This diversity grows directly and naturally from the changing nature of American society. Demers says critics misunderstood the how and why of corporate concentration; the trend is a natural outgrowth of a more pluralistic social system, he argues. This same pluralism leads to increasing diversity of thoughts and ideas. As a community or society becomes larger and more complex, citizens are less likely to feel a common identity with the interests of everyone else in society. They divide into special interest groups, each of which reflects and puts forth the views of a relatively narrow segment of society. This fragmentation creates more voices, not fewer — America today reflects this complexity and the diversity in viewpoints resulting from it.

Media managers know that competition is increasing for both audiences and advertisers, according to Lavine and Wackman. Audience fragmentation is rising. The existence of more radio stations, magazines, and TV channels results in narrower targeting of audience segments; this provides more choices for all consumers.

In spite of increasing concentration, media diversity cannot be seriously compromised because media owners remain too numerous and the public's media consumption is too fragmented. William B. Shew, visiting scholar at American Enterprise Institute, provides an example in *The American Enterprise* in 1996: "The magazine industry has seen almost a 30 per cent increase in the number of titles published over the last fifteen years, from roughly 9,600 in 1970 to over 12,000 by 1994. So it is difficult to believe that the recent spate of media mergers presents a threat to competition."

"Print is no longer the only rooster in the barnyard," Compaine observes. "And broadcasting is not its only companion." The new media involve some old names, but many new ones as well. Nor is competition limited to the traditional media or even intermedia competition, he points out. Among the new competitors are financial institutions (electronic data bases for home customers), retailers (home shopping), and computer time-sharing firms and service bureaus.

All those new forms of information would not have appeared if it were not for large companies with the resources to launch new media. Dramatic advances in television and computer technology could not have occurred without immense capital investment. The same need for the dollars and resources of huge companies can be seen in other new media.

"We must not be so idealistic as to believe that the small business entities of previous eras are as appropriate today," Compaine argues. "AT&T (whole or split up) may have awesome assets, but assets of sizable magnitude are necessary to keep a growing nation wired."

Competition does not necessarily increase diversity. Having two newspaper voices in one city does not radically change what the newspapers cover. The substance will be largely the same. Monopolies "do not substantially affect the contents of newspapers in the U.S." concludes Carlos Ruotolo. The author reviewed a number of studies of the relation between monopoly ownership and content for *Press Concentration and Monopoly.* "Monopoly alone is not likely to be a major cause of content homogeneity," he writes. "The need to cater to wide audiences, not marginal readers, appears to be a central influence."

Maxwell E. McCombs, in another study from the same book, describes the content of the daily newspapers in Montreal and Winnipeg, Canada, before and after they became one-paper cities. "Traditional democratic assumptions about newspaper competition and the diversity of content are not well supported by these content analyses," he concludes. After the death of the competing paper, the surviving newspapers still produced highly similar products because of similar professional values, beliefs, and practices.

Publicly owned companies care about profitability and value, not about using the media for power and influence. "Media owners, obedient to market demands or at least their sense of what the market demands, set limits on news coverage — notably, by setting budgets," observes Michael Schudson in "How News Becomes News." "But today they rarely seek to use the press as a soapbox for their own political views."

Compaine points out that many owners of corporate media are large institutional investors like trusts and pension funds who buy stock in publicly-held firms. "Institutional investors are most often looking for long-term growth," he states. "They are not overly concerned with the potentially controversial content of some successful movies or best-selling books, nor with the lack of intelligence evidenced in top-rated television shows, as long as these channels continue to produce revenues."

Media ownership groups explicitly protect the editorial autonomy of their products. Besides, individual owners are just as likely — perhaps more — to interfere with editori-

al policy and news decisions. Critics of media concentration and corporate ownership paint an image of owners who dictate their editors' opinions, protect advertisers, and promote their friends' interests. However, corporate ownership may have no impact in this regard, and in fact may free the media from outside pressures.

David Pearce Demers explains that as media reflect more corporate characteristics, power and control over day-to-day operations shift from the owners to the professional managers. As the owners' power to affect content declines, news and editorial content become more critical of social and political conditions. A study by Demers concludes that corporate newspapers are more critical of established power groups than locally owned newspapers and are more likely to promote or accelerate social change. Demers observes that locally owned newspapers traditionally had strong ties to the local community power structure. This "decreases the probability that the newspaper will challenge or criticize dominant groups and their ideas and values," he argues. He also claims that the non-corporate newspaper's smaller profit margin makes it less able to risk offending big advertisers.

The trade newspaper Publishers' Auxiliary reported a study by the American Society of Newspaper Editors, which concluded in 1980 that "chain editors called their own shots more often than did editors working day to day with a local publisher." More recently, Dennis Hale, writing in *Press Concentration and Monopoly*, analyzed twenty-eight newspapers' editorial pages before and after they were purchased by chains. Although he expected that chains would devote fewer pages to editorials and commentary, this did not occur. He concluded that editorial pages neither deteriorate nor improve under chain ownership.

His study did not explore other measures of editorial diversity, such as staffing, news hole, salaries or coverage of local conflict. However, Robert H. Giles, editor of the *Detroit News,* said in 1987, "I've been a Gannett editor for almost ten years. And in terms of my ability to run my newsroom in the way I think it should be run and to pick the issues and pick the agendas and pick the projects that we want, I have total autonomy."

Groups bring strength. Concentration of ownership in larger units generally helps individual media to endure hard times. Groups also have the resources to improve content and upgrade technology. Many smaller media could not have survived recessions and rapid changes during the last three decades without the resources of large companies. Tom Noonan, publisher in 1977 of a chain-owned suburban Denver weekly, noted in an editorial, "Thanks primarily to the large chains, today's newspapers are experiencing a technological revolution. Without that technology, many papers wouldn't have survived the monumental price increases of the past half-decade."

Groups also can provide more professional management skills and training. Alvah H. Chapman, Jr., former president and chief executive officer of Knight-Ridder Inc., left his family-owned papers because "resources were limited. Professional training opportunities and staff opportunities were less than today with those same newspapers which are now under Knight-Ridder stewardship."

Groups strengthen the "watchdog" role of the press. Groups can resist pressure from both the government and big advertisers to limit freedom of information and expression. A local media owner may not be able to afford to challenge a government agency that refuses to release public information. However, the editor of a group-owned paper can call upon the financial and legal resources of the parent firm.

Groups are also less likely to protect local sacred cows and more likely to pursue controversial issues. "Many, many newspapers across this country were pervasively mediocre, [un]professional and timid. They often lacked the economic strength — or will — to resist the special interests," Chapman writes. "Professionalism and commitment are the key factors....These factors are not a function of individual vs. group ownership."

Resolution

To speak of "resolution" of issues surrounding media concentration implies that there is room for consensus — some middle path. This seems unlikely; the only areas of agreement appear to be that media concentration is increasing and that diversity is a good thing. It would help if all sides were to focus the debate more narrowly. This controversy is mostly about the effects of ownership on news and public affairs information, not entertainment or other non-journalistic content.

Those who believe that media concentration is neutral or even beneficial in its effects will argue for letting the marketplace continue to sort out the difficulties. Competition, even among giants, will ultimately benefit consumers and the public good. In general, this argument will favor further changes like those embodied in the Telecommunications Act of 1996, which removed many restrictions on media cross-ownership and expansion.

Critics must accept that further concentration will occur unless Americans actively support drastic changes through legislation and regulation. Legislative remedies that have been suggested are aimed at either preventing or diffusing concentration. Among them:

• Strengthen and vigorously enforce antitrust laws affecting the media;

also eliminate the law that permits newspapers to evade antitrust regulation through "joint operating agreements." However, some scholars predict that even if changes in antitrust laws were to increase competition, they would not be likely to increase diversity of information and opinion.

- Limit the number of media outlets that can be held by a single owner or company.

- Restrict cross-ownership and interlocking directorates that involve media companies.

- Encourage noncommercial media as alternative voices to corporate-owned media. This presumably would require extensive funding by government sources, foundations, or other public interest groups.

- Provide tax incentives to encourage independently owned media to remain independent. For example, existing laws have forced many heirs to sell family-owned media to pay inheritance taxes.

Some would go further. Mazzocco would abolish a media system based on free enterprise, placing most media under ownership of public, non-profit foundations. He also recommends taxing commercial media to create a fund to support independent, alternative grassroots media.

However, significant legislative and regulatory changes seem relatively unlikely. The issues are laden with complexities requiring a high degree of technological expertise that may baffle and intimidate the average citizen. Also, consumers may not demand change when the diversity of media programming in general (though arguably not in news and public affairs programming) is expanding, not shrinking. In addition, efforts to legislate change will encounter powerful political opposition from corporate-owned media companies, as well as more general objection to any changes that seem to restrict freedom to gather or report information.

However, other alternatives may be more achievable because they do not depend on legislation and regulation. Some of these include the following:

- Increase public disclosure through schools, alternative media, and other outlets to encourage awareness of both the extent and effects of media concentration. Citizens who are aware of the private interests of media owners can better evaluate the news and comment they receive from those media.

- Encourage media companies to strengthen their own rules and internal processes to protect the independence of journalists and the newsgathering process; this would be not only in the public interest but also in the long term self-interest of the companies.

- Encourage formation of a foundation-funded national media council to monitor and promote awareness of institutional media behavior as well as specific abuses and shortcomings.

- Organize citizens' local and regional grassroots media councils with a three-pronged objective: to increase awareness of how the media work; to call attention through grassroots media (newsletters, the Internet, etc.) to media shortcomings or abuses of power; and to lobby both the media and government for change.

Controlling the growth of media concentration may be impossible. But greater efforts to understand, monitor and reveal the direction and effects of that growth are both possible and desirable. If those efforts are half-hearted or non-existent, the growing economic power of large media corporations will lead inevitably to overwhelming social and political power as well.

Recommended Readings

Books

Bagdikian, Ben H. *The Media Monopoly*, 5th ed. Boston: Beacon Press, 1997. In this new edition of the best known and most outspoken attack on the misuse of the power of media concentration to influence public opinion, the author has updated some statistics and added material on the Telecommunications Act of 1996.

Compaine, Benjamin M., Christopher H. Sterling, Thomas Guback, and J. Kendrick Noble Jr. *Who Owns the Media? Concentration of Ownership in the Mass Communications Industry.* White Plains, N.Y.: Knowledge Industry Publications, 1982. This massive study views media ownership patterns more benignly than do the better known critical studies.

Demers, David Pearce. *The Menace of the Corporate Newspaper: Fact or Fiction?* Ames: Iowa State University Press, 1995. Demers's book summarizes much of his research into media concentration in recent years. He argues that critics have misunderstood the how and why of corporate organization and that corporate newspapers benefit modern society.

Ghiglione, Loren, ed. *The Buying and Selling of America's Newspapers.* Indianapolis: R.J. Berg, 1984. The authors examine the effect of the ownership changes on the quality of newspapers through qualitative case histories of ten family-owned papers sold to chains. The editor concludes, "It's virtually impossible to generalize — good guys or bad? — about the groups' impact."

Herman, Edward S., and Noam Chomsky. *Manufacturing Consent: The Political Economy of the Mass Media.* New York: Pantheon Books, 1988. The authors argue that giant mass media companies are part of an "elite consensus" mobilizing support for special interests that dominate government and major power groups.

Kreig, Andrew. *Spiked: How Chain Management Corrupted America's Oldest Newspaper.* Old Saybrook, Conn.: Peregrine Press, 1987. The author, an investigative reporter, worked for the *Hartford Courant* for fourteen years. He recounts the story of management decisions that led to his resignation after Times Mirror bought the paper in 1984.

Mazzocco, Dennis W. *Networks of Power: Corporate TV's Threat to Democracy.* Boston: South End Press, 1994. A former television producer presents an angry expose' of the effects of concentrated ownership and monopoly in U.S. network television, focusing on Capital Cities/ABC, Inc.

McCord, Richard. *The Chain Gang: One Newspaper Versus the Gannett Empire.* Columbia: University of Missouri Press, 1996. This former editor, who fought Gannett in Santa Fe, N.M., and Green Bay, Wisc., presents three case histories describing in dramatic detail the competitive tactics of America's largest newspaper company.

Parenti, Michael. *Inventing Reality: The Politics of News Media,* 2nd ed. New York: St. Martin's Press, 1993. The corporate-owned news media do not live up to their claims of objectivity, balance, and truth, the author argues. Rather, they deliberately distort important aspects of social and political life in a repeatable and systemic way that reflects the ideological and economic interests of media owners.

Picard, Robert G., Maxwell E. McCombs, James P. Winter, and Stephen Lacy, eds. *Press Concentration and Monopoly: New Perspectives on Newspaper Ownership and Operation.* Norwood, N.J.: Ablex, 1988. This collection of research studies provides empirical evidence to help remedy what the authors call "the dearth of evidence about the actual impact" of chains and monopolies on journalists and communities. It includes a thorough and wide-ranging bibliography.

Squires, James D. *Read All About It! The Corporate Takeover of America's Newspapers.* New York: Times Books, 1993. The former editor of the *Chicago Tribune* describes what he sees as the journalistic decline of the paper, concluding that "the marriage of corporations and journalism is an unnatural, unhappy union."

Articles

Lacy, Stephen. "Effects of Group Ownership on Daily Newspaper Content." *Journal of Media Economics* 4 (Spring 1991): 35-45. This nationwide study of 114 newspapers examined a week's content and concluded that group ownership had no effect on how news space was allocated. Group-owned papers tended to give a smaller percentage of their space to news but had larger news staffs than independently-owned papers.

"Marketplace of Ideas Revisited, The: Competition and Concentration in Print, Broadcasting, New Technologies." *Journal of Communication* 35 (Summer 1985). This issue contains a collection of useful essays and studies of varied media under this theme title. Authors of individual articles include Benjamin M. Compaine, Ben H. Bagdikian, Paul M. Hirsch, Heikki Hellman and Martti Soramaki, Edward S. Herman and Robert M. Entman.

"Media Mergers." *Media Studies Journal* 10 (Spring-Summer 1996). This entire issue is a collection of relatively informal and provocative essays by scholars and media practitioners focusing on the effects of media concentration. It includes a brief bibliography of the most current books discussing media mergers and profiling the principal players.

Picard, Robert G., and Stephen Lacy. "Newspaper Economics Bibliography." *Journal of Media Economics* 4:2 (Summer 1991): 35-59. This bibliography, prepared for the Association for Education in Journalism and Mass Communication, is the most thorough listing of books, articles, and unpublished material on a wide range of media economics topics published prior to 1991.

Rosse, James N. "Economic Limits of Press Responsibility." *Studies in Industry Economics No. 56*, Department of Economic Stanford University (1975). Rosse's "umbrella model" has been widely used by other researchers. He argues that in urban areas, competition exists primarily between layers (such as between suburban dailies and weeklies) rather than within layers (such as between suburban dailies).

Shew, William B. "Are Media Mergers a Menace?" *The American Enterprise* 7 (March/April 1996): 69. This essay by a media telecommunications adviser argues that current mega-mergers will not eliminate competition or reduce content diversity. He opposes proposed public policy changes that might further restrain media competition.

Chapter Thirteen

Newspapers and Joint Operating Agreements

David C. Coulson
Stephen Lacy

Debate about the Newspaper Preservation Act has continued unabated since its passage by Congress in 1970. Its supporters maintain that the law preserves two independent news and editorial voices in cities that otherwise might have only one. Opponents charge that it is used to eliminate newspaper competition that otherwise might have been preserved. In reality, the act has had some success but has not saved the newspaper industry from its march toward single-newspaper cities.

The Newspaper Preservation Act gives an antitrust exemption to any two newspapers existing side by side in the same city, allowing them to merge business operations to reduce costs while retaining separate news-editorial departments. The combination is called a joint operating agreement (JOA). This chapter reviews the arguments concerning JOAs in light of developments in the newspaper industry since 1970 and examines the underlying assumptions about JOAs.

Although highly controversial, JOAs exist in only a small number of cities. In 1998, there were seventeen joint operating agreements, one less than existed when the NPA was passed. Eight joint ventures have folded and seven have started during the law's existence.

Except for Denver, Colo., the cities with competing daily newspapers are not good JOA prospects because of the great disparity in circulation between the dominant and weaker papers. Cities that seemed destined for joint agencies just a few years ago, such as Dallas and Little Rock, are now one-newspaper towns. Since the law was passed, the number of daily newspapers in the United States has dropped from about 1,750 to slightly more than 1,500.

Origins of the Issue

Even though the first formal joint operating agreement started in Albuquerque, N. M., in 1933, Edward Adams discovered similar agreements at E.W. Scripps newspapers fifty years earlier. Scripps papers typically trailed larger dailies in their markets, and combination agreements with other papers (e.g., agreements to fix advertising and subscription prices) were seen as ways of overcoming inferior market positions.

Combination agreements were fairly common in most industries during the late 1800s, which is why Congress passed antitrust laws in 1890 (the Sherman Act) and 1914 (the Clayton Act). As with most laws, passage did not necessarily eliminate the activity. So in 1933, the *Albuquerque Journal* and the *Albuquerque Tribune* signed an agreement to combine their business operations and leave their editorial departments separate. This became the model for JOAs throughout the country.

Three more JOAs were created during the 1930s, and an additional three were added in the 1940s. By 1965, eighteen cities had JOAs. The Justice Department incorrectly listed twenty-two cities as having JOAs, but subsequent evaluation of the lists resulted in the removal of Bristol, Tenn., Franklin-Oil City, Pa., Lincoln, Neb., and Madison, Wis., as JOAs.

In 1965, the Justice Department filed suit against the agreement in Tucson, arguing that it violated the Sherman and Clayton acts. Justice argued that the agreement involved price fixing and profit pooling and resulted in a monopoly. The federal district court agreed with these arguments, and its ruling was upheld by the U.S. Supreme Court in 1969.

Congressional efforts to protect the joint agreements began with the introduction of legislation in 1967, even before the Supreme Court ruled on the Tucson case. In 1970, Congress passed the Newspaper Preservation Act, which allows the Justice Department to grant exemptions from antitrust law to JOAs.

Since the passage of the Newspaper Preservation Act, pairs of dailies in Anchorage, Chattanooga, Cincinnati, Detroit, Las Vegas, Seattl,e and York, Pa., have had JOAs approved by the Justice Department. During the same period, JOAs have been dissolved in eight cities (Anchorage, Cincinnati, Knoxville, Miami, Pittsburgh, St. Louis, Shreveport, and Tulsa).

The Issues

During the history of joint operating agreements, debate has centered on a number of issues. During the Congressional hearings, supporters argued that the economics of the newspaper industry no longer allows two separately owned and operated dailies to survive in the same city. They said the Newspaper Preservation Act would provide a way for cities to keep two separate editorial and news voices. Critics of the NPA argued that the given city itself could support two dailies and that JOAs wouldn't necessarily preserve two separate voices.

Other observers took a more philosophical approach, saying that even if newspapers are more likely to survive as a joint venture, the NPA makes these papers beholden to the government. The NPA, they argue, is essentially a licensing of newspapers, which is inconsistent with the First Amendment.

More recently, criticism of the NPA has involved charges that publishers are more interested in preserving profits than two robust editorial voices as envisioned by the law. They argue that profit goals of large corporations run counter to the NPA supposed goal of providing communities with editorial diversity.

During the decades since passage of the Newspaper Preservation Act, research and experience have helped resolve some of the issues surrounding joint agreements. But other issues remain unsettled.

Supporters of JOAs

It has become evident during the past three decades that competition between dailies headquartered in the same city cannot survive. Only about a dozen cities continue to have two separately owned and operated dailies, and in at least three of these, a paper is subsidized by a religious or educational institution. Critics of the Newspaper Preservation Act who argued that intracity competition could continue were wrong.

However, proponents who argued that joint operating agreements would save competition are also wrong. There is one less JOA existing today than when the NPA was passed, and few cities appear to be good candidates for joint partnerships.

A major factor in the decline of daily newspaper competition is the circulation spiral that continues in most JOA markets despite the Newspaper Preservation Act. The phenomenon occurs because the newspaper that moves ahead in circulation attracts a disproportionate percentage of advertising in its market. Because readers read newspapers for advertising as well as news and editorial content, the greater amount of advertising in the circulation leader subsequently draws more readers, which draws more advertising, which draws more readers, and so on. The result is that a trailing newspaper may have 40 per cent of the circulation but only 25 per cent of the advertising lineage. Because advertising accounts for 70 to 80 per cent of newspaper revenues, the trailing newspaper will ultimately lack the money to continue publishing.

Industry analysts suggest that when a newspaper drops below 40 per cent in the market, its chances for reversing the downward trend and catching up with the leading newspaper are extremely slim. In 1998, a third of the seventeen JOA markets had trailing newspapers with less than 40 per cent of the circulation. In three markets, the weaker papers had less than 25 per cent.

David Lawrence Jr., publisher and chairman of the *Miami Herald*, defended the Newspaper Preservation Act in a 1997 article in *Quill*. He worked through what he calls the "painful years" in Detroit — as executive editor, then publisher of the *Free Press* — that led up to a joint operating agreement. He claims that the JOA saved a "distinctive and distinguished newspaper" as well as more than 2,000 jobs. His argument in defense of the Newspaper Preservation Act includes three major points:

- The legislation has largely preserved two separate and independent editorial voices in seventeen cities.

- Economic conditions change. What appeared "reasonable and feasible" at the time of NPA's passage in 1970 may not be so years later.

- Few publishers will run newspapers at a loss for long. Owners of publicly held companies who will do that are even more scarce.

Lawrence is correct that closing JOAs has a negative impact on communities. Unquestionably, terminating joint ventures results in newspaper closings and loss of jobs. In addition, the death of a JOA newspaper decreases the amount of news and opinion provided to the community. Two newspapers publish more news than a single newspaper regardless of whether the survivor increases its coverage after gaining a monopoly. Another undesirable outcome is a loss of circulation in the former JOA market. Research indicates that some readers stop taking a newspaper after one of the competing papers ceases publication.

The editor of the *Journal Gazette* in Fort Wayne, Ind., claimed in a recent *Quill* article that the partnerships have preserved several family-owned and family-controlled newspaper companies. Even the most adamant advocates of group ownership seem to agree, according to Craig Klugman, that diversity among newspaper owners, which includes having a number of family newspapers, is a good thing.

Klugman is not alone. Coulson found in 1994 that most journalists working at JOA newspapers claimed that joint agencies have permitted two newspapers to publish in cities that probably otherwise would have a monopoly daily. This response may be largely explained by their impression that a JOA saved either the newspaper they worked for or its joint partner.

This position has some empirical support. In 1986, Blankenburg studied the patterns associated with the closing of afternoon newspapers. He estimated that a daily in at least five JOA markets would have closed had the NPA not been in existence.

Klugman also argued that the joint operating agreement he is involved in does promote editorial diversity. And he doubts Fort Wayne is unique. He contends that the city's readers have a choice — the JOA offers them distinct editorial voices and different approaches to the news.

Research supports his claim. Hicks and Featherston found readers of JOA newspapers in Shreveport, La., got distinct products in terms of appearance and non-duplicated content, although there were similarities in the general kinds of news published. Shreveport was the site of two other case studies about JOAs. In 1991, Sylvie looked at the coverage of the 1988 riots in Shreveport by the JOA papers. He found that while the JOA papers had some similar coverage, they also were noticeably different in some of the areas of emphasis.

The diversity of coverage continued in Shreveport even after one of the JOA papers closed because the surviving daily, the *Shreveport Times,* agreed to contin-ue publishing the *Shreveport Journal's* editorial page after the *Journal* closed. Sylvie and Mueller concluded that the diversity of editorial content in Shreveport during the JOA continued afterward as a result of the two editorial pages in the *Times.*

The diversity of editorial material found in Shreveport's JOA papers is con-sistent with a comparison Lacy conducted in 1984 of editorial pages in Albuquerque, Charleston, Knoxville, and San Francisco. Editorial pages at these four pairs of JOAs showed distinct differences in the types of content they emphasized.

But what about news coverage? Litman and Bridges found that JOA papers carried more news services than monopoly papers in their 1986 study of 101 dailies. Lacy's 1987 study of 114 dailies showed that JOA papers had more reporters and fewer square inches of copy per reporter than dailies with no direct competition. JOA newspapers also carried more wire services, had a higher percentage of 1) news and editorial material, 2) news section given to newshole, and 3) newshole given to in-depth coverage.

It would be difficult to argue that having a JOA results in perfect journal-ism, but research indicates that having a joint agency provides a greater financial commitment to news and a second editorial voice that would not have been available without the JOA.

Critics of JOAs

During the past decade, critics have begun to argue that the high profit goals of some publicly held corporations run counter to the Newspaper Preservation Act's goal of providing communities with editorial diversity. They claim that these corporations ignore the public benefits the act once provided and increasingly exploit the NPA for their economic advantage.

The most recent example cited is in Detroit. During the first few months of the recent labor conflict, the *Detroit News* and *Detroit Free Press* combined their editions. This allowed the newspapers to continue to publish until they could hire enough replacement workers to return to separate daily editions.

Operating the dailies together seems counter to the intent of the Newspaper Preservation Act, which requires separate editorial products. However, Gannett and Knight-Ridder amended their agreement to allow joint publication of the Detroit dailies in the event of strikes. The NPA does not state that JOAs should be granted to bust unions, but this could be the result of the amendment that was ignored until the strike.

Detroit is just one example where newspaper management has used special government treatment to serve its own ends. In Miami, the agreement resulted in the single-daily market it was supposed to prevent. A 1987 renegotiation of the Miami JOA allowed the owner of the *Miami News*, which was losing $9 million annually, to share the operating revenues of the prosperous *Miami Herald* whether or not the *News* was published. Furthermore, the *News'* share of the profits was extended from 1996 until 2021. It was reported in *Editor & Publisher* that the paper's owner could earn $300 million under the new arrangement, although this amount has been questioned by the *Miami Herald*'s David Lawrence, Jr. Press critic Stephen Barnett charged in *Columbia Journalism Review* that the *Miami News* was "rubbed out" as part of the "JOA endgame in which the owner of the weaker paper is paid to kill it off."

Many observers also were troubled by what happened in Pittsburgh in 1992. Scripps' *Pittsburgh Press* was sold during a prolonged strike to its smaller-circulation JOA partner, the *Post-Gazette*, whose owners promptly closed the *Press*. It was reported, however, that Scripps received other comparable bids for the *Press*, a claim that has been denied by managers at the *Post-Gazette*.

Gene Roberts, former managing editor of the *New York Times*, framed the JOA debate in a 1997 *Quill* article as the obligation of newspaper corporations to put out two newspapers for as long as the agreements last.

Because the Justice Department must rule that the public interest is served before a joint venture can be formed, Roberts said there should be comparable standards to disband a JOA.

"In at least two instances — Pittsburgh and Miami — we can deduce that newspaper corporations can get out of a JOA without a by-your-leave to the community or the Justice Department or anyone else," Roberts said in a 1997 interview. "If these corporations made convincing cases to get approval for a joint agency, they ought to be required to get similar approval before they kill one paper."

When newspaper management ignores the basic premise underlying JOAs — that a community needs diverse voices — and increases its profits by doing in one paper and sharing income from the remaining paper, it makes the NPA "an absolute farce," according to Roberts.

Critics also argue that a JOA creates a connection between the newspapers and the federal government that can have a harmful effect on press autonomy. While the Detroit JOA application was pending before former Attorney General Edwin Meese, Knight-Ridder's *Detroit Free Press* "killed editorial cartoons and toned down editorials" critical of his official conduct, according to Barnett in a 1991 article. He also contended that the chain's flagship paper, the *Miami Herald*, cooperated by instructing its editorial cartoonist "to lay off Meese." This incident suggests that lobbying for JOA designation can prevent the press from performing its role as an independent watchdog of government.

Of course, the potential for influence from the federal government is based on acquiring or renewing a JOA. If a newspaper does not seek a license, the federal government holds no leverage. Because few dailies will seek JOAs and many existing JOAs are not opting for renewals, it is unlikely that the NPA will result in federal government influence in the future.

Resolution

When the Newspaper Preservation Act was passed in 1970, daily newspapers primarily competed against other dailies located in the same retail trade zone. Today, dailies face competition from an array of print and electronic media for audience and advertising. Technology has changed the way people acquire news and information.

Many metropolitan dailies face well-entrenched weekly newspapers in their central city and in the suburbs. For instance, in 1998 the San Francisco market included four alternative weeklies, two African-American weeklies, two gay and lesbian weeklies, and ten ethnic weeklies, with a combined circulation of more than 750,000. Nationally, weekly newspaper circulation doubled from 1970 to 1990, and a study of Michigan counties outside Detroit found readers were willing to substitute weeklies for dailies at an increasing rate during the 1980s.

JOA newspapers are also facing competition from dailies in other cities. As daily newspaper penetration declined and middle-class readers moved to the suburbs during the 1970s, 1980s, and 1990s, regional daily competition grew. Dailies expanded their markets with wider distribution patterns and zoned editions. In 1988, 69 per cent of all counties in the United States had no fewer than two daily newspapers with at least a 5-per cent household penetration. The average number of dailies in these counties was 2.76.

In addition, changes in the newspaper business in the United States have been accompanied by growth in city and regional business magazines.

But changes in the print industry have been minor compared with those in the electronic media. Using microwave and satellite technology, local television newsrooms in large markets have increased the length of evening newscasts and expanded local coverage. Cable programming devoted to public affairs — such as C-SPAN, local government, and public access channels — is available on most cable systems. The country has more than 230 commercial radio news stations, and most public radio stations provide a variety of news and information programs.

Despite the recent growth and development of alternative news and information outlets, the local daily may face its stiffest competition from new forms of computer-generated electronic media. The growth of the World Wide Web continues to increase people's options for news. In 1997, 1,000 newspapers in the United States and more than 1,800 newspapers worldwide had versions on the Web. Analyst John Morton explained the potential this way in a 1996 article:

> It is a contest in which local television will be shunted aside as the primary newspaper competitor. Instead, we will see new forms of electronic media that will attack, more forcefully than local television was ever able to do, the basic franchise of the newspaper business — delivery, price-and-item advertising and reader-specific local information. This new competition will come from the telephone and cable television industries.

Just how substitutable these various outlets are for the local daily newspaper can be debated. However, the continuing downward trend in daily newspaper penetration indicates that people are getting information elsewhere. The important impact of media developments during the past thirty years is that the daily newspaper has seen a decline in its monopoly power over its market. In 1970, supporters of the Newspaper Preservation Act argued that the interests of the public would be harmed by the closing of the second daily in a city. Support for this argument will continue to erode as fiber optics and computer technology merge and computers make publishing cheaper, offering people a myriad of options for news and information.

The potential for corporate abuse of JOAs is real, but another potential for abuse exists. A proposed joint partnership in Manteca, Calif., several years ago showed that the vagueness of the Newspaper Preservation Act might result in its application to daily and weekly combinations. The weekly applicant shut down, and a final ruling on the request was never made, but critics and scholars see such a potential arrangement setting a dangerous precedent. They fear dailies could force weeklies into joint ventures and then use their combined market power as a barrier to new weeklies, which have emerged as dailies' main competitors in most larger cities.

Even more harmful would be the application of the Newspaper Preservation Act to joint agreements between two weeklies. Entry by new firms into the weekly segment of the newspaper industry remains possible. For example, in Michigan between 1980 and 1986, Lacy and Shikha Dalmia found that weeklies stopped circulating in thirty-three counties and started circulating in seventeen counties. Joint agencies between weeklies would prevent new entry by weeklies into a market and limit the diversity of voices.

The passage of time has helped to clarify the impact of joint operating agreements on communities and newspaper markets. It turns out that the critics and supporters of the NPA were both right and both wrong. It did not save the newspaper industry; neither did it destroy competition and ruin the newspaper industry.

Perhaps Cathleen Black, former president and chief executive of the Newspaper Association of America, portrayed the Act in its best light when she said: "To what extent and forever long that JOAs prolong the presence of two independent editorial voices in communities around the country, they are worthwhile."

JOAs have helped readers in some markets and hurt them in others. The overall impact on the industry has been limited to the twenty-six markets that have had joint ventures since 1970. It appears that few if any other cities will have JOAs in the future, unless weeklies and dailies begin to form agreements.

However, the Newspaper Preservation Act remains law, and as such it continues to generate debate mostly because of the occasional managerial abuses that occur. The reality is that the NPA no longer serves society. It should be abolished. Any future benefit that might come from the Act has faded with the disappearance of potential JOA markets and the decision of newspaper companies to end the arrangements at their convenience and without regard to the public welfare.

Repeal of the NPA would lessen the public perception that government policy promotes special interest legislation for the press. It also might indicate to the newspaper industry that the government and the public will not accept the flagrant exercise of government-approved monopoly power. To avoid negative economic repercussions, however, existing joint agencies should be allowed to continue operation provided the agreements are honored for the complete duration of the contract.

Some observers argue that it is unnecessary to repeal the NPA because it does not appear there will be more JOAs, but the potential for daily and weekly combinations and weekly JOAs continues as long as the law exists. It seems prudent to avoid the potential obstacle to new editorial voices in a community that non-daily combinations might pose.

The Newspaper Preservation Act exempts newspapers from some antitrust laws and was justified because it retained an additional community voice. However, in the years since the NPA became law, JOAs have become another element of market strategy. The government extended special privileges to newspapers for public service — not for use as a corporate tool.

Recommended Readings

Books

Busterna, John C., and Robert G. Picard. *Joint Operating Agreements: The Newspaper Preservation Act and Its Application.* Norwood, N.J.: Ablex, 1993. Provides extensive historical background and discussion of the legal underpinnings and consequences of the NPA.

Gruley, Bryan. *Paper Losses: A Modern Epic of Greed & Betrayal at America's Two Largest Newspaper Companies.* New York: Grove Press, 1993. Contends that the Detroit JOA between Gannett's *News* and Knight-Ridder's *Free Press* has done more harm than good. He points out that the changing nature of media have made JOAs unnecessary.

Articles & Book Chapters

Barnett, Stephen R. "The JOA Scam." *Columbia Journalism Review* 30 (November/December 1991): 47-8. The author maintains that while JOAs probably have preserved some newspapers, it's likely that they kill more competition, and more papers, than they save.

Busterna, John C. "Newspaper Preservation Act: To be or not to be — That is Irrelevant!" *Newspaper Research Journal* 14 (Summer-Fall 1993): 2-12. The author argues that competing newspapers can form joint operations very close to what is permitted under the

Newspaper Preservation Act without having to deal with the NPA, or the costly litigation involved in the act.

Coulson, David C. "Impact of JOAs on Newspaper Competition and Editorial Performance." *Mass Comm Review* 21 (1994): 236-49. Attempts to determine not only whether joint ventures were viewed by journalists at JOA newspapers as preventing the demise of a second daily but also what impact they were perceived as having on new newspaper competition and other papers competing in the same vicinity.

Coulson, David C., and Stephen Lacy. "It's time to repeal the NPA." *Quill* (April 1997): 36. Asserts that any future good that might come from the Newspaper Preservation Act has faded with the disappearance of potential JOA daily markets and the decision of newspaper corporations to end the arrangements at their convenience and without regard for the public welfare.

Giles, Robert H. "NPA Is No Panacea, But It Has Worked." *Quill* (January/February 1993): 17. The commentary offers the perspective of an insider who participated in the planning and implementation of the Detroit JOA. The former editor and publisher of the *Detroit News* believes his paper and the *Free Press* will become the prototype of the successful joint venture.

Klugman, Craig. "In Fort Wayne, it works." *Quill* (April 1997): 38-9. The article provides an editor's insight into how a small daily newspaper operates under a joint agency.

Lacy, Stephen. "Content of Joint Operation Newspapers." Pp. 147-60 in Robert Picard, et. al., eds., *Press Concentration and Monopoly: New Perspectives on Newspaper Ownership and Operation*. Norwood, N.J.: Ablex, 1988. Reviews the performance of joint operating agreements and presents empirical evidence concerning the underlying assumption that the partnerships will preserve a second editorial voice and affect news content.

Lacy, Stephen. "Impact of Repealing the Newspaper Preservation Act." *Newspaper Research Journal* 11 (Winter 1990): 2-11. The commentary holds that most JOA cities would lose one of their daily newspapers if the Newspaper Preservation Act were repealed. According to the author, the result would be decreased competition for news, and readers less well served by the surviving newspaper than they are now by two newspapers operating jointly.

Lawrence, David Jr. "Act has saved voices." *Quill* (April 1997): 38. The publisher and chairman of the *Miami Herald* offers a defense of the Newspaper Preservation Act based largely on the contention that it has preserved two editorial voices in seventeen cities.

Morton, John. "JOAs: No Guarantee of Saving a Paper." *American Journalism Review* (April 1996): 52. The column argues that joint operation — while preserving competitive editorial voices, sometimes for lengthy periods — often only delays the inevitable.

Naughton, Keith. "JOAs: Is it Time to Lay the Funeral Wreath?" *Quill* (January/February 1993): 15-16, 18. The major point of the article is that the cause of a JOA death is strikingly similar to the factors behind the demise of most of the 162 newspapers that have folded since the Newspaper Preservation Act was made law in 1970. Increased competition from radio, television, cable, and other media draws readers and advertisers away from at least one of the papers in a joint agency.

Picard, Robert G. "Evidence of a 'Failing Newspaper' Under the Newspaper Preservation Act." *Newspaper Research Journal* 9 (Fall 1987): 73-82. The article reviews tests under which the courts and the U.S. attorney general may rule in favor of a joint operating agreement for newspapers. It then considers how well five newspapers that have sought JOA status met the specified criteria.

Roberts, Gene. "First order of business." *Quill* (April 1997): 37. The former managing editor of the *New York Times* discusses what he sees as the "JOA scheme." First, newspaper publishers argue that the public good demands that cities have two competing daily newspapers. Then, for reasons other than community service — mainly for increased profit — some of the same publishers decide that each of their communities shall have one paper.

Sylvie, George. "A Study of Civil Disorder: The Effects of News Values and Competition on Coverage by Two Competing Daily Newspapers." *Newspaper Research Journal* 12 (Winter 1991): 98-113. This study of riot coverage in Shreveport in 1988 found that despite some similarities, the two JOA dailies provided distinctive content.

Wendover, Ed. "JOAs: Anti-trust for Everyone but Me." *Quill* (January/February 1993): 19. The author insists that the Newspaper Preservation Act was intended to save independent family-owned newspapers. But instead, it is used by some of the largest corporations listed on Wall Street to stifle competition and extract monopoly profits.

4 Legal Issues

The area of media law is one that has been particularly exciting in the past several years. New media, for example, have forced us to reexamine traditional media laws; and trends in news, entertainment, and advertising have led to new laws and legal battles as well.

This section addresses some of those changes, carefully explaining the statutes, administrative regulations, and court cases that make up our current laws. As always with media law, the First Amendment takes a center stage, placing itself at the heart of the following debates. Its guarantee of a free press, and of free expression for all Americans, seems to pit itself against a number of other rights and ideals.

The right to a fair trial, for example, has equally strong standing as a right guaranteed by the Sixth Amendment. As David Arant, a specialist in communication law, explains, these two rights have clashed a number of times in American history, and the clash continues today whenever an extremely high-profile court case threatens to become a media circus and thus bias the justice system by influencing juries and potential jurors. The nation thought it had witnessed the trial of the century when Bruno Hauptmann was tried and convicted for kidnapping and murdering the baby of national hero Charles Lindbergh. As we discovered in the 1990s, however, the "trial of the century" was yet to come. Professor Arant addresses the infamous O.J. Simpson trial, discusses the public demand for constant media coverage that accompanied the trial, and presents the timeless debate over which civil right should take precedence in an increasingly media-saturated society.

Pam Tidemann writes of the similar tension that exists between free speech and the individual's right of privacy. With an omnipresent media system, both legal and ethical questions arise concerning just where to draw the line between what is and is not "newsworthy."

In the realm of advertising, the First Amendment hasn't been quite as strong because, as the Supreme Court has viewed it, advertising concerns matters of commerce — which simply aren't as vital to a functioning democracy as political and social expression. In chapter sixteen, Frances Collins and Timothy Smith trace the rationale the Supreme Court used to justify this status quo. They then present the modern quandary of advertising "sin" products that are either unhealthy or potentially dangerous. In a modern American culture that requires citizens to wear bicycle helmets and seatbelts, many are concerned that regulations affecting alcohol and cigarettes may soon extend to unhealthy foods and pastimes.

A similar debate can be found regarding the huge amount of information — including questionable material such as hate speech and pornography — that surfers can find on the newest medium: the Internet. In "Censorship in Cyberspace," Amy Robinson outlines the birth and demise of the Communications Decency Act, which attempted to make sending indecent and patently offensive material to minors a crime. Although the Supreme Court in 1997 ruled that the CDA was unconstitutional, the debate regarding children's access to sexually explicit material on the Internet continues. As Ms. Robinson points out, this debate will continue until an acceptable resolution is reached.

Chapter Fourteen

The Free Press–
Fair Trial Conflict

M. David Arant

U.S. Supreme Court Justice Hugo Black wrote in *Bridges v. California* (1941), "Free press and fair trial are two of the most cherished policies in our civilization, and it would be a trying task to choose between them." The Bill of Rights provides explicit protections for its citizens — for freedom of the press on one hand, and for a speedy and public trial by an impartial jury on the other. The First Amendment states that "Congress shall make no law ... abridging the freedom of speech, or of the press...." The Sixth Amendment says, "In all prosecutions, the accused shall enjoy the right to a speedy and public trial by an impartial jury." These constitutional protections have collided when the press covers crime and resulting criminal trials; and in an attempt to reduce the impact of prejudicial publicity on the defendant's right to a fair trial, the courts restrict press freedom. When media coverage has created prejudicial publicity, criminal defendants have appealed to higher courts to have their convictions reversed. To prevent publicity from affecting trials, judges have tried to limit coverage by restricting media access to the courtroom and lawyers' freedom to discuss the trial. And in a few rare instances, courts have imposed restraining orders to keep the press from publishing information about the trial.

The opening of many state courtrooms to electronic media has raised another important issue in the free press–fair trial debate: the impact of television cameras on a trial. In the aftermath of the O.J. Simpson trial, many have suggested that the intense media spotlight on the trial affected the outcome. In reaction to the Simpson trial, many judges have closed their courtrooms to cameras, and others have called for the press to exercise greater responsibility in reporting criminal prosecutions. When the media transmit images of sensational trials throughout the community and the nation, can a defendant get a trial by an impartial jury? Should cameras be banned because televised court proceedings create distractions that alter the trial and increase potential for juror prejudice?

This chapter explores these and other conflicts between the First

Amendment right to receive and report information about a trial and the Sixth Amendment guarantee of a fair trial to those accused of criminal activity. The chapter considers the three sides in this conflict: the defendant's Sixth Amendment right to a fair trial, the media's First Amendment right to cover criminal trials, and the courts' attempts to balance these rights. Then the chapter addresses these questions: Should the right to a fair trial take precedence over press freedom? Or is there no circumstance when fair trial concerns should be used to limit the free press guarantee? And do the media, which enjoy an almost absolute freedom to publish information about criminal and civil trials, have a moral obligation to restrict their own accounts in the interest of fair trials?

Origins of the Issue

The framers of the U.S. Constitution believed that a trial open to the public and the media increased accountability and thus the likelihood of a fair trial. The framers viewed public trials as a means of ensuring justice to the defendant in contrast to the evils of secret judicial deliberations, such as the Star Chamber court of seventeenth-century England, notorious for its secret sessions, lack of juries, and harsh judgments.

Crime and criminal trials have had a prominent place in news reporting since the earliest mass media publications. Especially sensational crimes have attracted widespread press attention. The early penny press publications were filled with reports of murder and mayhem, and later in the nineteenth century many newspapers were so eager to report the latest news of sensational crimes that reporters tried to get ahead of the police and solve the crimes themselves.

When a heightened concern for the rights of the accused emerged in the twentieth century, participants in the criminal justice system began to react to the impact of press coverage on the defendant's right to a fair trial. In 1935, when Bruno Richard Hauptmann was convicted of the kidnapping and murder of Charles Lindbergh's infant son, the media frenzy easily compared to that surrounding the Simpson trial. Media obsession with details of the case cast shadows on court decorum and the trial's fairness. Five film companies managed to sneak movie cameras onto the courtroom balcony in Flemington, N.J., apparently without the judge's knowledge. Before the trial was over, newsreels of the courtroom action were running in movie theaters across the nation.

The Lindbergh trial, *the* trial of the first half of the century in terms of press attention, provoked a backlash against excessive and intrusive media coverage of trials. Afterwards, the American Bar Association recommended a ban on cameras in courtrooms that lasted for about thirty years.

The difficulty in formulating a proper balance in the fair trial vs. free press issue was illustrated by a series of standards issued by the American Bar Association. In 1966, after another sensational murder trial, this one involving murder suspect Sam Sheppard, the ABA adopted the report of its Reardon Committee on Fair Trial and Free Press, which contained stringent restrictions on the release of crime news to the press. In 1978 another ABA committee issued a new set of free press–fair trial standards that came down more heavily on the free-press side of the balance. Then, in 1991, a third formulation of ABA standards for free press–fair trial sought a middle ground and incorporated the legal standards of the 1980s cases establishing the public's right of access to the courtroom.

The 1994-1995 murder trial of sports legend O.J. Simpson reignited the debate about the negative impact of intense media scrutiny on impartial deliberation in the interest of justice for the accused. In a survey of lawyers during Simpson's trial, most lawyers said that extensive media coverage of a criminal case jeopardizes the defendant's right to a fair trial and that Simpson was less likely to get a fair trial because of media publicity.

The Criminal Defendant's Perspective

For the criminal defendant, who faces a verdict that might take away his freedom or even his life, press freedom to cover his trial is a secondary consideration. Primarily, the defendant wants a trial setting that will be most conducive to his acquittal. The main problem that media publicity creates for a fair trial is the prejudicing of potential or actual jurors. The free press–fair trial conflict occurs when jurors do not base their verdict solely on the courtroom evidence but are instead influenced by pretrial publicity or the trial coverage itself. Potential jurors might be exposed to the information before the trial begins and be excluded from selection during *voir dire*, the questioning of potential jurors.

This was an issue in the jury selection for the murder trial of Timothy McVeigh, accused of the 1995 bombing of the Alfred P. Murrah Federal Building in Oklahoma City, and the deaths of 168 people. During the jury selection, several members of the jury pool acknowledged that they had learned in the media of an alleged confession by McVeigh. The *Dallas Morning News* somehow obtained the confession from defense files and published it just before jury selection began. McVeigh's lawyer denied that the defendant ever made such a confession. On an ABC *Nightline* broadcast that spring, criminal defense lawyer Elisabeth Semel said she found the media's publication of McVeigh's confession to be offensive. She believed that the extensive pretrial publicity would make an impartial jury difficult to find.

An impartial jury, the kind guaranteed in the Sixth Amendment, is one that is able to decide a case based solely on the evidence presented in the courtroom. When exposed to extensive media coverage, jurors might get accurate or inaccurate information about the crime, information that is not part of the courtroom testimony. Certain information, such as confessions by the defendant, his or her previous criminal record, pretrial lie detector tests, or evidence gathered illegally (including forced confessions), might be inadmissible in the actual trial. With additional information obtained outside the courtroom, jurors might vote to convict a defendant they would have otherwise acquitted.

Another problem created by intense media scrutiny is public and media pressure on the judge, prosecutor, and jury to convict the defendant. In some jurisdictions, judges and prosecutors are elected officials who must maintain popular support to remain in their offices. Even when judges and prosecutors are appointed, media publicity might affect the outcome of a trial. Appointed prosecutors might have aspirations to elected offices, and a televised trial could be a launching pad for a political campaign. Public opinion about a trial can be very powerful. For example, after a jury failed to convict four Los Angeles police officers of police brutality against Rodney King, dissatisfied Los Angeles citizens rioted. After escaping these state criminal charges, the officers were tried in a federal court for violating King's civil rights. Many Los Angeles residents feared that if the defendants were not found guilty in this second trial, another riot would erupt. In the federal trial, two of the police officers were found guilty of violating King's civil rights.

Another threat to the defendant's fair-trial right is the tactic of trying the case in the court of public opinion rather than simply the court of law. In the Simpson trial, the defense and prosecution were constantly appearing in the media, trying to sway the public to support their positions. Some judges have imposed gag orders on attorneys in highly publicized trials. In the civil suit brought by the families of murder victims Nicole Brown Simpson and Ronald Goldman against O.J. Simpson, the California Superior Court judge ordered the lawyers in the case to refrain from talking to the media.

Thus, when media coverage threatens to become excessive and prejudicial, a judge is obligated to stem the problems. But judges can employ one of a variety of means to limit the effect of publicity without infringing on the First Amendment rights of the press: change of venue, continuance, sequestration, *voir dire*, and admonition are all acceptable alternatives. Change of venue involves moving the trial to another part of the state in which the pretrial publicity is not widespread. A continuance is a delay of the trial while the publicity dies down. Sequestering the jurors prevents them from prejudicial media exposure during the actual trial. Conducting intense *voir dire*, jury questioning to weed out those affected by publicity, can also be effective. Jurors can also be admonished to disregard prejudicial information and decide the case based only on evidence presented at trial. A gag order on trial participants is sometimes used as well, when judges order court employees, police officers, lawyers, or witnesses not to discuss the case with the press.

Judges can also keep the press from publishing some incriminating information. If certain information might have a prejudicial effect on potential jurors, a judge can order the press not to publish what it learned about the defendant's past crimes, coerced confessions, or lie detector tests.

Another remedy to prevent prejudicial publicity is for the defense to ask the judge to close the courtroom. If judges cannot stop the media from publishing what they learn, then why not cut the flow of information to the press? Some judges have actually kicked the press and the public out of the courtroom when prejudicial information was being presented in pretrial hearings.

If the defense cannot exclude the media and public entirely, it can recommend barring cameras from the courtroom to limit information going to the public and thus prevent sensational coverage. Usually the defense attorney does not want a client's trial broadcast. An outspoken critic of courtroom cameras, defense attorney Gerry Spence says cameras change courtroom dynamics and present a false picture of the U.S. justice system. For most of the last sixty years Americans have not seen photographic or televised coverage of trials. For many years all they saw were artists' drawings of court proceedings because the courts had determined that the presence of cameras and recorders in the courtroom deprived criminal defendants of their Sixth Amendment rights.

In 1937, just two years after the sensational trial of Bruno Hauptmann, the American Bar Association recommended banning cameras because they detracted from the dignity of the court proceeding, degraded the court, and created misconceptions among the public. The federal courts and most state courts adopted rules banning cameras from the courtrooms.

Today, with cameras that are smaller and quieter, most states have reopened their courtrooms to the devices. In 1996 forty-seven states provided some access to cameras in courtrooms. While the U.S. Supreme Court allows cameras in state courts, it has not found any constitutional right of camera access. Therefore, most federal courts and some state courts remain off limits to cameras. In 1996 only two circuits of the U.S. Court of Appeals opened their appellate arguments to cameras. At the federal district or trial court level, cameras are barred in criminal cases, and only two district courts allow cameras in civil cases.

The American Civil Liberties Union, which has been a champion of both First Amendment rights and the rights of those accused of crimes, has adopted a policy supporting media access to all judicial proceedings, except when there is clear and convincing evidence of a specific danger to a competing fundamental liberty, such as a fair trial for the defendant, and no alternative exists to protect that right. The one exception to this rule in the ACLU policy is that in a criminal case, the accused should have an absolute right to exclude all broadcast coverage of any proceedings.

Empirical research provides some support that Sixth Amendment rights are damaged by prejudicial publicity. In *Chandler v. Florida* (1981), Chief Justice Warren Burger suggested that proof of prejudice must be offered by a defendant appealing his conviction because of cameras in the courtroom. Although defense attorneys have argued for closure of pretrial hearings based on the assumption of jury prejudice, only recently have empirical studies attempted to document the impact of prejudicial publicity. In "A Journey into the Unknown: Pretrial Publicity and Capital Cases," Sandys and Chermak found that the empirical evidence of the impact of prejudicial publicity on fair trials and the efficacy of procedural safeguards remains inconclusive. But twenty-three out of thirty studies they reviewed showed some evidence that pretrial publicity is prejudicial. A 1991 study by Norbert Kerr and others found that jury deliberation did not remedy but rather magnified publicity-induced bias.

In a 1970 survey, Fred Siebert found that many judges relied heavily on jury admonition and *voir dire* to minimize jury bias in high-publicity cases. However, a 1990 study by Geoffrey Kramer and others showed that judicial admonitions were ineffective on jury deliberations and argued that continuances may be the only means to protect defendants against adverse pretrial publicity.

In "Free Press–Fair Trial: Can They Be Reconciled in a Highly Publicized Criminal Court?" Stabile suggests that when a compromise between First and Sixth Amendment rights is necessary to prevent "a defendant's rights to a fair trial from being overrun by unrestrained media coverage ... an accommodation of these rights should favor the fair-trial rights of the individual over the media's rights to freedom of expression." Stabile proposes that the best way to achieve the balance is a ban on extrajudicial statements by trial participants when those statements present a clear and present danger to the defendant's right to a fair trial. Criminal defendants facing the loss of their freedom and even their lives make a strong case that their trials should be protected from the effects of prejudicial publicity by whatever means necessary.

The Free Press—Fair Trial Conflict

The Media's Case

The media, on the other hand, reject the arguments that when the Sixth and First Amendments collide, freedom of the press must give way. Journalists often argue that they represent the public's right to know and, in fact, have characterized themselves as the public's surrogate in the courtroom. In the above ABC *Nightline* broadcast, Reporters Committee for Freedom of the Press attorney Jane Kirtley said, "I think that the press gets into a lot of trouble if it tries to become the guarantor of somebody's right to a fair trial. That's not the role of the press. The role of the press is to report the news as it sees it as accurately and fairly as it can."

The news media have also argued that it is the judge's responsibility to ensure a fair trial but not at the expense of their right of access and right to publish. Journalists do not object to the judicial remedies, such as *voir dire*, that have little or no impact on their First Amendment rights. However, they reject the use of gag orders on either the press or the trial's participants, as well as restrictions on press access to the courtroom. In their brief in *Nebraska Press Association v. Stuart* (1976), attorneys for the press association argued against the Nebraska courts' assumption that the Sixth Amendment trumped the First Amendment. "Except in the most exceptional case," they said, "carefully selected jurors are fully able to exercise their independent judgment of guilt or innocence based on the evidence introduced in court, whether or not they have read or heard about the case before." Careful *voir dire*, they argued, is usually sufficient to seat a jury capable of rendering a fair verdict.

In his brief for the media side in *Richmond Newspapers v. Virginia* (1980), Harvard law professor Lawrence Tribe asserted that the Court should not allow the defendant's Sixth Amendment interests to overcome the independent public interest in an open courtroom. The public trial assures the victims of crime that justice is served, he wrote, and unless the trial is open, the people "can have no assurance that any of the Constitution's other guarantees for fair trial and due process of law are being complied with." Also, the open courtroom provides the public with information about how the criminal justice system functions.

Friendly and Goldfarb maintain that because both of these liberties are fundamental ones, neither can be absolute, and yet citizens cannot accept the diminution of either one. A free press serves the cause of justice by providing public scrutiny far more than it hinders it through prejudicial publicity. Friendly and Goldfarb suggest that because the conflict between these two rights is limited, usually to the occasional, sensational case, the remedy to the problem should be a limited one as well.

One legal analyst, who has consistently articulated strong support of First Amendment rights, has suggested that choosing to protect one right instead of another is a false choice. Former Oregon Supreme Court Justice Hans Linde argued that the courts should not choose between the two but should fully protect both. In "Fair Trials and Press Freedom — Two Rights Against the State," Linde said that "there is nothing unique, in principle, about freedom of the press to write about law enforcement, trials and courts as distinct from any other facet of government. You must insist on that freedom here if you want to save it for any other purpose." It is wrong for the government to take two rights that the Bill of Rights guarantees to individuals, such as fair trial and free press, and trade them off against each other, Linde argued. The government has an obligation to protect both the defendant's right to a fair trial as well as freedom of the press. The government cannot sacrifice the rights of the defendant to protect the rights of the press or vice versa. Therefore, no constitutional conflict exists between fair trial and free press. If the government cannot provide a fair trial to defendants while respecting press freedom, then it must let defendants go.

In "Cameras Belong in the Courtroom," Steve Brill, founder of Court TV, emphasized that cameras in the courtroom provide the public with effective access to judicial proceedings. Because the public has little chance of physically attending trials due to severely limited space in high-profile cases and the difficulty of getting to the courthouse even when space is available, televising a trial is the only way to ensure the public its right of access. Cameras offer the public the opportunity to see whether justice is served and thus counter rumors and speculation. Brill concludes that studies show that camera coverage has not impeded the process of justice or negatively affected the participants.

ABC News correspondent Catherine Crier told a National Judicial College conference on the media and the courts that cameras in the courtroom are not a problem when they portray the actual trial. However, in the Simpson trial, the media were too concerned with looking for a story that would sell in order to keep its audience. Crier said that instead of an accurate portrayal of the murder trial unfolding, the public was entertained with information about attorneys' personal lives, including prosecuting attorney Marcia Clark's hair.

Although some empirical research on jury prejudice indicates that judicial admonitions do not remedy the effects of prejudicial publicity, Robb Jones has maintained that the basis of this research is artificial. In these studies the admonition was on a video tape shown to a mock jury. In a real trial, Jones argues, jurors would take the judge's admonition against prejudice more seriously. According to Jones, other empirical studies on jury prejudice use simple, artificial methods, such as exposing mock jurors to prejudicial information, and do not show how actual media coverage of a pretrial hearing impacts potential jurors. Prejudicial information revealed in a pretrial hearing is usually already public and available to the media. Judicial remedies such as *voir dire*, change of venue, and continuance are effective in countering the effects of publicity, Jones has concluded.

Several states conducted studies about the impact of cameras in the courtroom as they began to reintroduce cameras in the 1970s and 1980s. Twenty-three of the twenty-four states conducting studies concluded that cameras did not alter the behavior of judges and attorneys. As part of the 1992 rewrite of its free press–fair trial standards, the ABA found that, according to recent empirical studies, pretrial publicity does not have the profound and pervasive effect it was once thought to have. The overall body of empirical research does not provide clear support for court decisions that limit press freedoms in the interest of fair trials.

The Supreme Court's Balancing Act

The U.S. Supreme Court has articulated its deep concern about the impact of pretrial publicity upon the Sixth Amendment guarantee of a fair trial by an impartial jury. In its landmark 1966 decision, *Sheppard v. Maxwell*, the Court expressed disapproval of the media frenzy that surrounded a high-profile murder case. In the Sheppard trial, similar to the Simpson case in the nature of the crime and intense media coverage, a Cleveland osteopath was charged with brutally murdering his wife, who was pregnant with the couple's second child. Sam Sheppard claimed to have been asleep on the couch when a bushy-haired intruder broke in and murdered his wife. Sheppard said he was knocked out when he confronted his wife's assailant and woke up the next morning without his shirt. There was no evidence of an intruder, and the media reported that Sheppard was having an affair. The press and the public were skeptical of Sheppard's story and anxious for the police to make an arrest. The *Cleveland Press* even published a front-page editorial titled "Getting Away with Murder" and a week later ran another inflammatory headline, "Why Isn't Sam Sheppard in Jail?" Police arrested him the next day.

When Sheppard's case came to trial, the press hounded the participants. The judge told a reporter that Sheppard was "guilty as hell" and allowed the press to sit at a table inside the bar of the courtroom. The judge failed to protect the privacy of jury deliberations. Both the judge and the prosecutor were up for election to judgeships, which might have made them susceptible to media pressure for a conviction.

When it reviewed the case, the Supreme Court reversed the conviction on the grounds that Sheppard had been denied a fair trial. The Court did so without requiring proof that the jury's verdict had been prejudiced by publicity; it just assumed improper publicity had created prejudice. Sheppard was in jail for twelve years before the Court reversed his conviction. After a new trial in which he was represented by a young F. Lee Bailey, Sheppard was acquitted.

The Court said the trial court judge had erred because he had not used his power to control the proceedings and the publicity surrounding the case. It recommended that judges use their powers to mitigate prejudicial publicity with continuances, changes of venue, careful jury selections, and admonitions to the jury to disregard extrajudicial information.

In *Sheppard* the Supreme Court criticized the judge for doing nothing to counter the prejudicial publicity. On the other hand, in *Nebraska Press Association*, the Court said the judge did *too much* to protect the Sixth Amendment rights of the accused when he imposed a restraining order to stop the press from publishing prejudicial material. After a Nebraska state court judge imposed a gag order on the media about what they could publish concerning a sensational rape and murder trial, the Supreme Court overturned the restraining order as a violation of the First Amendment. The Court said that "pretrial publicity — even pervasive, adverse publicity — does not inevitably lead to an unfair trial." In his opinion for the Court, Chief Justice Burger said that although none of the Court's previous prior restraint cases involved restrictive orders to protect a defendant's right to a fair trial, they all had the common thread that "prior restraints on speech and publication are the most serious and the least tolerable infringement on First Amendment rights." The press, in publishing information about criminal trials, played an important role in the judicial process by subjecting officials to public scrutiny and guarding against miscarriage of justice.

Burger said that although the plaintiffs wanted the Court to assign priorities between First and Sixth Amendment rights, the Court could not assign a priority applicable in all circumstances. To decide if preventing the evil done to Sixth Amendment interests by pretrial publicity should take priority over the injury to First Amendment protection against prior restraints, Burger offered a three-step test to determine whether "the gravity of the evil, discounted by its improbability, justifies such invasion of free speech as is necessary to avoid the danger." He said in order to assess whether prejudicial publicity presented a clear and present danger that might require infringing on First Amendment protections, the courts should examine the evidence to determine 1) "the nature and extent of pretrial publicity," 2) "whether other measures would be likely to mitigate the effects of unrestrained pretrial publicity," and 3) "how effectively a restraining order would operate to prevent the threatened danger."

In applying the test, Chief Justice Burger found that the Nebraska trial judge's judgment that pretrial publicity would endanger a fair trial was speculative and that the judge had made no specific findings that other measures to ensure a fair trial would not work. The Court found that a restraining order on the press would not prevent publicity about the trial from spreading throughout a small town. Burger said that the order's ban on publication of what the press learned at an open, preliminary hearing was unlawful. "[O]nce a public hearing had been held," he wrote, "what transpired there could not be subject to prior restraint." Finally, he maintained that the restraining order was defective in another respect: its prohibition against publication of "implicative" information was "too vague and too broad to survive the scrutiny we have given to restraints on First Amendment rights." Burger said that the Court's decision did not rule out prior restraint in every instance of pretrial publicity, but illustrated the difficulty of showing the heavy burden of proof necessary to justify the restraint. "We reaffirm that the guarantees of freedom of expression are not an absolute prohibition under all circumstances, but the barriers to prior restraint remain high and the presumption against its use continues intact," Burger concluded.

The Supreme Court has also sided with the press on the right of access to the courtroom. When faced with closure in criminal trials in the 1970s and 1980s, the press appealed the closure orders to the Court and won. In these cases, the Court established for the public and the press a strong constitutional right of access to criminal trials. Beginning with *Richmond Newspapers, Inc. v. Virginia* (1980), the Court recognized that the First Amendment embodied a right of access to the courtroom. Although no majority could agree on a single opinion, seven Justices agreed to overturn a state statute authorizing trial closure at the unfettered discretion of the judge or at the request of the parties in the trial because the law violated the public's right to attend criminal trials. In rulings on the First Amendment right of access to criminal proceedings after its initial decision in *Richmond Newspapers*, the Court has followed the two-part test developed by Justice Brennan in his concurrence in that case: a historical tradition of openness to the government function and the value of openness to the government process itself. Those wishing to deny access must provide compelling reasons to justify closure and must show that the closure was narrowly drawn and no alternatives existed. In subsequent cases, the Court established the presumption of openness for the public and press not only to the trial itself but also to preliminary hearings and *voir dire.*

Another way the courts have attempted to protect a fair trial from the impact of media coverage of the judicial process is by banning cameras and recording devices from courtrooms. In the 1950s and 1960s some state courts were permitting cameras in their courtrooms. The state of Texas, which in the early 1960s tried Billy Sol Estes for swindling investors, allowed television and still cameras in the courtroom. The sensational trial of this friend of President Lyndon Johnson created massive pretrial publicity. Estes' pretrial hearing was carried live on radio and television. The bulky television cameras were a prominent distraction in the courtroom; cables and wires were everywhere, and photographers roamed the courtroom. Estes appealed his conviction on the grounds that the presence of cameras in the courtroom had deprived him of his Sixth Amendment right to a fair trial. In 1965 the Supreme Court agreed with Estes and ordered a new trial. Estes was convicted again.

The Court said the presence of the cameras created several problems. First, it was concerned about the impact of the cameras on the jurors. It feared the jurors would be distracted or would feel pressured by their neighbors to render the popular verdict. The Court said cameras could jeopardize the chance of impaneling a second jury if a retrial was necessary. Second, the Court feared cameras would affect witness testimony. Witnesses might refuse to testify before the cameras or be affected by the testimony of previous witnesses. Third, the Court was concerned about the burden on the judge to control the cameras.

The Supreme Court decision in *Estes v. Texas* was used for two decades to keep cameras out of courtrooms. The Court refused to accept the argument that its ruling discriminated against broadcast journalists. It said any reporter could be in the courtroom — and each one could use the same news gathering tools. The Court did not require specific evidence of prejudice created by the cameras but rather presumed it from the circumstances. Although a majority of the Court did not agree that cameras should *never* be allowed in the courtroom, the case was widely interpreted this way by the lower courts.

As cameras became smaller and quieter, and thus less intrusive, some states began allowing cameras in the courtroom again in the late 1970s and early 1980s. Two criminal defendants convicted in a trial, about three minutes of which had been televised, challenged their convictions on the grounds that the televised coverage had deprived them of their Sixth Amendment right to a fair trial. In its *Chandler v. Florida* decision, the Supreme Court ruled that *Estes* was not an absolute constitutional ban on broadcast coverage of trials and did not bar states from experimenting with cameras in the courtroom. The risk of juror prejudice did not always justify a ban on broadcast coverage. The Court said it would not assume cameras impaired the judicial process but would require proof of the prejudicial impact of cameras in the courtroom. While not explicitly overruling *Estes*, the Court said that this case did not involve the same kind of circus atmosphere that occurred in *Estes*, and that there was no evidence this jury was exposed to sensational media coverage.

The debate about the harm caused by cameras in the courtroom resurfaced during the Simpson trial, open to media pool cameras. In its aftermath, Judge Robert Payant, president of the National Judicial College, said that the public received a skewed view of the criminal justice system from the Simpson trial. Likewise South Carolina Judge William Howard, who presided over the trial of Susan Smith for the murder of her children, said that he excluded cameras from his courtroom because they distracted the attorneys, increased the length of their arguments, and raised the level of anxiety in the courtroom.

Resolution

Because empirical studies do not provide consistent and definitive findings about the impact of media publicity on the courtroom and the efficacy of judicial remedies for prejudicial publicity, no easy conclusion can be drawn about the need to sacrifice freedom of the press in the interest of preserving a fair trial. The courts in the decisions cited above as well as many legal commentators have suggested that what is needed is a balance between these two rights.

In its cases involving the tensions between the First Amendment rights of the press to publish without government restraint versus the Sixth Amendment right of the defendant to a fair trial, the Supreme Court has not really reconciled the fair trial–free press conflict. All it has done is suggest there may be some restrictions on press access and publication in extraordinary situations. In the cases it has examined, the Court has not found many situations to merit limitations on the press.

However, the conflict of interests cannot simply be analyzed in terms of legal rights. Journalists must also consider the moral dimension of the free press–fair trial issue. On the one hand, the media are supposed to promptly publish what they know when it comes to matters of public interest and importance. On the other hand, the media share responsibility as citizens to protect the integrity of the criminal justice system.

Although, under the law, journalists have almost unlimited protection against prior restraint of publication and substantial protection against punishment in publishing almost any truthful information lawfully obtained about criminal activity, journalists can choose to withhold certain information in the interest of justice. That is, to protect the defendant's right to a fair trial, some journalists have decided not to publish confessions or criminal records of the accused. The 1996 Society of Professional Journalists Code of Ethics reminds journalists that although it is legal to publish, journalists may make ethical decisions not to publish certain information to protect the interest of a fair trial. The code includes under its "Minimize Harm" section the admonition to "balance a criminal suspect's fair trial rights with the public's right to be informed."

For journalists it is difficult not to publish legally obtained, factual information about a crime and the subsequent trial. For example, some bar–press guidelines suggest that journalists never publish defendants' confessions before a trial. However, publishing a confession only becomes a problem when it is declared inadmissible because it was obtained illegally, such as being coerced by law officers. If a confession is found to be coerced, the report of the confession is especially important to the public: law enforcement officials are using a heavy hand against a defendant. Not publishing the confession might serve to shield official misconduct from public scrutiny or at least minimize awareness of the abuse of power by the police. The impact of covering up abuse of power is worse than the potential prejudicial impact of published confessions on jurors.

Although it is difficult for journalists to withhold accurate information about crime and criminal trials from the public, those who publish unsubstantiated information about a criminal investigation, information that turns out to be false, engage in the worst type of dissemination of prejudicial information. On several occasions during the Simpson investigation and trial, media outlets published unsubstantiated information in an attempt to get the story first. Most of the problems of media coverage that Judge Lance Ito criticized in the trial arose from inaccurate publications. When the media tried to get ahead of the story, to scoop the competition, they reported many inaccuracies that could have tainted potential jurors.

In the 1997 trial of Timothy McVeigh, the *Dallas Morning News* published an alleged confession by McVeigh, in which he claimed to have bombed the building on a weekday to maximize the body count. The newspaper's editors refused to explain how it got the confession but assured the public that the information was gained lawfully and through routine newsgathering techniques. McVeigh's lawyer suggested the confession was a hoax or a fabricated document used when interviewing witnesses. The story about the confession was published nationally, and the public was left with the impression that this confession might have been leaked by insiders in the defense attorney's office or obtained through access to the defense attorney's computers. But the public, and the potential jurors, did not know what to believe about its existence.

Because the Dallas paper published the confession without being able to provide its source or verification of its authenticity, it acted irresponsibly. Essentially, the Dallas editors were asking the public to trust their judgment that the confession was authentic, although they would not or could not explain how they received the information or how they knew the confession was legitimate. If the Dallas newspaper believed that by publishing the confession the defendant would have no chance of getting a fair trial, then perhaps the editors should have delayed the publication until a jury was impaneled.

However, there is no reason why a court in this case, or any high-profile case, cannot find people who have not read or heard about the confession, or are able to put aside the prejudicial information and consider only the evidence presented in the courtroom. U.S. District Judge Richard Matsch rejected McVeigh's request to delay his trial in light of the media publicity about the confession. He said he was confident that a fair-minded jury would be impaneled and render a just verdict based on the law and evidence presented to it.

To protect the fair trial guarantees as well as the nation's concern for a free press, trial participants and media practitioners should renew their commitment to the integrity of the system of justice as well as the preservation of the press and public rights to attend and report on criminal trials. For the media's part, they should not publish unsubstantiated rumors. And the lawyers should try their cases in the courtroom and not use the media to sway the public to their side. The courts should not restrict media and public access to the courtroom, including cameras, except in the most exceptional situations. Broadcasting trials enhances the judicial process. Broadcast coverage of trials provides a more complete presentation than do journalistic reports, which by their very nature are selective presentations of what happened in the courtroom. Judges and attorneys under the camera's eye are more likely to be professional in their practice of law. Although a few witnesses may be intimidated by the thought of cameras in the courtroom, today's inconspicuous, wall-mounted cameras are soon forgotten by trial participants.

Certainly there are a few extraordinary instances when coverage of a trial might have to be limited. In some trials, the identity of a witness might need to be shielded. Assignment of pseudonyms, blurring the camera's image, or even a temporary closure might be in order to protect young sexual assault victims on the witness stand, for example. However, the norm of openness in the courtroom, as the Supreme Court has clearly established in the past two decades, need not fall to concerns about juror prejudice. We should not sacrifice one constitutional right, the press and the public right to attend trials, for another, the defendant's right to a fair trial.

Unfortunately we must also tolerate the ethical lapses of thoughtless, success-hungry journalists who ignore the concerns of fair trial in their higher allegiance to ratings and profit and who pander gossip and infotainment along with factual information about a trial. We must resist the urge to corral these journalists by restricting access to all journalists and their cameras. A steady flow of information from the nation's courtrooms is the best antidote to the skewed presentations of the system of justice, such as that created in the Simpson trial. Ultimately, it is the public trials, including televised trials, that ensure a public informed and justice served.

Recommended Readings

Books

American Bar Association. *ABA Standards for Criminal Justice, Fair Trial, Free Press*. Chicago: American Bar Association, 1992. Contains the most recent ABA recommendations on coverage of criminal trials.

American Bar Association. *The Rights of Fair Trial and Free Press*. Chicago: American Bar Association, 1968. Contains ABA recommendations on coverage of criminal trials adopted from a report of its advisory committee chaired by Paul C. Reardon.

Freedman, Warren. *Press and Media Access to the Criminal Courtroom*. New York: Quorum Books, 1988. Argues for access for the press and its cameras to all phases of criminal trials as well as urges responsible coverage by the press.

Friendly, Alfred, and Ronald L. Goldfarb. *Crime and Publicity: The Impact of News on the Administration of Justice*. New York: Twentieth Century Fund, 1967. Contends that protecting a fair trial is the responsibility of the courts and lawyers, not of the press, whose job it is to disseminate information. On the other hand, the press might refrain from publishing prejudicial characterizations and gratuitous judgments.

Gerald, J. Edward. *News of Crime: Courts and Press in Conflict*. Westport, Conn.: Greenwood Press, 1983. Examines American Bar Association guidelines to protect fair trials as well as press efforts to establish standards for reporting crime and criminal trials.

National Conference of Lawyers and Representatives of the Media. *The Reporter's Key: Rights of Fair Trial and Free Press*. Chicago: American Bar Association, 1994. This handbook analyzes the ABA Fair Trial/Free Press Standards from the media's perspective.

Siebert, Fred S., Walter Wilcox, and George Hough III. *Free Press and Fair Trial: Some Dimensions of the Problem*. Athens: University of Georgia Press, 1970. Prejudicial publicity is most commonly addressed through jury admonition and intense *voir dire*.

Articles

Brill, Steven. "Cameras Belong in the Courtroom." *USA Today Magazine* 125 (July 1996): 52. The founder of Court TV discusses the advantages of courtroom cameras.

Castenada, Laura. "O.J., other high profile cases benefit from Court TV, but controversy over televised trials is renewed." *Dallas Morning News*, 22 October 1995, 1H. Traces the success of Court TV and offers views of those for and against courtroom broadcasts.

Kerr, Norbert L., Geoffrey P. Kramer, John S. Carroll, and James Alfini. "On the Effectiveness of Voir Dire in Criminal Cases with Prejudicial Pretrial Publicity: An Empirical Study." *American University Law Review* 40 (1991): 665-91. Jury deliberation did not remedy but magnified publicity-induced bias.

Kramer, Geoffrey P., Norbert L. Kerr, and John S. Carroll. "Pretrial Publicity, Judicial Remedies and Jury Bias." *Law and Human Behavior* 14 (1990): 409-34. Judicial admonitions were ineffective on jury deliberations and a continuance might be the best way to protect against adverse pretrial publicity.

Jones, Robb M. "The Latest Studies on Pretrial Publicity, Jury Bias, and Judicial Remedies — Not Enough to Overcome the First Amendment Right of Access to Pretrial Hearings." *American University Law Review* 40 (1991): 841-8. Because empirical studies of juror prejudice based on mock juries are fragmentary in their findings and fail to recreate the real criminal trial setting, courts cannot draw definitive conclusions about the negative impact of pretrial publicity as a basis for closing courtrooms to the media.

Linde, Hans A. "Fair Trials and Press Freedom — Two Rights Against the State." *Willamette Law Journal* 13 (1977): 211-20. The government cannot trade off protection for free press for that of a fair trial but must protect both.

Stabile, Mark R. "Free Press-Fair Trial: Can They Be Reconciled in a Highly Publicized Criminal Court?" *Georgetown Law Journal* 79 (1990): 337-58. To protect a defendant's Sixth Amendment rights, a ban on extrajudicial statements by trial participants when those statements present a clear and present danger to the defendant's right to a fair trial is constitutional.

Sandys, Marla, and Steven M. Chermak. "A Journey into the Unknown: Pretrial Publicity and Capital Cases." *Communication Law and Policy* 1 (Autumn 1996): 533-77. Provides a comprehensive review of existing research on the effects of pretrial publicity on case outcomes.

Strossen, Nadine. "Free Press and Fair Trial: Implications of the O.J. Simpson Case." *University of Toledo Law Review* 26 (Spring 1995): 647-54. Cameras in the Simpson criminal trial made an invaluable contribution to public understanding of the criminal process and fundamental liberties.

Chapter Fifteen

Personal Privacy vs. Freedom of the Press

Pam Tidemann

Suppose someone is murdered. Let's say the victim was a private citizen who lived quietly in the suburbs, minding his own business, until a delusional lunatic chose his house at random to act out fantasies of revenge. You are the reporter sent to the scene, and the scene is full of details that would interest the reading public: blood spatters, insane scriblings on the wall, a victim who looked like everyone's favorite uncle. You find a great surplus of newsworthy data and compelling human interest touches. But, in a manner eerily reminiscent of afternoon soap operas, one additional tragic fact after another piles up in the family background: the wife's alibi is a local politician with whom she's been sleeping; the victim has left behind seven handicapped children whose Christmas presents were set on fire by the murderer; the blood at the scene is HIV positive; and a business rival of the victim had been sending blackmail letters accusing him of being a closet homosexual.

Well established precedents will guide you in choosing to publish the victim's identity, the time and place of the crime, and even the shocked reactions of his family and friends. The public has both a right and an interest in knowing such things, and the government certainly could not censor coverage. But what about the private and potentially damaging details that have been swept into the tragedy? Morning newspaper readers would be intrigued by allusions to the sexual activities, but should they be served every available piece of information regardless of consequences to the family? Signs of a dreaded disease and an unfaithful spouse in the household could disrupt and stigmatize the lives of the children. Rumors of homosexuality and blackmail could financially ruin any business interest existing after the victim's death. Survivors are already griefstricken without the trauma of airing family secrets. Assuming that you have gathered verifiable facts that may be legally published, what duties do you have to exercise restraint with such sensitive information?

The dilemma sketched here illustrates a classic conflict in reporting: freedom of the press versus the right to privacy. The media report events of significance and interest to their audiences. The public wants to be accurately informed, as well as occasionally entertained, surprised, and emotionally moved. But our democracy is imbued with a strong concept of individual dignity; we recognize a right to privacy about any personal details that are not essential within a given context. Imagine the repercussions if a medical office let patient records circulate freely on the street, or if a job interviewer was discovered badgering an applicant to reveal personal religious beliefs. Such activities are not only illegal, but also readily perceived by Americans as unethical violations of privacy. In the context of news reporting, the public would not tolerate clandestine investigations of private citizens' lives when undertaken in isolation from any newsworthy event. But when a crime or tragedy envelopes a previously unknown person, a free press makes judgment calls on what and how much to reveal in the name of news. Should the names of rape victims be automatically printed? If a plane crashes, should photographic close-ups be broadcast from a waiting room of hysterical relatives? Does a murder rightfully cast a spotlight on all aspects of the family's lives? The line between sensationalism and thorough coverage can at times become a razor's edge.

Origins of the Issue

The fine line of the privacy issue has been walked by mass communicators many times in the past. Yellow journalism burst onto the front pages of New York papers in the late nineteenth century, and debate over privacy and taste skyrocketed along with newspaper sales. The trend eventually ran its course, but remnants of sensationalism lingered into the twentieth century. Tabloid newspapers, movie magazines, even newsphotos of glaring celebrities boarding planes in frumpy clothes — all of these obviously involve invasions of public figures' lives for the entertainment of the masses. But "public figure" is a key concept in evaluating such invasions; celebrities have chosen careers in public arenas, surrendering much of their zone of personal privacy in exchange for fame and power. The law holds public figures to much higher standards of proof for defamation and invasion of privacy. Ethically, the media and the general public expect these famous people to tolerate a great deal of publicity, for matters both great and small, without taking umbrage.

In contrast, private persons overtaken by enormous events have always fallen into a type of twilight zone for media coverage. Jack London walked the streets of San Francisco in 1906 — almost a century ago — and reported the aftermath of the devastating earthquake. He interviewed residents who had lost everything they owned, but he chose to present them anonymously as he shared their despair with readers. His narrative was compelling partly because it was free of the tattletale quality of tabloid disasters. In 1925, an everyday citizen named Floyd Collins became the center of worldwide news coverage as he slowly died from a freak accident. He was imprisoned in the narrowest of passageways of a Kentucky cave, with one foot pinned hopelessly by a mountain of rock. All rescue attempts were failing, and each detail of his ordeal was chronicled by a 110-lb reporter who was able to crawl to his side to offer aid. The reporter, William Burke Miller, penned a series of reports that were genuinely compassionate, although melodramatic by today's standards, that aroused both interest and offers of assistance. Collins eventually died in the damp cavern, but the petite newsman won a Pulitzer Prize for his reporting.

Fifty years later, a photojournalist won a Pulitzer for his picture essay of inner-city dwellers trapped in a fire in 1976. Photographer Stanley Forman clung to a ladder truck as a fireman attempted to retrieve a woman and child from a fire escape. Suddenly, the ancient structure collapsed, and Forman instinctively clicked his camera as the woman tumbled downward in a free-fall to her death. He turned away before the moment of impact and spent the rest of the day in a nauseated daze. But the photos were captured: an everyday person, moments before sudden death. Forman's editor printed the pictures for an awe-stricken public. The victim's ordeal was newsworthy and possibly instructive in a civic sense — but should actual photos of her death plunge have been displayed on the front page? The resulting Pulitzer operates as a stamp of professional approval, but ethical issues of privacy could still be debated here, as they could be for many other personal tragedies in the news.

Legal and Ethical Parameters

What guidelines exist for handling privacy issues in media reports? The answers fall into two categories: legal and ethical. Case precedents give basic parameters for handling private information, while ethical guidelines cluster on the edges of the imprecise sciences of conscience, judgment, and human relations.

Legally, privacy is defined most succinctly as "the right to be let alone" and is recognized in a loosely related group of "privacy torts." Recalling that a tort is a civil wrong committed by one person against another, we might also note that privacy torts are relatively new to our system of law. They originated with an 1890 law review article in which a future Supreme Court justice and a colleague decided to take constructive action against the yellow journalism practices of that era. Ironically, the heyday of sensationalism would thus spawn some of its own remedies. Attorneys Louis D. Brandeis and Samuel Warren reasoned that privacy rights were already implied, but not overtly identified, in the common law of the respective states. They inferred protection of privacy to be reflected in areas such as trespass law and copyright regulations. Subsequent Supreme Court justices have visualized privacy as "emanating" from the Constitution, especially from passages such as the Fourth Amendment prohibition against unreasonable searches and seizures.

The result of this inference of privacy rights has been four torts familiar to most mass media professionals. "False light" is defined as portraying someone inaccurately, in a way that is offensive to that person, even though some people would find the portrayal flattering or neutral. "Appropriation" is unauthorized use of a name or likeness; it is essentially an advertising or public relations tort outside the context of this chapter. "Intrusion" is unique among the group because the wrong occurs at the information-gathering level without regard to whether the information is later published. As the name suggests, intrusion is an invasion of someone's legitimate privacy by means such as electronic bugging, hidden cameras, or physical trespass. Of most relevance is "publication of private facts," through which reporters may be liable for publishing true facts of a highly personal nature. The media usually, but not always, win lawsuits for publication of private facts with the defense of newsworthiness. In other words, the law accords reporters a thick safety net for inclusion of sensitive data related to a news event.

The legal utility of the newsworthy defense is similar in strength to "truth" as a defense for defamation. A publisher or broadcaster sued for libel could successfully defend an embarrassing revelation about someone — perhaps a past criminal record — by presenting evidence of truth. Personal information gleaned from the same person's private life — perhaps family members' descriptions of bizarre recent behavior — might be challenged as publication of private facts. But the broad defense of newsworthiness would probably keep the publisher on safe ground legally. For instance, he might simply show that the subject has been arrested for a crime similar in nature to the Satanic rituals he performs in his living room every Friday night. And since the public event of the arrest has provided the publisher a "newsworthy" umbrella, he might want to unearth other true facts as the subject awaits trial — perhaps a childhood babysitter's account of his bedwetting problem, or divorce-court testimony of his ex-wife on his lack of sexual finesse. After all, truth can shield the media from libel charges, and newsworthiness offers a broad legal defense for publication of private facts. Who cares if a few arrestees are embarrassed from time to time?

Reputable communicators care, and this is where the ethical side of private information comes into play. Ethical decisions are often complex; the word "privacy" itself is a relative term that depends partly on the context to which it is applied. The issue in a given news event usually boils down to the value of disclosure to society versus the potential damage to the private individual thrust into the spotlight.

In Favor of Disclosure

The American press is often symbolized as a roving watchdog that guards society from abuses by the government or unscrupulous individuals. Non-democratic systems thrive on personal rights infringements conducted in an atmosphere of secrecy and censorship. Disclosure of a wide range of events and opinions prevents harmful activities from thriving in relative darkness; the Constitutional principle of freedom of the press is based partly on this line of reasoning.

Additionally, most print and broadcast media are undeniably in business for profit, no matter how lofty their ideals or how kind-hearted their managers. Financial survival of a publication or station can become a formidable obstacle to purely altruistic presentations of information. A tasteful and completely objective report may not score as large an audience as a less restrained extravaganza on the same event. Bottom-line business imperatives can factor into editorial decisions on what stories to headline and how to portray the people involved. Even individual journalists' differences in background and judgment influence perceptions of when effective realism turns into morbid curiosity. And always foremost are the journalistic needs to be first to get the story and first to capture the roving attention of the mass audience. Ratings and circulation rule the account books, and completely cautious, softly treading media businesses risk becoming extinct.

Crime coverage is a key arena for the exercise of ratings savvy by producers and editors. Information on crime is valuable to the public for obvious reasons, such as personal awareness and revelation of the consequences meted out to lawbreakers. Crimes are frequently committed against private citizens who would otherwise lead lives invisible to the public eye. The violent and distasteful details of many crimes further blur any distinct dividing line between sensationalism and worthwhile information. Thus, the media often have reasons to spotlight personal information that would be grossly intrusive were it not in the wake of a crime.

Crime reporter Steven Chermak researched decisions on crime content in his 1995 book, *Victims in the News*. His statistical analysis showed not only that crime stories are emphasized in papers, but also that certain types of crime are more likely to reach print than others. Murders led the list, due apparently to the combination of their severity to society and inherent drama in print. Other violent crimes were not equally represented in headlines and coverage; their prominence depended on unusual aspects of "routine" burglaries and assaults. For instance, a neighborhood burglar was elevated to front-page coverage for his compulsion to break and enter for the purpose of raiding residents' underwear supplies. Similarly, a young assault victim landed in both the hospital and the headlines because two hoodlums threw him off his bicycle to steal his Mother's Day flowers. The news value of these incidents was audience fascination with life's bizarre occurrences, always a rich source of pathos and comedy. And a basic principle of covering such crimes is that victims' potential embarrassment takes a back seat to entertaining the audience.

Currency in public concern is another factor affecting the news value of certain crimes. Surges of alarm about drug abuse will elevate drug-related crimes above other serious offenses when editorial decisions come down to the wire. A rash of publicity on the problems of abusive relationships can lift domestic disputes off police blotters and into prominent places in print. Public exposure for people involved in crimes of popular concern is influenced by audience appeal, as well as the rallying cry of "political correctness," with decreased concern for factors such as actual severity and individual privacy.

Certain factors about a crime victim increase his or her likelihood of becoming front-page news. Children are perceived as innocents deserving special attention, as are elderly victims and bystanders caught in crossfire. Their ordeals are more likely to be prominently displayed, often with the mixed results of increasing trauma through exposure while simultaneously arousing public awareness and support. In contrast, drug dealers and career criminals injured in illegal events are often given passing attention as victims in the news, even though glaring publicity might be a more just result for all participants.

Defendants in the news are not only more frequently identified than some victims, they are also more likely to make headlines when they meet certain criteria for capturing public interest. A member of a helping profession, such as medicine or law enforcement, is likely to receive a lot of publicity when accused of a crime. An accused person will also experience more publicity if she is normally in a nurturing relationship to the victim, such as mother-child or teacher-student.

Along with crime stories, coverage of disasters leads news for sales and public attention. Disasters can come in big packages, such as a mentally unbalanced loner opening fire on a school, or an earthquake that devastates a major city. Disasters can also occur on a small scale, such as a series of deaths in one family. Regardless of the scope, any disaster necessarily involves human suffering in the context of events that interest the world. Coverage of these individual stories in a way that communicates the impact of the event while also preserving some personal privacy has proven to be a delicate balancing act.

One of the most analyzed instances of recent disaster coverage was the 1988 explosion of Pan-Am Flight 103 over Lockerbie, Scotland. There were no survivors, and many passengers were college students flying home for Christmas break. The press was largely perceived as descending on victims' families in a "wolf pack." A photojournalist filmed a recognizable body, still strapped into the airline seat, being lowered from a rooftop. A reporter was filming when the mother of one of the victims stiffened up like a board and collapsed on the floor of the airport. A number of classmates attending victims' funerals complained about reporters hovering ghoulishly over them for reactions. Reporters themselves described a scene of journalistic chaos as they scrambled over each other to transmit the critical copy to offices around the world.

However, a closer analysis reveals more than just a media feeding frenzy in the wake of the crash. Many press members interviewed later have described a feeling of identification with the families, as well as subsequent decisions not to use material that seemed to offend the privacy and dignity of the grief-stricken. Several spoke of trying to harmonize their desire to capture the reality of the disaster with their feelings of respect for the tormented families. One result was a number of compromises, intended for dramatic yet tasteful effects, where the more distant shots of wreckage were used and the more distant relatives spoke for family members agonized by grief. Part of the public outcry about compulsively filming and recording at the scene was based on a misunderstanding of media procedures: a lot of material was gathered by reflex as events developed, but not ever used if felt to be excessively graphic or intrusive.

Disasters occurring to individuals can also pose conflicts for the media. Public fascination may be high, while widespread value of publication may be minimal compared to mass disasters and criminal activity. The *Salisbury Post* in North Carolina struggled with such a decision in 1984 when it published the identity of an adoptive family who wished to remain unknown. Local news coverage of the biological mother's search literally involved a carnival atmosphere; the adopted baby had been abandoned seventeen years earlier by a carnival barker and his wife. The young carnival couple began leaving their infant with a loving babysitter named Mary Hall, a poor man's wife with three children of her own. The biological parents came to retrieve their baby less and less frequently as the carnival moved further away. Eventually, even their phone calls tapered away to nothing, and the Halls realized that baby Susie had been abandoned, albeit into their caring home. A legal adoption was arranged, with the knowledge of just a handful of local acquaintances, and Susie proceeded to grow up as a bona fide member of the Hall family.

Meanwhile, the young biological mother never forgot the child, whom she claimed her first husband had manipulated her into abandoning. She remarried and launched a search that began in Rowan County, N. C. Adoption records were firmly sealed by law in that state, and authorities gave her no information. The *Salisbury Post*, however, recognized a human interest angle in dramatizing the search. Obliging the natural mother's request for publicity, it published both a feature story and a follow-up. The feature story gave enough detail for acquaintances to recognize Susie Hall's unconventional beginnings, and their flood of tips enabled the woman to place a phone call to the very upset Hall family. The follow-up story identified Susie and her family, resulting in a period of personal and public discomfort for them. They eventually filed a lawsuit for publication of private facts.

Arguments in the case pitted privacy in family matters against unrestricted freedom of the press. The local paper argued that the published facts were neither highly offensive nor strictly private; what's more, they were very newsworthy. The Hall family, who had consistently refused to meet the adoptive mother, attempted to refute each of these claims. They took offense to publicity about the details of their daughter's abandonment by the traveling circus. They pointed out that knowledge of the facts among a small group of old acquaintances was not equivalent to having the entire county read the story in current newspapers. Additionally, they questioned the newsworthiness of their family's private history when there were willing subjects for adoption stories. Despite their arguments, North Carolina's Supreme Court ruled against any right to trial on a privacy claim. It also abolished any and all privacy cases against the press in North Carolina.

Advocates of the state decision in *Hall v. Post* argued that any restriction on the media's ability to report true information would lead courts down a slippery slope; the eventual result could be paranoia about publishing even routine local events. Opponents of the ruling argued that it obviously went too far in removing all legal barriers to publicizing details of people's lives. The only real deterrent to coverage of a private life in such a jurisdiction is the judgment of the editor, which media proponents feel is sufficient. But not all parties to the debate agree that the media always make sound decisions on possible violations of individual dignity.

The Case for Privacy

Juxtaposed against the ideal of freely disseminated information is the

American archetype of the proud individualist — the protagonist who braved the nineteenth-century frontier, who possibly immigrated from Europe with just a few possessions, and who was drawn to the land of opportunity in part by the inherent dignity recognized in each individual. Such a cultural archetype tends to discourage painful exposure of private events; the same American readers who peek into tabloids are actually quite guarded about the possibility of such prying and publicity in their own backyards. Exactly how can the media cover events on a personal scale, without crossing the line most of us would label as common respect for private citizens? There are no rigid guidelines, but many news events have certainly been covered tastefully without depriving the public of essential and enlightening information.

To the media's credit in the arena of crime coverage, considerable thought is given to the way certain victim factors are handled. Rape victims' overall ordeals are understood to include the probable humiliation of publicity, although good arguments have also been made for matter-of-fact identification in the news, in order to lessen the traditional stigma surrounding sexual assault. In practice, newspapers are found to be responsive to individual wishes and case circumstances. Only a small percentage publish names of rape victims regardless of situation. The majority of publications describe a policy of treading carefully in this sensitive area, weighing the benefits of identification against the possible compromise in the victim's safety and recovery. Child molestation cases are handled with even more discretion, on the basis of the child's need to resume his or her growth and development. Of course, some publications may also act to ensure their readers' goodwill, but, either way, sexual crimes are handled with more attention to privacy than is popularly imagined.

Safety is another consideration that has earned increasing influence in decisions about victim identification. Studies have shown a recent upswing in incomplete identifications of identity and location, presumably in response to the increase in predatory crimes. Many papers now decline to give the traditional news element of crime location or victim address when such information may pose further risk to victims or families. Some editors have a policy of giving approximate locations, by block or neighborhood, when pinpointing a locale that would tend to benefit the public. Similarly, some victims or witnesses are not initially identified by name. Safety issues handled well by the media show a public concern that balances some of the more sensational news items, and such handling also benefits victims' feelings of privacy and personal dignity.

Accused persons who are widely publicized, then later cleared of any suspicion, face the special dangers of fickle and inaccurate public memories. Readers and viewers may be vague about the official vindication, while forever remembering the name as "the man in that child molestation case" or "the woman arrested when her husband died mysteriously." Such undeserved reputations are not only a real injustice to innocent parties, but are also partially preventable through media restraint. Massive regurgitation of every scrap of information in the chaos of a fresh crime discovery can work against innocent parties, as well as against the station or newspaper publishing an indiscriminate scoop. Organization of crime data, with personal details selected carefully for impact and reliability, results in greater justice to parties involved and in greater authority for the news bearers.

Media authority can also be enhanced through a similar screening process in mass disaster coverage. One of the best results of the chaos in covering the Flight 103 disaster was media refinement of guidelines for future disasters. *CBS News* strengthened its interview suggestions for obtaining clear-cut permission, as well as for discerning which potential subjects might be actually in a state of shock. Professional discussion was stimulated on the art of portraying mass disasters accurately without resorting to gory shock-appeal. The BBC actually circulated a type of ethical essay to its members; some commentators have nominated it as a foundation for a practice code on disaster coverage. With typical British reserve, the BBC stated that dying people deserve dignity, and not all information uncovered should be paraded across the TV screen and the front page. The same document also gave specific practice instructions to members — on showing wreckage and bodies from a distance only, for instance, and on lowering one's voice respectfully to traumatized subjects on camera, rather than frantically shouting questions into their faces. The use in America of BBC guidelines may be an excellent starting point for increased sensitivity in mass disasters.

Further guidelines for sensitive situations include the arts of communication and compromise between reporter and subject. For example, the *Salisbury Post* in the North Carolina adoption fiasco could have contacted the Halls for permission and input; the editor also could have compromised by covering the topic of adoption in some way that did not single Susie Hall out for identification and public scrutiny.

The Susie Hall adoption case involved publication of long-standing background information, and this was a factor in the newspaper's victory in court. In contrast, immediately developing events present greater challenges in coverage of family crises, such as the painful crisis experienced by a middle-aged couple in Los Angeles. In what is an almost universal situation, the husband died and his wife was left to grieve. Their experience, however, was extraordinary in one respect: it was captured on film without their permission and broadcast repeatedly on the local news channel for part of a series on emergency services. The husband, Dave Miller, died from a heart attack in his bedroom, and paramedics were called to revive him as his emotionally fragile wife watched. There they all stood together in the bedroom of a dying man: the wife, the medical team — and a crew of cameramen. Local broadcast affiliate KNBC was filming a special in response to complaints about the performance of the 911 system, and such concerns are certainly related to the public interest. The problem began when the producer decided to follow an ambulance in action, without regard to the fact that medics often have to charge into private homes. The problem for the station intensified when the producer aired graphic sequences of Dave Miller's resuscitation scene. Mrs. Miller was not aware that cameramen had been part of the chaos on the worst night of her life, nor was she subsequently informed and asked for permission to have her husband's death broadcast.

The news station expressed amazement when Mrs. Millers and her children sued for a combination of claims that included intrusion and intentional infliction of emotional distress. As a media defendant relying on the First Amendment, KNBC considered the film to be newsworthy coverage of a socially significant issue. It claimed that anonymity was maintained by avoiding direct views of the stricken man's face and that entry into the home was legal due to lack of objection by anyone inside. Furthermore, it asserted that a ruling against its actions in *Miller v. KNBC* would strait-jacket media in the future from the spontaneous filming of any disaster of public significance.

The Millers' attorneys countered these arguments with ethical and common-sense considerations that they felt the news station had neglected. A tragedy in a private home should not have merited the type of automatic public coverage granted to larger scale disasters occurring in public areas; some sort of consent should be obtained from families like the Millers. Consent should be for both broadcasting of the film and initial entrance onto the private property. Rushing past an unprotesting resident was not equivalent to informed consent; people in situations like Mrs. Miller's should be assumed to be in a state of shock that precludes full awareness of surrounding events. Finally, identity of a person or situation is a complex grouping of clues to people who may view the film; simply skirting around the key figure's face or name does not render him anonymous when the inside of the home, complete with next-of-kin, is aired on television.

A long battle ensued over whether the Millers even had sufficient cause to go to trial, and the parties ultimately settled before reaching the California Supreme Court. The intermediate court denied any right to trial for the actual broadcast, but gave the Millers permission to proceed with their intrusion claim. The opinion went on record as an ominous warning to "ride along" camera crews: beware of crashing into private homes without residents' consent, as this act alone can meet the standard of "highly offensive to a reasonable person." Even without the full weight of a jury trial, the Miller case underscores an important privacy consideration for news teams interested in investigating socially significant topics: occurrences in private homes are not always a wise choice for illustration.

The Millers' situation has not been the only investigative report to raise privacy issues; the practice of investigative reporting itself sometimes poses ethical dilemmas. Increasingly popular in today's complex society, investigative reporting often involves penetrating the surface of entities to see how they really operate. Does a charity really give proceeds directly to the poor? Is that quaint little store on the corner actually a front for a drug ring? Reporters may try to answer questions such as these for purposes of exposing corruption and waste in their communities. To get the answers, they may have to resort to deception and invasion of privacy as they dig for secrets. Some loss of privacy for innocent people is considered justified when great wrongs are exposed. But investigative reporters have generally developed codes of ethics aimed at protecting truly innocent people by not publishing every detail they unearth, just those that hit the targets of their exposés.

Not all exposés, however, are targeted at an evil individual or a faceless institution. Some are researched and written to illuminate a destructive pattern that permeates the social fabric, such as drug abuse among the disadvantaged or the increased isolation of modern families. Certain individuals may surface in the foreground of a reporter's research and end up featured as prototypes, with debatable personal benefits from the publicity. Many such reports have been praised for successfully merging private events and social commentary.

Consider a cable television show presented in November 1995 that examined the impact of a single defining photograph. Titling the documentary "Leona's Sister Gerri," the *Point of View* social issues program presented a retrospective of the life and death of woman who died in the 1960s after an illegal abortion. This mini-biography was constructed from interviews with the young woman's family members, principally the sister who was her closest confidante. Their family tragedy inadvertently provided a rallying image for the pro-abortion movement of the following decade, with fluctuating reactions by Gerri's surviving family.

The focus of the controversy was a stark black-and-white coroner's photograph of Gerri slumped over in death on the floor of a cheap motel room. Naked and pale in a dark pool of blood, she was crumpled into a knee-chest position, with her arms stretched overhead in a manner similar to that of a prayerful supplicant. Her face was not visible to the camera, and *Ms.* magazine published the photo in 1972 as an anonymous example of the pathos and danger of backstreet abortions. The silent message of the picture crystallized a concept that words had not done justice to, and multitudes of pro-abortion demonstrators began to carry the image on signs with the terse caption, "Never Again."

Family members were stunned to recognize Gerri's body and intimate death scene in nationwide coverage of an emotional issue. Initially outraged by the invasion of privacy, they launched an investigation that traced the path of the photo from "anonymous" selection among morgue records to national media exposure. The *Point of View* documentary, in turn, traced the family's evolution from feelings of violation to recognition of a higher purpose in exposing Gerri's unnecessary death. The broadcast dramatically illustrated the tension between sanctity in personal tragedies and the unique value that some tragedies may have as symbols of widespread wrongs. In this particular privacy issue, Gerri and her surviving family represented not only the passion of a large social movement, but also the conflicts faced by investigative media in finding private griefs with the potential to personify larger social problems. The broadcast itself seemed to personify a successful use of personal tragedy, intimately detailed, to encompass larger dimensions of sadness and controversy.

Resolution

Can conflicts between freedom of the press and personal privacy find a balance? This complex question involves the exercise of many individuals' judgment and values, but some guidelines are possible. The substance of each guideline goes back to the key concept of benefiting the audience through disclosure versus protecting the individual from unjustifiable violation and harm.

First, is the event truly newsworthy? Purely private tragedies without some unique connection to an ongoing issue are best left alone. Similarly, unnecessary details may often be omitted without compromising a story of real public interest. Not all information gathered needs to be publicly regurgitated by reputable print or broadcast media. Thus, a murder in the community should be reported, but not with every agonizing detail of the family's shock and mourning.

Second, are there particularly fragile parties that stand to be damaged by full-scale revelations? News reporters have always tended to shy away from complete identification of child victims of sexual assault; and elderly or disabled victims of misfortune can be harmed in more ways than one by full disclosure. Embarrassment may be the least of the problem for vulnerable and fully identified victims; contemporary news reports have shown an increase in predatory and hate crimes. The complete name and address of a bereaved widow or a sexual assault victim may be the calling card for someone who preys on the weak.

Current editors are experimenting with ways to report significant personal crises without exposing innocent parties to stigma and physical danger.

Third, has thought been devoted to alternative ways of presenting an event that encompasses private parties? Obtaining consent to use even a certain portion of a film, or to enter private areas, is a critical move often overlooked in the chaos of emerging events. Consent to be filmed or interviewed has obvious legal value, but the value it can bring in goodwill and quality of coverage may yield even longer-term benefits for the publisher. A delay in airing or printing can also be an effective technique in managing extremely controversial material, although editors also have to be realistic in operating in a fast-paced news market. When possible, it is better to hold powerful private material long enough for reflection on its utility and manner of presentation. A slightly-delayed but more professionally edited piece may become the definitive version of a famous event. Additionally, there may be less intrusive ways of conveying the same meaning, such as longer distance shots of wreckage and bodies.

Finally, what do the dictates of conscience and common sense seem to suggest in covering a given event? Even through a filter of professional customs in covering news, and despite many variations in taste and abstract thinking ability, reporters are part of a larger culture of people who share many values and background factors. If a particular piece of reporting strikes a journalist at the gut level as belonging in a tabloid, next to a story about an Elvis sighting in outer space, his or her perception of unethical privacy violation would probably be shared by the public audience. Great stories that spotlight inner aspects of a private person's life should be chosen carefully for maximum social effect. Saturation of private details in the media cheapens individual dignity, but insightful focus on the right details can elevate subject and reader alike to new levels of understanding.

Recommended Readings

Books

Alderman, Ellen, and Caroline Kennedy. *The Right to Privacy*. New York: Alfred A. Knopf, 1995. Extensive discussion and case histories on privacy violations in America; see chapter on "Privacy and the Press."

Chermak, Steven M. *Victims in the News: Crime and the American News Media*. Boulder, Colo.: Westview Press, 1995. Discussion and statistical analysis of how crime victims are interviewed and publicized.

Christy, Marian. *Invasions of Privacy: Notes from a Celebrity Journalist*. Reading, Mass.: Addison-Wesley, 1984. Personal recollections of author's celebrity subjects, with comparisons to her own private crises.

Depa, Joan. *The Media and Disasters: Pam Am 103*. London: David Fulton Publishers, 1993. Extensive treatment of media coverage of the famous air disaster, with multiple viewpoints from reporters, victims' families, and the worldwide audience.

Protess, David L., et.al. *The Journalism of Outrage: Investigative Reporting and Agenda Building in America*. New York and London: Guilford Press, 1990. Incudes discussion of intruding into personal lives and when to conceal identities.

Articles

Bailey, Dennis. "Ghost Writers in the Sky." *Columbia Journalism Review* 28:1 (May-June 1989): 10-12. Tabloids create bogus first-person account of pilot's adventures in freak accident; pilot sues for invasion of privacy.

Cunningham, Richard P. "Seeking a Time-Out on Prurience: Curbing the Sensationalization of the Grief of Others Through Photographs." *Quill* (March 1992): 6. Urges restraint in photographing distraught survivors at death scenes.

Lipschultz, Jeremy Harris. "Mediasat and the Tort of Invasion of Privacy." *Journalism Quarterly* 65:2 (1988): 507-12. Most images beamed by satellites will be newsworthy — and therefore legally safe for media.

Paul, Nora. "Some Paradoxes of Privacy." *Journal of Mass Media Ethics* 9:4 (1994): 228-30. Examples include journalists wanting open government meetings and records while being secretive about their own sources and procedures.

Plopper, Bruce L. "Judicial Linking of Intentional Emotional Distress to Intrusion." *Journalism Quarterly* 67:1 (1990): 40-51. Compares and contrasts legal consequences of aggressive vs. intrusive techniques in reporting.

Siegal, John. "Privacy on the Poverty Beat." *Editor & Publisher*, 25 June 1994, pp. 92-95. Initially cooperative subjects sued poverty reporter for unflattering portrayals.

Von Hoffman, Nicholas. "Should the Press Play Vice Cop? Peephole Journalism." *The Nation*, 20 June 1987, pp. 835-8. Responsible publications should not let tattletale sex scandels dominate political coverage.

Wolf, Rita. "The Right to Know vs. the Right to Privacy: Newspaper Identification of Crime Victims." *Journalism Quarterly* 64:2-3 (1987): 503-8. Survey and statistics on newspaper trend toward caution in identifying various types of victims.

Chapter Sixteen

Selling Bad Habits:
Advertising Questionable Products

Frances L. Collins
Timothy D. Smith

After notorious bank robber Willie Sutton's luck ran out, and he was giving jail-house interviews, someone asked him why he robbed banks. Willie's legendary and apparently market-driven reply: "Because that's where the money is."

This is the concept behind target marketing — directing product advertising to the audience most likely to respond with a purchase. That's where the money is. Take a moment to think about who the target audience for a denture adhesive product would be....

Okay, time's up. You probably identified a senior-citizen audience. Logic would tell you that those are the people Dentu-Creme® is trying to reach with its advertising message. Where would you place magazine ads for such a product? In *Modern Maturity* or *Rolling Stone*? The answer should be obvious. But some marketers are being told that they can't or shouldn't advertise their products to the audience identified as being the most likely to be interested in those products.

As this chapter was being written, hearings were being held to determine what the marketers of certain products could and could not do to promote their wares to the most interested audiences. Appeals of lower court decisions are working their way to the Supreme Court, seeking final word on the constitutionality of proposed restrictions on advertising messages.

As you read this chapter, think about what you would do and how you would decide, if it were your responsibility to set the standards for identifying the most appropriate audience for specific products and for creating and placing the advertising for "habit-forming" products and services such as cigarettes, alcoholic beverages, or even access to the Internet. How would you balance the interests of the government, business, and consumers?

Companies want to produce the goods and services that people want and need. The connection between seller and buyer, sometimes regulated by government, is often made through advertising. Would it make a difference, for example, if advertising designed for and directed to adults would also be seen by children? Should the government be concerned if beer commercials are seen by recovering alcoholics, or prescription drugs to treat depression are advertised on television? Is there a difference, in principle, between an ad for toothpaste and one for condoms? Should the advertising of these products be regulated by the government to protect consumers? What interests are being protected? What interests are the legitimate concern of the government? And how can we balance the government's efforts to shield its citizens with the speech protections guaranteed by the First Amendment to the Constitution?

These are the issues at the heart of this chapter.

Origins of the Issue

Congress shall make no law respecting the establishment of religion,
or prohibiting the free exercise thereof; or abridging the freedom of speech,
or of the press; or the right of the people peaceably to assemble,
and to petition the government for a redress of grievances.

Generally, the "speech" recognized by the First Amendment has been defined as "political speech" — speech related to the business of governance. This concept was reinforced by a 1942 Supreme Court decision that introduced a subordinate category of speech called "commercial" — speech intended to promote a commercial transaction — also known as "advertising." That decision, *Valentine v. Chrestensen*, declared that the First Amendment did not protect "purely commercial speech."

In 1964 the Court decided *New York Times v. Sullivan*, a watershed case for freedom of the press. While it is cited as a landmark decision for "political" speech, it grew out of a full-page advertisement, not a news story, in the *Times*. The ad, with the headline "Heed Their Rising Voices," was designed to raise funds for the civil rights struggle in the South, but it contained some inaccurate statements about the way police in Montgomery, Ala., handled a civil rights demonstration. Even though there were minor factual errors in the ad, the Court said that because "Heed Their Rising Voices" was not strictly a "commercial" ad, because it included editorial information, the ad and the *Times* were protected by the First Amendment.

But those who support constitutional protection for purely commercial speech had to wait another decade for the Supreme Court to change its collective mind. This happened in a 1975 case concerning a newspaper ad for abortion services. Jeffrey Bigelow, the editor of a Virginia weekly newspaper, was fined by the state for running an ad for an abortion service located in New York. At the time, abortions were legal in New York, but not in Virginia. In overturning Bigelow's fine, the Court stated that the ad "did more than simply propose a commercial transaction" by providing "factual material of clear 'public interest,'" thus supporting its 1964 ruling that the First Amendment does, indeed, protect speech contained in an advertisement.

In 1976, the Court was even stronger in its affirmation of constitutional protection of commercial speech. In *Virginia State Board of Pharmacy v. Virginia Citizens Consumer Council*, the Court ruled that a consumer's interest in knowing the price of prescription drugs in order to comparison shop, "may be as keen, if not keener by far, than his interest in the day's most urgent political debate." For the first time, the Court also considered what consumers might want to know — rather than just what the government, a news organization, or an advertiser might want them to know — and introduced the concept of a citizen's First Amendment right to receive information.

In 1980, the Court introduced a four-part test to help determine whether the government could restrict an advertiser's speech. The Court outlined its criteria in *Central Hudson Gas & Electric Corp. v. Public Service Commission*. The four parts are as follows:

1. Whether the advertising itself is false or misleading or promotes an illegal activity. If the answer to any part of that question is yes, the ad deserves no constitutional protection. But, if the answer is no, the test moves to the second question....

2. Whether the state interest being protected by the regulation is substantial. This is the basis of most attempts to restrict advertising — the government's assertion that the issue affects the health, welfare, or safety of its citizens, which the government has a duty to protect. Assuming that the answer to the second question is yes — and it always has been — the next question is....

3. Whether the proposed regulation directly advances that state interest. To put this in less legal terms: If advertising for certain products is banned, or even restricted, will that support the government's interest? Government agencies trying to restrict advertising always answer yes, bringing us to....

4. Whether the regulation is "more extensive than necessary to serve that interest."

The last two points have been a source of continuing conflict since the adoption of the *Central Hudson* test.

The tide turned in 1986 when the Supreme Court stepped back from its favorable commercial speech rulings with its decision in *Posadas de Puerto Rico Associates v. Tourism Company of Puerto Rico*. In this case, dealing with the advertising of casino gambling, the Court deferred to what it later called "legislative judgment" in deciding what was best for citizens. The Court ruled, for example, that because the Puerto Rico legislature believed that its restrictions on casino advertising would, in fact, protect its citizens from the evils of casinos, the Court was bound (by parts three and four of *Central Hudson*) to accept that assertion at face value without further proof. In 1993, in *United States v. Edge Broadcasting*, the Court reaffirmed its belief in deference, supporting a federal law that forbid broadcasters licensed in non-lottery states from advertising lotteries to states that allow them.

But in 1996, in what is being hailed as a landmark decision for advertising, the Court disavowed its ruling in *Posadas* and seemed to question its decision in *Edge*. In *44 Liquormart v. Rhode Island*, the Court said that a state could not restrict truthful advertising about a product when the state's real interest was not related to the product, but focused instead on consumers' conduct. Rhode Island claimed that its ban on advertising the price of distilled spirits was needed to "promote temperance" among its citizens. Even though the state could have raised taxes on liquor to discourage drinking, the state instead chose to restrict advertising as the only method of achieving its goal. The Supreme Court said this was unconstitutional under the third and fourth parts of the *Central Hudson* test.

The long-range impact of the *44 Liquormart* decision, however, remains unclear. The Court has not agreed to hear enough new commercial speech cases to clearly signal its intent. For instance, the Court reversed a Baltimore ordinance banning alcohol and tobacco advertising on billboards and sent the case back for reconsideration. But when the appeals court again upheld the ban, the Court declined to review the decision a second time, allowing the ban to stand. Both sides in the ongoing tobacco wars (the Food and Drug Administration and the tobacco companies) have promised to appeal the parts of a District Court ruling that deal with the regulation of nicotine as a drug and the continued advertising of tobacco products. How would you decide whether to restrict or permit such advertising?

The next section discusses the perspectives — pro and con — for restricting the advertising of these habit-forming "vices."

Arguments in Favor of Ad Restrictions

Few products available legally in America generate as much controversy as alcohol and tobacco. Both are reputed to have addictive qualities; both, unquestionably, are linked to health problems; both are legal and suspect simultaneously.

For these reasons, both products have been the target of extensive regulation. Mandatory labels for cigarettes and super-majority age limits for drinking alcohol are just two examples. Both products are older than America itself. Tobacco was a gift from Native Americans, bestowed on European explorers when they arrived on this continent. Those explorers brought with them a knowledge of fermented beverages. The popularity of both products made them natural targets for taxation, and it is no accident that today they represent two-thirds of what are called "sin taxes," with gambling the final third.

Regulation was slower to develop than taxation, and it wasn't as uniform in application. The health hazards of tobacco had long been suspected, but regulation was confined, until recently, to a loosely enforced prohibition against sale to minors. Alcohol was dealt with more severely, probably because its detrimental impact was more visible, more quickly, with no intervening variables such as poor air quality or job-related health hazards. Alcohol abuse was so widespread, in fact, that Congress was persuaded to amend the Constitution in 1919 to ban the manufacture, sale, or transportation of "intoxicating liquors."

Americans, of course, did not quit drinking just because it was illegal. Where there is demand, someone will provide a supply. For an idea of how ineffective such regulation was, consider that the "Prohibition Era" was also known as the "Roaring Twenties."

Finally, after fourteen years, public disgust with the corruption produced by Prohibition, coupled with the recognition that the law simply wasn't working, led to the repeal of the Eighteenth Amendment by the Twenty-first in 1933, shifting the burden of regulation from the federal government to the states.

Now, almost sixty-five years later, anti-tobacco and anti-alcohol forces are again looking to the federal government to restrict the attraction, promotion and availability of these products. As this chapter was being written, the FDA had won the first legal round in its attempt to regulate tobacco as a drug-delivery system (the drug being nicotine) but lost its attempt to curtail the advertising. These are the portions of the decision, mentioned above, being appealed by the FDA and tobacco marketers. The appeals are complicated by several state lawsuits against the tobacco companies, trying to win monetary damages to offset the medical costs of treating those afflicted with tobacco-related illnesses. Another complicating factor is the settlement, negotiated by a group of state attorneys general, calling for concessions by tobacco companies, as well as major fines. President Clinton, members of Congress and other government officials are questioning various parts of the agreement, which must be approved by Congress and the President before it can take effect.

By the time you read this chapter, many if not most of these circumstances will have changed. But some things are expected to remain constant: Tobacco products will still be sold in stores and by machine; prohibitions on smoking in public places will continue to grow; limits on tobacco (and other "vice" products) still will be debated.

The one constant in all of this will continue to be the lure of advertising regulation. First, it is a highly visible aspect of any product marketed to the public, and a daily presence for anyone who travels on public highways, reads newspapers or magazines, or has access to any electronic media, including the latest: the Internet.

Advertising for most products, but especially for tobacco and alcohol, is not just pervasive, it is overwhelming. Critics enjoy citing a Georgia physician's study that found that children between three and six years old could identify Joe Camel and relate him to a picture of a cigarette as easily as they could identify Mickey Mouse.

As Prohibition proved, taking the direct approach and regulating conduct is sometimes beyond society's grasp, at least when the approach is as drastic as an outright ban on the product. Even enforcing the laws on product sales, a relatively simple element of conduct, appears to be beyond the government's grasp, although current negotiations between tobacco companies and the states are reported to include a provision to fine retailers a "substantial" amount for underage sales. Therefore, legislators, faced with public pressure to take action, but realistic enough to know that a frontal assault on questionable products won't work, are taking the more expedient path of regulating advertising, based on four primary criteria.

Advertising is misleading. This argument contends that advertising for "questionable" products is inherently misleading because the ads do not include full disclosure of the products' negative aspects. There is no litany, as accompanies print advertising for prescription drugs, that provides a list of ingredients, a complete rundown of the hazards and contra-indications of using the products, or detailed information about all possible, even if remote, health complications.

The tobacco companies might take issue with that argument, considering they've been placing warnings on their packages and ads for decades: "SURGEON GENERAL'S WARNING: Smoking Causes Lung Cancer, Heart Disease, Emphysema And May Complicate Pregnancy" or "Quitting Smoking Now Greatly Reduces Serious Risks to Your Health."

The FDA has proposed even stronger warnings, such as "Cigarettes Kill" and "Cigarettes Are Addictive." The Associated Press reported that Tobacco Institute Vice President Walker Merryman called these proposed warnings unnecessary because "it's virtually impossible to give people any more information about the health consequences of smoking."

The fact that state or federal government attempts to regulate advertising are constitutionally flawed does not, however, strip the government's underlying concern of all merit. For example, there can be little argument that alcohol is the root of many social ills. Drunk drivers kill thousands every year and destroy the lives of many others. Spouse and child abuse can frequently be traced to alcohol abuse. For those reasons, if not others, the industry has a moral obligation not to advertise its products in ways likely to compound these problems. For example, the well-known "Miller Time" ad campaign created the impression that it was all right to hit the bar at the end of a hard day's work. The campaign helped relieve the individual of responsibility for the decision by suggesting that the conduct was the norm — a deserved "reward." The campaign, although now long retired, created a phrase that has become part of our culture. The same is true of Miller's main competitor — Budweiser — with its "This Bud's For You" slogan and campaigns that featured vigorous sports activities followed by just as vigorous drinking. It is no secret why beer companies are inclined to sponsor major-league sporting events. The positive images of professional athletes go well with the message that drinking beer is a manly, athletic endeavor.

Ads entice those not legally able to purchase and/or use the product(s). The juvenile audience for tobacco and alcoholic beverage products is of particular concern. The thrust of the advertising regulations for tobacco products offered by the FDA is aimed squarely at children. Studies offered in support of the FDA's proposed regulations all cite evidence that 1) the smoking habit starts young and 2) younger children are more susceptible to the persuasive powers of advertising. The crunch comes in proving that advertising actually causes children to start smoking or drinking. Proponents of regulation repeatedly point to the Joe Camel/Mickey Mouse linkage. While the connection between recognition and causation has yet to be made conclusively, the issue gets thornier because of tobacco company memos that surfaced during litigation in 1996 and 1997 that clearly indicated the companies were targeting younger audiences with some of their messages. In fact, the Federal Trade Commission cited such RJ Reynolds memos in filing charges of unfair advertising practices against the company for its use of the Joe Camel character.

Further, there is evidence that young smokers choose the most heavily advertised brands. The question then becomes whether the advertising influenced the decision to start smoking or just which brand to smoke after the decision was made. The tobacco companies argue the latter; the FDA argues the former, citing a 1982 study on brand preference by adolescent smokers, published in the

American Journal of Public Health.

There can be no question that tobacco advertising throws into sharp relief the toughest issues concerning the delivery of a message by a manufacturer. Even if there is no solid proof that advertising is the mechanism that launches a life of smoking, there is little about advertising techniques in general, and specifically those used to sell tobacco and alcohol, that provides much comfort to the defenders of commercial speech. Advertising's "puffery" is accepted practice. David Ogilvy, one of the pioneers in the field, once called advertising "truth well-told." If that means that advertising tells the truth well, there's no problem. But if that means that advertising puts the best "spin" on a product's positives or minimizes its negatives, that could be problematic. Everything about the advertising of such questionable products as alcohol and tobacco screams "HEALTHY." Ads show outdoor scenes, populated by youthful, fit, attractive young men and women doing fun things that include these products. The message could not be clearer: This lifestyle and these products are made for each other.

A 45-year-old couch potato, catching the flood of beer ads during the Superbowl, knows he is never going to look like those athletic young men piling on in the backyard, no matter which name-brand beer he drinks. He isn't fooled. But the ads also subtly reinforce a belief not as clearly articulated as the beautiful-people-drink-beer theme: A few beers after your favorite activity is okay. This is a concept more insidious than whether six-year-olds recognize Joe Camel. Six-year-olds are not inclined to smoke. But many 18-year-olds play flag football on the weekend. They can't drink legally, but the ad message tells them that a few beers are appropriate nonetheless. Beer companies, no doubt, would deny any such intent. But that interpretation is possible, and regulators cite it as a reason to curb such messages.

Curbing advertising reduces demand. It seems axiomatic that advertising stimulates demand and just as logical to assume that reducing advertising would also reduce demand. That argument is embedded in the FDA's proposal to regulate tobacco advertising as part of an overall plan to reduce teenage smoking. If familiarity breeds contempt, it also breeds awareness. Given the volume of tobacco advertising available today, particularly in magazines marketed to young people, it is easy to see how government regulators can make an argument that a reduction in the message must have an impact. The argument is more intuitive than scientific, but there isn't any research that conclusively proves otherwise. Almost a century ago, department store magnate John Wanamaker said he knew that half his advertising was wasted; he just didn't know which half. In 1997, *Time* magazine reported ad agency CEO Bob Kuperman's assertion that companies waste a full 95 per cent of their advertising dollars because the audience doesn't listen to or believe their ads.

There doesn't seem to be the same level of pressure to curb alcohol advertising beyond a campaign to keep distilled spirits ads off television. This lack of pressure does not signify acceptance of the advertising, but more likely a one-vice-at-a-time approach. Alcohol advertising will also undoubtedly get its day in court.

Since some marketers have voluntarily agreed to restrain their advertising, why should they object to mandatory restraints that limit but do not ban their product advertising? As the tobacco industry's negotiations with state attorneys general progressed, it became abundantly clear that the companies were willing to negotiate to ward off government regulation. It is a lot easier to circumvent voluntary guidelines than to circumvent the law.

Although tobacco companies went along with a Congressional ban on advertising on television and radio in 1971, television has long been home to beer and wine advertising. However, distilled spirits marketers have voluntarily kept advertising for their products off television since 1948. But, as the business and news media reported extensively in 1996, Seagram Americas announced plans to advertise two of its brands through cable and independent broadcast stations on a market-by-market basis. The company claims it simply wants to "level the playing field" and be able to advertise its products through the same media as beer and wine marketers.

The *New York Times* reported that from 1970 to 1995, hard liquor's share of the alcohol market dropped from 44 per cent to 29 per cent, while the market share for beer rose from 45 per cent to 59 per cent. Commentators have questioned Seagram's motives: Could the "level playing field" actually mean the elimination of beer and wine advertising from television? Market analysts doubt that would be the result, given the Supreme Court's recent shift toward greater protection for commercial speech. Arthur Shapiro, executive vice president-marketing for Seagram Americas, has denied that that is Seagram's goal. In an interview with *Advertising Age* magazine, he noted that if beer and wine marketers were forced off television, they would simply apply those advertising dollars to the print media, outspending companies like Seagram. He added that company research showed that the general consumer saw no difference between hard liquor and beer or wine in terms of the appropriateness of television advertising.

Without legislative regulations in place, voluntary restraints have a way of loosening considerably, especially when marketers' profits are at stake. Consequently, there is pressure to convert the guidelines into law. It wasn't long after the Seagram Americas' commercials appeared that members of Congress introduced bills designed to make such television ads illegal.

Arguments Against Ad Restrictions

The ill-conceived concept of Prohibition also serves to highlight the primary argument against regulation of truthful, nonmisleading advertising for a legal product. Even though alcoholic beverages weren't advertised during Prohibition, people kept on drinking. Without advertising, comparison shopping was impossible, as was the development of brand loyalty, but no one needed to see appealing advertisements as an inducement to imbibe.

Advertising is misleading. The first part of the *Central Hudson* test squarely confronts this issue. Advertising is not constitutionally protected unless it is truthful, nonmisleading and promotes a legal product. In the event that an ad is found to be misleading, it loses its constitutional protection, and the FTC has broad authority to force the offending advertiser to cease such advertising, to levy fines against the advertiser or to require corrective advertising to repair any consumer misperceptions.

Some questions that should be asked are: Who is being misled by the advertising in question? Does anyone really believe that Keebler® cookies are baked by elves? Or that wearing a certain brand of cologne or designer jeans will bring Mr. or Ms. Right to one's doorstep? It's doubtful that anyone — regardless of his or her age — doesn't know that smoking cigarettes or abusing alcoholic beverages can be dangerous to one's health. Some would say the same about high-cholesterol, fast-food diets, but no one is lobbying Congress to restrict advertising for the Whopper® or Quarter Pounder® with cheese.

Ads entice those not legally able to purchase and/or use the product(s). The alternative viewpoint — beyond expecting ethical behavior from marketers — is for would-be regulators to focus on the behavior in question, not commercial speech that might encourage such activity. Research studies cited by those who oppose restricting tobacco advertising suggest that peer pressure and the presence of smokers in a child's family are more likely to lead that child to take up the habit than are advertisements.

In 1993 and 1994, *Advertising Age* reported on two surveys showing that, although the Joe Camel character was highly recognized by young people, the character wasn't necessarily well-liked. One study revealed that while 58 per cent of children between the ages of six and eleven recognized the Joe Camel character (compared with 91 per cent who recognized Tony the Tiger and 83 per cent who recognized the Energizer Bunny), only 22 per cent gave him a positive rating, versus 59 per cent who gave the character a negative rating. The second study found that the recognition level among ten- to seventeen-year-olds for the Energizer Bunny, Ronald McDonald, and Tony the Tiger topped the 73 per cent who recognized Joe Camel.

In 1997 *Advertising Age* reported New York lawyer Douglas J. Wood's assertion that no study has ever conclusively shown a causal connection between advertising and a child's decision to start smoking. "All the studies that have been done in various places in the world have shown that peer pressure and behavior of siblings and parents are the primary reasons kids choose to take up smoking."

There are penalties for drinking beer, wine or liquor, as well as penalties for selling any of those items to someone under twenty-one. If underage drinking is to be a focus of enforcement — and it seems to be a popular target — then perhaps the enforcement should be stiffened and the penalties increased. For example, the license to sell alcoholic beverages is a prized possession. The holders of these licenses might be much more careful about the age of their customers if a violation resulted in swift suspension of the license, and repeat violation meant a permanent loss. Licensing also has been proposed for tobacco product retailers. That would put some teeth into the laws against selling those products to minors.

Another way to curb consumption by underage drinkers is to reduce the number of outlets where alcoholic beverages could be purchased. It borders on insanity, for example, to allow gas stations to sell alcohol, especially when a mainstay of their trade is quart-sized bottles of beer. If ever there was an invitation to disaster, it is the combination of gassing up both car and driver in a single stop. There are other, fairly simple, easy-to-enforce methods available to reduce underage drinking and problem drinking among those old enough to legally purchase and consume the product: raise taxes on the product (and use the revenue to underwrite the cost of enforcement); set a minimum price to discourage discounting; curb the hours of legal sales. Many of these suggestions were proposed in the Supreme Court's *44 Liquormart* decision and are equally applicable to tobacco products.

These concepts relate to direct action against the misuse of the product, rather than indirect action against commercial speech about the product. Curbing speech, at best, simply shifts the focus away from the real problem. At worst, it is unconstitutional.

Curbing advertising reduces demand. On many fronts today, especially among regulators, it is taken as an article of faith that advertising — and advertising alone — creates demand for a product. This belief is so deeply rooted that its proponents, including some members of the Supreme Court, are incredulous that anyone would even try to deny its truth. As recently as 1993, Justice Byron White wrote in the majority opinion for the *Edge Broadcasting* case that "the Government obviously legislated on the premise that the advertising of gambling serves to increase the demand for the advertised product." He further noted that if "there is an immediate connection between advertising and demand, and the federal regulation decreases advertising, it stands to reason that the policy of decreasing demand for gambling is correspondingly advanced." The justice did not seem concerned that the North Carolina area he was protecting from the pernicious gambling advertising was already swamped with lottery messages — broadcast and print — all from media sources in Virginia, where lotteries were legal.

However, in 1996 the Court rejected this paternalistic approach in *44 Liquormart*, refusing to accept the claim that advertising the prices of alcoholic beverages would lead to increased consumption. As Prohibition showed, if the demand is there, advertising isn't essential. Demand exists separate and apart from any advertising. Despite the total lack of advertising for illegal drugs, and in the face of sustained law enforcement pressure on sellers and buyers, not to mention the widely known health risks associated with these "products," demand, purchase, and use invariably continue.

That is not to say, however, that advertising has no impact on demand. But the impact is not susceptible to the easy analysis usually offered by regulators. The cause-and-effect equation is more complex than "If X is advertised, then those seeing the ad(s) will buy X." First, this assumes that the consumer wants product X or has some need for it. If questioned, most consumers might balk at saying they want toilet paper, but there is little debate over the need. However, they might want a particular brand, and any advertising for the product category in general or that brand in particular could serve as a reminder the next time they go to the store.

The next faulty assumption is that product X is advertised in a vacuum. Suppose you suddenly realize that you want a burger and fries, but there are many brands to choose from. Those Wendy's® ads featuring company founder Dave Thomas may be entertaining, but if you prefer a Big Mac®, Wendy's has an uphill battle to get you to change. The demand for the fast food meal is already there; the advertising is aimed at helping you make or sustain your brand choice. One school of advertising thought contends that more advertising is designed to maintain brand loyalty than to encourage brand switching. Once you make your brand choice, advertising for that brand continually reinforces your brand preference. And advertising for a competing brand will do little to change it. (Of course, some would argue that a diet heavy with fast food is also heavy with harmful cholesterol, so maybe those ads should be regulated.)

The issue with smoking gets even thornier because of the confidential tobacco company memos that have surfaced, clearly indicating that the companies were trying to target younger audiences with some of their messages, despite repeated denials. Even if tobacco companies contend that such messages are just spilling over from campaigns aimed at legal smokers, there remains the question of whether the campaign influenced the decision to smoke or merely the brand selection after the decision was made.

Since some marketers have voluntarily agreed to restrain their advertising, why should they object to mandatory restraints that limit but do not ban their product advertising? One of the complicating factors in this equation is the willingness of tobacco companies to compromise their own commercial speech rights in return for being allowed to continue to sell their products without fear of future litigation.

Initial news reports of 1997 settlement discussions in the suits against tobacco companies by state attorneys general included suggestions that the companies would voluntarily give up certain types of advertising. For example, several print and broadcast news reports had RJ Reynolds and Philip Morris agreeing to kill off Joe Camel and the Marlboro Man. (RJR's offer was made before the FTC sued the company to force it to drop the character from its ads.)

This raises the question of waiving certain rights. The law recognizes that a person may waive a right, such as the Fifth Amendment right against self-incrimination or the Sixth Amendment right to legal counsel. So, to the extent that tobacco companies have a First Amendment right to advertise, they can waive it. But the waiver would be limited to only those involved in the suit, which includes the five largest tobacco companies (Philip Morris, RJ Reynolds, Brown & Williamson, Lorillard, and Liggett), but not all tobacco companies. And the reports did not suggest that the companies would be willing to forego all advertising, but just certain formats.

The bottom line is that even though a tentative settlement has been reached, a resolution of these issues is likely to take a long time, especially since both Congress and the White House must agree to the terms. The fact that a damage figure of $368 billion (to be paid out over twenty-five years) apparently didn't trouble the tobacco companies if they could get immunity from future lawsuits, relief from federal regulation, and the right to continue to sell their products should provide some clue as to the amount of money at stake. On the day information about the previously secret talks was "leaked" to the press, tobacco company stock prices actually rose. For the companies, the advertising issue is merely a sideshow. Although they spend billions annually to advertise, they claim this effort is aimed at maintaining brand loyalty, not generating new customers. Critics scoff at that notion, pointing out that the companies must continually recruit new customers, because their most faithful ones die prematurely. But the sad fact is that some bad habits don't have to be advertised to flourish. When was the last time you saw an ad for cocaine or heroin?

The trend toward greater protection for advertising found in the 1996 Rhode Island case noted above will face its greatest test in regulations on advertising aimed at curbing tobacco use by the young, even though the FDA suffered a first-round loss on that point in court. The appeal to protect children, which is also being invoked in discussions about alcoholic beverage advertising, is especially compelling, given the overwhelming evidence that use of cigarettes is often fatal and that the habit is almost always established during the teenage years. One question to ask regulators is: Why is the ban on cigarette sales to minors not more strictly enforced? Dr. Stanton A. Glantz, a harsh critic of the tobacco industry, writing in the *Journal of the American Medical Association*, points out that research has shown that 60 to 90 per cent of children who smoke report having been able to buy their own cigarettes.

One of the most heavily debated portions of the proposed FDA regulations deals with the look of tobacco product ads in magazines with a substantial underage readership. The FDA proposal (struck down at the trial court level and now on appeal) calls for black and white, text-only ads in magazines with an underage readership representing 15 per cent or more of the magazine's readership or a total underage readership of two million or more. Magazines cited as being affected by this requirement include *Sports Illustrated, Car and Driver, Motor Trend, Rolling Stone, Mademoiselle, Vogue,* and *Glamour.*

It is precisely because the "look" of advertising can be inherently misleading that suggestions for mandatory limits are being proposed. There is not a company on the market that uses unattractive models to sell its wares. The Disney company may have turned Quasimodo into a lovable character in its cartoon version of *The Hunchback of Notre Dame,* but no company would select Victor Hugo's original character to endorse its product. The outdoor, sporty scenes with glowing models suggesting that smoking is associated with athletic endeavors are not unique to cigarette ads. They also appear in ads for mountain bikes, four-wheel drive vehicles, and health clubs. The problem becomes: What happens if these mandatory limits are upheld? What products will be next?

Resolution

Whenever commercial speech freedoms come under fire, supporters of those freedoms warn of starting down the "slippery slope" of restricting truthful advertising. "Today it's cigarettes," they say. "Tomorrow, it could be...." Well, tomorrow, it could be your favorite fast food. Columnist Cal Thomas of the *Los Angeles Times* Syndicate, reminds us that heart disease is the number-one killer in America today. He also reminds us that fast-food burgers and fries contribute to heart disease. But no one has called for restrictions on the extensive television and radio advertising for these products ... yet.

Drunk drivers are responsible for a significant number of highway deaths and injuries each year. Citizen groups call for severe restrictions on alcoholic beverage advertising, yet no one calls for restrictions on automobile advertising. Logic dictates that DUI injuries and fatalities would drop significantly if drinkers didn't have cars to drive. If we accept the idea that advertising stimulates demand, restricting automobile advertising should reduce the number of cars on the road and, therefore, reduce the number of traffic fatalities. In the same vein, all states restrict their citizens from obtaining a driver's license until they reach a certain age — sixteen in most states. Perhaps we should restrict automobile advertising to keep those under the legal driving age from driving without a license.

Sound ridiculous? Perhaps, but the concept of a slippery slope is not. Once we are willing to accept restrictions on certain messages, what protections remain in place for other messages? We believe the logical course of action is to look at and address the abuse of certain products, not commercial speech about those products.

The solution may lie with the half of the case over the FDA tobacco regulations that the federal government won at the trial level. The judge declared that tobacco is a drug (a nicotine-delivery system) that can be regulated. FDA regulations now permit pharmaceutical drug advertising directly to consumers but require extensive disclosure statements to accompany the ads. Applying this concept to tobacco-product advertising would increase the cost of tobacco advertising in print media, because the required disclosure portion of drug ads currently takes up almost as much space as the sales pitch portion, if not more. Requiring these disclosures would benefit newspaper and magazine publishers, because of the additional advertising income that would be generated, and the disclosure statement requirement might also have the practical effect of eliminating billboard advertising for tobacco products — not because the speech is being restricted but, in fact, because more speech, not less, is being mandated.

In this same vein, as the Supreme Court pointed out in *44 Liquormart*, setting maximum purchase levels or minimum prices, or raising taxes on products like alcoholic beverages would do more to affect purchase patterns than keeping the public ignorant of prices. Strictly enforcing existing laws against underage purchase would make it harder for minors to acquire and use such products. Regulations aimed at the retail level, not the marketing level, are more likely to bring about positive social results without infringing on marketers' free speech rights.

That is not to say, however, that marketers should have free rein to say whatever they wish about their products or to misrepresent their products. If marketers can't or won't police themselves, there are agencies that will take on that role, from the FTC to voluntary groups like the National Advertising Review Board and the Better Business Bureau. Remember that the first element of the *Central Hudson* test that must be satisfied when someone seeks to restrict advertising is whether the advertising is truthful, not misleading and for a legal product. The authors believe that if the answer to this question is yes, the content of the message may not be restricted. However, regulation of the product and its availability is another matter.

Recommended Readings

Books

Fox, Stephen. *The Mirror Makers: A History of American Advertising And Its Creators*. New York: William Morrow, 1984. The author, a historian, provides a chronology of the development of advertising from the 19th century through the 1970s, focusing on the people and events that influenced advertising. Fox weaves the concept of consumerism — the consumers' influences on advertising — throughout his narrative.

Fritschler, A. Lee. *Smoking and Politics: Policymaking and the Federal Bureaucracy*. Englewood Cliffs, N.J.: Prentice-Hall, 1983. This book examines bureaucratic processes and agency policy-making by following the controversy over cigarette warning labels, first on the product and then in all product advertising. Included is a detailed chronology of the relationship between the government bureaucracy and the tobacco industry, from the first published report of the link between smoking and lung cancer (1939) to the early 1980s.

Hilts, Philip J. *Smoke Screen: The Truth Behind the Tobacco Industry Cover-up*. Reading, Mass.: Addison-Wesley, 1996. The author, who wrote about the Brown & Williamson "tobacco papers" for the *New York Times*, writes not only about B&W, RJ Reynolds, and Philip Morris, but also the FDA, its plans to regulate tobacco advertising, and the general political climate that has, historically, supported the tobacco industry.

Jacobson, Michael, Robert Atkins, and George Hacker. *The Booze Merchants: The Inebriating of America*. Washington, D.C.: Center for Science in the Public Interest, 1983. The authors evaluate the themes and impact of a variety of print and television ads for alcoholic beverages, based on their (presumed) intended effects on specific audiences: light drinkers, heavy drinkers, underage drinkers, and women. The authors contend that alcoholic beverage marketers are, indeed, trying to increase consumption among these groups, not simply take market share from the competition.

Kaplar, Richard T. *Advertising Rights: The Neglected Freedom. Toward a New Doctrine of Commercial Speech.* Washington, D.C.: Media Institute, 1991. Chronicles the history of the Supreme Court's commercial speech decisions from their beginnings in 1942 and makes a strong case against legislative and court-sanctioned paternalism that would restrict commercial speech, favoring instead legislative policies that would regulate product availability and use, rather than (advertising) speech about the product.

Kluger, Richard. *Ashes to Ashes: America's Hundred-Year Cigarette War, the Public Health, and the Unbiased Triumph of Philip Morris.* New York: Alfred A. Knopf, 1996. While the Philip Morris company is at the center of the narrative, this extensive history of the tobacco industry looks at the many companies, individuals, and social and scientific forces that have shaped the current dilemma and debate over the marketing of tobacco products.

Twitchell, James B. *ADCULT USA: The Triumph of Advertising in American Culture.* New York: Columbia University Press, 1996. Each of the five chapter titles is actually an advertising slogan, representing the degree to which such slogans, brand names and images have become part of our popular culture. "Where's the beef?" "It's in there," along with reproductions of print ads (historical and current) and discussion of advertising messages on radio and television.

Articles & Book Chapters

Annas, George J. "Cowboys, Camels, and the First Amendment — The FDA's Restrictions on Tobacco Advertising." *New England Journal of Medicine* 335:23 (5 December 1996): 1779-83. Provides a summary of the status of First Amendment protection of commercial speech and FDA's arguments for the legality of its proposed restrictions against tobacco-product advertising and the counter-arguments of the tobacco and advertising industries.

Boedecker, Karl A., Fred W. Morgan and Linda Berns Wright. "The Evolution of First Amendment Protection for Commercial Speech." *Journal of Marketing* 59:1 (January 1995): 38-47. The authors review the chronology of commercial speech cases and discuss commercial speech standards in light of the various points of view that the Supreme Court must balance when making its decisions.

Fueroghne, Dean K. "Advertising Concerns with Alcohol and Tobacco," Chapter 13, pp. 470-505, in *Law and Advertising: Current Legal Issues for Agencies, Advertisers, and Attorneys.* Chicago: The Copy Shop, 1995. Looks at the history of alcoholic beverage advertising from the end of prohibition to the present, including industry standards for beer, wine, and distilled spirits advertising.

Glantz, Stanton A. "Removing the Incentive to Sell Kids Tobacco: A Proposal." *Journal of the American Medical Association* 269:6 (10 February 1993): 793-4. Dr. Glantz introduces an unusual proposal to charge tobacco companies for encouraging smoking among minors, thereby discouraging the practice. He proposes annual government surveys to estimate the number of underage smokers and the per-brand annual sales volume represented by those smokers; tobacco companies would then be assessed double that amount, payable at either the state or national level, to reduce the economic incentive of marketing these products to children.

Hanson, Mark. "Capitol Offensives: Will the state attorneys general be able to do what no private lawyer has ever done, make the tobacco industry pay out its first dime in damages?" *ABA Journal* (January 1997): 50-6. Presents the arguments on both sides in the multistate lawsuits designed to recover the costs of medical care for tobacco-related illnesses from the tobacco industry.

Hernandez, Debra Gersh. "Tobacco Ad Debate Rages " *Editor & Publisher*, 7 September 1996, pp. 24-5, 36-7. Summarizes the federal government's proposed restrictions on tobacco product marketing, advertising, and sales and the arguments for and against such restrictions.

Reid, Leonard N., Karen Whitehall King and Peggy J. Kreshel. "Black and White Models and Their Activities in Modern Cigarette and Alcohol Ads." *Journalism Quarterly* 71 (Winter 1994): 873-86. Compares the depictions of minority and non-minority models in ads for cigarettes and alcoholic beverages in a cross-section of consumer magazines and asks whether these portrayals actually reflect the reality of black and white life.

Seelye, Katharine Q. "Trickle of Television Liquor Ads Releases Torrent of Regulatory Uncertainty." *New York Times*, 12 January 1997, p. 8. Reviews the conflict between beer and wine marketers' television advertising and the previously voluntary agreement by the distilled liquor industry not to advertise its products on television.

Teinowitz, Ira. "The politics of vice. Campaign '96: Once campaigns were decided in smoke-filled rooms; now the pols are lighting debates over product ads." *Advertising Age*, 8 July 1996, pp. 1, 26. Looks at the convergence of influences that made product advertising a target of both Democrats and Republicans in the 1996 presidential election. The combination of "family values," a renewed concern to protect children, tobacco industry campaign contributions to both parties, and the announcement that at least one liquor marketer would begin advertising on television took a leading role in setting the agenda for this presidential campaign.

Chapter Seventeen

Censorship in Cyberspace:
Unnecessary or Inevitable?

Amy Robinson

The Internet, a worldwide connection of computer networks, has become one of the most far-reaching, fastest growing communication tools available to the general public. A person can send e-mail to a friend across the room or across the ocean with the same ease. The Internet grows each time a new user connects, and there's no apparent end in sight. What started as the pastime of scientists, academicians, and "Star Trek" fans has begun to affect the lives of the general public. Students and employees access the Internet through their universities and companies; parents and children surf the Net through their home accounts. Those who call themselves computer-illiterate are out of the loop. Television commercials and print ads now feature not only company addresses and telephone numbers, but also the addresses of Internet home pages.

In fact, this medium has grown so fast it may have begun to outgrow the existing laws that govern other media. This situation was bound to create some kind of controversy, and it has. Among the issues that have evolved is the question of whether the Internet requires any form of content regulation. The Internet allows people to communicate more freely than ever — but this has some drawbacks. A University of North Carolina student working on a French degree can now access web sites in France, but an eleven-year-old can access pornographic material just as easily. The existence of some fairly dark material on the Internet has led some to believe that such material should be made illegal in order to protect minors from its harmful effects.

Origins of the Issue

The Internet itself is the product of almost forty years of technological advances. In 1957, the U.S. government formed the Advanced Research Projects Agency within the Department of Defense to establish its lead in military science and technology. In 1972, forty machines were connected as part of a demonstration. Soon universities were connecting and distributing information to each other. The Transmission Control Protocol (TCP) and Internet Protocol (IP) were established in 1982, becoming commonly known as TCP/IP for ARPANET. Because a connected set of networks, specifically those using TCP/IP, was called an "internet," a connected set of TCP/IP internets came to be called *the* Internet.

The Internet began to grow quickly, and this growth continues today. In 1989 there were more than 100,000 hosts, and by 1992, more than one million. By the end of 1997, there were approximately 35 million. The diversity of users continues to increase — the U.S. White House came online in 1993 — as does the diversity of the Internet itself. Web pages, which used to be primarily text, now include graphics, video, and audio. Internet Talk Radio began broadcasting in 1993, Internet shopping malls appeared in 1994, and Internet mass marketing began in the form of mass advertising e-mails.

This relatively new medium has begun to take on characteristics of traditional media. It has advertising, for example, and it's used for both information and entertainment. Yet, it has a fairly short history as a public medium, so the regulation issue is still an uncertain one, and the government's first attempt to regulate it resulted in controversy and a U.S. Supreme Court case.

In 1996, Congress passed the Communications Decency Act as an amendment to the larger Telecommunications Act. In its final form, the CDA made it a crime to disseminate indecent or patently offensive material to a minor through the Internet . The Act made violators subject to up to two years in jail and $100,000 in fines. On the day it was signed into law, a rather strange alliance of organizations — from the ACLU to the American Library Association — immediately filed an appeal that would ultimately become known as *Reno v. ACLU*. According to these organizations, the CDA violated the First Amendment, and when their challenges to the law were filed, the Justice Department agreed not to enforce the Act until its constitutionality had been determined.

At issue was the nature of the Internet as a medium of communication. The ACLU and its fellow plaintiffs were trying to prove the Internet is more like a newspaper than a broadcast medium. Why? The Supreme Court has, over the years, established a hierarchy of First Amendment protection given to various media. Print has received the most — any form of licensing or prior restraint is virtually unheard of for newspapers, books, and magazines, for example. Broadcast media, on the other hand, has received less protection. The airwaves through which radio and TV signals are transmitted are limited ones, and so the government took on the management of those airwaves in 1927, licensing stations in the public interest. Since then, the FCC has had a much greater role in the content of radio and TV broadcasts than would ever be acceptable for print media. The government cannot, for example, take away someone's printing press because that press churns out material that is racist, vulgar, or sexually explicit; but the FCC can certainly slap a warning on a broadcast station for airing such material. It can also take away that station's license altogether.

Another reason for this second-class status goes back to the case, *FCC v. Pacifica*, in which a radio station was issued a warning for airing comedian George Carlin's monologue, "Seven Dirty Words." The case had begun when a father complained to the FCC that he and his son had been effectively assaulted by Carlin's rambling string of expletives while driving in the car one morning. In its *Pacifica* opinion, the Court emphasized the "invasive" nature of broadcasting, noting that a quick change of the channel could expose the listener or viewer to something he or she didn't expect. Moreover, that listener could easily be a young child. With broadcast media, a child didn't have to know how to read in order to access whatever was being aired.

The same year that Congress passed the CDA, the Court was trying to decide where to place another new medium in its now well-established hierarchy. In *Turner v. FCC*, its members determined that cable had more First Amendment protection than broadcast. After all, cable isn't bound by finite airwaves. However, cable would receive less protection than print. So where would the Court place the Internet? Those who were appealing the CDA hoped it would be extended the high level of protection that print media have enjoyed. Those who wanted it to be regulated were counting on an assessment that was closer to the broadcast and cable status. In effect, most observers expected *Reno v. ACLU* to be a definitive ruling on the nature of the Internet as a medium. This would be a powerful case.

When Congress passed the CDA, there was a striking reaction from the Internet community. Many sites turned their home pages black in protest, and some continued to update their users on the progress of the appeal. One home page, for example, featured a link called "Why WAS this page black?" It went on to describe the Act: "What you see, read, and write in public will be curtailed because of this legislation." A protest organized by Voters Telecommunications Watch, Center for Democracy and Technology, and many other organizations asked people to turn their home pages black for forty-eight hours after that. It was a success. This particular web page listed almost seventy organizations that had joined the protest, including the ACLU, CyberQueer Lounge, Feminists For Free Expression, Hands Off! The Net, Institute for Global Communications, the Libertarian Party, Marijuana Policy Project, National Campaign for Freedom of Expression, National Coalition Against Censorship, Republican Liberty Caucus, and *Wired* Magazine.

In the days after President Clinton signed the CDA, the web sites devoted to pornography generally remained the same. Some tried to comply with the new regulations by setting up warning pages, but other sites were not so accommodating — on the night of the signing, a new Usenet group was formed called alt.f---.the.communications.decency.act.

The Supreme Court decided *Reno v. ACLU* just over one year later and overturned the law before it was ever implemented, giving it a tentative status that was clearly above broadcast in the First Amendment hierarchy, and possibly as high as print. Since then, legislators, parents, librarians, and libertarians have all tried to find a way to either keep minors from accessing questionable material on the Internet or keep the government from regulating what one U.S. District judge has called the most democratic medium in history.

Arguments for Content Regulation

When the U.S. government's lawyer, Seth P. Waxman, approached the nine Supreme Court justices to defend the CDA, he had the singular goal of proving that the Act was necessary to the wellbeing of America's youth. One characteristic that's common among today's children and teenagers is that they are often extremely comfortable on computers — much more so than their parents. This is even more true of their abilities on the Internet. It is the younger generation that is surfing through the ocean of information found in cyberspace — and this is what concerns many who realize how easy it is for kids to sit at a bedroom terminal and access everything from pictures of naked celebrities to discussions of sexual techniques. Unlike conventional red-light districts, with adult movie theaters, stages, and bookstores, those who present pornographic information on the Internet are unable to check their audience's IDs and, subsequently, their ages. Thus, minors now have the technological finesse to find material that they may not have the psychological maturity to see. The Internet, Waxman argued before the Court, "threatens to give every child a free pass to every adult bookstore or video store with the click of a mouse," and "threatens to render irrelevant all prior efforts" to shield children from that content.

What are parents so concerned about? When this was written, an Internet search using the AltaVista search engine and the simple word "sex," called up 9.1 million web sites that matched. A few examples:

- *Hardcore Hot Ladies! Here you will find: on-line sex with naked women, xxx pictures of nude girls, erotic videos of gay men, and hardcore adult pornography*

- *Young naked girls teen anal sex pictures!*

- *Most perverted weird and bizarre xxx pictures!*

- *Naked sex fiend! I love being a whore....*

Many of these sites had numerous sexually explicit terms listed in their description in order to be "found" by as many searches as possible. And some did in fact require either credit card payment or password, both of which would effectively lessen the number of underage visitors.

In *Reno*, the government tried to argue that it was in fact trying to preserve the exciting potential of the Internet by keeping it from becoming like a bad area of town, trafficked heavily by those peddling indecent and pornographic material whose presence left cyberspace a vast wasteland because parents would no longer allow their children to visit. Its future as the greatest library in the world, the government argued, would be supplanted by its ability to disseminate sleaze without any inhibitions.

One early red flag surfaced in 1995, when a University of Michigan student, Abraham Jacob Alkhabaz, a.k.a. Jake Baker, was charged for posting a sexually violent story on the Internet. Baker had sent three stories to a "sex stories" file in 1994. The problem was in the one that featured a character named after one of Baker's classmates. He had taken a Japanese class with the woman but had apparently never met her. In the story, "Pamela's Ordeal," she was portrayed as the object of violent sexual fantasies. The story then described how Baker and another man would kidnap the woman at gunpoint. It outlined how they would force her to strip; then rape and torture her with a clamp and a spreader bar; then kill her. A Canadian man, who was never named or charged, responded to this story. He and Baker began exchanging e-mail messages, discussing how they could kidnap the woman. One of Baker's messages read: "Just thinking about it anymore doesn't do the trick. I need to do it."

Baker did not deny writing the story or the messages that included such gems as: "Torture is foreplay, rape is romance, snuff [killing] is climax." Baker's lawyer, Douglas R. Mullkoff, said the offending quotes were taken out of context, and pointed out that the story began, "The following story contains lots of sick stuff. You have been warned." Baker said his story was protected by the First Amendment. Magistrate Thomas A. Carlson of the Detroit Federal District Court said that the twenty-year-old's free-speech rights were irrelevant because he discussed how to carry out *specific* threats against a *specific* woman. Carlson said that even though Baker never spoke to the classmate, his writings were those of a disturbed, potentially harmful man, "a ticking bomb ready to go off." FBI agents arrested Baker, who was charged with transmission of a threat across state lines, and he was to be jailed until his trial. The charges were later dropped, but the case's frightening implications reverberated throughout the country.

First Amendment lawyer Herschel Fink contended that Baker lost his free speech protection when he named a target for his crime and discussed how to carry it out, saying what Baker did was "potential criminal conspiracy." Assistant U.S. Attorney Kenneth Shoddily condemned Baker's actions, noting he used the name of a real person. He also argued that Baker was putting the woman in danger. "God knows who's going to hear this and like it and do something about it," Shoddily said.

With stories like this, it was not long before support for a bill regulating this kind of material gained support. Although the CDA was overturned by the Supreme Court, that support has not altogether dissipated — but neither has the resistance to regulation.

As conquerors of the CDA point out, the most viable alternative to government regulation of sexually explicit material on the Internet is that of filtering software, installed at the user's home, business, or library. One legal scholar, however, has actually argued that the CDA was less restrictive on free expression than these software packages. Harvard law professor Lawrence Lessig, in "What Things Regulate Speech," justifies the government's right to "zone" hardcore pornography, keeping it out of children's reach.

This analogy of real-world zoning — the red-light district notion — was used in *Reno*, but faced two problems. First, the government could not convince the Court that it was not yet technologically possible to "zone" cyberspace, to check the ages of site visitors. Second, the content that the CDA tried to zone was constitutionally vague — neither indecency or patently offensive material were defined clearly. Lessig, however, has limited his proposal to hard-core pornography, which is just one step down from the constitutionally unprotected category of obscene speech. In addition, Lessig agrees with the two Supreme Court Justices who didn't sign the majority opinion in *Reno*: he believes it will be technologically feasible to screen cyberspace visitors in the future.

The heart of his argument is that it is less restrictive of free expression to keep minors from accessing hard-core pornography than it is to use filtering software, which often filters out too much — discussions of AIDS or breast cancer, for instance. Moreover, the filtering software does not inform its user when it has blocked out information during a search. Lessig points out that the use of filtering software in schools and libraries amounts to government restriction on speech, and is thus unconstitutional. And perhaps more importantly, he believes the use of filtering software poses risks of spreading into more insidious versions of censorship — some forms of filtering technology can be put in place at any level, from a company to an Internet Service Provider to a whole country, without the person at home even realizing it. In short, Lessig believes the CDA, if more carefully crafted, would be much less likely to seriously violate the First Amendment.

In fact, a more carefully crafted bill has surfaced since the CDA was over-turned. In November 1997, Sen. Dan Coats announced that he would sponsor an amendment to the 1934 Communications Act that would require commercial distributors of material that's "harmful to minors" to restrict access with credit cards or personal identification numbers. It only applies to web sites; not news-groups, chat rooms, or e-mail, and Coats is optimistic that it will be constitution-ally sound. "Although I think that many opponents of the CDA, who are feeling very heady, want to call it CDA 2," he said, "it is really very different. CDA cast a very wide net. This legislation hunts with a rifle. It goes after one specific area." Violators would face six months in jail and a $50,000 fine, and the FCC would be brought into the fray, charged with regulating the access mechanisms of the relevant web sites.

Although it has dominated the debate, sexually explicit material isn't the only Internet content that has worried people. Some have voiced even more con-cern about material that results in harm to others. Although the Baker case brought hard-core pornography and sexual crime to the forefront, an even larger event — the bombing of the federal building in Oklahoma City in 1995 — prompted some to point out that detailed descriptions of how to reproduce the bomb could be found online in a guide called *The Big Book of Mischief.* There was a suspicion that the bombers had used the Internet to plan the attack. This theo-ry was later discredited, but the seeds of suspicion had already been planted. Even President Clinton admitted that the Internet "has a dark underside."

Hate speech has also been a concern. Debra Gersh Hernandez describes a Senate subcommittee debate about hate messages on the Internet in a 1995 *Editor and Publisher* article, "Mayhem Online." Witnesses and members of the subcom-mittee voiced concern over the destructive messages, although many still didn't want the First Amendment limited in any way. Some supported government regulation. Others wanted parents or networks to be responsible for policing, and for federal agencies to investigate seriously threatening messages.

A hate-speech controversy of international proportions occurred in early 1996. CompuServe, America OnLine, and T-Online (a German company) were warned about giving German subscribers access to the neo-Nazi writings of Ernst Zuendel, a German living in Toronto. Prosecutors warned America OnLine it could be charged with inciting racial hatred, because it's illegal in Germany to publish or distribute neo-Nazi or Holocaust-denial literature. It is still uncertain, however, whether posting information on the Internet would constitute publish-ing or distribution in terms of the German law.

In a related example, four Cornell University freshmen e-mailed twenty friends a message entitled, "75 reasons why women (bitches) should not have freedom of speech," including, "if she can't speak, she can't cry rape." The message found its way through hundreds of computer networks, and the Cornell students received furious responses, including death threats. After an investigation, the students were absolved of sexual harassment and misuse of computer resources because the list was originally distributed as a joke to friends who were not offended by the communication.

One of the legal issues brought up by the CDA concerned who should be held liable for material posted on the Internet. Providers or the individuals themselves? In January 1996, a rabbi named Abraham Cooper began sending letters to Internet providers and universities asking them not to carry messages that "promote racism, anti-Semitism, mayhem and violence," according to a 1996 *Chicago Tribune* story. "Internet providers have a First Amendment right and a moral obligation not to provide these groups with a platform for their destructive propaganda," said Cooper, associate dean of the Simon Wiesenthal Center, a Jewish human rights group. Although Cooper believed the providers were at least ethically responsible, he pointed out that he wasn't referring to chat rooms or news groups, but only to the World Wide Web itself, on which groups have posted racist documents, including pictures and sound clips that are accessible to millions of people.

Basically, there are a number of things that people would rather not have on the Internet — from pornography to hate speech. Those who advocate regulation argue that something must be done to establish and clarify legal rights and obligations regarding this new medium. Once these are in place, they contend, the Internet will be able to grow into a useful *and* user-friendly medium.

Content Regulation is Censorship

According to many in the U.S., however, any form of content regulation — regardless of the medium — violates the First Amendment. James Exon writes in a *CQ Researcher* article, for example, that opponents of regulation say free speech encompasses any communication between two consenting parties regardless of who else might be eavesdropping. Thus, even if children happen upon indecent or pornographic material on the Internet, they are probably not the intended recipients. Consenting adults should not have to tailor their exchanges to include the possibility of eavesdroppers.

Sen. Herb Kohl said at a 1995 Senate hearing that while instructions on bomb-making can be found online, those instructions can just as easily be found in libraries and bookstores. He said people who want such information will find it, and that it is the online communications industry, Internet publishers, and parents — not the government — who should be responsible for controlling children's access to Internet information.

Jesse Lemisch also examines the issue of hate-speech regulation in "The First Amendment is Under Attack in Cyberspace," a 1995 article in *The Chronicle of Higher Education*. Lemisch argues that Internet regulation would impede free debate, and that attempts to get rid of worthless messages would invariably lead to a loss of valuable messages as well. Not everyone, for example, agrees that hate speech should be banned. Bill Maxwell wrote in a 1996 *St. Petersburg Times* story that, as a University of Florida graduate student, he was harassed by skinheads and otherwise targeted with hate speech. He believes, though, racist speech is protected by the First Amendment. Similarly, Mike Godwin, staff counsel for the Electronic Frontier Foundation, has argued that regulation of the Internet would not eliminate anti-Semitism or revisionism. Godwin used the argument of the Jewish Supreme Court Justice Louis D. Brandeis, saying, "The best response is always to answer bad speech with more speech." David Abitbol, the operator of Net Hate, a web page that exposes hate speech on the Internet, said if hate speech was censored, his page would be affected, a possibility that he finds "offensive."

At this point it may be helpful to examine the First Amendment. There are two traditional theories associated with it: the positive and negative. Thomas Emerson's positive, value-promoting theory says that in a self-governing society, there must be a social mechanism for getting the truth and attaining individual self-fulfillment. Alexander Meiklejohn and Vincent Blasi have both argued that a free press is one such mechanism. Positivists, following the principles of John Stuart Mill, would say society is ultimately best served by those allowed to express and learn about themselves. Negative theory, on the other hand, is wary of the extension of government power to limit speech. This theory says that there must be social mechanisms for assessing the government and ensuring it does not curtail free speech. The main concern, upheld by the First Amendment, is protecting citizens' ability to govern themselves.

There are many books describing current opinions on the First Amendment as it relates to electronic media. *The First Amendment — The Challenge of New Technology* is a collection of papers presented at a conference hosted by the San Diego Communications Council. The conference addressed the way electronic technology would affect the media's First Amendment protections. The council was concerned with whether the First Amendment has the flexibility to keep up with new technology. In one presentation, J. Richard Munro, chairman and CEO of Time Inc., said the First Amendment was about "the people's right to know...

to choose for themselves what to believe, to hear every side, to weigh as much information and as many opinions as possible." Censorship of any viewpoints, no matter how hateful or offensive, would violate this crucial First-Amendment tenet by limiting citizens' access to all sides of an issue.

Craig R. Smith, president of the Freedom of Expression Foundation in Washington, D.C., said there has historically been a fear of new technology, leading to the danger of unnecessary regulation, especially in the area of information technology. He urged his audience members to "ask yourself why, if there are so many broadcast outlets in this country, so much electronic media, they have to suffer under content controls whereas the press does not." Richard M. Schmidt Jr., a partner in the Washington, D.C., law firm of Cohn and Marks and counsel to the American Society of Newspaper Editors, agreed that the First Amendment "should be applied whenever and wherever possible to all forms of communication."

David Laventhol, president of the Times Mirror Company of Los Angeles, cited a case in which an investor who lost money on a Canadian company sued Dow Jones because an article on the company did not clarify that some prices were in Canadian, not American, dollars. The investor, however, had read the information from his online Dow Jones News Service. New York Civil Judge Louis R. Friedman decided not to apply new rules to the online technology, saying, "If the substance of a transaction has not changed, new technology does not require a new legal rule merely because of its novelty." He continued that there was no reason to treat the investor differently because he read the information from a computer screen than if he had read it on paper. The Dow Jones News Service, the judge said, was a modern way for the public to get current news, and "it is entitled to the same protection as more established means of news distribution."

Today's First Amendment advocates can cite more practical reasons for their feelings. Many groups that regularly post messages or other information on the Internet are concerned about the effect of regulation, including, of course, operators and users of pornographic sites. Regulation of the Internet to keep it clean "is like the federal government deciding that too many people use 'filthy language' in their private letters and phone calls and then proposing to prosecute, fine and imprison anyone who curses," argued ACLU legislative counsel Donald Haines in a 1995 *CQ Researcher* article. Other groups have also been worried — particularly those who use the Internet for commercial purposes. Those who make money through the Internet fear their operations will suffer a chilling effect if future restrictions label even non-pornographic material illegal. In a 1995 *New York Times* story, Vanderbilt University business professor Donna Hoffman said the CDA frightened Internet entrepreneurs, who didn't even know what words they are allowed to use in their sales pitches. The greatest effect, however, would probably be on small companies or non-commercial individuals who couldn't afford court costs. Fearing prosecution, they might post only bland material on the Internet. Even larger companies have expressed concern. Scott Kurnit, president and chief executive of MCI/News Corporation Internet Ventures, said his company was less at risk than small businesses, but the law would mean his company could only offer a "sanitized" version of its products. "I'm not sure that product would be interesting enough to consumers that anyone would buy it," Kurnit said.

Some First Amendment supporters are particularly troubled because Internet providers are participating in self-censorship. According to the June 29, 1994, issue of the *New York Times,* America Online closed some feminist discussion groups that month because young girls might see the word "girl" in the group's headline, access the discussion, and be exposed to the "inappropriate" subject matter contained within. Another provider, Prodigy, has routinely found objectionable words in messages sent by users. It has warned the users to erase them or the messages will be censored. Its list of unacceptable words, according to the article, is in the dozens. Also, at one point during the Congressional debate about indecency, America Online censored the word "breast" from its system, even in the context of discussion groups between women with breast cancer. The company restored the word after women protested, but this incident caused concern that on-line services would give in to pressure of those advocating regulation.

Some argue that it is consumers who govern what is on the Internet. If there is pornography available, the reasoning goes, it is because people want it. If this is true, and people do want access to such content, then how can the First Amendment be used to bar them from it? Kenneth Roesslein, editorial page editor of the *Milwaukee Journal Sentinel,* said in a 1996 article that CompuServe blocked access to 200 sexually explicit Internet newsgroups in response to a German federal prosecutor who said the content violated Germany's pornography laws. Roesslein, as a member of the media, says he is expected to support unlimited First Amendment freedom. However, he expresses concern for the children involved in the newsgroup sites. "Are there no limits to what must be endured by the First Amendment and those who steadfastly defend it?" he asks, and says civil libertarians who defend "unfettered speech and display" do not have to answer to "the parent whose child was exposed to, or worse yet used, in one of these sleazy cyberspace productions." Yet CompuServe agreed to ban not only pornographic sites, but also news agency articles that mentioned sex.

Another twist to the free speech debate is that the Internet can be used to fight government censorship. In 1993 a Canadian woman, Karla Homolka, pleadedd guilty to murder and said her husband, Paul Bernardo, was also involved. The Ontario court imposed a gag order on the media so potential jurors in the husband's trial would not hear about the case. The Canadian media obeyed the gag order, but Internet users were not so compliant. Daily information about the trial began to appear in a newly created Usenet newsgroup in Toronto. Canadian police shut down local access to the bulletin board, but soon a similar newsgroup appeared, featuring the same information under a different name. This government attempt to regulate information had simply led to more innovative ways of distributing it, pointed out Stephen Kimber, a journalism professor at the University of King's College in Halifax. He called the ban a joke, considering the ease with which the Net citizens bypassed it, and he said that communication systems are now "beyond the short arms of narrow-minded Ontario judicial regulators."

Computer-law specialists say these types of cases test the current laws that were created for other media. In addition, the information on the Internet is often globally available, meaning that it goes outside local or national jurisdictions. The Internet can be regulated only to a limited extent, argued Karen L. Casser, general counsel at a Virginia telecommunications and technology firm, in a 1995 *CQ Researcher* article. "It is really a network of networks rather than any one network," she said, "and cyberspace doesn't have U.S. geographical boundaries. You can't stop people from sending any information in and out of the country."

Obstacles to Regulating the Internet

One problem with regulation is that no one owns the Internet. It is simply a connection of computers. In addition to home pages, users may communicate with each other by using computer bulletin boards. Users post messages on bulletin boards much as they would on physical bulletin boards. These bulletin boards are run by a system operator, who usually does not regulate or censor content, unless it is to satisfy some individual standard. However, web sites do not belong to any one person or group; so they are not governed by any across-the-board standard. As stated in a 1994 *Time* article, "Battle for the Soul of the Internet," many argue that no one owns or controls the Internet, it is a free space, and it may represent journalism's ultimate liberation.

Another problem is that users do not always use their real names. Subscribers to commercial on-line services such as America OnLine often use code names. So they can post messages anonymously. This gives users great freedom to speak their minds without fear of personal recrimination. Of course, this does not mean other users will not disagree with them; they do disagree, often vehemently. This is called "flaming" and can be quite intense; yet, it is not a personal argument if those arguing are hiding behind code names. This aspect of the Internet has unleashed a powerful drawing force: the ability for users to interact anonymously and thus say whatever they want without fear of embarrassment or punishment. Some, though, think this liberating situation has been abused.

In a 1995 case, Caribbean resort owner Arnold Bowker and scuba instructor John Joslin said they were defamed by an anonymous user on a computer bulletin board, and asked that America Online be forced to disclose the user's name so they can sue the person for libel. The user, identified as "Jenny TRR," posted a bulletin-board message saying her diving instructor at the Carib Inn used drugs. The message continued, "I won't mention his name but he's the only white instructor there." Bowker posted a message on the bulletin board saying the allegations were untrue and asking Jenny TRR to recant. There was no apology, and Bowker decided to sue for damages. His attorney, Lawrence Levin, said the user had "abused the privilege of being able to communicate with people worldwide."

Another obstacle to applying current laws to the Internet is that the medium is somewhat undefinable in itself. Its place in the First Amendment hierarchy was mentioned earlier and, again, the Supreme Court tentatively gave it high standing in that hierarchy. At the same time, the Court noted that the Internet's role in society was still developing, and left the door open for a future change of heart. Part of the confusion comes from the Internet's many uses. People can send e-mail to each other the same way they can send letters through the mail, except that e-mail travels much faster and is not subject to the same privacy laws as so-called "snail mail." People can also talk in "real time," making the Internet similar to telephone technology. On the other hand, newspapers and magazines can be found on-line, so the Internet would seem to be another method of publishing news and information for large groups of people. Its possession of visual and audio characteristics make it not unlike TV and radio — although, again, the Internet is, like cable, not constrained by a limited radio spectrum. In sum, it possesses the characteristics of all other traditional media and then some.

Another characteristic, perhaps the most important and difficult to assess, is its ability to create for its users an entire "virtual" world separate from the physical world. Users are able to join discussion groups in which they can simply "lurk," or "listen" without responding, or they can add their opinions and ideas to the discussion. It is possible to go into "chat rooms" with a few other people and have a more private conversation. Some people feel they benefit greatly from this activity; for example, a shy person who rarely goes out with friends may assume an entirely different personality under the cloak of anonymity, and a whole new exiting world opens up. On the other hand, some feel this virtual lifestyle can be carried too far, that such people lose contact with reality. At any rate, these examples illustrate the indefinable quality of the Internet. To some, it is simply a means of distributing information. It is a public forum to many people, in which they can exchange ideas with people all over the world through discussion groups. To others, it is an almost real environment.

This multifaceted nature of the Internet is, of course, further complicated by its global reach. Since the groundbreaking case, *Miller v. California*, the justice system has utilized the notion of "community standards" when determining whether something is obscene, and thus unprotected by the First Amendment. This means that a jury in Jackson, Miss., can find a film to be patently offensive, appealing to prurient interests, and subsequently obscene — whereas a jury in Las Vegas, Nev., can find that same film to be simply pornographic, and thus deserving of at least some First Amendment protection. This system wasn't problematic when it simply applied to traditional media. Its effectiveness grew murky, however, when new technology emerged.

One of the first major cases that highlighted this problem concerned the New York-based Home Dish Satellite Corporation. The company distributed R-rated films to about 1.2 million customers nationwide. It also distributed X-rated films to another 30,000 customers. But when some citizens in Montgomery, Ala., happened upon the X-rated material, it was not long before a jury of that city's conservative citizens were able to put the entire satellite company out of business by indicting it for distributing obscenity. The case never even made it to trial, however, because GTE Corporation, GTE Spacenet Corporation, and United States Satellite, which had been providing satellite transmission service to HDSC, withdrew their service and forced HDSC out of business.

Similarly, what is considered obscene to someone accessing a computer bulletin board in Memphis, Tenn., may not be considered obscene to a person in Los Angeles accessing the same bulletin board. Thus, a California couple who maintained a sexually explicit bulletin board were charged with distributing obscenity in Tennessee. Although the Supreme Court refused to address the issue of international community standards in *Reno*, the potential problems are exacerbated even further when one considers the conservative cultures worldwide, to whom the likes of Madonna and Howard Stern are unquestionably obscene.

Resolution

The debate over free speech and content regulation will probably never be resolved to adequately satisfy both sides. If the Internet were to enjoy total freedom, then many parents, religious groups, and others would be upset that children could be exposed to indecent material. On the other hand, if the government began to take an active role in regulating the Internet, then some sites would undoubtedly be banned, and many would feel that freedom of speech was being violated.

As it stands, the government has already instituted some programs for cracking down on child pornography — which has long been illegal — on the Internet. The U.S. Customs Service created Operation Longarm, an international weapon against child pornography distributed through computer networks. In May 1994 the agency had obtained thirty-one arrest warrants, and half the offenders had pleaded guilty to the charges..

As mentioned earlier, one likely solution to the quandary has been found in the software that filters out offensive material based on keywords and, potentially, "flags" on web sites. In 1996 Microsoft Corporation endorsed a voluntary ratings system for information on the World Wide Web. The system was first developed for rating video games and computer software. Retailers such as Wal-Mart have used it to help select the software they sell. Microsoft said it would incorporate an Internet version, an information filtering system, into its next version of Internet Explorer. Also endorsing ratings systems are Microsystems Software Inc., which makes Cyber Patrol, and SurfWatch Software Inc. The ratings system, developed by the Recreational Software Advisory Council and called RSAC-I, lets parents block a computer's access to certain web sites.

Netscape Communications Corp. and Spyglass Inc. have not agreed to support the RSAC-I ratings system, but they do support the Platform for Internet Content Selection. PICS is an industry-wide standard that would provide for numerous ratings systems. Companies that support it would provide in their software a means for parents to choose their preferred ratings system. The RSAC-I system is seen as objective and comprehensive. It assigns ratings based on Internet publishers' responses about the content of their web pages. Each page is rated from 0 to 4 in the categories of sex, nudity, violence, and offensive language. The RSAC-I system allows parents to block pages with higher ratings than they wish their children to be exposed to. The council's executive director, Stephen Balkam, told the *Wall Street Journal* that the council is devising ways to make sure Internet publishers accurately report their pages' content. One of these is already intact; the software allows parents to block access to any web site without an RSAC-I rating, giving publishers incentive to comply with the system. Other organizations may develop ratings systems. If so, parents will have an even wider choice of which ratings systems to use.

Despite the earlier criticisms of filtering software, its use, combined with a comprehensive ratings system, may be the best compromise. Using this method allows parents to protect their children from harmful influences without infringing on the First Amendment rights of others.

Because it is relatively easy to create a web site in the form of a home page or bulletin board, and because exchanges with other users may be anonymous, the Internet has been called a virtual marketplace of ideas. This marketplace should not be used to expose a child to indecent or pornographic material if the child's parents object. At the same time, it must not be censored. It is stretching the meaning of the First Amendment to claim that it protects everything that appears on the Internet. Yet, as many First Amendment supporters point out, cyberspace may be the most democratic arena of free speech ever discovered.

Recommended Readings

Books

de Sola Pool, Ithiel. *Technologies of Freedom.* Cambridge, Mass.: Belknap Press of Harvard University Press, 1983. Follows evolution of media freedom from print and broadcast media to cable television and electronic publishing.

Diamond, Edwin, Norman Sandler, and Milton Mueller. *Telecommunications in Crisis: The First Amendment, Technology, and Deregulation.* Washington, D.C.: Cato Institute, 1983. Arguments for keeping the government from regulating media, broadcast in particular, and predictions concerning the FCC and new media.

Emord, Jonathan W. *Freedom, Technology, and the First Amendment.* San Francisco: Pacific Research Institute for Public Policy, 1991. Protecting the First Amendment in the age of new media.

Gabbard, C.B., and G.S. Park. *The Information Revolution in the Arab World: Commercial, Cultural and Political Dimensions — The Middle East Meets the Internet.* Santa Monica, Calif: Rand, 1995. The impact technology will have on the Middle East, including whether the government will allow the free flow of information that could threaten its power or impose restraints on access to the technology.

Garry, Patrick M. *Scrambling for Protection: The New Media and the First Amendment.*

Pittsburgh: University of Pittsburgh Press, 1994. The First Amendment is approaching change because of new technologies and politics.

Martin, Shannon E. *Bits Bytes, and Big Brother.* Westport, Conn.: Praeger, 1995. The government's control of information in the technological age.

Mickelson, Sig, and Elena Mier Y Teran, eds. *The First Amendment — The Challenge of New Technology.* New York: Praeger, 1989. A collection of papers discussing the First Amendment's ability to adapt to changing communication technology.

Articles

Clark, Charles S. "Regulating the Internet." *CQ Researcher,* 30 June 1995, pp. 563-80. Examination of various points concerning Internet regulation, including government censorship of pornography and information that could potentially be used to commit crimes.

Exon, J. James. "Should the Government Crack Down on Pornography on the Internet?" *CQ Researcher,* 30 June 1995, p. 577. Debate between supporters of government regulation of Internet information and free-speech advocates.

Hernandez, Debra Gersh. "Bombmaking on the Internet." *Editor and Publisher,* 24 June 1995, pp. 38-40. A Senate amendment to anti-terrorism legislation specifies that circulating literature on making explosives is illegal if the information supplier intends the explosives to be used for criminal purposes.

Hernandez, Debra Gersh. "Mayhem Online." *Editor and Publisher,* 24 June 1995, pp. 34-8. Discussion of a Senate subcommittee's hearings on hate messages on the Internet and some proposed solutions.

Lemisch, Jesse. "The First Amendment is Under Attack in Cyberspace." *Chronicle of Higher Education,* 20 January 1995, p. A56. Examination of whether Internet speech should be regulated.

Rosen, Jeffrey. "Cheap Speech: Will the Old First Amendment Battles Survive the New Technology?" *The New Yorker,* 7 August 1995, pp. 75, 76. Discussion of rebuttals of the *Time* magazine story about cyberporn and overview of cases including the First Amendment, pornography, and government attempts at regulation.

Webb, William. "Too Much Pornography on the Internet — or in the Press?" *Editor and Publisher,* 22 July 1995, pp. 30-2. Discusses charges of pornography made by Internet supporters and newspapers/periodicals against each other, and whether First Amendment protection of free speech applies to online communications as well as print media.

5 Media Roles and Obligations

J n this section, the authors address issues that are probably the most often discussed among media practitioners and their audiences. The first five chapters are essentially about the blurring of lines between news and entertainment.

George Gladney asks the question of whether the news media should give readers what they *want* or what they *need*. His discussion outlines the quandary of whether to maintain traditional news protocol or give into what ratings and circulation figures suggest that the audience wants — particularly with regard to the choice of stories that go on the air or the front page. Professor Gladney examines the philosophical underpinnings of the debate. LeAnne Daniels adds to the discussion with attention to a cultural side of the debate, offering one side's notion that news is in fact a cultural product — and is thus acceptable in both its superficial and serious manifestations.

In an analysis of the impact of tabloid news, Emily Erickson Hoff points to one of the probable causes of the modern bent toward infotainment. The debate hinges on whether programs like *Hard Copy* have truly changed the media landscape and whether such an influence is necessarily negative.

According to Lisa Mullikin's discussion of mainstream television news, that first question seems to be answered in the affirmative. Ms. Mullikin presents the uphill battle waged by TV news since its inception, and the modern issue of whether network television utilizes its unique characteristics as a medium to serve the American public — who does, after all, prefer to get its news from TV over any other medium.

A practice that has become alarmingly *en vogue* in recent years — paying news sources for their stories — is discussed by Lorna Veraldi. She notes that both tabloid and network news organizations have been known to use the practice of "checkbook journalism" and presents the debate regarding what impact it has had on news credibility and, on occasion, the credibility of witnesses called to testify in criminal trials.

Michael Gouge provides a treatment of a public journalism, an approach of both growing popularity and growing controversy. In this issue, the value of objectivity is set against that of social responsibility. Mr. Gouge addresses the notion of public cynicism covered in earlier chapters and develops the argument that "public" journalism is more appropriate to the modern news industry in that it empowers readers and viewers to take a greater role in their community. But, as he shows, there are drawbacks to this journalistic approach, not the least of which is a compromising of traditional objectivity.

With such issues as these — along with numerous others that raise questions about media performance — it is only natural to think that media professionals would give close attention to them. Whether the media have the capability to criticize themselves, however, is a question that observers long have asked. Fred Bales takes up that every question. He asks whether it is possible for the media as an industry to diagnose and treat its ailments — many of which are addressed in this section — or whether it is only those outside the industry who can see well enough to suggest improvements. As Professor Bales shows, there have been various attempts — with varied results— at providing such mechanisms to assess problems and challenges as they arise.

Chapter Eighteen

Giving Readers
What They Want or Need?

George Albert Gladney

William Kovach's abrupt resignation in 1988 as editor of the *Atlanta Journal* and *Atlanta Constitution* created a stir in journalism circles. The reaction was even stronger six months later when the newspapers hired Ron Martin, executive editor of *USA Today*, to replace Kovach. What seemed to be at stake was the legitimacy of a potent but controversial trend begun in the newspaper industry in the mid-1970s. The trend went by the catch-phrase, "Give readers what they want."

Kovach, a former Washington bureau chief of the *New York Times*, was brought to Atlanta with great fanfare in 1986 to make the somnolent newspapers important and give them elite stature. Kovach's supporters claim he revamped and revitalized the papers, turning them into Pulitzer Prize winners. Under Kovach, the Atlanta papers adopted a hard-hitting reporting style, with emphasis on investigative, in-depth, and explanatory journalism and stories with strong public policy implications. The papers also took on the look and tone of *The Times* — elaborate lead paragraphs, stories that ran on for 70 inches or more, and prudent use of color.

With the hiring of Martin, many observers worried that the Atlanta papers would become the next McPaper, a pejorative reference to the Gannett Co.'s national newspaper, *USA Today*. Since its creation in 1982, *USA Today* had become known for its penchant for short, breezy stories; dazzling graphics; lavish use of color; offbeat, lightweight features; emphasis on news relevant to readers' personal affairs (hobbies, personal finance, careers, etc.); stories high in entertainment value but low in substance (e.g., news about celebrities, sports, and weather); and heavy reliance on marketing surveys to help determine content and format.

The concerns about Martin's hiring were heightened when Jay Smith, publisher of the Atlanta papers, owned by Cox Enterprises, said that "there are some things we could learn from *USA Today*." Smith said techniques borrowed from *USA Today* might provide the dramatic change needed to attract young readers and buoy sagging circulation. A number of top-flight reporters, disgruntled by Kovach's departure and Martin's hiring, left the Atlanta papers, but the flap soon subsided. Kovach moved on to become curator of the Nieman Foundation at Harvard University, and Martin brought his *USA Today* influence to the *Journal* and *Constitution.*

The controversy sparked in Atlanta is an old one, going back to the early days of American journalism, and it is alive in the late 1990s. At issue is the question: What is the primary mission of journalism? Is it, as Kovach argues, to inform citizens about important events and issues that are relevant to self-governance? Or is it, as Martin believes, to provide information that is both informative and interesting or entertaining? Put another way, should newspapers give readers what they need to make intelligent decisions in a participatory democracy, or should they give readers what they want, even if it means forgetting public policy considerations?

Philosophically, the issue has its roots in political science with eighteenth-century British statesman and orator Edmund Burke's distinction between the "delegate," whose role is to follow the dictates of constituents, and the "trustee," whose role is to follow the dictates of his or her own conscience. Traditionally, editors have favored the trustee model, claiming that their professional expertise, experience, and values qualify them to judge what is news.

Origins of the Issue

USA Today has been a paragon of change in newspaper form and content in the 1980s and 1990s, but the innovations cannot be credited wholly to the people at Gannett. Leo Bogart, in his influential book *Press and Public*, found that the idea of "giving readers what they want" was not a Gannett innovation, but had become a catch-phrase among editors in the late 1970s, before the birth of *USA Today*. Carl Sessions Stepp, a journalism professor who once worked as one of its national editors, observed, "I can think of nothing that *USA Today* invented. What I think *USA Today* did was take a lot of things that were on the edge of happening, or happening locally, bundle them together and then sort of dare everyone else to do them." Much of the experimentation in the late 1970s was guided by heavy market research, something new to the American newsroom. In 1977 the newspaper industry launched the $4-million Newspaper Readership project, a joint effort spearheaded by the American Newspaper Publishers Association, American Society of Newspaper Editors, and Newspaper Advertising Bureau. One study that especially caught editors' attention concluded that readers like good news as well as bad. Editors were urged to adopt "soft news" written in short, easy-to-understand stories that attempted to get readers personally involved. Editors were told that readers are busy and appreciate newspapers that are designed so readers can find and digest stories easily. According to Doug Underwood in his book, *When MBAs Rule the Newsroom,* these recommendations became "the hallmarks of the typical redesigned newspaper of the 1980s."

Why, suddenly in the late 1970s, all this interest in readers' wants? The answer: ominous circulation trends. According to journalism professor Robert L. Stevenson, between 1945 and 1970 newspapers saw a slow, steady rise in circulation, only to see it flatten and decline in the 1970s. The drop was slight — from 62.1 million total circulation in 1970 to 60.7 million in 1975 — but it alarmed editors who knew the population was growing at a fast clip. In 1946, circulation per 1,000 people was 382, but by 1975 it fell to 281 — a 26 per cent drop. In the 1980s circulation was mostly flat, despite peaking at 62.8 million in 1988, and then a recession in the early 1990s caused total circulation to dip below 60,000 for the first time since the 1960s. In 1995, total circulation was 58.2 million.

This background helps explain the motivation behind the massive changes in newspaper design, graphics, and packaging, and the shift to "reader-friendly" content. But reader-friendly journalism isn't new. Underwood states that modern marketing and packaging journalism may be seen simply as a more sophisticated way of doing what newspaper executives have traditionally done whenever they were worried about their market share — that is to try to build circulation by giving readers what they want, attract more advertisers by target-marketing customers, and produce a more attractive newspaper by packaging it in more enticing ways.

Journalism historian Gerald Baldasty notes that news did not become a commodity, shaped and marketed for profit, until the late 1800s. He quotes one editor from that era saying that "the man who manufactures the newspaper must as surely cater to the public taste as he who manufactures tobacco, or neckties, or candies, or groceries, or any other article of consumption."

Periodically, newspapers have experimented with things for which *USA Today* is known. For example, truncated or digest-form stories flourished in Chicago newspapers in the 1870s and again in the sensationalist "yellow press" papers in New York in the 1890s. The yellow press also was infatuated with use of color, graphics, and illustrations.

Other newspapers, more concerned about satisfying readers' informational needs, have concentrated on substantive issues affecting public life and the welfare of the community. The editors of these newspapers have viewed the newspaper as an important vehicle for disseminating opinion and criticism. This was the concern of editors of the Partisan Press Era in the early decades of the republic when newspapers were aligned with political parties and focused heavily on political affairs, and with the influential journals of opinion in the mid- and late-nineteenth century. In the late 1800s and early 1900s these editors used the press to further progress and reform and battle injustice and corruption. This brand of journalism is exemplified by the best work of Joseph Pulitzer's *New York World* and the investigative journalism of "muckraking" newspapers and magazines. While eschewing crusades, Adolph Ochs' *New York Times* probably focused on readers' informational needs more than any other paper of this era.

Give Readers What They Want

In a study titled "Reader Satisfaction: Are Community Editors Giving the Readers What They Want?" Guido H. Stempel III and Robert Nanney tell the story of how the late journalism professor Hal Lister once startled a group of news editing students when he suggested that a newspaper's first priority should be to make a profit, and its second priority — necessary to achieve the first — should be to know its audience.

Lister's pronouncements were rooted in two theories that have enormously influenced journalistic values: libertarian press theory and social responsibility theory. Libertarian theory, which harkens to the early days of the American press, enumerates two primary press functions: to inform and to entertain. A third function, a necessary correlate to the others, is for the press to ensure its own financial independence through sales and advertising. According to Fred Siebert, a co-author of the classic *Four Theories of the Press*, the media's purpose is to help discover truth and assist in solving political and social problems by presenting all manner of evidence and opinion as the basis for decisions. However, according to libertarian theory, press freedom was viewed as a purely personal right of press owners. The Founding Fathers believed that for truth to emerge, there must be a free marketplace of ideas; the best way to ensure that is to guarantee an unfettered press. If a newspaper does not satisfy citizen wants or needs (market demand) for information, presumably a competitor will.

Four Theories co-author Theodore Peterson wrote that social responsibility theory, which grew out of recommendations of the Commission on Freedom of the Press (Hutchins Commission) in the late 1940s, criticized the American press — then operating largely under libertarian theory — on a number of counts. Among its recommendations for change was a call for the press to provide a "truthful, comprehensive, and intelligent account of the day's events in a context which gives them meaning." Stempel and Nanney point out that many journalists believe that knowledge about readers' interests is necessary to fulfill this recommendation.

This background helps us understand the first and second arguments of those who believe the press should give readers what they want. These are the advocates of reader-friendly, or market-driven, journalism associated with *USA Today* and its many imitators.

The first argument embraces the libertarian claim that newspapers have a right or obligation to ensure their own financial independence. Advocates of this position argue that for the sake of a newspaper's owners, employees, stockholders, and readers, a newspaper has a right or obligation to survive and make a profit. Reader-friendly advocates argue that the newspaper industry today faces several trends that threaten its profitability and perhaps even its survival. The best way to buck those trends, they insist, is to give readers what they want.

The most worrisome trend is the significant decline in circulation, which was discussed earlier. Editors have been especially worried about the reader drop-off among baby-boomers, women and youth. For example, a Gallup Poll in 1965 found that 67 per cent of adults under thirty-five said they read a newspaper the day before; by 1990, the percentage had dropped to 29, according to a study by the Times Mirror Center for the People and the Press. The result: Since the late 1960s newspapers have struggled to attract advertisers, which explains why the newspaper share of total U.S. advertising expenditures has dropped significantly. All of this is part of a chain reaction, because without increases in advertising revenues and circulation, earnings per share cannot grow at an acceptable rate to attract investors. In turn, investors hold the key to raising capital for newspapers' equipment and plant modernization. Further, the deteriorating financial health of newspapers can damage the morale and well-being of workers in the newspaper industry.

Proponents of reader-friendly newspapers argue that these developments are connected to two other trends that are not likely to go away anytime soon. The first is concentration and consolidation of newspapers into the hands of a few large national and multinational corporations whose shares are traded publicly. As more and more family-owned newspapers have been purchased by these large firms, it has meant that more newspapers are components of large companies competing with the most profitable and speculative investments.

The second related trend is the proliferation of competing forms of media that are in an ideal position to give their audience — and advertisers — what they want. The impact of new competition began in the early 1920s, when newspapers peaked in number. While radio did not significantly affect newspaper circulation (and perhaps even stimulated it), radio did begin to cut into the pie for advertising dollars. TV cut into the pie even more and hurt newspaper circulation when Americans began to turn to television as their primary source of news. In the 1980s and 1990s, direct mail (catalogs and fliers delivered by mail) has competed successfully for newspaper advertising dollars, offering customers the advantages of precise targeting of the market, blanketing of zip codes, or 100 per cent market saturation. While newspapers' actual dollar volume of total U.S. advertising expenditures has gone up, it has not increased nearly as dramatically as for other media, i.e., magazines, direct mail, and broadcast outlets, particularly television. In the 1980s and 1990s newspapers have faced other threats in the form of sharply rising newsprint costs and rising competition from suburban and alternative newspapers.

Given all these fretful trends, proponents of reader-friendly journalism argue that newspapers must be marketed like any other commodity — soap, breakfast cereal, appliances. To do that, they say, newspapers must do market research to find out what readers want in a newspaper, and then satisfy those wants. If a little light fare and a splash of color are needed to lure readers, then so be it — the very survival of newspapers is at stake. A newspaper that's out of business can't be read.

The second argument favoring reader-friendly journalism relates to the Hutchins Commission's concern about placing news in context for readers. Stempel and Nanney point out that many journalists believe that if a newspaper is to place news in a meaningful context for readers, it must know readers' interests.

This argument also relates to the question of why population growth has outstripped newspaper circulation. It is said that because newspapers have been averse to change and market research, they have lost touch with readers. Newspapers, it is argued, are too boring and hard to read. People today, in an era of double wage-earner families, lack time to pore over comprehensive, in-depth, analytical, interpretive, explanatory, or critical reporting. Besides, if it is important news, it will be on the nightly TV broadcast.

But proponents of reader-friendly journalism say newspapers' problems go beyond mere lifestyle changes. What has happened, they explain, is a change in epistemology, or "ways of knowing." Young people today, they argue, have learned to process information differently, thanks largely to television. This is the notion that literacy, traditionally defined in print terms, needs to be rethought in visual terms. Thus, the terms "visual literacy" and "teleliteracy" have come into vogue.

Peter Prichard, in his book *The Making of McPaper*, makes it clear that designers of *USA Today* were mindful of this new type of literacy, and they made a conscious effort to attract a generation of readers weaned on television.

The same sort of thinking guides editors who have tried to emulate *USA Today*-style innovation in their newspapers. Media critic Howard Rosenstiel, writing in the *Los Angeles Times*, observed that many journalists consider the most important element of *USA Today* to be "its personality as a newspaper designed for the TV generation, with its hopeful tone, its mixing of entertainment and news and its quick-bit, non-linear way of delivering information." In 1986, *Los Angeles Times* media critic David Shaw quoted the managing editor of the *Orlando Sentinel* as saying, "We're in the Television Age and we're discovering how static print can be, especially to the younger generation, so we're actively seeking ways to make newspapers visually exciting ... as animated as possible."

With this sort of thinking guiding editors, many newspapers have developed new formulas to attract the visually literate. The changes generally include the following features: Shorter stories and a limit or complete bar on use of story "jumps" (continuation on another page); more use of color and visuals, including drawings, charts, and graphs (or "infographics") and more and bigger photographs; more news summaries and indices; front-page teasers about stories inside the paper; provocative quotations (similar to a TV "sound bite") lifted out of a story and played separately, in larger type, to catch the reader's eye; fewer stories on page one; use of extra-large, full-color weather maps; expanded sports coverage; more story "breakouts" (short abstracts, boxed and screened, positioned alongside a major story); increased use of first-person plural pronouns ("we," "our"); creation of distinct, topical sections; more stories about personalities and celebrities; more stories with soft news and upbeat themes; a bright, snappy prose style that uses short, declarative sentences; more human interest stories and seasonally related features; more "news you can use" (information about personal finance, health, career, beauty, relationships, etc.). If all of this sounds like the 10 o'clock newscast, it's intended that way.

The third argument for giving readers what they want can be stated simply: Newspapers are elitist and arrogant if they think that, in their wisdom, they can decide what's best for readers. This is a reaction to the view of network news broadcast legend David Brinkley, who once said, "News is what I say it is." This third argument clearly reflects Edmund Burke's distinction, noted earlier, between the roles of delegate and trustee. It says editors should be delegates who follow the dictates or interests of their constituents — not trustees who select news on the basis of their own judgments and conscience.

Subrata Chakravarty and Carolyn Tortellini, writing in *Forbes*, observed that the trend toward *USA Today*-style form and content — call it the "delegate model" — represents an effort by newspapers to "win back readers" after years of "telling readers what they should read and shoving the fare down readers' throats." Prichard notes that the creators of *USA Today* intended it to be edited "not for the nation's editors, but for the nation's readers."

One large effort to propel market-driven journalism is the Gannett Company's News 2000 project, which has involved surveys of more than 100,000 people to develop a program that tailors coverage to the topics that people say matter most to them. Stempel and Nanney report that the project's philosophy is simply "to improve content by meeting the changing needs of the readers" and "to deal with community concerns and not staff hunches."

Most newspaper editors will tell you that their hunches are fairly accurate, that they try to stay close to the pulse of their community and have a good idea of their readers' interests. However, Stempel and Nanney point out that empirical studies raise doubt about editors' claims of special powers of perception when it comes to their audiences. One study concluded that "there's little evidence that editors are especially privy to the thoughts of readers." Other studies have pointed out that journalists are not a representative sample of the public. This lends support to the argument that journalists are essentially elitist in their news judgment.

Give Readers What They Need

The argument that editors should give readers what they "need" informationally — call it the "trustee model" — is rooted in classical democratic theory and the First Amendment, as well as tension between libertarian and social responsibility theories. At heart is the notion that for a representative democracy to function properly, citizens must fulfill a civic obligation to be adequately informed about important public matters.

In theory, the government is a creation of the people, and the people elect representatives (servants of the people) to deliberate over public policy and administer the government. For the system to work, however, the people must: 1) take an interest in political matters, 2) have an adequate level of knowledge about political matters, and 3) participate in politics at least to the extent of voting in elections.

Supporters of the trustee model embrace the part of libertarian theory holding that the press should be a vehicle to present evidence and arguments on the basis of which people can check the actions of government and decide on public policy. These supporters further embrace the libertarian call for a free marketplace of ideas and information, with the press operating unfettered in a free enterprise system. However, they turn to social responsibility theory in the hope of fulfilling that call.

Modern social responsibility theory holds that, given the tremendous concentration of the media into the hands of a powerful few, the press too often fails to provide a free marketplace of ideas and information. Under these conditions, it is argued, the press has a duty to be socially responsible. That is, the press must ensure that all sides of important public issues are presented and that the public has enough information to make intelligent decisions in the polling booths.

This interest was expressed by William Kovach in an interview with the *Washington Journalism Review.* "The only interest I have is public service, public interest, and public information journalism," he said. "The business of journalism is protected in the Constitution for a reason ... and if you choose to publish a newspaper, you inherit that obligation." The same sort of thinking prompted William Hornby, an editor at the *Denver Post,* to declare in an oft-cited 1976 article in *Quill,* "The newspaper is a quasi-public institution with a constitutional purpose.... The press has never been and never should be in the business to give the people just what they want. The editor who does his editing predominately from market research isn't worth a damn."

While delegate advocates argue that the press should be absolutely free to ensure a free marketplace of ideas, trustee advocates support the Hutchins Commission view that, in an era when most newspapers are local print monopolies, newspapers have a special duty to ensure thorough and fair news coverage, taking care to present all sides to an issue.

Proponents of the trustee model rebut the three primary arguments of the delegate model this way:

First, they argue that no one is advocating withdrawal of a newspaper's right to make a profit, survive, and attract readers with news and entertainment. The issue is whether they can do that and simultaneously fulfill social responsibilities that transcend counting-house values. Harold Evans, former editor of *The Times* of London, once said the challenge of U.S. newspapers "is not to stay in business — it is to stay in journalism."

Further, trustee model supporters view editors' harping on their putative fear of declining readership as nothing more than crocodile tears. Underwood describes the long-time industry practice of "badmouthing" the industry's prospects despite profits pouring in. This "disingenuous ritual," he writes, was first labeled "hogwash" in Benjamin Bagdikian's 1973 essay with the telling title, "The Myth of Newspaper Poverty."

Trustee advocates point out that most newspapers are print monopolies, and pre-tax profit margins, which ranged from 15 to 20 per cent throughout the 1980s, have been, and continue to be, higher than most industries. Chakravarty and Torcellini observe that for all the worry about losing readers and advertising base, and prognostications of coming financial ills, the newspaper industry is still one of the nation's most prosperous. James Squires, former executive editor of the *Chicago Tribune*, has said the newspaper business is "the most profitable legal business in America." Actually, according to *Presstime*, the magazine of the Newspaper Association of America, the broadcast industry is more profitable, typically posting earnings margins in the 30- to 40-per cent range. But many media conglomerates and newspaper chains have invested heavily in broadcast stations and benefit from those lavish earnings.

In 1996, newspaper profits were at about 14 per cent, still at a level that *Presstime* reported "would make managers of many industries glow with pride." The magazine said that "many investors inside and outside the business remain bullish on newspapers." It added, "Investors continue to spend top dollar on newspaper acquisitions while newspaper companies pour millions into building their core business."

In response to the reader-friendly advocates' second argument — the charge that newspapers are too boring and too in-depth, and lack relevance to readers' personal lives — trustee advocates rely on classical democratic theory. They argue that newspaper readers, like all citizens, have a civic duty to be informed about important public policy matters. Classical democratic theory says nothing about allowing people to ignore certain issues because they are boring, or require too much effort to comprehend, or don't relate to people's personal lives. What is at stake is civic life, the broader community.

They further argue that if editors buy the argument that newspapers must emulate TV to accommodate the visual literacy and shortened attention spans of today's TV generation, they enable further shortening of attention spans and hasten the death of traditional literacy. This argument is forcefully stated by Neil Postman in his book *Amusing Ourselves To Death*. Postman argues that print is best for people who think conceptually and deductively, and engage in contemplative, deliberative, reasoned discourse. Print fosters introspective, analytical, and abstract thought; it is fundamentally propositional in character, inclined toward serious, rational argument and logical, orderly (linear, sequential) arrangement of facts and ideas. Postman maintains that TV, on the other hand, with its mosaic presentation of non-discursive symbols (pictures), presents the world as objects and images rather than ideas. "Thinking does not play well on TV," Postman says, because it does not permit pause for people to think and reflect. TV essentially trivializes serious discourse by presenting all subject matter as entertainment.

Delegate advocates may argue that a *USA Today*-style newspaper can adopt some of TV's attributes for reasons that have nothing to do with marketing and profits and everything to do with an informed public. To make readers willing to study complex tax law, for example, or to demonstrate the change in AIDs rates among various populations, a newspaper can make tedious statistical information more readable with charts and graphs.

Trustees advocates, however, counter that while charts and graphs may broaden and clarify public understanding, they are nevertheless biased against intellectual burdening and do not easily accommodate complex, in-depth information loaded with nuance and subtle meaning. In other words, charts and graphs nourish and sustain readers' inability to handle extended, complex thought through words. Instead of encouraging people to read a newspaper, infographics encourage people to "watch" a newspaper. As media scholar Joshua Meyrowitz observed in his book *No Sense of Place*, abstract ideas such as respect, patriotism, and the theory of gravity "cannot be pictured easily."

Trustee advocates say that giving readers a heavy doze of shallow, abbreviated news high in entertainment value and visual appeal is likely to develop in readers a weakness for things passive and pleasurable. Even more serious, in view of consequences for the public polity, is that newspapers emulating TV may accelerate the trend toward declining public literacy, lower SAT scores, and widespread voter apathy. In short, reader-friendly papers may become part of the problem rather than the solution.

Proponents of the trustee model also argue that if newspapers give readers only what they want, readers will not know what they're missing. Some observers have referred to this as the "loss of serendipity," the latter being the phenomenon of finding something agreeable or valuable not sought for. William Shawn, former editor of *The New Yorker*, once remarked that by giving the reader "only what they think they want," editors will "never give them something new they don't know about. You stagnate…. The whole thing begins to be circular. Creativity and originality and spontaneity goes out of it." Part of a newspaper's mission, then, is to educate readers, and that means educating them about things they are unaware of — not just what they think they want to know about. Newspaper researcher Leo Bogart explained, "Editors have to know what readers will tolerate, but their job is to push up constantly against the limits of that tolerance and thus to expand it."

Concerning the delegate advocate's third argument — that the trustee model is elitist and arrogant — trustee proponents counter by saying that delegate editors are arrogant as well, in a different sort of way. While delegate supporters sneer at editors who presume to know instinctively what information readers presumably need to know, trustee supporters argue that the "dumbing down" of newspapers to reflect the format and content of TV is essentially patronizing. In effect, the argument goes, delegate editors demonstrate little confidence in their readers' intelligence and ability to handle complex, extended exposition, and in-depth and analytical reports.

Delegate supporters argue that market research should guide the gatekeeping process so that readers get what they want rather than what some elitist editor assigns. But trustee advocates counter that readers are not always aware of what news is being made; readers are not out there on the front lines, like journalists, where the raw events of news are occurring. They argue that journalists, being close to the raw happenings and events, are able to track developments over time and gain perspective about which events are likely to be more important than others. Market research can't do that.

Further, Bogart points out that without someone to select, package, measure, and label information, it becomes random and chaotic and produces mental indigestion. Any newspaper, even *USA Today*, has to judge the day's events in terms of whether readers should be informed about them, and then it has to grade the news so that readers know what stories are considered to be more important than others. Bagdikian argues that when *USA Today* allows form to dominate content, stories are played up or down not because of their inherent importance but "on the basis of their potential for jazzy graphics or offbeat features." Readers thus get a distorted sense of the relevant importance of the day's news. With news that is relevant to public policy considerations being buried or ignored by delegate-minded newspapers, readers begin to get the impression that news dealing with sports and celebrities is more important, when, of course, it is not. News about sports and celebrities is important only as entertainment.

Resolution

No newspaper attends exclusively either to the wants or the needs of its readers; to some extent all newspapers, with the possible exception of the super-market tabloids, mix news and entertainment. It is a question of degree. Perhaps it is most appropriate to think of it as a continuum, with wants and needs at opposing ends.

If we are to seek resolution of the debate, we must look more toward the middle of the continuum. There is moral authority for this reasoning if we consider the wisdom of Aristotle's principle of the golden mean, which states that moral virtue is located between two extremes: excess and deficiency.

If we take that advice to heart, we should be open to the possibility that both sides of the debate, delegate and trustee, raise points that are valid and worthy. If we accept this view, we can proceed to resolve some of the differences between the two groups and reach a compromise resolution.

A compromise will acknowledge that newspapers should not eschew market research entirely, but at the same time they should not be slaves to research findings. Similarly, newspapers should attempt to balance their mission to inform and entertain, dual media functions identified by the Hutchins Commission. Too much emphasis on the informational needs of readers will repel some readers from newspapers, but too much emphasis on entertainment wants will accomplish the same.

A compromise also would ask newspapers to consider that they are not purely businesses, in the same sense as, say, a dry cleaning establishment or a sporting goods manufacturer. All newspapers will acknowledge a transcendent purpose of the press if they will seriously consider First Amendment concerns such as the public's right to know and the watchdog role of the press. The latter includes investigative and in-depth or explanatory journalism that educates the public about government and business. Lastly, a compromise would allow newspapers in truly competitive markets, where there is an ample assortment of newspapers, to ignore pleas to be socially responsible. But it would require newspapers that are true print monopolies — the only newspaper in town — to concede that monopoly status is not what the Founding Fathers had in mind when they guaranteed freedom of the press. It thus seems reasonable that monopoly status should impose a moral obligation to be socially responsible.

If editors insist on catering more to the one than the other (either wants or needs), there is a good argument that readers' needs should be served before their wants. Charles McCorkle Hauser, retired executive editor of the *Providence Journal-Bulletin,* asks: If newspapers don't take seriously the informational needs of readers, who will? He doesn't see television or any other medium providing enough serious coverage for people who are genuinely interested in a full accounting of the day's activities. On the other hand, if newspapers ignore their entertainment function, there are plenty of other media to fill the void.

Hauser argues that while some segments of the population are unconcerned about the future of newspapers — and could easily do without them — two significant segments of the population consider newspapers to be essential to their day. The first is "a literate, sophisticated and intellectually curious group that believes the printed word is the most efficient and most satisfying way to attain lots of information on subjects of importance." The second is "an intensely local and involved group that depends on newspapers as the only medium providing detailed coverage of hometown and home state news."

Hauser asserts that the dominate trend in the newspaper business is toward a small and loyal readership made up primarily of these two groups. But he points out that most editors remain in an acute stage of denial over the irrevocable loss of readers. "They keep searching for magic formulas to restore newspaper reading to the levels of the good old days when people had longer attention spans and fewer demands on their time." Hauser's prescription for newspapers: Drop the search for magic formulas and forget TV. Commit to serving core readers.

There is one final, important concern. We are beginning to see the emergence of electronic online newspapers. So far, these have taken the form of newspaper web sites that give online readers a sampling of the day's stories and photos.

As with most material available on the Internet, it is menu driven, meaning that online readers select from a variety of topics the content they wish to be exposed to. Online newspapers also can be tailored to give readers only what they want, or say they want. So, for example, when first subscribing to an online newspaper, subscribers list those topics they want to read about and those they are not interested in. A reader dossier or profile is then constructed, and only news pertaining to those topics is made available. It is technically possible for newspapers to go one step further and electronically monitor actual reading patterns, fine-tuning the reader profile. Another development that is emerging as of this writing is application of a broadcast, or "push" model on the Internet. Until now online readers have selected or "pulled" content from online sources, but with the broadcast model the online source broadcasts, or "pushes," highly customized information directly to the readers' personal computer.

To some extent, readers have always had their choice of what stories they want to read or ignore in a traditional newspaper. Readers typically browse a newspaper, skipping over stories and advertisements that do not interest them. However, the way a traditional newspaper is packaged and delivered makes it difficult for most readers not to be exposed to what's on the front page and the section covers, even if they only glance quickly at the headlines. With the development of electronic newspapers, and the prospect of the "push" model replacing the current "pull" model, exposure to the front page and section covers is threatened and may be lost entirely.

These developments have potent implications for our sense of community. They raise the possibility that the community will miss news that newspeople, in their professional judgment, consider to have important bearing on the welfare of the community or polity. Missing will be a newspaper that assumes broad interdependence among its diverse inhabitants and seeks to report the shared experience of the collective life. Without a common page to be shared by all subscribers — without a common frame of reference — how can a newspaper foster a civic spirit or shape a vision of public community?

Instead, what we will have is *The Daily Me*, electronic newspapers that are "personal newspapers." This is a solipsistic journalism, individualistic in focus, that views the community as a fragmented collection of private affairs.

Recommended Readings

Books

Meyrowitz, Joshua. *No Sense of Place*. New York: Oxford University Press, 1985. One of the best books explicating the epistemological differences between print and broadcast media and the attendant consequences.

Postman, Neil. *Amusing Ourselves to Death*. New York: Viking Penguin, 1985. A leading cultural critic provides an amusing yet serious look at how television is ending the reign of print and threatens culture decline.

Prichard, Peter. *The Making of McPaper*. New York: Andrews, McMeel & Parker, 1987. An insider account of what went through the creators' heads as they designed *USA Today*.

Squires, James D. *Read All About It*. New York: Times Books, 1993. A searing indictment of how corporate owners of U.S. newspapers have sacrificed the ideals of a free press at the altar of profits.

Underwood, Doug. *When MBAs Rule the Newsroom*. New York: Columbia University Press, 1993. Probably the best book on the corporate influence in America's newsrooms. Author blends journalistic storytelling with social science findings.

Articles

Bagdikian, Benjamin H. "Fast-Food News: A Week's Diet." *Columbia Journalism Review* (March/April 1983): 32-3. An early, incisive indictment of *USA Today* by respected press critic with impressive credentials as a former newspaper editor and journalism educator.

Bogart, Leo. "In Pondering the Customized Newspaper, Don't Lose Sight of Big Picture." *Presstime* (December 1990): 60. An early warning of the probable effects and dangers of the coming of the "personal newspaper."

Gladney, George Albert. "The McPaper Revolution: *USA Today*-Style Innovation at Large U.S. Dailies." *Newspaper Research Journal* 13 (Winter/Spring 1992): 54-71. Content analysis of 230 largest U.S. daily newspapers to determine the degree to which they emulated content and format of *USA Today*.

Hauser, Charles McCorkle. "Forget Hustling, Chiseling and TV; Commit To Serving Core

Readers." *Editor & Publisher,* 2 September 1995, 40, 30. A well-argued plea for a return to traditional news values by a veteran editor.

Hornby, William H. "Beware the 'Market' Thinkers." *Quill* (January 1976): 14-17. A respected editor provides an early warning and plea for newspapers not to let marketing executives encroach into the newsroom.

Lallande, Ann. "Alive and Kicking." *Presstime* (January 1997): 31-7. A special report on the financial state of the U.S. newspaper industry.

Rosenstiel, Thomas B. "We Take a Look at *USA Today.*" *Los Angeles Times,* 8 October 1987, 1, 20-21. A leading media critic provides an analysis of *USA Today*'s influence on the newspaper industry.

Rosenstiel, Thomas B. "Editors Debate Need to Redefine America's Newspapers." *Los Angeles Times,* 13 April 1991, A18. Excellent update on the debate about market-driven journalism.

Shaw, David. "Newspapers Going for a New Look." *Los Angeles Times,* 13 March 1986, 30-31. A leading media critic examines spread of *USA Today*-style innovation in U.S. newspapers.

Shumate, Richard. "Life After Kovach." *Washington Journalism Review* (September 1992): 28-32. Excellent wrap-up of controversy surrounding William Kovach's departure and Ron Martin's hiring at Atlanta newspapers.

Stepp, Carl Sessions. "When Readers Design the News." *Washington Journalism Review* (April 1991): 20-4. A respected journalism educator and editor tracks changes in newspapers and asks if they are dumbing down or wising up.

Stevenson, Robert L. "The Disappearing Reader." *Newspaper Research Journal* 15 (Summer 1994): 22-30. Excellent overview of circulation trends affecting U.S. newspapers.

"*USA Today,* Its Imitators, and Its Critics: Do Newsroom Staffs Face an Ethical Dilemma?" *Journal of Mass Media Ethics* 8 (1993): 17-36. Provides results of survey of newsroom personnel at forty large U.S. dailies (split between heavy adopters and non-adopters of *USA Today*-style innovation) to gauge attitudes about *USA Today*-style innovation in newspapers.

Chapter Nineteen

Is News Superficial?

LeAnne Daniels

Why does the news sometimes present the latest escapades of Madonna more prominently and thoroughly than the plight of refugees in Rwanda or the impact of Social Security reform on our elderly? Why are most newspaper stories ten inches or less, and why do broadcast soundbites average nine seconds when they used to be forty-three seconds thirty years ago? Why does news often play up the drama and sensationalism even in the most mundane of human events? Why is political coverage more image than substance, more horse race than issues?

These are all questions that frame one of the most contentious debates in American journalism. At the heart of the issue is whether human interest news and entertainment news deserve the same First Amendment protections historically accorded those responsible for producing information needed by citizens and institutions. Is traditional investigative journalism being sacrificed at the altar of profits and ratings? Was the 1968 Kerner Commission correct in criticizing the press for not putting the news in a context that gave it meaning, or writing about all of society's constituencies? People inside and outside the profession have outlined the negative effects they see when boundaries between news and entertainment begin to blur.

Watergate journalist Carl Bernstein warned about the consequences of this blurring in a *New Republic* article titled "The Idiot Culture." His essay described what he sees when he looks at American media today. "The coverage is distorted by celebrity," he wrote, "by the reduction of news to gossip, which is the lowest form of news; by sensationalism, which is always turning away from discourse that we — the press, the media, the politicians, *and* the people — are turning into a sewer." Bernstein said that because the industry-wide model for journalism has become Rupert Murdoch's sleaze and cynicism, "for the first time in our history the weird and stupid and the coarse are becoming our cultural norm, even our cultural ideal." The same message was presented by author Michael

Crichton to a lunchtime crowd at a 1993 National Press Club banquet. His most startling statement was that if news organizations don't abandon "sensationalistic junk-food journalism" in favor of a more sensitive, informed, and responsive journalism, traditional mass media will be extinct by the year 2003. In his book *Amusing Ourselves to Death*, Neil Postman has argued that the entertainment model of television has become the framework for all presentations of the media industry, including information. In his view, the result has been a serious decline in public discourse that society can ill afford if democracy is to be served. Debate is polarized — issues are presented in a dichotomous fashion with no shaded or multiple viewpoints. In his book, *Breaking the News*, James Fallows outlined how the notion that news has to be focused but entertaining narrows everything to politics. He says that issues such as crime, health, and the economy, which qualify as collective concerns of all Americans, become framed narrowly as issues for political battles. As a result of making social issues political debates, the public sometimes receives misinformation or little substantive information about more important issues that directly impact their lives.

The focus in this chapter on whether news is superficial goes to the heart of the function of news in our society. Lippmann in his 1922 book, *Public Opinion,* said it must offer "citizens information upon which they can act." This doesn't mean signalizing events as much as it means shining a beacon on all of society to discover truth. The themes of this chapter relate then to whether the current news product has those qualities. What is the evidence for and against the view that news is form over substance, personality-driven human interest stories more than social and cultural issue stories, brief stories without depth, and a product without diversity. To answer these questions is to determine to what extent news delivers on its public service promise to add to our public knowledge and our sense of community and shared values.

Origins of the Issue

Most media scholars concede that media do influence what people think about—a concept embodied in the agenda-setting function, first documented by Maxwell McCombs and Donald Shaw in a 1972 *Public Opinion Quarterly* article. But whether media effects are powerful or limited, or whether they can be directly linked to behavior, remains an area of considerable uncertainty. The unsettled nature of the issue means that the quality of news and its effects have been the subjects of a long historical debate. The impetus for such debate is, of course, journalism's role in democracy. News is the conduit between citizens and their institutions, particularly the government that works for them. It can help or hinder citizens' participation in civic life. A significant historical question has always been whether journalists should provide news and information that citizens need or news that they want. This dichotomy is reflected in the labels "hard" and "soft" news. Soft news is often considered less useful to our society because it emphasizes topics sometimes far afield from the kind of information citizens need to participate in public life. It has been described as often sensensational because of its focus on human interest and lifestyles or sex, violence, and gossip.

William Cullen Bryant (*New York Evening Post* editor, 1828-78) made an astute observation about how the journalist gets caught up in superficiality. He said, "The necessity of attending to many subjects prevents the journalist from thoroughly integrating any." As a result, journalism "begets desultory habits of thought, disposing the mind to be satisfied with mere glances at difficult questions and to dwell only upon commonplaces."

Mitchell Stephens in his book, *History of the News,* suggests that the public's appetite for stories of sex, crime, and gossip was documented as early as the sixteenth century. Pamela Shoemaker, in a *Journal of Communication* article titled "Hardwired for News," offers some further insight into why news has always been about the sensational. She argues that an explanation can be found in a biological as well as a cultural need for such news. In her view, monitoring bad and deviant news is primarily a survival mechanism, a way of dealing with possible environmental threats.

Michael Schudson offers a cultural explanation for the schism that has developed historically between entertainment or "tabloid" news and information news — often called "investigative reporting." In his social history of the newspaper, *Discovering the News,* Schudson credits the 1830s Penny Press with the "democratizing" forces that led to the storytelling tradition in news. The growth of a democratic market economy led newspaper publishers such as Benjamin Day to seek story formulas that appealed to mass audiences, which often resulted in tawdry tales of crime and passion. Such stories were meant to attract the new urban middle-class reader produced by the growth of literacy, the Industrial Revolution, and the growth of urban populations. As Schudson explains, James Gordon Bennett popularized "entertainment" news even more by instituting such modern newspaper devices as the "beat" system for covering court news and crime news. Schudson identifies two simultaneous news traditions surviving side by side in the Yellow Journalism period of the 1890s. Joseph Pulitzer and William Randolph Hearst had adopted the "entertainment model" of news by using personal stunts and crusades played out in the pages of their newspapers.

At the same time, Adolph Ochs was rescuing an economically weak *New*

York Times and distinguishing it in the marketplace by adopting an informational model of news. His paper's motto was an early reference to the idea that a gatekeeper in the guise of an editor knew what was best for the public to read. The slogan "All The News That's Fit to Print" was not selected by happenstance.

With the arrival of *USA Today* in 1982, the changing nature of audiences, and the push to adopt a more business-oriented approach to news organizations in the 1990s, it is a small wonder that even the *New York Times* has found its informational model softening at the edges. Twentieth-century journalism has been focused on the effort to democratize news — a push that has brought the labeling of *USA Today's* television-modeled news as the "McPaper" with bite-sized nuggets of information and the characterization of television news as "sound-bite journalism" and "happy talk."

Ben Bagdikian, author of *The Media Monopoly,* has been one of the most vocal critics of market forces that push journalism too far toward the "story-telling" model first introduced in the Penny Press period, and reborn in 1960s New Journalism. Bagdikian has expressed concern that concentration of ownership and monopoly forces are pressuring even "legitimate" news organizations to homogenize their content and imitate "tabloid news" providers. Witness the growth of tabloid newspapers such as the *National Enquirer* and tabloid news programs such as *Hard Copy* and *A Current Affair.* Then there are the programs that report on civil and criminal trials called *Court TV,* which further blur the lines between news and entertainment.

As audiences have made television their primary source of news and information, a concern has also been expressed that this medium is ill-designed for presenting the depth of information and context that citizens will need to cope in a multicultural, global world. Traditional news organizations such as CBS represent the golden age of television, when news was substantive and not so celebrity-oriented. In an *American Journalism Review* article titled "Saving CBS News," David Zurawik and Christina Stoehr explain that CBS balanced prestige and profits when Richard Salant and Reuven Frank — journalists, rather than businessmen — headed the news organization. Now CBS, like most news organizations, is in a battle for audience against cable offerings like Ted Turner's Cable News Network and C-Span, as well as with local news. In such an environment, it is hard to protect the journalistic mission.

In his book *Sound Bite News: Television Coverage of Elections, 1968-1988,* Daniel Hallin documented the shrinkage of television sound bites in election coverage to nine seconds, which raises the question of whether television news can ever inform citizens adequately. If audiences are getting most of their news from television, many ask, what does this mean for the safety of our democratic system?

The historical concern about the growing superficiality of news centers around many issues. Most important among them are whether dramatic and personal news crowds out more legitimate news and skews reality, whether it fuels people's fears, but most of all whether it makes people feel powerless at a time in our nation's history when we need them to participate most in political and social life.

News Is Superficial

Those who consider modern news to be superficial document its decline as a movement away from the muckraking traditions of Ida Tarbell and Lincoln Steffens and toward a journalism of outrageousness focused on personal drama, not public issues. Media researchers have found news inadequate in local, national, international, and specialized coverage.

The public would seem to agree. As editor Bruce Evensen notes in *The Responsible Reporter*, audience surveys show the public believes journalists do not take the interests of the audience seriously enough. "One of the most persistent criticisms of journalists," he writes, "has been their superficiality in understanding of issues, which leads to shallow explanations and errors in even the most elementary facts." Evensen suggests that journalists committed to excellence must make pursuit of knowledge their life-long goal, beginning with a liberal arts education in college.

John McManus, in his book *Market-Driven Journalism: Let the Citizen Beware?*, studied local television news and found market logic overriding journalistic logic in news gathering and presentation. In a case study analysis conducted at four television stations in the western United States, he found journalists seeking images over ideas, emotion over analysis, exaggeration to add appeal, and looking for shortcuts to researching stories. McManus also found an emphasis on news as a commodity — something to be sold and let the buyer beware — to be the most consistent theme of his qualitative analysis. When news was content analyzed to determine whether it maximized public understanding, the results were disturbing. In his view, two kinds of news would be most useful to public understanding: news high on orientation and, failing that, news high on both orientation and entertainment. But the news selected by the stations McManus studied generally avoided both. Following a profit model, the stations provided mostly pure entertainment stories and "filler news" of low cost and little journalistic value. McManus concluded that the stations chose audience appeal over consequence, and consistently cut back on news quality by making market choices instead of journalistic ones. In his assessment, news that gets covered in the local media environment is news that doesn't threaten the interests of advertisers and investors, news that is inexpensive to gather and report, and news with a wide appeal to a demographically "correct" audience. Investigative journalism was squeezed out by a more passive form of discovery based on use of wire services and public relations material. Dull but important stories such as economic trends and political apportionment debates were driven out by event news of a visual nature.

His findings raise the possibility of two plausible explanations for the superficiality of news. Either 1) most journalists are simply not deep thinkers (being concerned with doing more than thinking) or 2) journalists are usually generalists, not specialists who have a great deal of education or knowledge of particular subjects. McManus predicted the following consequences of a steady diet of market-driven news over normative news:

- consumers are likely to learn less from the news

- consumers may be misled by the news

- news sources may become more manipulative

- the audience will become more apathetic about politics

In his view, "most of the time, market journalism is an oxymoron, a contradiction in terms."

Doug Underwood, in his book *When MBAs Rule the Newsroom,* also documented the decline in normative journalism in newspapers, and the increase in superficial news based upon marketing principles such as story packaging. The author used his own research in newsrooms at West Coast newspapers and others' research of the newspaper industry to show that much news in newspapers is not news at all. In newsrooms across the country, he found an increase in boosterism stories of big business and stories aimed at the upscale readers that newspaper advertisers want to reach. He too was alarmed by the absence of investigative reporting. What he found replacing it was a safe news and "entertainment style" news that offered little depth, insight, or context into issues that American citizens must be concerned about. He specifically questioned the wisdom of newspapers abandoning investigative reporting, arguing that depth reporting is their franchise. It is this capability that sets them apart from the time-confined and visually driven television medium. Underwood expresses the hope that journalists with understanding of the public service function of journalism will not abandon the industry but fight internally to turn the tide against market-driven news. In his view, only such a circumstance (having journalists in the profession with enterprise reporting skills and commitment to truth telling) will shield the public from manipulation by government and corporate image makers.

Those who view news as superficial in traditional media don't necessarily place much faith in new technologies such as the Internet to improve the situation either. At a 1996 roundtable conference at Louisiana State University on new technologies and journalism education, one media educator pointed out the major weakness of unmediated news and information: its untrustworthiness. News or information that is not superficial has to be high quality, that is, accurate and contextual. Everette Dennis, executive director of the Freedom Forum, made it clear that the Internet is neither. "You have more and more providers out there fragmenting the market, he said at the conference, "How do you distinguish between and among them? I think we go off on the wrong tangent if we're looking at every home page on the Internet. There are 300 new ones a day, and most of it, frankly, is people reducing their sense of powerlessness. That should be identified as mental health therapy, not as communication."

As early as 1980 in his classic study, *Deciding What's News*, Herbert Gans argued forcefully that journalism may not be up to the task of providing news that binds citizens to the community and the nation. In a study of CBS *Evening News*, NBC *Nightly News*, *Newsweek*, and *Time* he found that news focuses on politics and limits its news frame to conflict stories about events rather than process stories about race and class and other social problems. For that reason, he said that national and international news is mediated through a filter of news values such as conflict and prominence, with bureaucrats monopolizing the news play. The news values represent a kind of para-ideology, a loosely defined and untested set of journalistic opinions and beliefs, which narrows news to topics such as the routine activities and routine conflicts of leading public officials. Thus news, whether intentionally or not, creates pictures in audiences' heads that support establishment views but distort reality. This worried Gans so much that in his book he called for taking the full responsibility for selecting news for society's needs out of the hands of journalists. His functional analysis concludes that news providers bring dysfunction into people's attempts to maintain contact with nation and society.

Gans concluded that news organizations were not providing news analysis, explanation, and news about America as a society. He argued that if news is to fit society's needs, it must include a greater variety of perspectives. He defined such news as more national (moving beyond government news), more bottom-up (focused on ordinary people), more accountable (describing how programs affected people's lives), and more representative (reflective of our society's diversity in age, income, education, ethnicity, religion).

Of course, Gans wrote his book before the market pressures of news had really begun. But in a prophetic passage he anticipated the coming age of corporate control of news. "News judgment is resistant to change and journalists will fight hard to preserve their autonomy," he said, "but if corporate economic well-being is threatened, executives may insist that their news organizations adapt."

Those who argue that news is superficial say that Gans' concerns about news have been realized. In his study of 3,000 stories appearing in the *Washington Post* and *New York Times,* Leon Sigal found little evidence of investigative journalism in the elite press. His 1973 book *Reporters and Officials* documented that about two-thirds of the stories came through routine channels — public sources such as bureaucrats or staged events such as news conferences. What were least represented were enterprise stories, those where journalists gathered news and validated facts through their own investigations. Only one-fourth of news stories fit the enterprise category. One reason for lack of enterprise stories is, of course, the expense in doing them.

And international news analysis hasn't fared much better. The superficiality of international news in American media (newspapers and television) has been well-documented beginning with a UNESCO report by the MacBride Commission in 1980. In that report, international news was characterized as "superficial, episodic and limited in range of topics." Newspaper and television research on the quality of international news coverage has shown similar results. Most international news coverage is about coups and earthquakes, not social and economic progress. Negative news prevails over positive. Those countries with the best chance of coverage have strong economic and political ties to the United States; so they are in the Northern hemisphere. International news centers primarily on war and defense, diplomacy, domestic politics, and crime. Little coverage is given to the soft news categories of culture, the arts, human interest, and social change.

Daniel Riffe and colleagues took a 22-year longitudinal look at international news in *The New York Times* and found even the most elite newspaper in America cutting back on its coverage of the world. In a 1994 *Newspaper Research Journal* article titled "The shrinking foreign newshole of the *New York Times,*" he and his fellow researchers found that the paper covered fewer international stories, although they were slightly longer. Michael Emery found a similar situation in his 1988 study of ten American prestige newspapers. Based on his results, published in the *Gannett Center Journal* the following year, he called the international newshole "an endangered species."

Roger Wallis and Stanley Baran discovered the same provincialism in their cross-cultural comparison of broadcast news in the United States, Great Britain, and Sweden in 1986. In their book *The Known World of Broadcast News*, they conclude that the American broadcast system is the least committed of the three countries studied to providing its listeners with a global outlook.

In a study of eighteen years of international news on U.S. television networks, William Gonzenbach and colleagues in a 1992 *Gazette* article also found a crisis-orientation in international news and a greater proportion of negative news stories coming from the Third World than developed countries. All news from developed countries was more varied than from developing countries. In fact, positive news about human interest, the arts, education, science breakthroughs, etc., was more likely to come from Western Europe and the United States than anywhere else.

This research evidence that international news is generally superficial underscores once again the connection between news and society that makes such findings matter. Poor performance in international news coverage contributes to an uneducated society unprepared to face the realities of a global marketplace. Furthermore, it keeps the citizens of the world unconnected and even isolationist in their views at a time when they have become connected by social and political problems that know no national boundaries: trade, health issues such as AIDS and world hunger, environmental threats, threats of nuclear war, and political crises.

A study of Cable News Network, Ted Turner's 24-hour cable news service launched in 1980, showed that more news was not necessarily better news either. A book-length study by the Media Institute in 1983 titled "CNN vs. The Networks" showed that CNN fared little better than the three broadcast networks on four tests of performance: balance, depth, sensationalism, and news priority. While content analysis did show CNN to have more balance and less sensationalism in its news coverage, it actually provided less depth than the networks.

Lack of depth has been a criticism of most specialized news coverage, including environmental news, science news, and political news. Barbara Moore and Michael Singletary in "Scientific Sources' Perceptions of Network News Accuracy," in the Winter 1985 issue of *Journalism Quarterly*, concluded that brevity of coverage and lack of depth were the most common objections of scientists about science coverage on network news. In a 1990 *Journal of Communication* article titled "A Question of Quality," Kandice Salomone and colleagues found differences between environmental scientists and journalists in what they considered a quality environmental story. The authors found scientists more likely to stress accuracy and risk information of a positive nature supported by science and devoid of controversy. Journalists placed a higher emphasis on stories that used negative risk information. This would suggest that editors find the dramatic elements of the environmental story less likely to bore audiences.

But for those who argue that news is superficial, perhaps the area of news coverage that poses most concern is political news. This news can be seen as the most vital because it has the potential to influence the quality of democracy. Thomas Patterson, in his book *Out of Order*, argues that there is a direct link between the media's fault-finding mentality about politics and the public's disenchantment with politicians and the political process. He also charges the media with a lack of knowledge about how politics works in our society.

A pack mentality that Larry Sabato identified in his book, *Feeding Frenzy*, leads to the framing of political issues without a context that gives them meaning, according to Patterson. He uses Whitewater as an example of a non-contextual story, which he says was incorrectly compared by the media to Watergate, Irangate, Iraqgate, and the Savings and Loans scandals. In his view, the watchdog press has lost its bite and does not have the "judgment to distinguish real abuse from normal political activity." Journalists' most serious failing in their news gathering and presentation is that they wrongly want to frame politics in terms of games and metaphors instead of substantive and cognitive schema that can help even disinterested citizens understand the basic issues of public discourse.

Recent public opinion polls seem to support those who argue that political coverage is too much about horse-race issues. Cheryl Arvidson reported in the *American Journalism Review* that the public shares this view. She said in "Partners and Adversaries" that a Roper public opinion poll conducted as part of a Freedom Forum study of Congress and the media in 1995 showed that 73 per cent of the public characterized the media's coverage of Congress as "often confusing and unclear." The public wanted more information about how legislation affects their lives; they wanted less coverage of the personal lives of politicians and partisan in-fighting. What all the studies on this side suggest is that news suffers from major structural inadequacies that leave it incapable of serving the body politic without improvements. The most striking need is to provide more balance in news coverage — toning down the sensensational, offering more stories with context and depth, and most of all not abandoning completely the investigative journalism that is the highest calling of journalism because it seeks truth. Interrelated issues like poverty, crime, and racial inequality have to be presented in context. Otherwise, audiences are prone to blame the individual rather than the system for many social problems.

News Is More Substance Than Superficial

Those who defend the quality of American journalism compare it to the press performance of the rest of the world. John Merrill, who has assessed the world's greatest newspapers in his books *The World's Great Dailies* and *Global Journalism*, finds the criticism of American news media content much as Mark Twain said of his premature obituary. It has been greatly exaggerated. In *Media Debates*, Merrill argues that if one looks at American media institutions in an historical and worldwide context, they are "relatively vigorous, thorough, competent, literate, appealing, and useful." He adds: "I know of no other country in the world with such a high proportion of reputable middle-level or 'mass newspapers.'"

Proponents of this view often cite some of the more notable examples of journalism's success stories in counteracting the entertainment model of news. One such story was discussed in Jay Taylor's 1993 article in *Quill*. It was a nine-part investigative series written and published in 1991 by *Philadelphia Inquirer* writers Don Bartlett and James Steele titled "America: What Went Wrong?" This long-form journalism piece on the poor government management decisions that have undermined America's middle class was one of the paper's most requested reprints. In a 1996 *American Journalism Review* piece titled "When to Go Long," Jon Franklin even sees some evidence of a return to narrative or long-form journalism based on a study done by the American Society of Newspaper Editors in 1993 titled "Ways With Words." But he says such a form must be used with caution. Narrative journalism works only for some stories, not all. The key is to do thoughtful journalism, which is knowing when to go long. He points out that no-jump journalism (stories so short they don't jump to inside pages) seemed to coincide with an unprecedented decline in readers and loss of prestige by America's newspapers.

George Gladney investigated the supposition by many media critics that all newspapers have come to imitate the fast-paced, brief, and television-inspired journalism of *USA Today*. In his 1992 article "The McPaper Revolution?" in the *Newspaper Research Journal*, he studied 230 of the country's largest newspapers and concluded that there is some reason to be optimistic about news quality for the future. Gladney looked at what he defined as McPaper traits: emphasis on color, pictures and graphics, trivia and fluff coverage, brevity, and simplistic coverage of topics and concepts. Such variables are similar to what this essay has defined as characteristics of superficial news. Gladney found that several papers were resisting the *USA Today* formula, specifically those prestige papers traditionally cited on Top 10 lists. Those papers scoring lowest on *USA Today* innovations included the *Philadelphia Inquirer* and the *Boston Globe,* among others.

Two authors represent several others who have found television news to be more powerful in passing on knowledge to audiences than critics from the other side have acknowledged. John P. Robinson and Mark R. Levy, in *The Main Source: Learning from Television News,* make the argument that television is not people's main source of news but it does have some cognitive strengths that have largely been overlooked in the news quality debate. One strength is to socialize Americans into the political life of the nation. Another is to teach even average citizens that minority viewpoints can be expressed safely in our culture. They concluded that "TV can help the information poor acquire the news and information that better informed and more affluent counterparts absorb from the print media. Where there is a will to be informed, there is a way."

The cognitive approach to news adopted by researchers W. Russell Neuman, Marion R. Just, and Ann N. Crigler supports the findings of Robinson and Levy. In their book *Common Knowledge,* they use survey research, content analysis, in-depth interviewing, and experiments to uncover the media's strengths in shaping people's common knowledge of politics. They conclude that the media do a good job of transferring shared knowledge of the world and political beliefs as long as the public is active in reinterpreting the media messages using their own cognitive skills. Contrary to other research, these authors did not find newspapers superior to television in promoting learning — just different. Learning seemed to have more to do with whether people possessed strong cognitive skills than what medium they used. Therefore, people with above average cognitive skills learned about the same from both mediums. In the authors' view, however, television had much more potential to help those with average cognitive skills. They found the structure and style of newspaper journalism (particularly the inverted pyramid) made it harder for people with average cognitive skills to learn information about political issues. Television was most effective for this group because it could make abstract issues more comprehensible with its narrative storytelling structure.

Doris A. Graber, author of *Processing the News: How People Tame the Information Tide,* argued in an article in *The Annals of the American Academy of Political and Social Science,* that televised news has a special ability to pass on information because of its visual nature. In her view, those who have argued that the visual components of stories are trivial in their contribution to content are simply wrong. Her research on the audiovisual elements of television news showed that pictures do enhance a story and add new information. She rates television high on audiovisual literacy and says it encourages, not discourages, the average citizen to participate in political life.

In "Useful News, Sensational News," C. Richard Hofstetter and David M. Dozier reported in their 1996 *Journalism Quarterly* article that even sensationalism as a news value has some positive benefits. In their examination of local television news, they found through content analysis that "sensational news contained elements of quality news, information which could serve as an opinion resource for citizens in their everyday lives." A majority of the sensensational stories provided background on the development of issues, events, or problems. The authors found more similarities than differences between sensational and non-sensational news.

Proponents of the view that today's news *is* substantial also take heart in the evidence that specialized reporting is not as bad as critics portray. A 1983 study by G. Cleveland Wilhoit and David Weaver published in the *Journal of Communication* found that U.S. wire service offerings of international news showed more balanced coverage of the Third World than previously reported. This finding has been supported by other researchers. Charles Ganzert and Don M. Flournoy in their 1992 *Journalism Quarterly* article found further reason for optimism that international news is not all episodic, violence-oriented and critical of the Third World. Their study of CNN, titled "The Weekly World Report on CNN," showed that the cable network was providing an alternative kind of news about developing countries. Turner was allowing journalists from other countries to present their own news to American audiences. It included less focus on politics, crime and military topics, and more arts, culture, and human interest news than the networks.

Finally, news analysts have also supported the view that political reporting is not as superficial and meaningless as others have claimed. Mark Miller and Bryan Denham's 1994 article "Horserace, Issue Coverage in Prestige Newspapers: the 1988 and 1992 Presidential Elections" in the *Newspaper Research Journal* showed that journalists can cover politics differently if they choose. Miller and Denham's research supported the contention that in 1992 journalists made a conscious effort to focus more on issues and less on polls. The prestige press used significantly more substantive issue terms (those about actionable government policy) than in 1988.

It's important to point out that those who believe news is more substantive than superficial take a more subtle approach to the communication process than the powerful effects models of the past. Audiences actively participate in news processing and bear some responsibility for their learning from the media. Researchers who study news from this approach look at the many strengths of the news media rather than dwelling on their weaknesses. In some respects, the differences between the first two viewpoints is like the difference in perceptions between those who look at a glass and see it as half-full and those who look at it and see it as half-empty.

News Is Culture; So It's Both

A final viewpoint about news, that it is both superficial and substantive, comes from those who view news as a product of a culture that is socially constructed in a negotiation between the journalist and sources. Those who adopt a cultural perspective on news do not recognize a firm line between hard and soft news, nor do they see any value in denigrating one form of news at the expense of the other. Both have societal functions.

Schudson lays out a similar argument. He explains that because news is embedded in the culture and very much subject to the same social forces that shape the culture at large, it is rather futile to talk about news in terms of high and low standards. News is a product of the interaction of people with the media. Therefore, there is no objective truth, only the best version of truth that can be negotiated between media and society.

In *The Power of News*, Schudson shows that, in many ways, journalism has myths that it protects, such as the view that television turned the public against the Vietnam War and that Nixon lost the presidency in 1960 because of his poor performance in the televised Kennedy-Nixon debate. In Schudson's view, the media mediate; they do not set the agenda or shape American consciousness. The media's responsibility is to simply present knowledge to the public and to let the public decide whether to use that knowledge. The public may indeed turn it into new and significant art forms. This argument would suggest that discussing whether news is substantive or superficial is somewhat fruitless. News is both, depending upon who is using it and to what purpose.

For Schudson, informational news will always be centered on an elite segment of society. It is only this group that really cares about being informed about politics and the inner workings of government. The media are not equipped to do more than make such individuals *informational* citizens. Being an *informed* citizen is up to the individual and will require more than simply paying attention to the media. Schudson argues that investigative news has never been a strong tradition in journalism, either before or after Watergate. It is another myth about the journalism profession.

He concludes that news will probably need to remain inconsistent to meet the needs of the culture. Journalists must strive to give all citizens the information upon which they can act, but they must also realize that some segments of the populace will invariably choose not to exercise their democratic rights and civic obligations. The most the media can do is mediate. In doing so, some news will continue to serve as myth. Because news is culture, Schudson says, Watergate as myth serves the social system. That myth, like others, serves the social system by maintaining socioeconomic and class divisions. On the positive side, it can also unite us in commonly shared experiences.

James Carey is another proponent of the view that news is culture. In his book, *Communication as Culture,* he argues that one cannot look at news content and judge its merit in our society. He says that news is not the transmission of information. It is a ritualistic process of symbols and ideas. Therefore, one must speak about its performance in terms of how well it maintains society, not how well it imparts knowledge. If the media help citizens connect with their community, then the media system is working properly. Once again the concept of high and low culture is irrelevant.

Based on this view, several scholars have begun to use a "news-as-social-construction" framework to assess media offerings. Matthew Ehrlich adopted this approach to news in his study of tabloid television news and investigative news in a 1996 *Journalism Monograph.* In "The Journalism of Outrageousness" he challenged the assumption that tabloid television news has no value to the public. In fact, he found similarities to investigative news.

One similarity was that tabloid news also occasionally engaged in "old-fashioned, roll-up-your-sleeves investigative journalism." Furthermore, while crime, sex, and gossip were the staples of tabloid television news, they weren't the only diet. Tabloid news also dealt with more serious topics. "Tabloid news and investigative news did indeed share a certain body of literary devices and lore in telling their stories," Ehrlich said. He suggested that mythological or tabloid journalism is a necessary balance to investigative journalism to sway public opinion in our society. An example might be the O.J. Simpson case, where much investigative news was first broken in the tabloids. In order to be meaningful to a wide public, though, the author states that modern society will probably have to adopt both forms. The tabloid tradition's strength is that it is less elitist and has the same "democratizing" elements that new technologies seem to have for audiences in the Information Age.

Maria Elizabeth Grabe in a 1996 *Journalism and Mass Communication Quarterly* article titled "Tabloid and Television News Magazine Crime Stories" reports similar findings. When she compared tabloid and broadcast news magazine programs on their emphasis on crime and the content of crime narratives, she found both types of programs gave crime stories similar prominence and the content was relatively similar. She concluded: "This study suggests that we should consider tabloid news as maintaining cultural distinction and diversity by catering to specific segments of the population. Thus, contemporary mass communication of crime stories may play an important maintenance function for society by creating diversification of values and rules through communicating somewhat different stories to people of different social standing."

Ted Glasser and James Ettema, in their article in *Critical Perspectives on Media and Society*, even trace the epistemology of investigative reporting to a cultural function. For "Investigative Journalism and the Moral Order," they interviewed investigative reporters about their work. They found that investigative reporters do more than uncover facts in an objective fashion. Their news frames really allow them to influence public morality and contribute to the moral order within the communities they cover. The objectivity standard allows their news judgments actually to be moral judgments.

The authors conclude that while objectivity distances journalists from audiences and can contribute to a failure of journalists to contextualize what they do, it can also have the unintended effect of bringing social change by consolidating community consensus around what are violations of social order. The latter is a good thing, but the weakness, of course, is that objectivity standards do not allow journalists to debate and discuss their decisions critically with the public. A cultural perspective, Glasser and Ettema seem to be arguing, at least allows the public to demand an alternative form between media objectivity and media as the public's conscience. The public has begun to resent how patronizing the latter approach can be.

Resolution

The debate about the nature of news would seem to be at an impasse if we are looking for pat answers about the nature of modern news. Most critics would acknowledge that news is superficial, subjective, and cultural. But the resolution of this debate requires that we move away from content questions and look at how well the media and the public understand the larger role of news in our society.

This focus is crucial because it is editors within organizations who understand journalism's mission. It is they who will ultimately keep news and information grounded in its obligation to be of use to people in their lives. One editor at a major metropolitan paper explained that he judges the output of his newsroom, not in daily snapshots but in a wide-frame look across a year or more. His goal, he said, was to present a mosaic to the public, a diversity of views and cultures and types of news that captured the complexity of our world. That meant having a balance of serious public affairs information but also giving audiences stories that show our society's humor and humanity.

This solution to judging news quality suggests that news must be a balance of short- and long-form storytelling. It must be accurate and trustworthy regardless what format it takes — online communication or the traditional avenues of print and broadcast. It must be about fairness more than objectivity, ensuring that all voices are represented, not just those who are attractive to advertisers. Furthermore, news must be contextual because our society's problems are systemic and not individual. But nowhere in this solution is the suggestion that news must be all substantive or all superficial. The better argument is that news must have at its core a commitment to truth-telling, so that resources will be found to investigate vigorously those issues that affect our citizens. Those resources must be used, even if lower profits will be the short-term result. In the long-term, news organizations that help society solve its problems will survive in the economic marketplace and build a base of brand loyalty, leaving other news delivery systems unable to compete.

One situation that has brought criticism of the news product is content providers who distance themselves from the people they serve. So in the future, news providers in particular must find new feedback mechanisms for interacting with audiences. This does not mean, however, that editors should turn over their franchise to audiences. Audiences want the media to take a leadership role in filtering out all the "white noise" out there and in giving them news of "high quality."

What it does mean is that news organizations must show respect for their audiences and not "dumb down" content or fail to explain why they make the news decisions they do. Attacks on news as being superficial would be lessened if journalists would take the time to demystify the news process for the public and freely admit to their own mistakes.

New technologies are fragmenting audiences more than ever before. This represents a golden opportunity for traditional media to step into the void. People want a common core of knowledge that binds them together as Americans and citizens of the global community. News organizations can deliver these collective memories while at the same time providing solid public affairs knowledge. The trick is to integrate all the delivery systems and pass the message through many channels. The Tribune Company is an example of an organization that has embraced the new technologies while maintaining its core commitment to journalistic values. It uses its traditional media to deliver a basic public awareness to its audiences. But it links this information to its on-line systems where readers can get even more depth on a topic than a newspaper or broadcast news program could ever provide. Television and newspaper journalists have come together at the Tribune organization to provide a legitimate extension of their traditional news product through cable and other delivery systems. But the key to their success is that the news product, regardless of its form, is all shaped by journalistic expertise and news, not marketing, standards. This, it would seem, is an appropriate approach and one best for staff morale and for public service.

Another way to begin resolving the news-quality debate is to fill news rooms with a diversity of viewpoints and a diversity of staff by race, ethnicity, and gender. This will improve the likelihood that news organizations will keep a focus on serving communities, not bottom lines. The successful news organization of the future will adopt a new paradigm of news, which in essence will really be the old. The message will still need the quality standards of journalism — truth, relevance, fairness. In the competitive, interactive environment of modern news, these standards are more important than ever to ensure a loyal audience that will improve journalism's societal image.

This focus on truth, relevance, and fairness in news is more important than any discussion of substance versus superficiality. Journalists must work to reconnect citizens to public life by using whatever delivery mechanisms and storytelling techniques they can to make news meaningful. That's the bottom line. This doesn't mean the boosterism of public journalism but embracing serious, in-depth journalism again and delivering it in new and more interesting formats. Doing so will end the shallow news debate once and for all.

Recommended Readings

Books

Boorstin, Daniel. *The Image.* New York: Athenaeum, 1961. The historian defines and describes the pseudo-event in American culture and how citizens and journalists use it to present news and information.

Cook, Philip S., Douglas Gomery, and Lawrence W. Lichty, eds. *The Future of News: Television, Newspapers, Wire Services, Newsmagazines.* Baltimore, Md.: The Johns Hopkins University Press, 1992. A set of essays by media scholars addressing how changes in technology, demographics, economics, and organizational structure of the media industry have affected the quantity and quality of information available to the American people.

Fallows, James. *Breaking the News: How the Media Undermine American Democracy.* New York: Pantheon Books, 1996. Discusses the weaknesses of political reporting, blaming such problems as the entertaining and personal nature of news for public lack of understanding of political issues and apathy and cynicism about politicians and politics.

Gans, Herbert. *Deciding What's News: A Study of CBS Evening News, NBC Nightly News, Newsweek and Time.* New York: Vintage Books, 1980. A classic study of how news decisions are made, tracing the presence of enduring values in news that entice journalists to use a narrow framework for telling the nation about itself.

Hallin, Daniel. *Sound-Bite News: Television Coverage of Elections, 1968-1988.* Washington, D.C.: Woodrow Wilson International Center for Scholars, 1991. Hallin documents the shrinkage of soundbites in election coverage and in television generally. He explains how such news lends itself to simplistic news frames.

McManus, John. *Market-Driven Journalism: Let the Citizen Beware?* Beverly Hills, Calif.: Sage, 1994. Documents the market-driven journalism prevalent in local news production and offers suggestions to counteract the negative effects such news has on journalistic quality.

Manoff, Robert Karl, and Michael Schudson, eds. *Reading the News.* New York: Pantheon Books, 1986. A series of essays about how news is constructed using the various personal, organizational, and external constraints of the journalism profession.

Postman, Neil. A*musing Ourselves to Death: Public Discourse in the Age of Show Business.* New York: Penguin Books, 1986. The media critic's exegesis on how the entertainment model of news is destroying serious public discourse.

Articles & Book Chapters

Bernstein, Carl. "The Idiot Culture." *The New Republic,* 8 June 1992. The Watergate journalist's take on the effects of having entertainment values replace journalistic values in news.

Ehrlich, Matthew. "The Journalism of Outrageousness: Tabloid Television News vs. Investigative News." *Journalism & Mass Communication Monographs* 155 (February 1996). A careful comparison of the characteristics of tabloid and investigative news. Ehrlich finds they share many similarities. Furthermore, tabloid news does not do such a bad job of informing the public about topics more serious than sex, crime, and gossip.

Gladney, George Albert. "The McPaper Revolution? USA Today-style Innovation at Large U.S. Dailies." *Newspaper Research Journal* (Winter/Spring 1992): 54-71. An assessment of 230 of the largest U.S. newspapers on their *USA Today*-style characteristics. Gladney sees hope that not all newspapers have gone too far toward this entertainment model.

Grabe, Maria Elizabeth. "Tabloid and Traditional Television News Magazine Crime Stories." *Journalism and Mass Communication Quarterly* 73 (Winter 1996): 926-46. The author tests whether tabloid news violates journalistic objectivity and fails at the journalistic ideal of giving citizens information of value to their lives. She found support for tabloid news being similar in its presentation of crime to traditional coverage. She argues society needs both forms.

Hofstetter, C. Richard, and David M. Dozier. "Useful News, Sensational News: Quality,

Sensationalism and Local TV News." *Journalism Quarterly* 63 (Winter 1986): 815-20, 853. The authors content analyze local news and find even sensational news has more in common with non-sensational news than differences from it. Their research suggests that even sensational news has some background information that can teach citizens.

Jamieson, Kathleen Hall, ed. "The Media and Politics." Special issue of *The Annals of the American Academy of Political and Social Science* 546 (July 1996). Discusses several important topics in the news debate: how voters learn about politics from the media, a comparison of the extent to which print media and broadcast news as sources of political information affect citizen learning, the underused and underestimated visual information in television news that carries information, and a new paradigm of news.

"Looking Over the Edge: The Impact of Technology on Communication Education." May 1996. A Roundtable report, Manship School of Mass Communication, Louisiana State University. A compilation of the best thinking of media professionals and educators about where the industry is headed. Roundtable participants argue that journalists will always be in demand even in this technological age because they have the skills to deliver the accurate and trustworthy information that the public demands. Only the packaging will change, but the message is all. Excerpts are available on the Manship School homepage at http://www.lsu.edu/guests/manship (Manship School Reports).

Tuchman, Gaye. "Making news by doing work." *American Journal of Sociology* 79 (1979): 110-31. Part of a pioneering study of the news media by a sociologist interested in developing a "sociology of news." Tuchman argues news routines are a kind of "strategic ritual" intended to protect journalists from criticism of their work and to help them meet deadlines. These are not always good techniques for bringing the highest quality of news to the public.

Chapter Twenty

The Legacy of Tabloid TV News

Emily Erickson Hoff

Media professionals and academics have been shaking their heads for a number of years, condemning superficial image-driven and story-driven news. They have decried a modern tendency to cater to the lowest common denominator, to be irresponsible in newsgathering, and to treat the news as entertainment.

The public has appeared to agree with this assessment. In the weeks following O.J. Simpson's arrest for the murder of Nicole Brown Simpson and Ronald Goldman, surveys showed that a majority of Americans thought the media coverage was unfair and excessive. But the ratings showed that many Americans were watching that coverage just the same.

Distraught mourners of Princess Diana helped illustrate this paradox when they pointed into camera lenses indiscriminately, crying out, "You killed her!" But precisely who were they pointing at? They would have said "the tabloids" or the "paparazzi," but their fingers were also aimed at respectable news organizations. And they were unwittingly pointed at the viewers who sat on their living room sofas, watching the spectacle on TV.

Who is to blame for this apparent crisis in journalism? By many accounts, the primary instigator of this crisis has been tabloid TV news programs — *A Current Affair*, *Inside Edition*, *Hard Copy*, and their progeny. Many questionable news practices can be found in these camps: strident sensationalism, celebrity-centered news, checkbook journalism, and a marked absence of careful verification regarding questionable information.

Some say that the heyday of tabloid TV news is over, simply a trend that is fading quickly from the scene in the face of waning public interest. Others argue that it has irrevocably seeped into the mainstream news media. Still others raise the question of blame. Who, after all, is responsible for the success of tabloid TV news, and how should Americans view an increasingly blurry line between the tabloids and traditional news programs? This chapter will address the strengths and weaknesses of tabloid TV news, its past, and the force of its legacy upon the mainstream news media of our future.

Origins of the Issue

To examine the modern tabloid TV phenomenon, it's necessary to look at its roots, which date back at least 150 years to the American penny press era — a time when newspaper owners first realized the untapped audience potential in the newly literate common man. It was during this era that a visiting Englishman reported that American newspapers were "dreadfully licentious" and expressed amazement that "cabmen, boatmen, tapsters, oysterwomen, porters" all read and discussed the news. In *Sensationalism in the New York Press,* John Stevens argues that this new working-class audience changed the news, infusing it with simpler, more sensational themes.

But that early dose of sensationalism paled in comparison to the infamous era of yellow journalism at the close of the nineteenth century. It wasn't until 1884 that the term "tabloid" was coined. It was, at the time, the trademark for a tablet of compressed medicine. "In other words," explains Terry Murphy, former *Hard Copy* co-anchor, "a tabloid is something small, easy to swallow and good for you." In the 1890s, this translated into huge headlines, tear-jerker news stories, and a number of frenetic attempts by editors and reporters to actually create news.

Joseph Pulitzer and William Randolph Hearst claimed center stage. Pulitzer sent Nellie Bly around the world, and Hearst sent Richard Harding Davis to Cuba to report on the Spanish-American war — which many historians blame the editors for starting in the first place with their jingoistic rally cries. The backlash was inevitable, and in 1898 *Life* magazine ran an editorial cartoon that portrayed King Kong, the words "yellow journalism" imprinted on his chest, flapping his arms angrily with newspapers flying everywhere. "Extra!" read the sheets, "Lies, Filth, Crime!" The Spanish-American War proved to be a watershed for yellow journalism, much like the O.J. Simpson trial would be for the modern TV tabloids, marking both a heyday and an inevitable ending.

Less than ten years later, American journalism was marked by "muckraking," a term coined by journalist-turned-president Theodore Roosevelt. "The men with the muckrakes are often indispensable to the wellbeing of society," Roosevelt conceded in 1906, "but only if they know when to stop raking up the muck, and to look upward to the celestial crown above them, to the crown of worthy endeavor." Most of this era's journalists claimed that the muck they dredged up — from the disease-ridden squalor of tenement housing to political corruption — was in itself a worthy endeavor. Cumulatively, it constituted a call for justice. And although the muckrakers often admitted to using sensational techniques, particularly in their colorful stories of personal woe, it was sensational for the express purpose of jolting the public out of its sense of complacency. Nevertheless, the journalists of the muckraking era walked a fine line between practicing investigative journalism and tabloid journalism.

After the days of the penny press, yellow journalism, and muckraking, tabloid journalism was able to carve out a niche for itself in modern American culture. The *National Enquirer*, for example, has existed for many years without causing much distress among mainstream journalists, by virtue of the fact that it functioned solely in that niche. Read in the checkout line, primarily by people who understood its *raison d'etre* was entertainment, it remained comfortably segregated from "real news," as did similar tabloid rags.

What, then, is new about today's tabloid news controversy? William Spragens, author of the book *Electronic Magazines*, defines the modern phenomenon as "sensation-oriented programming, mostly syndicated, which has pulled conventional broadcast programming in the direction of high ratings, personality-oriented content." Note in this definition that the tabloidism that's most controversial today is found on television. The line between the *National Enquirer* and the *New York Times* was always clear and solid and continues to be so. It is the TV tabloids that concern media scholars and professionals.

It was in July 1986, the middle of the cable revolution, that Australian-born media baron Rupert Murdoch launched *A Current Affair*, anchored by Maury Povich. In his autobiographical *Current Affairs*, Povich gives an account of the program's premier. After it aired, Murdoch expressed outrage at a reporter's inability to "bring in" a Chinese "Godfather." Povich describes the scene:

> A reporter [Murdoch] had in mind — his kind of reporter — would have clapped kindly Uncle Jimmy in irons, in full view of his henchmen — which would have made an interesting part of the show if the henchmen didn't gun down Miller and the cameraman and the soundman first — then march him to the Elizabeth Street police precinct, where he would present this known felon, this unrepentant villain, to the desk officer. Swear out a complaint. Press charges. A trophy from an aroused citizenry who were no longer going to tolerate criminals in their midst. It was an interesting twist on activist journalism.

Of course, it was also exactly the kind of stunt that William Randolph Hearst would have applauded one hundred years earlier. And like Hearst's *New York Journal*, *A Current Affair* was a success, and it gradually grew into national syndication. Soon after, two of its producers launched *Inside Edition*, hoping the new show would be a more upscale version of *Affair*. Other tabloid magazines joined in quick succession, fueled by the freakish cases of Robert Chambers, Amy Fisher, and Lorena Bobbitt. Thus, by the early 1990s, there was a new genre of TV news.

With David Frost as its original anchor, *Inside Edition* did strive to stay on a more investigative track. It was, by most accounts, the "cleanest" tabloid news programs. But its ratings didn't really take off until 1992, when it began going after the more sensational fare.

Meanwhile, *Affair* was trying to clean up its act, responding to sponsor pressure. Povich had left to begin his own talk show in 1991, and a string of producers and staff had desperately tried to hold onto its early success. In November 1992, its newest executive producer, John Terenzio, announced that this would be the first network sweeps on the show "where there's not one stripper swirling around a pole." The ratings dropped soon after.

By 1995, the tabloid programs had pocketed consistently good ratings but few friends. Among their enemies were celebrities like Paul Newman, Kevin Costner, and Robert DeNiro, who had experienced run-ins with the videorazzi or, as actor Will Smith has called them, the "stalkarazzi." Celebrities weren't the only angry ones, however. That year, former Education Secretary William Bennett, Sen. Joseph Lieberman, and Sen. Sam Nunn called tabloid TV "cultural rot" and waged a brief campaign against them as well.

It looked like the beginning of some sort of end. The programs reported a decline in ratings that year, which they blamed on the still ongoing O.J. Simpson trial, covered by Court TV. And in 1996, a number of developments seemed to further signal the genre's end. First, a number of periodicals — from *Variety* to the *Columbia Journalism Review* — described an increasing disinterest in the tabloids and radical moves the shows were making to survive. Even *Hard Copy*, the ratings leader that year, agreed to stop using unsolicited, invasive, or provocative footage of an enraged George Clooney and other celebrities. And although the Simpson trial's conclusion provided a boost — ratings skyrocketed as viewers tuned in for juror interviews and "what came after" coverage — that boost was a temporary one. In the two years that the Simpson case dominated news coverage, the public got exactly what it wanted — unlimited coverage — and ultimately grew tired of it.

And it was during 1996 that *Affair*, the "granddaddy of tabmags," was cancelled. Rosie O'Donnell, the new Queen of Nice, was launching her new talk show, and when a Chicago station decided to replace *Affair* with the new O'Donnell show, it signaled *Affair's* death knell.

It seems that the heyday of the tabloid news program is over. At this writing, only a handful of tabloid news shows have survived. But their impact on the mainstream news has been much more far-reaching. Is it any coincidence that an average NBC newscast today has only five or six "hard news" items in the first half, with features material dominating the second half? Compare this to twenty or so stories in the golden era of network news. That era's venerable anchor Walter Cronkite says today's news is forsaking an important role in democracy. But as this chapter will demonstrate, the verdict is still out on tabloid TV news and its legacy.

The End of Respectable Journalism

What clearly links modern TV tabloid news with its predecessors is its age-less appeal to escapism and a simple world of black and white, good and evil. "Tabloid programs are popular and profitable because they recycle a proven for-mula with widespread appeal — a mix of crime, sex, gossip, and human interest stories," says Matthew C. Ehrlich in "The Journalism of Outrageousness."

In his monograph, Ehrlich carefully delineates the differences between tabloid programs and similar investigative magazine shows like *60 Minutes*. Referring to Roosevelt's critique of the muckrakers, Ehrlich argues that tabloid TV news is gen-erally unable to raise its head to any celestial crown of good intentions. Rather, it "keeps its eyes resolutely downward, positively wallowing in the muck it dredges up, reveling in its disposable, interchangeable, ironic tales of outra-geousness." Rather than seeking social justice or even the simple exposure of truth, tabloid journalism is "a means unto itself, with the occasional piece of 'real' news, sentiment, or fluff served up to help mask the pungent odor of its main stock." In other words, the tabloids are guilty of sensationalism for its own sake — pure gratuitous sensationalism.

His assessment is echoed by others, such as Christopher Hanson, Washington correspondent for the *Seattle Post-Intelligencer*, writing in the *Columbia Journalism Review*. "In the old days of yellow journalism," Hanson writes, "little could top a U.S. invasion of some exotic Caribbean isle: lives at risk, Big Stick in action, world taking notice. Today such a story is evidently too sophisticated to please main-stream journalism's tabloid gatekeepers, who have O.J. on the brain."

Hanson supports this view by describing a scene in September 1994, when President Clinton was preparing the public for an invasion of Haiti. A brief inter-view between Dan Rather and Chief Lt. General Raoul Cédras concluded with a rather inane question from Rather: "Will you fight if invaded?" and ended abruptly to make room for the two-hour premier of *Due South*. "This is the same Rather," says Hanson, "who once complained: 'They've got us putting more fuzz and wuzz on the air.'" As bad as yellow journalism was, its actual content was often important and bona fide news. Hanson argues that the modern tabloid phenomenon — and, subsequently, today's mainstream news — has less to do with sensational *presentation* of real news than it has to do with sensational *content* itself.

Another difference regards the corporate communication context in which the tabloid programs were born. It is this new twist on the old tabloid theme that has many scholars and practitioners fearful of its endurance. Jeff Greenfield, media critic for the *Washington Post*, emphasizes the importance of today's myriad media outlets in creating and sustaining tabloid fare. It was the emergence of cable and satellite, he says, that "made it possible for network competitors to distribute tabloid TV shows like *Hard Copy* and afternoon talk shows that viewers lapped right up." With fifty or more channels, and a remote-control in a viewer's hand, it takes more to convince him or her to stay tuned.

It's also cheaper to produce these shows than it is to produce prime-time entertainment. On the flip side, these tabloid news programs have to compete with that entertainment. This in turn makes it even more vital to use sensational hooks and scandalous material — if the news can't beat the entertainment, then it must join it. And this is just as true for the local and network news as it has been for the tabloid programs; so the latter's demise may not matter now that the precedent of news competing with entertainment has been set. The ratings structure was already in place, and this new context of high competition among many players shows no signs of fading. In short, the tabloid tradition itself is a rather timeless one, but, according to the critics, the new rules of corporate media management have opened the way for sensational productions to flourish indefinitely.

But how exactly have the tabloid programs influenced the mainstream media? Most critics of tabloid news cite the increasing use of both tabloid techniques and tabloid content — both necessary because the tabloids set new lows in newsgathering and new highs in ratings. "Broadcast news has an important role to play in the democracy," said Robert MacNeil, former co-anchor of PBS's *MacNeil/Lehrer Report* in a 1996 speech at the University of South Dakota. But "the networks have felt forced to make themselves more entertaining and more popular."

It is often assumed, by virtue of time order (the tabloids arrived, the mainstream news became more sensational), that this was a direct result of the tabloids' success. "Those of us who remember a different tenor to broadcast news aren't indulging in hazy nostalgia or false memory," insists Greenfield in "Why relevance is obsolete." "It really was different: hour-long documentaries were commonplace in the '60s and '70s." But times have changed. With a hand from the ratings system, tabloids have had the ability "to 'launch' stories — often of the sleaziest kind — that the mainstream press feels it necessary to follow," according to *Washington Post* staffer David Broder.

For example, in Spragens' *Electronic Magazines*, CBS news producer Andrew Hayward admits that both tabloid and mainstream news share a basic need to pursue ratings and profits, which can force the networks to pursue otherwise distasteful stories. Hayward argues, however, that the network's shows "combine the profit-making necessity with a standard-setting goal; they must set a standard for public service while making a profit and staying competitive." CBS, for example, put stories about the Menendez brothers and John and Lorena Bobbitt into a framework of "finding an excuse" for criminal activity. This thematic organization, in Hayward's mind, was superior to "showing night after night coverage of the Menendez or Bobbitt cases without getting a real story."

But critics like Greenfield deride this argument, saying the network commitment to public good is just lip service. With this kind of rationalization, says Greenfield, "the divorce of Donald and Ivana Trump 'shed new light on the issue of prenuptial agreements.' The travails of Woody Allen and Mia Farrow 'shed new light on child-custody issues.'" And now even this transparent "relevance requirement" has fallen away, "like a booster stage that fires a rocket into orbit only to be jettisoned once it has accomplished its task." The mainstream news has indeed been felled by tabloidism. "Let's face it," says Edward Planer, former NBC news vice president and current chair at Columbia College's journalism department. "The news cycle has been dominated by JonBenet Ramsey, O.J. Simpson, floods and bank robberies.... They are doing what is easy to do."

Taking the easy — or tabloid — route to news has also contaminated bona fide topics, say critics, affecting even the coverage of politics and ultimately democracy. In a 1992 *New York Times* column, Alex S. Jones argued that the alleged Gennifer Flowers–Bill Clinton affair would have passed quickly except that "both wings of the press have effectively worked in tandem to keep the story alive. The sensational wing has kept stoking the flames and repeating the story with every mention of Mr. Clinton," Jones wrote. "The more mainstream press has reported on the impact the story is having on Mr. Clinton's candidacy, and in doing so they have repeated the accusations as well." Thus, a story that was initially presented by one of the tabloid programs gained further credence when it found its way onto a *60 Minutes* interview with Bill and Hillary Clinton. When the charges made by the tabloids are picked up by serious news organizations, Jones argued, they are "converted from dross into journalistic gilt." This single issue of trivializing and "tabloidizing" politics has stirred up significant concern and controversy among voters and journalists alike, causing many to worry that the sleaze will take over serious policy debate because extramarital affairs are easier to report than healthcare policy reform.

According to Christopher Hanson, the connection between news content and voting day involves more than coverage of politics itself. It can also involve the absence of that coverage. There is, Hanson says, a general sense of civic involvement and knowledge that can wither away when the public is given more tabloid content than substantive news. "Most people have little spare time and only finite space in their attention box," he argues. "When it is filled every day for years and years with wuzz and fuzz ... rational discourse on such matters as military intervention diminishes; civic ignorance mounts; and each time we play Russian roulette at the ballot box there is another round in the chamber."

In a *New Republic* article, "Making Sausage," William Powers addresses a consequence of utilizing tabloid techniques: lawsuits, such as *ABC v. Food Lion*, in which the supermarket chain won damages for fraud after reporters posed as employees and surreptitiously gathered evidence of negligent food handling. "One careful look at the ubiquitous magazine shows is all one needs to see why there are so many of these lawsuits, and why juries are coming down against newsgatherers," Powers says. "The news standards that guide these shows and the ethical standards that guide them as they gather that news ... are often terribly low. And as the magazines have proliferated and the number of story slots that must be filled has grown — NBC's 'Dateline' is on three nights a week — they are getting lower."

Indeed, *Dateline* is a program whose pieces would normally be labeled investigative. But it is these programs that have been most dramatically influenced by their tabloid cousins. Carl Bernstein, one of the two reporters who broke the Watergate story, has been one of tabloid journalism's most emphatic enemies, and the book he co-wrote with Bob Woodward, *All the President's Men*, serves as a prime example of the tedious footwork involved in solid investigative reporting. All allegations against Nixon's reelection campaign staff had to be confirmed by two or more reliable sources, and the two reporters even gathered physical evidence before printing some of their information. This painstaking newsgathering stands in stark contrast to the easier and sleazier means of using questionable sources, subterfuge, and hidden cameras in order to get a story. This technique has, according to critics, become much more prevalent since the emergence of the tabloid TV programs.

Another item that can be linked directly to the tabloid shows is the notorious practice of checkbook journalism — paying sources for their stories.

Jane Meredith Adams was a reporter for the *Boston Globe* in 1994, when Tonya Harding was helping the tabloid TV ratings skyrocket by her apparent participation in the attack on her competitor, Nancy Kerrigan. Adams was sent to Oregon to report on the sensational story. "I participated," she writes in the *Columbia Journalism Review*, "in the kind of bottom-feeding journalism ridiculed — even as we in the 'mainstream' do more of it — by virtually everyone." What amazed Adams in this experience was the amount of money that changed hands in order to capitalize on the story. "In more innocent times, under the rules of the media game, a tough-talking, Marlboro smoking skater with a tenth-grade education would spill her story to whoever got there first, or asked in the most empathic tones, or worked for the most prestigious news organization," Adams writes. "She would open her life to us, flattered that we asked. Not Tonya; not in the 1990s." Instead, Harding received well over six figures from *Inside Edition*.

Although most news organizations still refuse to pay sources for information, the practice of checkbook journalism has, according to many, created a greedy expectation of payment in return for information, which seriously hampers the newsgathering process. And this increasingly common attitude toward one's "story" was poignantly illustrated by the conviction of the young woman who tried to blackmail comedian Bill Cosby by threatening to tell a tabloid that she was his illegitimate daughter. If he wouldn't give her the money, she told him, she had the right to profit from her story.

At the heart of the moral repugnance toward checkbook journalism is the notion of news as a public service. It is an old argument that, because freedom of the press is protected by the Constitution, there is an appropriate expectation that the press should be responsible caretakers of that right and the presentation of news overall. This too is an area where the tabloid news shows have made enemies with their apparent dismissal of any such obligation by appealing to the base interests of their viewers. By making their stories center exclusively around sex, crime, celebrities, accidents, and tales of the bizarre, the tabloid programs do indeed seem to wallow in the muck described by Roosevelt.

Based on the ratings, of course, this rather dark fare has apparently been what the viewers want to see — this was particularly supported in the falling ratings that followed *Affair* producer Terrenzio's attempt to clean up the show. But the critics of tabloid TV argue that what the viewers want is not necessarily what they ought to get. Jeff Greenfield, for example, recalls the old TV show *You Asked for It*. The most common request sent in by viewers, Greenfield says, was to see a televised execution. "Sometimes, late at night," he says, "I conjure up a syndicator offering a new updated version of *You Asked for It* in today's marketplace. It is not a pleasant thought." Greenfield acknowledges the viewers' part in enabling the sensational material to thrive, and yet he holds the industry responsible as well. "Just sit back one afternoon, and turn on the set," he says, "and realize that what you are seeing is a result of the deliberate, conscious decisions of some of the most powerful, respected people in this business — that this is what we choose to put over the public airwaves ... and it would not be there if we did not want it to be."

Here stands the strange paradox of the ratings and the public's expressed criticism of tabloid content. According to Harvard fellow and former *New York Times* staffer Lee Daniels, cited by Jacqueline Sharkey in *American Journalism Review*, this is proof that news should be substantive and informative rather than sensational. The public believes this, Daniels says. This is why they will condemn the tabloid fare, even as their eyes are glued to it.

Again, critics maintain that this negligence of the media's obligation has seeped into the mainstream. In 1993, Howard Kurtz did a survey of local news shows and found that 46 to 74 per cent of their first half hour constituted tabloid coverage. This was defined as stories involving crime, sex, disasters, accidents, or public fears. If the death and destruction fare dried up, Kurtz said, the stations would turn to things like "a snakebite victim, a woman bitten by a deadly spider, a public school flasher, a third-grader hit with a BB pellet, 'satanic' activities involving cats and dogs and, inevitably, Gennifer Flowers, Joey Buttafucco, Madonna and the death of Elvis Presley."

The dominance of these topics and themes lead critics to perhaps their strongest point of contention. In a field informed by the theory of agenda-setting, which posits powerful media that dictate what issues the public thinks about, it should not be surprising that many are concerned with the warped version of reality being presented by the tabloids.

In George Garneau's *Editor & Publisher* article, "Trash Journalism," Carl Bernstein argues that, over the past twenty years, the mass media have "been abdicating our primary function — the best obtainable version of the truth — and allowed our agenda and priorities to become bastardized and dominated by ... the triumph of Idiot Culture." Although Bernstein doesn't lay the blame on tabloid TV news entirely, he has special vitriol reserved for *Affair* creator Rupert Murdoch. "Murdoch and the sleazy, cynical standards of the low end of his empire," he says, "which increasingly affects the standards of even the high end of our business, are an even greater threat to the truth than ... the lying and secrecy of a succession of American presidents and their governments."

What precisely constitutes truth in Bernstein's mind? According to him, it is an ability to provide context in a story. The aim of tabloids and their cousins, he says, is "to shock, to titillate, to distort, to give grotesque emphasis." And with increasing competition, "speed and accuracy and quantity substitute for thoroughness and quality, for accuracy and context." So here again, the critique goes back to what is easy to report — and giving a story context, rather than simply good visuals and sound bites, is not easy.

Another practice that critics say obscures the truth is that of teasing out a story as long as possible in order to keep viewers hooked. In his 1994 column "Tabloid 'News' Warping Views of Real Thing," John Kiesewetter argues that tabloids have no interest in giving balanced news coverage because, if they have another source, "they have another exclusive news story to prolong coverage another day." Similarly, William Powers criticizes the camera techniques used by the tabloids as being inadequate to explain the complexity of truth. "The footage," he says, "with its grainy cinema verité quality and its you-are-there evocations of FBI stings and bank robbery films, carries an associative suggestion of guilt powerful enough to override even scrupulously evenhanded writing."

Howard Kurtz has argued that this same vision of reality now exists in mainstream news. "It seemed almost a parody of journalism," he reported in his study of local news shows. "[There were] bold graphics filling the screen, melo-dramatic background music, correspondents reporting live from some darkened street corner that the police had vacated hours earlier." With the increasing use of these tabloid presentation techniques, local news programs are presenting a similarly skewed version of reality. Hyping these stories each night "presents a distorted picture of the community," Kurtz writes, "creating a sense of anarchy and chaos with precious little context."

Instead of providing viewers with context, which is often difficult and "messy," the tabloid means of presenting reality is — according to both critics and supporters — through story form. In "The Tao of Tabloid," Bert Briller explains this: "When traditional journalists say 'I've got a great story,' they usu-ally mean they've uncovered a newsworthy development," he says. "But the tabloid journalist thinks of the story as *story*, a narrative with plot, characters, conflict, emotion, and a moral." When tabloid TV news first began, it inherited a tradition of storytelling already well-established in the medium of TV. As early as 1984, TV had been labeled the most popular storytelling form in the United States, over both books and movies. Tabloid news had a similar tradition, partic-ularly visible in the era of yellow journalism. Reporters would often construct news stories similar to fictional ones, emphasizing archetypal characters and plotlines. This practice has been a trademark of modern tabloidism as well. Both Bert Briller and Matthew Ehrlich have demonstrated how tabloid news stories conform to conventional storytelling style — morality playlets, for example, in which a subject's greed or arrogance results in his or her downfall; stories in which good and evil are pitted against each other; "cautionary tales," in which the story serves to warn the viewer of falling prey to scams.

Many are critical of portraying the news as a story because, they argue, it forces reality into a set mold that is both inaccurate and oversimplified. When people are cast as villains and heroes, for example, the journalist must omit or overemphasize some information in order to portray these black-and-white characters. Ehrlich has also pointed out that today's villain may be tomorrow's victim, as was the case in *Hard Copy*'s coverage of Prince Charles and Princess Diana over the course of their marriage — their discord was always blamed on one of them, but not always the same one. This points toward an indifference or lack of belief in any real "truth." A story's plotline can also be manipulated, which can sacrifice its depth and complexity in order to follow the format of, say, a morality play or cautionary tale.

Forcing news into the framework of a story, using questionable newsgathering techniques, and pursuing sensational fare are all part of the tabloid tradition. Critics today are most alarmed because TV has seemingly exacerbated all of these practices and because these practices have in turn seeped into mainstream news. Even *Affair* creator Peter Brennan has confirmed the influence of the TV tabloids on their more respectable counterparts. "Once upon a time there was just 'A Current Affair' going after these stories," he said in a 1993 *Variety* article. "Now you not only have four syndicated shows going after the same story but you have all the network primetime newsmagazine shows as well."

In 1996, Robert MacNeil made an ominous observation in his speech at the University of South Dakota. This is "the end of news," he said, "or at least the end of news as we know it, because [news] as we know it is already changing so rapidly that it could be said to be ending."

TV Tabloids Are Being Scapegoated

Of those who disagree with the TV tabloids' critics, most would be quick to point out that Robert MacNeil's job as a PBS newsman puts him in the top 1 per cent of the nation's intellectual elites. In fact, one of the most common means of defending the tabloids is through a critique of its critics, whose abhorrence of the genre is based in large part upon elitism. In Jacqueline Sharkey's 1994 *American Journalism Review* article, "Judgment Calls," ABC's Senior Vice President of News Richard Wald defends the coverage of "popular" topics, such as the O.J. Simpson case. "There's an elitist attitude that because it's interesting, it must be wrong," he says, "[or] because we do well with it, there must be something wrong." He is joined by both Ted Koppel and Sam Donaldson in this anti-elitist line, although the two anchormen are also quick to raise their eyebrows at ratings-driven programs. Nevertheless, Donaldson finds it "terribly elitist" when journalists "sit around deciding what is good for people to know, or what is responsible for people to learn" and to use that "as the major criterion for doing something in the news business."

The fact is that, demographically, the TV tabloid's audience comprises mostly lower-middle-class Americans, and even some elites like Donaldson and Koppel are hesitant to condemn those programming tastes out of hand. Those behind the tabloid programs recognize where their audience members are as well. *Affair's* Maury Povich and John Terenzio have both, in different contexts, referred to their viewers as those in America's "heartland." Thus, when people vehemently criticize the TV tabloids, it is much like criticizing any other pastime of this group — it is inherently and unabashedly elitist. Those who argue against this elitism point out that the tabloid programs are only a handful of a large and diverse collection of available news.

In "Tabloid and Traditional Television News Magazine Crime Stories," Maria Elizabeth Grabe examines the line separating high culture and mass culture in terms of tabloid and mainstream news. Her study shows that the crimes reported on tabloid news programs are more likely to be white-collar crimes — and, alternately, crimes reported in the mainstream news are more likely to be blue-collar crimes. In other words, the villains of tabloid TV are likely to be its audience's societal superiors, thus reinforcing class lines. Grabe also notes that the content of tabloid news reflects the realities and problems of its viewers. Thus, criticism of the tabloids "assumes that international and esoteric matters, such as the world economy or politicians' competition for the Nobel Peace Prize, are more legitimate and more worthy of news coverage than the events that impact the lives of ordinary people," she says.

Taking this argument a step further, many say that tabloid TV and its influence on mainstream news have actually represented an evolution of American culture and have made the news media more democratic.

In a 1997 *Newsweek* column, for example, Meg Greenfield noted that tabloid fare "may be prurient, unelevated and unbecoming, but it is also eminently understandable." Calling the genre "high-wire TV without the net," Greenfield wrote that tabloid TV news has taken the place of old-fashioned back-fence neighborhood gossip. "We get what we seem to need — gossip, drama, diversion, reinforcement in our prejudices and justification in our conceits — from the seemingly unending series of ordeals our fellow humans undergo." From this view, the tabloid phenomenon has little to do with "real" news; rather, it serves a more social function and should be judged accordingly.

Douglas Rushkoff also takes a more cultural approach to sensational news in general. In his *Futures* article, "Life in the Tube," he argues that tabloid TV tends to "promote our culture's natural, unexpressed agendas.... [W]hen approached from an evolutionary perspective, [these shows] reveal themselves as the process by which closeted social issues are brought out into the cultural conversation exactly when they need to be."

Defenders of tabloid TV note that, in this light, putting news into a traditional storytelling format seems more innocuous because its function is different from traditional news altogether. If, for example, the news stories are not only *presented* as morality plays, but are actually *functioning* as morality plays as well, then perhaps the increasing prevalence of tabloid practices is not so disastrous.

Louise Mengelkoch, a university journalism instructor, argues that tabloid TV news has functioned to make the media arena more democratic as well. In a *Columbia Journalism Review* article, Mengelkoch tells her account of a Minnesota family who was struggling financially and legally after the father shot and killed the man who raped his daughter. It was only through tabloid TV — first *Sally Jesse Raphael* and then *Hard Copy* — that the family members were able to tell their story and get both financial and legal help.

"The tabloids' greatest virtue," Mengelkoch now tells her journalism students, "is exactly that which makes people sneer at them — they're often foolish and not very selective. As gatekeepers they're lousy, and that's often fortunate for those who need them most. They will listen to your story when nobody else will, if it has the elements they're looking for." Menglekoch sees the tabloids as contributing to a more democratic marketplace of ideas. "If we truly believe in access, that journalists should be dedicated to comforting the afflicted and afflicting the comfortable," she argues, "[then] the tabloids must be recognized as sharing that mission."

Others who think tabloid TV has gotten a bad rap don't try to circumvent its news function at all. They believe it has actually improved modern news. Fred Young, a Hearst Broadcasting news executive, defends his use of media consultants in the creation of news, and attributes this move to the tabloids. "Tabloid news is this year's T.B. scare," he says. "Frankly, it has forced all of us to become more interesting programs. Our writing is better, our content is more sophisticated, our video is better and we have better sets and graphics."

But most who defend the face value of tabloid news seem to be within the industry itself. Maury Povich, for example, has been the genre's biggest advocate. "Tabloid journalism strikes at the heart," he said in Spragens' *Electronic Magazines.* "It doesn't make forays around the subject. It peels away layers of the superficial. It's readable. Better yet, it's watchable." Like many who defend the quality of tabloid news, Povich emphasizes the value of personalizing events, showing the audience how a given development affected people, or, even better, how it could affect the viewers themselves. *Hard Copy*'s Terry Murphy, for example, has described how the program decided to "play" one story:

> We put a personal emotional touch on much of what we do. When Magic Johnson announced he was HIV positive, my producer said, "Isn't your son a Magic fan?" My eight-year-old Justin idolizes Johnson, practically has a Magic shrine in his room. And so the producer had us do the Magic/HIV story through the eyes of Justin, who's like many kids for whom Magic is a hero. Viewers said they were really touched.

Not surprisingly, those who applaud the more personal approach to news found in the tabloid programs feel that traditional, objective news treatments would at least remain unharmed, if not better off, with a bit of that "personal emotional touch" poured into the mainstream media.

The third view of tabloid TV's function is the most prevalent: tabloid TV news is essentially entertainment, just as its newspaper counterparts are. John Stevens tells of a man who found "this parallel universe" while waiting in line at the grocery store. It's like our universe, said the man, "but with more gusto." In reading the "rag," the man learned that "tabloidworld had no problems with national debt, ecological blight, or nuclear tension but was overrun with invaders from outer space, vampires, and above all, exclamation points." Stevens argued that the author took the tabloid no more seriously "than have many — perhaps most — Americans of many eras who lay down their coins for the escapism provided by sensational papers."

Those who view tabloid news as functioning as simply entertainment liken it to the features side of the news, which is in itself an important part of American culture. Celebrity news, for example, has a long history in the United States. The video camera has simply made celebrities more accessible to viewers, who want to follow the stars' glamorous lives in order to escape the mundane realities of their own. The public, in this view, consists of individuals who are savvy enough to recognize tabloid stories and the "news lite" of mainstream news as entertainment rather than reality. Again, the anti-elitist vein runs through this argument.

Not everyone who defends tabloid news, however, actually thinks the genre is a good one, or that its influence on the mainstream has been positive. Some simply see few differences between the tabloid and mainstream press. Deborah Norville, for example, worked for a number of years at the top of network news and then took a job at *Inside Edition*. "I've ridden the backs of both ponies," she said in a History Channel interview, "and I've got to tell you — there's not that great a difference."

According to some, even checkbook is a practice more common in the mainstream than some would admit. J. Max Robins points out that, although the networks refrain from paying the likes of Joey Buttafucco for an interview, they have their own versions of checkbook journalism — CBS, according to Robins, paid $300,000 for three Lyndon Johnson interviews and the same amount for a ninety-minute conversation between Richard Nixon and an aide. "It's a story that's as old as news," Robins quotes an unnamed tabloid news producer saying. "You do whatever you have to in order to get the interview. The only thing that's changed is that it's gotten a lot more expensive."

Legal analyst Jeffrey Toobin has even gone a step further and called the Supreme Court's venerable members accountable for runaway checkbook journalism. According to Toobin in "Buying Headlines," the Court's decision to rule unconstitutional New York's "Son of Sam" law opened the floodgates for those who wanted to profit from their stories. The law was passed in 1977 to keep a convicted serial killer (who called himself Son of Sam) from profiting from a book about his crimes by making such profits illegal. "Once that law was gone, we knew that the day would come when the Jeffrey Dahmers of the world would make a bundle," Toobin quotes John Terenzio as saying. "I wouldn't pay a convicted criminal, but it opened our eyes to what was out there — the deals to be made."

Along a similar line, some believe that external events are responsible for creating the public appetite for tabloid news. In a 1997 *American Journalism Review* article, for example, James McCartney argues that the fundamental nature of news — mainstream or otherwise — has changed because there is no longer a Cold War or world war, a civil rights movement, or a Watergate to rouse the public from its happy slumber. "Let's face it. One of the things that's happened is that there is very little news," McCartney quotes Reuven Frank, former president of NBC News. Today, continues Frank, "we've got stories that aren't as compelling, that aren't worth much. We are no longer threatened with annihilation. There is less news of any crisis. We have more and more news outlets, and less and less news. Whether what's going on is 'dumbing down,' I don't know. It is certainly softening."

Media critic Joshua Gamson supports this argument as well, pointing to a dwindling sense of political efficacy among the public. It is for this reason, says Gamson in the *Prospect* article, "Incredible News," that infotainment has flourished. "There is no important information," Gamson writes, "no world filled with injustices to fight, complicated truths to mull over, powerful people whose actions change everything; only me, the couch, the fun simulations of a world that doesn't much matter."

The Legacy of Tabloid TV News

Many of those who decline to vilify tabloid news also emphasize that it is just one of many forces that are reportedly contributing to the "dumbing down" of America — forces that are led by new technologies and a host of virtually unlimited information outlets. Although few of today's college students will remember the "golden era" of network news, there was a time when, in the evening, one's choice of TV programs was limited to the news of CBS, ABC, and NBC. These networks didn't have to claw desperately for the attention of viewers. The viewers had nowhere else to go. Today, the national pastime of surfing through a hundred channels makes talking heads and complex policy issues difficult to sell, and it is the explosion of these outlets that has created the pressure for ratings that has driven the mainstream press toward more tabloid content and presentation. Tabloid news programs themselves have thus been a natural result of the increased outlets and subsequent competition.

Moreover, the public itself is responsible for its digestion of news content, whether it's on *Hard Copy* or *60 Minutes*. In a 1994 *Editor & Publisher* column, Professor Joel Kaplan defended the media's coverage of the O.J. Simpson case and argued that it was fulfilling its traditional role in spite of incredible pressures of competition. It was, Kaplan said, informing the public so it could make informed decisions — by showing viewers important issues like spousal abuse and the Sixth Amendment right to a fair trial. "The fact that most Americans haven't the foggiest idea of why we're considering military action in Haiti, yet know every intimate detail of Brian Kaelin's life, says more about the news reader than the news writer," Kaplan wrote.

Finally, those who refuse to condemn the modern tabloid phenomenon raise the flag of free marketplace. Jane Kirtley, executive director of the Reporters Committee for Freedom of the Press, argues that packaging news as a profitable product — presumably even if that product is tabloid — certainly beats the alternative of government regulation. In Jacqueline Sharkey's article "Judgment Calls," Kirtley maintains that the present system, with its proliferating venues and frenetic competition, still has the advantage of giving the public "a powerful voice" in deciding what's news. And in a democratic country whose free-market economy is as strong as it is, the practical "solution" is obvious: there is nothing that can or should be done about tabloid TV or its potential impact on mainstream news.

"You know," said Diane Sawyer in a History Channel interview, "I think we can call it good, bad, we can think about it — it won't make any difference. It's about human nature. In the end, we're saying people shouldn't be interested in what they're interested in. But they are."

Resolution

In facing the quandaries posed by tabloid TV news and its influence on the mainstream press, the easiest approach is the laissez-faire one hinted at by Sawyer. In practical terms, she is right that elite media reporters and academics cannot change the public's appetite for sensational tabloid fare. Nor should the U.S. government intervene in the media marketplace. So, left on its present course, the legacy of tabloid TV journalism could leave the news landscape changed in three possible ways.

First, American news could end up resembling a number of European media systems, in which the line between low and high journalism is actually quite clear — a tiny intellectual segment of the population tunes in to drab, serious talking heads on the public stations and the rest of the country watches the sensational ratings-driven material on commercial stations. Popular culture expert John Fiske warns against this scenario, in which a wall has been erected between the low and high journalism that very few people will cross over.

Second, the landscape could end up as many have been predicting — with the lines blurring even further between serious and tabloid news, leaving no program or station untouched. Those who fear this future point to a cynical society whose sense of civic involvement has reached a sofa-engulfed sensation of numbness.

The third potential future is the most optimistic and seems increasingly viable. "I sense that we are now coming back from a dangerous precipice," anchor Sam Donaldson said in a History Channel interview, "where we might have gone over and just done the funny farm, and just done the three-headed cow, and yes-we-found-Elvis-in-a-supermarket-in-Sheboygan-last-week type of thing. [I think we're] coming back to a steady, more sober look at events." Donaldson's sentiments are echoed by journalists Dan Rather and Katie Couric, who also see the pendulum swinging back to a less sensational status quo.

Nevertheless, the debate over tabloid TV's influence upon the mainstream press still poses questions about what role TV journalism should play in the new world of virtually unlimited media outlets and ratings pressures. And there are arguably some things that news organizations *should* hold onto from this tabloid TV phenomenon.

There should, for example, be a heightened awareness of the ways in which news can improve and broaden its content and presentation. Fiske, for example, argues that instead of trying to increase its objectivity, depth, or authority — which are better done by newspapers — TV news should try "to increase its openness, its contradictions, and multiplicity of voices and points of view." TV has made visual and oral transmission of information an integral part of the news. Tabloid TV news, in turn, has capitalized on and exacerbated these qualities in a sensational way, but traditional TV journalists can learn to better utilize them by 1) following Fiske's suggestion to present a multiplicity of voices and 2) working with interesting presentations of news without sacrificing serious content. TV news can be so much better than a light version of traditional newspaper news — it simply needs to redefine itself within the framework of its unique medium.

Similarly, something can be lifted from the storytelling tradition used by the tabloid programs. After all, traditional news writing is a storytelling formula unto itself. Those in TV news should stretch that formula without, as Matthew Ehrlich puts it, "pandering or descending into sleaze."

The hand-wringing critique of tabloid TV news is certainly elitist, and the tabloid phenomenon should not be forgotten once it has run its course. Nevertheless, just as low-brow news — the *National Inquirer,* etc. — has always had some small niche in society, so should the voices of critique. The two sides of this debate are part of an American tradition that keeps a pendulum swinging back and forth in many facets of our culture. And although there are eras of seeming extremism, that pendulum usually hovers fairly close to a modestly centrist position that, in the end, is fairly acceptable to a remarkably diverse population.

Recommended Readings

Books

Campbell, R. *60 Minutes and the News: A Mythology of Middle America.* Urbana: University of Illinois Press, 1991. This is useful in offering points of contrast and comparison to the history and techniques of today's tabloid programming.

Povich, M., and K. Gross. *Current Affairs: A Life on the Edge.* New York: G.P. Putnam's Sons, 1991. An entertaining book about the creation of *A Current Affair,* the original TV tabloid news program, written by the show's first anchor, the self-congratulatory Maury Povich. The book does succeed in depicting the exuberance with which he embraced what he felt was a fresh and honest approach to news.

Stevens, John D. *Sensationalism and the New York Press.* New York: Columbia University Press, 1991. A well-written account of several sensational eras in New York journalism, correcting to some degree the view that Yellow Journalism was an anomaly.

Spragens, William. *Electronic Magazines: Soft News Programs on Network Television.* Westport, Conn.: Praeger, 1995. This book outlines the evolution of TV magazine journals, from *60 Minutes* to modern "soft news" programs. It also has a helpful chapter titled "'Tabloids' versus Magazine Programs," which illustrates some of the ways tabloid practices have seeped into the mainstream press.

Articles

Ehrlich, Matthew C. "The Journalism of Outrageousness: Tabloid Television News vs. Investigative News." *Journalism and Mass Communication Monographs* 155 (February 1996). Probably the best, most thorough treatment of tabloid news to date. Ehrlich compares the two genres and critically assesses the cynicism that's within and promoted by the tabloids.

Gamson, Joshua. "Incredible News." *The American Prospect* (Fall 1994): 28–35. Takes a sociological approach to tabloid and sensational news, pointing out the cultural implications of watching news that simply isn't important.

Garneau, George. "Trash Journalism." *Editor & Publisher,* 29 October 1994, pp. 8–11, 38. Reports the scathing words of Watergate journalist Carl Bernstein, speaking at the Southern Newspaper Publishers Association convention. Bernstein has been one of tabloid TV's biggest critics.

Glynn, K. "Tabloid television's transgressive aesthetic." *Wide Angle* 12:2 (1990): 22–44. Something of a literary critique of tabloid TV that dismisses "the high-minded elitism of moralistic culture critics" in favor of the nation's popular voice. Very academic treatment.

Goode, E., and K. Hetter. "The Selling of Reality." *U.S. News & World Report,* 25 July 1994, pp. 49–56. Describes the process of tabloidesque newsgathering by recounting a story of two American children abandoned in Mexico. The process in which reality is packaged as entertainment/news has, the authors show, become an industry unto itself.

Grabe, M. E. "Tabloid and traditional television news magazine crime stories: Crime lessons and reaffirmation of social class distinctions." *Journalism & Mass Communication Quarterly* 73:4 (1996): 926–46. In this content analysis, Grabe finds that tabloid shows depict crime among the upper-class more often than mainstream news and that mainstream news depicts crime as a more working-class phenomenon.

Greenfield, Jeff. "Why relevance is obsolete." *Time,* 24 February 1997, p. 18. One of the biggest critics of tabloid news and its influence, Greenfield argues that journalists have discarded any pretense of reporting relevant news.

Greenfield, Meg. "Real-Life Mini-Series." *Newsweek,* 2 June 1997, p. 84. Although not endorsing tabloid news, Greenfield says she understands its appeal and argues that its daily "plotlines" are often more compelling than the fictional dramas on TV.

McCartney, James. "News lite." *American Journalism Review* (June 1997): 18–25. Discusses the ratings competition that has forced network news to favor sensational stories over hard news and argues that the press has served the public interest less since 1993.

Mengelkoch, Louise. "When Checkbook Journalism Does God's Work." *Columbia Journalism Review* (November/December 1994): 35–8. Mengelkoch gives an account of her experience in helping a Minnesota family use the tabloids to voice their side of a legal battle. She argues that the tabloids' lack of standards ultimately democratizes the media.

Powers, William. "Making Sausage." *The New Republic*, 20 January 1997, pp. 14–16. A critique of *20/20* and its Food Lion coverage. Powers argues that the court ruling against the magazine show was well-deserved.

Rushkoff, Douglas. "Life in the Tube." *Futures* (February 1996): 87–90. Rushkoff defends the tabloid genre, saying it enables certain taboo issues to be included in society's "cultural conversation."

Sharkey, Jacqueline. "Judgment Calls." *American Journalism Review* (September 1994): 19–26. Considers the O.J. Simpson trial and the issues it has raised with regard to celebrity and sensational news — and whether the public should get what it wants or needs.

Tharp, M., and B. Streisand. "Tabloid TV's blood lust." *U.S. News & World Report*, 25 July 1994, pp. 46–8. Summarizes the view that tabloid news programs have influenced the mainstream press and "coarsened" American culture and distorted reality.

Toobin, J. "Cash for trash." *The New Yorker*, 11 July 1994, pp. 34–41. Legal analyst Toobin examines the impact that checkbook journalism has had on the American legal system and offers some interesting insights into its emergence.

Weiss, P. "Bad rap for TV tabs." *Columbia Journalism Review* (May/June 1989): 38–42. A fresh look at the tabloids that includes straightforward analyses and critiques of individual programs, and then offers a persuasive defense of the genre.

Chapter Twenty-one

Television News:
For Better or Worse

Lisa Mullikin

"One of the basic troubles with radio and television news," wrote Edward R. Murrow, "is that both instruments have grown up as an incompatible combination of show business, advertising, and news. Each of the three is a rather bizarre and demanding profession. And when you get all three under one roof, the dust never settles."

Although broadcast news has come a long way since its introduction in the late 1940s, it remains unable to shake its entertainment image. Walking this fine line between entertainment and serious news has been a great challenge for broadcast news. Americans love to hate television. They love the entertainment it provides and hate it for the same reason. Television news is trapped somewhere between *I Love Lucy* and the *New York Times*. Is television news serious journalism developed with the same integrity and dedication of its print cousins? Or does its heart lie in entertainment and ratings, where sensationalism, action, and drama determine what makes it onto the screen?

Despite our animosity, almost all of us watch it. Most Americans claim they get their news from television. We were watching when Neil Armstrong set foot on the moon, when President John F. Kennedy was shot, when the space shuttle Challenger exploded, when the Berlin Wall was torn down, when the Persian Gulf War broke out, and when O.J. Simpson was acquitted for murder. When anything happens in the news across the world, most people reach for the remote. We want to know what's going on, and we want to know right now. So, is network television news the good guy or the bad guy?

Origins of the Issue

Television owes its birth to radio. Radio, the wireless wonder that fascinated the country by bringing the entertainment shows of *The Shadow*, the *Grand Ole Opry*, and *Lux Radio Theatre*, as well as news reports from home and abroad, right into America's living rooms, formed the foundation of what would soon overshadow its father medium: television.

RCA introduced the world to television at the 1939 World's Fair in New York. Standing before this early television, Chairman of RCA David Sarnoff said, "It is with a feeling of humbleness that I come to the moment of announcing the birth in this country of a new art so important in its implications that it is bound to affect all society. It is an art which shines like a torch of hope in a troubled world. It is a creative force which we must learn to utilize for the benefit of all mankind." With the onset of World War II, the government forced RCA to halt further developments and investments in this new technology. But when the boys came home, the technology and dream of television were picked up again.

CBS and NBC, building on the strong economic foundations of the radio industry, became the two major players in television. ABC later became a distant competitor, focusing its initial energies almost solely on entertainment, but as the years progressed ABC increasingly contributed new ideas, concepts, and visions. Although broadcast stations had to be licensed by the Federal Communications Commission (FCC), the networks had so far avoided this regulation. Networks believed that if they provided public services, the FCC would not require them to be licensed. The networks quickly realized that giving a news broadcast was a public service. This was advantageous for both the public and the networks. A fifteen-minute news broadcast was an economical and easy way to show compliance with the FCC rules.

Most of television's founding fathers began their careers in radio. Radio greats like Edward R. Murrow, who covered World War II from his post in London, were at first reluctant to have anything to do with this new technology. As the best known voice of radio and one of the most respected newsmen of the time, Murrow feared a close association with the new technology, especially one with such a strong background in entertainment. Finally convinced that television could have a positive and profound impact, he adapted his popular radio show *Hear It Now* to a television version called *See It Now*. In the first broadcast of *See It Now* he pledged to the audience that he and his fellow television news people would "learn to use it and not to abuse it." Television news was successfully launched, but the industry was only beginning to understand the power of the medium.

Early news broadcasters were called "readers," men hired for their voice and presentation skills and not for any journalistic background. As news departments grew in stature, "readers" were replaced with experienced newsmen. In 1948 CBS introduced *CBS Television News* with Douglas Edwards. It was quickly followed the next year by NBC with John Cameron Swayze's *Camel News Caravan.* Before long, CBS and NBC began building up their news departments with radio news reporters and print newsmen. In the early days, to be respected in television news, one had to be trained in print. By the middle of the 1950s, news "personalities" began to emerge with both a strong presentation style and a news background. The NBC news anchor team of Chet Huntley in New York and David Brinkley in Washington, D.C., resulted from a fortuitous internal disagreement over which of the two should be the sole anchor. It was settled by pairing the men — a compromise so successful that NBC beat CBS in ratings for years. Not until the golden years of Walter Cronkite did CBS overtake NBC in ratings. (Ratings, published every quarter, measure the number of people tuned in to each broadcast or entertainment show. Advertising rates are then based on these rankings.) Popularly know as Uncle Walter, Cronkite became such a trusted man by the American people that he became the personification of CBS News until his retirement.

Although network evening news continued to improve in ratings, it remained almost the step-child of the networks. Working in cramped quarters with cumbersome equipment, early television newsmen had to prove their worth to their own networks as well as the public. Given only fifteen minutes to present the world's news was proof enough of their status. In the 1950s, these short news broadcasts were positioned in the early evening time slots, where they remain today. Not until 1963 for CBS and NBC and 1967 for ABC would television news producers, anchors, and reporters finally break through the fifteen-minute time barrier and extend the evening news broadcast to half an hour.

Television news took a giant step toward receiving equal respect with newspapers during the 1952 presidential election. In June of that year, General Dwight Eisenhower planned to announce his bid for the presidency at an open rally in his hometown of Abilene, Kan. Mother Nature ruined the event with a cloudburst, and Eisenhower's announcement was postponed until his scheduled press conference the next day. As Eisenhower prepared for his announcement, print reporters and columnists protested television's advantage in getting news to people faster. They demanded television reporters be excluded. The Eisenhower staff bent to pressure and banned cameras from the room. Fed up, CBS and NBC told the candidate's staff that their cameras would be in the room and ready to go, and if the staff wanted them moved, they would have to do it themselves. Eisenhower decided to leave them there. Sig Mickelson, then head of CBS News, later wrote, "For the first time in its short life, television had insisted on equal rights with the printed press and won.... The new boy on the block had stood up to his peers and had signaled a demand for respect." Since then television has been an important player in covering politics and the government.

In the 1960s and 1970s the three networks continued to expand their news operations and increase their credibility in the eyes of the public. They also sharply increased the amount of news on television in various forms. CBS debuted its morning news show named *CBS Morning News* in 1963. NBC continued to run its morning show *Today*. ABC introduced *Good Morning America* in 1975. Documentaries, in particular *CBS Reports* and *NBC White Paper*, became popular. News magazines, talk shows, political focus group programs, special reports, scheduled debates, mini-documentaries, and other special public affairs programs were born during this period. Trustworthy news programs made the networks look good; but especially important, they began to make money.

When Walter Cronkite retired in the early 1980s, more had changed in network news than just a face. Satellite technology had made possible instant links to almost anywhere in the world for breaking news. Anytime and anywhere news happened, television could and would be there to instantly report to Americans. The same decade that saw Dan Rather replace Cronkite at CBS also saw Tom Brokaw replace John Chancellor at NBC, and Peter Jennings become the sole anchor (down from three) at ABC. The combination of satellite technology and expanded cable operations enabled Ted Turner to launch the Cable News Network (CNN). The cable network offered 24-hour television news and was the channel most Americans turned to for coverage of the Persian Gulf War. In recent years, local television stations have used the expanded network feeds and access to CNN to go beyond local news to cover national and international news. Running before network news, these local broadcasts now have the technology and ability to "scoop"the networks.

The Bad

The stepchild status of television news people to their older cousins in newspapers has eased some since television's birth, but not completely. In the 1960s those in television news still looked to the wire services and newspapers for the story. Barbara Matusow, in her book *The Evening Stars*, tells a story that sums this up best:

When Tom Pettit was covering Alabama governor George Wallace's attempt to block the integration of the University of Alabama, an NBC editor in New York telephoned Pettit and told him he could get much of the material that he needed from the Associated Press report. When Pettit replied that he did not have access to the AP, the editor told him to use the United Press International report instead. When Pettit explained that he didn't have UPI either, the exasperated editor declared, "Good Lord. Well, go out and get a copy of the *New York Times*. The story's on page twenty-three." Pettit then informed him that the *New York Times* was banned in Tuscaloosa. "After a pause," Matusow recounted, "the man in New York said, in disbelief, 'You don't have the AP? You don't have the UP? You don't have the *New York Times*? How in the hell do you know what's going on down there?'"

The biggest and oldest criticism of television news revolves around its credibility. The charge of sensationalism bangs an ever-growing dent into the credibility of broadcast news. Sensational stories of fires, accidents, and crime make much better television than stories on the economy, legislation, and health care. The economy is often boring and difficult to personify on television. Murder trials, on the other hand, make great television. For proof, look at the amount of national attention focused on the O.J. Simpson murder trial. What makes good television also produces better ratings, which increases profits. This makes network owners happy. Unfortunately, these stories are not always the most important news pieces of the day. Often they just serve to boost ratings. Using these stories caters to what the viewers want and not to what they need to know, one of the oldest tenets of good journalism.

Other blows to broadcast journalism's credibility, charges Av Westin in his book *Newswatch*, come from the practice of reenactment. Reenactment can occur in many forms, but essentially involves repeating an action for the camera. While networks scorn blatant reenactment, some borderline practices continue. For example, some networks use the reverse question tactic in interviews. This involves reshooting the interviewer asking the questions once the guest has left. The news person can now smoothly ask the questions and look more poised on camera. These shots are later edited into the interview. A second and related technique, called the phony reaction shot, involves reshooting an interviewer's response to a guest's answer after the interview is over.

Critics also accuse networks of distorting reality through the shots and locations of stories chosen. Since the networks are based in either New York or Washington, D.C., a disproportionate number of stories are done from that vantage point. For example, some argue that a piece on gang violence will likely focus on the problems in one of these two cities and not stretch out to include "Hometown, USA." Similarly, a piece on the increasing use of crack cocaine would probably again center on New York and D.C., not the neighborhood town of "Central City." The problems that network executives and news people living in New York or Washington, D.C., run into every day become the problems of the nation. In other words, what is happening in New York and Washington is represented in the news as what is going on across the nation, and that's not necessarily so.

The shots the camera first picks up, which are later flashed across the screen, often distort the real situation. When covering a story, camera operators try to capture the moments of action in each story. If the president delivers a speech to Mothers Against Drunk Drivers, and he once raises his fist to show his anger at drunken drivers, that is the shot that will probably appear on the evening's news. This one outstanding gesture will upstage him outlining his plan to stop the problem or reading off a list of names of young people killed on the road that year. Once this material hits the editing room, the distortion becomes more pronounced. Film editors intensify the action by cutting out "dead," or inactive, scenes. In the typical murder story, the camera operator generally arrives on the scene while the police are still questioning witnesses and looking for evidence. Hours go by while everyone waits for the police to wrap it up and clear the scene. When the video is taken back to the network, this "boring"material is cut away and all that remains is a shot of the body being carried away and the suspect being stuffed in a police car. After the camera operator and the film editors complete their jobs, the finished product little resembles the complete story that unfolded before the reporter's eyes.

What makes it on the news isn't always really news, explains Horace Newcomb in *Television: The Critical View*. Pseudo events like signing legislation, arrivals, departures, and walks about town are staged for the television camera. These non-news events offer a way to inject some excitement and visual drama into what is really happening. Instead of a long explanation of how the new crime bill will affect the public, viewers get a great shot of the president signing the bill with a pen from a police officer killed in the line of duty. Crammed around the president is every politician trying to form a connection to the bill, along with the widows and children of other officers recently killed. A touching picture full of patriotism and hope, but what does that really tell us? Not much.

No longer are we in the golden days of broadcast journalism when CBS President William S. Paley and his counterpart at NBC, David Sarnoff, allowed the profits from entertainment programming to help carry the news departments. The 1980s in particular saw an increase in new network owners demanding cost-cutting measures designed to please stockholders but not necessarily news viewers. "Streamlining" became the buzz word. What resulted, charges Edwin Diamond in *The Media Show* and other critics, was an attack on expenses and staff cutbacks that crippled the news departments and limited news coverage. More videotaped packages were added to save networks the cost of sending film crews and correspondents. Straight pool footage transmitted directly to New York and voiced-over by the anchor was a cheaper substitute. In the end, many critics claim, cost saving results in news cutting.

In fact, the audience gets only 22½ minutes of network news per program. That's it. It's impossible to cram the news of the world into that short a time, according to many in the business, including former president of CBS News Fred W. Friendly. What we get instead is headline news. Short blurbs of the top stories with video footage to back them up. News stories average only two to three minutes. One often repeated statistic says that the nightly newscast set in type would cover less than the front page of the *New York Times*. For crisis reporting or historic events short, up-to-the-minute news works well, but for more complex issues like civil rights, the economy, health care, or welfare we are left with only part of the story, and even that is sometimes confusing. As Friendly put it, "what we don't know could kill us."

Not only do we get just headlines, but the ever lamented sound bites are growing even shorter. According to research, the average sound bite is now limited to only two or three sentences. These little blips don't contribute much to defining an issue. This is particularly a problem when covering an election. Short sound bites rob the candidates of enough time to define themselves and their platforms. The networks have generally agreed not to shorten candidates' sound bites further, but they still remain too short to completely express ideas.

These abbreviated stories and short sound bites also cause a problem for viewers trying to absorb the news. Unlike reading a newspaper, when television material becomes confusing, the viewer cannot go back and re-read the story. What he or she missed is missed. And the short pieces are confusing. Walter Cronkite recognized this in a speech he gave at the RTNDA Conference in 1976. He believes there is "...inadvertent and perhaps inevitable distortion that results through the hypercompression we all are forced to exert to fit one hundred pounds of news into the one-pound sack that we are given to fill each night."

The length of news pieces isn't the only thing making them confusing. The way television news is presented, viewers often pay more attention to the anchors, reporters, computer graphics, and video tricks than to the news itself, explain critics. The presentation distances the viewers from the news. Instead of concentrating on the words coming out of the reporter's mouth, we are noticing the color of her suit, the design of his tie, the graphics dancing across the screen, and the colorful banners stretched along the bottom. The "news" gets lost somewhere in the presentation.

When Dan Rather took over the anchor position for CBS, he took over more than a chair. His contract awarded him the title of managing editor. Whereas in the past the producer had the final say in what made it onto the news, now Rather has an equal if not stronger voice. If he says he won't do it, it won't be done. Some argue (in particular Barbara Matusow in her book *The Evening Stars*) that this "star" power that now Brokaw and Jennings have as well, coupled with seven-digit salaries, gives anchors more power and control than is good for the broadcast or the country. In other words, for each broadcast, one white, wealthy, middle-aged celebrity now decides what is "news."

The advent of satellite technology and instant footage from almost anywhere on earth opened up a new set of problems. As the "live" story becomes even more popular, reporters are more and more often thrust in front of the camera with the action behind them to bring the viewers the exciting drama unfolding before their eyes. But the problem is just that. The news is unfolding before them, and by reporting live we get coverage of only a select point in time and space. No longer do the viewers get the benefit of the traditional filters of the story being shaped and edited to include background, analysis, predictions, and consequences that help explain the story, explains critics Westin and Diamond. "Live" coverage may be exciting, but it doesn't always tell us very much.

The combination of terrorism and television coverage is problematic at best. No one is really sure what role television should play in covering an act of terrorism or a hostage situation. Most people agree that initial reports of hijackings, hostage situations, and other acts of terrorism are well done and sound journalism. It's the continuous coverage that presents the problem, claims Diamond in *The Media Show*. Hour after hour and even night after night television brings us the latest footage of terrified husbands and wives pleading to the camera or microphone for agreement to terrorists' demands and emotional fathers, mothers, and children at home expressing their fear and desire for a quick resolution. This heart-wrenching drama plays right into the hand of the terrorists. What better way to get a message across to the United States than to have it sent directly into every home across the country through television? Many argue that this extensive coverage just encourages terrorists to repeat the acts. Once faces are put on the story and the issue becomes more personal, government military action is no longer an option. During the 1985 hostage crisis of TWA Flight 847, CBS White House correspondent Lesley Stahl explained on *CBS Morning News*: "We [the television networks] are an instrument for the hostages.... We force the administration to put their lives above policy."

The Good

Many of the major criticisms of the network evening news are the same elements that form the basis for its benefits. Television provides news to the masses in an enjoyable and even entertaining way. When breaking news occurs, we all turn to television news. A story repeated in Robert J. Donovan and Ray Scherer's book *Unsilent Revolution* symbolizes the importance of television news to most Americans and even the newspapers:

As the late-edition deadline approached, Eugene Patterson, then managing editor of the *Washington Post*, sat with his staff watching the television screen for any last-minute developments in the Apollo Space Mission. A young employee entered the office, looked around, and said, "I always wondered how a great American newspaper covered a space mission." "Well, you know," Patterson observed long afterward, "that is how we kept up with the story."

Newspapers, the medium television reporters turned to in the 1960s for the story, now also rely on television to keep abreast of breaking news. When it comes to breaking news, television has a virtual monopoly.

Television is a universal medium. Almost everyone, even the nation's poor, has access to a television and the three networks. You don't need to be literate to get your news from television, explains Gene F. Jankowski and David C. Fuchs in *Television Today and Tomorrow*. People who never finished high school can generally watch and understand most television news. The combination of narration and video makes the news story relatively easy to understand. More importantly, most people enjoy watching television, probably because it is easy. Watching the network evening news is a relaxing way to push your own problems out of your mind and become wrapped up in the larger problems of the nation and world, claims Mark R. Levy in his research article "The Audience Experience with Television News" in *Journalism Monographs*. If you enjoy something, you will continue to use it. By increasing your use of television, you will increase the amount of news information to which you are exposed. More knowledge creates the desired "informed citizen" in a democracy. Since research shows people don't really rely on only one source for information (conversations with friends, listening to the radio in the car, chatting around the coffee pot at work, etc., all contribute to our overall store of information), any knowledge gleaned from television just adds more value to us as voting citizens.

Many people even make television news part of their daily routine for the information, entertainment, and reassurance it offers each day, according to Levy's research. Watching the news allows viewers to become a distant participant in ongoing history. Through the filter of a respected and trusted anchor, viewers are able to keep up with national and world events. Most serious news junkies prefer one network evening news program over the others and organize their schedule around that broadcast. Why people select one broadcast over another varies from person to person, but all seem to select a network evening news broadcast based on its ability to help them find out what they want to know and then present it in an understandable, concise, and entertaining way.

The way television presents the news often makes it easier for some of us to absorb the details (if we are active and not passive in our viewing). Television presents news pieces as a story. Each story includes a beginning, middle, and end and is narrated by the anchor with a supporting group of correspondents fleshing out the details. The anchor ties together the individual news pieces to create one 22 1/2-minute long synopsis of the story of the world on that particular day. Ongoing news events like elections, crises, and legislation in Congress become a continuing part of the overall story. As the election story progresses, for example, we are given a small amount of background information each day to find our place in the saga and then an update to keep the story line moving. Stories are familiar to us. We communicate with each other in story form, not the inverted pyramid of newspapers. Presenting the news in story form makes it easier to relate to and, subsequently, understand. By the end of this long woven story of the world's news we believe we understand what is happening and maybe even where we are heading. Walter Cronkite even closed each *CBS News* broadcast with the words "And that's the way it is...."

The old adage "a picture's worth a thousand words" has often been applied to television. While the words of the correspondent or anchor may not add up to the amount of copy in a newspaper story, the accompanying video may tell the story just as well or even better. Watching video footage, the viewer gets a sense of "being there." Television covers certain news stories better than print, according to many critics, in particular Robert J. Donovan and Ray Scherer in *Unsilent Revolution*. Emotional stories — riots, protests, homecomings, celebrations — make great television. The printed word was no competition for watching the East Germans spill over the Berlin Wall to freedom. That scene held so much conflicting emotion, words could not describe it. Television took the audience to the scene and showed what was happening.

Having the news stories strung together into a 22 1/2-minute package forces the audience to watch all the news pieces, explains Edwin Diamond in *The Tin Kazoo*. Unlike newspapers, where readers can skip over articles or entire sections that do not interest them, the television format pulls the viewer through every news item. Viewers learn information that they probably need to know, even though they did not actively seek out the material.

Friendly and most other critics agree that crisis situations provide television's finest hour. Television has the unique ability to make a continuous story easier to understand by simplifying the complex details around a few easily understood pictorial symbols. People turn to television during a crisis not only to keep abreast of the latest developments, but also for more psychological reasons. Over the years viewers have grown to know and trust the network anchors. In times of crisis they turn to these men, as former president of ABC news Av Westin wrote in his book *Newswatch*, to find out if the world is safe and if they are safe. They want to know the latest to judge their own security. Newspapers just can't keep up. By the time the delivery boy drops off the paper in the morning, most people consider the printed word old news in a crisis.

Breaking news is another area in which television shines, even in the face of some criticism. The news break and longer breaking-news special give television news the opportunity to do what it does best — provide instant coverage at any time on any day from anywhere. When breaking news occurs, people tune in to see their favorite anchor present the latest video and information as it is received. Westin and other critics argue that breaking news coverage opens the door to too many mistakes. Breaking news goes on the air almost the instant it is received, and this increases the odds for mistakes. Instead, critics say, news updates should be delayed from broadcast until a more rigorous editing and clarification process can occur. But, Westin recognizes, the American public has come to expect, even demand, instant news coverage. Even newspapers, with their longer editing process, make serious mistakes. One example was the printed announcement that former President Ford would become Ronald Reagan's vice-presidential running mate in 1980. No matter how much time is allowed to check facts, mistakes can and will still be made. Americans have learned to expect a fair share of mistakes in return for fast news. Breaking news is one of the best services television provides — giving the country the news almost instantaneously.

Television news also receives high marks for covering special events. Inaugurations, funerals, political conventions, election days, and the like are all staged for television — and television makes the most of the opoportunities, according to Westin. Long before the event, network production staff and researchers accumulate and coordinate piles of background information, old footage, interesting tidbits, experts willing to be interviewed, analysts ready to explain the consequences, and correspondents prepared to arrive on the scene. The day of the big event, the networks are so organized they are able to smoothly cover the story from beginning to end and even include extra information that makes the event more than just a giant photo opportunity for the people involved.

One little known or recognized service that network television news provides is protection of the president. Through the system known as a "pool," the three networks take turns covering the president every time he sets foot outside the White House, explains Judy Woodruff in *This is Judy Woodruff at the White House*. (Pool coverage can also pertain to anytime television news teams agree to have one camera crew cover the event and the other parties pay for the footage.) When the president leaves the security of that building, a camera crew and a news correspondent travel along with him. This not only gives the networks footage if anything newsworthy should happen, but it also provides video should any attack or other tragedy occur. For example, when Ronald Reagan was shot outside the Hilton Hotel in Washington, D.C., the CBS news team captured the would-be assassin on video. Not only were CBS White House correspondent Judy Woodruff and her camera crew on the scene and able to broadcast the story almost immediately, but they were also able to supply the authorities with video of John Hinkley.

Television journalists play an important role during hostage situations in saving lives. During the TWA Flight 847 hostage crisis mentioned above, the networks kept the situation in the forefront through continuous coverage. This coverage probably saved the lives of the other hostages. During the Iranian hostage situation, Walter Cronkite counted the number of days the Americans had been held hostage at the end of each nightly news broadcast. This constant reminder that these men were American sons, fathers, and husbands precluded, however, any agreement that would sacrifice them in the name of policy.

Resolution

Has network television news become the creative force utilized for the benefit of all mankind that David Sarnoff envisioned in 1939? Or has it become a ratings-driven headline service that entertains more than it informs? The true situation is probably, not surprisingly, somewhere in the middle.

Network television news has worked hard since its birth to overcome the shadow of the entertainment industry. Former senior vice-president of CBS News Gording Manning even tried to use terminology to further distance the news department from the entertainment side of CBS. He refused to allow anyone to call the news a "show" or a "program." Shows, Manning explained, were what people like Ed Sullivan produce. CBS News produces "broadcasts." For the most part, network news departments today produce "broadcasts" and not "shows." Certainly, each network can recall more than one time it leaned a little too close to the entertainment side. But what other news gathering medium can't say the same?

All of the above criticisms of network television news are true, however. Though each problem may vary from night to night and station to station, broadcast news as a whole does have some severe limitations. Yes, television news distorts reality. Yes, television news often selects stories based on what will look good on television. Yes, television news only gives part of the story and often goes by too fast. Yes, television news still has problems with credibility.

The first order of business for network television news needs to be putting a stop to sensationalism in news coverage. Recent research shows that sensationalism in local news has increased dramatically. Critics now charge that the networks are mirroring this trend. Tearjerkers, explosions, sexual sagas, gruesome murder cases, and other dramatic news stories all make their way onto the three network newscasts. The tabloids or "trash tv" thrive on this sensational news, and their success may be the cause of growing sensationalism in network news. The gates need to be closed to stem the tide of lurid and stimulating material flowing from tabloid television into network news. This increase in sensationalism certainly moves television news closer to the very industry it tries to avoid, the entertainment industry.

Networks no longer have the advantage of being the only provider of national and international news. Today a combination of local stations' access to feeds, electronic news gathering (ENG), satellite news gathering (SNG), and other technology allows broadcast stations to be as current as the networks. Network affiliates now cover national and even international stories on their local broadcasts. The ever expanding CNN also satisfies many Americans' needs for news. Viewers no longer have to wait for the network evening broadcasts to get national and international news; they can catch up on the latest — twenty-four hours a day.

No one now knows what the future will hold for the three networks. The viewing audience becomes more fragmented every year. The time is long gone when the nation could sit down together to watch the evening news on the three networks. Most people in the industry believe the time is approaching when consumers will be able to dial up entertainment programs, movies, or news whenever they want. Each year brings new cable stations and further subdivides the viewing audience based on personal interests. With the addition of every new form of technology in mass media, ABC, CBS, and NBC will have to redefine their niche.

Network evening news now maintains an undefined role sandwiched between local news broadcasts and in constant competition with CNN. Many believe this is the end of network evening news. More realistically, the networks need to reexamine their mission. Just as newspapers redefined themselves after the advent of television, television must recreate its role. There are several ways this can be accomplished.

First, the networks should continue to feed the local stations with national and international news. Local stations, in general, do not have the expertise or manpower to independently cover all national and international news. For this, networks provide a valuable service. Local stations, on the other hand, have what networks do not — time. Some local stations run newscasts both before and after the network news and another broadcast later in the evening. Not enough local news exists to fill this time, but add in national and international news and newscasts can go beyond mere headlines.

Second, networks should adopt a more in-depth and analytical look at the news. PBS has produced its own in-depth round-table discussion of current events for years. The networks should produce their own expanded version. Instead of providing headlines of what's happening, correspondents should delve into the reasons behind what's happening. Experts across the country and around the world could be interviewed. News analysts could answer questions such as what does this mean to the United States? Where are we going? What does this mean to me? In the age of information-overload what the public needs is explanation and analysis. The networks have already begun moving in this direction. NBC, for example, features a report called "NBC In-depth, Information Beyond the Day's Headlines." The report covers one topic or issue by offering analysis by an expert, different angles of the story, and often explanations of "what this means." The anchor ties together the whole package. With this more in-depth coverage the news breaks out of the constraints of black and white, good and evil and goes deeper into the real issues and meanings.

Third, if more breaking news is left to the local stations, networks should concentrate on (but cover more completely) a smaller number of stories. One five-minute news piece would replace five one-minute pieces. The "headline news" days would be over. Viewers wouldn't be left with just a taste of each story; they would be left with an understanding. Longer pieces on the more complicated issues would certainly benefit viewers trying to keep up in the information age. If networks hand over the shorter, more routine news pieces to the affiliates, CBS, NBC, and ABC will be free to do a more thorough examination of confusing news events.

In some capacity, networks will always do what they do best — cover breaking news, crises, and pre-planned events. The public still trusts network anchors and relies on them in times of crisis. People will still turn to them for coverage of inaugurations, election days, and other big media events. After all, what would Super Tuesday be without Tom, Dan, and Peter to carry voters through the night and predict the results?

Overall, television news is here to stay, problems and all. It is America's common denominator. It's a universal medium with the ability to grab viewers and involve them in a story. It is impossible to say what form television news will take twenty years from now, but it should still be here, and the networks will play an important part.

Recommended Readings

Books

Diamond, Edwin. *The Media Show: The Changing Face of the News, 1985-1990*. Cambridge: MIT Press, 1991. A good history of television news, discussion of its problems, and analysis of its future.

Donovan, Robert J., and Ray Scherer. *Unsilent Revolution*. Cambridge: Cambridge University Press, 1992. An analysis of both the advantages and disadvantages of television news done by examining multiple news events covered by television.

Jankowski, Gene F., and David C. Fuchs. *Television Today and Tomorrow*. New York and Oxford: Oxford University Press, 1995. Both CBS executives, Jankowski and Fuchs cover the history of television, how programs are created, the role of advertisers, the impact of government regulations, the problem with television news, and the future.

Lowe, Carl, ed. *Television and American Culture*. New York: H. W. Wilson Co., 1981. Argues that what television shows is not necessarily reality.

Matusow, Barbara. *The Evening Stars*. Boston: Houghton Mifflin, 1983. Look at the rise of the anchor "star" and its impact on the news and the industry.

Newcomb, Horace. *Television: The Critical View*. New York, Oxford: Oxford University Press, 1979. Discusses the way television news distorts reality and why people watch the news.

Nimmo, Dan, and James E. Combs. *Nightly Horrors: Crisis Coverage by Television Network News*. Knoxville, Tenn.: University of Tennessee Press, 1985. A strong analysis of television's coverage of crisis situations with an in-depth look at the networks' coverage of the People's Temple, Three Mile Island, Flight 191, Mount St. Helens, and the Iran hostages.

Westin, Av. *Newswatch*. New York: Simon and Schuster, 1982. An insider at both CBS and ABC, Westin covers the evolution of broadcasting, the anchors and commentators, immediacy and accuracy in crisis coverage, documentaries, magazines, and local news.

Woodruff, Judy, with Kathleen Maxa. *More Vast Than Wasteland: The Influence of Television*. Reading, Mass.: Addison-Wesley, 1982. Lists common criticisms of network news and defends them one by one. See particularly pp. 203-21.

Articles & Book Chapters

Cronkite, Walter. "Remarks by Walter Cronkite at the RTNDA Conference, Miami Beach, Florida." Pp. 191-8 in Marvin Barrett, ed., *Rich News, Poor News*. New York: Thomas Y. Crowell, 1978. Cronkite pushes news people to make stories longer, expand the time of the broadcast to an hour, keep quotations in context, and use longer soundbites.

Bliss, Edward, Jr. "The Meaning of Murrow." *Feedback* 24 (Winter 1983): 3-6. Discusses the vast contributions of Murrow to the standards of broadcasting.

Friendly, Fred W. "The Nightly News: A Leap of Faith Versus the Bottom Line." Pp. 69-96 in Michael P. Beaubien and John S. Wyeth, Jr., eds., *Opinion*. New York: New York University Press, 1994. Argues that television news should be longer, explains the relationship between networks and affiliated stations, and discusses what television news is good and what is not.

Gunter, Barrie. "The Growth of Television News." Pp. 1-18 in *Poor Reception: Misunderstanding and Forgetting Broadcast News*. Hillsdale, N.J.: Erlbaum, 1987. Covers a history of television news, who is watching television news, why they are watching, and what media are best for doing what stories.

Levy, Mark R. "The Audience Experience with Television News." *Journalism Monographs* 55 (April 1978). Looks at the different reasons people watch televison news.

Zurawik, David, and Christina Stoehr. "Money Changes Everything." *American Journalism Review* 15 (April 1993): 26-30. Discussion of the influence that financial pressures have on the quality of television news.

Chapter Twenty-two

Checkbook Journalism

Lorna Veraldi

In the summer of 1994, on the opening day of the preliminary hearing to determine whether O.J. Simpson should be tried for the murder of his former wife, Nicole Brown Simpson, and her friend Ronald Goldman, witnesses from Ross Cutlery in downtown Los Angeles testified that earlier that spring Simpson had bought a fifteen-inch stiletto at the store. Before Simpson left the store, these witnesses testified, he had asked that the knife be sharpened. Potentially important testimony. No murder weapon had been found; and, according to these witnesses, Simpson had paid cash for the stiletto and had taken the only paper receipt documenting the purchase.

But the store employee who testified that he had sold a knife to Simpson also testified that, prior to the hearing, he had sold the story to the *National Enquirer*. Would jurors believe such a witness if he were called to testify at trial? Or would they harbor reasonable doubts about whether the witness had really sold Simpson a knife or had embellished a story to sell to the *Enquirer*?

Like layers of an onion, media coverage of the Simpson arrest and murder trial peeled back to reveal many of the dilemmas that confound journalists and news organizations. One of these is "checkbook journalism." Should the press ever pay for news?

As the Simpson coverage gathered momentum, Henry Weinstein reported for the *Los Angeles Times* Service, "The dramatic nature of the O. J. Simpson case has intersected with the growth of tabloid media to produce a landmark moment in checkbook journalism." The editor of the *National Enquirer* predicted that more money would be spent on exclusive interviews with the key players in the Simpson story "than ever before in the history of the press."

Origins of the Issue

Prior to the Simpson murder trial, the issue of checkbook journalism had periodically ignited debate — most notably over coverage of the Watergate scandal twenty years earlier. Much had changed in the news business, however, in the years between Watergate and the Simpson trial. Tabloids, both print and broadcast, had multiplied. Although it was not clear just how often the tabloids pulled out the checkbook, there was no question that many newsmakers and "trained seal" experts were being paid for their interviews. According to Richard Zoglin in his 1993 article, "Easing the Sleaze," even before the Simpson trial, the television tabloids had "changed TV news."

But it was *CBS News*, not *Hard Copy*, that first triggered national debate over checkbook journalism when in 1975 it paid key Watergate conspirator H. R. Haldeman $100,000 for an interview. The network claimed it was paying for "memoirs," not "news." But to many critics, that sounded like rationalization.

Gary Paul Gates, in *Air Time*, referred to the Haldeman interview as "an embarrassing fiasco." Not only did CBS open itself to criticism for paying, but Haldeman, who had worked in advertising, "knew exactly how to play the interviews to his own advantage." The result, opined Gates, was that "the biggest news to come out of the Haldeman interviews was CBS's folly. The network had shelled out all that money for a huge load of nothing, and in addition to all the sanctimonious scolding, there now was the sound of mocking laughter in the air." Norman E. Isaacs, in *Untended Gates*, noted that the National News Council, in response to CBS's payment to Haldeman, suggested calling for disclosure of any payment beyond actual expenses "so the public could draw its own conclusions."

CBS had not been the first to pay. A decade earlier, *Life* magazine had bought stories from the NASA astronauts. And half a century before that, one of the surviving *Titanic* crew members reportedly received $1,000 (no small amount in 1912) to tell his story to the press. Indeed, as S. Elizabeth Bird noted in *For Enquiring Minds*, once the penny press in the 1830s began to use interviews in crime reporting rather than court documents, the stage was set for modern checkbook journalism. Bird reported that supermarket tabloids spend thousands of dollars every year for information from a network of contacts — from hairdressers to lawyers — paying anywhere from $50 to the "high five figures."

Checkbook journalism played a part in a number of high-profile crime stories during the 1980s and 1990s. Payments were made for interviews concerning the story of Amy Fisher and Joey Buttafuoco, the William Kennedy Smith rape trial, and accusations of child molestation against singer Michael Jackson, to name only a few.

As Louis Day noted in *Ethics in Media Communications,* for the establishment press "the commercial link to newsworthy subjects is sometimes more subtle than direct cash payments." For example, after an airline hijacking in 1985, some families of hostages were flown to Europe by TV news crews who hoped to gain exclusive coverage when the hostages were released. Some American reporters working in foreign countries pay bribes to officials or corporate executives for information, a practice they defend as accommodating cultural norms "to increase the flow of information to their American audience." Some have suggested that network payments to "so-called consultants" or "deals between entertainment units and news sources that spill over to interviews for the news division" are in truth little different from the tabloids' cash payments. But according to *Broadcasting & Cable* reporter Steve McClellan, the television tabloids' straightforward admission that they pay cash for stories has brought the issue "into the realm of respectable debate."

Marilyn Matelski noted in *TV News Ethics* that the 1980s explosion in camcorder sales added the dimension of purchases of amateur video by professional news organizations. Most payments to amateurs started small — $25 to $100 — but they came at a time when the availability of video increasingly determined what television stations called news. As D. M. Lindekugel noted in *Shooters,* "With reporters more likely to reserve judgment until they see the pictures, the pictures take on an increased importance to the story, and, consequently, so does the photographer." By 1991, an organization called the Amateur Video News Network had been formed to serve as a clearinghouse and broker for amateur photographers.

Checkbook journalism has given rise to several legal disputes. For example, responding to outrage over media payments to potential witnesses in the Simpson trial, California in 1994 enacted a law that would have prohibited future witnesses from accepting money for such disclosures before a judgment had been rendered. However, a federal court soon found the California law unconstitutional. In another case, the amateur photographer who sold videotape of police beating Rodney King to a Los Angeles station sued unsuccessfully over rebroadcasts of the tape. And after the mass suicide of members of the religious cult Heaven's Gate in 1997, NBC News bid $45,000 for the cult's farewell video, which for unexplained reasons had come into the possession of a Michigan minister. NBC said it would sue after the minister reneged on his promise and sold the tape instead to ABC for $50,000. For the most part, however, checkbook journalism has remained an ethical issue, rather than a legal one.

Is Checkbook Journalism Wrong?

In the wake of growing controversy over checkbook journalism, the Code of Ethics of the Society of Professional Journalists has been amended to warn journalists to "be wary of sources offering news for favors or money" and to "avoid bidding for news." Long before it was directly addressed in the code, checkbook journalism was denounced by many journalists. As the Simpson story unfolded, former *Washington Post* editor and journalism educator Ben Bagdikian was quick to condemn such payments. "If the practice of paying for interviews became widespread," he told correspondent Henry Weinstein, "the whole process of reporting would be distorted." Reporter Theo Wilson told Weinstein she was "disgusted" by the practice. In 1994, when former *Today* host Deborah Norville took a job with tabloid *Inside Edition,* she was reportedly "not terribly comfortable" with the program's practice of paying for interviews. That same year, a Miami television reporter surprised "the people in the control booth" by announcing in a live report that she had paid five dollars apiece for interviews with prostitutes while covering a story on a serial murderer who was targeting prostitutes. Her colleagues were reportedly "aghast," and her station quickly pointed out that it had a policy against paying for news. Earlier that same year, it should be noted, the same station had declined to comment on whether it had paid to broadcast a videotape supplied by the lawyer of a former Miami commissioner turned fugitive from justice in a sex and drug investigation.

John M. Kittross, in "Checkbook Journalism: The Final Marketplace," wrote that "treating news as a commodity eventually will destroy journalism as a public benefit" by eroding both the media's credibility and their access to information. Kittross admitted that journalists may traditionally have traded a cup of coffee, lunch, or even a few dollars to "those who need it or need to feel that the reporter is a fellow human being." However, he argued, such small amounts "would never be thought of as conveying exclusive rights to the part of the story that the source is telling the reporter between refills." However, when thousands or hundreds of thousands of dollars are changing hands, "the bean counters in media management insist on written contracts and exclusivity — the ability to prevent other media organizations and consequently, the public, from using the story." Kittross expressed particular concerns when those selling exclusive rights to their stories are government employees, like those astronauts who "made particularly advantageous deals with *Life* magazine."

H. Eugene Goodwin discussed checkbook journalism under "dubious methods" in his book, *Groping for Ethics in Journalism.* he wrote that only a "very small minority of journalists have even a slightly kind word to say for checkbook journalism." Jeffrey Toobin echoed the same sentiment in a 1994 *Quill* article, "Buying headlines," in which he dismissed checkbook journalism as "cash-for-trash." He pointed to case after case in which potential prosecution witnesses had damaged their credibility by selling their stories to tabloids in deals brokered by what he called "the cash-for-trash bar." In the same special ethics issue of *Quill*, Emerson Stone argued that media covering the Simpson case relied too much on "speculation by armies of paid consultants" — at the expense of the traditional standard: "Report. Report. Report." Louis A. Day, in *Ethics in Media Communications*, stated flatly that checkbook journalism is "not a standard practice among American news organizations."

According to attorney Robert L. Shapiro, a member of the Simpson defense team, paying for information destroys a news organization's credibility. In "Secrets of a Celebrity Lawyer," he distinguished between "legitimate members of the press" and tabloid reporters. He admitted that sensational headlines in the tabloids "can have a severe impact on a high-profile criminal defendant." But he has countered damaging tabloid stories by simply pointing out "that most [tabloid] stories are bought and paid for."

Perhaps ironically, while Shapiro shuns the tabloids, he goes out of his way to notify the "legitimate working press" in advance about what to expect in court "so they can adjust their schedules and avoid going to court when nothing will take place." He noted that "such consideration helps to develop a relationship of trust which will be greatly appreciated." For all their seeming disapproval of checkbook journalism, high profile defense lawyers have accepted substantial sums for their comments on the Simpson murder trial and others. Lawyer Roy Black, who as William Kennedy Smith's defense attorney discredited a prosecution witness because she had taken money for an interview with a television tabloid, was reported by the *Miami Herald* to have earned $250 an hour for "consulting" on the Simpson trial on NBC, though neither he nor NBC would confirm the amount. Black was quoted by *Miami New Times* reporter Steven Almond as saying he had been courted by all three networks before signing with NBC, which "offered the best contract."

Paying People To Do the Right Thing

Richard Zoglin admitted that when crime stories break, for all their "dicey" tactics, the tabloids "get the scoops" and "are doing a lot of old-fashioned, roll-up-your sleeves journalism." But he expressed concern that as bidding for major interviews has escalated, the press is finding it hard to get anyone to say anything except for a fee.

Paul Martin Lester, in his book *Visual Communication,* expressed concern over the motives of the amateur photographer who sold the tape of police beating Rodney King to a Los Angeles television station and set off a chain of events that would become a major international story. Lester acknowledged that the sale of the tape led to redress of an incident of policy brutality. But he was skeptical of the statement by amateur photographer George Holliday that he sold the tape because he "just wanted someone to know about it." "To 'know about' the beating would cost some money," wrote Lester, decrying the "hedonism" reflected when "financial gain and not civic duty motivates individuals to donate tapes to news organizations and to tell their stories to the press."

After King was taken away by police, Holliday called the LAPD to report the beating. However, according to Lester, Holliday did not tell police he had made a tape of the incident. Instead, the next morning he sold the tape to a local television station for $500, which Lester wrote was "three times the normal freelance rate." Lester noted that Holliday believed he would get the tape back after the station had aired it. But the station had an agreement to supply newsworthy amateur videotape to CNN, and did so. After CNN aired the tape, both King and Holliday became celebrities. And both King and Holliday, Lester wrote, "tried to profit from the tragedy" by filing civil suits — King against the city of Los Angeles, Holliday against KTLA and all the major television networks and individual television stations that had shown the tape without his permission after KTLA fed it to CNN.

Holliday's lawsuit failed. A federal judge dismissed his claims, on the grounds that news organizations had a First Amendment right to air the newsworthy tape. Holliday did profit from the sale of rights to the tape to director Spike Lee for use in the movie *Malcolm X* and the commercial distribution of the beating video. And he earned a royalty from promoting a commercial videotape called "Shoot News and Make Money with Your Camcorder." A jury awarded King almost $4 million in damages, and King also sold the rights to his story to a movie company. Several of the officers involved in the beating were able to sell television interviews, and two of them published books.

Lester acknowledged that Holliday's video focused attention on an important issue, quoting the Reverend Jesse Jackson as saying "there are many other police beating victims without the benefit of a Holliday videotape." Lester admitted the contents were "unusual, dramatic, and important — a common definition of news for most journalists." However, he suggested that the ubiquitous amateur photographer, spurred on by cash from news organizations, may intrude too far into ordinary lives with little thought to the societal benefit to be served. Violent images taped and sold to the media for replay to casual viewers far removed from the event may not be representative of or responsive to deeper social issues. While televising such images could help spur reforms, Lester argued that it could also add to television's sensationalism. "[T]he broadcasting of violent home videos supplied by a growing number of eager, camcorder-holding neo-journalists distorts reality," he declared.

More important, Lester argued, paying for news encourages "looking out for number one ... one of the most dangerous social trends in the United States or any other country." Ordinary citizens should recognize a civic duty to disclose information about important events. Buying stories or tapes from individuals trains them to think only of their own gain, not of the benefits to their community. And the huge amounts both King and Holliday originally demanded in their lawsuits- — $56 million and $100 million, respectively — in Lester's view reflect a growing opportunistic streak fed by news organizations all too willing to pay for news.

Only Fair in an Information Age

Not everyone is troubled about creating cash incentives for amateur photographers or others who provide information to the media. Television anchor Ted Koppel has reportedly said that using home video in news is creating a revolution in that "television has begun falling into the hands of the people." Television's narrow vision has long been the subject of criticism. Edward Jay Epstein noted in his 1973 study of television news, *News from Nowhere,* that in the days before the camcorder, "organizational needs" largely determined what television news covered. When a limited number of network crews covered "conveniently located" events "wired for television," the result was what Epstein described as a "functional neglect of events with less advance warning." Giving amateur videographers a cash incentive to broaden television news coverage could make television "democratic in a way that it never has been in our history," Marilyn Matelski has argued. She quoted a broadcast journalist praising the advent of amateur video, "You never have enough eyes and ears out there." In addition to the Rodney King tape, for example, home video of alleged police brutality has resulted in other calls for reform. In 1994 a Compton, Calif., grandmother sold a Los Angeles station a video of her grandson being beaten by police, spurring protests that led to an investigation of alleged racial bias against Latinos by community officials.

"How to transform governance in an age of instantaneous and simultaneous information transfer to a population accustomed to having the press distill and process its information is a daunting task," concluded Anne Wells Branscomb in her 1994 book, *Who Owns Information?* She noted that legal scholars Arthur Miller and Alan Westin have proposed protecting privacy by granting greater property rights to personal information. Treating genuinely personal information (e.g., medical records) as private property and requiring payment or permission for its use would give the individual greater control over that use. Legal principles emerging from this idea, wrote Branscomb, include "publicity" ("the right to release information into the public domain at a time and place of one's own choosing"); "commerciality" ("the right to sell information for fair value"), and, perhaps most importantly when considering checkbook journalism, "reciprocity" ("the right to receive value in exchange for value given").

Jack Landau, former director of the Reporters Committee for Freedom of the Press, has found little justification for newspapers' paying for the memoirs of the famous and the syndicated columns of non-employees, but refusing to pay for eyewitness accounts of news events: "Checkbook journalism may be a bad practice economically, but I can't see the distinction between purchasing the kind of information publications do from one category of person but not another." Organizations that make a profit from selling information seem self-serving at best when they claim that paying for that information would be "unethical."

A. David Gordon, in a counterpoint to Kittross in "Checkbook Journalism: The Final Marketplace," pointed out that "news has always been an economic commodity, at least since the advent of moveable type." While paying for information may be a relatively new phenomenon, it isn't in Gordon's view "automatically any less ethical" than other means of gathering news. Instead, Gordon argued, the debate should focus on the difference between public and private information. No public official has the right to demand payment for public information. However, argued Gordon, there is nothing unethical about paying or accepting payment for private information, interviews, photographs, or video tapes. Journalists have often engaged in questionable or even illegal practices to get stories — for example, "palming a picture from the home of its owner." Instead of stealing in the name of the "public's right to know," the media would be more ethical if they respected the owner's right to compensation (and control). "In offering to pay for such pictures or videotapes, the media are at least giving the owners both an option to refuse to release them and an opportunity to be compensated if they agree to their use." Gordon further pointed out that sources who do not wish to sell information can always say no. And even if an "exclusive" interview is sold to one news organization, he noted, other journalists are free to cover the story as aggressively as their resources allow.

In fact, competition and coverage by the tabloids can spur mainstream media to better reporting. Louise Mengelkoch, in "When Checkbook Journalism

Does God's Work," tells what happened when a small town rape and murder, largely ignored by the mainstream press, caught the attention of the producer of a nationally syndicated talk show. The coverage until then had been shallow and one-sided. Once the tabloids got into the act, the other side had an opportunity to tell its story. Equally important, in exchange for sharing their personal story with a national audience, the rape victim's family earned $3,000, enough to hire a lawyer and ensure a fair trial for a father accused of murdering one of his daughter's alleged rapists. Mengelkoch wrote that "the impact on those lives from their willingness to 'sink' to the level of tabloid journalism has been nothing but positive." While admitting that checkbook journalism has potential for harm, Mengelkoch argued that "for the powerless in our culture who knowingly open themselves up to very personal stories that should be told — and that have a real message for the public — it seems only fair that they should be compensated for their willingness to go public. My only complaint is that [the family in question] didn't get more."

Maria Elizabeth Grabe's research supported the theory that the poor are less likely to have access to the establishment press than to the tabloids. Grabe found that traditional television news is more likely to portray criminals as members of the working class, and tabloids to portray criminals as members of the middle or upper classes. "The highly publicized condemnation of mass culture," including tabloids, suggested Grabe, "may actually be a device whereby social class divisions are publicly drawn."

Journalist Darcy Frey, in his book about basketball and inner city poverty, *The Last Shot*, grappled with the ethical issue of writing the intimate story of inner-city high school teenagers without sharing the profits from his book with his impoverished subjects and their families. Frey was prompted to consider the issue of information equity by an encounter with the father of one of the boys about whom he was writing, who in exchange for an interview said he expected compensation. Frey was at first taken aback: "all I could think to say at the time was that most journalists considered it unethical to pay people for information." Yet Frey began to have second thoughts. His subjects and their families had given up a substantial degree of privacy in allowing him to interview them and observe their private lives over many months. He had to admit that, over the time he had spent with his young subjects, he had already handed over money for a vending machine here, a meal at a fast-food joint there. He knew that these families' lives were hard and that they could use the money. Finally, he explored whether the NCAA's rules would allow him to share the book's proceeds with these high school players without jeopardizing their chances for college basketball scholarships. Any such deal, he was told, would mean the player would lose his eligibility to play college ball. Frey scrapped the idea of compensation. But his story raised questions about whether the tradition of never paying sources might be exploitation passing for ethics.

Everette Dennis, executive director of Columbia University's Freedom Forum Media Studies Center, has conceded that the traditional stigma against checkbook journalism may be hard to defend against arguments of equity and just compensation for value. "It's hard to argue that the ordinary person shouldn't share in the benefit of what's going to be a commercial product," Dennis was quoted by Zoglin. O. J. Simpson's friend Al Cowlings reportedly turned down a million-dollar offer for an interview with the tabloids, yet set up his own 900 number to communicate directly with the public for $2.99 a minute. "Everybody else has been making money off of me.... So why not?"

Some argue that payment for information went on in one form or another long before television tabloids arrived on the scene, and that the frank admission of television tabloids that they pay for interviews has simply brought the issue "out of the closet." Journalist Jerry Nachman told *Broadcasting* that the key issue is not whether payment is made, but whether it is disclosed. "If you pay for it, say so, so the viewer can draw whatever inferences are appropriate about the veracity of what the paid [source] is saying." Stephen Coz, editor of the *National Enquirer,* has been admirably frank, many would concede, about the publication's practices. "Let me state our policy," he explained candidly. "We pay for truthful information, we don't make any bones about that."

In contrast, it has been argued, the major networks have done television's credibility more harm by obfuscating than the tabloids have in admitting that they do pay. After *60 Minutes* killed a story on the tobacco industry when Brown & Williamson threatened to sue over a confidentiality agreement signed by the former employee on whose interview the story was based, CBS initially refused to comment on reports that it had paid the interviewee a "consultant's fee" and agreed to pay his legal fees if he were sued. According to commentary by Michael McMenamin in *Reason,* reporter Mike Wallace "was less than forthcoming" about the facts even with some of his colleagues at the network. As with the Haldeman interview twenty years earlier, the network found itself having to rationalize practices that didn't seem to comport with policies. It is hard to see how a payment for information, fully disclosed to viewers, would have been as damaging to credibility, especially in a case like this one, where the source apparently put himself at substantial risk to provide an interview.

Branscomb has suggested that we need to develop not only a new law of information, but a new ethics of information as well. "The difficulty with today's information society is that we have not had enough experience to agree upon acceptable behavior." The issue of whether (or when) news organizations ought to pay for information is only one reflection of an uncertainty over what the new rules ought to be.

In his 1995 essay "Cyberights," Max Frankel proposed a principle for the Information Age that seemed to sum up, albeit facetiously, the view that checkbook journalism, though unconventional, may be both ethical and equitable. Frankel was interrupted one evening during dinner by a telephone call from someone taking a survey. After ascertaining that the interviewer was being paid to ask the questions, Frankel asked how much he was to be paid for his answers. "I decided that information about me, like anything created by me, is valuable property. You want it for your business, let's deal." Paying for news, like any other cost of doing business, may be only fair in the Information Age.

Resolution

Whether money goes to a former policymaker turned "consultant" or to an amateur with a camcorder who happens upon history, common questions arise about whether to pay for news. Whenever the press pays for a story, it risks undermining both its credibility and its future access to information. On the other hand, every time the press profits from publicizing private lives, or ignores the rights or dignity of those whose stories it tells, it loses respect. In an age when the lines between tabloid journalism and traditional reporting are blurring, should mainstream media hold fast to policies that forbid checkbook journalism? Or do they invite ridicule by insisting that real reporters don't pay for news and then engaging in the hypocrisy of calling news "memoirs" or "consulting services" when they violate their policies to compete for information.

Sources who watch the press wiggle around its own policies learn to play the same game. A childhood buddy who never escaped the impoverished neighborhood where O. J. Simpson grew up quickly came up with his own bargaining strategy when hordes of reporters converged to find a new angle on the murder story. He accommodated journalists who "don't pay for news" by arranging interviews only for reporters who agreed to buy his old snapshots of O. J. Was it ethical for reporters to buy the snapshot they didn't use to gain access to the information they wanted? More important, did this private citizen have a duty to share his memories with reporters free of charge? The duty of the informant to speak, as well as the value of the information he provides, should both be factors in determining whether it is acceptable to pay for news.

News is a competitive business. Right or wrong, to some extent the press has trained sources to think of themselves as a salable commodity in that bazaar.

After all, if the press has paid a former president and his staff to tell us about how they conducted themselves in office, as it did in the case of Watergate, why should the man in the street who happens to witness history being made, or who captures history with his camcorder, have any greater duty to share that information?

Even if journalists could presume that checkbook journalism represents a passing lapse in standards, rather than a shift in how we define, gather, and distribute news, there are other, more compelling reasons to develop a framework within which journalists can make better, more honest decisions on whether to pay their sources.

Each of us has a stake in guarding against the cynicism of a citizenry too jaded to believe that government or the courts can work — or to believe very much of anything the press reports. Each of us has a stake in protecting rights to privacy and preserving the rights of the individual and the press to benefit from the value of their property — including information they may create, own, or distribute.

The press must recognize and weigh the conflicting issues raised in deciding whether to pay for news and to address them honestly — case by case. Is it proper for television to buy "memoirs" — even from former public officials? Probably. Book and magazine publishers have a long history of paying for memoirs. Royalties are a good way of giving history makers the incentive to record and preserve their stories. In a video age, it would be silly to frown on paying for the television equivalent of the autobiography. If a source expends substantial time or effort or shares information that the source has no duty to make public, the press has the right, and perhaps the obligation, to pay for that.

Is the answer different when a potential witness in a criminal case has a story to tell and a duty to testify? A blanket prohibition on checkbook journalism may not serve society's interests. But neither would a selfish refusal by the media to consider the impact a checkbook can have on individual rights or society's interests in justice and fairness.

Resolving the debate over checkbook journalism may revolve not so much around the issue of payment in and of itself as around questions of fairness and full disclosure, respect for privacy and property. With technology promising increasing competition in the news media, there is little reason to expect that the competition for information will ease, or that the pressure to pay for stories will let up. Nor will it be confined to the peripheries of journalism. In the Information Age, it may become increasingly acceptable to compensate owners of information for the value it represents. If journalists and the news organizations for whom they work expect to profit from gathering, writing, editing, producing, and distributing information, why should they object to paying for the information on which these enterprises depend? Just as it is acceptable to pay higher salaries to the best reporters or to buy the newest computer or satellite equipment, so it ought to be acceptable, where appropriate, to compensate for private information. A press that once decried "checkbook journalism" may do better to consider more complex questions of whom, when, and how much to pay.

Recommended Readings

Books

Bird, S. Elizabeth. *For Enquiring Minds: A Cultural Study of Supermarket Tabloids*. Knoxville: University of Tennessee Press, 1992. Looks at the tabloid, its cultural roots and its current practices, including checkbook journalism.

Epstein, Edward J. *News from Nowhere, Television and the News*. New York: Random House, 1973. Studies the organizational structures and processes that determine, and limit, what is "news." Before the advent of portable amateur video, news was largely limited to what could be gathered by a handful of network film crews, covering predictable events.

Frey, Darcy. *The Last Shot, City Streets, Basketball Dreams*. New York: Houghton Mifflin, 1994. Frey considers dividing profits from his book with his subjects and their families — impoverished urban teenagers hoping to escape their neighborhoods and parlay their basketball talent into college scholarships.

Gates, Gary Paul. *Air Time, The Inside Story of CBS News*. New York: Harper & Row, 1978. Describes the aftermath of CBS's decision to pay for a 1975 interview with Watergate co-conspirator H. R. Haldeman.

Lester, Paul Martin. *Visual Communication, Images with Messages*. Belmont, Calif.: Wadsworth, 1995. Considers the positive outcome of a television station's decision to pay an amateur videographer for tape of the Rodney King beating, but laments the commercial motives of those who would seek to benefit from such events.

Articles & Book Chapters

Day, Louis A. *Ethics in Media Communications: Cases and Controversies*. Belmont, Calif.: Wadsworth, 1991. In a chapter on "Conflicts of Interest," Day suggests that paying for exclusive interviews undermines the credibility and accuracy of the press.

Frankel, Max. "Cyberights." *New York Times Magazine*, 12 February 1995, p. 26. Ciscusses the principal of "no pay, no say."

Goodwin, H. Eugene. *Groping for Ethics in Journalism,* 2nd ed. Ames: Iowa State University Press, 1987. In a chapter titled "Dubious Methods," Goodwin concludes that the majority of journalists find checkbook journalism an unacceptable practice.

Gordon, A. David, et al. *Controversies in Media Ethics.* White Plains, N.Y.: Longman, 1996. The chapter "Checkbook Journalism: The Final Marketplace," pp. 280-4, contains pro and con essays on checkbook journalism. John M. Kittross argues that treating news as a commodity erodes both the credibility of the media and access to important stories. David Gordon counters that paying private individuals for information about private matters may in fact be more ethical than invading privacy for the sake of a story.

Mengelkoch, Louise. "When Checkbook Journalism Does God's Work." *Columbia Journalism Review* (November/December 1994): 35-8, reprinted in *Mass Media 97/98,* Joan Gorham, ed. Guilford, Conn.: Dushkin/McGraw Hill, 1997, pp. 123-5. Considers the impact of tabloid coverage on a small-town rape and murder story and argues that, for all its potential abuse, checkbook journalism can give the powerless access to the media and the resources to tell their side of the story.

McMenamin, Michael. "Tobacco Row." *Reason* (February 1996): 42-4. Criticizes Mike Wallace of CBS's *60 Minutes* for misleading the public about whether an interviewee had been compensated for his willingness to make disclosures about his former employer, Brown & Williamson, in a story on the tobacco industry.

Shapiro, Robert L. "Secrets of a Celebrity Lawyer: How O. J.'s Chief Strategist Works the Press." *Columbia Journalism Review* (September/October 1994): 25-9. High-profile defense lawyer denounces ethics of tabloids that pay for stories.

Stone, Emerson. "Simpsons gone hellish, Case offers textbook challenge for media." *Quill* (November/December 1994): 24-5. Decries the media's decision to replace traditional reporting with the "speculation of paid consultants" in covering O. J. Simpson murder trial.

Toobin, Jeffrey. "Buying headlines, Journalism and justice clash over the checkbook." *Quill* (November/December 1994): 20-3. Toobin, labeling the tabloid's practice of paying for interviews "cash-for-trash," cites numerous examples of high-profile criminal cases affected by paid interviews with witnesses and discusses the role played by attorneys in brokering the deals.

Weinstein, Henry. "Tabloids have cash to lavish on Simpson stories." *Miami Herald,* 3 July 1994, p. 6A. As the Simpson story began to gain momentum, Weinstein discussed the impact that checkbook journalism could have on this and other high-profile trials.

Zoglin, Richard. "Easing the Sleaze." *Time,* 6 December 1993, pp. 72-3. Zoglin looks at tabloids, the "disreputable stepchildren of TV journalism," as they make a bid to gain respect. One of their most controversial practices has been checkbook journalism.

Chapter Twenty-three

Public Journalism:
Sin or Salvation of News?

Michael E. Gouge

As newspapers struggle to reverse the downward spiral of readership, and as opinion polls find the public's distrust of the media rising, many editors are exploring a new way of practicing journalism. Public journalism, also known as civic journalism, has sparked debate as to how newspapers should try to bridge the widening gap between the press and the citizenry. Public journalism blurs the line between reporting and editorializing.

Public journalism supporters believe that the press should take a more assertive role in trying to make democracy work and that journalists should work to improve public discussion. Public journalists believe something basic has to change because journalism's traditional practice of detachment isn't helping solve society's problems. They urge newspapers to stop "telling the news" and start creating opportunities for civic participation. Large and small newspapers across the country are joining with radio and television stations to promote civic education projects and sponsor town meetings to address public concerns in the hopes of both revitalizing public discussion and stemming a decline in newspaper readership.

Critics of this new movement denounce public journalism as merely a fad or marketing gimmick. They maintain that the traditions of objectivity and neutrality should not be rejected. If improvements are needed, they should come within the framework of good, solid journalism. Traditional journalists contend that experimentation in public journalism threatens to cross the line into unethical behavior. Letting the public guide news coverage, they argue, would inherently "dumb-down" newspapers. They contend that this new direction in news coverage is merely "advocacy journalism" or "boosterism" and may cost newspapers their credibility.

A 1994 survey by the Times-Mirror Center for the People and the Press found that 71 per cent of those polled felt the news media get in the way of society solving its problems. That statistic shows the problem facing today's newspapers. The same survey showed declines in the public's trust of government and other institutions. What this is telling journalists is that they are not helping their readers solve their problems. In fact, journalists are becoming the problem, many citizens say. At the 1996 convention of the American Society of Newspaper Editors, outgoing president William B. Ketter, editor of the *Quincy* (Mass.) *Patriot Ledger*, said newspapers are getting tarred with the reputation of shock-trash journalism on TV or in supermarket tabloids. Readers like the traditional journalism values of accountability, accuracy, and thoroughness, but Ketter says the public's perception is that newspapers don't practice those elements very well.

The dissatisfaction with journalism is not limited to readers. In newsrooms across the country there is a great deal of anxiety, frustration, and an evaporation of idealism. A recent survey found one in five journalists plan to leave the industry in the next few years. Industry observers say journalists, too, suffer from the cynicism and angst of the general public. Furthermore, some feel they cannot sit by passively while the public turns away from civic life in frustration and disgust. Added to this is the economic crises of diminishing newspaper readership coupled with corporate mandates to keep up profit margins. How can journalists produce a product that people will continue to purchase in order to make important decisions as an electorate?

"Journalists are now creating the coverage that is going to lead to their own destruction," says Kathleen Hall Jamieson, dean of the Annenberg School for Communication at the University of Pennsylvania. "If you cover the world cynically and assume that everybody is Machiavellian and motivated by their own self-interest, you invite your readers and viewers to reject journalism as a mode of communication because it must be cynical, too."

Geneca Overholser, editor of the *Des Moines Register*, says, "The public is right to question whether newspapers are acting in the public interest. I think what readers are asking is, 'Are you really giving us a reflection of what is happening or are you just discouraging us?' We're so good at reporting all the negatives and all the infighting that we give people a sense it is all hopeless."

Traditionally, journalists have been trained to distance themselves from the events they cover. The standard credo is: the journalist's job is to cover the news, not to make it. Most papers require reporters to refrain from any public or political activity in order to maintain objectivity and avoid conflicts of interest. Journalists are taught not to interfere or intervene in the public discussion. Their role is of detached observer and chronicler, not a facilitator of civic discussions.

An ever-changing newsroom has become another difficulty in connecting with the public. Transience has increased among professional journalists as they strive for upward mobility. The allure of higher paying jobs has made moving on a symbol of success and staying in one place a mark of failure. The problem of transience is that journalists have no stake in the community. The problems of the town need not be resolved, only reported. Then, when the reporter moves on to a larger market, the next new hire with little knowledge of the community steps in and must rebuild rapport and credibility with the public.

Chain ownership, mergers, and shutdowns made most cities one-paper towns by the 1990s, decreasing the competitive urgency for enterprise reporting. What some editors now fear is that newspapers are becoming irrelevant in the lives of ordinary citizens. The great traditions of journalism, such as fostering public debate in a marketplace of ideas, are giving way to the practical and economic demands of running a deadline-oriented, profit-making business.

Davis Merritt Jr., editor of the *Wichita* (Kan.) *Eagle* and a pioneering force in public journalism, says the limits on time and newspaper space often restrict journalists from telling citizens what is really going on beyond a fleeting episode. At its best, Merritt says, journalism can provide the shared information and the place for discussion that is essential to the democratic process. But all too often, journalism is practiced by reflex in order to meet the restrictions of time and space. These reflexes have become journalism's culture. A uniform way of telling the news has developed, guided by traditional rules. Some have dubbed it "one journalism," the concept that there is one way of thinking, one way of practicing good journalism. This one journalism is guided by detachment and the longtime practices of elevating conflict, episodic coverage, and taking an adversarial stance toward all institutions.

What editors like Merritt fear is that people will have no need for journalists if they have no interest in the concerns of their community and the democratic process. Newspapers should move beyond cool neutrality and detachment, treat people as citizens rather than consumers, and start acting as if they belonged in the communities they serve.

While newly arrived reporters and editors bring little local knowledge, they do bring objectivity, which traditional journalists contend makes them effective in any situation. The "our difference is indifference" pun has become something of a panacea, Merritt says. Objectivity practiced uniformly by all journalists means that, in theory, local issues can receive the same quality of coverage regardless of the individual reporter or his/her background. Although journalists strive to remove themselves from events to do the job, they in fact cannot be removed, Merritt argues. They are unavoidably caught up in societal, political, and technological changes. And they bring their preconceptions and values to every story they write.

Origins of the Issue

While the phrase "public journalism" only emerged in the early 1990s, the ideas driving the movement have always been a part of journalism. Early American newspapers were dedicated to political discourse. Newspapers during the Revolutionary War rallied the public toward the cause of independence. Later, during the period of the party press, editors became activists for their political parties encouraging political activism. They had no desire to be impartial, but to put forth issues for debate, explains historian David Sloan in *The Media in America*. The rise of the 1830s penny press brought with it today's journalism principle of impartial, objective reporting. Even with this new dedication to objective reporting, the penny press took sides on timely issues such as abolition and westward migration. The penny press made newspaper readers of a whole economic class of citizens previously untouched by the earlier party press. The penny press gave them a voice in society. Along with the penny press' desire to inform the general public of news was the desire to expose abuses. Later, during Theodore Roosevelt's presidency, journalists bent on bringing about social reform were labeled "muckrakers." During this Progressive era, the muckrakers made detailed inquiries into unchecked business expansion, corrupt politicians, and labor abuses. The exposé became a powerful tool of the press. This "gotcha" journalism became particularly pervasive after the Watergate scandal of the 1970s.

Throughout the nineteenth century, journalists generally believed facts were not human statements about the world, but aspects of the world itself. This was due to the faith in empirical science. But in the 1920s and '30s, many journalists observed that the facts themselves could not be trusted. What then arose was an allegiance to rules and procedures that surrounded objectivity. This ideal of objectivity meant that a person's statements about the world could be trusted if the statements were submitted to established rules deemed legitimate by a professional community.

Two nearly forgotten traditions in journalism that stand against objectivity found renewed support in the 1960s — a literary tradition and a muckraking tradition. The literary tradition seeks to write a good story, not a safe or objective one. It aims to create a finely crafted work with emotional impact. In the '60s, the literary tradition inspired "new journalism," a kind of journalism that aimed to remove the barrier between reporter and reader. *Rolling Stone* magazine became one of the best-known vehicles for new journalism. Writers such as Norman Mailer, Tom Wolfe, and Truman Capote incorporated this new style of writing into their books. Regardless of the subject matter, "new journalists" were always implicitly writing about reporting itself. Hunter S. Thompson's "gonzo journalism" is a new journalism spinoff. "New journalism rewarded flair, personality, style and insight and trains the tastes of journalists and their readers away from objective reporting," says the sociologist Michael Schudson.

What had a greater impact was the revival of the muckraking tradition. What began during the Progressive era of the turn of the century, when reporters became socially responsible reformers, returned as "investigative reporting" or "enterprise reporting" during the '60s and '70s. The legendary model of such journalism is of course Woodward and Bernstein's Watergate reporting. It prodded journalists to delve deeper into stories and issues.

Where public journalists find an historic mandate is in the 1940s. After World War II, social responsibility became the standard most institutions sought. Democratic leaders criticized the press as unfair, slanted in its political coverage, and guilty of presenting gossip and trivia rather than information useful to the public. Publishers, largely Republican, were fearful of possible government regulation. Henry Luce, publisher of *Time* magazine, organized what became known as the Hutchins Commission, which was a panel of experts headed by University of Chicago chancellor Robert Hutchins. Their report, *A Free and Responsible Press*, concluded that press freedom was endangered due to the media's increased importance and visibility, lack of contributing to the needs of society, and preoccupation with sensational news rather than supplying information and discussion for the average citizen. The Hutchins Commission asserted that the public has a right to expect five basic services from the press: 1) an accurate, comprehensive account of the news, 2) a forum for the exchange of comment, 3) a means of projecting group opinions to one another, 4) a method of presenting and clarifying the goals of society, and 5) a way of reaching every member of society.

Public journalism also finds an ally in the participatory journalism movement of the 1970s. Delegates to the United Nations Educational, Scientific and Cultural Organization (UNESCO) began to complain about what they saw as a "one-way flow of communication." Developing nations felt the press of the industrial nations did not sufficiently cover their issues and seemed to be speaking down to them. The new nation states of Asia and Africa, which felt their colonial governors had denied them a free flow of information, supported efforts to increase worldwide press freedoms. A resolution calling for a free flow of information also called for the media to contribute to the preservation of peace and human rights, to aid in eliminating prejudice, and to be responsive to the concerns of people. It urged participation of the public "in the elaboration of information."

A one-way flow of information tends to maintain the dependence of poorer countries upon richer ones, a UNESCO committee said, and this prompts a "cultural imperialism." Although the committee was speaking of international news agencies, a similar dominance of American media can be seen with large newsgathering organizations like the Associated Press, Knight Ridder-Tribune, and the New York Times News Service. As newspapers large and small trimmed their staffs as part of the '90s trend of downsizing, they became more dependent on wire service copy to pass on to their readers.

But a change in the information flow is not enough, participatory journalists said. The conventional criteria for judging news, ingrained in modern journalists, are not sufficient for tackling the big issues. Helping to solve world problems such as hunger, overpopulation, and the environment requires more than the impact of spot news coverage.

The Public Journalists

One of the foremost scholars of public journalism is New York University professor Jay Rosen. He defines public journalism as a set of practices in which journalists attempt to reconnect with citizens and improve public discussion. Along with Arthur Charity, Rosen and other journalism scholars have formed the Project on Public Life and the Press, a public journalism advocacy group.

"Public journalists are not (as they are sometimes portrayed) radicals departing from the canons of their profession, but traditionalists attempting a return to first principles," Charity says.

In one of the first public journalism efforts, the editors at the Columbus (Ga.) Ledger-Enquirer decided to combat their city's problems. In 1988, they launched an eight-part series on the future of Columbus. They exposed a host of persistent difficulties long avoided by elected leaders such as traffic flow, low wages, a faltering school system, and a controlling elite running the city government. The series met with silence. Wishing to do more, the paper took an active role in stirring town debate. It organized a town meeting to provide a forum for citizens to speak. Three hundred people turned out. The paper's editor, Jack Swift, served on a steering committee of a newly formed citizens group. The newspaper and the civic movement worked together to open up the political process to more people and revive public discussion. Instead of reporting from a detached position, the paper took the bold move of placing itself in the problem.

Public journalists believe something must change because journalism isn't working now. Citizens who want to participate more intelligently in public life are finding newspapers, by adhering to old habits of newsgathering, have placed hurdles in their way. Citizens should have a larger role in the reporting of news, and papers should re-orient themselves around citizens' concerns such as crime, race relations, drug use, education, prison sentencing, and other issues.

Supporters of this movement say journalists should be full-time citizens. The average citizen cannot attend every city council meeting or research every issue and every candidate during election season. Crusades by journalists out to expose scandal offer little in the way of building a public discussion. Journalists who started off representing the people have replaced them. "Gotcha" journalism should not be the main principle of journalism, advocates say, but to help society operate smoother. Journalists, as citizens, also have a stake in the future of their communities. "A society that considers journalism to be only an irritating appurtenance or a negative burden rather than an interested stakeholder will look elsewhere for ways of getting the information necessary for that society to function," says Merritt.

The fast-paced temporary nature of newspapers makes problem resolution a difficult order on a nightly deadline. Resolution of public problems requires a working through, a sorting out of opinions and often a slow compromise. Journalists often ignore the working-through process and the compromising and rely on the quick quote from polarized experts and absolutists. To balance the limited coverage of an issue, journalists tend to go with the easily explained extremes, leaving the average citizen whose views fall in the middle ground unable recognize a middle position. Journalists are good at raising consciousness on issues. Agenda setting has become so widespread that journalists rush to find new problems to thrust into the spotlight, leaving the previous ones unattended and unresolved. Readers, bombarded with more and more problems and seeing few of them resolved, begin to see the media as just reporting more negative news.

"Conventional journalism," said Cole Campbell, editor of the *Virginian-Pilot* in Norfolk, "too often emphasizes conflict and polarizations rather than the search for common ground. It quotes ordinary people as colorful characters rather than as authentic participants. It exalts experts and public opinion over citizens and public judgment."

Public journalists should look for ways to strengthen their community's goodwill. They should maintain a "proactive neutrality," Rosen says, to engage citizens in the political process and encourage people to work together.

"Journalism should advocate democracy, without advocating particular solutions," Charity says. "Traditional journalism tries to serve the public in essentially two ways. It seeks to inform on the one hand, and act as a watchdog over government on the other. Public journalism ... tries to strengthen the community's capacity — the key word is capacity — to recognize itself, to converse well, and make choices." The vision of public journalism is a well-connected community where everyone who should be talking, regardless of race or social class, is in fact talking. "I do not believe journalists should be solving problems," Charity says. "I think they should be creating the capacity within the community to solve problems." Investigative reporting of political scandals, while going beyond detached reporting, may prompt legislative action, but often the citizens are uninvolved in the process. The results of investigative journalism often leave no new capacity for citizens to make decisions or solve problems.

Traditional journalists worry about getting the separations right. What they should be turning more attention to, Rosen says, is getting the connections right. They should draw connections between problems, rather than isolating issues; use emotion, shunned by traditional journalists, as a way of forming relationships with the public concerns and discussions; and inject community values into news coverage. "The people we seek to inform," Merritt says, "filter virtually everything they learn through their own value systems. By reporting and writing as if that does not happen, we create yet another major disconnection between us and our product and the citizens at large."

Journalists should develop the skills needed to help people recognize how personal core values affect their view of issues and how failure to resolve conflicts between values hinders problem solving. In a world filled with facts and events, readers want not only information, but opinion about the relative importance of things. They trust journalists and their viewpoint, Merritt says, only if they believe they are based on some broad, shared values.

In his book, *Doing Public Journalism*, Charity describes some recent public journalism experiments around the country:

- The *Charlotte* (N.C.) *Observer* focused on a single high-crime neighborhood for six weeks, reporting on the reasons for the area's problems and drawing help and suggestions from across the city. The paper helped volunteers and local organizations coordinate efforts to improve the area.

- The *Cape Cod Times* in Hyannis, Mass., consulted a panel of representative citizens to set priorities in covering the 1992 election. It also surveyed readers and promised long-term coverage on the public's six areas of greatest concern.

- Ohio's *Dayton Daily News* and the *Spokane* (Wash.) *Spokesman-Review* offered free pizza to any family or group who discussed a certain issue and completed a questionnaire. The Dayton paper used the pizza parties to find out more about juvenile violence and then offered a series of forums on how to deal with violence.

- The *Wisconsin State Journal* in Madison staged mock legislatures and grand juries composed of citizens to deliberate property taxes, the national budget, and health care reform and then reported on the deliberations to encourage public discussion.

- The *Virginian-Pilot* in Norfolk replaced its beat system with teams of reporters organized not around institutions like schools and city councils, but around issues as citizens see them such as "public safety" and "public life."

- The *Huntington* (W.Va.) *Herald-Dispatch* followed up a special section on economic renewal by sponsoring a town hall meeting with the local university and TV station. When six task forces were recommended in the meeting, the paper rounded up volunteers for the panels.

What journalists can do to build a closer relationship with citizens is to move from seeing concerns depicted through masses of fragmented facts to the citizen's view of wanting to know the whys and hows, the history, and all sides of the debate. Instead of using expert-driven facts to establish authenticity, journalists can look for people and issues to reflect a sense of reality. Citizens are spurred to discuss and act on public concerns as individuals in their daily lives, not by experts seen by the media as catalysts for engaging citizens. "Our obligation as journalists in a free society, " says *Virginian-Pilot* editor Cole Campbell, "is to help readers find out what is going on — by reinvigorating the best of traditional journalism — and help them discover how they can take responsibility by devising new ways of listening and exploring community connections. This is public journalism."

Public journalism assumes that readers want to be active citizens. Citizens would strive for solutions if they only had the time, money, and access of professional news media. The journalist's task then is not to report the news in a vacuum, but to figure out how to round up a community's agenda and questions, and then to produce a newspaper with answers citizens need. Some civic leaders agree. "Newspapers hide behind the idea that they're not supposed to become involved in the community's business," says Duluth, Minn., mayor Gary Doty. "I think they have a corporate responsibility and a personal responsibility to be a part of that community and help find solutions, and not just go digging around for all the dirt they can find and then sit back and say, 'Lets see if the people can solve this.'"

Public Journalism: Sin or Salvation?

By crossing the line between detached observer and a participant in community events, public journalists argue that the mainstream's rule on noninvolvement is the one that threatens the public. When social problems grow unchecked and citizens are angry and frustrated, some editors are breaking tradition and stepping in to advocate intelligent discourse. "Which form of journalism is really more flawed and dangerous in a free society," asks Charity: "the one that sits passively by while people grow divided, or the one that finds ways of bringing them together?"

The Traditional Journalists

The tenet of objectivity in modern journalism is sometimes credited to the demise of the party press system in the 1830s and the rise of wire services. As newspapers became more commercial, they found objectivity beneficial in serving heterogeneous audiences without alienating a large portion of the audience. The penny press set forth its objective creed, according to historian Frank Luther Mott, that "the newspaper's first duty is to give its readers the news, and not to support a party or a mercantile class." With the advent of the telegraph, wire services could cover news events for several newspapers. Their use of nonpartisan, unbiased accounts allowed them to serve several clients. Also in the late nineteenth century, the empirical scientific method became widely respected. Journalists, seeking to emulate scientists, developed a deep reverence for the facts.

Critics of public journalism say this new movement raises serious ethical concerns. The traditional journalism code of ethics frowns on involvement in news events. Under public journalism, newspapers sometimes end up reporting on themselves or creating the news, issues that chafe many editors. "Much of what is commonplace in business or politics, many of the social conventions that make the wheels of progress go around — the fancy dinners and tickets to the luxury box — are expressly forbidden by our codes of conduct and ethics, " says William Woo, editor of the *St. Louis Post-Dispatch*. "When the editor and the real estate broker, the banker and the elected official form a team, whose ethics, whose culture prevails?"

One of the things traditional journalists have against public journalism is what critics call "advocacy journalism." Rallying behind an issue contradicts the long-held adherence to objectivity. "As a practical matter," Woo asks, "can a paper objectively report on a burning community issue when the editor sits on the commission that is promoting a particular point of view on the matter?"

Public journalism's enthusiasm for giving citizens more of a say in editorial content draws sharp reactions. Critics say public journalists are letting focus groups tell editors what to cover and that editors are acting like the mayor and taking over the business of running the town. Public journalism may endanger journalistic credibility, traditionalists fear. "Newspapers are not to take sides — even for Mom and apple pie and the flag, " says Michael Gartner, editor of the *Ames* (Iowa) *Daily Tribune*. "That stuff should be saved for the editorial pages.... It ultimately will cost newspapers their credibility."

Many newspaper publishers believe the credibility of the news department is crucial to their success as news providers, but also as an advertising carrier. John H. McManus in his book, *Market-Driven Journalism: Let the Citizen Beware*, says that if a newspaper damages its credibility with readers, its advertisers will also lose the factual environment that by association adds to the credibility of advertisements. Any erosion of a paper's market share among consumers will quickly affect advertising revenues.

Many traditional editors believe newspapers should not be convening community meetings, writing legislation, or soothing their readers, as public journalism does. "Newspapers are supposed to expose the wrongs, not campaign against them," Gartner says. "Reporters and city editors are not supposed to write legislation or lead campaigns or pass moral judgments. They are supposed to tell the truth, and God knows, that's hard enough to do all by itself."

Some critics dismiss the movement as a new age cult for the press. This dogma of political correctness, writes Hiley Ward in an *Editor & Publisher* article, begins with fermenting a sense of guilt in the journalist for all of the problems of the modern world. Journalists are blamed for contributing to the decline of society and failure to stimulate the Greek agora of political debate. Made to feel as if they have sinned, journalists are encouraged to make amends and seek out problems to remedy. Their conversion gives them new eyes to view the public, not as readers and consumers, but as citizens and voters.

Public journalism has also been dismissed as merely a marketing gimmick. Its pandering to community groups is a way of stimulating readership, which stimulates circulation, and leads to higher ad revenues.

Critics warn that public journalism can go too far in encouraging debate. The decision to publish the Unabomber manifesto "was public journalism run amok," said the editor of the *Daily Tribune* in Ames, Iowa. Newspapers became the pawn of the FBI in catching the elusive terrorist.

Most editors feel that a major change in the industry is not needed, only a renewed commitment to the practice of quality journalism. Good journalism does inform the public. Good journalism does create avenues of discussion without the newspaper sponsoring a media event. Len Downie Jr., executive editor of the *Washington Post*. says good journalism provides citizens with as much information as possible for them to conduct their lives without sacrificing objectivity. More investigative reporting, more context, more clarity, more reporting on solutions as well as problems will keep newspapers alive and will keep them credible.

Public journalism is really nothing new, Downie says. Much of what public journalism advocates is a gimmicky, repackaged parcel of basic journalism principles. Editors have used polling and focus groups effectively to explore issues without giving up objectivity or editorial control to the public. In-depth interviews with candidates and even sponsoring debates all fall within normal journalism practices.

"Public journalism crosses the line for me," says Downie, "when the newspaper and its editors and reporters become actors on the political stage, by forcing candidates to participate in dialogues with voters, by staging campaign events, by deciding what good citizenship is and force feeding it to citizens and candidates, by pressuring citizens to register and vote when, as I say, non-voting can also be viewed as an honorable and honest way to participate in a democratic process."

Another opponent of public journalism may be the media owners. Shareholders, ever hungry for higher dividends and faced with the persistent increases in newsprint costs, may be reluctant to fund "community building" town meetings and focus groups. Appeals to fund measures to bring small communities closer and to hire additional staff members to closely follow through on complex civic issues are unlikely to succeed as distant stockholders are insulated from community problems.

Is it the job of newspapers to subsidize events to get citizens involved in civic affairs? "I don't think the press should be an alternate arm of government," says *Pittsburgh Post-Gazette* editor John C. Craig. "I don't see that it's Rupert Murdoch's responsibility to make the American people more connected, and I clearly don't want the Disney corporation and Time-Warner to get together to see what they can do to make the American people more connected."

Resolution

As society and politics change, surely journalism should be flexible enough to adapt. The long-standing tenets of journalism have served newspapers well for years, evolving as technology and world events dictated. Journalists should be concerned about the current problems of an apathetic electorate, disenchanted communities, and ineffective leadership. How far should they go to help solve the problems?

The solution is to become more attentive to newspaper readers. When newspapers begin staging public events and then covering what happens, public journalism critics have valid ethical concerns. Forcing issues on the public and creating media events out of neighborhood complaints pushes journalism into a questionable realm. But newspapers shouldn't wait for a traditional "news hook" to get involved with an issue. It is a tricky path to navigate. Using focus groups is a widely accepted and beneficial practice, but staging pizza parties in order to generate stories, and thus boost readership, is not good journalism.

Newspapers should not be posturing citizens to get out there and fix the system or cheerleading for civic groups. And neither should they be constantly crying wolf over community problems without taking the added step of following up on what is being done to address them. These are aspects of public journalism editors are correct in questioning.

But public journalism has many merits that editors should consider. Public journalism raises the point that newspapers today are not doing as good a job as they could. The daily strains of news space and tight deadlines make it all too easy to fall into the trap of episodic storytelling. The dominance of wire services, which helped to originate objectivity and detachment, contributes to one journalism, making experimentation a suspicious activity among newspapers. And the heavy reliance on wire services makes most newspapers almost carbon copies of each other. The fact remains that newspapers are losing readers. They must become more attuned to what the public wants from a news provider. If readers find they like what public journalists are doing to bring their communities together, the graying of traditional lines of reporting is worth the effort. However, if the public views the newspaper's intervention as pandering or playing up social ills to boost circulation, editors must be careful not to damage their organization's reputation as credible information providers.

Public journalists defend themselves from accusations of unethical and improper practices by noting that the movement is still in its infancy. No code of ethics has yet been established for practicing civic journalism. Given time, critics may lessen their opposition to the movement and see value in getting closer to the subjects that concern readers.

Perhaps what public journalism can do best is convince the reader that journalism is a human endeavor and not an ideological conspiracy. When reporters become public advocates, when the average citizen can read an article and see a reasonable and recognizable source quoted instead of ivory-tower experts and government bureaucrats, journalism — and communities — will benefit. The public will see that journalists have a stake in how common problems are addressed. Reporters and editors live in the same communities as their readers, yet many people feel their newspaper is a product of a distant corporation and not the work of their neighbor.

What traditional journalists can learn from this new movement is to be more responsive to their readers. They should put wire stories in a context that keeps readers from asking, "What's this got to do with me?" Newspapers should try to cover stories from viewpoints other than official sources and to connect with the average citizen. All of these things can be done without violating the canons of journalism objectivity.

What public journalists need to be more cautious about is becoming lobbyists for social causes. Newspapers run the risk of returning to what historian Frank Luther Mott described as the "dark ages" of party journalism when they get too close to a civic movement and cross over into advocating social change or becoming the mouthpiece for a social movement.

Public journalists' questioning of journalism's sometimes overzealous adherence to the ideals of objectivity is healthy. Recognizing the forgotten journalistic styles of the literary tradition and the social-reforming muckrakers can keep newspapers from falling into the "one journalism" trap. By combining the best points of objectivity — the search for facts and impartiality — with public journalism's desire to move beyond dispassionate detachment, newspapers can rest easier about the status of their credibility while bringing their communities closer together.

With increasing pressure from stockholders to increase earnings and the dismal future of declining readership, newspapers must abandon the status quo mentality they have operated on for so many years. The future of the medium depends upon the ability of journalists to adapt to changing attitudes and demands from their consumers. Selling a new form of journalism to frugal publishers may be a difficult battle. Justifying the expenses of organizing town meetings, sponsoring focus groups, and dedicating manpower to new beats is hard without the assurance that the newspaper will benefit in both image and circulation. Yet, public journalism may hold the key to winning back readers. If newspapers can give them the information they need, framed in a context that has meaning and engages citizens on public concerns, 71 per cent of the people may no longer feel that the media get in the way of solving society's problems.

Recommended Readings

Books

Charity, Art. *Doing Public Journalism.* New York: Guilford Press, 1995. A comprehensive book on the origin and practice of public ournalism as it stands today. Offers how-to instructions for adapting newsrooms to the public journalism practices and examples of what papers have done with public journalism.

Lappe, Frances Moore, and Paul Martin Du Bois. *The Quickening of America: Rebuilding Our Nation, Remaking Our Lives.* San Francisco: Jossey-Bass, 1994. Shows how public citizens are reshaping workplaces, schools, and media by grassroots movements. This self-help book is filled with tips aimed to help readers apply the art of democracy to reshaping public life.

Merritt, Davis. *Public Journalism and Public Life: Why Telling the News Is Not Enough.* Hillsdale, N.J.: Erlbaum, 1995. An easy to read and understand primer on public journalism by a working journalist and pioneer in public journalism. It's part memoir, part argument for solving some of the problems newspapers now face.

Articles

Albers, Rebecca Ross. "Whose Newspaper is It, Anyway? Editing for Readers Shakes Up Journalism's Status Quo." *Presstime* (December 1995): 38-40. As a result of readership research, newspapers are changing their coverage.

Fitzgerald, Mark. "Decrying Public Journalism." *Editor & Publisher*, 11 November 1995, 20. Some common criticisms of public journalism.

Hoyt, Mike. "Are You Now, or Will You Ever Be, a Civic Journalist?" *Columbia Journalism Review* (September/October 1995). Public journalism takes heat for straying from long-standing practices.

Merritt, Davis. "Public Journalism — Defining a Democratic Art." *Media Studies Journal* 9:3 (Summer 1995): 125-31. Good outline of public journalism's philosophy and practice.

Rosen, Jay. "Public Life and the Press." *Quill* (November 1993). Journalists should take a more active role in encouraging public debate.

Shepard, Alicia C. "The Gospel of Public Journalism." *American Journalism Review* (September 1994). Pros and cons of the public journalism movement.

Stein, M.L. "Beware of Public Journalism." *Editor & Publisher*, 6 May 1995, 18-19. Cautions against viewing public journalism as a cure-all.

Chapter Twenty-four

Can the Media Criticize Themselves?

Fred Bales

Because the mass media are obligated by tradition to print and broadcast criticism of other major American institutions — and many do so frequently and zealously — it might be assumed that they cover and criticize themselves to the same degree. Not so. Newspapers, magazines, and broadcast stations assign reporters to state capitols, city halls, courts, businesses, sports venues, and the like, but relatively few have full-time reporters to monitor the news and public affairs products of their own field. Many employ reviewers of television entertainment fare, but rarely do media staffers examine news and public affairs performance, either in their own markets or nationally, as a way of enhancing accountability in their field. As Maxwell King, former executive editor of the *Philadelphia Inquirer*, has said, "We have been much better at self-righteousness than self-criticism."

Granted, the mass media do sometimes engage in self-criticism. For example, magazines from print and broadcast professional associations not only educate their members about improving their products but also discuss problems and shortcomings in news and public affairs coverage. And in recent times, newspapers, magazines, television stations, and broadcast networks have been more diligent in correcting errors — although television may seem to do less of this because viewers have a more difficult time detecting errors than in print, where information can be reread and scrutinized.

Many practitioners would say that the first duty of a journalist in a free society is to monitor public institutions and reveal their shortcomings. Typical are the comments of the late CBS correspondent Charles Kuralt during a 1991 speech at the University of Colorado. "Our kind of country cannot work," he said, "unless we persist in pointing out everything that can go wrong in the country. That is the essential job of journalism. If we don't do it, nobody will." True. But if this attitude has currency among journalists, then journalists cannot, without blushing, object to the general principle of having the errors and omissions of journalism exposed. This idea seems even more imperative when one remembers that the First Amendment has generally shielded the media from government interference.

Origins of the Issue

From their early days, but more particularly from the advent of modern mass communication in the late nineteenth century, American media have engaged in self-criticism. In her review of American press criticism, *Civilizing Voices: American Press Criticism 1880-1950*, Marion Marzolf concluded that this criticism has revolved around two major issues: the role of the free press in safeguarding other democratic freedoms from government interference, and the press' socio-cultural role in promoting higher ideals and moral behavior. The latter was especially trenchant at the dawn of the twentieth century when mass circulations were built upon sensational content, exemplified by "yellow journalism," and played out in its most dramatic form in the New York circulation wars between Joseph Pulitzer and William Randolph Hearst.

The issue of sensationalism arose against a backdrop of American industrialization and urbanization and was echoed in journalism by the passing of the erudite owner-editor's personal style of journalism. Limited-circulation newspapers and magazines were overshadowed by mass-circulation publications fueled by large staffs of reporters and editors who, as employees in a big business enterprise, were more faceless than their predecessors.

One witness to this development was newsman Will Irwin, who in 1911 wrote an authoritative fifteen-part series titled "The American Newspaper" for *Collier's* magazine. Standing as a milestone between the "old" journalism of the editor-owner and the "new" journalism of mass audiences and corporate structures, the series not only related a history of the medium and criticized unethical practices but also set standards for modern press criticism.

As journalism became a powerful institution in society, the individual journalist sometimes sought professional status as one positioned between society's interests and commercial necessities. In 1910, the Kansas Editorial Association adopted the first code of American journalism ethics, and in 1922 the American Newspaper Publishers Association embraced its famous "Canons of Journalism," later renamed "Statement of Principles." In the same era Sigma Delta Chi, a professional journalism society, was founded at DePauw University in Indiana. Its successor, the Society of Professional Journalists, survives as a professional organization committed to improving journalism practices through its code, special activities, and *Quill* magazine.

The advent of radio broadcasting caused critics to worry about its entertainment content while its news functions were subsumed under those categories and concerns developed for newspapers and magazines. With television arriving in the mass market after World War II, and its ascendancy in the 1950s as an entertainment medium and a news medium, critics took notice — but rarely from within the medium itself. Regular broadcasts where practitioners assess media performance have continued to be rare, left mainly to public television or odd time slots on commercial venues. Examples from public television are *Behind the Lines* in the 1970s, hosted by Brendan Gil of *The New Yorker*, and *Inside Story*, hosted by journalist Hodding Carter in the 1980s. Also in the 1980s, Ted Koppel's ABC *Nightline* launched *Viewpoint*, a program addressing audience complaints about network news and public affairs coverage. In the 1990s CNN aired *Reliable Sources* with former network newsman Bernard Kalb as moderator.

Among the more innovative attempts at media criticism on the air was Don Hollenbeck's radio program, *CBS Views the Press*, which ran on the network's New York City affiliate, WCBS, beginning in 1947. Today, media criticism on the radio can be found in many markets through National Public Radio's half-hour program, *Counterspin*.

In the wake of the Vietnam War and the Watergate scandal, and the media's prominent role in each, journalism in the 1970s was among those callings emphasizing ethical practices. Subsequently, a flood of books, articles, college courses, textbooks, seminars, and codes have given journalism self-criticism a new standing. But today, critics may wonder whether all this activity benefits the marketplace's profit-making goals, rather than promoting ways for the media to better serve a diverse populace. Related to this issue is the oft-heard complaint that the collective media are merely an entrenched institution protecting and defending the status quo.

Assumptions and Perspectives

What constitutes mass media self-criticism and whether it is worth doing at all remain in dispute. For this chapter, a strict standard is favored, requiring that such criticism be "of the media, by the media and in the media." This means that the ideal media self-criticism will appear in mass media outlets, such as newspapers, broadcast stations and networks, and mass-circulation periodicals and be performed by mass media practitioners. As seen below, this will discount some meaningful vehicles of criticism, especially limited-circulation periodicals.

The general perspectives can be divided into three categories:

Proponents

In modern times, media self-criticism was brought into focus by the Hutchins Commission on Freedom of the Press, which in its 1947 report called for enhanced media responsibility, including establishing press councils. Many practitioners have defended the mechanisms of self-criticism ever since. Among these was syndicated columnist Arthur Rowse, who embraced self-criticism more than a quarter of a century ago. He argued that the best criticism had originated from within the media and would continue to do so because — among other reasons — those inside were the most knowledgeable about the subject and, second, were most likely to be listened to by their colleagues.

Traditional Opponents

Opposing not so much the idea of self-criticism as advocating better sources, some commentators have argued that meaningful press criticism could emanate only from outside the institution. Among these was Harry S. Ashmore, Pulitzer Prize-winning editor of the *Arkansas Gazette*, who believed that the best criticism could be initiated from those wholly independent of the mass media. Specifically, he argued for the academic world to be the seat of criticism and for a press council to be the means.

Structural Opponents

Going a step further than the traditional detractors are structural analysts, who say that the very capitalistic orientation of American media make self-criticism meaningless. One such intellectual is the linguist Noam Chomsky. He asserts that the media too often "get it wrong" because they act like propagandists dedicated to defending the dominant power groups and their political, economic, and social agendas. According to this outlook, no institution so tied to the status quo could possibly produce significant criticism of itself.

The Mechanisms of Self-Criticism

One way to categorize self-criticism is by differentiating between *internal* and *external* criticism. The first pertains to activities such as correcting errors or analyzing coverage at a critic's own media outlet. The second relates to looking at other media outlets' performances, although it may include the critic's as well.

Two other categories are *direct* and *indirect*. Self-critics often take on specific coverage or issues, directly citing violations of good practice while suggesting improvements. But indirectly, self-critics can contribute to the field by praising positive press performance and thereby chastising those who fail to measure up.

This tone of criticism says, "Here's what we should be doing. And incidentally, I need not add that some of you obviously are not doing it." Journalism codes might be considered self-criticism under this definition because they attempt to promote good practices in advance of problems and create an atmosphere of "right conduct" in the workplace.

Vehicles of criticism have taken several forms. The most prominent are the following, and each has had its own advocates and detractors.

The National News Council

The National News Council was formed in 1973 with a major grant from the Twentieth Century Fund. A similar body had existed in Great Britain for many years, and among its American champions were the Hutchins Commission members and journalist Herbert Brucker of the *Hartford Courant.*

In a 1970 *Saturday Review* article, Brucker called for a U.S. version of the British council to promote credibility and better news media coverage. Among a council's other benefits, Brucker and others said, would be heading off petty but costly libel suits and shielding newspapers from legislated controls. Advocates of more stringent industry standards had also invoked the specter of the "big stick" of government awaiting an excuse to impose responsible media conduct if they refused to do so themselves. Brucker's article was published at the height of Vice President Spiro Agnew's spirited attacks on the public affairs content of the major television networks and major print news operations. Despite Brucker's practical tone, however, he ended his call for a news council with a straight appeal to journalists' higher instincts. "There is a better reason," he said. "It is right."

New York Times publisher A.O. Sulzberger, *Boston Globe* editor Tom Winship, and Wayne Godsey, president of the Radio Television News Directors Association, were among media representatives criticizing the council concept. Their views were shared from the academic side by Professor John Merrill, then at the University of Missouri. These critics said that a council would threaten press freedom by forcing more conformity and restrictions on an endeavor meant to enjoy maximum freedom. They also argued that such a council would ultimately invite government interference by creating an atmosphere of regulation. Some specific complaints were that the council would effectively make aggressive news media timid through council criticisms while the less aggressive would be spared any criticism, even though the latter's sins of omission were more damaging to journalism's proper public role. Critics further argued that the council was too powerful, acting as both judge and jury without any mechanism for appeal. They also feared that council decisions against media organizations would bolster future legal actions — such as libel suits.

With backing from professional organizations such as the American Society of Newspaper Editors, but without the backing of some media giants, the National News Council was established at the Columbia School of Journalism in New York City. It included eighteen members, eight of them representatives of the communication industry, although criticism was raised that some of the ten "public" members had close ties to the media. Cases were generated by dissatisfied citizens who contacted the council about major questions of coverage. The council heard evidence from the complainants and news media and then issued findings, not unlike court decisions, duly noting whether the action had merit and which members voted in the majority and minority. Minority views were printed following the majority decisions.

Supporters hoped that council deliberations and decisions would be widely disseminated among the mass media as a means of censuring offenders. But in practice few media carried the results, which were initially printed in the *Columbia Journalism Review* and later in *Quill* magazine. Some media members, including NBC and the *New York Times*, refused to cooperate, even when their own cases came before the council.

Despite its members' efforts, the council died in 1984 when foundation money ran out and no other institution rose to support it. The council had served a limited usefulness, but it failed to gain the broad support of media practitioners necessary to make it viable. It hardly acted as a hanging jury against the media, however. Of 242 complaints considered during its eleven years, 120 were found unwarranted and eighty-two warranted in whole or in part, while thirty-seven were dismissed and three withdrawn. In any event, the National News Council files housed at the University of Minnesota remain fertile ground for study.

The idea of a national news council endures. From time to time voices inside and outside the media call for the resurrecting of a council, perhaps in a different form. Among them have been General William Westmoreland after his unsuccessful libel suit against CBS News in the 1980s, and John Sigenthaler, former editor of *USA Today* and longtime executive with the Gannett newspaper chain. More recently, during a 1996 speech at the Media Studies Center in New York City, CBS newsman Mike Wallace urged the formation of another news council. "I'm convinced," he said, "that more state news councils and/or a renewed national news council could strike a blow for a better public understanding in a time of skepticism about us, of who we are and what it is we do."

There is one particularly successful news council that functions at the state level today. Minnesota's news council, a vibrant organization founded in 1971, gained a national audience in late 1996 when CBS' "Sixty Minutes" aired a segment about its deliberations over coverage of Northwest Airlines safety practices. And a handful of other local news councils have existed over the years.

Ombudsmen

Another means for audiences to confront the media involves designating someone within a specific media outlet to take complaints. The representative of media audiences takes the title "ombudsman," a Scandinavian term that means "go-between" or "intermediary." Sweden is credited with having the first ombudsman, a person appointed in the early nineteenth century to hear citizen complaints against the government. Although the office has grown in America to include corporations, hospitals, and universities, few media outlets have ombudsmen, and they exist almost exclusively at newspapers. In the late 1990s, the National Organization of News Ombudsmen listed thirty-seven members in the United States, all at newspapers except one at NBC news. The organization also listed members in ten countries abroad. Despite its masculine name, about one-third of the American ombudsmen have been women, and the position sometimes goes by more descriptive titles, such as "readers' representative," "readers' advocate," "public editor," or "public-contact editor."

Ombudsmen gather complaints through telephone calls, letters, or personal visits from readers or viewers. Then ombudsmen become reporters themselves, investigating through interviews with editors and staff members. If a complaint concerns factual errors, the ombudsman may oversee the preparation of corrections.

The ombudsman idea was advanced in a 1967 *New York Times Magazine* article by A.H. Raskin, who said that the major threat to newspapers was the smugness of their owners and editors. One way to counteract this threat, he said, would be for newspapers to utilize ombudsmen. Norman Isaacs, executive editor of the Louisville newspapers, read Raskin's article and succeeded in appointing the first ombudsman at a major U.S. newspaper that year.

Proponents say that ombudsmen can serve to improve reporting quality by monitoring accuracy, balance, fairness, and taste and can heighten credibility by giving audiences easier media access. Included is the increased coverage of deserving community activities historically ignored by the media. Further, the position is said to increase awareness by news professionals of public concerns and to save time for publishers and editors who cannot meet all of the public's demands on them. Finally, it is argued that by resolving complaints in the early stages, media may head off costly legal actions.

Critics contend that the ombudsman idea is too radical because it confuses the media obligation to maintain maximum freedom from interference in their operations. Specifically, antagonists such as Robert Haiman, former managing editor of the *St. Petersburg Times* and later president of the Poynter Institute for Media Studies, said that ombudsmen get between editors and their audiences, blocking direct dialogue between them. The critics point out that in almost all cases, the ombudsman is a veteran news hand who is "institutionalized" and incapable of maintaining an impartial perspective when the media outlet is attacked. This reality may also mean that the audience misconstrues who controls a media outlet while staff members question who their boss really is. And it is admitted that many organizations cannot afford to pay someone attached to the newsroom while not producing or processing the news product. Another telling objection is that the ombudsman is akin to a coroner, brought to the scene after an offense has been committed rather than intervening earlier.

Where ombudsmen exist, they need the power of publicity to print or broadcast regular reports explaining or criticizing their medium. This is particularly important because they function as advisers rather than as administrators.

Media Critics

Although both involve media cooperation and support, ombudsmen and press councils operate essentially as conduits, carrying media criticism originated by media consumers, and could thus be judged as falling short of pure self-criticism. No such ambiguity exists with media critics. They produce stories for public consumption, and their tasks should not be confused with the ombudsmen's. Both are attached to a particular media outlet, but critics can act as self-starters, professionals who undertake their own appraisals of media content rather than waiting for public action. Also, critics are not limited in reach, and often they survey media operations other than their own. Although most are veteran news hands, they often have a broader mandate for material, covering not just news operations but also entertainment fare and media personnel changes.

Few media operations have a full-time media critic, although many incorporate the function under an arts and theater assignment. Also, many editors view the role of the media critic as a constricted one, devoted mainly to covering media celebrities or the media as a business. But a number of large newspapers employ true media critics, including the *New York Times*, *Washington Post*, and *Los Angeles Times*. Some major media critics, among them Tom Shales of the *Washington Post* and David Shaw of the *Los Angeles Times*, write syndicated columns, and their work addresses why certain stories are deemed newsworthy and how they are handled. Shaw's books include *Press Watch*, a collection of his newspaper columns.

The introduction to *Press Watch* presents a strong rationale for the press critic. Shaw argues that the media have done a poor job of explaining themselves, saying, "Until relatively recently, about the only time newspapers wrote about themselves was when they won a Pulitzer Prize or when the publisher's son got married or his wife was placed in charge of one important social group or another or, heaven forbid, when the newspaper was sued for libel." And he concludes, "We must stop acting as if what we do everyday is either an arcane secret, too complex for the reader to understand, or a state secret that's none of the reader's business. We should tell you how we function and why, and how we sometimes malfunction and misfunction."

Despite Shaw's observation, some media without ombudsmen or critics still manage to explain particular episodes or issues of coverage to their audiences. These explanations can be found under a standing headline, such as "Letters from the Editor," or appear on the editorial page or op-ed page as a kind of column with a topical headline, such as "Why the *Times* Used an Anonymous Source in the Smith Murder Story."

Some criticisms aimed at ombudsmen apply to media critics as well. Critics are veteran journalists and part of the institutions paying their salaries. Also, they arrive on the scene after the fact, so that in the popular jargon they are more "reactive" than "proactive." Likewise, they fail to answer the criticism of Chomsky and others that the very nature of the media's economic base prevents in-house critics from broadening their outlook to structural issues.

Professional Associations

Like all major businesses, the mass media have formed national associations to foster better practices and to represent them to wider audiences. Some representative examples of these organizations are the Public Relations Society of America (PRSA), the National Association of Advertisers (NAA), the National Association of Broadcasters (NAB), Radio-Television News Director's Association (RTNDA), the International Association of Business Communicators (IABC), the Society of Professional Journalists (SPJ), the American Society of Newspaper Editors (ASNE), the Associated Press Managing Editors (APME), the National Newspaper Association (NAA), and the National Press Photographers Association (NPPA).

Most media associations publish periodicals dealing with issues of media personnel and professionalism. A 1994 *Quill* article reviewed some of these publications and found improved content, both by way of serving their primary audience — association members — and by offering better access to the general public. Part of the improved content was criticism of writing techniques. And one new voice of criticism, *Forbes MediaCritic,* from the publisher of *Forbes* business magazine, was noted.

Critics complain that publications by professional groups are geared mainly toward improving practice and boosting members' business volume and bottom-line profits. In the case of journalism groups, a constant theme logically centers on maintaining freedom of speech against government interference, and there should be no quarrel with this. Nevertheless, the reach of self-criticism is seen by some as circumscribed, and few national groups openly criticize specific members or welcome significant philosophical discussions about the social utility of their work. How often, for instance, would one expect to see an article in the ASNE News advocating "reporter power" — the practice in some European nations of reporters' participating in newsroom administration?

Journalism Reviews

External, independent publications that criticize the media exist in various forms. Two of the best known are *Columbia Journalism Review* and *American Journalism Review* (formerly *Washington Journalism Review*). These publications have earned wide respect and rank among the best examples of media criticism. However, their standing as organs of pure self-criticism can be disputed. *Columbia Journalism Review* operates from offices at Columbia University and *American Journalism Review* from the University of Maryland campus. Each depends directly on subscription sales and other financing outside mass media organizations, their content a mix of contributions from working journalists, academics and free-lancers.

A direct vehicle of comment and criticism by journalists themselves is *Nieman Reports*, published by the Nieman Foundation at Harvard University. This quarterly contains essays and short articles by news people chosen in national competition for one year at Harvard to pursue — without concern about deadlines — in-depth study of a media subject of their choosing.

In the 1960s, several local journalism reviews sprang up in San Francisco, Chicago, and other large cities in response to rising social and political activism. Often these reviews were edited and written by media workers. However, over time these local and regional efforts have dwindled, and in the 1990s the *St. Louis Journalism Review* was one of the few survivors from that earlier spurt of critical activity.

Independent reviews from ideological bases also are marketed. Among them are *AIM Report*, published by Accuracy in Media, and *Extra*, published by FAIR, Fairness and Accuracy in Reporting. Both are national in scope and seek to correct media bias and imbalance, FAIR from a liberal perspective and AIM from a conservative one.

These publications contribute significantly to the field of media criticism, particularly when juxtaposed against one another on particular issues of perceived media bias. Like the other periodicals mentioned in this section, *AIM Report* and *Extra* enjoy dedicated and influential followings but not particularly large circulations when compared with mass media organs.

Resolution

Self-criticism constitutes a major theme running through the fabric of mass media analysis: the tension between freedom and responsibility. Those accentuating freedom are less likely to accept formalized efforts of self-criticism than those emphasizing responsibility. While this issue often defines disputes between government and media, it also pits media practitioners against one another.

In an abbreviated way, this question can be framed as an intramural contest between journalism practitioners — particularly those in newsroom journalism — who focus more on their right to publish and broadcast versus those who focus more on the people's right to know.

The word "professional" also has to be used cautiously. Because of its applied nature and the requirement to learn specific skills for its practice, journalism resembles a craft. Yet its most thoughtful members maintain that journalism embodies a calling, demanding devotion to a higher purpose than earning a paycheck, and even its most cynical adherents must admit that journalism practice has major political and social implications in a democracy. Where journalism fails as a profession primarily, however, is the absence of any formal means for controlling entry into and exit from its ranks. Journalists are not licensed, even by themselves. Most critics inside and outside of journalism accept this as proper because practitioners under a "free" press should not be licensed by government representatives or anyone else.

Still, if journalism should amount to more than a disassociated group of money-makers performing a craft, then what should it be? One answer is offered by Professor Edmund Lambeth of the University of Missouri. He suggests that journalism be defined as "a craft with professional responsibilities." In that way the onus of accepting or even promoting self-criticism falls upon the serious journalist accepting the need for public accountability.

Another comment should precede the following suggestions: One standard of criticism in an applied field requires suggesting changes that have a realistic chance of success. And because this chapter has chronicled media shortcomings in self-criticism, realistic propositions for effecting change will be advanced.

First, although inconsistently applied, the practice of editors and station managers or news directors speaking directly to their audiences through something like "Letters From the Editor" or "A Message to our Viewers" holds promise. The very sources of these messages would lend authority to self-criticism, bypassing the resistance that an ombudsman sometimes encounters from harried and recalcitrant news hands. Second, the format would give the sender "creative control" because the editor or broadcaster could choose topics of major import and relevance. What needs to occur aside from wider use of this technique is its systematic and regular presentation — once a week or bi-weekly or monthly — in a fixed place in a publication or at a fixed time on a broadcast station. A possible time slot for broadcasters would be two minutes or so concluding a weekend newscast when news flow customarily slows significantly.

In the longer run, education through specific courses of study in higher education — and books like this one — and continuing education of professionals beg wider adoption. Much has been made of journalism programs offering "mid-career" help to working professionals. Often these endeavors concern the skills side of the business. Perhaps more important is an academia–newsroom connection for deliberating the larger roles of media in society and of a particular medium in its community, along with contributions from academics to foster media self-criticism.

Throughout this chapter reference has been made to methods of self-criticism and arguments for and against such measures. Also, historical background and some general comments about the nature of criticism have been presented. What has not been advanced is a formal and systematic means for accomplishing meaningful criticism.

Even those media supporting and implementing self-criticism are likely to do so on a seat-of-the-pants, ad-hoc basis, addressing problems as they surface, from covering the legal problems of O.J. Simpson or President Clinton, to the naming of a rape victim, or any of the myriad issues found in this book.

Proper critical approaches anywhere demand more than a hit-and-miss approach, however, no matter how frequently performed. Sustained and cohesive self-criticism in journalism can spring only from a defined critical perspective. That perspective can be assisted by following the classic steps of obtaining a factual grasp of a situation, defining the related issues, applying fundamental moral principles, and ultimately reaching a decision about a course of action. This model leaves aside the earlier question as to whether journalists are as capable as non-practitioners in producing significant journalism criticism. Also, the exercise can be performed either by journalists deciding how to handle a particular story or by critics coming along after a story has appeared.

By definition this activity is a process, an ongoing operation in thinking and decision-making described by several commentators, including Ralph Potter, a theologian. Potter presented a "box" to help visualize the progressive mental steps required. First, the critical process requires a firm factual knowledge of a case. And just like reporters, journalism critics should do their own reporting to understand as many facts as possible. Then the critic is prepared to consider the values and principles related to the case. Here, definitions become important and some commentators talk of values where others talk about principles. Some distinguish values and principles.

Whatever one's preference, knowledge of news values and an elementary understanding of classical ethical philosophy is necessary. Philosophy serves to point the way toward broad principles relevant to journalism, particularly promoting such "big-ticket items" as truth-telling, humaneness, maximum freedom, and credibility.

Under Potter's model, after one follows the trail of facts, values, and principles, one final check is applied: loyalty. Potter suggests that the analyst reach a decision and then ask one last question: If I handle this story this way, whom am I being loyal to? Looking honestly at that question may yield an unacceptable answer such as "myself" or "my company's reputation" or "other journalists" or "a powerful politician." If those narrow outcomes result, a newsroom decision-maker will be vulnerable to justifiably harsh criticism.

Although the goals and practice of media criticism often overlap between self-critics and outsiders, the critic's role should be expanded from its current limited core. While academics and others outside the profession can generate useful material, such output usually reaches a select audience segregated from the public at large. Yet, it is the public at large that increasingly needs access to channels of media criticism, and this will be realized only when those with built-in mass audiences, the mass media, present a consistent and voluminous body of work analyzing their product.

Regardless of the type of criticism — direct/indirect or local/national — the gateway to all self-criticism is the media's willingness to practice it. Whether the media directly start the process or join others to facilitate it, journalists need to change and "buy into" the idea that historically has offended or alienated so many of their members. Finally, it is hoped that even the most pragmatic media operator will recognize that self-criticism is vital to shaping media content, and if that element is absent then only market forces will prevail within an institution where the public and its best traditions mandate accomplishments beyond the bottom-line.

Recommended Readings

Books

Brown, Lee. *The Reluctant Reformation: On Criticizing the Press in America*. New York: David McKay Co., 1974. One of the first and best books about criticizing the press, including theories of criticism. Acknowledges press improvement, but suggests that the press too often, and to its own detriment, has ignored its critics.

Chomsky, Noam, and Edward S. Herman. *Manufacturing Consent: The Political Economy of the Mass Media.* New York: Pantheon, 1988. Press treatment of issues and ideas is inevitably determined by the political and economic structure of the press itself. Thus, the press cannot adequately criticize itself because it is trapped in itself.

Clurman, Richard. *Beyond Malice.* New Brunswick, N.J.: Transaction Publishers, 1988. This sharp critique of the mass media, by a *Time* editor who became chairman of Time-Life Broadcast, could serve as a model for other practitioners' attempts at criticism. Among his more controversial ideas: letting sources review the contents of a story before publication.

Lemert, James B. *Criticizing the Media: Empirical Approaches.* Newbury Park, Calif.: SAGE CommText Series, 1989. Argues for the need for empirically-based critical analysis of the mass media. Contains many practical examples of social science techniques.

Lippmann, Walter. *Liberty and the News.* New York: Harcourt, Brace & Howe, 1920. The renowned political writer makes a case for better trained journalists and for a voluntary "Court of Honor" where media professionals would have to prove their assertions or face the prospect of being humiliated by prominent publication of the court's findings.

Shaw, David. *Press Watch.* New York: Macmillan, 1984. Examples of a range of columns from the press critic of the *Los Angeles Times*. Examples include critiques of both news and entertainment content.

Articles

Alter, Jonathan. "New Questions — That's What Media Critics Need." *Media Studies Journal* (Spring 1995): 19-24. In an issue given over to media criticism, a *Newsweek* columnist and veteran media critic contends that most media critics tend to chastise those who fail to live up to the standards of journalism instead of challenging the standards themselves. The central task demands "scrutinizing the folkways and first principles of the news business."

Case, Tony. "Ombudsmen Overboard?" *Editor & Publisher,* 25 May 1996, pp. 8-9. Cost pressures and downsizing in the newspaper industry threaten the numbers of ombudsmen at a time when they are needed more than ever.

Ferry, W.H., and Harry S. Ashmore. "Mass Communications." Santa Barbara, Calif.: Occasional Paper of the Center for the Study of Democratic Institutions, 1966. Included is the argument by Ashmore, a former *Arkansas Gazette* editor, that the press cannot effectively criticize itself because of built-in biases against publicly discussing the media's "grave deficiencies." Ashmore's position was countered by syndicated columnist Arthur Rowse in a Fall 1967 *Columbia Journalism Review* article. (See below.)

Isaacs, Norman. "Why We Lack a National Press Council." *Columbia Journalism Review* (Fall 1980): 16-26. The editor who appointed the first newspaper ombudsman and later was a National News Council member during his tenure at Columbia University outlines the issues surrounding the national news council idea.

Pardue, Leonard. "Hard times be damned." *Quill* (January/February 1994): 50-3. A long-time newsman reviews changes and upgradings, amidst an overall industry-wide recession, at *Columbia Journalism Review, American Journalism Review, The Bulletin, Editor & Publisher, Quill* and *Presstime.* Also considered is Forbes *MedicCritic.*

The Quill (April 1987, February 1988 and April 1988). Taken together, articles from the publication of the Society of Professional Journalists outline various viewpoints over the censure clause formerly contained in the society's Code of Ethics.

Rowse, Arthur E., et al. "Hutchins Commission: Responses." *Columbia Journalism Review* (Fall 1967): 52-5. The lead author replies to Harry Ashmore's contention that the best press criticism necessarily has to originate with outside sources.

Wallace, Mike, and Joseph Lelyveld. "News Councils: The Case for and Against." *Columbia Journalism Review* (March/April 1997): 38-9. CBS correspondent Wallace and Lelyveld, of *Time* magazine, debate news councils. Wallace follows up earlier pronouncements about the need in light of eroding public trust in the media.

6 News Practices

A number of chapters in this book have critiqued the media, challenging their approaches to news, entertainment, and advertising; posing questions about how practitioners can best behave ethically, how they can fulfill a duty to their audiences by providing them with the best "product" possible. This section, devoted to news media, examines both traditional and new practices found in today's newsrooms.

The section begins with the debate over objectivity, the time-honored practice of neutral reporting, which has been challenged by new trends such as public journalism. Like other authors in this book, Bruce Evensen cites the growing pressures of media competition as the force behind today's more colorful, less neutral journalism. Moreover, he outlines the argument that news should loose itself from its traditional objectivity, allowing journalists to draw their viewers and readers into a story by making that story more compelling. Professor Evensen concludes that objectivity, according to this argument, has failed.

Another traditional practice under attack is the that of pursuing news stories based on the newsworthy value of conflict or controversy. In an analysis of that issue, Margot Hardenburgh describes three views: some think there's an appropriate emphasis on conflict, others think there's too much, and still others think journalists' emphasis is determined largely by their own political agendas.

Robert Dardenne follows with an analysis of the growing use of storytelling devices in news writing, in which he points out that one part of the pursuit of conflict may come from the drive to construct a good story. Professor Dardenne addresses the practice of teasing a good tale out of news events in order to keep an easily distracted audience in place. As some have argued, this may be an acceptable way of surviving in the news industry today. At the same time, though, it may also compromise the complexity and accuracy of news stories — and the credibility of journalism as well.

Using unattributed sources also may have consequences for media credibility, as Lori Bergen illustrates. Alternately, rushing to name the suspect in a crime, while good for headlines and circulation figures, poses ethical quandaries when it's uncertain whether the suspect is going to be charged for the crime. The hapless Richard Jewell serves as an illustration for both issues. He was revealed as a suspect in the Olympic Park bombing by a source who, not surprisingly, chose to remain anonymous. Clay Calvert discusses the different viewpoints that news organizations have taken on the decision to reveal Jewell's name, as well as implications for similar decisions in the future.

Our final chapter, on the use of video news releases, discusses the ethical and practical considerations that TV news organizations face when one part of the communications profession — public relations — meets with another. Many TV stations use VNRs, stories packaged in video form by PR practitioners, without identifying their source. Anne Owen provides the arguments on both sides of a debate about whether using VNRs without source identification compromises a station's integrity — and whether the practice deceives viewers.

Some of these practices are traditional ones, being challenged by a changing media industry and culture. Others are new practices, being eyed suspiciously by the traditional side. Whether it's because of new technology, proliferating media outlets, or giant corporate ownership, it seems clear that the mass media are changing rapidly. As this book attempts to show readers, there isn't any clear pathway marked for the industry's future. However, an understanding of the many viewpoints articulated by practitioners, scholars, and the public will help the mass media move in a positive direction.

Chapter Twenty-five

The Debate
Over Objectivity

Bruce J. Evensen

The reaction to Joe Klein's admission in 1996 that he wrote the best-selling *Primary Colors*, a political satire of the 1992 Clinton presidential campaign, is as intriguing as Klein's decision to do the book and lie about having done so. *Newsweek*, where Klein works as a political columnist, saw no evil in his repeated public denials that he was the "Anonymous" behind the $6 million seller. His editor noted that Klein had said he was working on an outside writing project and that a book lambasting the Clintons by a former insider wasn't "a matter of national security." CBS News, where Klein worked as a consultant, was "obviously disturbed" that Klein had told *Newsweek* what he was up to without telling his supervisors, and they fired him. *Washington Post* assistant managing editor Bob Woodward, after congratulating his paper "on a great piece of detective work" in unmasking Klein's deception through handwriting samples, thought the author should do "a one hundred percent grovel" and publicly apologize for impugning the honesty of all journalists by his decision to lie repeatedly. Most in the press, though, failed to see the significance of the Klein caper. The *Chicago Tribune* spoke for many when it said "Klein probably deserves a medal for keeping his mouth shut so long." As for Klein, he couldn't imagine why the book and his lying about the fact he wrote it should affect his credibility.

It's not only Klein's credibility but public confidence in the press as an institution that should worry journalists. A survey by the Times-Mirror Center for the People and the Press cited lack of objectivity, emphasis on bad news, sensationalism, invasion of privacy, over coverage, and inaccuracies as the six major reasons the public distrusts the press. A Gallup media specialist notes in the second edition of *The Responsible Reporter* that only 2 per cent of all respondents believe newspaper reporters have very high ethical standards, and fewer than one in five think journalists are honest. Both findings are a twenty-year low. When the 1980s began, more than half of all Americans said they had "a great deal" or "quite a lot" of confidence in newspapers. Today the number is fewer than one third. The rating of broadcast journalists is little better. In fifteen years newspaper reporters have seen the number of people who thought the press had very high ethical standards nearly halved. One in four Americans now say they have very little or no confidence in newspapers or television news.

Journalism's fall from grace is all the more remarkable when one considers that less than a generation ago this country's best known journalist, Walter Cronkite, was annually voted the most trusted man in America. Today, journalists are in a statistical dead heat with Congressmen and car salesmen in terms of public perception of their honesty and ethics. Twice as many people think funeral directors have very high ethical standards as think that journalists do. The nation's much maligned police force outpaces journalists for honesty and ethics three to one. Americans have as much confidence in journalists as they do big business or organized labor and half as much confidence in journalism as they do the nation's military.

While it's true that Americans are increasingly skeptical about many institutions of national life, it's also true that few occupations have absorbed the hit journalism has taken in terms of public credibility. The Pew Center for the People and the Press notes that while three Americans in four are satisfied with their standard of living, more than nine in ten are satisfied with their family lives. That puts these numbers at a quarter-century high. But when asked about their attitude toward national life, Americans are deeply pessimistic. More than four in five express concern about crime. More than half express similar sentiments about health care and the economy. Whether one mentions the criminal justice system or Congress, the public schools or the presidency, a great majority of Americans are distressed by what they see and hear, and feel powerless to fix what must be repaired.

Seventy-five years ago Walter Lippmann observed that the picture Americans had of the world was increasingly mass-mediated. The complexity of twentieth-century living, Lippmann reasoned, would force more and more readers to turn to the press to give them something they could no longer get for themselves, and that was a picture of the world that would be the basis for how one saw the world and one's place in it. At century's end, that picture has rarely been so bleak. Andrew Kohut of the Pew Center and Derek Bok, author of *State of the Nation*, both see the press playing its part in turning people off to public life. The appetite for scandal and the search for the sensational has, in the mind of former New Jersey Senator Bill Bradley, created conditions where the public no longer sees a connection between one's personal life and the life of the nation as a whole. In the mad dash to sustain one's share of a diminishing audience, the press has abandoned previous patterns of objectivity, balance, and fairness that made the press an indispensable instrument in linking the electorate to its democracy. As a consequence, citizens in record numbers opt out of the process. They do not vote. They do not participate. And they watch the passing spectacle with growing derision and anxiety. That is why not only the future of the press but the future of a republican form of government is implied in the current crisis gripping the news business.

Origins of the Issue

From *Publick Occurrences* to the rise of the penny press, few readers ever expected the press to be fair, impartial, or balanced in what it reported. That 140-year period generally saw the press as a mouthpiece for whoever was paying the bills. Sometimes it was the crown. Sometimes it was the colony or interests within the colony. Benjamin Franklin had urged a kind of neutrality on colonial printers, but that wasn't in the interest of objectivity. As David Sloan and Julie Williams demonstrate in their book, *The Early American Press, 1690-1783*, the concept of newspaper neutrality developed out of the earlier notion that printing was simply a business and should be done for customers despite their point of view. Furthermore, running a newspaper could sometimes be such a marginal enterprise that printers were reluctant to alienate readers. That neutrality, however, was more and more difficult to maintain as the colonies lurched toward rebellion. Those newspapers that encouraged caution were seen as Tory. They risked having their presses confiscated and their printers tarred and feathered. The threat, understandably, curtailed genuine conversation. Thomas Leonard has noted in *The Power of the Press* that revolutionary editors reported British leaders were part of a "criminal class." And regardless of George Washington's initial incapacity to lead the revolutionary army, Carol Sue Humphrey observed in "Media and Wartime Morale" that he was nevertheless portrayed as our heroic general. Alternate opinions rarely saw their way into print.

After the revolution had been won, editors opposing the centralization of power through a chief executive were locked out of the constitutional convention. Only papers favoring a strengthened federal government were welcome. They got out the news that those fashioning a new nation were to be trusted, while publicizing the contention that without power sharing the country could not stand. Politics was a shouting and sometimes violent matter in the 1790s and was fueled by competing newspapers that called each other names. Federalist papers were certain the Republicans under Thomas Jefferson were anarchists. The Republican press was positive the Federalists were monarchists. And so it went. The Adams administration attempted to silence the Republican press.

Jefferson praised the power of a free press, but that didn't stop him from encouraging state prosecutions of Federalist editors when he took his turn in the White House.

The political press of the eighteenth century remained the pattern for the first third of the next century. Separate worlds existed for what was said and what was published. Politicians of the period agreed with John Quincy Adams that it was bad enough to have to make a speech and worse yet to have it printed. Politicians expected and were often able to report their own speeches. In 1820, the Missouri Compromise was seen as too controversial to report. When Andrew Jackson emerged later in the decade, he royally rewarded through patronage those editors who had been with him and succeeded in breaking a great many who had been against him.

It wasn't until the Industrial Revolution had helped to create a democratic marketplace that a new kind of newspaper remotely approximating the one we now know began to emerge. A high-speed press made it possible for editors to sell their papers for a penny to urban audiences who were newly literate. Political partisanship no longer paid as well as delivering a significant readership to advertisers. Editors were now able to claim that their papers were free from special interests and sought only to serve "the people." In doing so, these editors cloaked their enterprises in the role of civil servant, claiming they gave readers the unvarnished information the public needed to encourage their participation in the political process. Now that they were about the people's business, editors argued, they should be given the widest latitude in public comment without fear of government intrusion.

The Founding Fathers had seen a free and unfettered press as fundamental to the promotion of public dialogue that made self-governing possible. That was why they made the press the country's only commercial enterprise worthy of First Amendment protection. Historians, though, have been divided on the question of whether editors were to be taken seriously when they later said "objectivity" would guide the stories they ran. The sociologist Michael Schudson, among others, has argued, in *Discovering the News*, that editors had an economic incentive to serve the interests of working class readers by giving them information that furthered their participation in public life. Dan Schiller, however, claimed in *Objectivity and the News* that penny press editors used objectivity as a strategic ritual to serve not the public but the powerful. Schiller argued that claims of balance, fairness, and impartiality in journalistic storytelling disguise the press' true purpose, which is to reinforce the status quo and to make sure that those who have power continue to hold it.

Objectivity has remained a professional paradigm in journalism since the

1830s, although reporters in any era would be the first to admit that fairness suffers in times of national crisis. Louis Starr's *Bohemian Brigade* depicted one-sided, hyperbolic reporting by Northern newsmen during the Civil War. Quintus Wilson saw the same bias in Southern newspapers in the Confederate Press Association. The news media willingly demonized the German Hun during the First World War, wrote James Startt in "The Media and Political Culture," and the press was little more than a mouthpiece for Franklin Roosevelt in the war that followed, claimed Richard Steele in "News of the Good War." The Vietnam and Persian Gulf wars appear to have followed this pattern. Michael Scherer and Daniel Hallin have shown that a negative press followed public opinion more than it led it during the Vietnam war. Hallin and Todd Gitlin have noted in "The Gulf War as Popular Culture and TV Drama" that the Persian Gulf War was so brief and was won so decisively that Americans had little time to consider the one-sided media coverage of that campaign.

There is a temptation even in peace for reporters to make facts fit prevailing sentiment and to sacrifice objectivity to the winds of public or official opinion. But that is where a journalist's training and reward system must prevail. When tabloids arose in the interwar era with their emphasis on sex and crime stories painted in purple prose, the country's leading editors embraced a professional code of conduct that reiterated journalism's long courtship of objectivity, balance, and fairness in getting at the truth. State press associations stated the same ideals, and journalism schools were launched to prepare reporters for careers in public service where they took their social responsibility seriously. Conservatives produced books, academic journals, and articles in the popular press hoping to reassure readers that the journalistic establishment was not about to abandon the standards of fairness and balanced fact-finding that had long won them a favorable following.

As veteran newspapermen in the 1920s were attempting to win back reader trust in journalism's professionalism, changes in technology threatened to undermine and overwhelm them. First radio, then television, took audiences to events the written word could only approximate. And their craftsmen and craftswomen had no histories of professional objectivity to overcome in telling stories as they saw them. William Stott observed in "Documenting Media" that readers distrusted what reporters wrote, but as listeners, believed everything Edward R. Murrow told them about the Battle of Britain. That same audience, Robert Stam would write in "Television and Its Spectator," liked its TV news both shocking and reassuring. The world's bloodletting needed to be viewed at a distance and from the safety of an easy chair. Defenders of this entertainment model of newsgathering now argue what has worked for broadcast media can be made to work for print. They would like newspapers to look more like magazines and magazines more like television if they are to attract and hold an audience. In an era of contracting audiences and rapidly rising costs, news departments find themselves forced to justify the bottom line to businessmen with little or no experience in journalism who will make the decisions affecting journalism's future. Bill Gates and other key Internet figures argue that cyberspace is the twenty-first century's democratic marketplace. Journalism's critics, though, are left to wonder whether objectivity, balance, and fairness will be the values embedded in this worldwide web.

The Failures of Objectivity

There are no shortage of defenders of advocacy journalism. Carol Simpson, a longtime ABC news anchor, puts it simply. "I think the public now wants us to take a position," she told *Equal Time*, a talk show on CNBC. "I think people really kind of want you to direct their thinking on some issues." Simpson claims objectivity leads to audience uncertainty. "If you say on the one hand this and on the other hand that, it's boring." Journalism with a point of view "can make people care about an issue" and gives the journalist far greater freedom "to reach people and touch people, millions of people." Advocacy may mean the journalist substitutes his or her own judgment for that of readers in the presentation of information. As Thomas L. Friedman of *The New York Times* sees it, "I gather all the information I can. I cross out what I don't believe. And I write up the rest. And that's news."

The Enlightenment ideal had the reporter gathering all the information relevant to an issue, organizing it, and reporting it in context, trusting the audience to do the crossing out. But trusting the rational powers of readers and watchers to think for themselves and come up with the "right" answer has come in for a terrific beating in the academy and the classroom. *The News People*, a sociological study of American journalists and their training in the 1970s, noted what has since become all too obvious. Journalists-in-waiting came to distrust "facts" as a matter of educational philosophy. Their introductory college courses told them there was no knowledge without a knower. This implied all truth statements are statements of power and the struggle of someone's vision of reality over competing visions. This dominant reality might be called the metadiscourse, or the taken-for-granted, or the conventional wisdom. The freshmen humanities courses gave it different names, but each name seemed to say the say thing: a reporter's best detective work resulted not in truth-finding but in competing, interest-bound approximations of the truth.

The shift in elite understanding of the reportable universe is reflected in the textbooks of the journalism profession. Joseph Pulitzer emphasized "great powers of concentration and sustained effort" in outlining nearly a hundred years ago the need for journalism training. As late as the 1960s, Curtis MacDougall's *Interpretative Reporting* still likened the skill of the reporter to the training of the concert pianist who learns "Bach's two-part inventions." But by the 1980s the ninth edition of MacDougall's book was certain editors and reporters could "no longer pretend that the news does not involve their interpretations." MacDougall's book has plenty of company. Journalism textbooks in the 1990s tend to view objectivity as a "myth," according to Macmillan Publishing's *Getting the Story*, "that failed to meet society's needs for information." Clifford Christians, writing in *Media Ethics*, notes that "there is not a serious journalist who believes in objective truth anymore." "You can only give your perception of the truth," agrees Louis Hodges, an ethicist, from Washington and Lee University.

At a recent meeting of journalism historians, an editor for the *Philadelphia Inquirer* observed that the shift to greater subjectivity in the news sections of today's newspapers was a necessary and irreversible response to television's success in weaning audiences away from urban dailies. To survive, he told his audience, newspapers would have to read more like magazines and look like television. That meant less text and more pictures, less tiresome attribution, and more storytelling with the reporter-narrator as novelist. At annual meetings of the American Society of Newspaper Editors and the American Newspaper Publishers Association, the defense of subjectivity is the same. Three quarters of all Americans get all or most of their news from television, these executives reluctantly admit. By implication, these viewers already know what happened, if not why it happened. That means if newspapers are to survive they must be in the business of offering explanations and merchandising opinions of those they interview and those who report those interviews.

Part of this merchandising is increasing the visibility of print reporters on television. Thomas Rosenstiel and Alicia Shepard have written about the lengths leading newspapers and news magazines will go to get their star reporters on stage. There they often say what has or will appear in print. In so doing these trusted translators may achieve celebrity status, while serving to promote their publications as well as themselves. Punditry pays reporters for opinions — their own. Readers and viewers, admittedly, may have some difficulty separating a reporter's opinion from the opinion of those he or she reports on. But it is better for the reporter to be honest and on the record about opinions he holds, proponents of punditry suggest, than having the reporter hide behind sources who agree with him. The circuit of thirty TV talk shows assures print media and their consultants the kind of access necessary in keeping up with the competition.

Edwin Diamond and Stephen Klaidman have noted how *The New York Times*, long a leader in the establishment press, has adapted itself to the new environment in which newspapers are forced to operate. In "All the News That's Fit to Interpret," Klaidman details a growing "subjective tendency" in the *Times*, characterized by a high percentage of articles that interpret events in a critical tone in the absence of sourcing. Diamond traces the change in tone to editor Max Frankel's insistence the paper find more ways of being "user friendly." This meant making the paper easier to read and creating for under-40 readers a "with it" image. A search for younger readers and improved advertising revenues now made America's journal of record report the news with an attitude. Nancy Reagan and Frank Sinatra upstairs at the White House would make the front page in the new *Times*. So did stories on Utah polygamy, do-it-yourself sex videos, and sleepovers. Publisher Arthur Ochs Sulzberger, Jr., called the pieces "sociology" while reaffirming in a promotional video that the new *Times* was still "newspapering of the highest order." Klaidman saw it as an effort to compete with television on its own terms.

Matthew Ehrlich has written that "taking sides" is central to the new journalism. It uses irony and innocence to tell tales of celebrity gossip and sex crimes. Human interest stories of victim and victimizer play well to audiences inattentive to the daily run of political reporting. Jon Katz of *Rolling Stone* is one of the most enthusiastic advocates of what he calls "new news." He points out that fewer than half of all Americans in their twenties read newspapers and only a third in their thirties read one daily. The only way to win them back, Katz asserts, is to abandon the "old news" practices of the establishment press with the "dazzling, adolescent, fearless" reporting of "new news." To do this, he insists, the tone and substance of reporting must change. Sex, race, crime, celebrities, and spiritualism, he argues, are the pop culture themes that win. The president, the Congress, and the courts are the preoccupations of the white male establishment media that is increasingly out of touch with youth, women, Blacks, Hispanics, gays, and Asians.

Veteran CBS anchor man Dan Rather summed up the position of advocacy journalism and tabloid TV by admitting the competitive pressures of "a volcanic era" in newsgathering required new approaches to win and hold an audience. Rather told CNN's Larry King in January 1997 that news organizations were not as free as they once were to operate with a blind eye to the bottom line. The realization that news could turn a profit had led to the triumph of entertainment values in the news. In other words, the networks now did news not for prestige but profit. He wondered whether media preoccupation with the Jon Benet-

Ramsey case wasn't an exercise in "kiddie porn" and whether the O.J. Simpson case was not "terribly overdone," but suggested news directors and news anchors felt "their pants were on fire" if they failed to follow the stories others were following.

More than half of all journalists responding to the *Times-Mirror* survey agreed that journalists were too cynical, and two-thirds admitted they were too focused on the misdeeds and personal failings of public figures. Two-thirds of national journalists and more than one-half of those in local media markets said they paid too little attention to good news. But *Washington Post* media critic Howard Kurtz observes that journalists are less cynical than the general public. National journalists were three times more likely and local reporters twice as likely to give federal officials high marks for honesty compared to their readers and viewers. Kurtz finds these citizens have a "growing sense of alienation" from politics and public life in America. He sees the subjectivity of the press as an effort to break through the tide of public indifference.

Christiane Amanpour, the London-born CNN correspondent who won an Emmy and a Peabody Award for her reporting in Bosnia, argues that advocacy in times of tragedy is necessary to awaken public opinion. "In certain situations," she explains, "objectivity can mean neutrality and neutrality can mean you are an accomplice to all sorts of evil." To her mind "genocide and crimes against humanity" required reporters to take a stand and to name those guilty. To do less was to evade her responsibility as a reporter. The United Nations and the Clinton administration may have been uncertain who was responsible for shelling a Sarajevo marketplace in February 1994 that killed sixty-eight, but she wasn't. She was "disgusted" by the "flip-flop" of the Clinton administration on the war and told the president so in a televised press conference. Amanpour saw the war in terms of "a clear aggressor and a clear victim," and her reporting reflected that certainty. Reporter Mary Battiata, writing in the *Washington Post,* agreed. She also identified with those in Sarajevo who had suffered under the shelling. To do less, she argues, would have made reporters "cows chewing their cud."

Editors are not unaware of public disenchantment with current press practice, and a majority see sourcing patterns as a big reason why. Attribution in nearly half of all assertions appearing in print in big city dailies barely a decade ago have been reduced by a third. Sometimes interpretation is substituted for a sourced assertion. Sometimes "anonymous sources" are cited. Four of every five editors answering an Ohio University survey said using unnamed sources made stories less credible, but a majority of these said competition forced them to do it. More than half of these editors thought anonymous sources would go on the record if reporters pushed harder but admitted that deadlines did not always make this possible. Managing editor of the Associated Press Darrell Christian acknowledges "putting names with the facts" might solve a reporter's credibility problem, but the *Washington Post's* Bob Woodward believes that would leave a lot of important news unreported. The problem, he admits, is that so many reporters have become comfortable with anonymous sources that it is difficult for the reader or the viewer to know the difference between when an unnamed source is necessary and when they're being lied to.

There is still a certain amount of self-consciousness in journalism's romance with the subjective. Few seem fully satisfied that the embrace of advocacy with its abandonment of previous standards of fact-finding is a good thing. But the perceived realities of the news business, with its contracting and indifferent audience, along with intense competition and attention to the bottom line, have led reluctant reporters, editors, and correspondents to submit themselves to the inevitable. The entertainment model of newsgathering, long on point of view and telling a good story, is where journalism is headed, they argue, if it is to continue to attract and hold the attention of its audience.

In Defense of Objectivity and Sourcing

When Walter Cronkite briefly appeared in a sketch on the *Mary Tyler Moore Show* in 1974, it was only over the strong objections of Richard Salant, his boss at CBS News. Salant was certain that Cronkite's appearance as himself on the popular comedy show would confuse viewers and detract from Cronkite's image as the most trusted man in America. Cronkite appeared on the show in a well received two-minute segment that did little to tarnish a reputation for objectivity and fairness developed during four decades' work for wire services and CBS. But the story shows how far the news business has come in promoting the celebrity of its reporters as a means of maximizing the visibility of its on air talent. The current ad campaign for CBS News, for instance, promotes its news operation by running a montage of reporters' faces. It's actually unclear what Dan Rather, Randall Pinkston, Eric Engberg, Scott Pelley, Vicki Mabrey, Ray Brady, David Martin, Rita Braver, Jim Stewart, and Bob Simon are saying. There's little time for that. The point of these close-up shots is that these are the authorities to be trusted. The climax of the ad is a wide-eyed Dan Rather speaking over a drum roll. "All in a day's work," he tells the viewer. The claim appears clear. Each of the networks tease in more or less the same way. MSNBC is more contemporary in its approach. Its talent indicates a desire to "get connected."

Cronkite feels frankly uncomfortable with efforts to promote the reporter over the story. The celebrity culture of network commentators that he helped create with his work on Kennedy, Vietnam, and Watergate leaves him cold. Cronkite holds to an Enlightenment Model of the press that claims the reporter is not more important than the story and is not an important part of the story. He now notes that on the rare public occasions where he spoke his mind, his comments were always labeled news analysis. He sees no harm in reporters feeling passionately about a story, but believes the time and place to erupt on air or in print should be clearly indicated. To do otherwise, he warns, is to invite the drop in journalistic credibility that is now all too apparent. "The people's doubt that they are getting the truth can turn to cynicism," Cronkite worries, "which spreads through the populous like a virus. It eats away at confidence in all the nation's institutions and threatens the very foundation of democracy."

The media writer for the *Los Angeles Times,* Thomas Rosenstiel, agrees with Cronkite. "Today the idea of straight reporting is giving way to something else," he says. That something else, he fears, is "a new era of subjectivity." Rosenstiel feels highly interpretative journalism is an exercise in self-promotion for the reporters writing or airing these stories and for the companies they represent. Writing in *The Future of News,* he notes that some reporters might achieve "celebrity status" as a result of this approach, winning better assignments and higher pay but at a terrible price. A "culture of assertion journalism," he argues, "mirrors the devaluation of substance" in reporting that has alienated much of 1990s journalism from its audience. The campaign of big time reporters and their organizations to increase their visibility in a crowded, competitive media marketplace blurs the lines between reporter and the reportable universe, Rosenstiel argues. It reduces the reporter to little more than professional "kibbitzer," whose findings on a story are viewed with the same skepticism as any other news source.

Rosenstiel's warning is confirmed in an analysis of news content by Matthew Ehrlich. His *Journalism Monograph* article, "The Journalism of Outrageousness," shows how more and more of the values of tabloid television news seep into the self-respecting journalism establishment. Its conventions include a cynical story-telling that makes the reporter the authority over the characters and issues that ostensibly are the subject of the story. Crime, sex, and celebrity gossip are at the center of this journalistic gaze, Ehrlich writes, with irony, sarcasm and heavy doses of sentiment the customary tone of these reports. Ehrlich finds storytelling formulas of victim and victimizer consistent in tabloid and establishment journalism. Each relies on the personality of the storyteller to walk audiences through a sensational maze of fact and innuendo. Ehrlich has no doubt this dramatic model of news narrative gains an audience's attention but wonders what its overall impact is on journalistic credibility.

David Broder, a nationally syndicated columnist for the *Washington Post*, believes the rise in celebrity journalism and advocacy storytelling has created a "crisis in confidence in journalism" with "serious people asking whether we have lost our way." Broder deplores what he sees as a growing cynicism among reporters, who substitute their distrust of public people and institutions for journalism's traditional calling "to check it out." The cynic, Broder told students at the University of Minnesota, "never expects candor or truth," or anything other than "self-interest narrowly pursued." Paul Starobin, writing in the *Columbia Journalism Review*, senses the same contemptuous tone in much of contemporary journalism. He describes it as an "ethos of disgruntlement" that doesn't serve the public well. Broder worries what readers and viewers are to believe when there is "no longer a clear distinction between journalists and civic leaders." Starobin sees reporters substituting cynicism for the curiosity that once drove the investigative process. A "search for hypocrisy" is both hip and dismissive. When reporters complete this "seductive retreat from belief," he says, they "produce little that is enduring" and even less for their readers and viewers to believe in.

The country is awash in "punditry," Alicia Shepard warily observes in *American Journalism Review*. More than thirty "shout shows" are now on the air with highly visible reporters from leading newspapers and news magazines telling viewers what they may or may not have told them that day or week in print. The "journalist as performer" accelerates journalism's "waning credibility," Shepard argues, and rewards reporters "for the wrong reasons." "Punditocracy" reminds Broder of "the last scene from Orwell's *Animal Farm*. You can't tell the journalists from the politicians, the watch dog from the running dog. It's not just that they're in bed with each other, it's that they have become one in the same." The result, according to Shepard, is that audiences tend to deride the fact-finding mission of the news media.

James Fallows, the veteran media critic for the *Atlantic Monthly* who now edits *U.S. News and World Report*, finds the high profile of some reporters a professional "pestilence." Self-promotion, he is certain, "is directly at odds with what you are supposed to be and do as a reporter." The "journalist as performer," he argues, is not "more important than the topic he covers." When he tries to be, he sacrifices his credibility and a bit of the profession's at the same time, while driving a widening wedge between the press and its public. The occupational absorption of coming to a conclusion on a story often substitutes a reporter's opinion for fact-finding, Fallows suspects. The *Times-Mirror* only serves to show the great perception gap in what reporters think the public thinks of them and what the public does think. "Americans hate the media," Fallows concludes, because a journalism of self-promotion "gets in the way of solving the nation's problems."

First Amendment authorities Marc Franklin and Vincent Blasi note that the relationship between the press and the public, as outlined in the First Amendment, is founded in a mutual faith. The public trusts the media to live up to their watchdog role in checking government abuses, these authors write, and to provide the electorate with information it needs to fully participate in public life. The information is not prescriptive and relies instead on competing sources of information, carefully and thoroughly contextualized, to facilitate the widest possible public participation in decision-making. Fundamental to this approach is the confidence of the press in the public's ability to make rational decisions when provided with the necessary information.

The authors' old-fashioned faith in the common sense of ordinary Americans may strike many young reporters as Capraesque, if not Kafkaesque. What it suffers in idealism, they would argue, it more than makes up for in its absurdity. Two world wars, seventy years of Freud, Camus, Sarte, Vietnam, Watergate, the celebration of the unconscious, the irrational, and the perceived malleability of audiences seen in effects research is more than enough to per-suade many reporters coming into the profession that readers and listeners are guided by sentiment when they are paying attention at all. Journalism that attempts to reach them through a sober summary of conflicting positions only frustrates and alienates them. Diminishing circulations and contracting audi-ences, they argue, only prove their point. And so senior editors, who once knew better, in an act of desperation, fail to blue pencil the very utterance that would have been laughed off the front page or the evening news just a few years ago.

The problem with the advocacy and entertainment model of storytelling, according to Frank Rich, a *New York Times* columnist from the old school, is that it crowds out the legitimate news that then fails to get a hearing. First-ness takes precedence over substance. "Journalists used to have a two-source rule," says Howard Kurtz of the *Washington Post*. "Now we have a no source rule." Kurtz notes that the drive to be first, exaggerated by the immediacy of television and radio, has put "even the most serious news organizations into the position of publishing or airing information that often tends to be half-baked." Osborn Elliott, a former editor at *Newsweek* now teaching at Columbia University, notes that "in the race for readers, ratings and advertising dollars, it's become all too tempting to sensationalize and to trivialize." Nowhere is this temptation clearer, Elliott says, than in the tendency to abandon clearly defined standards in sourc-ing and objectivity. Elliott's colleague at Columbia, Henry Graff, concurs. "We now have a new judgment of what constitutes news," he says. "More and more opinion leaks into news reporting" with the public unaware of whose opinions these are and what weight they should attach to them.

Bill Kovach, the curator of Harvard University's Nieman Foundation, told *American Journalism Review* that when reporters become advocates they "lose their unique and irreplaceable standing" as the sole source of information that can be trusted in accessing and assessing the problems of the day. Balance, fairness, and impartiality "does not mean that all sides in a conflict are presented in a context of moral equivalency." But it does mean that "all sides do have standing in a story and that standing rises and falls of its own weight." He sees advocacy journalism as the easy way out. It allows reporters "off the hook" by allowing them to substitute their emotional opinion for a carefully reasoned sourced assertion. David Binder, a veteran foreign correspondent of *The New York Times,* observes that reporters "play God" when they abandon objectivity as an occupational value. "Our job is to report from all sides," he says, "not to play favorites." He urges reporters to report and to leave propaganda to those in the propaganda business. Even Bob Steele, the director of the Poynter Institute's ethics program, who sees a proper place for advocacy journalism, believes when reporters take positions based on personal beliefs, it is up to the editor to bring out the blue pencil.

One editor who insists reporters go the extra mile before their copy appears in print is Mary Hargrove of the *Arkansas Democrat-Gazette.* She told *American Journalism Review* that the proliferation of anonymous sources further erodes whatever confidence the public had in the press. Reporters need to be told to "take that extra step," she says, in getting sources to go on the record. If they don't "it's just cheap shot heaven." Michael Gartner, former president of NBC News and now editor and part owner of the *Daily Tribune* in Ames, Iowa won't accept anonymous quotes under any circumstances. Readers deserve to know where the information came from, Gartner maintains. How else can they determine whether or not to trust it? Gartner warns that anonymous sources can "lie without accountability" and further damage journalism's shaky alliance with its audience.

W. Lance Bennett, a political scientist at the University of Washington, is among those who maintain the news we're getting "isn't fit for a democracy." In *News: The Politics of Illusion,* he castigates the narrative devices designed to interest and entertain an audience in hopes of delivering numbers to an advertiser. He agrees with Blasi and Franklin that news is not like any other good or service. It has an exclusive constitutional protection from government infringement because of the unique relationship it has to an informed electorate. This makes news unlike any other commodity, and the men and women who search for and present the news as a living have a greater obligation than any movie star or talk show panelist to provide audiences with what they need to make sense of the world.

Resolution

It isn't likely that Dan Rather, Peter Jennings, or Tom Brokaw will go on network television tonight or any other night, look into the studio camera, and implore viewers to tune in tomorrow because each enjoys their seven-figure annual salary and would like to keep it. And even if they did, it is unlikely viewers would be moved by the admission. The claim that the networks and their print consorts are pouring over every delicious detail in the O.J. Simpson case, or the Jon Benet-Ramsey case, or the Richard Jewell case, or the Bill Cosby case because they seek to serve their audience with what they need to know, is a pose few take seriously. Big city dailies and the small town weeklies are stuck with the same predicament that affects the big networks and the minor ones, radio news in big towns and the headline service in small ones. For 160 years journalists have justified their existence by making the claim of civil servant. The only claim that's ever stuck is that the public's business is its business and that's why it's in business. That is not to suggest that press practice always or even often reflected this reality. But the problem for the press is that is the only explanation it can give for enjoying a constitutional protection other businesses would kill for. Any other claim is sure to sound sour to an American public that feels betrayed by a press that has betrayed it.

This sense of betrayal is why journalistic credibility is sinking like a stone and why Americans feel so passionate about the fix they find themselves in. The problem they see in the press is not one of style but substance. That's what reader and viewer surveys are saying, if only those in the news media had the eyes to see it. The public is neither stupid nor inattentive. It sees what is happening and is switching its remote, putting down its paper, and moving its mouse in other directions. The harder it tries, the more superfluous the media becomes. Candidates are taking their messages directly to the American people through television and radio talk shows and town meetings, and the public likes it that way. The networks bail out of reporting national nominating conventions, and few seem to care.

If the press continues to promote itself as more important than the stories it is covering, readers and listeners will continue to get their information elsewhere. The more news organizations attempt to raise reporters to celebrity status the greater will be the public's disdain. When Geraldo Rivera issues his "official statement" to viewers as the jury returns its verdict in the O.J. Simpson civil trial, one is moved to painful laughter. The anonymous reporter who once played the role of civil servant is now the actor at the center of the stage. The play is simply a pretext for him to perform, and the implication is that the audience is paying for the privilege of seeing him act. Audiences who might be moved by great actors can be forgiven for not taking the performance of star reporters seriously. When celebrity reporters became persuaded the lines they delivered mattered more than the play itself, audiences understandably began to feel more than a little used. And audience surveys show that's what once faithful readers and listeners are feeling in unprecedented numbers.

The only recourse for journalists interested in the future of the profession is to stop selling personality and to get back to serving their audience. The celebrity culture, in part created by the media, is a trap for those reporters who tumble into it. How can viewers believe a reporter's standup on the White House lawn when a talk show appearance by the same reporter implied the president is a bum? The Gospel notes that the messenger must decrease, so that the message may increase. That is good news for the journalist also. Journalists are not more important than the stories they cover or the public they serve. News is decidedly not like any other commodity. Producing news is not the manufacture of corn flakes or soap bubbles. It was once taken far more seriously because it saw its responsibility far more clearly. Journalists owe readers and listeners now what they've long required from the profession—a story that is fair, balanced, and as objective as a reporter and editor can make it. When the story's over, no one should know, and few will care, what the reporter thought about the story. That's an unequivocal exercise in fantasy. Fantasy. Ultimately, it's the story that counts. The only thing that is important is when given all the available and relevant information, what do readers and viewers think and what do they plan to do about it? That's all journalists can or should do, and that's all their audience requires they do. After journalists have done that job, they need to trust them to do theirs.

Recommended Readings

Books

Bennett, W. Lance. News, *The Politics of Illusion*. New York: Longman, 1988. A political scientist attacks newsgathering and storytelling practices that he does not consider fit for a democracy.

Diamond, Edwin. *Behind the Times: Inside The New New York Times*. New York: Villard Books, 1994. Villard describes a "wild streak" that appears in the *Times,* with editor Max Frankel urging greater interpretation in the paper's news pages as a way of attracting and keeping a younger readership.

Evensen, Bruce J., ed. *The Responsible Reporter*, 2nd ed. Northport, Ala: Vision Press, 1997.

Twenty journalism educators and journalists offer practical advice to students about to enter the profession in light of Gallup Poll data indicating a withering of audience confidence in journalists. Michael Buchholz's Chapter 2, "History of Reporting," provides a particularly useful overview of the development of objective and interpretive reporting.

Fallows, James. *Breaking the News: How the Media Undermine American Democracy.* New York: Pantheon, 1996. The author examines what the erosion of objectivity means to American democracy.

MacDougall, Curtis D., and Robert D. Reid. *Interpretative Reporting,* 9th ed. New York: Macmillan, 1987. This journalism textbook shows the shift in abandoning objectivity as a professional paradigm.

Schudson, Michael. *Discovering the News: A Social History of American Newspapers.* New York: Basic Books, 1978. An examination of the rise of objectivity as a professional value among nineteenth-century journalists.

Schulte, Henry H., and Marcel P. Dufresne. *Getting the Story: An Advanced Reporting Guide to Beats, Records and Sources.* New York: Macmillan, 1994. This textbook for journalism students is typical of dozens of manuals now on the market deploring objectivity as a nostalgic and self-limiting practice of yesteryear's journalistic establishment.

Schiller, Dan. *Objectivity and the News.* Philadelphia: University of Pennsylvania, 1981. Schiller considers nineteenth-century claims of journalistic objectivity a strategic ritual by which journalists served the powerful.

Startt, James D., and Wm. David Sloan, *The Significance of the Media in American History.* Northport, Ala.: Vision Press, 1994. An excellent summary of the historical development of American journalism that includes an analysis of the rise of objectivity as a journalistic standard.

Articles & Book Chapters

Ehrlich, Matthew C. "The Journalism of Outrageousness: Tabloid Television News vs. Investigative News." *Journalism Monographs* (1996). The author compares and contrasts the values of television news with that of traditional, investigative reporting.

Evensen, Bruce J. "Journalism's Struggle over Ethics and Professionalism during America's Jazz Age." *Journalism History* 16 (Autumn-Winter 1989): 54-63. The manufacture of celebrity and civic spectacle by jazz age journalists anticipates the contemporary tendency towards tabloid journalism and storytelling as entertainment.

Fallows, James. "Why Americans Hate the Media." *The Atlantic Monthly* (February 1996): 45-64. The essayist examines the primary reasons why the news media establishment has become so unpopular.

Ricchiardi, Sherry. "Over the Line?" *American Journalism Review* (September 1996): 25-31.

An Indiana University professor analyzes advocacy journalism in the reporting of the war in Bosnia.

Rosenstiel, Thomas B. "Talk-Show Journalism," chapter 5 in Philip S. Cook, ed., *The Future of News*. Washington, D.C.: Woodrow Wilson Center; and Baltimore: Johns Hopkins University, 1992. The chapter analyzes the rise of celebrity journalism at the expense of public confidence in the news media.

Shepard, Alicia C. "The Pundit Explosion." *American Journalism Review* (September 1995): 24-9. The analyst interviews journalists and gets their reaction to the rise of punditry in television journalism.

Starobin, Paul. "A Generation of Vipers: Journalists and the New Cynicism." *Columbia Journalism Review* (March/April 1995): 25-32. The author describes five kinds of cynicism he finds in the contemporary news media and examines its consequences.

Chapter Twenty-six

Conflict and Controversy as News Values

Margot Hardenbergh

Judging from current media practices, conflict and controversy are the essence of news. The stories of conflict drown out those of resolution. News of unrest in Albania, civil war in Zaire, and tensions in the Middle East emblazon the front page, while news of a brief tranquility in Communist China is buried in the middle pages. Stories of cooperation and amiable resolutions are saved for the last few minutes of a newscast, if carried at all. Tradition and training support this emphasis on conflict and controversy. In their definition of news, journalism textbooks state that a combination of qualities determine whether or not something is newsworthy: timeliness, significance, proximity, prominence, controversy, and conflict. But conflict is what marks most news stories: conflict in war, politics, and crime.

The emphasis on conflict and controversy has created its own controversy. Many critics call for a change in our news values because the emphasis on conflict and controversy leads to superficial and even pernicious journalism. Critics contend that journalists cover an issue or event only if there is opposition. The media cover politics as a horserace, for example, instead of discussing the complexities of policy. Some say that politics is a fight for power, so that the coverage of politics would necessarily be the coverage of conflict. But that very coverage of the conflict of politics has a negative impact on the citizenry. Because there is so much news presented as conflict between opposing interest groups, the public has become cynical and any sense of community has been destroyed.

Others criticize the media for ignoring the important controversial issues. A news story covering a government agency's dispute with a private business over water pollution fails to let readers know if the water's safe to drink. The journalists cover the votes taken on either side of an issue, rather than delving into the new policy's implications.

Most journalists acknowledge their obligation to help the citizenry make decisions, to report on what is happening, to get ideas out into the public forum.

Most are committed to objectivity and dread being criticized as biased. However, to protect themselves, journalists report two opposing sides of an issue as if the truth were somewhere in between. They frame the issue as a conflict.

Some critics have suggested that journalists eliminate conflict and controversy as news values, while others urge journalists to approach conflict and controversy with more depth, claiming that to report the news is to report conflict. The defenders of journalism's emphasis on conflict and controversy respond that journalists are obligated to cover politics as controversial issues; they need to include drama in their stories to attract the readers; and their professional tenets force them to include opposing points of view. Their arguments imply that if conflict and controversy were deemphasized, journalism would have no beneficial function for society.

Origins of the Issue

This journalistic dilemma emerged prior to the formation of an American free press and the development of professional journalism. News of war victories, road races, and violent crimes have always traveled fast and been received eagerly. Before print and broadcast technologies, messengers ran marathons to announce war victories; tales of far off disasters were quickly disseminated by word of mouth and by songs; and people listened voraciously to the horrors of other people's strange behaviors, in public meeting places and behind closed doors.

Conflict has been the essence of news historically, but not all conflict has been published. Despite many attempts to censor information, the news of conflict and controversy would still get through. As Mitchell Stephens notes in his *History of News*, in the sixteenth century, for example, the predecessor to the newspapers, newsbooks, did not carry any of the sensational news of Queen Ann Boleyn's execution — but people knew about it nevertheless.

War coverage was also mollified for readers, tending to carry only victorious news. The British only read reports of their few successful battles against the Ottoman Empire in the sixteenth century, but news of the tragic battles would also be heard and discussed in the coffee houses.

Wars and journalism have often been intertwined. The French Revolution may have been ignited by the authorities' attempts to squelch all publications. For the American Revolution, the press unified the colonies by urging its readers to fight. The Civil War made newspapers a habit for Americans as they sought information on their loved ones. World War II contributed to the rise of broadcast journalism, as Edward R. Murrow and his colleagues brought the sounds of war back home to Americans.

Conflicting ideas have also been the grist of news. In her book *Journalistic Standards of the 19th Century*, Hazel Dicken-Garcia describes how the press had maintained a political bias, starting with passage of the Constitution: each side of a controversial issue would establish its own newspaper to promote its viewpoints. Newspapers were started as vehicles for people to wage political campaigns, then closed down after the election. In order to read many viewpoints, the reader would have to read many publications.

Despite debate about whether to maintain a partisan press or publish papers that served all political viewpoints, conflict remained the core of news. During the penny press era, as newspapers appealed to larger audiences, they began reporting events, not only political ideas. Journalists began to see themselves as guardians of the public good, or watchdogs. In 1883 Joseph Pulitzer, publisher of *New York World*, charged his staff to consistently challenge authority, for the good of the public, whether that authority came from economics, politics, or class.

As news became increasingly more competitive in the nineteenth century, conflict and controversy continued as major news values. By the 1890s the narrative form became the norm for many journalists. As journalists became storytellers, including drama as a device to hold the reader, conflict and controversy became more entrenched in news. And the search for the dramatic led papers to cover one crisis after another, one crime on top of another crime. Publishers were known to create controversy, simply to help sales. William Randolph Hearst has been accused of instigating the Spanish-American War to increase his paper's circulation.

By the twentieth century, newspapers had become big business, and the best way to improve that business was to increase circulation with coverage of more conflict and controversy. Broadcast journalists inherited these news values and further increased the emphasis on conflict and controversy. Not only would newscasts open with stories of violence and catastrophe, but they also highlighted opposing points of view and shifts in power in terms simple enough to understand via oral transmission. The first radio newscast by a licensed broadcaster covered the presidential election of 1920. And later, it became obvious that television could make or break political candidates, as it did during the Kennedy-Nixon debates of 1960. Even more dramatically, journalists could help unseat the President of the United States, as *Washington Post* reporters and the televised Watergate hearings did with President Richard Nixon in 1974.

Most journalists have defended their emphasis on conflict and controversy as a necessary component of good journalism. They need to report all sides of political issues and all political candidates. They need to frame reality into a story to make reality comprehensible to their audience, and the story form calls for the inclusion of conflict. And the coverage of conflicts leads journalists to uncover more issues for the public.

Appropriate Emphasis on Conflict

Most agree that news is appropriately about conflict and controversy. If journalists cover politics, for example, they will be need to reveal the differences among candidates and to describe the various aspects of policy issues to help inform the citizenry. In his introduction to *Newsmen & National Defense: Is Conflict Inevitable?* Lloyd Matthews notes that journalists in a democratic society have the obligation to cover and report on war. It is their duty to cover conflict and controversy, to inform the public about what their government is doing and the different points of view from which they can gauge an issue.

The Constitution guarantees freedom of speech to encourage public debate and freedom of the press to cover that debate. In *Reporters and Officials*, Leo Sigal wrote that he studied newsmakers and sources because he saw news as a forum for the competition for power. In her study of the profession of journalism, *A Place in the News*, Kay Mills found that politics was the best beat for a reporter to have, because politics is about power and where people want to be led.

Journalists and politicians depend on each other. Journalists need politicians to supply content for their outlets; politicians need news coverage to win votes. Politicians understand that the easiest way to get coverage is to bring a counter argument to their opponent's position. Political scientist Christopher Arterton, in *Media Politics*, refers to the campaign as a power struggle between the press and the candidates, in which each side has a major source of influence: the press through its control of what gets reported and the candidates through their control of what is said.

The desire of journalists to be fair or objective also encourages the use of conflict and controversy as news values. Herbert Gans in *Deciding What's News*, a study of the practice of journalism in print and broadcast, describes how journalists protect themselves from criticism and from the consequences of the news by seeking to balance stories and report a variety of opinions. (This is a sharp change from the partisan press era of the early nineteenth century, when each paper represented a specific ideology.) To avoid any appearance of bias in covering controversial issues or in anticipation of protest from a vocal minority, the reporter attempts to look for opposing viewpoints and report each in an equitable way. Gaye Tuchman, in her book *Making News*, found that reporters may actually create conflict by interviewing those whom they know to disagree with each other. She cites an example of a reporter who created an issue by searching for a senator willing to criticize a bill that most senators supported. Through this newsgathering process, the media create, cover, and control the controversial coverage.

Others note that conflict is news by definition, because news is that which is out of the ordinary. News is exciting; it's dramatic. In *Interplay of Influence*, all the elements that Kathleen Hall Jamieson describes as criteria for long-term or ongoing issues in the news are phrased as conflicts: 1) appearance versus reality, 2) little guys versus big guys, 3) good against evil, 4) efficiency versus inefficiency, 5) the unique versus the routine. And Jamieson finds that the journalist will frame the information into a story about conflict to make it coherent and to gain attention.

Many think that a good journalist is a good storyteller. The journalist must be able to provide an interesting narrative that attracts and holds the audience's interest. In his classic 1963 study, *The Press and Foreign Policy*, Bernard Cohen found that reporters believe that stories written in terms of sharp conflict increase the sale of newspapers. In 1974 Edward J. Epstein, in his *News from Nowhere*, reported how a major television news producer wrote a memo to his staff, telling them to be sure to include the attributes of drama in their stories: to have conflict with rising and falling action, a beginning, middle and end. In the 1975 article, "Writing News and Telling Stories," Robert Darnton writes of his experiences as a newspaper reporter. The very conception of news derived from the tradition of storytelling and has taken its form from storytelling techniques. In a recent article in the *Investigative Reporters & Editors Journal*, Dawn Hobbs called for the reporter to use literary techniques to make a story more meaningful to readers. Don't simply tell the truth, she suggested. Use foreshadowing, flashbacks, conflict, and resolution to explain ordinary incidents.

Hunter McCartney studied newspapers, news magazines, and television newscasts looking for the type of conflict and emotion most strongly represented. He used the five conflict divisions identified for literature:

- Conflict between people, such as wars, gang fights, political races
- Internal conflicts, people against themselves, such as someone overcoming addiction, or a religious turmoil
- Struggles with the unknown, such as people fighting off mysterious pressures from outerspace or ghosts
- Conflicts with nature, such as natural disasters
- Social conflicts, such as civil unrest, or a person's fight against the internal revenue service as a way to dispute national policy.

In "Applying Fiction Conflict Situations to Analysis of News Stories," McCartney found conflict to be the major aspect of news, but only in some of its forms. Internal conflicts, for example, were rarely depicted in the news, while conflicts between people were most common.

Too Much Conflict

It is the incessant interest in conflicts that has concerned many critics. In a brief article, "Journalism History and Women's Experience: A Problem in Conceptual Change," feminist scholar Catherine Covert argued that the emphasis on conflict and controversy was a male perspective and that journalism historians should also include the feminist perspective — studying journalism history as stories of the bonding of individuals and the forming of communities. And Third World countries have called for a New World Information Order to allow for news about their successes in development rather than only covering the civil wars and catastrophes in their countries.

But the most virulent criticism about the journalists' emphasis on controversy and conflict emanates from the coverage of our own our political process.

Critics argue that the struggle between political candidates and the press has led to superficial journalism. Columnist Ken Auletta in the *New Yorker* article, "Why did both candidates despise the press?" found that the coverage of the 1996 presidential campaign was covered as a horserace and that the journalists were only looking for controversy. Both candidates scorned the media, and their press secretaries concurred that the "reporters prefer a quick headline to deeper understanding" and have allowed news to "surrender to opinion."

Political scientist Thomas Patterson has constructed a timeline of journalism's descent to opinion reporting in his article "Bad News Period." In the 1960s, for example, reporters started to cover not only what the newsmakers said, but what they did as well. But by the late 1970s this disintegrated into a reporting style that favored controversy over accuracy. Because time and knowledge were lacking, the reporters let themselves slip into a quick and easy form of criticism. When a politician made a statement, they promptly reported the adversarial critiques but only as quick countercharges, not as thorough investigations into alternatives.

Robert Lichter and Richard Noyes, in *Good Intentions Make Bad News*, also found that reporters covered the 1992 campaign and the policy issues as a horserace. They covered the power plays or the process of the competition, not the policy issues that actually differentiated the candidates from one another. According to Lichter and Noyes, the public has been getting a description of the candidates' moves or poll standings instead of discussion on the contrasting points of views, or alternative solutions.

Some critics go so far as to say that this controversy-based coverage ultimately destroys the political process. In his book *Breaking the News,* James Fallows finds that the public mistrusts its political leaders because journalists have been covering politics as a battleground.

In *Out of Order,* Thomas Patterson states that there can't be a "sensible campaign if it's built around the newsmedia." The issues brought forward by the press tend to be the controversial ones. Foreign policy was not controversial during much of the 1992 campaign, for example; so President George Bush's strong suit, foreign policy, was not reported. In 1980, presidential candidate John Anderson took a strong stand on the controversial issues of taxes and gun licensing; his campaign platform was reported.

Some critics find that the way journalists dramatize events and issues is the problem. The molding of reality into story form means journalists will omit some aspects and exaggerate other aspects as they seek to present conflict to shape the story. W. Lance Bennett, in *The Politics of Illusion,* argues that news is not fit for democracy because it is essentially superficial and does not encourage critical debate or citizen action. News does not advance the cause of democracy, he says, because it over dramatizes.

In a study of news reported as a series of stories, "The Function of Form in Newspapers' Political Conflict Coverage," Karen Olson found that reporters would look for potential conflict and controversy to advance their stories. Conflict and controversy between the protagonist and antagonist allowed for plot complications and development, resulting in a unified narrative.

Researchers have found that the more dramatic story, not necessarily the more significant story, will get coverage. Carol Liebler and Jacob Bendix reported on the coverage of an environmental issue in the article "Old-Growth Forests on Network News: News Sources and the Framing of an Environmental Controversy." They found that journalists took the stories that the two sides handed them and that the less dramatic one lost support. They conclude that because journalists were not enterprising and did not cover the research and debate on the ecological and economic aspects of the story, it was easier for the reporter to go with the dramatic framing used by one side.

The medium cited as the one most people use to get their news is also the one found most guilty of overemphasizing conflict and controversy. In "See Jane Watch. Watch, Jane. Watch: Students Discuss TV News," Susan Maushart describes television as craving controversy.

Many blame television for the emphasis on conflict and controversy. In *Amusing Ourselves to Death,* Neil Postman has argued that television is a medium of exposition and naturally elicits an emotional response from its viewers. Television does not encourage argumentation and debate as the printed word does. Television is a medium of images, and the viewer is only allowed to accept or reject the image. A television newscast can be full of controversy and conflict, but what the viewer really sees is a show. In *How to Watch Television News*, Postman and Steve Powers warn that the show is well planned; the story order is constructed as a way to keep the viewer tuned in through the commercials, to increase ratings, not to explain the issues in depth or give the stories context.

In *The Media and the Mayor's Race*, Phyllis Kaniss reported on her study of the media's role in the 1991 Philadelphia mayor's race. Here, the "horserace" aspect of the coverage obscured the reporting of the substantive issues and the real differences between the candidates. Television was particularly vulnerable to this criticism. If the candidates did not provide the conflict, the personal attacks, there wouldn't be coverage. Philadelphia TV loved covering Frank Rizzo's biting personal attacks on the other candidates, but when Rizzo died, the coverage of the race shrank to almost nothing.

Even PBS, the network bold enough to have a daily one-hour newscast, most of which is discussion by talking heads, is criticized for its shallow political coverage. In the monograph "The Political Diversity of Public Television," David Croteau, William Hoynes, and Kevin Carraggee find public television's political coverage concentrated on the drama of the race. They conclude that the media's focus on the race keeps viewers from feeling they can take part in the decision-making process, making them just observers of the race. As a result, the public is not encouraged to make the connections between events in Los Angeles and issues such as racism and poverty in American cities.

Shanto Iyengar has found that political issues are framed either episodically or thematically. Television leans to the episodic. In other words, it focuses on individual instances or events that represent the issue. The visuals are more interesting for the viewer in episodic coverage, but consequently the viewer is less likely to hold politicians or public policy responsible for a given situation. When framed thematically, the background and context of the issue would be covered, but that entails discussion or talking heads, and commercial television news is less likely to rely on this static format. Iyengar found that TV frames unemployment and racial inequality thematically, while it frames poverty episodically. When television is dealing with poverty it tends to cover the black, single adult mother, and the viewer then holds the individual portrayed as responsible for her own poverty. Television thus portrays an example to represent the largest segment of poor adults in America, but it inhibits an understanding of the societal implications.

Being Politically Selective with Conflict

Not only are the media criticized for covering politics as just a horse race, or the quick, easy to find stories but they are also criticized for limiting what opinion, which conflicting ideas, which controversies they will cover.

Some critics find that journalists will cover conflict and controversy only if it brings a return to the status quo. Their studies show the media serving as a thermostat, as a leveler, or as a neutralizing agent. Because journalists attempt to bring order out of the chaos of events, their coverage of conflict is limited.

In his book *The Power of News*, sociologist Michael Schudson argues that the limitation on the coverage of controversy is because the media are part of the culture. The media cover the culture they are in, but they are also framed by the culture. Journalists are influenced not only by the professional culture, but the culture at the time and the nature of the events themselves that are to be covered. All these forces constrict which conflicts will be covered.

Donohue, Olien, and Tichenor have studied the role of the media in community development, questioning their influence. In *Conflict, Community and the Press*, they take a systems approach and find the press to be an integral subsystem of the community. Often the community affects the press more than the press affects the community. Donohue and his colleagues found in "Reporting Conflict by Pluralism, Newspaper Type and Ownership" that as the community became more pluralistic, the media were more ready to cover conflict. In a recent article, "A Guard Dog Perspective on the Role of Media," they suggest that the media be considered guard dogs performing as sentries more for those already in power who can guard themselves, than for the whole community.

There have been further studies testing the theory that the media serve to maintain the social system of the community and therefore cover only some conflicts. Kim Smith found that the media in small communities were less likely to report conflicts, because they could disrupt the tight-knit community. Instead, the media would tend to emphasize stories that would bring the community together. In the larger communities, the media could feel free to report conflict within certain groups. Here the media would act as a controlling agent, allowing for feedback among groups. Douglas Blanks Hindman found that when communities are in the process of changing, the newspaper content reflects the concerns of powerful groups within and beyond the community. He concludes that ultimately, newspaper reports of both internal conflict and conflict with outside groups contribute to the maintenance of community stability and community adjustment to change in the larger social environment.

Similarly if the conflicts are of an internal nature such as riots, or external such as wars with another country, the media will have different roles. In *Social Conflict and Television News*, a study of newscasts from five countries, Akiba Cohen, Hanna Adoni, and Charles R. Bantz found that conflict news stories were dominant and prominent and that foreign conflicts were more complex, intense, and difficult to solve than domestic conflicts. They concluded that society is generally characterized by consensus and that, as a consequence, news serves as a means of regulating social conflicts, thereby either reinforcing the status quo or creating conditions for a nonviolent social change.

Douglas McLeod, William Eveland, and Nancy Signorielli studied how the media directed public opinion during the Gulf War and found that the media enhanced the sense of solidarity among the public at the height of the war. Then, as the external conflict subsided, coverage of the congressional squabbling, the internal conflict, led to the questioning of government policy and ultimately criticism of that policy.

Some critics, often writing from an ideological point of view, claim that the reported conflicts and controversies only include those of the dominant power system. In *Inventing Reality*, Michael Parenti has found that journalists don't cover the conflicts or controversies important to the poor, or the liberals, or the women, or labor unions in any depth. Journalists, he argues, are part of a poorly organized system that works very well in maintaining the status quo for its owners, the conservative corporate and government elites. The coverage of campaigns as trivial races, or labor disputes as just opinions, helps maintain those in power. And those in power will only allow discussion of issues that have no impact on their power.

One study reported that coverage of criminal activity will not get balanced coverage. Fred Fico and Stan Soffin, in their article "Fairness and Balance of Selected Newspaper Coverage of Controversial National, State, and Local Issues," report that only half of the controversial stories are reported in a balanced fashion. In an earlier study, "Covering Conflict and Controversy: Measuring Balance, Fairness, Defamation," Todd Simon, Frederick Fico, and Stephen Lacy found that if the story was about crimes or law enforcement, the press rarely contacted the defendant and instead reported the police's point of view. W. Lance Bennett, in *News: The Politics of Illusion*, has found that moral conflicts such as abortion, gun control, or civil rights get in-depth coverage because the participants are willing to discuss them. But the economy, foreign policy, or energy are less well covered because the politicians and elites are guarded about them; they don't openly share information about those issues.

Some find that journalists are not covering the controversies that are significant for their readers. Rob Anderson, Robert Dardenne, and George M. Killenberg wrote

The Conversation of Journalism as a plan for how community journalism could save the profession. They called on journalists to be guided by the concerns of everyday people as they make their economic, religious, educational, and other important decisions. Journalists should not turn to the people on the street only when there is a change in government policy that might affect them; they should always be investigating the public interest. Anderson and his colleagues find that the values of conflict and controversy, among the other values of timeliness and proximity, are appropriate values, but journalists need to be addressing readers more directly. The use of stories is an effective writing device, as they are the only place where conflict can be fully addressed.

Some critics argue that cultural and professional tenets lead journalists to ignore some sides of the controversy. Patricia Aufderheide claims that newspaper coverage of the controversy surrounding the airing of an African-American gay video program, "Tongues Untied," on PBS's *Point of View* series didn't go far enough. Newspapers only saw it as a controversy limited to public television station managers and not one that involved the various publics such as the gay community. Aufderheide concludes that the limited coverage of the controversy can be blamed on the rituals of journalism, the formulas of objective, daily, event-based journalism, and conventional sourcing strategies.

Resolution

Conflict and controversy are news values that cannot be dismissed quickly, nor can they be cherished easily, and the issue is important for journalists to grapple with. The criticism can point to ways the profession can improve.

Conflict and controversy cannot be avoided entirely. It's almost impossible to write a story about harmony or unity and not include conflict and controversy, and vice versa. The opposite value is usually inherent in the framing of the story, for that is what gives it the frame. The passage of a new law usually means there were different viewpoints on the need for the law. The economic success of a developing country usually means hurdles were surmounted, and having people come together to solve problems means there were serious differences in the first place.

A representative democracy calls for debate and deliberation — a robust, open exchange of ideas to help eliminate flawed notions and reinforce the valuable ones. However, if journalists just run from one conflict to another and only cover crises, they risk losing the context, the details, the depth that make stories meaningful.

In response to those who call for an end to the presentation of conflict and controversy because it makes the public cynical, journalists should instead give the conflicts more context. Jim Fallows has noted that journalists in the 1992 presidential campaign intended to ask the candidates to identify how their stands would affect the citizenry, but didn't. They should. Covering politics as a race has merits for journalism, but the citizenry needs more. Instead of just reporting about politicians fighting among themselves, journalists need to provide more details about their differences, to help the citizenry consider the implications of their votes. Journalists need to inquire as to what a political stand on an issue will mean for the future, what the implications of a new healthcare policy will be for all, how a new family-leave policy will affect all families and businesses, or whether mandatory prison sentences will reduce crime.

The narrative force behind journalism should mean that journalists cover the conflicts in more depth. However, more consideration is needed to make the selections that help advance the narrative and also impart the significance of the story for the reader or viewer. Journalists should seek stories that will welcome the audience further into the decision-making process.

An alternative solution to the dilemma that storytelling presents is to have many different types of stories available to the audience. As valuable as objectivity is, it is also an ideal that may not be unattainable. Polysemy, or the presentation of many meanings, would also serve the audience.

Often journalists are avoiding coverage of those controversies that are most significant, the conflicts that are most disruptive to the community, and those that may be most productive in solving problems for society. News coverage is similar to television programming: it caters to the lowest common denominator. And journalists are abiding by the same maxim as television programmers: in their attempt to reach as many people and to offend as few as possible, network television programmers choose the least objectionable program. That is the very antithesis of good journalism and of the function of free speech. Journalists need to report all the controversies, all the conflicts. They need to put them into a context, to put them in narrative form, but they must be sure to search for all points of view.

It would be too dangerous for society to not have conflict and controversy as significant news values. They attract the attention of journalists as well as the citizenry. They point out areas of differences, and they allow the opportunity for further coverage. The flooding of a major river allows for the opportunity of another environmental science lesson; the economic difficulties of a foreign country allow for discussion of the value of capitalism or socialism within different societies; civil unrest allows for attention to be drawn to deep social problems that society must address and attempt to solve. For the citizenry to arrive at a consensus, it needs in-depth coverage of as many conflicts as possible.

Recommended Readings

Books

Cohen, Akiba A., Hanna Adoni, and Charles R. Bantz. *Social Conflict and Television News.* Newbury Park, Calif.: Sage, 1990. A study to see the relationship between social conflict as presented on TV news and how people perceive social conflicts and the extent to which there is a relationship between these two phenomena.

Fuller, Jack. *News Values: Ideas for an Information Age.* Chicago: University of Chicago Press, 1996. A former reporter, editor, and publisher calls for a new description of newsworthiness, one that would include timeliness, significance, and interest for a given community. He gives lengthy theoretical reasons, including a discussion of the role of journalists.

Herman, Edward S., and Noam Chomsky. *Manufacturing Consent: The Political Economy of the Mass Media.* New York: Pantheon Books, 1988. Through case studies of media coverage of foreign news, from the Vietnam War to elections in Nicaragua, the authors attempt to prove that their propaganda model works. The news media carry out their assignment of keeping the American public informed about U.S. foreign policy in a way that is supportive of that policy.

Iyengar, Shanto. *Is Anyone Responsible? How Television Frames Political Issues.* Chicago: University of Chicago Press, 1991. Shanto presents his evidence gained from content analysis, surveys, and experimenting with television newscast viewing, that television news causes viewers to assign responsibility for social problems to individuals rather than to society as a whole.

Kaniss, Phyllis C. *The Media and the Mayor's Race: The Failure of Urban Political Reporting.* Bloomington and Indianapolis: Indiana University Press, 1995. A study of the day-to-day reporting of the journalists covering a mayoral campaign to determine how shifting economic forces in local television and newspaper reporting would affect the election.

Parenti, Michael. *Inventing Reality: The Politics of News Media,* 2nd ed. New York: St. Martin's Press, 1993. A study in how the news media distort important aspects of social and political life to benefit the corporate owners and power elite.

Postman, Neil. *Amusing Ourselves to Death: Public Discourse in the Age of Show Business.* New York: Viking, 1985. Entertainment is the supraideology of all discourse on television, and it has worked so well that viewers don't even care. Television has brought in an age of exposition rather than syllogism

Contemporary Media Issues

Articles

Aufderheide, Patricia. "Controversy and the Newspaper's Public: The Case of Tongues Untied." *Journalism Quarterly* 71 (Autumn 1994): 499-508. A study of how the rituals of objective journalism limited the way newspapers covered a controversy within public broadcasting.

Auletta, Ken. "Inside Story: Why did both candidates despise the press?" *The New Yorker*, 18 November 1996, pp. 44-61. A detailed description of the 1996 presidential campaign underlining how both the candidates and the press were viewed negatively.

Diamond, Edwin, Steven Katz, and Cara Matthews. "Conflict v. Context in Covering Clinton's Health Care Proposal." *National Journal*, 19 November 1994, pp. 2738-9. How the media contributed to the demise of President Clinton's health care package.

Frankel, Max, "Where There's Fear, There's News." *New York Times*, 29 June 1997, p. E-22. Reiterates journalists' constant search for conflict and controversy.

Hindman, Douglas Blanks. "Community Newspapers, Community Structural Pluralism, and Local Conflict with Nonlocal Groups." *Journalism & Mass Communication Quarterly* 73 (Autumn 1996): 708-21. In periods of change, newspaper reports of both internal conflict and conflict with outside groups contribute to the maintenance of community stability and community adjustment to change in the larger social environment.

Liebler, Carol M., and Jacob Bendix. "Old-Growth Forests on Network News: News Sources and the Framing of an Environmental Controversy." *Journalism & Mass Communication Quarterly* 73 (Spring 1996): 53-64. A study of how television networks frame or portray disparate views when covering ecological controversy, particularly the old-growth forest-spotted owl controversy.

McCartney, Hunter. "Applying Fiction Conflict Situations to Analysis of News Stories." *Journalism Quarterly* 64 (Spring 1987): 163. An analysis of front-page news stories, national news magazines, and television newscasts for type of conflict and emotion most strongly represented.

Olson, Kathryn M. "The Function of Form in Newspapers' Political Conflict Coverage: The New York Times' Shaping of Expectations in the Bitburg Controversy." *Political Communication* 12 (1995): 43-64. Drawing on the example of President Ronald Reagan's 1985 visit to the Bitburg war cemetery, this article agues that form, in the Burkean sense, can operate in a body of conflict coverage to shape expectations for subsequent developments in the controversy and to help judge the appropriateness of news characters' subsequent choices in the drama.

Patterson, Thomas E. "Bad news, period. (negative political coverage)." *PS: Political Science & Politics* 29 (March 1996): 17. A description of how and why news has increasingly covered the negative.

Chapter Twenty-seven

News as a Narrative

Robert Dardenne

Mary was a survivor. She had to be in a home dominated by a drunken father and a screeching, critical mother. In her 13 years she had learned how to get out of their way, to avoid their wrath, to become invisible. She also learned how to take care of herself. She was strong, building a wall of invincibility around the hurt little girl inside. She knew she would make something of herself. She got babysitting jobs and saved her money. She worked hard in school and earned excellent grades.

Then she met Paul, the first person who ever seemed to love her. And then Mary got pregnant....

Wanting to know what happened to Mary next constitutes the power of story. That power makes it a wonderfully appealing form for journalists. It is intrinsic to humanity — a way people try to understand the world. Two of our most compelling questions are, What happened then? and What will happen next? It's no wonder that the mythical Scheherazade escaped death at the hands of her husband, King Shahriyar, by telling him stories each evening, interrupting each one at its most interesting point. She kept him listening by telling him what happened then, and she kept him coming back by promising to tell him what was to happen next.

We live in an interesting, confusing, and complex world, and like King Shahriyar, we all want to know what happened then, and we are waiting to see what will happen next. Among the people charged with telling us are journalists. Together, the journalists who produce the news and the citizens who share it create stories about what has happened and about what is going to happen. Some stories are more immediately complete; others take longer to materialize. But all of them potentially have the power that kept Scheherazade alive.

Most news tells stories about people in conflict, like Mary in the example above. That is journalism's great strength, and to some, its great weakness.

People are interesting; they take action, often unusual and unexpected action; they make the world go round. The president's latest trials and tribulations, whether involving women or money, add another chapter or at least footnote to a long and apparently popular narrative about the president, his family, and his administration. Writing about the president in narrative form — that is, covering his actions as a story in which he is the hero, the villain, or both — provides drama, suspense, pathos, conflict, and many other qualities of a good story. Mary, for example, could be a victim, a heroine, or a tragic figure; she could be some part of all of those, another person struggling against the odds to survive. Her story and that of the president are part of what might be called a narrative form of news.

Individual people, alone, don't make the world go round. They are buffeted by events, engulfed by groups, elevated and defeated by seismic changes. When journalists think of news only in terms of narrative (that is, essentially, stories about individual people and the drama of what happened to them next), then great social, cultural, political, and environmental forces tend to be ignored, or at best glossed over, at least until some crisis brings them to the fore. Several of these forces are at work in Mary's life. Some may be mentioned in her story, others not. Mainstream news coverage of anti-intellectualism, capitalism, global economics or democracy, race and gender, neo-liberalism or conservatism, or the conditions that result in pregnant teens usually highlights specific instances or human actions. It rarely, before a crisis, offers explanations and analyses. Consequently, we as readers and even journalists are often surprised.

We are, however, usually highly entertained. In fact, some critics, such as Neil Postman in *Amusing Ourselves to Death*, argue that entertainment values dominate journalistic values in the news media. It is possible that narrative forms of news — stories that feature heroes and villains, for example — can endanger journalistic credibility when its entertainment value overshadows its news and information value, a condition more likely in an environment in which the dramatic, sensational, and trivial pack far greater economic wallop than more analytical or even conventional reporting.

All news forms, however, can be problematic, in part because they are rarely recognized for being the potent force they are. News is as much a product of its form as it is a slice of some reality. In the course of telling Mary's story, for example, a reporter might be likely to link Mary's own imperfect childhood with her current circumstances. One "story line" could be that the sins of the parents are visited upon the daughter. Another could emphasize Mary's strength and willpower in overcoming obstacles to succeed under circumstances in which so many fail. Yet another could illustrate the dysfunction of an alcoholic family. Each of these might be a valid approach to Mary's story. We like to think that news, because it reports what's happening in the world, is above manipulations common in fiction and drama. News, in portraying the world accurately, is supposed to tell itself. But as we see, it doesn't and can't.

Conventional news forms, because we're so used to them, give the illusion that news tells itself. We see them as the "natural" way to present news because they are the way most news has been presented. However, today's unconventional "literary" journalism, which resurrected the narrative form from the remains of the New Journalism of the 1960s and 1970s, shifted the focus to form and revived discussions of the strengths and weaknesses of news narrative.

The most basic issue strikes at the heart of journalism — its credibility as a source of truth. In the early 1970s, New Journalism adherents stretched journalism's credibility with reconstructed scenes and dialogues, symbolic interpretations, and dazzling prose from multiple points of view. Critics, urging caution, demanded that the stuff of journalism be nothing but fact and truth. These notions conger up shadowy forms of journalism's near past — a flamboyant Tom Wolfe waving a sheaf of quotes reconstructed from ancient events (by journalism standards) and WHIZZZZZZZZZ, VOOOOOOMMMMMM prose shouting in the face of John Hersey, who calmly chants, "Thou shalt not lie, thou shalt not lie, thou shalt not lie...."

The current news narrative thrives without flamboyant adherents and, unlike New Journalism, is found in newspapers and television as often as it is in magazines and books. Its increased presence has shaken up the news business. With its focus on color and its tendency to keep readers wondering what happens next, it stands out from the more predictable inverted pyramid.

Many reporters when writing conventional articles adopt narrative devices, especially the anecdotal leads that pepper most papers in the country, and several others make careers out of narrative approaches to journalism. The approach invigorates news pages, appeals to readers, and expands notions of newsworthiness but is controversial when it threatens journalistic credibility.

Origins of the Issue

Neither new journalists nor literary journalists invented story as a form of news. Some of the earliest U.S. newspapers published "news" in story form, which was popular although never dominant well into the 1800s. These earlier stories were usually based on faith, charity, love, honesty, abstinence, perseverance, frugality, hard work, and other qualities. The *Connecticut Courant*, for example, urged these qualities on its readers through stories, some probably not based in fact, in which good, faithful, hard-working, sober, poor-but-proud men prospered, whereas intemperate, slothful, unfaithful men failed or perished.

These stories were published not just for entertainment, but because they best expressed the human qualities editors and publishers thought important. As objectivity and journalism's "scientific method" became increasingly common in the late 1800s and early 1900s, the news report and its inverted-pyramid offspring dominated news reporting. These did not tell stories in the traditional sense but offered continuing coverage of an issue or event that eventually became the story of that issue or event. More traditional story forms and approaches reappeared during various periods and at various newspapers, especially during the yellow- and jazz-journalism eras.

But the inverted pyramid and objectivity were solid, unassailable American journalistic standards through the 1950s. In the 1960s, a few reporters and writers, following practices going back well before Charles Dickens and Mark Twain, "discovered" non-fiction writing styles that relied on certain literary devices. As competition for news increased, among newspapers and then among newspapers and electronic media, journalists used the story form not to emphasize cherished qualities, but as a way to provide more context and information in an entertaining manner.

Wolfe, New Journalism's outspoken and self-promoting proponent, wrote in the now famous introduction to his and Edward Johnson's *New Journalism* that he discovered four narrative devices central to any literary journalism — scene-by-scene construction, recording dialogue in full, presenting scenes through the eyes of characters, and offering richly detailed descriptions symbolic of people's status in life. Using these and other devices and relying on a reporting that frequently put reporters in the middle of events, Wolfe, Hunter Thompson, Gay Talese, Norman Mailer, and others shook up and perhaps altered notions of familiar forms and conventional content and, for better or worse, loosened up journalistic practice. Perhaps too much for some, who accuse it of leading directly to the blurred lines between journalism and entertainment today.

Today's literary journalism resulted from, among other things, increasing criticism that news is boring and irrelevant, the encroachment of entertainment media into territory once occupied by traditional news alone, burgeoning competition, and a less attractive bottom line at even highly profitable newspapers. Story forms now seem to be an appealing and effective accommodation for news organizations under more pressure than ever to make news more entertaining.

The New Journalism is often linked to style, mostly as Wolfe laid it out. The devices he highlighted are still central to virtually any literary journalism work, but literary journalism is more frequently talked of in terms of substance. Its journalists seem to concentrate on subjects, sources, and content, often spending long periods reporting. It doesn't benefit from a controversial, powerful, and prominent voice defining and promoting it, but it does have vocal proponents. Norman Sims, in *Literary Journalism*, edited with Mark Kramer, acknowledges that some appeal of literary journalism is indeed narrative technique such as structure and voice, but also immersion reporting, high standards of accuracy and responsibility. Sims says literary journalism often concerns the feelings and experiences of ordinary people, a quality associating it with public journalism.

Arguments for Narrative

Narrative is an inseparable part of people's lives. We tell stories to each other about our work, play, spouses, children, sports, shopping — about all aspects of our lives. As Barbara Johnstone points out in *Stories, Community, and Place*, stories are a comfortable and familiar form for conversation; and, in fact, it is rare when our conversations do not take on story forms. Scholars and storytellers have gone so far as to say that storytelling is essentially understanding, that story structure is innately a part of the human mind, and that stories give people their conceptions of life. Roger Schank in *Tell Me a Story* argues that the ability to tell the appropriate story at the appropriate time is, essentially, the measure of intelligence. In other words, story, as a form, is crucially important to human beings.

It's also often interesting and entertaining, capable of turning the mundane into the exciting, transforming boredom into interest. These things make journalists and scholars sit up and take notice. Narrative is, in fact, too ingrained in human interaction and too compelling as both a form and a structure for gathering information for journalists to resist.

Use of narrative devices and story helped free journalistic writing from confining forms and paradigms and opened opportunities for reporting. Story provides, for better or worse, greater context than the conventional stripped-down and often discrete inverted pyramid and other report forms, and embodies more than just the traditional news values. It is through story forms that journalists can more readily give voice to those left out of the mainstream and present more positive, rather than negative, human action. When news covers ordinary people, it is often as victims or perpetrators of crime. More commonly, the news focuses on the actions of leaders and politicians, celebrities, and the rich and powerful. But as both new and literary journalists have demonstrated, everyone has a story, or several stories, often rich and rewarding. Narrative is a gateway to the ordinary as well as the exotic. People overcome obstacles, solve problems, work together, have moments of triumph and joy. Because it requires reporters to seek dramatic and suspenseful elements and order them in something resembling a plot line, narrative form allows these moments to be shared in the community as readily and in as compelling a manner as the latest murder or scandal.

A narrative or story can work remarkably well in situations not obviously "newsworthy," that is, situations lacking strong news qualities such as timeliness, proximity, consequence, and so forth. In the earlier example, barring some sensational turn or criminal twist, Mary would likely not be "newsworthy" without narrative form. Therefore, as Rob Anderson, Mike Killenberg, and I argue in *The Conversation of Journalism,* narrative forms can be a foundation in a more inclusive, inviting journalism that comes closer to representing and engaging the communities in which it is practiced.

The ordinary isn't always news, but a storyteller would argue that life has few ordinary moments, only ordinary tellings of those moments. Story's great power is that when done well, it transcends the ordinary, encouraging if not forcing people to recognize each other in similar and dissimilar situations. As readers, we might also come to see common things in uncommon ways. Mary's plight is common in some ways, but her story of persevering against such odds might inspire some readers to re-evaluate their own situations, while the story of Mary bludgeoned by abusive parents and perhaps used by an irresponsible man might force readers to rethink their positions on relevant social issues. Donald Drake, the *Philadelphia Inquirer* narrative writing editor, says he fought conventional newsroom wisdom when he argued for the newsworthiness of the seemingly even more mundane story of a South Philly girl getting ready for a high school prom. The usual news article is often about life's extremes, he says in *The Oregonian* newsletter *Second Takes,* but reporters can write about most of the rest of life through narrative. The prom story, he argues, was essentially "about" all the 90,000 Philadelphia high school youth getting ready for their proms, about to shed their adolescence.

The narrative form through the years has essentially broadened journalism's horizons, and it may help solve problems of lagging reader and viewer interest. Story as a news form is powerful, compelling, inviting, interesting, and often dramatic. It has tremendous potential to give voice to the voiceless, to make the familiar strange (or make the strange familiar), to offer new and valuable perspectives and insights, and to revive interest and relevance in news that reports on a narrow world too many see as mundane, bureaucratic, and political. In a news world that sometimes seems indistinguishable from entertainment, story, as a form that presents information or news in an entertaining way, can be intoxicating.

Even though he's a narrative or short-story form proponent, Jon Franklin warns in the December 1996 *American Journalism Review* article, "When to Go Long," that literary journalism is specialized, complex, difficult, and time-consuming and therefore expensive. When it's done well, it's great, but once they get beyond anecdotal leads, reporters don't often do it well. Given the form's popularity, success, and potential to entertain, it will take much more than mild cautions to put journalists off narrative.

Wolfe has practiced and touted narrative forms, arguing that they infuse journalism with an "artistic excitement." Ronald Weber in *The Literature of Fact* talks of a "higher" journalism in which the writer fuses "observer and maker, journalist and artist." Thomas Connery in his introduction to *A Sourcebook of American Literary Journalism* says the higher journalism (or something similar to it) merges events and feelings, the look and feel of the world, and the general and the specific. Sims, in *The Literary Journalists*, says that through narrative forms journalists demonstrate that people's lives contain great drama and substance. And Franklin himself has won two Pulitzer Prizes in part because of his considerable nonfiction narrative talents. In *Writing for Story*, he notes that many Pulitzer Prizes for feature writing have been awarded to articles written in narrative short-story form. It captures a large intelligent audience, he says, because it combines fiction's good qualities with nonfiction's information content.

Evidence of narrative journalism's popularity abounds in the news industry. The *Philadelphia Inquirer*, for example, is one of a number of news organizations that have writing coaches and host or send reporters to seminars that stress narrative techniques. *Editor & Publisher* and other trade journals, as well as news organizations' newsletters, often have narrative writing tips. "Writers" at some newspapers don't have the same deadline pressures as reporters. Tom French, the resident story writer at the *St. Petersburg Times*, took more than a year to write a hugely successful series on high school seniors and more than three years on a complex series of stories.

On a practical level, narrative is one answer to flagging interest in traditional news. People like "stories," and reporters can deliver them. Writing coach Jack Hart, in *Editor & Publisher*, says that novelists make millions and traditional journalists make peanuts because the story form "captures the popular imagination in a way that most newspaper writing never does." He says that learning to recognize and write journalism stories with a protagonist, antagonist, a conflict, dramatic tension, climax, and denouement will help and maybe save journalism. In *Second Takes*, Daniel Fricker explains why narratives work: they are visual, use scenes to show rather than tell, use theatrical devices such as foreshadowing to propel readers through the story, use dialogue rather than quotes, build to a climax, and "plumb the emotions." For these and other reasons, he believes that narratives, not investigative pieces, build newspaper readership. Perhaps that's why investigative reporters like narrative too. Erin Hayes, writing in *The IRE Journal* on how television investigative reporters can make viewers care, suggested they tell stories by using the lives of compelling victims. People are at the core of stories, and Hayes says some information is interesting only if it is made personally compelling.

Writing in *News/Inc.*, David Simon argues that traditional non-narrative coverage of crime is not only bad journalism but exactly what journalism shouldn't be: anesthetizing and simplistic. Journalists, he says, have given up as storytellers to their detriment, and only by returning to storytelling will they return this "lost sense of tragedy and even reality" to newspapers. The best stories, he says, are those in which "real people think and feel."

Some reporting and writing textbooks emphasize a literary-style writing. In Bruce Evensen's *The Responsible Reporter,* R. Thomas Berner quotes a practitioner of literary journalism saying that journalists must compete with video by giving readers "vivid stories" that supply their own "soundtrack and internal visuals." Berner provides a variety of literary tools, including detail, scene-by-scene construction, dialogue, foreshadowing, flashbacks, and epilogues. In the same book, narrative writing editor Drake says the form requires detailed reporting, beautiful writing, and hard work, but it's worth the effort because good narratives are read more than any other articles in the newspaper.

Michael Johnson, in his introduction to *The New Journalism,* puts it another way: narrative or "new" journalism is "fresher and more helpful" and often more thorough, honest, and intelligently critical than traditional journalism. This may be true, and perhaps this newest move to stories represents a shift in journalistic values, a movement to bring context to the news, to enrich it through tales of the lives and experiences of ordinary people like Mary. It could be an effort to transform the dry facts of daily journalism into entertaining, readable, and thus more effective information.

Arguments Against Narrative

However, in a period of declining readership and increasing pressure for profit, journalists may turn to narrative primarily for its entertainment value. Writer/journalist John Hersey, who, like Franklin, used fictional devices readily, sensed danger years ago. In contrast to Wolfe's enthusiastic proselytizing about journalism's story potential, Hersey has written in *The Yale Review* that in fiction nothing is forbidden; in journalism, nothing can be made up. Journalism's credibility as a reliable source for news and information constitutes the essential difference between the two. Hersey aimed his comments in *The Legend on the License* at the "nonfiction novel," but many literary journalism works have similar characteristics, including the reconstructed scenes and dialogues that so worried him. When entertainment is a dominant incentive for journalism and the report becomes a performance, Hersey says, "reality" blurs into the background and ends up "fuzzy, vague, unrecognizable, and false."

Hersey's comments applied to books by writers he thought violated journalism's major tenet, that "the journalist must not invent," a sentiment echoed by Janet Malcolm in *The Journalist and the Murderer*. The journalist, she says, is "under contract to the reader" to write without embellishment about real people doing real things. However, news in story form doesn't have to be invented to require caution. For example, confusion exists in the term "story," which is equated with the childhood admonition, "Don't tell me a story (lie)," and with fiction, because just as the inverted pyramid is journalism's "natural" form, story is fiction's natural form. Readers can confuse the two.

Support exists for this conclusion. In a work unrelated to journalism, *The Reader, the Text, the Poem: The Transactional Theory of Literary Work,* literary theorist Louise Rosenblatt argues that texts (we'll include news) offer clues as to how they should be read. Use of literary devices in newswriting doesn't necessarily make the work literary but may provide cues for readers to shift reading modes from what Rosenblatt calls efferent, most associated with fact, to aesthetic, most associated with fiction.

The following lead of a news article ("Thief leaves cash register, steals rabbit-eating snakes") comes from the May 28 edition of the *St. Petersburg Times:*

> TAMPA — A burglar broke into Erin Cunningham's store late Monday and ignored the cash register for a different goal: snakes. Three were stolen from the shop, the Snake Pit, at 1302 W. Busch Blvd., and Cunningham is angry — and worried.

In reading this more or less conventional news article in the "efferent" mode, we look for what the text can teach or tell us, what information it can provide. We seek guidance for our actions and solutions to our problems; we use news not only to orient ourselves to and make sense of our world, but also to be informed.

The following is from a series ("Rosa Lee's Story") in the October 10-16, 1994, national weekly edition of the *Washington Post:*

> Rosa Lee Cunningham guided her 10-year-old grandson through the narrow aisles of the Oxon Hill thrift shop, past the crowded racks of second-hand pants and shirts, stopping finally at the row of children's jackets and

winter coats. The boy picked out a mock flight jacket, with a big number on the back and a price tag stapled to the collar.

"If you want it," Rosa Lee said, "then you're going to have to help me get it."

"Okay, Grandmama," the boy said nervously. "But do it in a way that I won't get caught."

Also about a theft, this piece is written in story form, which is read in the "aesthetic" mode. Here we appreciate style and structure; we read more for the story than the information. In reading a "story," even in the news, we may have more difficulty with the events' relationship to reality, because in fiction we know "real" is created by the author's words and may have little or no basis in "real life."

Reporter Leon Dash wrote these paragraphs four days after the theft occurred. He didn't witness the scene, but he based it on Rosa Lee's account. It was a small episode in a larger story that seemed real, but often read like a novel. We usually don't confuse the contrived reality of fiction with actuality, yet here we're faced with a fiction-like story that claims to be true. If literature, as Rosenblatt says, invites confusion about its relation with reality, then journalism as literature may do the same. Journalists, for better or worse, strive to make such relationships unambiguous. One might argue that a more literary approach defeats this purpose, or that because it projects a more ambiguous relation with reality, it is a more honest journalism.

News stories, however, are not usually ambiguous in their assignments of motivation and their endings. In a traditional story, good people doing good things overcome bad people doing bad things, resulting in the story's end. Journalists and readers are generally clear as to who are the villains and heroes or heroines, or who they should be. Editors and coaches often say that those clear distinctions characterize good literary journalism. In the example above, a news story form more or less requires that Mary's motivations be understood or at least identified, that her actions and those around her be explained, and that they result in an appropriate ending. But clear motivations and endings, however common they are in stories, are rarer in real life. What led Mary's mom and dad and Mary and Paul to do what they did may be, when all is said, unfathomable. Therein lies the issue.

The recent frenzy of publicity about what Forbes *Media Critic* called "Church-Fire Fever" also illustrates motivation and closure issues, as well as narrative's role in both. In May and June 1996 newspapers and television throughout the nation devoted considerable space and time to cover the "story" of fires at black churches in the South. Most coverage blamed racists or a racist environment for the burnings, but later articles reported that both white and black churches had burned and that the rate of fires was no different from past years. Only news coverage increased. The *Media Critic* article offered several reasons why: Reporters had been lazy, and such a story is easy to construct, leading to pack journalism; many reporters disliked the country's conservative trends and connected them to the burnings; reporters were concerned, guilty, and self-interested; competition inflamed such coverage; and government officials, including the president, "authorized" the race storyline through their public comments.

Another explanation is that the media needed a story; they needed motivation and closure. Having black churches burned by white racists sets up a plot with good and evil, and a potential for closure — the capture of those responsible and the censure of all who think like them. In a 1996 *Columbia Journalism Review* article, Joe Holley argued that the church-burning story, besides being important with national implications, offered easily identifiable issues of good and evil, heroes and villains, and mystery. Further, it "resonated with the heroic tones of civil rights history." In other words, it was a terrific story. Such a story requires motivation, and as Byron York says in the *Media Critic* article, reporters and presumably readers found the "climate of hate" storyline entirely plausible.

The story form is such a powerful force in gathering as well as presenting information because it requires certain elements whether or not they exist in real life. The world does not often present itself in a manner convenient to journalists. They must create some kind of order. Story is one of the orders they create out of the disorder of the world. That night-riding racists burned African-American churches in ever-increasing numbers was, for many, a better story than if the burnings were random, common, and often without racial motivation. York notes in the *Media Critic* article that another plausible story was that a black thug murdered the pregnant wife of Charles Stuart in Boston in 1989. Certainly racial politics helps determine the direction of these stories, but sometimes the required beginnings, middles, endings, motivations, and plots are determined by convenience and an ever-increasing need for entertainment.

People and their motivations and actions are at the core of all stories. Journalism textbooks, instructors, and editors insist that reporters write about people. As professor and writing editor Hart says in the *Editor & Publisher* article, "We've all heard it to the point of numbness: 'Get people into your stories. Tell it in human terms.'"

People do breathe life into issues and make articles more entertaining. But a journalism of stories about people, as public journalism advocate Davis "Buzz" Merritt argues, is often anecdotal and shallow and generally fails to get to the heart of society's problems. Significant issues, he says, drown in a sea of stories and anecdotes. Supporting him is Shanto Iyengar, who in his 1991 *Is Anyone Responsible: How Television Frames the Issues,* says that news readers and viewers often connect problems to people. Reporters find it easier and quicker to write about complex issues in terms of the personalities most closely associated with them. The national health-care issue, for example, was first connected to Sen. Edward Kennedy and then to Hillary Clinton, and it was generally covered in terms of their personal battles with its opponents and, in Hillary Clinton's case, in terms of her legitimacy as a policy-maker. In Mary's story, writing about an articulate teenager caught in such a trap might illuminate larger social and cultural issues, but often it substitutes as coverage of them.

Resolution

Journalists writing narrative must weigh the advantages of a form with the power to draw audiences against the potential disadvantages that come from its close association with fiction and entertainment. In the end, as a form, narrative has as many pitfalls as the much-maligned inverted pyramid. Both story and inverted pyramid impose an order on the world. That story does so chronologically or "naturally" doesn't mean it requires any more or less contrivance than the inverted pyramid to shape the world's events, issues, and people into its mold.

Story as a journalistic form has enormous potential, but it is highly volatile. It can bring a freshness and vibrancy long missing from a repetitive and increasingly bureaucratic, political, and some say irrelevant news. But it can tie "news" to fiction and entertainment in ways that many deem unhealthy; it can stir emotions in ways that many find manipulative; and it can focus too heavily on people and their actions and motivations rather than on broader social forces.

Yet story may be our most powerful and promising means for making sense of the world. Journalists who use story forms to explain and even analyze can harness narrative's extraordinary powers to enlighten as well as entertain. For these and other reasons (including economic ones), journalists will and should continue writing news in narrative forms. Maintaining and emphasizing traditional journalistic values of truth, accuracy, and fairness can overcome the credibility objections voiced by Hersey and more contemporary critics.

Credibility is journalism's currency, and it must be spent carefully. Creating and maintaining credibility must not be sporadic, but constant. Narrative form alone doesn't necessarily damage credibility; however, given its wide use, its association with fiction, its focus on people and their individual actions, and its absolute need for specific elements, it is always potentially damaging. It remains, as Franklin reminds us, a dangerous journalism.

But journalism narrative form is too powerful to abandon or fear, and owners, publishers, editors, and reporters can take specific actions to ease the danger. Here are four such actions:

• *Understand that not all news should be written as story or even with narrative devices, including anecdotal leads, and realize that not every journalist is capable of writing in narrative form.* Franklin in *Writing for Story* clearly indicates that appropriate topics and situations are notoriously difficult to find at least for what he calls the "short story" narrative form. News as story is most effective when an appropriate topic is reported and written by a competent journalist storyteller.

• *Explain in detail to readers what you did to produce the story.* If it's a series, do it at the beginning and perhaps again each day. While some stories come easily, producing most news narratives is arduous and can consume much more time and resources than producing a conventional piece of journalism. It also requires skill and experience. Readers and viewers should know the kind of attention paid to detail, the time spent questioning and learning and even writing, the records pored over, the books read, the people interviewed and observed, and the care expended to make sure the story is true, accurate, and fair. Tom French of the *St. Petersburg Times* goes over what he has written with sources, giving them a chance to respond and comment, and protest if they think he has erred. It can be troublesome, he says, but in the end he has a much stronger and more accurate story. Journalists might tell readers something of themselves as well — their background and experiences, and perhaps what they thought and felt as the story was assembled.

• *Incorporate analysis, explanation, and multiple viewpoints in the narrative form.* Journalists frequently use an individual's story to highlight a larger issue. Mary's story, for example, could be about children of alcoholics, children in an emotionally abusive home, or teenage pregnancy. Critics argue that such individual stories often replace thoughtful coverage of the larger issue. Editors and reporters could make sure that doesn't happen by creating forms that include a range of per-spectives representing viewpoints of people as well as institutions. They could, for example, explain Mary's plight not only as a result of her individual actions, but also as a result of working-class values, gender or racial issues, addiction, or whatever larger social or cultural issues were relevant. It is impossible to write everything in one story, but it is both easy and inaccurate to let Mary's plight be explained solely by her own or other's individual actions.

• *Don't select facts and information to meet the demands of a preconceived story.* Know that stories generally demand clearly defined heroes and villains with understandable motivations. When reporters have a larger storyline in mind as they gather information, they are more likely to end up with information they need to provide the elements of that storyline. Reporters and editors who understand that individual action isn't the only force that drives society, that stories are created and not gathered whole, and that not everything is explainable through stories (or explainable at all) will be less likely to use narrative form in a manner that endangers journalistic credibility.

In the end, we are all King Shahriyar. We must hope that the tellers of our stories — business people, scientists, historians, journalists, and all of us charged with creating some kind of order out of the chaos — will at least understand that story helps us get closer to answers, but is not the answer itself.

Recommended Readings

Books

Anderson, Rob, Robert Dardenne, and G. Michael Killenberg. *The Conversation of Journalism.* Westport, Conn.: Praeger, 1994. Argues that narrative is a valuable journalistic form because it not only is more inviting to more readers, but enables more voices to be heard.

Franklin, Jon. *Writing for Story.* New York: Mentor, 1986. Franklin instructs and inspires in this book known not only for its instruction on writing news in story form, but for its detailed explanations of Franklin's own work.

Sims, Norman, and Mark Kramer. *Literary Journalism.* New York: Ballantine Books, 1995. Tries to do for "literary" journalism, with some success, what Tom Wolfe did for New Journalism. This anthology includes writers such as Joseph Mitchell, Calvin Trillin, Tracy Kidder, and John McPhee. Sims and Kramer define and explore "literary" journalism in separate introductions.

Sloan, Wm. David, and Cheryl S. Wray, eds. *Masterpieces of Reporting*, Vol. 1. Northport, Ala.: Vision Press, 1997. An anthology of excellent news stories exhibiting a variety of story structures.

Weber, Ronald, ed. *The Reporter as Artist: A Look at the New Journalism Controversy.* New York: Hastings House, 1974. Weber and more than twenty others provide an early critique of the New Journalism that considers not only its advantages and disadvantage, but also some of the continuing problems of the narrative form.

Wolfe, Tom, and Edward Johnson. *The New Journalism.* New York: Harper & Row, 1973. A classic anthology of New Journalism work from Hunter Thompson, Gay Talese, Truman Capote, Norman Mailer, and others. Widely known for Wolfe's introduction in which he defines the New Journalism and claims its ascendancy over the novel.

Articles & Book Chapters

Bird, Elizabeth, and Robert Dardenne. "Myth, chronicle, and story: Exploring the narrative qualities of news," 67-86 in James Carey, ed., *Media, Myths, and Narratives: Television and the Press.* Beverly Hills, Calif.: Sage, 1988. Discusses news, narrative, and story and their relationships to myth. The chapter also discusses the seductive powers of narrative, contrasts story and chronicle, and explores the complexities and possibilities of narrative form.

Darnton, Robert. "Writing News and Telling Stories." *Daedalus* 104 (1975): 175-94. In writing about his days as a reporter, Darnton explores newsroom structures and traditions, how reporters operate, and how information becomes story, connecting news to story's mythic qualities.

Franklin, Jon. "When To Go Long." *American Journalism Review* (December 1996): 36-9. Pulitzer Prize-winning Franklin says he's pleased that narrative form is popular, but he warns that it shouldn't be taken lightly, that it's not easy, and in the end, it could be dangerous.

Fricker, Daniel. "Making Stories Tell Stories." *Second Takes,* a newletter of the *Portland Oregonian* (November 1996): 8. An argument that narrative can build newspaper readership in ways that even investigative journalism cannot. Fricker says in prospective narratives reporters follow events as they occur, and in retrospective narratives they use interviews to reconstruct events. Either narrative expands traditional news content.

Hart, Jack. "Storytelling." *Editor & Publisher,* 5 February 1994, 5. A writing coach explains the value of narrative in journalism in a one-page primer. He says narrative shouldn't replace the inverted pyramid, but it could add a valuable new dimension to daily journalism and may help keep readers from flocking to TV, magazines, and other media.

Hayes, Erin. "Writing Tips for Television News." *IRE Journal* (September/October 1994): 13-15. A TV journalist provides suggestions for the process and style of TV news writing. Among the things Hays suggests is making stories personally compelling by telling stories about victims.

Holley, Joe. "Who was burning black churches? The anatomy of a story that got out of hand." *Columbia Journalism Review* (September/October 1996): 26-32. A demonstration of the power of narrative in creating a "story" out of an issue.

Liebes, Tamar, ed. "Narrativization of the News." *Special Issue of Journal of Narrative Life History.* Hillsdale, N.J.: Lawrence Erlbaum, 1994. Eight scholars discuss news and media narratives in an introduction (Liebes) and seven articles in this special double issue of the journal. In an appealing argument, Justin Lewis in one article contends that people find television news difficult to comprehend or retain because it is not narrative, but a peculiar structure all its own.

Roeh, Itzhak. "Journalism as Storytelling, Coverage as Narrative." *American Behavioral Scientist* 33: 2 (November/December 1989): 162-8. Roeh says that Western journalists and scholars refuse to deal with journalism as storytelling. While arguing, among other things, the similarity between news and fiction (stories have to be told to exist), he makes a good case for studying journalism as storytelling.

Simon, David. "Making the Story More Than Just the Fact." *News/Inc.* (July/August 1992): 37-9. A reporter argues that conventional crime coverage is bad journalism, bloodless and cold, reducing tragedy and anesthetizing readers. He pleads for journalists to reduce their fixation on objective analysis and return to storytelling, providing readers with stories from real people who think and act and feel.

Sloan, Wm. David. "The Ingredients of Good News Writing." Chapter 13 in Bruce J. Evensen, ed., *The Responsible Reporter*, 2nd ed. Northport, Ala.: Vision Press, 1997. Discusses the characteristics of effective newspaper writing, including a favorable treatment of narrative devices.

Chapter Twenty-eight

Revealing and Concealing a Suspect's Name

Clay Calvert

When journalists publicize the name of a suspect in a criminal investigation, their action carries consequences. The publicity affects the suspect, the journalism profession, the public, and potentially the criminal investigation itself. The harms can be dramatic.

The *Atlanta Journal* published an "Extra" edition on July 30, 1996, that named security guard Richard A. Jewell as the focus of the government investigation in the bombing at Atlanta's Centennial Olympic Park. The story triggered a media feeding frenzy that left Jewell — now cleared by the federal government — vilified, without a reputation, and stripped of privacy. As Max Frankel wrote in *The New York Times Magazine*, there was "an irreparable media assault on reputation and privacy." Furthermore, the incident launched a barrage of criticism against the press for giving publicity to leaked, off-the-record accusations that left Jewell forever sullied.

The public revelation also jeopardized the government's investigation, diverting attention to one individual who, had he been the real perpetrator, might have destroyed evidence or fled. The media spotlight on Jewell left the public confused about the status of the case, leading many people to believe that he planted the bomb and that the case was solved.

The Jewell incident should make journalists pause to consider when they should reveal or conceal the identity of a suspect in a criminal investigation. Alternatively, the question is: When, if ever, should journalists reveal (or conceal) the identity of an uncharged suspect or target in a criminal investigation?

Reporters and editors face choices when confronted with information that ties an uncharged individual to a crime. They can ignore it completely, or they can investigate it for possible use in a story. If they choose to use the information, they still have the option of withholding the alleged suspect's name. In other words, a newspaper might run a story that states that the police have identified a possible suspect but that does not reveal the suspect's name.

A crucial distinction, at this stage, must be made between an individual who merely is a suspect and one who either is arrested or formally charged or indicted with a crime. A suspect may simply be a person of whom police are asking questions or focusing an investigation. The person may be one of several suspects. It may be, as was the case with Richard Jewell, that a suspect is merely someone who fits a profile. Jewell seemed to fit the pop-psychology profile of the "wannabe" policeman who feigns his own heroism, and his story, in turn, fit nicely into the hero-turned-villain narrative device that makes for easy journalistic storytelling. At no time, however, was Jewell either arrested or formally charged in the bombing incident during the 1996 Summer Olympic Games.

A number of questions must be considered in resolving the complex issue of suspect revelation. For instance, what standard of proof is sufficient before a media organization should print or broadcast the name of a suspect? Is off-the-record information enough to justify publishing a suspect's name or should the name be confirmed by sources willing to go on the record for attribution? Alternatively, should a newspaper never identify an uncharged individual, regardless of the reliability of the information, and instead wait until either formal charges are filed or an arrest is made before revealing the name?

In addition to questions regarding standards of proof or confirmation about suspect status, other issues are relevant. For instance, is a news organization's only obligation to accurately report allegations or is it to investigate the truth behind those allegations? For instance, the *Atlanta Journal* was accurate in reporting that Richard Jewell was a suspect, but did it also have an obligation to investigate and report on whether that accusation was true? In other words, should the newspaper have investigated for itself whether Jewell in fact planted the bomb?

How much influence should the goal of "scooping" the competition play in the decision to print a suspect's name? When does a journalist's obligation to serve the public's right to know give way to what Jay Black and his colleagues in *Doing Ethics in Journalism* term the principle of minimizing harm? This principle requires treating subjects as "human beings deserving of respect, not merely as a means to ... journalistic ends." An additional factor is whether journalists should withhold a suspect's name if public revelation might jeopardize a criminal investigation by tipping off the suspect and causing the person to flee.

This chapter addresses these questions in the course of considering when journalists should reveal or conceal the name of a suspect. First, it provides background on suspect revelation, including a description of the critical difference between an individual who is a suspect and one who is arrested or formally charged with a crime. It then describes three alternative viewpoints and arguments regarding the publication of an uncharged suspect's name. The chapter concludes by presenting suggestions and guidelines for journalists on this complex issue.

Origins of the Issue

The Richard Jewell incident was a high-profile case, but it certainly wasn't unique. It has merely brought into high relief the question of what standards and guidelines journalists should consider when deciding whether or not to reveal a suspect's name.

In determining the level of proof that a journalist should have before giving publicity to a suspect's name, it's worth considering for purposes of background and analogy the legal standard of proof that must be satisfied before an individual can be arrested. The Fourth Amendment to the United States Constitution provides that before a warrant can be issued by a judge or magistrate to arrest an individual, the district attorney or law enforcement agency seeking the warrant must have "probable cause" to believe that the individual committed the crime in question. Legal scholars Jerold H. Israel and Wayne LaFave observe in *Criminal Procedure* that the probability required for an arrest "may generally be stated that it must be more than 50% probability that a crime has been committed, and at least sometimes a more than 50% probability that the person arrested committed it." The probable cause determination is based on the totality of the circumstances, the U.S. Supreme Court announced in 1983 in *Illinois v. Gates*. The Court observed in *Gates* that the veracity and basis of the knowledge of an informant is highly relevant in making the probable cause determination. Should similar standards apply when journalists consider naming uncharged suspects?

The legal distinction between an uncharged suspect and an arrested individual charged with commission of a crime may be a highly important consideration for journalists considering whether to reveal an individual's name. As was the case with Richard Jewell, it may turn out that a suspect is never charged and is, instead, completely cleared in the incident in question. The potential for harm, therefore, is much greater when an individual remains an uncharged suspect.

Three viewpoints regarding suspect name revelation are described below.

Publicity with Accuracy and Independence

Under this first perspective, a journalist's duty to accurately and objectively report facts that concern the public interest takes priority over other considerations. This duty trumps concerns for harm to a suspect who ultimately may be cleared in the incident, and it outweighs any potential harm to the criminal investigation that might be caused by name revelation. Factual accuracy also takes precedence over any investigation of whether the facts themselves are indeed truthful. The name of a suspect must be reported, in service of the public's right to know, provided it is reported accurately. In brief, journalists must report the name of a suspect if 1) they have reliable evidence that the individual is a suspect and 2) they accurately report the suspect's name as conveyed by a reliable source or sources.

The question of evidence reliability, for instance, arose in the *Atlanta Journal's* decision to publish Richard Jewell's name. The paper had information from several unnamed sources, but it also sent reporters to Jewell's apartment where they confirmed that FBI agents had placed him under surveillance. In other words, there was physical evidence that Jewell was a suspect. Furthermore, as Alicia C. Shepard wrote in the *American Journalism Review,* several reporters obtained similar information from a number of different sources. The newspaper thus complied with the admonition in the Society of Professional Journalists' new Code of Ethics to test "the accuracy of information from all sources and exercise care to avoid inadvertent error." Once questions of reliability and accuracy are resolved, the publicity with accuracy and independence viewpoint mandates publication of a suspect's name.

The free-speech and free-press clauses of the First Amendment support this position. The First Amendment provides in relevant part that "Congress shall make no law ... abridging the freedom of speech, or of the press." The Supreme Court reasoned in *Richmond Newspapers, Inc. v. Virginia* (1980) that the First Amendment has a "core purpose of assuring freedom of communication on matters relating to the functioning of government."

Crime affects the functioning of government. A criminal case involves the police, the courts and, of course, taxpayers' money. The public wants justice to be served, and it wants to know what is transpiring in a particular case. Revealing the status of the investigation — including publishing a suspect's name — furthers the public's knowledge about the incident. As Louis A. Day writes in *Ethics in Media Communications,* "[i]nformation is the lifeblood of democracy, and where certain knowledge is essential either to rational consumer choice or collective political decision making, the arguments favoring publicity over confidentiality assume critical dimensions."

Closely linked to this line of reasoning is the argument that publishing a suspect's name serves the public's right to know. Writing in the *Journal of Mass Media Ethics,* Christopher Meyers observes that "an appeal to the public's right to know serves as the core element of the journalism ethos." Meyers states that "[o]ne of the fundamental tenets of democratic political systems is that the citizenry must have access to relevant information about their government, their social institutions and so forth."

Indeed, the *Atlanta Journal* subscribed in wholesale fashion to the right-to-know principle in the Richard Jewell incident. After Jewell was cleared by the federal government in the case, the newspaper ran a statement in its October 29, 1996, editions explaining the decision to publish his name. The newspaper wrote that the "public had — and has — a strong interest in the progress of the bombing investigation. They had a right to know when authorities' doubts about such a prominent figure in the bombing story led them to suspect him."

The public's right to know a suspect's name, in the first viewpoint, overshadows or outweighs any harms caused to the suspect or to the criminal investigation. Meyers writes that "[a]lthough individuals will sometimes be harmed by the pursuit and coverage of news, these harms are said to be justified by the promotion of a more powerful moral good — satisfaction of the public's right to know."

The press must not be concerned, under this viewpoint, with whether reporting a suspect's name may harm the criminal investigation by causing the suspect to flee or destroy evidence. Journalism and law enforcement are two distinct professions with two distinct sets of goals and purposes. Black and his colleagues write in *Doing Ethics in Journalism* that journalists "have an obligation first to inform the public. Law enforcement is charged with protecting the public." The journalist must act independently of the needs or desires of law enforcement.

The danger of not acting independently of law enforcement agencies is made clear by Black and his co-authors. "As watchdogs of the police," they argue, "journalists who squelch news to cooperate with law enforcement invariably reduce the public's opinion of their tenacity and erode press credibility." The press, in brief, is not a tool of law enforcement. Instead, it often serves, as Vincent Blasi writes in *The Checking Value in First Amendment Theory*, a watchdog function on government abuses. How can the press keep government abuse in check if it bows to the wishes and desires of government agencies like the police or FBI?

The truthtelling function of journalism in the first perspective considers, as Edmund Lambeth puts it in *Committed Journalism*, "truth in the sense of factual accuracy." Essentially, in this view, the journalist's role is reduced to little more than a mouthpiece or megaphone for the sources who feed them information about suspects. Stanford University's Theodore L. Glasser writes in his *Quill* journal article, "Objectivity Precludes Responsibility," that the reporter functions in this mode "as a translator — translating the specialized language of sources into a language intelligible to a lay audience."

The journalist assumes no responsibility for the consequences of his actions, provided he accurately reports that a person is a suspect. Considering the consequences and harms caused by reports of accurate information is not the reporter's job. The reporter is merely a messenger, not a soothsayer who predicts speculative outcomes or a social engineer who strives to report only news that will help society. The journalist who becomes bogged down in a consequentialist quagmire is the journalist who has forgotten his or her overriding duty — to accurately and objectively inform the public about information that affects the general welfare. It is far too difficult to predict whether or not a suspect will ultimately be cleared, and it is not the job of the journalist to worry about this potential outcome. For every Richard Jewell who is cleared and left reputationless there is a suspect who will be charged and convicted. Viewed in this light, Glasser writes, the ideal of objective, accurate reporting promotes "a disregard for the consequences of newsmaking."

Another aspect of the first perspective — one that was the case in the Richard Jewell incident — is that the desire to scoop the competition is a valid concern in the decision to publish a suspect's name. As reporter Ron Martz of the *Atlanta Journal* told Alicia C. Shepard in the *American Journalism Review,* "If we'd gotten beaten, we'd have been the laughing stock of the industry." A newspaper shouldn't need to see what other media outlets will do before publishing the name of a suspect. If information about the suspect's identity is reliable, the quicker that information is published the better — both for the public's right to know and for the sake of the newspaper in beating the competition.

Once the suspect's name is given initial publicity by one media outlet, other news organizations are relieved of any burden of deciding whether to publish the name. The "it's-out-there" rationale justifies republishing the name. Journalists in this perspective, to quote Carlin Romano in his essay, "The Grisly Truth About Bare Facts," believe that "facts are like sea shells to be scooped away and taken home." In other words, republishing the facts — the suspect's name and identity — is non-problematic because the facts already exist independently of the republishing news media outlet. The facts were published once before; they are "out there" ready to be gathered and used again. Provided the other media outlets accurately attribute the information to the news organization that broke the story, they have satisfied their obligation to serve the public's right to know. Giving further publicity that may cause harm to the suspect is not their concern — these "repeater" or "downstream disseminator" news organizations are merely conduits for information already disseminated by another source. They carry no responsibility for its consequences.

This was certainly the case with Richard Jewell. Thirty minutes after the *Atlanta*

Journal's story hit the streets, CNN read the story — including Jewell's name — on the air, and the three major television networks each led with the story that same night on the evening news.

In summary, the first viewpoint privileges and honors the public's right to know and journalistic independence. It downplays concerns for harm that might be caused by giving publicity to a suspect's name. The first viewpoint also relieves journalists of any duty other than to accurately report the suspect's name.

Publicity with Accuracy and Caution

This perspective starts, like the first viewpoint, with a presumption that the press must publish a suspect's name if it has reliable information that a person is a suspect. That presumption, however, may be rebutted or overcome if there is clear and convincing evidence that giving publicity to the suspect's name will threaten an ongoing criminal investigation. This perspective also requires that a news organization does more than just accurately publicize the name of a suspect. A newspaper also has the duty to investigate whether or not the suspect indeed committed the allegedly criminal act in question.

The possibility, under the second perspective, that the journalist may conceal a suspect's name suggests a balancing approach. The journalist must weigh the potential benefits of exposing a suspect's name against the potential harms that it may cause to a criminal investigation. In brief, a cost-benefit or risk-utility balancing occurs. Because there is a presumption — under the rationale of the public's right to know — that the suspect's name should be revealed, however, the level of evidence of harm to the investigation must be high to rebut the publication presumption. The evidence must be clear and convincing that the investigation will be harmed. There must be more than mere speculation that the suspect could flee or destroy evidence or that the investigation will otherwise be impeded. Instead, there must be an articulable, substantial basis on which the fear is based. For instance, it may be that the suspect in question has a past history of fleeing or that the gravity of the crime in question — its seriousness and the possible penalties for a conviction — suggests a substantial danger that the suspect will flee. There is, however, no precise fixed formula or mathematical percentage for this calculation, making it somewhat difficult to apply. This is a weakness that afflicts any approach attempting to weigh or balance competing interests.

Under the second viewpoint, the journalist acts not only in his or her role as a journalist but also as a citizen of the community, state, or country in which he or she works. As a citizen, the journalist has a vested interest in assuring that justice is served and his or her community is safe. This may entail sacrificing some level of journalistic independence that is so prized under the first perspective. It may require not publishing the suspect's name. The journalist may need to shed, as Davis Merritt puts it in *Public Journalism and Public Life*, "the armor of detachment" to enhance the public's safety and the community's well being.

The journalist also has a duty, in addition to giving publicity to the name of a suspect fed to it from reliable sources, to investigate the truth behind the allegations. As the Commission on Freedom of the Press, chaired by Robert M. Hutchins, reported in 1947 in *A Free and Responsible Press*, "It is no longer enough to report the fact truthfully. It is now necessary to report the truth about the fact." This admonition and the report itself suggest, as Lambeth writes in *Committed Journalism*, "the concept of the social responsibility of the press." The press must do more than simply print facts.

If the press, for instance, is going to name Richard Jewell as a suspect, then it has a concomitant duty to investigate whether or not Jewell in fact planted the bomb in Olympic Centennial Park. It must present the facts about Jewell, in the words of the Hutchins Commission, in a "context which gives them meaning." In other words, it must be made clear that although an individual is a suspect, it may be that the person did not in fact have anything to do with the crime in question. Furthermore, the press must take steps to determine whether or not this is indeed the case.

In a nutshell, there are two major differences between the first and second perspectives. The second perspective is not afraid to sacrifice journalistic independence from law enforcement agencies if there is clear and convincing evidence that revealing a suspect's name would harm an investigation. The second difference involves the obligation of truthtelling. In the second perspective, truthtelling means more than mere accuracy or conveying information like a stenographer that was handed a set of facts by sources to transcribe in verbatim fashion. If a news media outlet gives publicity to a suspect's name, it also incurs an obligation to investigate that accusation and to present the allegation in a context that makes it clear that suspect status is not the same as arrest status.

Concomitant with the consideration of these two additional elements, each of which requires reflection and investigation by the journalist, is the preclusion of the scoop mentality as a driving force behind publishing the suspect's name. When journalists take the perspective of citizen-journalists, as they do when weighing the harms and benefits of concealment of a suspect's name, the desire to "beat" the competition takes a back seat. The primary concern is determining whether the public's right to know outweighs the public's need to further the investigation. The issue is not to beat other media organizations to the story.

Non-disclosure Until Arrested or Charged

The beauty of the third viewpoint is its absolutist nature. A suspect's name cannot be printed until that individual is formally charged with a crime or actually arrested. It is a bright-line policy that reduces the need for on-the-spot decision making by journalists in times of crisis when the ability to meet and discuss choices may be scarce.

A guiding principle for this viewpoint is that it minimizes harm to the suspect who may never be charged with a crime. The types of harm a suspect may sustain include invasion of privacy, loss of reputation, emotional pain and suffering, job loss, and physical harm. For instance, Richard Jewell was repeatedly hounded by journalists who camped outside his apartment and gave widespread publicity to his suspect status. As Jewell told reporter Kevin Sack of *The New York Times*, "the media almost destroyed me and my mother."

Max Frankel, writing in *The New York Times Magazine*, articulated the kind of black-and-white absolutist policy embodied under the third viewpoint. "Whatever the source of the suspicions about Jewell, he was at least owed respect and privacy until formally charged, let alone convicted," Frankel opined.

The Society of Professional Journalists' newly adopted Code of Ethics published in the October 1996 edition of *Quill* admonishes journalists to minimize harm and to "recognize that gathering and reporting information may cause harm or discomfort. Pursuit of news is not a license for arrogance." Under the heading of minimizing harm, the new code specifically addresses the topic of suspect-name revelation. It states that journalists should be "judicious about naming criminal suspects before the formal filing of charges." Although not an absolutist position, this maxim is nonetheless served by a blanket policy that prohibits the use of a suspect's name prior to arrest or indictment.

In contrast to the first viewpoint that justifies publishing a suspect's name under cover of the public's-right-to-know rationale and the First Amendment's protection of the press, the third perspective makes a critical distinction between the right to publish and the need to publish. As Robert Ellis Smith writes in a recent issue of the *Journal of Mass Media Ethics*, although there may be "an absolute right to publish, there is not always an absolute need to know." Put another way, although some members of the public may want to know the identity of any and all suspects, this is not the same as the public needing to know that information.

Although the press may have a right to publish a suspect's name, this viewpoint questions whether there really is a need to do so. An article can reveal that the police or other law enforcement agency have identified or narrowed their search to several suspects without specifically revealing the identity of those suspects. The information value added by using suspects' names is outweighed by the potential reputational, emotional, and economic harm to those suspects. Some of these harms may be short term, but others are irreparable and may follow the individual for the rest of his or her life. Labeling Richard Jewell a suspect, as David Johnston writes in *The New York Times,* made him "guilty by suspicion even though he [had] not been arrested or accused of any crime." Once a suspect is formally charged or arrested, then the person's name may be revealed. At this stage, the government has satisfied its initial burden of proof — described in the introduction — to bring the matter to resolution in a courtroom.

A major criticism of the third perspective, however, is that it forces the journalist to keep a secret. Philosopher Sissela Bok observes in her book *Secrets: On the Ethics of Concealment and Revelation* that to keep a fact secret is "to block information about it or evidence of it from reaching [a] person, and to do so intentionally: to prevent him from learning it, and thus from possessing it, making use of it, or revealing it." Concealment and hiding, Bok observes, are the defining traits of secrecy.

When journalists choose to intentionally conceal the name of a suspect, they are keeping secrets from the public. This conflicts directly with the truthtelling obligation of journalists. Journalism is not about keeping secrets, but about public dissemination of information that serves the collective welfare. Although journalists sometimes maintain the confidentiality of sources to enhance their newsgathering ability, sources and suspects are very different classes of individuals. Sources supply information for a story while suspects often are the story.

The *Seattle Times,* writes Alicia C. Shepard in the *American Journalism Review,* has an absolutist written policy that "suspects should not be named until they are charged." However, in the Richard Jewell situation, an exception was made because the paper would have appeared "foolish for being the only medium in the country not to name Jewell." This seems to reflect the "it's-out-there" rationale for publication described earlier. The *Seattle Times* makes exceptions to its general rule, Shepard writes, if "there's a smoking gun situation or a person is apprehended in the midst of a crime in a public place."

The danger with carving out a few exceptions and caveats to an absolutist policy, of course, is that those exceptions may create a slippery slope that allows for the creation of more exceptions to the rule. Eventually, the exceptions swallow up the general rule until the absolute prohibition on naming suspects until charged is meaningless. Those who adopt an absolute rule must therefore be vigilant in its enforcement and guard against erosion-by-exception.

In summary, the third perspective privileges minimizing harm to the suspect and protecting the criminal investigation. It sacrifices truthtelling for secrecy and creates a standard that can blur when organizations begin to create exceptions to what at first appears as bright-line rule.

Resolution

Each of the three viewpoints described above has merits and weaknesses. Is one necessarily better than the others? We return to the question raised in the introduction: When should journalists conceal or reveal the identity of uncharged suspects in criminal investigations?

This section adopts the viewpoint of the second perspective that there should be a rebuttable presumption in favor of publishing a suspect's name once a media outlet obtains reliable information that the person is a suspect. This presumption privileges the truthtelling function of journalism and serves the public's right to know information that affects its well being.

Before publishing a suspect's name, however, journalists should consider a number of factors to determine if the presumption of publicity can be rebutted. No single factor is determinative in the decision whether to reveal or conceal. Instead, each must be considered in a totality-of-the-circumstances approach.

First, journalists should consider the amount of evidence known that actually links the suspect to the crime. Is the evidence merely speculative, based on a pop-psychology profile like the one that was used to make Jewell a suspect? Is there some tangible physical evidence that links the suspect to the crime? Are there several pieces of evidence that link the individual to the crime or is there only one? The greater the amount of evidence, the more reason there is to publish a suspect's name.

Second, journalists should consider whether the source or sources of information are willing to have their names attributed to it. The more willing a source is to speak for attribution, the more likely it is that he or she has real information about the person. More important, however, is the principle that naming the source promotes and fosters public accountability. Readers and listeners who know the source or sources of information can better evaluate the veracity of that information. Providing a source's name gives the public more information — it serves the truthtelling function — on which to weigh the credibility of the accusation against a suspect.

Third, journalists should consider if the police or government agency investigating the crime has asked the press not to publicize the name of the suspect. If no specific request is made to keep the identity of suspects in a particular incident secret, then journalists do not need to consider this factor. If, however, there is a specific request that asks journalists to conceal suspect identity, then the journalist should ask the government agency for specific details about why the suspect's name should be concealed. Ultimately, it is up to the journalist — not the government agency — to evaluate the strength and weaknesses of these reasons.

Fourth, journalists should consider the number of suspects under investigation. How many individuals are suspects? If there is more than one suspect, then the journalist should consider holding off on publicizing names until there is more information that pinpoints the investigation to one specific suspect. When a half-dozen suspects for a single crime exist, for example, publication of all six names will wrongfully harm the reputations of at least five (and possibility six) of the suspects who were not involved. The amount of harm caused by publication in this case is much greater than when an investigation targets one suspect and that lone individual's name is publicized.

This quartet of factors should be considered as a whole with no one factor receiving more weight than the others. It is up to practicing journalists to thoughtfully consider these factors on a case-by-case basis. If, for example, the evidence against the suspect is speculative at best, sources are not willing to speak for attribution, the police have offered substantial reasons for withholding a name, and there are multiple suspects, then the journalists should not disclose a suspect's name. On the other hand, if the investigation pinpoints one individual and features several pieces of tangible evidence that link the person to the crime, this may militate in favor of publicizing the suspect's name.

Absent from this list of factors is the goal of scooping the competition. This should be irrelevant in the consideration about whether to reveal or conceal a suspect's name. Journalism is not about "beating" others to the punch; it is about providing well researched information that serves the public's interest. Beating others to the punch may increase corporate profits, but it does not necessarily serve the public. Often, the rush to publish first becomes a "race to the bottom" in which the value of the information distributed quickly is minimal. Sometimes, in fact, the information may prove false, and an extra day spent investigating that information would have prevented the dissemination of false information.

If journalists decide to publicize the name of a suspect, their duties should not end there. They have an affirmative obligation, until the person is formally charged or arrested, to 1) explain the difference between suspect and arrest status, 2) investigate the truth behind the accusation, and 3) explain whether there are other suspects who the police or government are also investigating. These three factors serve the Hutchins Commission's twin admonitions to place the facts in a context that makes them meaningful and to investigate the truth about the facts.

Applying the second viewpoint and the factors identified here to the

Richard Jewell case, it is clear that the presumption of publicity would have been rebutted at the time the press revealed his name. Why? First, there was no physical evidence that connected Jewell to the crime, only a psychological profile. According to *The New York Times*, the FBI affidavits used to obtain search warrants for Jewell's apartment "had only the most circumstantial of evidence against Mr. Jewell at the time it named him a suspect."

Second, although journalists had firsthand observations of the FBI's search of Jewell's residence, the official government sources that provided information to the journalists were not willing to have their names attributed to that information. Third, the fact that the FBI was focusing on Jewell did not mean that it was not focusing on other individuals. The journalists should have asked their sources whether other individuals were under investigation. Whether they ever did this is not clear. Fourth, what seemed to drive the publication of Jewell's name was the goal of scooping the competition. As a reporter for the paper that publicized his name said in the *American Journalism Review*, "if we'd gotten beaten, we'd have been the laughing stock of the industry." In brief, Jewell's name was published for all of the wrong reasons. Cases similar to Jewell's will arise the future. How journalists will react remains to be seen.

Recommended Readings

Book

Bok, S. *Secrets: On the ethics of concealment and revelation*, 2d ed. New York: Vintage, 1989. Provides an in-depth analysis, from the perspective of a non-journalist, on the benefits and harms of keeping secrets.

Articles

Frankel, M. "An Olympian injustice." *New York Times Magazine*, 22 September 1996, 60-1. Frankel criticizes the majority of media outlets for their coverage of the Richard Jewell incident, and he suggests that Jewell's privacy interests were owed more respect.

Meyers, C. "Justifying journalistic harms: right to know vs. interest in knowing." *Journal of Mass Media Ethics* 8 (199): 133-46. Meyers argues that too often journalists fail to distinguish, when attempting to justify potential harms caused by publicizing information, between the public's right to know and its mere interest in knowing.

Shepard, A. C. "Going to extremes." *American Journalism Review*, 29 October 1996, 38-43. This article does a thorough job of providing background information and analysis of the media's coverage of Richard Jewell and the bombing at Atlanta's Olympic Centennial Park.

Chapter Twenty-nine

The Use of
Anonymous Sources

Lori Bergen

Officials say, and spokesmen confirm. Experts, aides, and authorities reveal. Specialists report, and insiders admit.

Who are these anonymous providers of much of the news presented to Americans today? They are the unnamed sources, the off-the-record newsmakers who occasionally request, and often demand, the promise of confidentiality from the media in exchange for information of public interest.

Don't tell anyone I told you so. It's on deep background. And not for attribution.

There's no question that journalists rely heavily on blind sources, especially when it comes to news that happens in Washington, D.C. The ubiquity of unattributed sources is documented in study after study. Some have shown that as many as 55 per cent of all network television news stories and 80 per cent of newsmagazine stories contain at least one anonymous source. And while it's common practice for journalists to use unnamed sources in their work, nearly all news organizations have policies discouraging their use.

When and under what conditions should a journalist use anonymous sources? Reporters argue that granting anonymity to a source can help them gain access to information that would otherwise remain unobtainable. But one of the criticisms against giving the protection of confidentiality to a news source is that it often undermines the public's trust and confidence in the accuracy and veracity of the reporter's information. The public's ability to make a judgment about the believability of a story is compromised when the source is unknown. And damage can be done by unsubstantiated accusations made by people unwilling to be identified.

What are the rules governing the use of unnamed sources? Who decides that it's appropriate to grant anonymity — reporters or their editors? Is the reporter obligated to protect the secret identity of a source when circumstances change? On occasion, a reporter has gone to jail to keep the promise of confidentiality. And sometimes, when a reporter breaks that promise, the cases have landed reporters and their news organizations in court.

Given the crisis of credibility for journalism today, it would seem wise to call for an examination of journalists' routine use of unnamed sources in the news. First, let's consider the role that anonymous sources have played in the American media over the past several decades.

Origins of the Issue

Journalists have always used unnamed sources, but the practice was unremarkable until the early 1970s. Publication of the Pentagon Papers in 1971, when whistle blower Daniel Ellsberg was the anonymous provider of documents outlining America's involvement in the Vietnam War, was a prelude to the first notable journalistic use of unnamed sources. In 1973, *Washington Post* reporters Robert Woodward and Carl Bernstein relied heavily on journalism history's most famous unnamed source, "Deep Throat," for their coverage of the Watergate cover-up. Deep Throat's identity remains a mystery, although he (or she?) was only one of many anonymous sources who contributed to a series of stories that led to the resignation of President Richard Nixon and the prosecution and conviction of several members of the White House staff.

After Watergate, journalists used anonymous sources with increasing frequency, but without the corresponding caution required to prevent criticism. John L. Hulteng has written in *The Messenger's Motive* that, when other reporters began to pursue the Watergate story, they "tried to emulate the tactics used by Bernstein and Woodward but without the same care and professionalism." They didn't check out secret leads or verify independently the reliability of their sources. The result was what Hulteng called "shoddy, indefensible journalism."

A new standard was set for reporting about everything from government to gardening. Some reporters considered it "sexier" to use an unnamed source than one on-the-record. Disguising source identities could add prestige to some reporters' stories. Sources came to expect anonymity, and reporters were quick to offer it. Anonymous sources were used as a matter of style as opposed to a matter of content.

But the unchecked use of anonymous sources after Watergate lasted less than a decade. It ended abruptly in 1980 when another *Washington Post* reporter, Janet Cooke, wrote a compelling story about an eight-year-old heroin addict, "Little Jimmy." The problem, of course, was that Jimmy did not exist. Although Cooke had convinced her editors that she was protecting her sources in refusing to reveal the identity of Jimmy, the truth of her fabrication was revealed only after she won — and then was forced to return — a Pulitzer Prize. In this most notorious case of a reporter's deception, Cooke's use of a source both unnamed and unverified by editors led to significant criticism of the media.

News organizations responded with evaluations of their policies on granting confidentiality to news sources, and efforts to prevent their abuse and overuse were widespread. Douglas A. Anderson studied newspaper managing editors after the Pulitzer Prize hoax to gauge the effect on newsroom practice. He reported in a 1982 *Journalism Quarterly* article that 92 per cent agreed that editors would scrutinize stories with unnamed sources more carefully in the future. Journalism scholar Ted Glasser has suggested it was "cool" to use anonymous sources during the 1970s, but called 1981 "a watershed year," recounting the mood of self-examination and restraint that resulted. "Every journalism publication came out with these long essays saying we can't use anonymous sources anymore," he is quoted in a 1994 *American Journalism Review* article by Alicia Shepard. "Everyone beat their breast and said we are going to do better. But I don't think anything's really changed." Indeed, Shepard observed that "many journalists feel about anonymous sources the way people in troubled relationships feel about their partners: can't live with them, can't live without them." So although some organizations prohibit their use, most permit them, under certain conditions.

Examples of significant stories that rely on blind sources abound. Consider the story published by the *Seattle Times* in 1992 based on charges of sexual misconduct made by eight women against former Sen. Brock Adams. The award-winning newspaper ran the story with allegations that ranged from sexual harassment to rape and spanned a twenty-year period, but they didn't run the names of the accusers. Michael R. Fancher, executive editor for the *Times*, said the paper tried for years to persuade the women to go on the record, but the women all feared reprisals and refused. The paper was convinced of the truth of their stories because all were corroborated and checked. The senator's reelection campaign was in progress, further complicating the issue. The paper's decision to publish was based on a new standard — that a "critical mass" of women agreed to sign affidavits agreeing to come forward if a trial was necessary.

Although Fancher and the *Times* were criticized for their coverage and reliance on unnamed sources, many supported their decision and commended the meticulous procedure they used to ensure the truth of the story. But not all recent cases bear up under such scrutiny. The story published by the *Atlanta Journal and Constitution* on July 30, 1996, is a case in point. Olympic security guard Richard Jewell went from hero to villain status after the newspaper reported he was the focus of a federal investigation in the Olympic Park bombing case. The basis of the story, however, was off-the-record information obtained by a police reporter and reports that the FBI had Jewell's apartment under surveillance. The media frenzy that ensued cast Jewell as the prime suspect, and for months the networks and leading newspapers (with the notable exception of the *New York Times*) embellished the story with profiles of Jewell as a frustrated cop with psychological problems. Media stake-outs of his apartment and ambush interviews wherever he went deprived him of his privacy. The story, of course, later proved to be false. Congress held hearings investigating media behavior in the case. Jewell's lawsuit against the Atlanta newspaper was filed in January 1997, and he settled out of court with NBC, CNN, *Time* magazine, and an Atlanta radio station.

Other recent cases have further cast the media's use of unnamed sources in an unfavorable light. The media's reliance on unnamed sources in the reporting of the O.J. Simpson criminal trial brought further charges from critics about the use of unnamed sources. A string of unsubstantiated stories ensued, including, for example, that of a local Los Angeles television reporter who told viewers that DNA tests showed a match between blood on a sock found in Simpson's bedroom to his former wife's blood. The story was later retracted.

The frenzy in use — and criticism — of unnamed sources surrounding the O.J. Simpson case led some to hope that the practice would diminish due to public outrage. But the Jewell case followed, as did subsequent stories such as the two Dallas Cowboys football players accused of rape, and the *Dallas Morning News'* on-line publication of a pretrial confession of accused Oklahoma City bombing suspect Timothy McVeigh. These recent high-profile stories based on anonymous sources indicate that the practice continues and may even be increasing.

Although journalists must make ethical decisions when using anonymous sources, they must also be aware of the legal constraints and responsibilities they have with regard to their use. Granting a source anonymity can place reporters in a compromising legal position. They may be subpoenaed to testify about the identity of an unnamed source, be served with a search warrant for notes, videotapes, or other information gathered in pursuit of a story that may also contain information about criminal activity or that may be central to a libel suit. Journalists have some protection from having to provide confidential information under these circumstances, but it is not absolute.

It's ironic that a Supreme Court decision in 1972 against three reporters who asked for such protection actually helped to bring about a qualified privilege for journalists. In *Branzburg v. Hayes*, the court's 5-4 opinion was ambiguous and left open the opportunity for state legislatures and courts to establish through common law and state constitutional law a qualified privilege for journalists.

Twenty-nine states have enacted shield laws to protect journalists' privilege to maintain secrecy in shielding their sources, and many other states have extended similar protections to journalists through case law.

This historical overview highlights the development of two opposing points of view on anonymous sources. If actions do indeed speak louder than words, we can conclude that even though many journalists protest the practice of using anonymous sources, the practice continues. David Johnston wrote in a 1987 article in *Columbia Journalism Review* about the "syndrome" of using anonymous sources: "Complaining about the excessive use of unnamed sources has become a cliché in American journalism," he said. "The editors of the most respected papers have denounced it, but their front pages — and, increasingly, even their feature pages — continue to be forums for people who want to express their point of view but request anonymity."

Now, let's examine this paradox by considering the major criticisms directed against the use of unnamed sources and the evidence to support those concerns. Then, let's look at the arguments made to support their use and address the conditions under which most news organizations allow them.

Criticisms of Using Anonymous Sources

Many critics of anonymous sources argue that the costs of using them are so great that journalists and their news organizations should abandon them. Geneva Overholser, ombudsman for the *Washington Post*, has said that "the use of unnamed sources is among American newspapers' most damaging habits." Overholser's word choice — habit — is telling. It describes a behavior that one engages in without thought — a generalized, automatic reaction to a specific situation. And Overholser isn't the first journalist to see it that way. Gene Miller, Pulitzer Prize-winning reporter and associate editor for the *Miami Herald*, once said anonymity "is an invitation to exaggerate, embroider, embellish, slant. Or to take the cheap shot. This is true for the reporter, as well as the source. It is a bad habit and it is getting worse."

What are the concerns that critics have about this "habit" of granting anonymity? They include the possibility that reporters are too lazy to find on-the-record sources, or fail to work hard enough to persuade a source to talk for attribution. Other concerns are that reporters have made things up and are passing them off as unattributed facts, and that too many anonymous sources have self-serving agendas and intend to use the media for their own ends. The ultimate harm these problems cause, of course, is a diminution of the public's trust in the news media.

"There's not a place for anonymous sources," Allen H. Neuharth, founder of *USA Today* and chairman of the Freedom Forum, told *American Journalism Review*. "I think there are a few major historical developments that happened in journalism — the Pentagon Papers, maybe Watergate — where anonymous sources had a more positive influence than a negative impact. But on balance, the negative impact is so great that we can't overcome the lack of trust until or unless we ban them."

In a column she wrote in the *Washington Post* in late 1995, Overholser criticized the *Post's* use of anonymous sources, suggesting that the cost is not just to the quality of public dialogue about issues of importance or public confidence in the press. The lack of public confidence in government increases as well when the media fail to make officials accountable for information they provide.

The use of anonymous sources undermines the already shaky credibility of journalism. The public is less likely to trust the accuracy of the news reports that result and more likely to question the ethics of the reporter. Because anonymity masks the hidden motive or agendas of the source, the public is less likely to know how reliable the information may be. If used too routinely, sources come to expect anonymity and won't be willing to provide information unless they can do so in confidence. The relationship between the press and "one high government official" illustrates some of these concerns.

Although Deep Throat remains the most famous — and still anonymous — source in journalism history, former Secretary of State Henry Kissinger is one legendary Washington anonymous source who was never really quite anonymous. In his 1992 book *Kissinger, Time* magazine Assistant Managing Editor Walter Isaacson recounts the relationship Kissinger had with the press — one he characterizes as manipulative, insular, and symbiotic. Kissinger was adept at feeding headline-grabbing news to the "Kissinger 14," as the press corps who traveled on his plane were dubbed. Kissinger was always thinly disguised as "a senior American official," and he used background briefings to control the nature of the news coverage he received. "He refined a set of ground rules that fell between on the record (in which the speaker can be quoted) and off the record (in which the information cannot be used at all)," Isaacson wrote. "Usually he would speak on 'background,' which meant that he would be quoted merely as 'a senior American official' or some such label. Occasionally, he would speak on 'deep background,' meaning that reporters could use the information, but not quote or attribute it in any manner."

Isaacson suggests that few people were fooled and recounts "the time that humorist Art Buchwald, who was along for the ride on one trip, referred in his column to a "high U.S. official with wavy hair, horn-rimmed glasses and a

German accent." But a real danger exists under such conditions. As Isaacson wrote, the backgrounders "often replaced rather than supplemented real reporting, and their popularity arose from two great journalistic sins, coziness and laziness." Isaacson noted that these Middle East shuttles were usually reported by the press from Kissinger's plane, which meant that he was the source for most of the information. "Only a few of the more enterprising reporters consistently tried to supplement the background nuances gleaned on Kissinger's plane with hard reporting on the ground," Isaacson wrote.

David Shaw, media reporter and critic for the *Los Angeles Times*, has argued that naming sources is an important part of the story and necessary to maintaining public trust. "Reporters who write stories based on statements they do not identify for their readers are, in effect, asking their readers to trust them, to assume that the reporters (and their editors) have evaluated the source's credentials and credibility. Good reporters from good newspapers figure they have earned that trust."

To use an unnamed source, the reporter and editor must be doubly confident of the accuracy of the information they provide. When sources are named, it's easier for the public to decide for themselves if the source is credible and the information is likely to be true. When the source is anonymous, the reporter assumes responsibility for both credibility and truth. The source is no longer accountable, because the reporter and his or her news organization have assumed that responsibility. This "transfer of accountability" for the veracity of statements of opinion and fact means that reporters must confirm and verify the information.

To illustrate this concern, consider the critiques offered by several scholars and journalists about the books written or co-written by Bob Woodward, the Watergate reporter who is today a *Washington Post* editor and author. He relies heavily on unnamed sources in many of his books, which include *All The President's Men*, the book about Watergate he wrote with Carl Bernstein, and others about the Supreme Court, John Belushi, the CIA, the Pentagon, and inside the Clinton White House. As Stephen Banker wrote in a 1991 commentary for *Washington Journalism Review*, "the building blocks of the narrative [from Woodward's books] rest on air. There are no attributions, no footnotes, no list of sources. The reader is asked to accept what he reads because it comes from Bob Woodward."

Banker suggests that Woodward creates a harmful precedent in adopting a reporting technique that in and of itself is hazardous. "The danger is that success breeds imitators," Banker wrote. "Even if we grant that every word Woodward has written is valid (and that is demonstrably not the case), the public service of his disclosure is outweighed by the influence his methodology might have on other writers, and consequently on other subjects."

Let's consider one final argument against using anonymous sources — the difficult legal and ethical situations that can result. As a purely practical matter, journalists should be cautious in using anonymous sources because of the potential for tremendous consequences. Anyone who's ever heard a secret knows how difficult it is to keep it. Journalists should be aware that in granting anonymity, they create both a moral and legal obligation to maintain that trust. Yet doing so is not always easy.

Several visible cases where the press used unnamed sources illustrate this dilemma: what happens if the journalist is compelled to break the promise? As Stephen Klaidman and Tom L. Beauchamp have written in their book *The Virtuous Journalist*, competing values may at times override the obligation of confidentiality. The risk of disclosure is present in any such promise. But, in general, journalists break promises of confidentiality under two circumstances. The first is when a judge orders them or their news organizations to provide confidential information that may be relevant to a criminal or libel case. The second is when reporters and editors decide to break the promise themselves because of the overriding news value of the source's identity to a story.

In the book *Communication and the Law*, University of North Carolina journalism professor Cathy Packer writes that courts are insisting that journalists offer evidence that their relationship with a source was, in fact, confidential. And recently, courts have begun to treat these agreements like contracts.

In *Cohen v. Cowles Media Co.*, the Supreme Court's 1991 decision emphasized journalists' obligation to keep their promises of confidentiality. The case involved the *Minneapolis Star Tribune*, the *St. Paul Dispatch*, and a political party worker, Dan Cohen, who provided documents to reporters at both newspapers with information damaging to the opposing party's candidate for lieutenant governor. Cohen's information disclosed that, over a decade before, the candidate had been charged with unlawful assembly when she protested on behalf of minority workers and had once been convicted of shoplifting $6 worth of sewing materials. Cohen received promises of confidentiality from the reporters, but editors at the two newspapers decided that his identity and the political "dirty trick" he was playing on the opposing candidate was itself newsworthy. They ignored the reporters' promises of confidentiality and identified Cohen as the source in the subsequent stories they published.

Cohen sued the two newspapers for breach of contract and misrepresentation after he lost his job on the day the stories were published. Although the Minnesota Supreme Court refused to find that contract law protected the promise of confidentiality to a news source, the U.S. Supreme Court held that under Minnesota's common law of promissory estoppel (which protects people from injustice when they rely and act on a promise), a source could sue for damages against a news medium that broke its promise of confidentiality. The court said publishers of a newspaper "have no special immunity from the application of general laws." The case was sent back to the state court, where a $200,000 damage award was upheld.

In their book *Fundamentals of Mass Communication Law*, Donald Gillmor, Jerome Barron, Todd Simon, and Herb Terry suggest that this case gives journalists reason for concern. "[T]he Court has opened the door to alternative theories of liability, and the decision is likely to encourage other sources who have been 'burned' to consider suing," they wrote. These authors also identify the key point to remember: "In many ways, however, the newspapers have no one but themselves to blame in *Cohen*," they wrote. "If the editors had honored the promises of confidentiality and chided the reporters later in private, there would have been no case."

The *Cohen* case emphasizes the *gravitas* journalists should assume when promising confidentiality and underscores the seriousness of such a pledge. The promise of confidentiality, once granted, cannot be easily violated by the media. And such a constraint provides a compelling argument for avoiding the use of anonymous sources.

In Defense of Using Anonymous Sources

The potential benefits for using unnamed sources are the value they provide in uncovering information that otherwise would go unreported and in the protection that confidentiality affords when the source could be harmed by providing information. In some cases, granting anonymity to a source might protect that person's job, property — even his life. When the source's livelihood or safety is in jeopardy, anonymity provides the protection required for him to provide information of importance.

Bill Blankenburg, a professor in the School of Journalism and Mass Communication at the University of Wisconsin-Madison, has suggested that anonymous sources are critical to American journalism because they both are functional for newsgathering purposes and help to foster diversity in public opinion by presenting critical and controversial views. In a 1992 article in *Newspaper Research Journal*, he wrote that anonymous attribution "is integral to newsgathering in a variety of settings and vital in some circumstances. Prohibitions fail because anonymity works. The source-reporter relationship is a set of transactions, and one of the coins is attribution."

Blankenburg studied several samples of news stories submitted to the Nexis database by searching for the terms "sources said" and "official said." Not surprisingly, he found the incidence of anonymous sources was ubiquitous. In three prestige newspapers — the *New York Times*, *Washington Post*, and *Los Angeles Times* — anonymous attribution was used in 23 to 35 per cent of national and international stories.

Some circumstances may require an increased use of anonymity. Blankenburg also compared stories about the Gulf War with non-war stories appearing at the same time and found that war stories were more likely to use anonymous sources. This suggests that certain characteristics of war and its coverage led to the increase in usage. "The usual responses to a threat of unfavorable disclosure are suppression and manipulation," Blankenburg wrote. "In the Gulf War, this meant censorship and spin control. To counter these limitations, the news media resorted to a tool of necessity, anonymous attribution. The more significant the events, the more likely its use."

Many journalists concur. *American Journalism Review* in 1994 quoted author and *Washington Post* Assistant Managing Editor Bob Woodward, who still says — in spite of the criticisms often levied against him — that anonymous sources are crucial for some important stories. This is especially true for stories that deal with Washington and government. "The job of a journalist, particularly someone who's spent time dealing in sensitive areas, is to find out what really happened," Woodward said. "When you are reporting on inside the White House, the Supreme Court, the CIA or the Pentagon, you tell me how you're going to get stuff on the record. Look at the good reporting out of any of those institutions — it's not on the record."

David Shaw, the media critic for the *Los Angeles Times*, also argues for the essential role that anonymous sources play in providing fuller coverage. In his book, *Press Watch*, he wrote:

> People in power — in government and private enterprise alike — do not like to read stories critical of their programs, practices, policies, and personalities. If everyone who told a reporter about the flaws in a Defense Department plan or a power struggle in the White House were identified in print (or on the air), the certainty of immediate retribution by superiors ... would surely discourage all but the most hardy (or foolhardy) from speaking to the press on controversial matters.

It's the mission of journalists to serve as "a conduit of information" to the public. And the flow of information would be diminished if reporters were prohibited from writing anything that they could not attribute by name and title.

That's the argument made by Gene Foreman, managing editor of the *Philadelphia Inquirer*, in a 1984 article in *Social Responsibility: Business, Journalism, Law and Medicine.* "One of the strengths of the press," he said, "is that our reporters can talk with people that government investigators often cannot or will not consult; they give us information only if we keep their identities confidential. Their status in the community, their careers, perhaps even their lives might otherwise be in jeopardy. When we accept the conditions of confidentiality, it is a sacred trust. We decide that the information is more important than the identity of the provider."

It's clear that even those who support the use of unnamed sources do so with reservations and limits on the circumstances and conditions under which such anonymity should be granted to a source. One of the best pieces of evidence for that concern is the preponderance of newsroom policies and ethical guidelines that specify when and where unnamed sources should be used.

For example, in 1994 the Associated Press Managing Editors Ethics Committee adopted a policy proposal for newsroom ethics after holding discussion and debate among their membership as well as with readers at town meetings in nineteen cities. Their proposal suggests guidelines for the following policies related to the use of confidential sources and is useful as an illustration of the kind of limitations that professional organizations, working with the public, regard as appropriate limitations on the use of unnamed sources. Their proposal suggests:

> The use of confidential sources should be rare rather than routine. It is the obligation of newspapers to resist their use.
> - Editors and reporters should seriously consider whether the information received from confidential sources is vital to readers before deciding to print.
> - Pledges of confidentiality by reporters should be given only as a last resort.
> - Every effort should be made to get the information on the record before publishing it without attribution.
> - When a source must remain unidentified, the reason should be stated in print.
> - The responsible editor should know the identity of the source before publication.

Journalism ethics scholar and Indiana University professor David Boeyink provided seven guidelines for using anonymous sources in an article on the abuses of anonymous sources that appeared in the *Journal of Mass Media Ethics* in 1990. His position is that, although journalists routinely use unnamed sources in television newscasts, news magazines, and newspapers, the standard should be for full attribution. "The source of the information is critical to understanding the meaning and significance of the message," he wrote. Exceptions to the standard should only occur with ample justification to limit abuse of the practice.

Boeyink's guidelines are these:

Promises of anonymity must be authorized by the editor. Journalists learned their lesson after Janet Cooke's deceptive story about "Little Jimmy," the nonexistent eight-year-old heroin addict. Benjamin Bradlee, her editor at the *Washington Post*, has said it's impossible to catch a deceiver like Cooke. But if the newspaper had required that *at least one editor* knew the identity of Jimmy, Cooke's deception would have been exposed and the story stopped before publication. Boeyink argues that "involving a second person is a crucial check within the system to ensure that the story is accurate and fair in the face of the potential for error or abuse."

Anonymous sources should be used only for a just cause. Boeyink argues that one of the fundamental operating principles of journalism is the attribution of sources. So overriding is that principle that anonymity should be used only if the alternative has significant value: exposing public corruption or publishing information needed for citizen involvement in democratic government. "The burden of proof rests with those who want to use anonymous sources to demonstrate why a story is important enough to allow the use of unattributed information to override the preferred standard of attribution," Boeyink wrote.

Using anonymous sources in unexceptional stories — cases where the risk of distortion is low or the story is simply interesting and not really important — sets a worrisome precedent. Why not use anonymous sources whenever it seems convenient?

Again, Boeyink argues the consequence is that

> readers and viewers are denied a critical prerogative: the ability to judge for themselves the validity of the information they are given. They have no way of knowing if the source of the speculation is a low-level bureaucrat or the Secretary of Defense. The risks of manipulation grow, the risks to credibility and accountability are real, and the value of the news is diminished.

Anonymous sources should be used only as a last resort. Meeting this criterion means working harder to get information on the record. It also means, often, spending more time and more money. But reporters should turn to reasonable alternatives to get the information — including shifting the emphasis from human sources to documentary sources — and include the cost of damage to the media's credibility and the public's knowledge of the issues in the calculation, Boeyink suggests.

Identify sources as fully as possible, with reasons for anonymity explained in the story. News stories should provide the reasons for granting anonymity so that audiences can make judgments about the credibility of the source, the possible motives for not wanting his name used, and whether the source is a low- or high-level official.

Balance potential harms and benefits of anonymous sources. The possible harm that may occur to an individual or institution should not outweigh the importance that a story has to the community. It won't always be easy to measure the benefit to society against the harm that might be done to one individual, but Boeyink's argument is that journalists are obligated to consider those competing outcomes whenever a story involves anonymous sources.

The reporter, media, and source should have just intentions. Journalists shouldn't use anonymous sources to "win prizes, sell newspapers, or to be the first to get a news story," Boeyink wrote. Nor should sources be allowed to use anonymity in the media to advance their own ends. Journalists must be cautious of serving a source's agenda in granting anonymity, and they have the added obligation of knowing enough about the source and the circumstances to be capable of making that judgment.

Get independent verification by a second source. Confirmation of information from a second, independent source makes good journalistic sense — even when journalists don't use anonymous sources! Journalists need to be even more certain of the accuracy and completeness of information when they provide anonymity to a source, because publishing something that's untrue is an even greater sin when the source is unnamed. "When stories are based on unnamed sources," Boeyink wrote, "the heightened risk of half-truths, distortions, and mistakes elevates the need for independent checks on accuracy."

Resolution

Should the use of unnamed sources continue as a legitimate journalistic tool? Probably so, but with caution and care. Given the preponderance of the practice among American journalists, it would probably be unreasonable to suggest that the practice be simply abandoned. The overriding argument that legitimate stories would remain in obscurity without some measure of confidentiality between reporters and sources seems to have struck a cord with the public as well.

Although Americans may continue to criticize the press for inaccuracy, lack of fairness, and sensationalizing the news, they endorse the practice of investigative journalism. A full 80 per cent of Americans interviewed in 1997 by the Pew

Research Center for The People and The Press approved of the news media's practice of uncovering and reporting corruption and fraud in business, government agencies, and other organizations. When Americans were asked about their approval of four specific investigative reporting techniques, the only technique to garner more than 50 per cent support was that of running stories with unnamed sources. The three other common investigative techniques — using hidden cameras and microphones, reporters not identifying themselves as reporters, and paying informers for information — received 42 per cent, 31 per cent, and 29 per cent support, respectively.

Although not actually a plebiscite on whether the public endorses the use of unnamed sources, there is enough indication from results such as these to indicate that when journalists pursue investigative stories with significant impact, the public approves of at least one of the quills in their quiver.

Most news organizations do have rules about the use of unnamed sources, although rules may not always be followed. From reviews of newsroom policies, we know that most maintain certain conditions for granting anonymity. These generally include that an editor have knowledge of the source, that the story is important, that anonymity was used only as a last resort, and that reasons for granting anonymity are included in the story.

One solution to the problem of unnamed sources is simple: follow the rules. Reasoned minds have considered the pitfalls and weighed the consequences of using unnamed sources. Most newsroom policies and ethical guidelines concur that the standard should be to avoid anonymous attribution. When used responsibly, in moderation, when circumstances require them, journalists can be confident that they haven't fallen into the trap of habitual use.

David Johnston, in a 1987 article in *Columbia Journalism Review*, provided techniques that some of the best reporters in the nation have used to avoid the habit. The first technique is to use documents. Reporters can find written material in libraries, government records, and today in on-line data bases and on CD-ROM. CAR, or computer-assisted reporting, makes short order of tracking down information that can be used either to confirm information provided by a source who wants anonymity or as a starting point to keep sources from requesting it in the first place. Johnston wrote that sources are more inclined to go on-the-record when they know a reporter already has substantial information that's verified.

Johnston wrote that another approach is to initially promise sources not to quote them by name, but after gathering important information, the reporter suggests that if the sources want to see such information in a news story, they must help the reporter document the assertions, or go on the record themselves. Another technique is to read back quotes to sources. This reassures sources that a reporter wants to be fair and accurate and can help establish a rapport based on trust with the source. Yet one more technique is to bounce one side against the other: get sources on one side of a story to talk off-the-record and then use the information to get verification from another source.

Critics point out that thorough investigative reporters don't have to cite anonymous sources in the stories that are ultimately published. The trend for good investigative reporting has been toward use of unnamed sources as a beginning point for covering a story. An investigative reporter may initially receive information from a source who requires confidentiality as a condition for providing the information, but the reporter proceeds to independently confirm that information through other sources. Once the story is published, all sources are attributed.

But all reporters do not enjoy the luxury of many months and other resources to conduct such extensive investigations and multiple source confirmation. More often than not, the use of anonymous sources occurs when reporters are, as some have charged, simply lazy. Or they are working on deadline, feeling competitive pressure and the need to get the story before somebody else publishes it first. Those situations may prompt a sidestep of the rules that might otherwise have required more careful and full verification of facts.

The trick to kicking the habit may be in weighing the relative costs associated with using unnamed sources. News organizations need to balance the economics of more thorough and conscientious reporting with the risk of losing credibility. We may not see the end of anonymous sources, but a more responsible approach by journalists who are aware of the costs of using them.

Recommended Readings

Books

Bok, Sissela. *Secrets: On the Ethics of Concealment and Revelation.* New York: Pantheon Books, 1982. Features the moral and ethical issues associated with secrecy in society; includes several chapters relevant to the use of secret sources, whistle blowers, and investigative journalism.

Callahan, Joan C. *Ethical Issues in Professional Life.* New York: Oxford University Press, 1988. An anthology that examines ethical issues as they apply to many professions. Chapter 7, "Privacy and Confidentiality," pp. 207-259, includes "The Limits of Confidentiality," a case by Sissela Bok, pp. 230-239, and several other essays related to whistle blowing that are relevant to the media's use of unnamed sources in such cases.

Goodwin, Gene, and Ron F. Smith. *Groping for Ethics in Journalism*, 3rd ed. Ames: Iowa State University Press, 1994. The authors argue for a prescriptive ethical code for journalists and deal with several issues related to secret sources, including arguments for and against their use, the rituals of confidentiality, and the legal problems related to protecting sources.

Articles & Book Chapters

Blankenburg, William B. "The Utility of Anonymous Attribution." *Newspaper Research Journal* (Winter/Spring 1992): 10-23. Examines the ways anonymous attribution serves a reporting function and a moral function by providing divergent, critical views. Based on a word search for "sources said" of three prestige newspapers on Nexus database.

Boeyink, David E. "Anonymous Sources in News Stories: Justifying Exceptions and Limiting Abuses." *Journal of Mass Media Ethics* 5:4 (1990): 233-46. Considers current practices and policies on anonymous sources, and justification for and danger of using them. Seven guidelines for editors and reporters suggest when and under what conditions such sources should be used.

Foreman, Gene. "Confidential Sources: Testing the Reader's Confidence." *Social Responsibility, Business, Journalism, Law, Medicine* 10 (1984): 24-31. Considers the damage the media suffer from the use of unnamed sources; offers guidelines for their use.

Howe, Russell Warren. "Reveal The Name or Go To Jail: How a Reporter's Anonymous Source Worked Out a Novel Ploy to Save Him." *Washington Journalism Review* (January/February 1991): 29-31. The author's promise of confidentiality to an Irish diplomat, necessary to protect his life and family from IRA reprisals, is creatively resolved with cooperation from the source and prevents him from being in contempt of court.

Hulteng, John L. *The Messenger's Motives: Ethical Problems of the News Media.* Englewood Cliffs, N.J.: Prentice-Hall, 1985. Chapter 6, "Reporters and Sources," pp. 81-106, covers the relationship between the two, with emphasis on the use of official sources and reporter privilege, illustrated with relevant cases and examples.

Johnston, David. "The Anonymous-Source Syndrome." *Columbia Journalism Review* (November/December 1987): 54-8. Offers techniques for reporters on how to avoid the use of anonymous sources.

Klaidman, Stephen, and Tom L. Beauchamp. *The Virtuous Journalist*. New York: Oxford University Press, 1987. Chapter 6, "Maintaining Trust," pp. 154-79, discusses the relationship of reciprocity between journalists and their sources. Provides examples of cases involving confidentiality.

Packer, Cathy. "Confidential Sources and Information," chapter 14 in W. Wat Hopkins, ed., *Communication and the Law*. Northport, Ala.: Vision Press, 1998. A good primer on the legal aspects of confidential sources.

Salisbury, Bill. "Burning the Source." *Washington Journalism Review* (September 1991): 18-22. The *St. Paul Pioneer Press* reporter tells the story of his promise of confidentiality to Dan Cohen, his editor's decision to reveal the source in a news story, and the subsequent Supreme Court case ruling that the First Amendment does not protect a newspaper from a lawsuit if it breaks such a promise.

Shepard, Alicia C. "Anonymous Sources." *American Journalism Review* (December 1994): 18-25. Updates the practice and continuing arguments, both pro and con, on the use of anonymous sources in light of the O.J. Simpson criminal trial. Features interviews with leading journalists.

Chapter Thirty

The Use of
Video News Releases

Anne Owen

Should television news programs that use video news releases identify the VNRs' sponsors? Over half the stations airing VNRs don't identify the source as being any other than the station itself. VNRs represent a mix of story topics, and they look and sound like news packages. They are supposed to look as if the television news station produced the package so that viewers will not be able to distinguish between station-produced stories and VNRs. The debate has been particularly acute in the case of political and pharmaceutical VNRs because they are aired regularly on newscasts without any type of source identification.

VNRs are the logical extension of the printed press release, and organizations use both to distribute information to the news media. Like press releases, VNRs are produced by outside firms, known as "source material producers." The one- to three-minute video packages are then sent to stations by mail, courier, or satellite feed. Included with the VNR package is "b-roll," story footage with natural sound and shots of the organization's expert answering questions. Stations can use this b-roll video to give the story a local angle, making their reporters appear to ask the organization's expert questions. Source material producers notify stations of upcoming VNRs via wire or computer services, fax, and the Internet.

After a television station receives a VNR, the news executive decides whether and how to air the information. By broadcast journalism standards, the producer should watch the VNR package, send reporters to check facts and get original video, compile the material, and identify any VNR footage aired. However, as the use of VNRs has increased to the point where they are a ubiquitous part of television news, stations are increasingly using VNR footage without any form of source identification.

While VNRs may represent the future of integrated marketing communications (IMC) in a video age, they have generated considerable controversy between television news executives and the producers of VNRs. This PR material does not receive a warm welcome in all newsrooms, and according to Bob Sonenclar in his article, "The VNR Top Ten: How Much Video PR Gets on the Evening News?" some news directors "would sooner admit to insider trading than to extensive use" of VNRs. Several news executives have refused to use VNRs, apparently believing their organization's credibility would be eroded.

However, source material producers contend that as news stations' budgets and staffs are cut while news blocks and media competition expand, VNRs can provide a welcome solution to staffing and financial problems. They can supply stations with a convenient source of needed video and in-depth approaches to stories that news departments may not be able physically or fiscally to get otherwise. And although news executives may not like to admit their use of VNRs because of the backlash, according to one source material producer, "television stations do air VNRs in one form or another."

The issue of VNR use is exacerbated because the news format in which VNRs are used lends credibility to the video's content. At the same time, the viewing audience is most likely oblivious to the message's commercial intent. Subsequently, the debate turns to the issue of VNR identification.

News executives argue that stations should always inform viewers when VNRs are aired. Otherwise, according to one executive, "If you put it on the air and pretend it is your own product, you are leaving yourself wide open" for criticism. If the viewing audience discovers that some news stories are actually produced by source material producers, then the credibility of television news as a whole is eroded.

VNR producers, however, argue that news programs need not identify the source of news footage since, as with printed press releases, television news stations have the option of editing or rejecting VNR material. In addition, according to author Lowell Frazier, "VNRs supply television stations with real news that addresses real issues and impacts real people."

Origins of the Issue

The use of VNRs by television news has consistently remained high. In recent surveys, as reported by Nielsen Media Research Television Newsroom Survey Reports, almost all of the television stations responding reported using VNRs. These figures compare to usage rates of 86 per cent in 1992 and 83 per cent in 1988. According to representatives from Medialink, one of the largest VNR distributors in the United States, a minimum of 2 to 2.5 million viewer impressions should be generated for a VNR to be considered successful. Three million viewers with forty-two station airings is the Medialink median.

To determine when, where, and how much of a VNR is aired, their producers use electronic tracking systems. In 1991 Nielsen Media Research introduced Sigma, the first electronic monitoring system for VNRs, which encodes video with pulses of invisible light. While Sigma has the ability to track 212 markets, the code may be stripped during editing in television newsrooms. In his article, "VNRs: Who's Watching? How Do You Know?"Adam Shell observed that "Sigma also can't detect a hit if the video is 'squeezed' into a still frame, nor can it record a 'read-only' story." To overcome this, producers supplement the electronic tracking of VNRs with phone calls, reply cards, video monitoring services, and database searches.

VNRs may be aired in their entirety or edited by television stations. According to recent surveys and interviews with Medialink representatives, most news stations — approximately 85 per cent — edit VNRs to some degree. After editing, the stations generally use about thirty to forty seconds, or approximately one-third of the VNR.

As the use of VNRs by television stations has increased, so has the number of VNRs. In the mid-1980s approximately 500 VNRs were produced each year. Current annual production totals are over 5,000. Medialink representatives expect this number to continue rising.

The increasing number of VNRs produced and aired is attributed to several factors: station budget and staff cuts, an increase in news time to fill, an increase in media competition, and the availability of sophisticated broadcast technology. Small stations and stations in smaller markets tend to use VNRs more frequently than large stations or stations in larger markets. Smaller-market television stations have been affected by cost pressures. By incorporating VNRs into their newscasts, they can compete more effectively with stations that have larger staffs and budgets. According to one VNR producer quoted in the *Los Angeles Times*, "It's not always physically or fiscally possible for a station to send a camera to an event, but we can send them footage via satellite or on tape, and it's like they were there." This symbiotic relationship between producers and television news stations can provide some relief for the stations. A number of stations have even built video libraries by saving VNRs, and many have reported using VNRs as file footage.

Not only do VNRs provide television news stations a convenient source of needed video, they also offer sponsoring organizations a means to get on the newscast at a cost far less than that of comparable advertising time. The range of production costs for most VNRs, according to Medialink representatives, falls between $15,000 to $25,000 while distribution costs average $6,500. While these prices have remained fairly constant, in July 1995 overall VNR costs rose an average of 5 to 10 per cent because satellite time became a premium. The current shortage of satellite time was due to extensive coverage of the O.J. Simpson trial, the formation of new networks, and the retirement of old satellites. With the launching of new satellites in 1996, this time shortage was alleviated somewhat. Comparable advertising production and media placement costs are significantly higher. In 1998, the cost of a single thirty-second commercial on prime-time network television averaged $100,000, but the spot could have cost as much as $575,000 if placed during a highly rated show.

No Identification Needed

Source material producers argue that VNRs, one of the fastest growing, most controversial IMC tools, constitute legitimate news and include newsworthy material. When organizations use IMC, their marketing efforts are coordinated and integrated to convey a unified message and image. While the content of VNRs is similar to that of the organization's communications campaign, they have the added credibility of being placed in newscasts. Thus VNRs enable organizations to integrate or use messages consistent with their IMC campaigns while receiving the benefits of newscast placement and the subsequent third-person credibility that the news format lends.

To effectively expose television audiences to IMC messages, organizations have implemented a number of communication tools. One of the most commonly used tools is television commercials. But they may lack credibility, as audiences have become skeptical about advertising. To compensate for this skepticism, organizations use other types of messages, such as VNRs, which hide their commercial intent. Subsequently, IMC messages appear in news programming, which then lends third-person credibility to the content of the message. Thus, the IMC message is reinforced through frequency, consistency, and credibility. The audience views the message more than once in differing formats — as a commercial message and as a VNR — and in differing environments — as a commercial between programming and during the newscast, with the added third-person credibility that the news format lends.

But where do VNRs fit within the larger mosaic of IMC messages aimed at consumers in a communications campaign? In a broad sense, organizations employ, to varying degrees, two forms of non-personal communication: advertising and publicity. "Advertising" describes communications that are controlled by, identify, and are paid for by a sponsor. Commercial time or space is reserved and paid for by the organization. "Publicity" describes communications that are not paid for and may or may not identify a sponsor. The organization does not pay for time or space. Instead, the message is used at the discretion of television news stations.

VNRs may be considered publicity vehicles, since organizations don't pay the stations to air them and don't directly control how or whether they are used. Moreover, when used, VNRs are often not identified as having been produced for a sponsor. Given the high degree to which VNRs are used and not identified, VNRs, likewise, contain some advertising element. The sponsoring organizations are, in a sense, maintaining a large measure of control over the communication.

Messages that are used for advertising purposes but are non-commercial in character and do not use stimuli to alert viewers to the message's true commercial purpose are termed "hybrid communication messages." Such messages are paid for but do not identify the sponsor.

Thus, hybrid messages can be particularly advantageous for sponsoring organizations. Organizations maintain some measure of control over the message, and because VNRs benefit from the credibility lent by the surrounding news content, they are more effective than traditional television commercials. According to Anne Owen and James Karrh in their article, "Video News Releases: Effects on Viewer Recall and Attitudes," when VNRs are presented but not identified in the newscast, viewers give a higher credibility rating to the message versus a similarly structured television commercial.

Thus, before the question of whether VNRs should or should not be identified can be addressed, VNR producers argue that their benefits should be discussed. First, VNRs are successful IMC tools. They are more cost efficient than comparable commercials, and sponsoring organizations can create a news story from their communications campaign and distribute it to television news stations rather than having to spend thousands of dollars producing and buying television commercial time.

Second, newscasts lend VNRs the credibility that similar television commercials simply may not have. From such positioning, organizations get key placements and may increase brand equity. Brand equity is the worth of the brand to the organization and the target audience. With a VNR, the featured information, product, or political candidate can be positioned legitimately as the "next, best, biggest" thing without looking like a commercial plug for the sponsoring organization. The sponsor can appear as the authority on a certain topic, industry, or issue, as well as defining its position on controversial topics. The news environment lends VNRs credibility while the sponsoring organization is hidden from viewers.

Third, while organizations want to expose viewers to their IMC campaigns, their messages will fail if the target audience does not learn something about the name of the product, product features, or the relationship of the product to its competitor. Viewers tend to pay more attention to newscasts and VNRs embedded within news programming than to similarly structured commercials. Even if the VNRs are edited, they allow the sponsoring organizations to cut through commercial clutter and effectively reach their target audience.

By producing and distributing VNRs, organizations not only save money, but have an audience that is attentive and considers stories within a newscast to be more credible than advertisements. Through the use of VNRs, sponsoring organizations increase their opportunity to raise viewer knowledge about their current IMC campaign. According to Laurence Moskowitz, president of Medialink, "More than half of all America saw Medialink's top VNR on their local newscasts. That is more than the total circulation of the nation's most widely read daily newspapers."

VNRs are also of importance to television news stations. Stations must find ways to compete effectively with a growing news hole and demand for higher ratings while news budgets and staff are reduced. Through the use of VNRs, news departments can attract viewers with newsworthy stories and visually appealing video at no monetary cost to the station. VNRs allow stations to air stories they may not have otherwise been able to obtain. In this manner, stations can increase viewership and subsequently attract additional advertising dollars.

Because of threatened governmental guidelines in the 1990s, the Pharmaceutical Manufacturers Association planned to develop guidelines for pharmaceutical VNRs. But it steadfastly contends that no guidelines can replace news executives' editorial judgment in weighing each VNR's potential benefit or harm to the viewing audience.

As a result of mounting fear about possible government regulation of VNRs, the Public Relations Service established voluntary industry guidelines in its Code of Good Practice for VNRs. The following guidelines can serve as an industry reference for producers.

- The objective of a VNR is to present information, pictures, and sound that TV journalists can use and rely on for quality, accuracy, and perspective.

- Information contained in a VNR, to the extent possible, must be accurate and verifiable. Intentionally false or misleading information must be avoided.

- A VNR must be clearly identified on the video's opening slate and any advisory material and scripts that precede or accompany tape distribution.

- The sponsoring company, organization, or individual must also be clearly identified on the video slate.

- The name and phone number of a responsible party must be provided on the video for journalists to contact.

- Persons interviewed in the VNR must be accurately identified by name, title and affiliation on the video.

VNR producers argue that the video content should be treated as station-generated information, and as such the sponsoring organization need not be identified. If VNRs were identified, sponsoring organizations would lose the third-person endorsement the news lends.

Additionally, VNR producers argue that television news stations have complete control over the information and can edit or reject the video package. According to the Public Relations Society of America (PRSA), the news executive is ultimately responsible for making the decision to identify the source of the video. "Every once in a while there's a story expressing the outrage about newspeople using footage that viewers think was produced by a news station, when actually it was sponsored by a corporation or political candidate," noted one producer. "But it's no different from a printed press release. They have the option of accepting or rejecting, editing or changing it."

Identification is Imperative

Some news executives and VNR critics argue that stations should inform viewers whenever VNRs are broadcast. Image-hungry news stations and the convenience of ready-to-use VNR footage has led to an increase in exposure for sponsoring organizations. Critics argue that since the primary purpose of VNRs is to generate exposure on newscasts for sponsors, when viewers of news programming believe that they are watching the work of objective journalists who only air their own reports and video, it is imperative that VNR material be identified. For example, Mary Trudel, in an article titled "PR Professionals and TV Producers: The New Alliance for Good Television," quoted one news director as saying that VNRs are good for political candidates because of the exposure they can get on the news, "but they're terrible for viewers because they're biased." VNRs not identified during a newscast lend sponsoring organizations third-person credibility because the video packages have seemingly been approved by the news station. As observed by researchers Owen and Karrh, this type of exposure can effectively augment IMC campaigns. But according to VNR critics, the exposure does not enhance the credibility of television news.

Critics argue that while the speed and sophistication of communications technologies increase and the news hole grows, news department budgets are cut, staff is reduced, and competition from other stations, networks, cable, and pay-per-view programming becomes more fierce. Concurrently, television news executives are faced with producing newscasts that deliver high ratings. The situation makes VNRs particularly appealing, and television news stations may develop a dependency on material provided by source material producers.

According to John Pavlik and Mark Thalhimer in their report, "From Wausau to Wichita: Covering the Campaign via Satellite," news stations have a particular reliance on VNRs supplied by political candidates. They quote one news director as saying that VNRs "are the way most people find out about the candidates," while another director said that for the primaries "VNRs were the only way a candidate could get exposure." Craig Winnekar in his article "Live, Via Satellite from Houston," described staffers assembling daily VNRs designed to promote candidates at the 1992 Republican Presidential Convention. "These VNRs consisted of 90 seconds worth of highlights of the day's convention footage with commentary provided by the GOP. A separate version of the VNR was available with natural sound, so that the local stations could provide their own commentary (with help from handy GOP press releases, of course)." The exposure received by candidates, and the credibility the news lends, augments many IMC campaigns.

Critics claim that VNRs raise fundamental public policy and regulatory questions because they are virtually indistinguishable from regular news stories and, as such, their commercial intent is hidden. In addition, they point out that VNRs are produced, not by television news stations, but by VNR producers for sponsoring organizations that pay for the cost of production and distribution. Critics contend that VNRs are not bona fide news packages but IMC messages with their commercial intent deliberately hidden to unduly influence unsuspecting viewing audiences.

The issues of what is bona fide news, the validity of third-party produced news pieces being classified as bona fide news packages, and the responsibility of television news stations have been debated for over thirty years. For example, in *Oliver Productions, Inc.*, 1989, the FCC said that a news program qualifies for the bona fide newscast exemption "based solely on whether the program reports news of current events in a manner similar to traditional newscasts." However, if third-party produced news segments and newscasts are used only to promote particular candidates, they will not qualify as bona fide newscasts. According to recent studies, over half of the stations surveyed had some type of policy about the use of political candidate VNRs. However, the policies were mostly informal. Only about one-third of those surveyed had a policy prohibiting the use of candidate VNRs. The decision to promote candidacies rests with the broadcaster rather than the candidate. Thus, if a news station aired VNRs to promote a particular candidacy, then the broadcast would not qualify as bona fide news and the station would have to comply with the equal opportunity requirement.

The equal opportunity rule, Section 315 of the 1934 Communications Act, directs broadcasters to show the same considerations to all legally qualified political candidates. For example, if broadcasters allow one candidate to use their facilities, they must give all legally qualified candidates for the same office equal opportunities. But broadcasters don't have to meet the equal opportunity requirements when a candidate's appearance occurs during a 1) bona fide newscast, 2) bona fide news interview, 3) bona fide news documentary, or 4) on-the-spot coverage of bona fide news events (including but not limited to political conventions and other such activities). The FCC has consistently denied an exemption to self-initiated appearances by political candidates on newscasts where the candidate has control over the information.

For example, in 1962 Clark W. Thompson wrote the Commission to inquire if his pre-produced news packages would trigger the equal opportunity rule. The FCC informed Thompson that his pre-produced news packages would trigger equal time obligations because, while Thompson's packages were aired during a bona fide newscast, he controlled the content.

In a 1991 Notice of Proposed Rulemaking (NPRM), the FCC reiterated its decision that candidate-controlled, preproduced news packages would trigger the equal opportunity rule while station-produced packages would not. "Third-party produced newscasts featuring candidates not for their newsworthiness, but to promote a particular candidacy" would not qualify for the bona fide newscast exemption. Thus, if stations air third-party produced news segments to promote a particular candidacy, then they must comply with Section 315. But the FCC has taken no direct steps to regulate VNRs. Other governmental regulatory agencies, such as the FDA, have tried to take some preliminary action.

The importance of VNRs as IMC tools for pharmaceutical companies resulted from stringent federal restrictions on television advertising of prescription drugs. Companies are less constrained in their use of VNRs, as the FDA has not established any formal VNR guidelines. Therefore, VNRs are a tool by which pharmaceutical companies can effectively reach their viewing target audience.

Because of increased VNR use, the FDA tried to develop a comprehensive policy on VNRs and supporting materials about prescription drug products. The proposed guidelines, which were later withdrawn, came as a result of VNRs being aired that 1) promoted prescription drug products not approved by the FDA, 2) touted products approved by the FDA for one use but promoted for an unapproved use, 3) implied product superiority when there was none, or 4) criticized competing products. Under the proposed guidelines, pharmaceutical companies falsifying information about prescription drugs would have been prosecuted and would have had to correct any misinformation. Additional penalties could have also been imposed.

In 1991 the FDA began requiring pharmaceutical companies to submit VNRs for review, along with enclosed scripts, press releases, and package inserts. According to the Director of the FDA's Division of Drug Advertising and Labeling, "There is no doubt that these materials many times are highly promotional and need to be dealt with as most other promotional materials are."

The FDA was concerned about the lack of verbal or on-screen identification of pharmaceutical VNRs and contended that unsuspecting viewers could be misled by their content. "Virtually none of them state that they came from the drug company but rather imply a third party," the FDA reported. VNRs that use on-screen testimony from doctors hired by the pharmaceutical companies to test the products rarely point out this information.

These concerns led to the FDA's plans to develop guidelines for medical VNRs and other material promoting pharmaceuticals. The FDA was worried that some VNRs had a hidden agenda or secret backing or would present a conflict of interest. The FDA's concerns were heightened by an increase in the use of pharmaceutical VNRs by television news stations. According to studies, about 50 per cent of the news directors responding said that they used medical/health VNRs in the newscast and one-fourth used environmental or scientific VNRs.

However, because of criticism and the prohibitive cost of reviewing all medical VNRs and related materials prior to airing, the FDA's plans and guidelines were withdrawn. Some executives remain cautious about the claims made in medical VNRs because the source of the information is often left to speculation.

Resolution

The use of VNRs by television news stations will continue to escalate as more are produced annually by source material producers. This increase opens VNRs to greater criticism. According to one producer, "Media scrutiny of any growing industry, especially one that has the power to influence public opinion as VNRs do, is inevitable." The debate over whether VNRs should be identified will continue with each side asserting the legitimacy of its arguments. It is a fact that many stations air VNRs without any form of identification. Nonidentified

VNRs are beneficial to their creators as well as television news stations. Through the news format, VNRs are lent credibility; and with those same VNRs, the news hole is filled with programming.

Conversely, identifying VNR material could be detrimental to producers, sponsoring organizations, and television news stations. For example, if VNRs were identified, sponsoring organizations would lose the credibility that the news format provides. Stations could lose their credibility as well if viewers were aware that the stories they were watching were not produced by the stations' reporters. A loss in credibility with viewers would lead to a loss in ratings that would subsequently mean a loss in advertising revenue. Thus, identifying VNR material is not in the interest of anyone involved.

However, one concern is that stations may be transferring their control of the treatment of public issues and information to sponsoring organizations when they air VNRs without any form of identification. Even if the VNR package is edited, without identification the viewing audience cannot determine the source of the material. When VNRs are aired without identification, is the public interest paramount or subordinate to the whims and profits of the sponsoring organizations? Their producers and sponsoring organizations argue that no control has been transferred because it is the stations that make the decision whether to use VNR material or to identify any video. They argue it is ultimately the responsibility of the news station to serve in the "public interest, convenience, and necessity" as mandated by the Communications Act of 1934.

The only way to guarantee the identification of all VNR material would be if governmental regulation were enacted that required the on-screen or voice-over identification of all third-party produced material. If the issue of identification were brought by a citizen's or consumer advocate group to the FCC or FDA, then discussion of possible regulation may again be raised. At the present time, no such regulation has been enacted, and past attempts at labeling requirements have failed. But if any governmental regulations were to be adopted for political or pharmaceutical VNRs, they could serve as a precedent for other types of third-party produced material.

VNRs are big business in the United States, and VNR distributors are extending their reach globally. The VNR is here to stay, and this fact opens it up to possible regulation. But because of the benefits of VNRs to producers, sponsoring organizations, and television news stations, the answer of whether to identify or not identify VNR material lies in the congruence of industry self-regulatory guidelines with news station programming responsibility. VNRs need not be identified if source material producers, sponsoring organizations, and television news stations are vigilant in the production and screening of the veracity of VNR content used in daily news programming. As long as VNRs remain free from irresponsible practices, governmental regulatory policy will not be written. However, if stations air VNRs without identification and fail to take the responsibility for determining the truthfulness of the VNR content, then some sort of regulatory practice may have to be enacted by the FCC, FDA, or another governmental agency.

Recommended Readings

Articles & Book Chapters

Balasubramanian, Siva. "Beyond Advertising and Publicity: Hybrid Messages and Public Policy Issues." *Journal of Advertising* 23 (December 1994): 29-46. Explores a growing genre of marketing communication, labeled "hybrid messages," that creatively combines key advantages (and avoids key disadvantages) inherent in advertising and publicity messages.

Cameron, Glen, and David Blount. "VNRs and Air Checks: A Content Analysis of the Use of Video News Releases in Television Newscasts." *Journalism & Mass Communication Quarterly* 73 (Winter 1996): 890-904. Forty-seven television news stories generated by a VNR were content analyzed to determine how television gatekeepers use various elements included in VNRs.

Cronin, Karen. "Video News Releases from the Gatekeepers' Perspectives." In *Proceedings of the Sixth Conference on Corporate Communication* (May 1993): 357-67. Reviews television stations' use of VNRs.

Frazier, Lowell. "Video News Releases Overcome Era of Criticism, But Use and Value Questions Still Unresolved." *Southern Public Relations Journal* 1 (Winter 1995): 13-17. Reviews criticism of VNRs in the media over the past three years, analyzes the impact, and reports the results of surveys of the 75 top public relations firms and 112 television assignment editors.

Gordon, July. "FDA to Scrutinize Pharmaceutical VNRs." *Public Relations Journal* 47 (October 1991): 6. Describes the FDA's efforts to regulate VNRs on medical subjects.

Owen, Anne. "Reaching the Television Audience: The Use of Video News Releases in Integrated Marketing Communications." *Business Research Yearbook: Global Business Perspectives* 4 (1997): 62-6. Identifies and describes the subject matter of VNRs that pass through news gates.

Owen, Anne, and James Karrh. "Video News Releases: Effects on Viewer Recall and Attitudes." *Public Relations Review* 22 (Winter 1996): 369-78. Viewers assign significantly more credibility to VNR-based messages than to similar advertisements.

Pavlik, John, and Mark Thalhimer. "From Wausau to Wichita: Covering the Campaign via Satellite." In *The Media and Campaign '92, A Series of Special Election Reports.* New York: Columbia University, Freedom Forum Media Studies Center (June 1992): 36-46. Suggests that while voters may have the opportunity to see more of the candidates, what they will increasingly be exposed to is candidates' self-promotional VNRs paid for out of campaign coffers, not newsroom budgets.

Sonenclar, Bo. "The VNR Top Ten: How Much Video PR Gets on the Evening News?" *Columbia Journalism Review* 29 (March-April 1991): 14. Explores television stations' use of VNRs.

Thalhimer, Mark. "Video Sources in the Newsroom." P. 35 in *Covering the Presidential Primaries. In The Media and Campaign '92, A Series of Special Election Reports.* New York: Columbia University, Freedom Forum Media Studies Center, 1992. Discusses how local television stations balance between their need for high-quality, timely video against the rising cost of getting that material.

Trudel, Mary. "PR Professionals and TV Producers: The New Alliance for Good Television." *Public Relations Quarterly* 37 (1992): 22-3. Discusses the symbiotic relationship between public relations and television news.

The Editors

Wm. David Sloan, professor of journalism at the University of Alabama, is a leading historian of mass communication. Along with history, one of his specialties is journalistic writing. He is the author or editor of seventeen other books, including such works as *The Media in America* and *Masterpieces of Reporting*. In addition to his books on history and writing, he has published such general books in the communication field as *Makers of the Media Mind* and *Mass Communication in the Information Age*. He has authored more than eighty research articles and papers, received a number of research awards, and served as editor of the history research journal *American Journalism*. He is the founder of the American Journalism Historians Association, a national organization with a membership of more than 400, and of the Southeast Journalism Conference, a student-oriented organization of journalism programs at forty universities. Along with a variety of other academic and scholarly activities, he is president (1998-2000) of Kappa Tau Alpha, the national honor society in mass communication, and in 1990 received KTA's national award as outstanding chapter adviser. Before going into teaching, he worked as an editor on four newspapers. He received his Ph.D. in mass communication and United States history from the University of Texas.

Emily Erickson Hoff, a doctoral student in mass communication at the University of Alabama, specializes in media history, communication law, and political science. She teaches law, history, and research methodology and has presented a number of conference papers on the media and foreign policy and has written book chapters on the press in the late 1800s and during the Cold War period of the 1950s. Before beginning her graduate studies, she was employed in public relations.

The Authors

David Arant, associate professor of journalism at the University of Memphis, has written several book chapters and articles in scholarly and professional journals on media law, ethics, and history. Before going into teaching, he worked three years as associate editor of a weekly newspaper. He has a Ph.D. in mass communication research from the University of North Carolina at Chapel Hill.

Fred Bales, professor emeritus at the University of New Mexico, is print sequence coordinator in the Department of Communications at Xavier University of New Orleans. Before going into teaching, he worked as a reporter and editor at the *Louisville* (Ky.) *Courier Journal*. He was a Fulbright lecturer in the Philippines and holds a Ph.D. from the University of Texas at Austin.

Lori Bergen, an assistant professor at Kansas State University, teaches media research, communication theory, news and feature writing, and media studies. She does research on newspapers, journalists, and the role of media in communities and produces a television news and public affairs program. She worked as a newspaper reporter and magazine editor before she received a Ph.D. in mass communication from Indiana University.

Judith M. Buddenbaum, professor of journalism and technical communication at Colorado State University, is the author of journal articles and book chapters on religion and the media. She is also the author of *Reporting News about Religion: An Introduction for Journalists* and, with Daniel A. Stout, *Religion and Mass Media: Audiences and Adaptations*. A former general assignment and religion reporter, she received her Ph.D. in mass communication from Indiana University.

Hugh C. Cate, III, is a major in the United States Army, where he works as a public relations officer. He did his graduate work in journalism at the University of Alabama.

Clay Calvert, assistant professor and associate director of the Pennsylvania Center for the First Amendment at the Pennsylvania State University, has published extensively about First Amendment issues. He teaches news media ethics, media law, and mass media studies. He received his J.D. from the University of Pacific and Ph.D. in communication from Stanford University.

Kenneth Campbell, associate professor in journalism and mass communication at the University of South Carolina, specializes in minorities and the media. He received his Ph.D. in mass communications from the University of North Carolina. Before going into teaching, he worked for the *Greensboro* (N.C.) *News and Record*, *Miami Herald*, and *Philadelphia Inquirer*.

Frances L. Collins, assistant professor of advertising at Kent State University, is the author of several papers and newspaper commentaries on First Amendment and commercial speech issues. Before joining Kent State, she was an advertising agency media planner/buyer and media director, as well as a bank marketing director. She received her M.A. in journalism from the Ohio State University.

David Copeland, assistant professor of mass communication at Emory & Henry

College, is the author of *Colonial American Newspapers: Character and Content*, as well as journal articles on the colonial press and religion and media. He is co-editor of *Media History Monographs*. Before teaching, he worked as an editor, reporter, and photographer for daily and weekly newspapers. He received his Ph.D. in mass communication research from the University of North Carolina.

David C. Coulson is a professor and director of graduate studies in the School of Journalism at the University of Nevada, Reno. He has authored numerous articles on news media management and economics issues in scholarly and professional publications. His media experience includes working on seven metropolitan dailies and stints in television news and public relations. He received his Ph.D. in mass communication from the University of Minnesota.

LeAnne Daniels, assistant professor of mass communication at Louisiana State University, has had articles on media and society issues published in *Quill* and *Journalism Quarterly*, as well as the 1997 Business Research Yearbook for the International Academy of Business Disciplines. She has written about media managers' news decisions, public opinion of investigative reporting, and managing change in the journalism business in the 21st century. She worked as a university public relations writer for six years before completing a Ph.D. in mass communication from Indiana University and becoming a teacher.

Robert Dardenne, associate professor of mass communications at the University of South Florida at St. Petersburg, is co-author of *The Conversation of Journalism*. He has written book chapters and articles in scholarly and professional publications. He worked for ten years as reporter, editor, and feature writer in Baton Rouge, La.; Mexico City; Rochester, N.Y.; and Washington, D.C. He received his Ph.D. in journalism and mass communications from the University of Iowa.

Bruce J. Evensen, professor of communication at DePaul University in Chicago, is the author of two books, *Truman, Palestine, and the Press: Shaping Conventional Wisdom at the Beginning of the Cold War* and *When Dempsey Fought Tunney: Heroes, Hokum, and Storytelling in the Jazz Age*, and editor of *The Responsible Reporter*, now in its second edition. His articles on journalism history and ethics have appeared in scholarly journals, and his articles on history and journalistic credibility have appeared in numerous anthologies. Before going into teaching, he wrote for twelve years as a broadcast journalist and bureau chief in Washington, D.C., and Jerusalem. He received his Ph.D. in mass communication from the University of Wisconsin-Madison.

Anthony R. Fellow, professor of communications at California State University, Fullerton, is the author of *The Copy Editors' Handbook for Newspapers* and articles

505

in scholarly and professional journals. Before going into teaching, he was an editor and reporter with the Thomson Newspaper Group for ten years. He received his Ph.D. in communication from the University of Southern California. He is a city councilman, water board director, and member of the Metropolitan Water District of Southern California.

Robert S. Fortner, professor of communication arts and sciences at Calvin College, is the author of two books, *International Communication* and *Public Diplomacy and International Politics,* and a number of articles in scholarly and professional journals in communication. Before entering teaching, he worked in radio and public relations. He received his Ph.D. in mass communication research from the University of Illinois in Urbana-Champaign.

George Albert Gladney is an associate professor and director of graduate studies in the Department of Communication and Mass Media at the University of Wyoming. He has authored more than a dozen articles in scholarly journals related to journalism and mass communication. Earlier in his career he worked as a reporter for the *Los Angeles Times* and *Colorado Springs Sun* and editor of the *Colorado Springs Gazette Telegraph* and *Jackson Hole News.* He received his Ph.D. in communication from the University of Illinois at Urbana-Champaign.

Michael E. Gouge is a newspaper editor in North Carolina. He received his master's degree in journalism at the University of Alabama.

Margot Hardenbergh, assistant professor of communication at Marist College, is the author of book chapters and papers about the role of women in journalism, news values, and television history. Before going into teaching, she spent ten years producing television documentaries and public affairs programming on the regional and national level. She received her Ph.D. in communication studies from New York University.

Stephen Lacy is professor of journalism at Michigan State University. He received a Ph.D. in journalism from the University of Texas at Austin. He has worked as a weekly newspaper editor and a daily newspaper reporter. He has co-written or co-edited four books on newspaper and media economics and management and has written numerous articles about newspaper economics.

Val E. Limburg is associate professor of communication at Washington State University, where he has served on the faculty since 1967. He is the author of *Electronic Media Ethics* and *Mass Media Literacy.* He has written numerous book chapters and journal articles. He has served as an officer for the Washington State Association of Broadcasters for more than twenty years. He did graduate work at Brigham Young University and the University of Illinois.

Lisa Mullikin, a Ph.D. student at the University of Alabama, is the author of several book chapters and research papers in journalism history and media effects. She also advises rural community newspapers and researches the effects of curriculum-based television on children.

Anne Owen, assistant professor of advertising at Florida International University, is the author of several articles in scholarly journals in advertising and public relations. She also has presented papers at meetings of the American Academy of Advertising and other scholarly and professional organizations. She received her Ph.D. in mass communication from the University of Florida.

Mark Popovich, professor of journalism at Ball State University, teaches mass media law and graduate research methods. He is co-author of *The Process of Media Writing* and has contributed a number of articles and book chapters to scholarly and professional journals. He has worked as a sports writer, free-lance photographer, and high school journalism teacher. He received his Ph.D. in journalism from Southern Illinois University at Carbondale.

Paul Alfred (Alf) Pratte, a professor of communication at Brigham Young University, is the author of *Gods Within the Machines: A History of the American Society of Newspaper Editors, 1923-1993*. His research articles have appeared in *American Journalism, Journalism Quarterly, Newspaper Research Journal,* and other publications. He worked as a newspaper reporter in Utah and Hawaii before going into teaching. He is a former president of the American Journalism Historians Association.

Garrett W. Ray is an associate professor of journalism and technical communication at Colorado State University, where he teaches reporting, editing, and media ethics. He is a columnist for *Publishers' Auxiliary* and focuses his research on community newspapers. Before joining Colorado State, he spent twenty years as a weekly newspaper editor and publisher. He received his Ph.D. in journalism from the University of Wales.

Amy Robinson did her graduate work in journalism at the University of Alabama.

Timothy D. Smith, professor of journalism and mass communication at Kent State University, is the author of several articles on access to public information. He is director of the Ohio Center for Privacy and the First Amendment and editor of the Center's semi-annual newsletter, "On the Record." Before joining Kent

State, he was managing editor of the *Akron Beacon Journal*. He received his J.D. from the University of Akron.

J. Douglas Tarpley is professor and chair of the School of Journalism at Regent University.

Pam Tidemann did her graduate work in journalism at the University of Alabama.

Lorna Veraldi, associate professor of journalism and broadcasting at Florida International University, has written articles about media and law for both scholarly and professional journals. Before joining the FIU faculty, she worked for twelve years in radio and television as a writer, producer, reporter, and lawyer. She received her M.A. in mass communication from the University of Utah and her J.D. from New York Law School.

Index

Index

Index